Cold War Tech War

The Politics of America's Air Defense

Mockup of John Frost's
All-Wing Supersonic Project Y
also known as "The Spade"

We acknowledge the financial support of the Government of Canada through the Book Publishing Industry Development Program for our publishing activities.

Published by Apogee Books, Box 62034, Burlington,
Ontario, Canada, L7R 4K2, http://www.apogeebooks.com
Tel: 905 637 5737

Printed and bound in Canada
Cold War Tech War by Randall L. Whitcomb

ISBN 978-1-894959-77-3
Cover art by Randall Whitcomb, color plates by Randall Whitcomb.

COLD WAR TECH WAR

The Politics of America's Air Defense

by
Randall L. Whitcomb

An Apogee Books Publication

CONTENTS

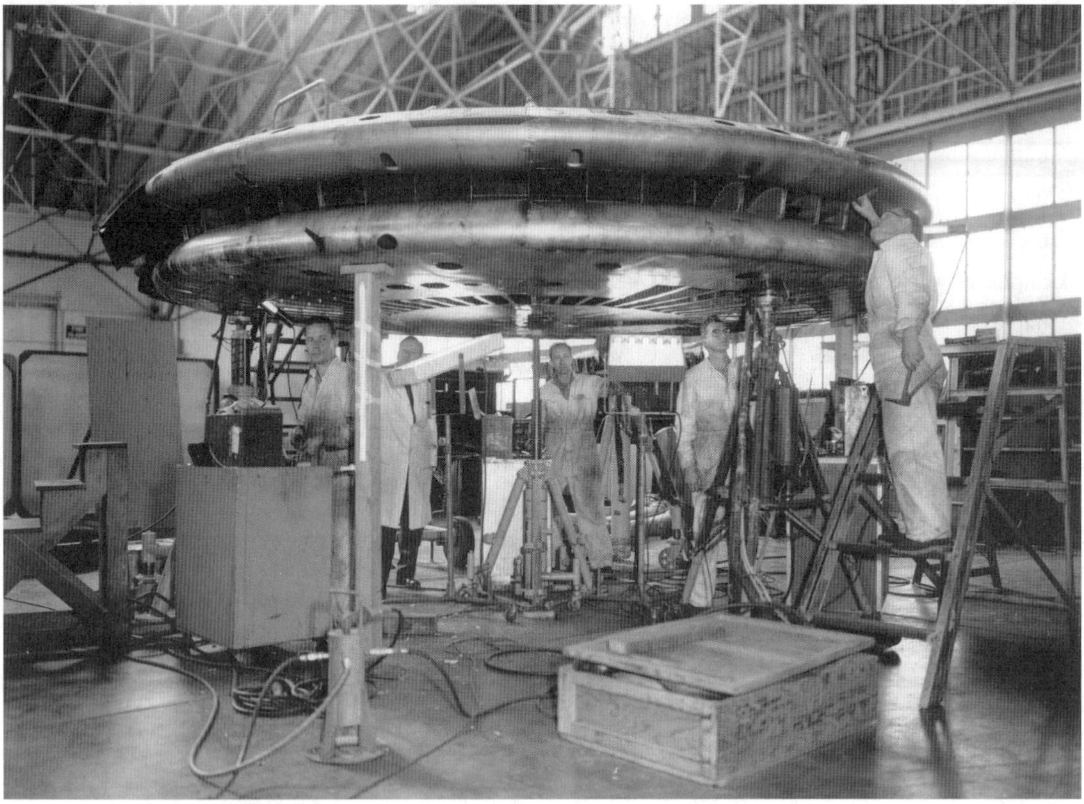

The Avrocar being inspected at Ames research Center

FOREWORD

Randall Whitcomb, the author of this book passed away in early 2008. He was only 44 years old. I didn't get to know Randall very well, we only met about a year before he submitted this manuscript for publication. However, I knew Randall by reputation. I owned his previous book *Avro Aircraft and Cold War Aviation*, and hanging proudly in my house is a print of one of Randall's remarkable portraits of the *Avro Arrow CF-105* aircraft.

Being an editor can often be a difficult task. You read a manuscript and you try to divine the author's intentions while sifting for mistakes, both grammatical and otherwise. As an editor of non-fiction you are often also held responsible for errors of fact. Frequently you find yourself riding a fine line between what you believe is right and what the author wants. I've never been comfortable with censoring a manuscript, in fact in 25 years only once or twice have I persuaded an author to remove something from their original draft (usually for legal reasons.) This book presented an entirely new set of problems for me. It is the only time that I have found myself with a contract, a finished manuscript, and no author. Randall was waiting for me to read it and provide some input. I never had the chance.

Randall's unexpected death just weeks after completing this book was a shock to us at Apogee Books. We had spent time with him at an open house in late 2007 at the Toronto Aerospace Museum. We watched as people flocked to him to buy his extraordinary array of aircraft paintings and to ask him questions. He evidently had a formidable store of knowledge. I didn't realise it at the time but Randall was more than just another aviation enthusiast, he was an excellent artist and one of the most respected authorities in Canada on the history of the Avro Arrow. In this book you will find that he also had a deep interest in the political significance of that ill-fated and superlative aircraft, and that he had a complex vision of its legacy inside the bigger picture of the Cold War.

In the following pages you will find a dazzling array of data and facts, but sadly no one will ever be able to challenge Randall to elaborate further on those facts. Thankfully, I can say that because Randall was an enthusiast, a meticulous researcher AND a technically adept Air Force pilot, his grasp of the complexities of this most controversial story may have been unparalleled. Randall dug deep into government documents in three countries, he interviewed the key players and analysed the hardware with a pilot's eye. It may be that no one will ever be able to do as much again, with so much palpable enthusiasm.

Randall was obviously a passionately patriotic Canadian, his willingness to sign up to defend his country clearly demonstrates this fact. The pages ahead will reveal a man who was evidently *upset*. He was upset because he could see, thanks to his extensive research, that lies have been told which hurt his country. Even more upsetting were that the lies were told by many of his own countrymen, and those same lies apparently continue to be perpetuated today; either through ignorance or malice. Since politicians can rarely be relied upon for their candour, it becomes the job of the historian to try to unravel the truth, but as we know history is often only reported by the victorious. In this observer's eye, there is much truth to be found in the following pages.

This may be an important breakthrough book *particularly for the average Canadian*, who for decades have been fed the "evil American cabal" story as the principal reason for the Arrow's demise. As much as Randy clearly concludes that some prominent American politicians had dirty hands in this story, he also proves, for the first time, that the US Air Force was quite happy to buy planes from Canada (a major recent discovery which he was particularly pleased about) and that Howard Hughes (the prototypical American capitalist industrialist) was also a very smart and generous man who tried to support Avro. Randy also makes no attempt to shy away from blaming no less than four prominent Canadians for their wilful negligence and flip-flopping (Howe, Foulkes, Pearkes and Diefenbaker). An American reading this book is likely to be upset, *especially if they don't read it through to the end*, but the average Canadian is likely to be completely surprised to find plain evidence of dirty hands in their own country. One thing is certain, as is so often the case with politics, this is not a simple story.

Within these pages you will find all of the traditional excuses for the demise of Canada's greatest aviation company. They include planes that were too expensive, didn't live up to specifications or were obsolescent. Characters with inadequate social skills. Markets that didn't exist, foreign tampering, incompetent politicians, scheming intelligence agents, devious Soviet spies, corporate greed and a host of other reasons. What becomes clear, however, is that the paper evidence dug up by Randall completely negates many of these shallow platitudes that are so frequently repeated ad infinitum by the media. My limited experience with the law and judicial system lead me to believe that there is enough evidence here to merit an official inquiry. I'm not fond of conspiracy theories, and I can't speak with authority to Randall's conclusions, some of them seem pretty harsh, but if I found myself on a jury in the court of public opinion and I was presented with so much documentary evidence, I would find many of his assertions difficult to rebut.

The security of the North American continent may well have been drastically improved had the forces at work in Ottawa in the late 1950's operated differently. There seems little doubt that those who say the Avro Arrow would never have lived up to expectations need to read this book. Right or wrong, there is so much information here it would be an act of almost moronic hubris to dismiss the contents out of hand.

As for the history of commercial aviation? Well, after reading this book, *I wanted to fly in the Avro Jetliner*. Not only was it a thing of beauty, it was, thanks to the new evidence presented herein, apparently *everything* it was cracked up to be.

Avro's forays into flying discs, SSTs and hypersonic spacecraft, previously the stuff of legend, are only now being discussed and understood by space and aviation historians; thanks to the efforts of people like Randall who worked hard to get the paperwork declassified.

Posterity has already shown that the team who worked at Avro Canada were a formidable group who, once dismantled, went on to help the United States pull off what was probably the greatest technical accomplishment of the 20th century, the manned moon landings. They were also instrumental in bringing Concorde to the world. It hardly seems likely that given those qualifications, Jim Floyd, John Frost, Mario Pesando, Jim Chamberlin and the other geniuses who brought us the *Arrow* and the *Jetliner* would have built a lemon.

Whether you can stomach Randall's condemnations of the various players or not, it seems to me that this could be an important book, and if the truth is ever revealed, in years to come may even be seen to be an important work of history.

I deeply regret not having had the opportunity to engage in conversation with Randall about this book. I didn't have the usual opportunity to have an informed dialog. So like the rest of you I will have no occasion to challenge or question the things that confuse me. However, I will make no apologies to anyone for the content found herein. Out of respect to Randall and his family I have changed nothing of substance. All I can say is that Randall mentioned to me, more than once by email, that he was sincerely concerned that his conclusions might be perceived as being too tough on certain of the players, and that particularly, he thought the readers in the United States might misconstrue his intentions. It is my opinion that the reader should not jump to any conclusions without completing the entire book. In the end, even if Randy had lived, I think it would have been very difficult for me to have sorted this book out to make it work for everyone. If I had removed the politics it would have totally diluted the point of the book. If I had moved the anti-Canadian material to the front and moved the anti-American material to the back it would have required a complete re-write. And so it remains; as it was written.

If nothing else, I feel, speaking as neither a natural born Canadian or American, that the evidence shown in Randall's book clearly illustrates that *somebody* did the world a great disservice by gutting Avro Canada. It was a mistake, plain and simple, regardless of who was to blame. Although Randall places his pieces firmly in place and makes no attempt to shy away from his own verdict, I at least will leave the reader to draw their own conclusions about who might have benefitted from this mistake.

I would love to have seen an *Arrow* or a *Jetliner* in the air. In hindsight, I will have to settle for having stood shoulder to shoulder with the Arrow's most ardent fan, Randall Whitcomb, as he watched the full size Arrow replica roll out of its hangar in Toronto in October of 2006.

Robert Godwin
(Editor: Apogee Books July 2008)

Author's Introduction

If you have had any exposure to the many books, articles and visual media generated over the Avro story, you are probably saying to yourself "Yet another book on Avro? What possibly could be added to this half-century old story?" The answer is, a great deal.

Nearly all the books to date have ignored the larger geo-political and economic issues surrounding A.V.Roe Canada Ltd., particularly those related to national presence in strategic industry and resources, and how this presence, or lack thereof, effects political independence and economic prosperity. It seems there is a determination, among Canadians in positions of corporate, financial and governmental authority (and in the media and education system), to ignore the vastly more important economic aspects of what A.V. Roe Canada Ltd. really was: *public investment in strategic industry and resources.* Avro represented a unique private-public partnership in terms of being a wilful creation by the government as part of a national industrial strategy designed to physically protect Canada from war by providing a domestic source of primary armaments. But the strategy of the leading civil servants and industrialists who founded the company was also to make the company a component of a technical foundation that would keep Canadian industry in general competitive in high-technology. In a real sense A.V. Roe Canada Ltd. was founded to also protect Canada economically. Part of this aspect was a hope that a solid industrial and technical base available to Canadian companies would help stem the increasing buy-out and foreign ownership of industry and technology in Canada. Certainly the directors and many politicians hoped Avro and allied companies would reverse the trend and increase the number of majority-Canadian-owned companies. Since most foreign capital investment in resources and industry came from the United States, the company and its supporters couldn't help but be seen by portions of American industry and finance as inimical to their interests. Through re-investing every dollar of profit that both the government of Canada and private sector fed Avro, back into the infrastructure of the company, Avro and Hawker Siddeley went from a standing start to being Canada's largest employer and third-highest capitalised corporation in thirteen short years. To some Americans interested in expanding in Canada, this would be seen as an alarming growth rate, and the company was expanding beyond aircraft and engines into resources and other heavy industry—with the apparent support of the national government. This book presents precedents showing how American politicians allied with their multinational industries and financial houses have often pursued foreign policies that serve those commercial interests. In fact, motive, precedent and opportunity are shown regarding the influence of certain powerful American politicians and industrialists in seeing the Avro Arrow, and with it Avro Aircraft Canada Ltd., curtailed. That this was part of the American national military-technical *and commercial* strategy is the thesis of this work. Unfortunately, for those sympathetic to the company at least, this American political strategy had many witting and unwitting accomplices in Canadian politics and the media, with this continuing to skew the debate to conclusions which, in this author's opinion, unnecessarily degrade the legacy of the founders, leading executives and certainly the engineers of A.V. Roe Canada Ltd. Government secrecy and classification of documents surrounding the company, particularly regarding the cancellations of the Avro Jetliner and Arrow, have also led to the publication and repetition of many incorrect assumptions derogatory to the company.

Popular historians have thus far failed to see the rightful potential of the Avro Jetliner, and what it should have meant for Avro and Canada in industrial, economic and political terms. We now, thanks to the tireless work of people like Palmiro Campagna, have *proof* that overturns the consensus of most prior historians on the sales interest in the Jetliner. Formerly restricted government documents now reveal, incredibly, that the United States Air Force, as Avro executives always insisted, tried to place an initial order for a dozen Jetliners. These were to be used for trials in a number of roles and were requested by the USAF early in the Korean War, with an eye to acquiring fleets of the plane. This order and others were, according to formerly-classified government documents, prevented "at the high political level". Howard Hughes interest in the Jetliner has been described previously, but Avro's world-leading SST designs, which were also produced partly to satisfy Hughes' interest, have been virtually ignored by the aviation fraternity, again because documentation on Avro projects has remained classified or was destroyed due to circumstances surrounding the destruction of the company. National Airlines in the United States tried to buy four Jetliners, (to be expanded to a full fleet if found satisfactory in trial service), and this order was prevented by the actions of a leading Canadian politician;

Clarence Decatur (C.D.) Howe. From comments by Howe and other sources, it appears there may have been an American political aspect influencing this decision.

In the late-1950s it appears that J.C. Floyd's team of engineers at Avro Canada led the world in designs for commercial supersonic transports (SSTs), and again, the dynamic Mr. Hughes entered the picture. In fact, the rivalry between Hughes' TWA and Pan American airlines (itself no stranger to global political and economic intrigue in collaboration with the state department), as portrayed in "The Aviator", is mirrored by the interest of both TWA and Pan Am in Avro's SST designs of the late 1950s. It will be revealed here, for the first time, that the SST design Avro Canada settled on in the months after Black Friday, and that had emerged from discussions with TWA and Pan Am, became the very first industry submission to the British Supersonic Transport Advisory Committee (STAC). This group was responsible for helping establish the government requirement that led to the British production of the legendary Concorde SST. While the initial Hawker Siddeley submission to the STAC was conceived, in large part, by Avro Canada engineers led by first Jim Chamberlin and then Frank Brame—with liberal use of Avro's IBM 704 mainframe and other computer facilities—but were revealed after the Arrow cancellation by the new Hawker Siddeley Aviation Advanced Projects Group (HSA/APG), headquartered at the Hawker Aircraft complex at Kingston U.K.. This new team, charged with design and engineering leadership for the entire Hawker Siddeley Group, was formed shortly after the cancellation of the Arrow, and was led by the head of the Arrow's engineering team Jim Floyd. The HSA/APG also included five former Avro Canada Arrow design section heads. In revealing this aircraft an enormous gap in the development that led to the Concorde is filled, in the process overturning a great many previous assumptions about the evolution of technology regarding SSTs. The solid-state IBM 704 would go on to fame for its significant role in the NASA space program. Some of the leading Avro computing, guidance and telemetry experts would play leading roles in developing systems for Mercury and Gemini that they had first conceived for the Arrow program. Indeed, Jim Chamberlin and Robert Lindley, chief of aerodynamics and chief engineer of the Arrow respectively, would assume senior guiding positions within the NASA space program.

It is also generally unknown that Avro Canada produced a design for a Mach 2, vertical take-off and landing (VTOL) fighter for the US Navy in the mid-1950s. This radical design incorporated four wings in an X-wing configuration, with a turbojet engine at each wingtip. This appeared to fill the US Navy requirement for which it was designed better than any competing design offered by American manufacturers, yet the requirement, and the Avro design, were dropped. Avro drawings and data are published herein for the first time.

And what of the Arrow? While many leading historians have denigrated the plane and its systems, an objective analysis of the aircraft design and, signally, of its demonstrated flight performance, suggest that the Arrow 2 would have remained the top performing aircraft/engine combination for at least a quarter century. Performance curves acquired by this author (revealed in *AA&CWA*) demonstrate that even the Arrow Mk. 1, armed and at combat weight, would have been a superior interceptor to most planes in service today. The more powerful Mk. 2, it turns out, would have had performance surprisingly analogous to that of the new F-22 Raptor, now entering service in the US.

However, had the Arrow been built, this author believes the evolution of military aircraft would have been radically altered by its presence. Almost overlooked previously are the advanced Arrow designs Avro was evolving for speeds past Mach 3, and altitudes in the sub-orbital range. Also ignored is the sales interest and potential of the Arrow 2 and successors. On examining the Arrow 3 design, and the ramjet-augmented version designated the Mk. 4, it seems plausible that Avro Canada could have produced Mach 3 to 5 interceptors by the mid-1960s. Even the Mk. 3 would probably have significantly out-performed the current holder of the world speed and altitude records for jet aircraft: the Lockheed Skunk Works SR-71 Blackbird.

It should come as no surprise then, that there appears to have been some interesting political gyrations between American defense specialists and politicians, and their Canadian (and British) counterparts over which concepts of air defense should have been pursued. Bombers were, and then weren't, the threat. Fighters weren't needed, in fact, manned military aircraft were to be replaced by missiles according to CIA intelligence and recommendations. Then, when every air defense chief in the West stepped forward in the summer of 1958 to say that manned interceptors would be required "as far into the future as we can foresee", the Canadians were told that one capable of Mach 3, long range, and high altitude, virtually an American Arrow Mk.3, was said to be the only future plane required. This plane, the F-108 Rapier, also involved an interesting technology exchange between Avro, Canadian defense planners and politicians, and American agents. The Chief Scientist of the United States Air Force (USAF), Dr. Courtland Perkins, sought and received information on Arrow variants Avro was planning, and used these for purposes related to the American Long Range Interceptor Experimental (LRIX) program, which North American Aviation had already been selected to fulfil with their Rapier. It appears that the design of the Rapier went from a rather ungainly canard-delta configuration to one resembling the Arrow Mk. 3, right around the time that Avro submitted the aerodynamic information, including lift-drag ratio graphs, of the Arrow, and information on the evolving Arrow Mk. 3 design.

With aerial refuelling designed into the Arrow 3 (but not included in the F-108 design), the American program looked somewhat redundant and inferior, yet Canadian defense leaders and politicians were convinced that it made the Arrow "look like something the might be picked up in a department store", in the words of the US Undersecretary of the Air Force, James Douglas, to the Canadian Ambassador, in January of 1958. Propaganda as to its performance (with Mach 5 being touted as its potential top speed—a hypersonic long-range aircraft) could not be challenged by the Canadians since no data was made available. Indeed, no flight test data on the F-106 was made available to Canada until the Arrow program was cancelled. With the available, "off the shelf" Curtiss Wright ramjets envisaged for the sub-orbital, hypersonic Arrow 4, with their integral fuel stowage, the Arrow program seemed poised, in hindsight, to produce aircraft capable of outperforming the SR-71 by a significant margin, never mind the F-108 Rapier. It had double the thrust-to-weight of either aircraft and comparable or lower drag. But then, the Canadians received mission specifications for the F-108, no hard design, materials, propulsion or aerodynamic information. (The same was true of the F-106 Delta Dart, the closest thing to the Arrow the United States was developing at the time—an aircraft the USAF acknowledged would be inferior to the Arrow.) Had they received the design and performance information on these aircraft, they would have seen that the Arrow 2 was in fact a world-beating aircraft, and a bargain as well. The future Arrow versions promised to keep Canada at the forefront of long-range, all-weather air superiority fighter technology.

Research and development efforts related to the Arrow's intended radar/fire-control systems, ASTRA 1 and 2, also seem to have benefited the American state of the art, and are described within. Some aspects of US-British-Canadian interaction relating to the various technologies, particularly relating to jet propulsion are discussed, as is British interest in the Arrow, which was highly developed in certain influential quarters. Arrow-competitive programs in Britain are also mentioned, along with Avro UK designs, which were sometimes fielded in competition with Avro Canada's Arrow. A much more interesting picture of cold war aviation emerges, with Avro Canada and Avro UK seemingly poised, as of 1956, to play a much more dynamic role in it.

By 1958-'59, Avro was proposing the development of a new interceptor capable of excelling the heady performance envisioned for the sub-orbital Arrow 4. Avro's Space Threshold Vehicle (STV) study described a hypersonic delta-winged "lifting body" of mixed-propulsion to serve as a research vehicle to investigate hypersonic speeds and sub-orbital to orbital altitudes. Initial versions were to take off using the main oxygen-kerosene rocket engine and climb to 40,000 feet and refuel. After detaching from the jet-refueller, the STV would throttle the rockets up, perhaps dive slightly to achieve supersonic speed, and light two large auxiliary ramjets. Using a combination of rocket and ramjet power, the STV was to climb to suborbital altitude and hypersonic speed, with its range and altitude being dependent on the thrust and fuel available.

This program was intended to culminate in an *orbital* interceptor/strike-reconnaissance vehicle that would provide its users with the ultimate in 'top cover' and also provide a satellite-deployment capability. Like all the Arrow variants, it was being developed with an eye to launching Avro's P-13 anti-ballistic missile (ABM) weapon, and that would provide some ability to intercept hostile nuclear missiles while they were in space, and to destroy hostile satellites at will. The STV project was intended to provide a protective radius to cover at least half the world, and would take the battle into sub-orbit or even space. It would have also provided a much more credible defense, indeed, *some* defense, against intercontinental ballistic missiles (ICBMs), than what history shows to have followed. Using then-available engines, the STV would not have proved capable of orbital operation and Avro pointed out this fact in their study. Subsequent scramjet (supersonic combustion ramjet) development has been discouraging, to say the least, although finally achieved in the early 21st Century. But the STV was meant to be an airframe in which to try different emerging propulsion technologies. Ducted rockets were considered even for the Arrow 4, and were an intriguing option under consideration. Subsequent disclosure of secret propulsion work undertaken in the United States, along with the STV design study, indicate that Avro may have thought they had an ace in the hole capable of making the STV truly orbital; a nuclear hydrogen-plasma, or nuclear-thermal rocket (NTR) main engine. They mentioned such an engine in the study. Perhaps Avro's own intelligence operations had brought to their awareness certain highly secret developments in the US. In 1956 the US government funded Project Rover under the Atomic Energy Commission, for a nuclear engine, resulting in the KIWI and NRX engines. KIWI 1 was fired in July, 1959 and from it a much larger engine was produced, the Phoebus. In the early 1960s, NASA merged its program to develop a practical flight engine with the Rover program. The NRX engine project emerged from NASA's NERVA and the Atomic Energy Commission's Rover. It began tests in 1964 and culminated in the EX engine, which produced 75,000 pounds thrust (lbt) and was considered for an upper stage of the Saturn V 'moon-rocket'. It seems that reactor cooling and radioactive-shielding problems, related to materials technology, prevented NTRs from being deployed. This and the problems with scramjet technology seem to rule out an STV capable of much over Mach 5 using these systems. Certainly the in-flight re-fuelling capability proposed for the STV was a novel approach, only proposed again recently as a credible and economical means of achieving long-range sub-orbital or orbital flight. Obviously, this kind of technology would have had, and would have today, serious implications on the global diplomatic front.

So equipped industrially, militarily and technologically, the Commonwealth may have adopted a more independent role in the Superpower confrontation, with the probability that many nations, presented with a third option in terms of political, military and economic allegiances, would have aligned themselves with this, presumably somewhat more moderate, power bloc. That possibility would concentrate the minds of powerful members of the intelligence and industrial/financial community, particularly in the most affected business and political communities of the dominant Western power. Indeed, the independent-minded activities of Canadian diplomat Lester Pearson were causing apoplexy among leading elements of the CIA, head of counter-intelligence James Jesus Angleton particularly. "The CIA took great personal offence at Pearson's independent stands in foreign policy, his grain trades with the Soviet Union, his anti-war positions on Vietnam, and especially his friendly stance on Cuba."[1] Avro Canada was offering the Commonwealth an independent space capability, offering profound possibilities in terms of intelligence gathering, communications and military capabilities. Satellites providing signals and communications intelligence (SIGINT and COMINT), deployed independently by the Commonweath could have precluded dependence on US assets, which, it appears, may have better suited the interests of the British and Canadians.

A.V. Roe Canada was not only involved in strategic military-industrial spheres related to aerospace and propulsion. While voices were heard decrying the buy-out of Canada by profiteering American interests, Roy Dobson and the Directors of A.V. Roe Canada Ltd. had rolled back into the company every dollar earned, to build the value of the enterprise and allow a stock issue to Canadians. With a stock issue in 1956 that allowed Canadians to acquire, by 1958, a 43% stake in the company, A.V. Roe Canada set out to diversify and thereby reduce their dependence on government contracts, while at the same time securing their sources of supply for their high-technology ventures. With their acquisition of DOSCO's steel, mining and industrial operations, by 1957 A.V. Roe also assumed responsibility for the design and production of the Royal Canadian Navy's anti-submarine frigates through ownership of Saint John Shipbuilding Ltd.. With Canadian Applied Research (which later merged with de Havilland Canada's Special Projects Division to form SPAR Aerospace; makers of the Shuttle's Canadarm), DOSCO, Algoma Steel, St. John Shipbuilding, Canadian Steel Improvements, Canada Car and others, they were the largest single presence in high-tech and strategic industry and resources in Canada. With DOSCO, the companies' operations included mining, particularly in iron ore and coal, steel production, automotive and rail car production, aircraft and turbine engine design and manufacture, advanced metallurgy, electronics, computation, guidance and telemetry and more. Avro had grown from one man with the world's largest office to become a major player in strategic resources, industry and technology.

Besides the 39 companies of A.V. Roe Canada Ltd., they had formed an alliance with 650 subcontractors, sharing technology to allow them to contribute to the product, thus providing high-tech jobs and the related management infrastructure within Canada. By 1959 A.V. Roe Canada was employing over 25,000 Canadians, Americans and Britons on the Arrow and Iroquois projects, 14,000 of these representing one third of the manpower of A.V. Roe Canada Ltd., by far Canada's largest employer. Those 14,000 Avro and Orenda engineers, technicians, and workers formed the top of the pyramid of the design and production capabilities described herein and this integrated group was lost to Canada after Black Friday. With the brain removed, naturally the rest of the A.V. Roe *corpus* didn't long survive, nor did many of the companies that were its suppliers.

A.V. Roe's XA-20 Bobcat prototype.

Since, by 1956, A.V. Roe Canada was generating 45% of the cash turn-over of the Hawker Siddeley Group, Sir Roy Dobson's Canadian venture had grown to become a significant element of the larger concern.[2] Including A.V. Roe Canada, Hawker Siddeley was a very significant asset of the British Commonwealth in terms of technical and industrial capability for defense and transportation. After all, they were producing much of the hardware of the RAF and RCAF (and, by the late '50s, the RCN with St. John Shipbuilding) and were one of the top 100 valued assemblages of talent and hardware, not to mention financial assets, on the globe. They were a *strategic asset, on the Geo-political level, of the remnants of the British Empire.* They represented the largest cooperating collection of industrial high-tech design and production assets outside the Soviet bloc and United States. By the time the Soviets launched the first ICBM in the fall of 1957, Avro Canada was much more like its parent, comprising significant holdings in iron and coal, shipbuilding, rail equipment, gas turbine engines, buses and trucks, steel, alloys, electronics, license aircraft construction, all weather day or night interceptor design and production, and much, much more.

The XA-92 Bobcat pre-production version. Too many cooks...

But little, and in some cases nothing, has been heard of many of the projects the company had planned for transportation in fields apart from aviation. By the mid 1950s Avro and Orenda had ambitious plans for turbine-powered high-speed monorail transit, turbine powered trucks, flying cars and military saucers, and were studying nuclear energy, electronics, hydrofoil warships, missiles, spaceplanes, satellites, space stations, mobile wheeled drilling platforms and much more. Avro's proposal for an inter-city turbine-powered mono-rail rapid transit system has seen little light. A.V. Roe Canada's program for an amphibious, tracked, armoured personnel carrier that could be airlifted has also received little attention.

The Bobcat program also seems to reveal the problems which can be encountered from having too many chefs contributing to the broth. Canada Car's original private-venture XA-20 design seemed to correspond roughly with what modern armoured vehicle experts think is the optimum design for such a vehicle. However, due to input from the various government and army research and development establishments, efforts to make the vehicle do almost anything resulting in it doing nothing very well, and it too was curtailed by the Diefenbaker Conservatives.

Orenda would eventually develop the OT-4 turbine engine which had been conceived to power some of Avro's transportation concepts. An experimental installation, using an Allison transmission, was made in a White 7000 transport truck. Former Orenda executives note how the program was purchased by American interests and then cancelled-despite evident promise.

Orenda's OT-4 turbine-powered transport. (courtesy AHFC)

Orenda would modify an M-48 Patton tank to accept this powerplant, long before the American Abrams tank would deploy turbine power. Despite evident promise, none of these programs came to fruition. When the Arrow was cancelled design studies into high-speed hydro-foil warships were also underway, with twelve core engineers on this program going on to lead the design team on the Bras d'Or hydrofoil, designed by de Havilland Canada. This ship was eventually powered by an engine similar to the Iroquois and set open-ocean speed records of almost 65 knots. Despite its performance and economy, it too was cancelled in the late-1960s.

The Bras d'Or hydrofoil, fastest open-ocean warship ever. (public archives of Canada)

Avro documents show they were also involved in research and development related to atomic power and electro-gravitics (or anti-gravity), and magneto-hydrodynamics which include electrical and ion-propulsion techniques. When this interest is viewed alongside Avro's flying saucer designs and STV program, a better appreciation of the vision and capabilities of the company emerges. Nuclear electricity generation was also being developed.

Avro and Orenda were also involved in investigating solar and other environmentally-friendly projects. A concept to cheaply derive huge quantities of fresh water from the fogs that engulf the south shores of Newfoundland was studied.

1 Miller, Nathan. FDR: An Intimate History, New York: Doubleday, 1983 p.p. 114, 115
2 See Roberts, John G. Mitsui, Three Centuries of Japanese Business

Chapter 1

A STORMY BACKGROUND

At the end of the Second World War and through most of the 1950s, the development of *Canadian ownership* of domestic industry and resources was a means to strengthen Canadian influence in the world. This was seen as a way for Canada to help prevent major wars by deliberately acting as a "middle power", not as a junior, and all too often silent, partner to either Britain or the United States. This concept has subsequently been abandoned as a national policy, purportedly because it was unrealistic. This belief is arguable however, since Canada did succeed for a time in this role, as shown by Lester Pearson bucking Britain, Israel and France over the Suez Crisis and winning a Nobel Prize in the process–coincidentally occurring near the apogee of A.V. Roe Canada's operations. In hindsight, Canada was probably never so influential and respected as it was between 1945 and the mid-1950s. Perhaps the real reason the 'middle power' policy became unrealistic is because, over time, nearly all the other fundamental trappings of an independent nation had been abandoned–A.V. Roe Canada Ltd. itself, an independent military, technical and industrial policy, and the separate service arms of the Royal Canadian Air Force (RCAF), Royal Canadian Navy (RCN) and Canadian Army all becoming casualties over the years. Subsequently, Canada has also allowed approximately 80% of its strategic resources and strategic industry (and, in fact, most sectors of the Canadian economy) to be purchased by foreign, mainly American, investors. It could be said, then, that Canada has given up economic, and with it, political independence as a result of a change of political philosophy which occurred around the time of the Arrow program and shortly afterward.

This writer feels the true importance of A.V. Roe Canada Ltd. is in terms of the geo-economic and geo-political synergies that accumulated around this company and its British parent and what they meant for the independence and prosperity of Canada, and of the geo-political power of both Canada and the British Commonwealth. Herein is a body of mostly primary source documentation suggesting that Avro, and indeed British defense and high tech industry, were targets of an American drive for global technical, economic, military, and, ultimately, political supremacy.

That A.V. Roe Canada Ltd. was *much* more than just an aviation company is also largely lost on critics and advocates alike. This company was intentionally established by leaders of industry and the government of Canada to provide the nation with a strategic industry to be used to increase the level of technical design and production capability within the Canadian economy. It wasn't just a strategic company in terms of the defensive purposes of its initial products, (not including the Avro Jetliner) which were primarily military in intent, but it was also a strategic company in terms of ensuring that the rest of Canadian industry was able to benefit and develop further through the kinds of technology transfer that A.V. Roe Canada and the British parent company were able to provide. A reflection of this success is the fact that Avro Canada, by the mid-1950s, was providing technology to the British, technology that often wasn't immediately appreciated. Aerospace was known to involve all the major sciences at the world-class level and, rather than select a niche technology, Canada chose aerospace to remain competitive in *all* technologies. Canadian independence in military, economic and ultimately political terms would be enhanced as a result, with a concurrent rise in Canada's influence on the world stage.[3] With the loss of A.V. Roe Canada, as it stood in 1958, Canada literally went from having a high-tech based economy to being dependent on resources—hewers of wood and drawers of water once more.

Missed in the 'studied ignorance' of Canadian professors, historians and politicians, are the most interesting and vital aspects of the story: Cold War Strategy and what interests concerned at the geo-economic and geo-political levels do to wage their own wars and protect their investments. Being able to classify facts and selectively release them, through various means, and thereby to manipulate opinion to arrive at desired outcomes are the tools of the intelligence and influence-peddling trades—and not just with intelligence agencies like the CIA and KGB. The latter two obviously had a direct interest in the Iroquois engine and Arrow interceptor programs since they were widely acknowledged to be the highest technology and performance examples of either in the world. It was their *job* to find out about design and technology to ensure their side didn't lose the Cold War. This was also the job of 'researchers' in competing industry to ensure the profitability of their companies. As such, political, financial and industrial spies were everywhere, and not just at Avro but throughout banking and industry and government in all the industrial nations. That was their job—to protect their employers' interests. To assume these various geo-political and geo-economic interests and their agents weren't at least attempting to do their jobs within Canada is, as a Canadian government source once wrote (while discussing this issue and the fact that his department was *not* releasing pertinent information to the CBC for a documentary on Avro), "somewhat naïve".

An important, related area will also be explored: American media manipulation at home and abroad. Primary sources right from the CIA are sourced.

Unfortunately, there have been yet more books and articles to come out in the years since the publication of this author's first book (*Avro Aircraft & Cold War Aviation)* that continue to ignore the primary-source information on the Avro Jetliner (and thus the true and inspiring story of this charming aircraft), given in Jim Floyd's *The Avro Canada C-102 Jetliner,* my own work, and the recent work of Palmiro Campagna: *Requiem for a Giant.* The negativity inherent in these epistles are, however, now obvious and should be put to rest once and for all. Due to the efforts of various parties associated with Trans Canada Airlines and the government of Canada (especially through C.D. Howe), and others involved in competing aircraft and research agencies in Canada and abroad, many utterly false assumptions still pollute the literature of aviation history regarding the *orders* that were attempted on the Jetliner, (and thus its saleability) and on the reasons given for the stop work order by C.D. Howe. Commentary by some Canadian "experts" (who should really know better) is negative in regards to the reception the Jetliner received in the United States, yet the record *clearly* shows, particularly thanks to document release by the tenacious Palmiro Campagna, that the reasons given by Howe, *and the negative comments of TCA* (recorded in many still-extant documents available in the Public Archives and thus several poorly researched books), are finally proven false, and these matters need to be put to right, for the sake of history, and for the sake of the people who designed, built, flew and experienced this ground-breaking airliner: CF-EJD-X– Avro's Jetliner. We can now show that National Airlines in the USA, the United States Air Force (USAF), and Trans World Airlines (TWA) all tried to buy the C-102 Jetliner, and this author, through personal experience, can attest that everyone he has met who had any direct experience with this aircraft, considers it to be the sweetheart experience of their flying or engineering careers, and this includes some Americans who had been associated with it.

Another crucial item that has remained classified, and which belies Howe's reasons for Jetliner termination, is a Canadian Air Transport Board (ATB) evaluation. Ordered by C.D. Howe's own department, the report showed the Jetliner to be a quantum leap in terms of value for the dollar (two Jetliners being able to replace three prop-liners for example), and offered vastly improved comfort and speed. The ATB report stands in stunning contrast to the TCA and related government reports that have long been available to the public, and which appear to be the foundation of the current 'popular history' of the subject. TCA's conduct in the affair and indeed the conduct of Mr. Howe himself do not stand up to scrutiny by any morally stringent code. As a result, many sources today, who have based their public pronouncements on the Jetliner on these and similar documents, are tragically resistant to simply acknowledging their misconceptions, and the reasons for them, and giving Avro's engineers and designers their due. After all, plenty of primary source evidence exists to support the idea that the Jetliner, allowed access to by potential suitors, would have become one of, if not *the,* best-selling commercial aircraft in history.

Another example of freshly declassified government documentation has added a further dimension to the decision by Canada to adopt the Lockheed F-104G Starfighter as the RCAF contribution to the NATO standing forces in Europe. Firstly, this decision was based on an American inspired decision by Canada to abandon its former defensive role in Europe, specialising in all-weather and night interception, in favour of an offensive low-level strike-reconnaissance role. It becomes clear that Minister of National Defense (MND) George Pearkes made the unilateral decision, in cooperation with the Chairman of the Chiefs of Staff Committee, (CCSC) Canadian Army General Charles Foulkes, to cancel the Arrow interceptor and Iroquois engine programs, *and to also deny Avro any further contracts* (such as for the Starfighter)—in favour of policies promoted by the US government. (CIA intelligence was a major factor in key decisions relating to all of these air defense programs.) In fact Avro's bid on the Starfighter license-production contract was several million dollars lower than the successful bidder, Canadair. Cabinet minutes show the contorted logic and methods used to deny Avro this contract. Worse, it is shown that the government of Canada made it its official policy to kill Avro Aircraft

Canada Ltd.—presumably because the company was British aligned and therefore not suitable for a US-proposed free-trade pact on armaments (Defense Production Sharing or DPS), while Canadair, which was then 100% US owned, was.

All of Foulkes' and Pearkes' decisions were 100% in alignment with the advice of US Secretary of State John Foster Dulles and US Secretary of Defense Neil McElroy (a former CEO of Proctor & Gamble). It emerges that the intelligence on which most of the Canadian defense policies were based largely came from the CIA, which was run by John Foster's brother, Allen Dulles. It emerges that a great many promises were made to certain Canadian politicians, particularly Prime Minister John Diefenbaker and MND Pearkes, if Canada cancelled the Arrow. One of these involves the DPS agreement, which was a US-Canada free trade agreement on defense products. Contrary to American sales pitches, this was a total failure for Canada. The government of Canada agreed, at American behest, to further integrate the military, and to also integrate defense industries with the Americans. It now appears abundantly clear that Diefenbaker's subsequent and decided souring on the Americans was due to the fact that the United States *reneged* on many of the promises made to offset the sacrifice of the Arrow, *and ultimately of Avro,* along with the total failure of DPS.

The critics like to point out that the cancellation of the Arrow was justified merely because there were comparable American aircraft available for a fraction of the price. The facts suggest otherwise. There were no comparable aircraft or engines in the world compared to the Avro Jetliner, the Arrow or the Iroquois engine. The Arrow also proves to have been cheaper than the smaller and significantly less capable American alternatives. When the facts are empirically examined, Avro's products are shown to have been considerably cheaper, for both development and production, than *inferior* foreign offerings. The Canadian 'experts' have, inexplicably, completely ignored the balance of payments problem inherent in buying foreign (mainly American) product and kissing those dollars goodbye. They have ignored the economic and political implications of exporting millions of Canadian dollars and thousands of Canadian *high-tech* jobs to the United States. They have ignored the strategic implications of being dependent on another country for technology, intelligence and defensive equipment (and thus, to greater or lesser extents, military, economic and political policy). They have ignored the implications of being *dependent,* even subservient, period. Worse, they have ridiculed those who *have* taken those implications to heart. Included in those ridiculed are men such as Fred Smye, James C. Floyd, Crawford Gordon Jr., author Palmiro Campagna and others. This book is an attempt to document those issues in such a scholarly manner that even the most reticent critics will be denied the intellectual 'wiggle room' to avoid truths which should by now be obvious.

The following reasons, given for cancellation by the decision's supporters, are examined:

a) Canada just couldn't afford the Arrow. (The only possible basis for this argument is that there existed, in the United States, better aircraft for the money–which there weren't.)

b) Manned fighter aircraft like the Arrow were obsolete compared to defensive missiles which were better or at least as effective, and vastly cheaper. (It emerges in this book that *not one* serving military air defense expert was saying this at the time. History also shows the fallacy of this idea through the reality of interceptors and fighters still being designed and produced by the leading industrial nations.)

c) The role of the manned interceptor was rendered superfluous because the threat had changed from that of manned bombers with nuclear payloads to nuclear-tipped ICBMs. (Again, not one serving air defense expert said that at the time, and history proves this assumption wrong through continued military aircraft design and production.)

d) Even if there was a threat, it was cheaper (and thus better) to allow USAF weapons onto Canadian territory for the defense of North America. (This ignores the fact that any country that is defended by another becomes the defender's 'protectorate', and loses its sovereignty.)

e) Canada is too small, too poor, too destitute in terms of the kinds of minds required, to compete in such a technically all-embracing field. (How then, can Sweden, with a third of Canada's population and comparatively few natural resources have its own aerospace *and* automotive industries?)

All of these 'red herrings' will be debunked herein through primary source documents and testimony of the people involved. If the above reasons are, then, invalid, logic suggests there must have been other reasons. These will also be suggested, using primary source documentation, within.

Regarding the Arrow decision making process in particular, the reader will be guided through the pertinent primary source materials in a 'play by play' on what can only be characterised as petty, faithless, dishonest and, indeed, vindictive behaviour by the very leaders involved in the cancellation of the aircraft and destruction of the company. Herein is evidence that shows that the government of Canada made it national policy to see Avro Aircraft Canada Limited fail. It is also shown that they probably didn't believe their own excuses, and knew full well that they were sacrificing a measure of Canadian independence in the process. So why did they do it? Because they thought they could classify the evidence and, by hiding the truth, remain in power. Saving face has, unfortunately, often been the overriding factor in the decision making processes of various levels of government in Canada. They are quite prepared to 'sell out' their constituents if it means they can retain the diminished levers of power (and perhaps particularly prestige) in their grasp. But this is nothing new, particularly in the business and political communities. Thousands of Canadians in business, commerce, and the media, work to secure advantage over Canadian competitors for their American head offices on a daily basis.

Your scribe believes, however, that the most valuable aspect of this book is pointing out *why* particular American interests *wanted* not just the Arrow and Jetliner dead, and the answer is most relevant to the current global situation. A situation where the United States government, serving the same *particular interests*, invents pretexts to invade a resource-rich country, completely in violation of the international laws and the standards the US helped to enforce at Nuremberg during the Nazi war crimes trials.

Also discussed are antecedents and precedents in terms of American actions against even its allies throughout the 20th century. For example, the American National Security Agency (NSA), by far the largest and most technically-advanced intelligence agency in the world, receives intelligence from installations in Canada that are manned by Canadians and subsidised by Canadian tax dollars, while the agency is well known to spy on friends and foes alike, most definitely including Canadians and Britons. They are well known to do so for *commercial* reasons where bids, particularly for aircraft, are undercut by US manufacturers through the gathered intelligence. American industry has been well served by US government intelligence in technical matters as well. The admitted job of the USAF and US Army foreign intelligence branches is to acquire foreign military technology—with the target countries by no means being limited to those that display a hostile political attitude towards the United States.

> "…more and more emphasis is now placed on economic intelligence. NSA was primarily oriented toward diplomatic traffic down through the years, said a more than thirty-year veteran of the Agency. "The sudden switch to economic traffic was a Johnny-come-lately because of the drying up of the diplomatic sources [caused by] higher [capability cryptographic] machine systems. So in later years we've gone to exploiting the economic, commercial end."[4]

In fact, the parties on the American side involved in bi-lateral (in fact global) defense issues relating to Avro were the principle members of the US Planning Coordination Group—a tiny triumvirate in Washington directing policies of the NSA, CIA and military intelligence branches—with their thousands of agents. The gentlemen in these positions have, historically, also been linked to what Eisenhower sagely termed, during his alarmist farewell address, the "Military-Industrial Complex". One must wonder about the influence and tactics of those powers considering that "Ike" was no dove, having been, among other things, Supreme Commander of the Allied Forces in Europe from D-Day to VE-Day.

Ike has also been shown to have participated in, and/or approved, most of the more questionable policy decisions and practices of the United States during his administration—one of those having been sanctioning the dismemberment of Viet Nam into North and South along with the installation of a US-friendly puppet government in the latter. His bogus "Open Skies" offer to the Soviets, whereby they could "end the Cold War", was also proposed in bad faith according to excellent sources, and allowed the US negotiators to withdraw virtually all the arms limitation proposals they had made in the preceding years. In fact Open Skies was designed expressly for that purpose, since Khrushchev had just agreed to all of those proposals as part of his de-Stalinisation program, and seemed to very much mean business. Of course, had the US taken the Soviets up on their disarmament offers, defense spending and the need for US bases worldwide, not to mention integration of western defenses with US systems, would have been greatly reduced. Unburdened by the need to compete with the West in military spending, the Soviet Union would have had a much better chance of improving the standard of living of its citizens. Open Skies, it might be noted, was formulated by a member of the Planning Coordination Group: Nelson Rockefeller. Of course, the Rockefeller banking, industrial and oil empire has been involved in many of America's international adventures, especially those that made money for their banks (Chase and Citi) and oil companies (Exxon-Mobil and the host of affiliates), and other major industries. Nelson in particular led the US charge in Central and South America to buy up resources and industry,[5] a practice that was pursued with such zeal and cunning that it resulted in a general backlash and many revolutions in this part of the world—including Castro's in Cuba. Other right-wing revolutions were also facilitated by these same so-called 'Yankee-Capitalist' powers, with the assistance of the US government's State Department and intelligence community—the Chilean military coup of the fascist General Augusto Pinochet being a popular example. This demonstrates a traditional support on the part of the US Executive, State Department, Department of Defense and intelligence community for American industry.

Which leads one to wonder what kind of forces have been applied to Canada over the years in order to secure American access to raw-materials, energy, water and industry. Most Canadians, or so the corporate media would have us believe, are all for Free Trade and closer ties with the United States. They seem to display a vast innocence and very naïve view of American intentions, tactics and actual manipulation of political events in foreign countries, *particularly their own.* But then, the truth of many American adventures and pressure campaigns has been well concealed from the general public—a public that is encouraged to concentrate on their own problems and goals. Due to this 'benign neglect', as the Mulroney Conservatives (who brought Canada Free Trade) termed and exploited it, the Canadian economy is about 80% owned by Americans. Hardly any Canadians seem to know this, which is surely a testament to where the heart of Canada's major corporate media lies—where the money is. It is unlikely that the corporate owners of Canadian corporate media are going to criticize these policies because, for one thing, they naively think that they have the financial might to compete and greatly enrich themselves through unfettered access to the American market. They are doubly unlikely to criticise the United States or accurately describe the results of Free Trade because if 80% of the economy is US-owned, then about 80% of their advertising revenue will also be American based. You don't bite the hand that feeds you. Even the Canadian Broadcasting Corporation (CBC), which is publicly-owned, relies on corporate advertisers for a good portion of its revenue. Furthermore, the CBC, faced with huge cuts in government funding during the implementation of Free Trade under both the Mulroney Conservatives and Chretien/Martin Liberals, is likewise unlikely to bite the government hand that feeds it, and every government since Mulroney's has been pro-free trade. (Today the CBC is in process of losing one of their last bastions, Hockey Night in Canada, due to the policies of another Conservative government.) In fact, after some of the Arrow files were declassified by the exiting Liberals in 1979 (after the traditional 30 years had expired), Mulroney immediately had them reclassified upon taking office. He apparently feared a nationalist backlash (or perhaps a backlash against the Conservative Party?) had the truth behind the Arrow story been revealed. Perhaps that in itself is adequate proof that there was something to hide and that those who, despite the annoyances of reality and history, insist that closer ties with the United States, (even 'deep integration', customs union, a common currency or annexation), is the best option for Canada.

It is surely a sign of the core strength of the Canadian economy that Canadians are doing as well as they are considering the fact that if you don't own it, you can't make anything from selling it, and that if you have Free Trade, you cannot even tax it when it leaves the country. This strength is underlined when one considers that most Western nations, including the United States, Britain, France and Germany, have less than 10% of their economies in the hands of non-resident owners. Yes, Europe has a Free Trade agreement through the European Union, but it, unlike the North American Free Trade Agreement, does not allow unlimited capital investment (buy-out of businesses and resources) from outside their borders. As former Deputy Prime Minister and MND Paul Hellyer notes, the FTA, NAFTA and other "free trade" agreements aren't about free trade in goods and services but really are Trojan horses meant to secure legalised and unrestricted capital investment by dominant (mainly

American) investors in resources, industry and infrastructure in foreign lands. Even if European trade agreements included unrestricted capital investment across their borders, the nations of Europe are much more evenly matched than Canada and the United States, in which case the US outweighs Canada by about ten to one. A pertinent question the neo-conservatives seem incapable of asking is this: can a nation one tenth the size of its partner ever possibly hope to compete financially, or to be treated equally, by its much larger 'partner'? As Canadian history clearly shows, only legislation can possibly redress the imbalance, and even then it is an uphill battle.

In the 1950s however, Crawford Gordon Jr., while at the helm of A.V. Roe Canada Ltd., considered it his duty to the Commonwealth and even the free world to secure Avro's (and Canada's) sources of supply. He embarked on what could only be termed a crusade to repatriate ownership of strategic resources and industry, and not just from American ownership—although in a speech to the Canadian Club in New York Gordon described American investment and industrial strategies as 'selfish'. He appears to have been referring to the US preference for direct capital investment (i.e. buy out) as opposed to operating loans. When it appeared that the Canadian industrial giant Dosco (with steel, shipbuilding and mining operations) was going to be purchased by German steel concerns, Phoenix Rheinrohr and Mannesmann International, Sir Roy Dobson ordered Crawford Gordon to "get cracking" to prevent this. German steel cartels (in which the American Bush and Harriman clans were financially involved) were an integral part of the Nazi war machine, and certainly used concentration camp labour. In part due to the Dosco merger (Dosco was Canada's largest employer at the time) by 1957 A.V. Roe Canada Ltd. was the largest employer in Canada and the third highest capitalised corporation in the land. It was also one of the top 100 corporations on the planet and one of the top 80 in North America.[6] Today, with the flattening of Nortel and other buy-outs, not a single top-200 corporation remains Canadian owned. In the 1980's there were six of them.

So, while this book focuses on the Avro story and its implications for North American air defense, it has several subplots relating to intelligence, economics and *real* history. In all cases the author has tried to quote from the primary sources themselves, including government documents, politicians, industrialists, intelligence agents and economic experts from several nations. In the process a solid body of evidence emerges to suggest that those who control the American economy, and thus its government, aren't nearly as altruistic as some of the media, many professors (perhaps dependent on endowments from US corporations), and political parties (dependent on a sympathetic media and donations from US corporations) would have us believe. There is a price to be paid when a country gives up ownership and control of its economy, and, by extension, political apparatus. Ironically, a similar predicament may be facing the United States in the years ahead.

But, in 1957, the Canadian dollar peaked at 1.11 U.S..

3 For a good examination of this concept, see MGen E.L.M. Burns' book, Canada in the Age of the Superpowers

4 Bamford, James. The Puzzle Palace, Inside the National Security Agency, New York: Penguin Books, 1983, p. 495

5 Open Skies information from Collier & Horowitz's authoritative, The Rockefellers, An American Dynasty

6 Stewart, Greig: Shutting Down the National Dream: A.V. Roe and the Tragedy of the Avro Arrow. Scarborough: McGraw-Hill Ryerson Ltd., 1988

Chapter 2

WHY A NATIONAL MILITARY INDUSTRIAL COMPLEX?

Many moral people dismiss any promotion of the A.V. Roe Canada story because, to their minds, they were another groping corporation involved in the international arms trade. Such suspicion of global cartels and other concentrations of money and power is not unwarranted, considering the history. In today's corporate, media and political culture, free trade and unrestricted global Capitalism are the accepted frames of reference. Most discussions of why Avro Canada was formed concentrate on the positive aspects; Canada wanted to compete as a world class economy and in high technology. Missing from the politically-corrected lexicon of today's corporate media are references to the old arms and banking cartels and their influence on many geo-political events, including wars, revolutions, coups and engineering of "democratic" elections. The history of the last half of the 19th Century and all of the 20th are replete with examples of sometimes sinister manipulations of events by global high-Capitalists—yet are absent from mainstream North American political and economic debate. Due to a lack of public exposure to some of these bona-fide conspiracies, this book will present examples as background for the readers' consideration. This is intended to help the reader decide if Canada was better off with, or without, A.V. Roe Canada Ltd., and also decide if the company was a good corporate citizen or not. It is also intended to provoke thought on just how truly democratic our nations are...or aren't.

The experiences of Franklin Delano Roosevelt, as Assistant Secretary of the Navy in WW I, as Governor of New York State, and as President of the United States are illuminating. Throughout his career he was consistently bumping heads with wealthy industrialists and financiers who were circumventing or manipulating the policies of the government. During World War I Roosevelt had worked under Secretary of the Navy Joseph Daniels in Woodrow Wilson's administration. "...[Daniels] tangled with the three steel companies—Carnegie, Midvale and Bethelehem—that had a monopoly on the production of armour plate for the Navy. In August 1913, contracts were advertised for armour for the battleship *Arizona*, and all three firms submitted identical bids... Upon learning that Bethlehem Steel habitually sold armour plate abroad at prices considerably lower than those charged to the U.S. Navy, Daniels angrily rejected the bids. [They were replaced by three more identical bids.] ...Daniels instructed Roosevelt to open negotiations with a British steel company...Enforced competitive bidding reduced the cost of the Arizona's armour by $1.1 million..."[7] A book on the vast Mitsui industrial cartel, Japan's largest commercial entity at the time of WW II, indicates that the cartel for armour plate didn't stop in the United States but included British and Japanese firms as well.[8]

Post-war, while FDR was President, another example of corporate-monopolistic greed presented itself: "Impressed by the evidence gathered by the Nye Committee, indicating that Wall Street and the munitions makers had helped propel the United States into World War... Angered by the high price [for explosives] charged by the American company that monopolized the importation of nitrates...[FDR] bypassed the State Department and upon his own authority entered into a contract with the Chilean government for five million pounds of nitrate."[9] The American company in question was almost certainly DuPont, which had faced an anti-trust suit in 1911. It wouldn't be the last time DuPont was charged with anti-trust violations. A few comments from the Nye Committee report describes the amoral activities of many large American companies, including Electric Boat Ltd., which absorbed Canadair in 1947—with C.D. Howe's support due to his professed belief that the company would bring Canada technology and contracts from the American parent corporation. (As the Diefenbaker Conservatives noted during the Arrow cancellation debates, the parent brought no contracts to Canadair.)

> "The committee finds...that there is no record of any munitions company aiding any proposals for limitation of armaments, but that, on the contrary, there is a record of their active opposition by some to almost all such proposals...and of violation of such controls whenever established, and of rich profiting whenever such proposals failed.
>
> "Following the peaceful settlement of the Tacna-Arica dispute between Peru and Chile, L.Y. Spear, vice president of Electric Boat Co. (which supplied submarines to Peru) wrote to

Commander C.W. Craven of Vickers-Armstrong (which supplied material to Chile): 'It is too bad that the pernicious activities of our State Department have put the brake on armament orders from Peru by forcing resumption of formal diplomatic relations with Chile.'" A later section of the report mentions "from official documents which it has not entered into the record, that the sales of munitions to certain South American nations in excess of their normal capacity to pay, was one of the causes for the defaults on certain South American bonds; and that the sales of the munitions was, in effect, financed by the American bond purchasers, and the loss was borne by the same people."[10]

[Discussing a Geneva arms limitation agreement of 1925:] "State Department documents not entered into the record, give credit to the American delegation to the Geneva Conference for weakening the proposed draft in two important respects [after consulting with the du Ponts and other arms makers. Allen Welsh Dulles was a member of the US delegation in 1925 and his papers always pleaded for a relaxation of the arms limitation elements of the Treaty of Versailles.[11]]. The du Pont representatives…later remarked of the final draft of the convention regarding the arms traffic signed at Geneva in 1925: 'There will be some few inconveniences to the manufacture of munitions in their export trade, but in the main they will not be hampered materially."

[The tactic of playing off one side against the other, while selling both arms, is also described:] "In China the munitions companies report that there was a certain amount of feeling between the Central [Nanking] Government and the Canton Government. The Boeing agent was able to sell 10 planes to the Canton Government. Referring to the Nanking (recognized) Government, he wrote: "Their anger at us in selling airplanes to the Cantonese is more than offset by the fact that the Cantonese have gotten ahead of them and will have better equipment than they will have. In other words, the Canton sale is quite a stimulant to the sale up here [in Nanking]." Boeing replied to their agent: '…it is to our advantage to successfully conclude the business if for no other reason but for the effect it would have on the Nanking Government."[12]

At that point in time, the Canton (Wuhan) government consisted of a Soviet supported hard-communist faction split from Chiang Kai-Shek's campaigning Koumintang government army—officially located in Nanking. Some say that Western activities to profit from the division and wars in China convinced Stalin of the West's duplicity, and affected his policies for the worse. Be that as it may, Boeing was certainly intent on cashing in on the conflict, and hoped to escalate it.

The Nye report also discussed the effects of the munitions companies on the policies of the government of the United States and found "that the munitions companies have secured the active support of the War, Navy, Commerce, and even State Departments [the CIA, NSA, etc. did not exist then] in their sales abroad, even when the material was to be produced in England or Italy."[13] John Foster Dulles was directly involved in DuPont's questionable dealings in the 1920s—deals that were "winked at" by the State Department.[14]

Perhaps worst of all, certain munitions and chemical companies had assisted future belligerents arm themselves to fight their home countries—and had profited from *both sides* in the process. Several US aviation companies had helped arm Japan for their conquest of Manchuria. It found that "the international commercial interests of such large organizations as du Pont and Imperial Chemical Industries [the British Empire part of the global Nobel interests] may precede in the minds of those companies the importance of national policy… [S]uch considerations of commercial interest were apparently foremost in the [illegal] rearming of Germany beginning in 1924, and in the sale of a process [for] cheaper explosives in Japan in 1932, shortly after Secretary of State Stimson had [expressed] his disapproval of this Nation for…military activities in Manchuokuo [Manchuria]."[15]

It noted that "the licensing of American inventions to allied companies in foreign nations is bound to involve in some form the recurrence of experiences similar to those in the last war in which Electric Boat Co. patents were used in German submarines and aided them in the destruction of American lives, and ships, and that in peacetime the licensing involves the manufacture abroad, at lower costs, of

American material."[16] It would appear that the Nye Committee was cognisant of the possibility of global corporations exporting domestic technology to another land for manufacture, thus providing no benefit to the country of origin—in this case the United States—but providing a possible threat instead.

In Canada, Nobel's ICI and DuPont had established something of an explosives and chemical monopoly. In an arrangement where DuPont was reserved the American market, ICI the British Empire, and combined cartel operations, such as Canadian Industries Limited (CIL) in Canada and Duperial in South America, to share the rest of the available world market. It is interesting that ICI itself had been formed partly because of the formation of the I.G. Farben cartel, consisting of many of the German industries involved in explosives and chemicals in WW I. It was interrelations on the part of leading British and American firms with a very clearly Nazi I.G. Farben after 1933 that drew the attention of a Canadian industrialist living in Britain named William Samuel Stephenson. Actually, he'd been following the re-establishment of militarist industrial power in Germany during her not-very-secret illegal re-armament of the 1920s—long before Hitler took power in 1933.

Ironically, it was this same Canadian, operating from New York's financial district under the code-name INTREPID, who would lead the effort to expose the worst American financial and industrial collaboration with not just German industry, but apparently with Nazi political goals as well. DuPont Canada's history shows that, in Canada, CIL management (under Arthur Purvis, from England and ICI) not only accepted, but suggested that the government set up a nationalised explosives industry under CIL technical management to prevent any questioning of CIL's allegiances during the coming conflict. Defense Industries Limited was duly established in Canada in 1938 to produce explosives and other munitions—nevertheless, profits for CIL's American and British owners were maintained at their healthy level of 1938 throughout the war. While ICI and CIL had dabbled in trying to get some I.G. Farben patents, (particularly for dyestuffs) their involvement with the Nazi company appears to have been innocent. The same cannot be said for du Pont involvement in Germany, or that of General Motors, then over one-third owned by the du Ponts.

In fact, wealthy capitalists were among the least willing to abandon investment and collaboration with Nazi Germany. Their sentiments were expressed by the privately-funded "America First" movement, which proclaimed sympathy with mothers and their sons, but really fronted rather more selfish motives on the part of some of its leading sponsors: industrialists and financiers. John Foster Dulles was known to be friendly and share views with some prominent "America Firsters" like Charles Lindbergh, but denied giving financial support. While heading the Sullivan Cromwell law firm, he was known, even to his supporters, to have persistently collaborated with Nazi industry and finance long after it became unfashionable to do so. According to a biography of the Dulleses, during the 1930s the Sullivan Cromwell firm represented about 70% of German municipal governments and handled a large proportion of American industrial and financial investment in Nazi Germany. Even the Bush family is implicated in reciprocal investments involving Brown Brothers-Harriman and the Union Bank in the United States, and various Nazi industrial cartels—some of whom employed slave labour during Hitler's reign.

Len Deighton describes one motive guiding some Western capitalists' tolerance and assistance to Hitler. "The view that Nazi Germany—whatever its faults— had to be supported because of the 'protection' it provided against the spread of Russian Communism was echoed by the rich and powerful everywhere."[17]

What distinguishes this group politically is that it prefers that all economic and political power be entrusted to a wealthy ruling elite—i.e.; the owners of the economy. This is, of course, fairly far to the political right. Unfortunately too often the ultimate result is fascism: State Capitalism. It is also fairly obvious that the United States has been a leading champion of pure, unbridled capitalism since early in the 20th Century.

Canadians working in C.D. Howe's Munitions and Supply empire during WW II also worked intimately with many of the leading American industrial and financial powers. Through Sir William Stephenson's (INTREPID's) work as a spymaster in New York, particularly in the financial district, they also knew about the corporate entanglement of many American (and even some British) concerns with the Nazi I.G. Farben cartel, and the difficulties this presented to make America understand the threat and respond to it. The Nazi-I.G. Farben campaign of industrial integration and political, financial and technological pressure, including in the corporate media, demonstrated the danger to democracy of one of the pillars of today's "free trade" movement: unrestricted foreign capital investment in strategic industries, resources and the media. In 1941 at Camp X in Canada a magazine was published describing some of the entanglements of American financiers and industrialists with Nazi Germany. The book *A Man Called INTREPID,* mentions this magazine being smuggled across lake Ontario and onto the newsstands of America. Also described is how Rockefeller agents were immediately dispersed to buy up every copy of the magazine *Sequel to the Apocalypse.* Within this magazine is described the involvement of William S. Farish, then head of Standard Oil (today Exxon and its host of affilates including Canada's Imperial Oil) with supplying the Nazis with petroleum. William Stamps Farish III is today described as George W. Bush's financial angel while his grandfather, Prescott Bush, is well known to have been involved in a Nazi steel cartel that used concentration camp slave labour. As a result some of their assets were seized early in America's involvement in WW II under the Trading with the Enemy Act.

This relates to the previously unspoken "dark side" as to why A.V. Roe Canada was invited to develop, for Canada, a strategic industry capable of providing Canada with its primary weapons of defense. This had two aspects: the provision of the actual weapons, plus the industrial and design infrastructure and patent access, to reduce dependence on foreign suppliers with their own geo-political and financial agendas. Canada had also witnessed the constant expansion of American ownership in Canada, and the entanglement of such huge American corporations as Standard Oil (Exxon, Mobil, Imperial, Esso and a host of others) and Ford Motor Company in the Nazi war effort. Focke Wulf FW-190 fighters used American Pratt & Whitney engines built by BMW under license. Boeing had fomented instability in China for fighter sales. Vickers in England had been involved in geo-political manipulations in the past in efforts to sell machine guns and other armaments. A.V. Roe in England, and Hawker Siddeley generally, appeared to be loyal to the ideals of the British Empire, including the values of the enlightenment and concepts of respect for the individual and duty of the state to provide for the general welfare, not just that of the rich. But then, A.V. Roe had been started by people who worked with their hands, not with other peoples' money.

7 Miller, Nathan. FDR: An Intimate History, New York: Doubleday, 1983 p.p. 114, 115
8 See Roberts, John G. Mitsui, Three Centuries of Japanese Business
9 Miller, FDR, footnote, p. 125
10 Nye Committee Report, section V. para. 8
11Mosley, Leonard: Dulles: A Biography of Eleanor, Allen, and John Foster Dulles and Their Family Network New York: The Dial Press, 1978 p.p. 71-72
12 Nye Committee Report, section V. paras. 16-18
13 Nye Committee Report, section V. para. 2
14 Mosley, Leonard: Dulles, p.92
15 Nye Committee Report, section VI. para. 4
16 Nye Committee Report, section VI, para 5
17 Deighton, Len. Blood Tears and Folly, An objective look at World War II. 2nd Edition. London: Pimlico, 1995 p.142

Chapter 3

AVRO CANADA COMPANY ORIGINS

Alliot Verdon Roe was the first Englishmen to design and fly his own airplane. He'd actually lived in Canada for a couple of years as a teenager before returning to Britain to become a railroad apprentice. He got tired of this and joined the Merchant Marine and began to sail the seven seas. One day, plowing through the ocean far from land, Roe became fascinated watching an Albatross dancing in the air behind his ship seeking a meal churned up by the ship's wake. Thus was Roe smitten by the idea of building and flying a heavier-than-air flying machine.

Alliot Verdon Roe

In 1907 Roe and two hundred other contestants entered a London model airplane competition with Roe being judged the victor. He used the £75 prize (a not insignificant sum in those days) to build a full size version of his model and then "flew" it on 8 June, 1908 at the Brooklands race track in England[18]. By 1910 the company was registered as A.V. Roe and Company Ltd. with the short name of Avro. The company went on to produce the famous Avro 504 for both operations and training in WW I. Canada kept using them until 1929 at its only air base for many years, Camp Borden, and elsewhere they served as *ab initio* trainers until WW II.[19]

Roe wrote a letter to the London Times urging Britons to take a more active interest in aviation. The Times published his letter with the following disclaimer:

"It is not to be supposed that we in any way adopt the writer's estimate of his undertaking, being of the opinion, that all attempts at artificial aviation on the basis he describes are not only dangerous to human life, but foredoomed to failure." So goes the pioneering spirit of the conservative establishment.

In the early 1920s Thomas Sopwith's aircraft company was liquidated despite so much fame and production in World War I. Sopwith Aircraft had produced many of the classic British fighters of the Great War, including the Sopwith Dolphin, Triplane (which Fokker emulated with his Dr.1), Snipe, Pup and the most notable of all, the famous Camel. Sir Thomas, undaunted by the financial collapse, immediately formed a new company and named it H.G. Hawker Engineering (and later Hawker Aircraft) after his late and legendary test pilot: Harry G. Hawker. The Australian Hawker had helped Sopwith improve his designs through his scientific test flying and was the major proponent of the Camel–showing what that plane could do in the hands of a capable and daring pilot. British Empire pilots showed what it could do in combat. More enemy aircraft were destroyed by the Camel than by any other allied fighter.

A 1936 Armstrong Siddeley coupe—offering twelve horsepower.

John Davenport Siddeley had been a cycle racer and designer who went to work for a bicycle manufacturer before switching to automotive pursuits. After starting a dealership selling French cars, he started Siddeley Autocar Company in 1902. By 1905 the enterprising Siddeley had a dozen models for sale, when Wolseley Motors bought the company. Siddeley remained as general manager, soon changing the name to Wolseley Siddeley. He resigned in 1909 to manage the Deasy Motor Company, changing its name, in 1912, to Siddeley Deasy. During the war the company was awarded a contract to produce the BHP, or Beardmore engine for British aircraft, along with ambulances, and, in the process, grew to employ 5,000 people. (The Beardmore engine was based on a captured German engine.) After the war, Siddeley Deasy and Armstrong Whitworth merged to form Armstrong Siddeley Motors. By the 1920s this company was involved in aero engine design and manufacture. In 1935 Avro Aircraft, Hawker Aircraft, Armstrong Whitworth, Armstrong Siddeley and Gloucester (later shortened to Gloster) Aircraft decided to pool their engineering and financial resources and amalgamated into the Hawker Siddeley Group—a real presence in British high-technology and heavy industry. Another factor in the consolidation was the growing challenge from German aerospace progress and expansion under the support and encouragement of the Nazi government. Ten years later, the Hawker Siddeley Group was one of the largest industrial alliances in the world, and was the world's leading manufacturer of aircraft. In fact for a time they were known as the General Motors of aviation.

Roy Hardy Dobson was born in Northern England in the Yorkshire "moors" area and joined A.V. Roe Ltd. in Manchester England at the age of 14, as a mechanic. He quickly became an engineer and was involved in all the WW I and 1920s Avro designs—working with Roy Chadwick, Avro's chief designer. By 1930 Dobson was Works Manager, overseeing all the work that went into physically building Chadwick's designs. When Avro joined Hawker Siddeley in 1935, Alliot Verdon Roe decided to leave his own company, (he joined Saunders, making Saunders Roe, aka SARO) and Dobson was made Managing Director. In 1958 he became Managing Director of the entire Hawker Siddeley Group, with his Canadian creation, A.V. Roe Canada Ltd., then providing 45% of the receipts of the entire group. The entire Group was already severely diminished by the loss of the Avro 730 Mach 3 strike-recce aircraft, the 720 jet/rocket interceptor, the CF-105 Arrow, the contract for the "Concorde" SST, the STOL/VTOL heavy-lift transport, the supersonic Harrier, and the TSR.2 contracts, by the time of Dobson's death in 1967. One would say not due to Dobson's management, but by deluded and misled British and Canadian governments. In 1977 Hawker Siddeley merged with British Aircraft Corporation thereby forming British Aerospace.

Sir Roy Dobson on a visit to Avro Canada.

By 1945 Dobson knew a great deal about airplanes and people, and had ideas on how to build both. (Dobson was a Freemason, and one of the aims of this esoteric group is an ongoing effort at self-improvement and a facilitation of that in others.[20] In fact, both the Avro and A.V. Roe logos and corporate colours are highly Masonic.) He was also fair-minded and known to have a not altogether inaccessible 'soft spot' and would do anything for someone who had earned his trust. Dobson was head of Avro in Britain and was also on the board of directors of Hawker Siddeley. Canada's performance in building his company's famous Lancaster heavy bomber had captured Dobson's imagination. The realities of an essentially bankrupt and exhausted Britain didn't escape him either. He knew that the United States had made a fortune during the Second World War, and therefore comprised most of the global market for aircraft, in the short term at least.

In Britain, the situation was much worse. Due to a chronic shortage of funds, which had been exacerbated by the expenses of WW II, the British government decided to try to adapt wartime aircraft to the commercial market for the short term, and concentrate their money on one major project, the enormous Bristol Brabazon. The Brabazon was a two-deck 12-piston-engined behemoth that was cancelled as something of an anachronism. It was a major setback for the airframe division of Bristol (which also produced aero-engines), and for the villagers of Charlton, which was flattened to make way for its enormous runway. It was also a setback for the whole British industry, with stop-gap aircraft like the Avro adaptations proving the only reliable domestic airliners—until the Vickers Viscount entered service in 1955.

The Avro Lancastrian, York, and Tudor were all stop-gap transports based, more or less, on the Lancaster and/or Lincoln bomber and Rolls-Royce Merlin engine. All of these designs were produced under Avro Chief Designer; Roy Chadwick, and most involved Stuart Davies, Jim Floyd, and later, Bob Lindley, in the Special Security Design Office—also known as Avro's "holy of holies", with Edgar Atkin from Boulton Paul aircraft joining in a senior position for the York project. Being adaptations of wartime designs they were 'tail-draggers'; nose-gear aircraft were preferred by civil airlines due to improved passenger comfort and pilot visibility. The unpressurised Lancastrian and York also had very narrow, rectangular fuselages, that greatly limited their passenger capacity.

Avro was also developing the Tudor airliner, which used a modern circular fuselage of good capacity but still employed the Lincoln wing and Merlin engines, while also retaining the taildragger configuration. With the failure of the Brabazon, Avro's hopes for the Tudor rose. It would be Britain's first pressurised airliner. Unfortunately, it would have a bad reputation for crashes, with a few mysterious losses over the Bermuda Triangle and other places, plus a take-off crash at Avro where Chadwick was killed, all making the headlines. Rather antiquated features compared to the American competition all made for a lack-lustre sales performance.

Jim Floyd circa 1950 at Avro Canada.

James Charles (J.C. or Jim) Floyd had joined the Avro company in 1930, just after turning sixteen, on a special apprenticeship scheme Dobson had introduced.[21] Bob Lindley joined the same scheme later, at around the same age. After a short lay-off brought on by the Great Depression, Floyd was promoted into the Special Security Design Office in 1934. Despite riding to work every day with Roy Chadwick, Lindley persuaded Floyd to plead his case to Chadwick to let him into the 'holy of holies'. He was successful. Most of these men worked on the Avro Manchester bomber, which became the Lancaster, with all of the Avro designs, discussed above, owing something to the engineering work that dated back to the Manchester. Stuart Davies came to Avro from Hawkers after having led the section that adapted the Hawker Hurricane into a two-seat aircraft, called the Hotspur.[22] Jim Floyd was loaned to Hawkers for this project and worked under the fiery and profane Davies. He describes a paradigm-shifting moment in their relationship: "He once said to me 'You know, there are days when I'd just like to *strangle* you." Apparently Jim's response was "Well Sir, there aren't very many days when I wouldn't like to strangle *you*." He was pleasantly surprised when Davies, rather than exploding, brightened and roared with laughter. In 1947, after Floyd left for Canada, Chadwick was killed in the crash of a Tudor on a test flight for which the ailerons had been cross-wired, making the plane roll opposite to input on take-off. Stuart Davies somehow walked away from this tragedy, which killed Avro test pilot Billy Thorn and others, and he took over as Chief Designer.

It was due to Dobson's leadership that the new Canadian arm was named Avro, since the Hawker Siddeley Group comprised numerous companies at the end of the war, including Avro U.K., Gloster Aircraft, the famous Hawker Aircraft, Armstrong Whitworth aircraft, Armstrong Siddeley Motors, High Duty Alloys, and others. Some involved in these decisions were heartened to know that Hawker Siddeley were involved in the design and manufacture of nearly everything related to transportation. This conglomerate was involved in the production of military fighters, bombers, transports and patrol aircraft, plus civil aircraft of all descriptions, engines to power many of them, jet engines, luxury-sports cars, rail equipment, and much more.

Hawker Siddeley would produce thousands of aircraft for WW II including the Lancaster Bomber, Anson trainer, Hurricane, Tempest, Typhoon and Sea Fury fighters, plus the Meteor jet fighter and others. The Gloster Meteor was the only allied jet fighter to see combat in WW II and, after setting several speed records and proving its adaptability, became the top-selling fighter in the world in the late 1940s—making Hawker Siddeley a fortune and in the process helping Britain's chronic balance of payments problems. In the case of the Gloster design team and management, however, it made them somewhat over-confident and complacent, resulting in Gloster's next aircraft, the delta-winged Javelin, being a disappointment. By the time this was glaringly obvious, the Group had the Canadian Avro Arrow in development, and all indications were that it would be a mighty success.

An Avro Tri-plane is prepared for flight.

18 In fact, according to later standards it wasn't a flight but more of a hop. His next aircraft, a triplane (with triplane tail as well) did fly not too long after. The main problem with his early designs was a lack of power, due to the J.A.P. engines he initially used giving poor performance for their weight.

19 Floyd, J.C. The Avro Canada C-102 Jetliner. Erin: Boston Mills 1986

20 Information from Jim Floyd interviews. The corporate logo of A.V. Roe Canada Ltd. is also strongly Masonic. It consists of a pyramid superimposed by a compass, with three stylised bars crossing it.

21 Avro's special apprenticeship program involved a student working through every department of the company, while the company paid for a special, accelerated education program, right through University.

22 After having included information on the Hotspur in AA&CWA, some criticism was received that the Hotspur was a glider, and that the two-seat adaptation of the Hurricane was called the Henley, all of which is true. However, there was a two seat adaptation of the Hurricane called the Hotspur, which was not produced even as a prototype. On this project J.C. Floyd became associated with Stuart Davies and Robert Lickley, who would later design the Fairey Delta 2.

Chapter 4

SONS OF PRIVILEGE

Since this book is a geo-political examination of the history *and* demise of Avro Canada and, indeed, of Avro U.K. and Hawker Siddeley, and of the implications this had on North American air defense, it is time to introduce some of the geo-political actors of the day. The patient reader may be surprised by the conclusions.

Central to the story, on the American political side, are John Foster and Allen Welsh Dulles; the Dulles brothers. Usually neglected is the fact that they also had a sister, Eleanor Lansing Dulles, named after their uncle: Secretary of State under Woodrow Wilson; Robert Lansing. While Eleanor would become an important State Department envoy to post-war Germany, her uncle Robert Lansing had been fired by President Wilson for undermining the League of Nations and the President, and participating in the coverup of the fact that the Lusitania was, indeed, carrying munitions in violation of the neutrality act before her sinking. This, of course, prevented the families of innocent American civilians on board the Lusitania from securing insurance coverage.[23] John Foster Dulles was named for their maternal grandfather, John Watson Foster, also a Secretary of State under President Harrison and a "personage of great influence in both the Republican Party and the business and banking world... John W. Foster joined the boards of several rich and powerful Wall Street corporations. He had built himself a lodge and…important guests—senators, big banking magnates, statesmen, like William Howard Taft, John W. Davis, Andrew Carnegie, and Bernard Baruch—came to stay with him…"[24]

John Foster Dulles

Taft would serve as Republican President from 1903 to 1913, having defeated the arch-progressive William Jennings Bryan on a largely disingenuous progressive platform. Taft's presidency would be characterised by 'dollar diplomacy'—the acquisition of U.S.-favourable foreign relations through direct capital investment; i.e.; buyout as opposed to lending operating monies. Similar to the Reagan administration's activities in Nicaragua, on December 19th, 1909, U.S. Marines invaded the tiny nation, installing the U.S. corporate-friendly Diaz regime.[25] While a strong proponent of competition at home, and while promoting world peace as a presidential mantra, Taft's administration is also noted for its involvement in the construction of the Panama canal. France had a commercial and strategic interest in constructing and administering the then non-existent canal, however the American Monroe doctrine guaranteed a conflict. After a civil war in Colombia (of which present day Panama was then a part), France began construction of a canal, yet was forced to abandon it due to political, financial and other pressures. British interests also became involved.

> "Before his assassination, President McKinley had persuaded the British to give up their claim on the isthmian canal… But when the Americans indicated that they would go to Nicaragua to build their canal, the Panama price suddenly dropped to about thirty-five percent of the original. The Americans bought the holdings and rights, but then had to get the Republic of Colombia to lease its Panama territory 'forever'. Colombia balked; it wanted a lot of hard cash. Teddy Roosevelt blustered that he felt like invading Colombia, but he did not. Instead he smiled benevolently on a rebellion of "Panamanians," backed by American and other capitalists interested in the canal; he sent American warships to the area to help out, and generally guaranteed the rebellion… Since there were only about fifty marines ashore, as compared to several hundred Colombian troops, the situation was difficult until November 5, when the

> USS *Dixie* arrived... The Colombian commander was bribed ($8,000 bought a Colombian troop commander in those days)... On November 6, 1903, the United States recognized their new government of Panama, and two weeks later Panama gave the United States control of the Panama Canal Zone... 'in perpetuity'".[26]

Baruch was a successful stock market speculator who served Wilson's administration as Chairman of the War Industries Board. He had earlier purchased a seat at the New York Stock Exchange for the then-princely sum of eighteen thousand dollars—and made a fortune speculating in the sugar market. Those were the days (somewhat like today) of the big sugar cartels, whose exploitation of Latin, South American, and Pacific nations, while profitable, didn't leave a sweet taste in the mouths of those toiling in the fields, nor their more nationalistically-inclined leaders.

Carnegie, of course, was the steel magnate and robber baron-cum-philanthropist, and founder of the tax-free foundation bearing his name. John W. Davis was the son of a Virginia politician who had opposed the abolition of slavery. John became a successful lawyer and ran for president as a Democrat (losing in a landslide to Coolidge), became Ambassador to the U.K. after WW I, was the founding president of the Council on Foreign Relations in 1921, and a trustee of the Rockefeller Foundation.

John W. Foster had "graduated from the University of Indiana in 1855, attended Harvard Law School, and, though never formally admitted to the state bar, joined a law practice in Evansville, Indiana. [He] fought in the Civil War, first as a major and then as a colonel, but left the military following the end of the conflict [returning] to his home state, where he worked as editor of the Evansville Daily Journal, ultimately transforming the paper into a forum for Republican politics."[27] Later he served as U.S. Ambassador to Mexico, Russia, and Spain.[28]

American foreign policy during Foster's diplomatic career was characterised by "gunboat diplomacy"; the opening of markets, acquisition of productive assets, and establishment of global coaling stations for the U.S. Navy through real or implied force. Hawaii was coveted by American sugar and fruit interests, and by the Navy for Pearl Harbour: an ideal naval base. "A succession of Republican administrations looked with approval at this yearning, and made it a diplomatic matter. ...Then, on November 3, 1896, Republican William McKinley was elected president, and Manifest Destiny was once again the foreign policy of the United States. ...on Friday, August 12, 1898, at 11:30 A.M., the flag of the republic was hauled down from the staff at the Executive Building in downtown Honolulu and the flag of the United States was run up. Hawaii had gone from coaling station to colony in twenty-three years, with scarcely a drop of blood shed."[29] Needless to say, this was achieved against the wishes of the Hawaiian monarchy and the native populace they represented. The acquisitions of Hawaii and the Panama Canal zone, the subjugation of Nicaragua, Mexico and other nations in the Western hemisphere through covert, and, where necessary, overt economic, military and political pressure would be a template for many of the CIA's nation-rebuilding schemes. To put it succinctly, the Dulles siblings were born into a bloodline that circulated with generally imperialistic pecuniary and political power. While their political affiliations crossed party lines, (thereby helping to explain an expansionist element of continuity in American foreign policy), their loyalty to the elitist concepts favouring the concentration of wealth and power in the hands of a ruling elite, as opposed to more egalitarian and democratic models, proves remarkably solid. Born to wealth and power, there are few 'class traitors'—few, but not zero.

23 The facts regarding the Lusitania are held in Secretary of State William Jennings Bryan's papers in the Library of Congress. See Mosley, Dulles, p.p.36-37
24 Mosley: Dulles, p.p. 18,19
25 Wikipedia
26 Hoyt, Edwin P. America's Wars and Military Excursions, New York, McGraw-Hill, 1987 , p.p. 336,337.
27 University of Virginia website: http://www.millercenter.virginia.edu
28 Information on John W. Foster and his "guests": Wikipedia
29 Hoyt, America's Wars and Military Excursions, p. 290-301

Chapter 5

CANADIAN GENESIS

Previous to the twentieth century, American forces had attacked Canadian territory many times, sometimes involving forces which outnumbered the entire population of Canada. Amazingly, through luck and sometimes military prowess, the invaders were always turned away. A superficial analysis of the history of Europeans in North America demonstrates that the peoples originally known as les *Canadiens* had staved off domination and annexation by the thirteen American colonies, first with the assistance and deterrent influence of Imperial France, and later that of the British Empire. It should come as no surprise, then, that previous to WW II Canada's primary war plans called for defense against US invasion. This was backed up by vigilance against US domination of Canadian foreign and economic policy. This stance on the part of the Canadian 'establishment' reflected the economic interests of those with power. These policies cannot be considered an extreme response because America's war plans up to 1931, were primarily concerned with displacing the United Kingdom as the most powerful global actor, envisioned invading Canada with four armies and removing it from the British Empire. Concurrently depriving Britain of control of Canada's strategic resources and gaining these enormous assets for themselves was the "win-win" situation envisioned.[30]

In Canada a review of Statistics Canada summaries reveals that up until the 1920s, the ownership of the Canadian economy had been held by mostly British and Canadian investors. By the 1930s it was about one-third each, split among American, British and Canadian interests. During the Second World War however, American investment almost totally displaced British, and became dominant over the combined British-Canadian share. While Britain was content to lend operating and other monies to Canadian enterprise, American investors preferred to own and manage these enterprises.

"In 1900…85 percent of Canadians' external [financial] obligations were owed to Britons, only 14% to Americans; by 1916 the figures were 66 per cent and 30 percent, respectively.

"American funds came largely as direct investments—that is, in connection with American ownership and management…in Canada. In 1909 American direct investments seem to have been worth about $254 million, as against $121 million worth of British direct investments… By 1900…Imperial Oil had come under American ownership…soon after…Ford of Canada began operations…"[31] Already the American predilection for buyout, as opposed to loaning operating monies, was evident. Britain wasn't nearly as fiscally imperialistic as the United States.

This change of hands of Canadian industry and resources largely resulted from the policies of the various Mackenzie King governments which, of course, came to include, in various portfolios, the American-born Mr. Clarence Decatur Howe. American imperialists were, perhaps, congenitally-disposed to favour King, due to his grandfather and namesake's being William Lyon Mackenzie. Mackenzie had been one of the leaders of a revolt against British Colonial rule, known as the Upper Canada Rebellion of 1837. "Mackenzie, Duncombe, John Rolph and 200 supporters fled to Navy Island in the Niagara River, where they declared themselves the Republic of Canada on December 13. They obtained supplies from supporters in the United States resulting in British reprisals (see Caroline Affair). On January 13, 1838, under attack by British armaments, the rebels fled. Mackenzie went to the United States where he was arrested and charged under the Neutrality Act."[32]

Canada had been governed by McKenzie King's Liberals off and on since 1921 and Knowlton Nash, journalist and author, wrote that John. D. Rockefeller Jr. "underwrote King's entire future career, enabling King to be free of financial worry."[33] This was in return for King's valuable assistance as a PR and labour relations advisor to John D. Rockefeller Jr. over the Ludlow Massacre, where Rockefeller coal miners had struck for improvements in their abominable conditions and pay, and where Rockefeller money paid for a band of mercenary "deputies" who promptly imposed terrorism, (exemplified by shooting deaths and burnt dwellings), on the suffering miners and their families. King advised a 'kinder-gentler' approach and sophisticated media manipulation and propaganda to calm the shocked population and avert a public retaliation that could have, in those days, resulted in a real backlash against Rockefeller. For helping avert a potential catastrophe, Rockefeller was, apparently, eternally grateful. Peter C. Newman has also mentioned in his writing that King would not make any major policy decisions without consulting Rockefeller.[34] Of course, King became well known for his highly developed political survival instincts.

Before King returned to power in 1935 there had been a liberalised trade agreement under discussion between Canada and the United States. Three weeks after being elected, King signed an agreement in Washington that was, according to the then US Undersecretary of State, "vastly more favourable to the United States than the one which was being considered by [King's predecessor] Mr. Bennett."[35]

> "The U.S. ambassador in Ottawa, Norman Armour, reported to Washington that King made it clear to him 'that there were two roads open to Canada, but that he wanted to choose 'the American road' if we made it possible for him to do so.' The prime minister was not advocating annexation, because, as he told Armour, 'certainly you have enough troubles of your own without wanting to add us to them.'
>
> "In his long memo on King's attitude to the State Department, Armour set out the importance for his government of signing the trade agreement with Canada, 'not so much from an economic standpoint as from, well let us say, a political or international viewpoint if you will.' In addition to being profitable for the American exporter, a trade agreement would have 'the long range effect of bringing Canada not only within our economic but our political orbit.' In recent years, Armour warned, Canadian industry, by protecting its economy had developed the capacity to produce goods 'destined to compete sharply with our exports on the markets of the world.' If such a trend were to continue, Canada 'may become before long our most intensive competitor. There is still time,' the ambassador continued, 'while the Canadian economy is in a formative stage, to shift the impetus away from highly competitive production to complimentary production [i.e., the provision of raw materials for US manufacturing] Is it not vitally important for our political future that we have next to us a Canada…supporting our policies in regard to Latin America…the Far East and elsewhere, and feeling that in a thousand and one ways that they are bound to us in practical things[?]'""[36]
>
> On November 11th, 1935, Prime Minister King and President Roosevelt signed the Canada–U.S. Reciprocal Trade Agreement.
>
> In four years, Canada's trade deficit with the United States tripled from $39 million to $107 million, meaning Canada imported almost three times more from Americans than it exported to them. John Hickerson of the U.S. State Department called the benefits "staggering" for the United States and said the agreement was "so favourable to us that…it will be recognized generally as a great economic and political asset." By 1942 the United States had surpassed Britain as Canada's major customer for the first time. U.S. control of the Canadian economy grew so rapidly that by the time King understood the full meaning of developing 'closer ties' with the United States, he was having second thoughts. He came to feel that "the long range policy of the Americans was to absorb Canada," and that "it might be inevitable for us to have to submit to it."[37]

Due to King's refusal to re-arm, prior to the German invasion of Poland, Canada was woefully unprepared once hostilities commenced. "King hoped an outbreak of war in the 1930s could be averted and he therefore supported the appeasement policies of the British. He met with Adolf Hitler who, he remarked in his journal, came across as 'a reasonable and caring man ... who might be thought of as one of the saviors of the world.' Telling a Jewish delegation that Kristallnacht "might turn out to be a blessing," he refused to allow Jewish refugees who were attempting to leave Nazi Germany entry into Canada."[38] Since Nazi intentions were obvious from even before Hitler's election to the Chancellor's office in 1933, one might suggest that King's partial mobilization of Canada five days before Hitler's invasion of Poland was hardly a visionary response. His tardiness suited some American interests though, many of them connected to the isolationist or pro-Nazi America First (and similar) movements in the United States. Rockefeller's Standard Oil empire, by now in ownership of Canada's Imperial Oil Ltd., being one particularly enthusiastic corporate supporter of Hitler's brand of State Capitalism. One Canadian businessman, founder of the National Steel Car company, saw the coming weather and built a modern aircraft production facility in Malton Ontario; just north of Toronto.

Due to the apparent need to supply Britain by sea, and Canada's inability to protect such traffic,

Prime Minister King sought assurances from the Americans that they would assist Canada by taking over most responsibilities for policing the North American coasts. King also, no doubt, sought access to American capital and industry as well, both for Canada's immediate needs and also for Britain. FDR and King met secretly at a railway siding in Ogdensburg New York in 1938 and agreed to set up a joint board on defense. At Queen's University in August FDR said:

> "I give to you assurance that the people of the United States will not stand idly by if domination of Canadian soil is threatened by any other empire."

It was not lost on some that America was herself an empire, and that what Roosevelt declared was no different in real form than the more obviously hawkish Monroe Doctrine—a doctrine that stated that the countries of the Western Hemisphere were part of US strategic interests whether the countries concerned liked it or not. The Ogdensburg Declaration and the policies that followed it were known to pose a threat to Canadian independence, but such was the price of being unprepared—besides, in this case the Nazis seemed to be a more immediate threat to Canada than US expansionism. Canada established, often under American ownership thanks to the Reciprocal Trade Agreement, many munitions factories for the war effort. During the Second World War however, American investment rose to dominate the combined British-Canadian share. This change took place under the premiership of Mackenzie King with Clarence Decatur (CD) Howe managing Canada's wartime industrial strategy through his omnipotent Ministry of Munitions and Supply. Within Howe's empire were many aspiring young professionals who viewed the astonishing advance of American ownership with alarm, and having participated in global industrial and economic matters, felt in a position to do something about it. As with King's apparent change of heart in how he viewed American investment, others in the Liberal Party also began to wonder if trade was already too free for Canada's long-term prospects as a prosperous, independent nation. By the mid-1950s, there was a growing split in the Liberals, with a band of up-and-coming 'young Turks', led by Pearson, adopting a more nationalistic line towards diplomatic and economic activities, as compared to the 'old guard', exemplified by CD Howe's "Continentalist" approach.

As a result of currency policies that, in today's world, would be scorned as pure socialism, and unrestricted US capital investment (buy-out) and loans, the government was able to implement the equally-scorned 'planned economy' for war purposes. With comparatively limited debt costs to the nation, the Canadian Gross National Product doubled between 1939 and 1945. In the process Canada's Crown jewels of agriculture and resources were augmented by a new gem: industry. Following what neo-conservative pundits would condemn as outrageously socialistic policies, Canada also put out more war production on a per-capita basis than *any* of the combatant countries. It would do so whilst providing the highest proportion of its prime working youth to uniform for service overseas. Surely an impressive contribution, by any standard, towards what most Canadians agreed were sound moral goals.

A result of the Ogdensburg Declaration was the establishment of the Permanent Joint Board on Defense (PJBD). In these agreements it was understood that each country would produce in the areas of "greatest capability" and the other partners would purchase such products there from. These principles were established in 1938 yet they were officially re-established several times over the years. Perhaps this is an indication that, despite the policy provisions, they weren't generating meaningful results—particularly for the smaller partners.

30 Granatstein: paper on US influence on the Canadian military
31 Bothwell, Drummond and English. Canada; 1900-1945 p.p. 78-79.
32 Wikipedia
33 Nash, Knowlton, Kennedy and Diefenbaker, Fear and Loathing Across the Undefended Border Toronto, McClelland and Stewart, 1990, p. 31
34 Newman, Peter C. Distemper of Our Times, 2nd Ed. Toronto: McClelland and Stewart, 1978
35 Phillips to Franklin Delano Roosevelt, November 7, 1935 Roosevelt Presidential Library PSF 25, Diplomatic Correspondence, "Canada."
36 paras from: Orchard, David. The Fight for Canada, Toronto: Stoddart Publishing, 1993, pp. 94-96, Armour's comments ibid.
37 ibid. Hickerson and King remarks: letter to the State Department by LaVerne Baldwin, November 9, 1935, quoted in Boucher, Politics of Depression, p.35
38 wikipedia

Chapter 6

BIRTH OF A CANADIAN GIANT

National Steel Car, a Hamilton, Ontario rolling stock maker, had built a large aircraft production facility in Malton, (current site of Pearson International Airport in Toronto), where Westland Lysanders and Avro Ansons were soon in production. Unfortunately, when Robert Magor, the president of National Steel Car died, the remaining company directors, perhaps particularly the new CEO, R.S. Hart, became hostile to the aircraft production division. Fred T. Smye was by this time working for C.D. Howe under the Director of Aircraft Production, Ralph Bell, and recommended that the government nationalize the Malton facility. Dave Boyd, hired to run the operation, also wrote a letter to C.D. Howe pointing out the interference of Hart, and suggesting that if the government of Canada hoped to receive any more warplanes from the operation, that they best nationalise it. This they did and renamed the new Crown corporation Victory Aircraft. J.P Bickell, a wealthy Canadian industrialist allied with the Canadian Imperial Bank of Commerce became the new chief executive of the operation.[39]

An expansion had been undertaken to suit the plant for production of the Martin Marauder twin-engine bomber. This didn't materialise due to some rather glaring safety problems with the Marauder which were never really overcome. "No damn good." wrote, succinctly, an RCAF expert sent to fly and technically evaluate the Marauder. The main problems were a very high wing loading for a bomber, and an alleged centre of gravity problem. When Glenn Martin himself was called on the carpet of the US Congress to explain the shortcomings of this aircraft, he stated that he felt the investment required to correct the aircraft was not worthwhile and that the plane was good enough as it was. This placement of profits before human lives was corrected, to some degree through a modest increase in wingspan, by an angry Congress. Canadians in Howe's Ministry of Munitions and Supply (perhaps Fred Smye himself) had, by this time, already been bragging about their industrial abilities and are rumoured to have said that they could produce a Lancaster bomber better, faster and cheaper than the company that designed it in Britain. The bluff was called and Victory Aircraft was contracted to build one of the largest, most complicated and advanced aircraft in the world. Roy Dobson, by this time in charge of Avro in the U.K., was convinced to take a much-needed working holiday to Canada to see for himself the Canadian operation. He was accompanied by Frank Spriggs, managing director of the Hawker Siddeley Group.

It was estimated that the Canadian Lancaster was, in many respects, a superior machine to the British, although the American Packard Motors license-built version of the Rolls-Royce Merlin engine had a time between overhauls of half that of the British original.[40] It was also estimated that Canadian workers were 15% more efficient than British on Lancaster production. Compared to the Boeing B-17 Flying Fortress the Avro Lancaster flew to the target 45 knots faster, and returned 75 knots faster. It also had a bomb load, on a long-range mission to Berlin, of three times its American competitor.

While the Lancaster program had been a great success, not all bi-lateral defense issues had gone smoothly. Hawker Hurricane fighters, built in Canada, were not available when Canada needed them in the face of the Japanese invasion of the Aleutian Islands. The British Purchasing Commission assigned them to the Red Army for the Russian fight against Hitler. Considering the fact that as of 1941 the Japanese Imperial Navy dwarfed the US Pacific Fleet (while there was practically no British Pacific Fleet), the Canadians, including Air Marshal Wilf Curtis, may be forgiven for feeling a little jumpy.

By 1944 eyes were turning to the future of the Victory Aircraft facility and of Canada's new industrial capability. An Advisory Committee on Aircraft Manufacture was established in Canada, while Avro U.K, under Dobson and Stuart Davies, with J.C. Floyd as the Chief Project Engineer, formed a company project to begin looking at the future of the industry. Fred Smye's boss, Director of Aircraft Production Ralph Bell, wrote Howe in March 1944:

> "The Ministers of Munitions and Supply and of National Defense for Air have the honour to report that an aircraft industry is of the utmost importance to Canada from the standpoint of National Defense, to supply the demands of both her internal and external transport lines and as part of her industrial economy. Such an industry would be organized as a compact, efficient and progressive nucleus capable of speedy and adequate expansion in an emergency. It must

> be based on keen, able and highly trained design staffs and the development of such staffs should be commenced immediately and pushed energetically."[41]

Due to the fact that rapid industrialisation had equipped Canada with considerable state-of-the-art industrial facilities and know-how that would be wasted once wartime contracts evaporated, the private sector was encouraged, through tax incentives and low pricing, to take on as much of it as possible if they would convert the industries to post-war production.

Hawker Siddeley, under the leadership of Avro UK's newly-knighted Sir Roy Dobson, was invited into Canada, in part, to preserve some of that industrial infrastructure and employment. They were also courted because they had the ability to provide Canada with the kind of technology that would allow Canadian industry to compete in all high technologies.

It was an interesting pairing of socialist policies with private industry, but then, in those days, Britain and the Commonwealth, indeed most European countries, used public investment in industry and research and development to ensure strategic national needs were met. In Canada and Britain, companies like Trans Canada Airlines (now Air Canada), BOAC (now British Airways), the CBC, the BBC, Avro Canada, Power Jets (where Frank Whittle invented the centrifugal flow jet engine), Turbo Research (leading to Orenda), and a host of other enterprises, got their start through government investment. The willingness of European countries, and the Commonwealth, to engage in quasi-socialistic industrial policies related to the 'planned economy' was anathema to some powerful practitioners of global capitalism and finance. Any objective resource on the history of private banking, the CIA or the US State Department will bring to light their running interference in the media and political arena (as a minimum), especially in the 1950's, to thwart the 'creeping socialism' that they felt was such a menace to classical, *laissez faire,* capitalism. Public enterprise, as rejected by current banking, industrial, media (and thus political) powers, runs against the new tide of inevitable globalisation, we are told. Perhaps the true problem with public investment and public ownership and creation of currency, is that this removes at least one layer of interest payments on debt, and thus removes one source of profits from one small sector of society. It certainly removes a major element of political power from powerful private bankers and financiers.

The RCAF's Wilf Curtis has been credited with leading the process that had Canada decide to build its own jet interceptor suited to Canada's unique requirements. Yet Roy Dobson of Avro UK apparently also had a leading hand in this unusually bold decision.

> "I went with Bob Leckie, head of the RCAF, to the Department of National Defense. Oh, lumme, I got a cold reception there. 'Canada doesn't want to embark on aircraft design and research,' they told me, 'Canada is too small and should only build on licence.' That's rubbish, I said, Canada *does* want an aircraft industry. What you want is to see poor old Bob here being a kept woman and having to rely for his livelihood on other people's resources."[42]

Leckie had been leading a movement in the RCAF, practically since its inception, to have Canada design and build her own aircraft. He believed it was naïve to think a country was armed (or independent) unless it could take care of its own equipment needs. Once the war ended, Avro Canada, the airframe manufacturer, was timidly established at the old wartime facilities of National Steel Car and Victory Aircraft. In a deal between the British Hawker Siddeley Group, led by Avro UK's Sir Roy Dobson and the government of Canada, (represented by C.D. Howe), Hawker Siddeley took possession of the plant in the fall of 1945, with its first employee being Fredrick T. Smye. The meeting Dobson referred to had been set up by Fred Smye as a means of bringing together the main potential customers' experts, the government, and some of the leading brains of Hawker Siddeley.

Fred Smye was born in Hamilton, Ontario, and had owned and operated the first cardboard milk carton production facility in Canada while in his early twenties. When war loomed he felt he had more to offer Canada in industry than in uniform and secured a job in C.D. Howe's Department of Munitions and Supply in 1940. His first posting was working in the New York City office of the department, trying to cajole production out of the officially-neutral Americans, and also did work related to the lend lease agreement. He then took on a job under Ralph P. Bell, who was the Director General Aircraft Production in the Howe Munitions and Supply empire. Fred was later promoted, at the age of 27, to the position of Director of Aircraft Production—an exceptionally challenging position. In 1944 Smye was appointed Assistant General Manager of Federal Aircraft Limited, which was the Crown agency overseeing wartime Avro Anson production in Canada.

Frederick Timothy Smye (via Jim Floyd)

Smye made a major impression on Roy Dobson who hired him in the same month as the Ottawa meeting. At this meeting from Hawker Siddeley were W.G. Carter, designer of the Gloster Meteor jet fighter; WWW Downing, another design engineer from Glosters; and Joe Lindsay, a gas turbine expert from Armstrong Siddeley engines who had been involved in their early efforts to design a turbo-prop engine. Greig Stewart wrote: "…that Fred Smye had literally dragged [these men] away from Roy Dobson to reassure the Canadian government and C.D. Howe that Dobson wasn't getting cold feet on the Victory Aircraft deal."[43] The meeting was chaired by A/V/M A.L. James, with Wilf Curtis and John Easton also representing the RCAF, with Turbo Research engineers, (two of whom had been involved with Power Jets) Ken Tupper, Paul Dilworth, and Winnett Boyd present on behalf of the National Research Council (NRC).

Engineers at Victory Aircraft had informally been developing a design for a Canadian jet fighter since 1943. This was a modest single-seat, single-engine design based on a thrust of about 4,000 lbs—all comfortably within the state-of-the-art. This had been done under Chief Engineer William Shaw. The meeting opened with Air Marshal James outlining an RCAF Operational Requirement based on an aircraft that resembled the Victory design, and an axial-flow engine in the 5,000 lb. thrust category to power it. A/V/M Jack Easton recalled that they couldn't find an axial engine meeting the thrust requirement. This is odd considering Rolls had the Avon turbojet, designed for at least 6,500 pounds thrust (lbt), under development. Also under development in Britain was the Metrovick F.9 axial turbojet, a promising design in the same thrust class as the Avon. Since they were on the Secret List in Britain, they may not have been apprised—this perhaps indicating that even wartime alliances as close as that between Canada and Britain only go so far.

Downing expressed horror that such a modest fighter should be thought sufficient to defend a nation as enormous as Canada. He suggested that Canada needed a two-seat fighter with very long range, meaning it would need two powerful engines for safety and to carry enough fuel and armament to achieve its mission. He suggested to Boyd, Dilworth and Tupper they "design the best engine you can to fit a 32-inch nacelle". His engine specification meant he wasn't trying to sell Canada his company's Meteors. The specifics of his engine recommendation might have meant that he knew of the Avon and F.9, but couldn't reveal their existence. By suggesting such, he helped prevent Canada from designing an obsolete engine (and thus fighter), whilst also facilitating the possible acquisition of a competitive engine program for Hawker Siddeley, should their collaboration in Canada bear fruit. The Canadians were suitably impressed and, essentially, wholly accepted the recommendations of the Hawker Siddeley experts. The Operational Requirement Air-7-1-Issue 1 was overturned and a new one started. The end result would be the Avro CF-100 all-weather, long-range, day-or-night interceptor, and the TR-5 Orenda turbojet engine.

39 Dow: The Arrow, p. 26, and Floyd:The Avro Canada C-102 Jetliner.
40 WW II pilot's notes for aircraft equipped with either engine, interviews with former RCAF and RAF engine technicians.
RG 28A, vol. 156, Public Archives of Canada.
42 Earl, Marjorie: "How Roy Dobson Pushed Us Into the Jet Age", Maclean's, 20 July, 1957,
43 Stewart, Greig. Shutting Down the National Dream, A.V. Roe and the Tragedy of the Avro Arrow. Scarborough: McGraw-Hill Ryerson Ltd., 1988 p.59

Chapter 7

A PRIMER ON INTELLIGENCE

Besides political cover-ups and document destruction that has prevented an accurate appraisal of Avro's place in history, *popular* historians, by definition, tend to be non-critical and present a cheerful and un-intellectually challenging "it was all for the best" view of history. Wars and other disasters and aberrations are dismissed, seemingly being caused by some sort of unavoidable 'random error' programed into the very fabric of the universe. Of the harsher truths many well-intentioned journalists and media executives think the public is better off unaware. Certainly, most individuals and groups act to prevent the disclosure of their less than glorious achievements, perhaps especially politicians, financiers, industrialists, and security and intelligence agents. Suffice it to say that it seems that those who control the money, control policy, and thus control history. The implications of this are that Western governments dating in an almost uninterrupted stream back to the cradle of civilisation—ancient Sumer (centuries before the Babylonian empire)—have quite often operated in the best interests of a dominant wealthy elite, by which the rulers were tolerated and, usually, sponsored.

The very reason nationhood was established was to give some kind of resistance to domination (and exploitation) by foreign elites, whatever their political creed. To do so, the successful ruling elites have always constructed a security and intelligence apparatus. But there are many elements involved in the 'ruling elite', and so one needs to consider that not only national governments employ secret intelligence and security forces. Churches, banks, royal and wealthy families, industrial empires and fugitive knights, at least the successful ones, have all employed sophisticated security and intelligence agencies. History resounds with tales of professional and freelance intelligence agents and their empire-saving (or toppling) exploits—Lawrence of Arabia, and his establishment of the house of Saud as the British oil-interest-friendly rulers of Arabia, spring to mind.

Intelligence agencies also exist to protect nations from domination and exploitation. However, the classic intelligence agencies have generally wielded a double-edged sword because their protective function is mirrored by a subversive aspect in selected foreign countries. As Chapman Pincher, a British journalist who specialised in intelligence and government affairs throughout the Cold War, wrote in his impressive book *Too Secret Too Long:*

"The most effective channel for misleading an adversary government is through its intelligence service on which it depends for info to guide its foreign policy decisions."[45]

National intelligence agencies aim to manipulate foreign policymakers while protecting their own from the same and in the process become well versed in conspiracy and the black arts. The various 'Black Chambers' associated with national mail services since before the Venetians dominated trade and banking have routinely been used to protect the economic interests of their country's ruling elite. Unfortunately, this kind of information theft, and its use for national commercial purposes, has only increased in sophistication and pervasiveness over time. The National Security Agency in the United States, which monitors virtually all global electronic communications systems, is the ultimate evolution of this form of spying, with a global reach that would have made Stalin blush. Yet at the top of Western intelligence and policymaking are always agents associated with global banking. John Foster and Allen Dulles, most of the Rockefeller brothers, members of the Rothschild, Warburg and Harriman banking clans, Prince Bernhard of the Netherlands and the House of Hesse,—all very powerful political and financial powers were also active in intelligence. It doesn't take a leap of logic to consider that, to some varying degree, these interests were using intelligence to further their own interests, while promoting policies that favoured the interests of their own. How this relates to their influence on foreign governments and policies to which they were opposed would appear to be a crucial missing piece in understanding not only the story of A.V. Roe Canada and even Hawker Siddeley, but in understanding the Cold War itself.

The scope, objectives and tactics of Soviet espionage against the ABC (America, Britain and Canada) countries are probably better known than those of their Western counterparts thanks to interest and fear generated by Hoover's FBI, Dulles's CIA, and McCarthy. Less emphasised are the operations of Britain and the USA in spying on Western countries. Repressed are official acknowledgements of the fact that, during and after the Cold War, the USA was using signals intelligence (SIGINT), and other methods, for commercial and political purposes against its closest allies. The popular press seems blissfully unaware of this area of inquiry, and, by implication, so does the majority of the public. Obviously if one hasn't been detected, one has much greater room for manoeuvre—legal or otherwise.

Under Stalin the Soviets developed such a militarist 'establishment', enforced by the KGB, that the subsequent premiers were under continual threat of removal, should their policies have been deemed insufficiently stern. The circumstances of Khrushchev's ouster are a prime example of how an intelligence agency can act against its own government, and, no doubt, against its own peoples' wishes and best interests. The CIA and many of those dominating politics and business chose to attack the communist ideology as though Communism and Capitalism were like matter and anti-matter, good vs. evil, and co-existing on the same sphere could only lead to total annihilation. This was, unfortunately, also the official view of the Leninist creed—because Lenin believed that Western capitalist and financial powers would not allow an alternate economic system to proliferate. Evidence from the time of the Crash seems to indicate that many leading capitalists had become convinced that socialism had the potential to destroy the capitalist economies through currency and investment reform. Instead of enterprising individuals having to be financed by private interests who always demanded a stake in the venture, government could provide financial help, expertise and property, reducing both the risk and costs of development. Any foreign sales would help the country's reserves of foreign currency, needed for countries reluctant to accept the national currency, and to provide some insulation against currency speculation. Unfortunately, the Soviet system never resembled socialism, with Stalin and the Soviet security and intelligence system ending any hopes of anything but a blundering command economy sustained by political and economic repression and raw military might.

However, the business and political elite in the Western countries, especially in the USA, chose to take the same 'all-or-nothing' view in economic theory and policy. They chose not to view the socialist experiment with an open mind but as anathema to their very being. In making their public pronouncements on socialism, they were blessed with the opportunity to associate Stalinist and Red Chinese atrocities with the socialist economic model, successfully evoking the desired emotional response: fear. The fearful citizens were encouraged to put their trust in Capitalism and to distrust government involvement in the economy. In fact, after the Bolshevik revolution the presidents of the United States were also under considerable pressure from the right wing and financial elite (and their newspapers) to avoid any taint of "socialistic" character in their administrations. General Smedley Butler disclosed a plot whereby an assassination of Franklin Roosevelt would have made him the military dictator of the United States. This effort was lead by industrial and financial interests unhappy with the egalitarian and interventionist character of Roosevelt's "New Deal". In 1947, in response to increasingly strident and alarmist Republican attacks, President Truman initiated a Civil Service Commission loyalty investigation of its two-million members. The results included 212 dismissals, thousands of resignations, and the conviction of precisely zero spies.

Clark Clifford, a presidential aide, described the rising Red hysteria: "The President didn't attach fundamental importance to the so-called Communist scare. He thought it was all a lot of baloney. But political pressures were such that he had to recognize it… We did not believe there was a real problem. A problem was being manufactured."[46] There were many victims of the witch hunt for 'Commies', with the Hollywood Blacklist, which targeted, of all people, Charlie Chaplin (and others), as perhaps the best known example. Certainly these measures served the purpose of moving the civil service, and media, somewhat to the right of the political spectrum. US oil, chemical, electronics and military equipment manufacturers, and their financiers, were well served by escalating tensions with the Soviet Union and China. This perhaps explains why imperialist impulses are most intensely displayed by the Republican Party in the United States: they represent the most right wing elements of American society, which includes bankers, industrialists and oil men. Truman himself said it well: "They [Republicans] did not understand the worker, the farmer, the everyday person… Most of them honestly believed that prosperity began at the top and would trickle down in due time to the benefit of all the people."[47] And people think Ronald Reagan invented "trickle down" economics?

That US government agencies would sometimes act against their own government, in line with the wishes of the wealthy right, is indicated by the behaviour of the FBI during Truman's election campaign. According to Truman historian David McCulloch, J. Edgar Hoover had put the resources of the

FBI at the Republican candidate's disposal months before the election in the expectation that when Dewey became President, he would name Hoover as his Attorney General. William C. Sullivan of the FBI was tasked with the duty of culling FBI files (including information gained through widespread illegal FBI wiretaps of the era) to find dirt on Truman and members of his administration. Sullivan recalled: "The FBI helped Dewey during the campaign itself by giving him everything we had that could hurt Truman, though there wasn't much... We even prepared studies for Dewey which were released under his name." Surely not an appropriate use of public funds.

The US State Department is another federal agency that often displayed a mind of its own—generally in line with the interests of the wealthy elite. Roosevelt had identified this problem and it was one reason that he set up an intelligence network somewhat outside the normal American institutions. As President Truman later expressed the situation:

"The difficulty with many career officials in government is that they regard themselves as the men who really make policy and run the government. They look upon the elected officials as just temporary occupants. Every President in our history has been faced with this problem: how to prevent career men from circumventing policy... Some Presidents have handled this situation by setting up what amounted to a little State Department of their own. Roosevelt did this... I wanted to make it plain that the President of the United States and not a second or third echelon of the State Department is responsible for making policy."

Interestingly, one of the leading career men in the department Truman was complaining about at the time was noted Republican John Foster Dulles. Dulles pro-German sentiments and those held by other representatives of the ruling elite were one reason Roosevelt had earlier set up his own State Department: he wanted to prevent financial and industrial collaborationists with dealings in Nazi Germany from circumventing his pro-British policies. Distrust of the entanglements of some members of the British aristocracy, which is responsible for British Intelligence, led Churchill to take similar measures regarding his intelligence apparatus. For this reason Sir William Stephenson served as "an invisible man directing four major British intelligence departments—SOE, SIS, Security Executive, and now MI-5—plus a communications-intelligence [COMINT] web...and a secret police force on American soil."[48] Roosevelt and Truman were no innocents when it came to understanding the motives and tactics of the wealthy right. FDR's maternal grandfather, for example, was a somewhat unrestrained capitalist. "The financial panic of 1857 wiped out Delano's investment, and he returned to China to make a second—and larger—fortune in the opium trade."[49] For his pseudo-socialistic programs of the New Deal, and interference with industrialists and financiers assisting the Nazis, there was an assassination attempt against FDR. Shady elements allegedly associated with the du Ponts and J.P. Morgan (and other members of the extremely wealthy elite) funded the Liberty League, and other organisations dedicated to the overthrow of Roosevelt and his policies. During the assassination attempt General Smedley Butler had been chosen as a possible Fascist Dictator to replace the office of the president. Butler was confidently expected to take the job since he had led many imperialist missions in Latin and South America to overthrow democratic governments in favour of those sympathetic to the interests of American financiers and industrialists.[50] Butler must have had a crisis of confidence, for he went to the appropriate authorities and revealed the plan.

Efforts to deter politicians with economic and other policies to the left of the right wing were taken by the CIA and other agencies towards leading and up-and-coming politicians in virtually all the Western countries, Canada and Britain included. Even British Intelligence got into the act. Lester B. Pearson served as Canadian Ambassador to the United States during WW II. He also served as Canada's Ambassador to the United Nations, and won the Nobel Prize for Peace in 1956 for his daring stand during the Suez Crisis. He was, of course, later the Prime Minister of Canada. He was under repeated surveillance and suspicion by, as a leading example, James Jesus Angleton and his Counter-Intelligence department within the CIA. Peter Wright, who worked intimately with Angleton during the time of the Arrow program, mentions how a significant cadre of MI-5, in sympathy with CIA efforts, conspired against Harold Wilson, the soon-to-be PM of Britain, and his Labour party, in an effort to sabotage their election chances. The book *Agent of Influence,* describes how Angleton was pressuring the security agencies of Canada and the UK to act against both Pearson and Wilson. Leslie Bennett, head of the RCMP's counterintelligence branch, mentioned to an impassioned Angleton that the problem his agency had was that they couldn't tell a Communist from a socialist. "For his pains, he was suddenly physically assaulted by one of Angleton's aides."[51] The proposed arrangement was, it is written, that if the RCMP and British arrested the two leading politicians, the CIA (i.e., Angleton) would deliver the proof that would make such an arrest tenable. According to an MI-5 head at the time, the CIA had lost all perspective due to a "rotten harvest" from spurious defectors and the paranoia and declining mental health of Angleton himself. It wasn't until the defection of Vitaly Yurchenko in 1985 that Bennett, who had run RCMP Counterintelligence for 15 years without a notable success, was cleared of suspicion.

> "Yurchenko was also able to set the record straight on a suspected spy who, in fact, had been entirely innocent. Leslie James Bennett, who had worked for British Signals Intelligence during WW II, had emigrated to Canada in 1954 and joined the RCMP, eventually becoming head of the RCMP Security Service Counterintelligence section monitoring Russian espionage operations in Canada...Yurchenko was able to reveal that the real author of these failures was a genuine Soviet agent within the RCMP security service named Gilles G. Brunet, a native Canadian whose father had been the first head of the security service!"[52]

It is fascinating to contemplate how successful Soviet espionage was during the Cold War, yet how utterly unsuccessful Soviet-style Communism itself ultimately was. The reason is that it didn't produce a decent standard of living or quality of life (particularly in rights to privacy), and once this was realised, both the supply of willing spies and of party members in the West dried up. Hard-line Communism was its own worst enemy.

It is now abundantly clear that the CIA, in particular, included leaders and planners who, to be blunt, conspired to manipulate intelligence given to various governments, including their own, to achieve goals shared by right-wing elements of America's ruling class. Canadian spymaster Sir William Stephenson "had always deplored the institutionalising of intelligence. This encouraged elitists who made their own secret organizations, engaged in separate diplomacy, followed their own laws."[53] Some of the tactics, successes, and excesses are now well known yet, without doubt, the majority of operations remain hidden due to policies that ensure the destruction of evidence being standard procedure among intelligence agencies—even the legally constituted ones. The worst of the CIA 'dirty tricks' are also said to have occurred in the late '50s and early '60s under planners Bissel and Helms, and under Director Allen Welsh Dulles. During the Eisenhower era Allen Dulles' brother, John, was Secretary of State of the United States of America. J.J. McCloy, another Wall Street star, had been considered for this post but was seen by planners as being too linked to Wall Street interests to be publicly acceptable. At the time and since, critics have claimed that the right wing of the Republican Party, led by John Foster Dulles, controlled the Eisenhower administrations. Even frankly apologetic biographies of the Dulles brothers describe John Foster and Eisenhower's relationship as being more that of equals, rather than of Dulles being guided entirely by the Chief Executive. Ann Whitman, one of Eisenhower's secretaries, wrote that Ike was Dulles's "chattel". Primary sources now acknowledge that these administrations were particularly prone to manipulation through secret intelligence.

Allen Welsh Dulles

In today's world, society seems to accept that governments, the military, and the security forces routinely keep a great many secrets, and do so for a great variety of reasons. In virtually every case, tyrannies, oligarchies and plutocracies have used secrecy against society to remain in power. Secrecy, therefore, can be the enemy of freedom and democracy. It is hard to make educated political choices without a balanced and comprehensive education. In a vigilant democracy, say of the kind envisioned by the American founding fathers, secrecy is used only to protect citizens from possible harm, and the nation from external attack, of whatever kind. It is not, ideally, supposed to be used to prevent accountability or to falsify the historical record. In fact, for a government to do so is, in some cases, an international crime. But there is also the old adage: 'It isn't illegal unless you get caught.' As Chapman Pincher, a long-time British investigative journalist specialising in espionage and foreign affairs wrote: "[S]candal could be safely concealed from the public because should investigative writers, for example, seek out such information they could always be threatened with prosecution under the Official Secrets Acts, which were passed to deter and to punish spies, but have been monstrously misused to prevent the disclosure of official information of any kind." [54] John Ralston Saul (the accomplished Canadian writer who is husband to a former Governor General of Canada) makes an excellent study of this highly-developed self-protection reflex among the class he calls the "technocrats" in his book *Voltaire's Bastards.*

In Canada and, presumably, Britain, it is thought that most official secrets are released after a thirty-year period has elapsed. This is not the case. In Canada sensitive information relating to the Gouzenko defection of 1945 still remains unavailable. Enormous quantities of information on WW II are still classified, including the role of many current global corporations in Hitler's planned "New World Order". Key ministerial documents on the Avro Canada Jetliner are simply missing. In December 1978, regarding documentation on Avro's Arrow interceptor, it was put to a CBC Executive Producer, George Robertson, that "Almost all the documents in both categories are highly classified i.e. no lower than SECRET. It is possible that a detailed page by page review of the technical files could result in some or all of the material being declassified. On the other hand, it is highly unlikely that many documents from the second category could be declassified... In any event, the detailed review that would be required of each document in both categories is well beyond the capability of our staffs because of their involvement in the day to day business of the department."[55] In other words, where politically sensitive information is concerned, the government of Canada feels absolutely no compunction to release information to the public. This evidently still includes huge amounts of technical and political information on the Avro Arrow and related topics.

History also shows that secrecy has been used to do more than cover incompetence and prevent accountability. *Spycatcher* mentions how the CIA, under James Jesus Angleton and Allen Dulles, took measures in violation of the spirit and letter of the wartime ABC accords. These agreements on intelligence and other aspects of US/British (and by extension Canadian) cooperation, were advanced in the summer of 1941 as the Atlantic Charter. It was not until April, 1943, however, that the United States was apprised of the true extent of British successes in German code-breaking. The May 17, 1943 signing of the secret BRUSA (Britain/USA) agreement was the first formal agreement on sharing communications intelligence (COMINT). This remarkably successful wartime intelligence alliance was continued, albeit much more quietly, and was strengthened in the face of obvious Soviet hostility, by the UKUSA agreement (USA, Canada, Britain, Australia and New Zealand). Although dating from 1945, no participant government has yet acknowledged its existence. The UKUSA agreement, augmented by others, essentially integrated the intelligence services of the United States and the British Commonwealth. The United States was recognised as the dominant partner by its "first party" ranking in the agreement, while Britain, Canada and others are second parties. More recent joiners, such as Japan, are third parties. A stipulation, particularly where Britain and other second parties are concerned, is included which states that, concerning items of mutual interest, all data was to be shared openly.[56] While this represented the spirit and trust inherent in the arrangement, there exists plenty of evidence showing that data, perhaps particularly commercial, has been withheld from other parties, particularly by the first party. A copy of this letter was sent to the Minister of Defense at the time of the Arrow cancellation, MGen George R. Pearkes V.C.. This pointed out the request of the CBC documentary producers for any documentation confirming rumours they had heard that it was actually Pearkes himself who had ordered the destruction of the extant Arrow aircraft following Black Friday (20 February, 1959). In a separate personal letter to Pearkes it was mentioned that they had found documentation showing who had ordered the aircraft to be cut up, and that it was *unclassified.* Nixon pointed out that his department was not releasing this information because he felt it would be a "breach of trust".[57] It is clear that the letter to the CBC full of mumbo-jumbo about lack of resources and the classification of information was a pure smokescreen. In other words, as of 1978 the government was still covering up who ordered the destruction of the Arrows. It appears to have been Pearkes himself.

Considering the signals-gathering capabilities of the nations involved, it is evident that the amount of raw intelligence gathered was, (and is) gargantuan. Equally gargantuan, then, must be the resources applied to process the data gathered. The National Security Agency (NSA), the US SIGINT agency, (the mere mention of which was an American federal offence for many years), is capable of monitoring virtually any kind of wire or wireless telephonic, data, computer or satellite communications, on a global basis.[58] The NSA employs thousands of people, and the largest concentration of supercomputers and mathematicians in the world, to do just that. The inability of the smaller nations to apply such resources to collection and analysis places them at a serious disadvantage when it comes to exploiting the information available. Various revelations, beginning with the famous 1959 double defection to Moscow of two NSA agents, Martin and Mitchell, (made famous by the movie *"The Falcon and the Snowman"*) revealed that the NSA was spying on the Allies as well as the Soviet bloc.[59]

> "What has only recently become apparent is that under...the U.K.U.S.A. agreement...the British cables and telex messages were also made available to the American...National Signals Agency (N.S.A.) [later renamed the National Security Agency]... The forerunner of the N.S.A. had made a secret deal with the three American cable companies, which undertook to supply the cables daily in the national interest, though [supposedly] with much reluctance because it was illegal."[60]

Clearly then, America's wartime ally, Britain, was, in the 1950s at least, a target of US intelligence. But it didn't end with Britain. In 1957 an NSA representative approached Boris Hegelin, an important developer and manufacturer of cipher machines. "[I]t appears likely that Hegelin was asked to supply to the NSA details about various improvements and modifications made to the cipher machines his company had supplied to other governments, especially, the member countries of NATO."[61] Why, in 1957, would the United States be especially interested in spying on NATO allies? Perhaps the answer is given below:

> "On July 18, 1957, a handful of the nation's top scientists crowded together in NSA's windowless Situation Room to present a blueprint for the Agency's future technological survival.
>
> ...They recommended the initiation of a Manhattan Project-like effort to push the USA well ahead of the Soviet Union and all other nations in the application of communications, computer science, mathematics, and information theory in cryptology."[62]

Peter Wright, the veteran MI-5 electronics and signals intelligence and technology expert, mentions that by 1961 the CIA was secretly monitoring the diplomatic corps, intelligence and security agencies of various allied nations. A Jack Daniels fuelled Bill Harvey, with Angleton present, bore into Wright over MI-5's having kept advanced surveillance technology, codenamed RAFTER, from the CIA. When Wright added that MI-5 had shared the technology with the FBI and RCMP, Harvey, in drunken rage, profanely mocked the security of the technology in Canadian hands. Harvey was head of "Staff D", the clandestine branch of the CIA involved in secret SIGINT work in violation of the UKUSA agreement. He sarcastically added that Wright best tell the Canadians to get a new cipher machine—thus implying, without subtlety, that they had broken Canada's codes and were monitoring government communications. As Harvey coughed up this gem, Angleton "kicked him hard under the table".[63]

"As well as having a drinking problem, Harvey was short, fat, and hideous looking; he had bulging eyes, attributed to a thyroid condition, and a froglike voice. His agents called him 'the Pear'. Harvey was a memorably bizarre figure, out of place in any kind of normal world yet at home among double agents."[64]

According to Wright: "Harvey's Staff D was almost certainly a department designed to bypass the terms of the UKUSA agreement, which specified the total exchange of SIGINT intelligence between the [American] NSA and [British] GCHQ. If the Americans wanted to mount a cipher attack and did not wish to share the product with us, or if they wanted to operate against the UK, or a Commonwealth country, *as we were sure they were doing*, Staff D was the obvious place from which to do it." [italics added] This occurred right around the time of the Avro Arrow cancellation, it might be added.

> "Apparently not even the British were spared in the embassy monitoring, as one former Vint Hill [an NSA listening post] employee secretly confirmed to the House Government Operations Subcommittee on Government Information and Individual Rights. 'We had a whole bank of machines, the Vint Hill [operative] revealed. 'I was one of a whole team of men whose only job was to read and process intercepted British communications.'"[65]

This was, of course, right before Diefenbaker, heading into his third election campaign, suddenly faced what Knowlton Nash (an iconic Canadian journalist turned CBC news anchor, author and political follower), an American PBS documentary and other sources described as a US-inspired and CIA-led currency devaluation crisis. Such runs on currency and raising of interest rates on government bonds, with attendant 'currency flight' from the country, are tried and true methods in which the Western financial and intelligence elites have manipulated governments—foreign and domestic.

45 Pincher, Chapman: Too Secret Too Long, p.301
46 McCulloch, David. Truman, p. 552
47 Ibid. p. 553
48 Stephenson, A Man Called INTREPID, p. 140
49 Miller, FDR: An Intimate History, p. 13
50 See Hoyt, America's Wars and Military Excursions.
51 Adams, Ian, Agent of Influence, p. 231
52 Owen, David. Hidden Secrets: A Complete History of Espionage and the Technology used to Support It. Firefly: Tor onto 2002, p. 153
53 Stevenson, William: Intrepid's Last Case, p. 266
54 Pincher, Chapman: Too Secret, Too Long, p.156
55 Nixon, C.R. National Defence Headquarters, reply to Mr. Geo. Robertson of the CBC, 5 December, 1978
56 Bamford, James. The Puzzle Palace, Inside the National Security Agency, New York: Penguin Books, 1983 p. 399
57 Nixon, C.R. letter to MGen (ret'd) George R. Pearkes V.C., 4 April, 1978
58 Ibid. If you read and pay attention to the advances in capability, minus losses (what losses?), over the last 50 years, you'll get the picture.
59 Kahn, David. The Codebreakers, The History of Secret Writing. New York: Macmillan, 1967
60 Pincher, Chapman: Too Secret, Too Long p.p. 458-59
61 Bamford: The Puzzle Palace, p. 408
62 Ibid. p. 429
63 Wright, Peter: Spycatcher
64 Thomas, Evan: The Very Best Men; The Daring Early Years of the CIA, Ney York: Simon & Schuster, Inc. 2006 p. 130
65 Bamford: The Puzzle Palace p. 213

Chapter 8

MONEY CARTEL

As Niall Ferguson writes of Europe in the 19th century:

> "Government bearer [bonds] were, it might be said, a kind of daily opinion poll, an expression of confidence in a given regime. Of course, they were an opinion poll based on a highly unrepresentative sample... only the wealthy–the "capitalists"–got to vote. These capitalists were thus, to a large extent, Europe's political class in a stratified, undemocratic society. If investors bid up the price of a government's stock, that government could feel secure. If they dumped its stock, that government was quite possibly living on borrowed time as well as money." [66]

During the 1962 election campaign, and again after Canadian PM Pearson's first budget, destabilising runs on the Canadian currency actually took place. In the first instance, in a radical response, Diefenbaker pegged the value of the Canadian dollar at 92 cents American for the duration of the campaign, and survived with a minority government. In other countries, such as Nazi Germany, the imposition of currency controls similar to those taken by Diefenbaker had an alarmist effect on the leading financiers in the West. Government interference in the realm of global financiers and central bankers and the response of those financial powers has been neglected as an area of public historical debate. Of course, had the government of Canada not given up its responsibility for creation and valuation of currency to private bankers, it would never have been an issue.

Another example of FDR's resistance to the monopolists came during his tenure as Governor of New York. He studied hydro-electric generation problems and thought the private utilities were gouging consumers. "...the Morgan interests were in the process of merging three of the largest upstate power companies—a merger that was expected to lead to a boost in electricity prices. ...Roosevelt warned that if the private companies refused to transmit electricity generated by publicly-owned power companies to the consumer at low rates, the state might construct its own transmission lines. The Republicans rejected the proposal, but had been outmanoeuvered by the governor... Louis Howe was assigned to compare the rates paid by Canadian consumers for public-generated electricity with those paid by New Yorkers, who got theirs from private utilities. As he expected, there was a large discrepancy in charges with the Canadian rates being substantially lower."[67] That, in Canada and Britain, a more recent wave of privatisations of utilities, predicted to lower rates, hasn't, should perhaps serve as an indication of the interests being served by the politicians responsible, particularly considering the many historical precedents. This might suggest that privatisation, *laissez-faire* economics, and so-called 'globalisation' are ultimately dysfunctional if not destructive to the interests of the majority.

When the Great Depression came, FDR became a hero of the poor for actions in line with statements such as: "I wish our banking and economist friends would realize the seriousness of the situation from the standpoint of the debtor class—i.e., 90 percent of the human beings in the country—and think less from the point of view of the 10 percent who constitute the creditor classes." Contrast that with the current view of neo-conservatives and business magnates and their captive politicians and media. FDR's predecessor, Herbert Hoover, "...was the last defender of the doctrine that the government should not interfere with the marketplace... In face of charges that the 'trickle down' theory constituted a dole for corporations, [Hoover was having American taxpayers bail out failing corporations yet nobody was bailing out the American taxpayer] Hoover argued that restoring prosperity to the banks and corporations would, in turn, reinvigorate the economy...Americans were puzzled—and then angered—that a president who handed out relief to corporations could ignore the misery of people grubbing in garbage cans..."[68] "The nation's business leaders were summoned before the Senate Finance Committee and asked for their solution to the crisis. If there was a consensus, it was... 'Balance budgets, stop spending money we haven't got... Tax, tax everybody for everything.' And yet these hide-bound and rather dim luminaries were the people that neo-conservatives and 'economic royalists' consider the engine of economic growth: *themselves.* Herbert Hoover Jr. would be the Undersecretary of State under John Foster Dulles in the 1950s. The key to the President elect's (FDR's) program was the restoration of consumer purchasing power and a sales tax, reducing the amount available for spending [a tight money policy], would be counterproductive."[69] A couple of comments around the time of his acclamation to run for the Democrats for a second term are indicative:

> "We have invited battle, we have earned the hatred of entrenched greed." On a modest reform of the Federal Reserve system: "We have driven the money changers from the temple." And on accepting the nomination: "The royalists of the economic order have conceded that political freedom was the business of Government, but they have maintained that economic slavery was nobody's business. They granted that the Government could do anything to protect the citizen in his right to vote, but they denied that Government could do anything to protect the citizen in his right to work and his right to live... These economic royalists complain that we seek to overthrow the institutions of America. What they really complain about is that we seek to take away their power."[70]

And, to some extent, he and Truman did. However, during the Eisenhower Republican administration, the tables were again turned. Roosevelt privately disclosed the magnitude of the power held by a tiny ruling elite in America in a letter to Colonel House, an advisor to Woodrow Wilson: "The real truth of the matter is, as you and I know, that a financial element in the larger centers has owned the government since the days of Andrew Jackson—and I am not wholly excepting the Administration of W.W. [Woodrow Wilson]. The country is going through a repetition of Jackson's fight with the Bank of the United States—only on a far bigger scale and broader basis."[71] This had been the first attempt to set up a central bank in the United States and had been seen by Jackson and others as an attempt to make the US government subservient to international bankers. Woodrow Wilson had allowed just that to happen in 1913 with the passage of the Federal Reserve Act, which placed control of the American currency in the hands of a consortium of 12 private banks—quite literally a cartel. It is redundant to point out that cartel's generally do not favour economic liberalism and healthy competition, nor, indeed, other democratic principles. Cartels are concentrations of power and capital in the hands of a tiny, unelected, undemocratic elite.

The role of central banks in Canada, Britain the United States, and other Western nations and their defacto ownership of the currency are suppressed truths. Despite protests from the US Federal Reserve, it was shown in a lawsuit in 1986 to actually be privately owned. Logically the citizens of a nation own all the wealth in the nation therefore the currency should also be owned by them, and controlled by their democratically elected representatives: the government. It was held that the owners of the currency, the people, should be the ones responsible for creating and loaning money, through the government, to lower-order enterprises and individuals. Under this system, big banks have to borrow from the people at interest, improving revenues for the treasury, thereby reducing the requirement to tax the people. Governments would thereby borrow from themselves, with no need for interest on national debts to further inflate the tax burden on the citizens. In 1913 this changed in the United States, at the behest of, in part, James Warburg, a banker associated with the Wall Street firm of Kuhn Loeb (and M.M. Warburg in Germany), and the Morgan, Rockefeller and other similar 'economic royalists'. From that time forth, anytime the US government needs to spend money above what is in the treasury, they have to borrow it at interest from the private banks comprising the Federal Reserve. One can see the difference in revenues between banks borrowing from government at interest to the opposite. Not only did this revenue now become a liability, but compound interest ensured an even heavier, and previously non-existent, tax burden on the public. It also vastly expanded the power of the wealthy elite and changed the government from being the top economic authority in the land to a second order entity. Obviously this was highly undemocratic, which is why the American people never got the opportunity to vote on it.

Closer to home, the Conservative government of Leslie Bennett adopted similar policies at the behest of similar special interests in Canada. By this time about half of Canadian manufacturing and most of Canadians' external debts were owed to the United States, so the probability of American influence in this decision is high. "R.B. Bennett inherited a system in which the chartered banks could borrow newly printed dominion notes from the Department of Finance... When the Depression began, the Canadian dollar was theoretically convertible into gold at a fixed price, but the King government had quietly suspended that arrangement in the winter of 28-29, and in autumn 1931 the Bennett government made the suspension public and permanent."[72] In other words, as of 1929, since the currency was no longer supported by reserve metals, the government could produce money at virtually no cost.

Then, in 1935, McKenzie King's Liberals formed the Bank of Canada as a *private* institution to control the Canadian currency. Through this the government now had to borrow money from the dominant shareholders of the Chartered Banks, not the other way around. As of this date the owners of the chartered banks could, since there was (and is) no reserve metal requirement, create money at virtually no cost and lend it at interest (and principal) to the government, businesses and individuals. Today is the era of debt-based currency. If you want a loan, the money is created as a ledger entry for basically nothing, and loaned to you at interest. Obviously this is highly profitable to those granted the ability to create money merely on your promise to pay it back, with interest, and requires no real productive effort on the part of the lenders. The formation of a Canadian central bank was probably done as part of the measures included in King's reciprocal trade agreement of the same year with the United States—thus harmonising the Canadian and American systems. With the coming of WW II and due to the objections of populists to the privatisation of the central bank, King nationalised the Bank of Canada in 1938. This gained for the Government the right to borrow money for itself or the provinces at little or no interest, and through an agreement with the Chartered Banks money was created at low interest for the purposes of the Second World War. *This*, and the hard work of Canadians, allowed the economy to double in size during the war. Yet, subsequently, the Bank of Canada has rarely been imposed upon to lend the government money at low interest and operates in the same way as the US "Federal" Reserve. As a result, we have a large national debt. Neo and other conservatives like to blame the government for these deficits and debts—because they presumably cannot manage their spending. Perhaps had currency creation been left to the government, and the banks to borrow from this source, national debts wouldn't be such a problem, and the largest single item on which revenue is spent and taxpayers are taxed—interest on the national debt—wouldn't be such a problem. That these facts are suppressed are a good indication of where power really flows from, and who our top leading politicians really represent: those who can afford to lend money at interest. As the book *The Money Spinners* states, in Canada the directors of the Bank of Canada, all leading executives of the chartered banks, really run the economic policy of Canada with the minor meddling of the politicians being tolerated—unless they are really at odds with the bankers' agenda. In those cases they are sufficiently powerful and well connected to the corporate media and other power brokers to cause the politicians unbearable difficulties.

66 Ferguson, Niall: The Rothschilds; Money's Prophets, p.6
67 Miller, FDR, p. 233
68 Miller, FDR, p.p. 252, 253
69 Ibid, p.p. 292, 293
70 Ibid, p.p. 379-384
71 Ibid, p. 334
72 Bothwell, Drummond and English, Canada; 1900-1945, p. 250

Chapter 9

DAWN OF THE JET AGE

While several inventors postulated on gas turbine, (jet) engines, even going to the point of producing some working models, Frank Whittle is credited with having patented the first practical jet-engine for aircraft propulsion. Whittle was born the son of a mechanic in 1907 and joined the RAF as an apprentice in the same trade in 1923. His skill in producing replica aircraft models, obvious mathematical gifts and his general conduct so impressed his commanding officer that he was recommended for Cranwell, the RAF's officer training college. In those days, the British military was ruled, like most other areas of professional endeavour in Britain, by people from the upper class, making Whittle's acceptance a rare event. It must have been sobering to realise that this guaranteed nothing—candidates from apprentice backgrounds historically faced a 99% failure rate.

Whittle made the grade however, and for his master's thesis attacked the problem of high-speed flight and showed that existing technology (i.e., propeller-driven, piston-powered aircraft) were unlikely to get much past 500 mph. He was correct in this conclusion, and to top off a masterful performance, proposed a solution in detail: a gas turbine, or jet engine and aircraft. Yet Whittle had been enrolled to train as a pilot, and his flying also proved excellent, with Whittle graduating in 1928 with an "exceptional to above average" flying rating, and second in his class over-all. In 1936 he graduated with a First in Mechanical Sciences.

Industry, finance, and government, failed to grasp the potential of his concepts at first, and so public funding and/or official sanction was hard to come by. Private funding was equally elusive. This was in part due to the fact that the Ministry of Supply (MOS) had referred Whittle's 1929 ideas to A.A. Griffith, who had actually published a paper on axial-flow jet powerplants for aircraft in 1926, somewhat ahead of Whittle. Griffith criticised Whittle's selection of a centrifugal compressor, and suggested its inherent design would make it too large, in terms of frontal area, to be practical for aircraft. He also suggested that to use the exhaust directly for thrust, rather than to drive a propeller, would also be inefficient. While correct that the axial flow principle was better, Whittle proved him wrong on the other counts, but only after many trials and partnerships of convenience (and desperation?) in the process. When the RAF turned Whittle down on the development of the engine, it meant that he was free to patent the idea himself, and was convinced to do so by, of all people, a man who would go on to fame as one of the top Allied aces of WW II: Johnnie Johnson. When his patent lapsed in 1935, he was convinced by three other RAF officers familiar with his work to form a joint venture company to develop his engine. Power Jets was duly formed. They managed to run the "Whittle Union", or "WU" engine, in April, 1937. Interest was still anaemic until the war started, although the British government provided some modest funds, and a contract, to develop a flyable engine: the W.1.

In April 1941 the first jet-engine to fly in the West propelled the Gloster E.28/39 to velocities faster than the RAF's vaunted Spitfires—recently triumphant in the Battle of Britain. Interestingly, the W.1, which powered this plane, was built around a crucial piece of technology in the Spitfire itself: the centrifugal compressor disc of the Spitfire's Rolls-Royce Merlin engine's supercharger. This performance occurred, no doubt, to the chagrin of Griffith who had teamed with Metropolitan Vickers to develop his axial-flow turboprop concept into a flyable engine: the F.1. This was set aside when Whittle's centrifugal W.1 proved so fast, right off the mark, in a Gloster-designed research aircraft that Griffith turned to the F.2, which deleted the propeller and gearbox from his F.1 turboprop design making it a pure jet engine. This culminated in the successful Metrovick F.2 Beryl, Britain's first axial jet engine. In terms of low frontal area and thrust output, the Beryl vindicated Griffith, yet, when the RAF and MOS people viewed it they were somewhat aghast at the complexity of the engine and its requirement for extreme precision in the fabrication of its many parts. The compressor section of Griffith's axial design comprised nine discs with a multiplicity of precision-machined and finished blades on each disc, rotating between ten stationary rings of similar blades. That is 19 sets of blades, and nine discs, to accomplish what one, cheap, cast steel disc was doing in Whittle's engine.

Wartime gave impetus to production and technology-sharing of Whittle's ideas which precluded his dream of founding an industrial concern that would lead in jet engine development and production. The Air Ministry offered development and production contracts to Vauxhall, British Thomson Houston (which, interestingly, had merged with Metrovick) and Rover. Rover accepted the challenge. In 1941 they set up a laboratory and production line at one of their facilities, but also set up a parallel operation, using their own engineers, at another site. Here Adrian Lombard dispensed with the 'reverse flow' combustors Whittle was using on the W.1 and new W.2 designs, and modified Whittle's W.2B/23 into the W.2B/26.

Rolls-Royce got more directly involved in the jet-engine game through Stanley Hooker, a design engineer who ran their supercharger division and had been called upon to help devise solutions to surging problems encountered with the early centrifugals based, more or less, on his compressors. (One of the reasons their Rolls-Royce Merlin held such a competitive advantage to most engines produced during WW II was due to the superiority of the Merlin's superchargers.) Rolls had also been contracted by Whittle to produce a few W.2 engines, leading to an interesting blending of interests. It was no secret that Whittle himself was incensed by Rover which had taken his technology and developed it on their own into the "straight through" W.2B/26, perhaps leading him to look to Rolls as a possible means out of his situation with Rover. The end to the situation unfolded at the Swan and Royal Pub where Rolls-Royce's managing director Ernest Hives, Stanley Hooker, and Rover's Spence Wilkes met over a few pints and decided to do a swap. Rover would trade Rolls their jet operation for a division of Rolls-Royce involved in the production of a Merlin-derived engine that powered armoured vehicles. Power Jets and Frank Whittle suddenly found themselves without production capability. Perhaps knowledge of this deal helped prompt Sir Roy Dobson to exclaim, after Hives backed out of a promise to provide Avon engines for Avro Canada Jetliners in 1947; "That's Rolls-Royce for you, they'll screw you every time." Dobson had nearly lost Avro's heavy bomber program (for the Manchester/Lancaster) due to problems with Rolls-Royce's Vulture engine.

The deal was consummated on January 1st, 1943, although not officially. Rolls closed Rover's "parallel" operation, but continued development of Lombard's W.2B/26, *and* Whittle's W.2B/23. They would eventually emerge as the Derwent and Welland engines respectively. And so Whittle's brainchildren were adopted by Rolls-Royce, and Stanley Hooker embarked on a prodigious career in gas-turbine engineering.

Whittle's technology came to the United States more directly. In 1942 he was sent to assist the General Electric gas turbine program in Boston. They were licensed to produce a version of the W.2 and did so, for America's first experimental jet fighter, the Bell Airacomet. Pratt & Whitney would produce under license the Rolls-Royce Nene, which, being an enlarged Derwent, also owed a great deal to Whittle's work. Nevertheless, the British centrifugals were considerably superior to early American efforts.

De Havilland also came by their jet-engine technology through inspiration derived from Whittle's efforts. Frank Halford had modified an enemy WW I piston aero engine into the British BHP, which Armstrong Siddeley produced as the Puma (in the process helping introduce this future Hawker Siddeley component company into the aero engine field). Enthused by the rpm (and thus power) offered by the sleeve-valve, he collaborated with Napier engines to produce the amazing Sabre engine, which produced over 1.5 hp per cubic inch of displacement (modern high performance automotive engines are finally achieving this today). With Whittle's successful running of the W.1, Halford developed an interest in jets, and proceeded to produce a simplified "straight through" centrifugal engine design based on Whittle's engine. The resulting Halford H.1 ran in April, 1942 and was soon taken up by de Havilland who developed it into the Goblin engine which would power de Havilland's Vampire jet fighters. This, and de Havilland's other jet-engine, the Ghost, would prove disappointing compared to Rolls-Royce's Derwent and Nene engines however. Also in 1942, an unemployed English engineer named Harry Keast would join Power Jets. He soon showed a real flair for aerodynamic and thermodynamic design. He would later become a mainstay of Canada's Orenda Engines design team.

Following the Puma in-line engine from WW I, Armstrong Siddeley produced a series of air-cooled radials also named after big cats, like the Cheetah and Lynx. They started work on gas turbine engines in 1939, and soon produced the Mamba and Double Mamba turboprop powerplants. A larger turboprop, the Python, was also produced, as well as the Adder, which was a pure turbojet version of the Mamba—dispensing with the latter's propeller, gearbox, and power turbine. Having been left in the cold with their promising F.2 Beryl, Metrovick's jet-engine operation was ripe for take-over in 1947, when the British government encouraged them to join Armstrong Siddeley. In the process, Hawker Siddeley gained some brilliant engineers, and the emerging F.9 engine, which was then dubbed the Sapphire. In 1947 it produced 7,500 lbs of thrust during testing, far outstripping the Rolls-Royce Avon, or any other engine for that matter. Due to its superiority many were soon built under license in the United States by Curtiss Wright, and used, to the chagrin of Pratt & Whitney, Allison, Westinghouse and General Electric, in many US aircraft.

The Armstrong Siddeley Sapphire ASSa.7 jet engine

Chapter 10

TURBO RESEARCH

Not wanting to be left behind in the new field of gas turbine engines, in 1942 Canada's National Research Council (NRC) sent a team of scientists, including Paul Dilworth and Ken Tupper, to Britain to work at Power Jets and to study Whittle's concepts. By January 1944, a Whittle engine was running in a government facility at Stevenson Field (now Winnipeg Airport) for cold weather research purposes.

In July 1944 the Crown company Turbo Research was established to direct gas turbine research, and a team of engineers, Dilworth and Winnett Boyd, were involved in designing some engines of their own. The TR-1 was a centrifugal flow engine similar to Whittle's engines and the Rolls-Royce derivatives thereof, with the TR-2 being an axial. Boyd later remarked;

> "I submitted these proposals to a team of three people…and they decided on the axial compressor… Detailing work did commence on a design known as the TR-3, but it was crude…and I was delighted when the opportunity came in the autumn to abandon it. For the record, it might be worth noting that the TR-3 was designed for 4,200 pounds thrust and was 40 inches in diameter."[73]

The design study for the TR-3 resides in the Toronto Aerospace Museum and a perusal thereof indicates that Boyd wasn't exaggerating when he says they had detail designed much of this engine. It is very similar to the Chinook and Orenda, yet at 40 inches in diameter it had a low output—especially since the Iroquois would eventually produce over five times this thrust from a nacelle size only two inches larger. Finally an axial flow design named the TR-4 Chinook was accepted as an engine to cut their teeth on. Considering the modest thrust expectation, of around 3,500 lbs, and the existence of the German axials and the Metrovick F.2 Beryl axial, it seems the government was being, at best, conservative. But, at this time, for the allies at least, axial flow turbine engines were exotic technology and about the best engine in terms of performance (at around 3,500 lbs thrust) and reliability was the Rolls-Royce Derwent, which was based on Whittle's W.2. Whittle's engines were centrifugal flow, and this was proven technology by 1945, however axial flow designs were known to hold more promise, but probably more development headaches too. Indeed, Rolls-Royce ambitiously set out to produce an axial flow engine of 6,500 lbs thrust, the Avon, in 1943. It would be ten years before that engine was meeting expectations in thrust and reliability. In the same year, Griffith and Metrovick embarked on their next axial, the bigger F.9. Both Metrovick designs would use an annular combustion section, compared to the more complex 'can' type employed on all the centrifugal flow engines, and also on most early American axials. While Hawker Siddeley was inheriting Metrovick's operation, it had acquired another axial flow jet-engine effort in Canada: Turbo Research. The Chinook turbojet was A.V. Roe Canada's first design success and ran in 1948.

Post-war, as Director General of the Department of Reconstruction, Crawford Gordon Jr. advised his minister, C.D. Howe, that the government could not justify sustaining Turbo Research in peacetime and therefore the government should try to find a private firm to take on the enterprise and make something of the government's investment.

> "It is my understanding that Turbo Research have proposed a five-year program for the manufacture and development of prototype jet engines and that this program will cost some eight million. It is also my understanding that Turbo Research was formed to (a) develop and manufacture jet engines for aircraft and (b) provide the nucleus of a new industry in Canada… Following my discussions in the last two weeks, I cannot help but feel that these two objects cannot be attained under the present plan of operating a Crown Company working solely on aircraft jet engines.
>
> "As I see it, the jet-engine will be used in many fields, i.e. locomotives, stationary power units, ship propulsion units, aircraft engines and possibly for the automotive industry…
>
> "Similarly, I cannot see how Canada can hope to establish an aircraft jet-engine industry to compete on world markets…
>
> "To sum up, if A.V. Roe is able to bring a group into Canada to work on aircraft jet engines, I feel Turbo Research should be disbanded, A.V. Roe and Company and the National Research Council absorbing the majority of the skilled personnel…"[74]

The government didn't accept the suggestion of A.V. Roe immediately, however. According to Fred Smye:

> "The first time I told Howe and Scully we wanted Turbo, they told me to hold my horses. They both wanted an established company to take it on. So they put out proposals to Pratt & Whitney, Rolls-Royce, and Bristol with the condition that any and all technical data in the hands of these existing companies would be made available to the Canadian companies. The first to fold was Pratt & Whitney. The next to go was Rolls-Royce who cracked, 'Tell the Canadians they can put a maple leaf sticker on the Avon if that'll make them happy.'
>
> "So that left Bristol and ourselves. Bristol sent a team to look things over...[and] said that Canada wouldn't know how to even manufacture an engine, let alone design one, so count them out...
>
> "In the meantime, Dobson went to the Ministry of Aircraft Production and met with Sir Archibald Rowlands, the Deputy Minister, and said he wanted him to authorize Armstrong-Siddeley and Bristol to provide us with all their data so when we took over Turbo we would have all the latest tech data available to us from England. We got the permission. Turbo was ours."[75] And Dobson's ability and dedication to his Canadian venture were underscored.

The acquisition provided a seed by which to fulfil an earlier promise made to C.D. Howe when he took over the Victory Aircraft facilities, to get into the design and production of gas turbine (jet) engines in Canada. The Hawker Siddeley Group had Armstrong Siddeley engines, who, with the Metrovick merger, were leaders in axial flow design, and now they had a nucleus in Canada on which to build. Turbo Research became Avro Gas Turbines Ltd., and the first success of the corporation was their TR-4 Chinook axial flow turbojet engine. It should be noted that some of the British investors and directors, along with some politicians and members of the British 'establishment', were against Hawker Siddeley's (and thus Dobson's) venture in Canada. Industrial and technical pride where at stake in some cases, and competition for money, resources and jobs was fierce in Britain. Dobson's vision won the day however, and within thirteen years his tiny rent-to-own venture had become Canada's largest employer and one of the top 100 companies in the world. Initially Avro produced whatever it could get contracts for. Hairbrushes, oil-furnaces and cookware were early gap-fillers. The company was granted maintenance, repair and modification contracts for the RCAF by the government, and by 1948 the Victory Aircraft facility had been paid off–before the company had produced a single airplane.

In Canadian officialdom all were not unanimous in their support of the new venture. J.H. Parkin of the National Research Council (NRC) was not forwarding to A.V. Roe Canada many of the technical reports being sent by Bristol to Canada for the jet-engine effort. After hearing complaints from Paul Dilworth, Fred Smye went to C.D. Howe who arranged a meeting between Smye and the head of the NRC, Jack Mackenzie.

> "So I went over and told him the story. He brought in J.H. Parkin and he said, "Mr. Smye is missing a few reports,' and as soon as he mentioned Howe, Parkin started to shake. It seems Parkin had been sending some of the reports from Bristol back to England by surface mail, questioning whether the material should be made available to A.V. Roe.
>
> "He explained this to Mackenzie who turned about six shades of red and asked how many of the reports had been returned. It turned out to be many.
>
> "This was one of the things we had to put up with occasionally—the technical jealousy of Parkin and his guys in the NRC. They felt that if anybody was going to develop airplanes and engines, it should be them."[76]

Unfortunately for Smye and Avro, Parkin was soon to replace Jack Mackenzie.

73 Stewart, Shutting Down the National Dream, p. 80
74 Stewart, Shutting Down the National Dream, p.81
75 ibid p. 82
76 ibid p. 85

Chapter 11

BACK IN THE UK

It is easy to forget, 60 years on, that after the war the British economy was devastated. Prior to the war, in fact, all through the 1920s and 30s, Britain had been experiencing a continual drain on her treasury–thanks in part to Churchill returning Britain to the Gold standard, largely under the advice of international bankers closely associated with or working for the treasury. Due to exasperbated currency flight, Churchill was forced to abandon it. After being somewhat deprived of currency in the inter-war period, Britain went on to spend a fortune in WW II in the United States for war supplies and equipment. The US had also driven a hard bargain with lend-lease in accordance with advice given by Nelson Rockefeller and other interested financiers and industrialists, with them particularly interested in inheriting the remnants of British (and indeed European) colonialism in the Western Hemisphere.[77] Suffice it to say that post-war Britain, deprived of her money, markets, and sources of raw materials, was suffering. Rationing was still on, and many things we take for granted, such as creamery butter, eggs, fresh vegetables and fruit, were still almost unheard of luxuries. Britain was even having a hard time keeping warm in the winter. A reluctance to export money for fuel made them concentrate on coal, and when a hard winter blew onto the Isles and stayed for a few weeks in 1946-47, the weather nearly achieved what Hitler had failed to do with the U-Boat wolf packs of a few years earlier. Due to this situation Avro Canada became a Mecca for British (and European) engineers seeking to avoid the rationing and other problems of post-war Europe. In fact the flood of engineers migrating to the A.V. Roe Canada operation became unofficially termed "the British airlift".

All was not well on the diplomatic front between America and Britain in 1947.

> "Peace also complicated financial relations between the United States and Britain. Both countries tentatively decided during the war that postwar prosperity would be best served by liberalizing international trade. Cordell Hull, America's wartime secretary of state, promoted liberalized trade as one of the world's most urgent needs. Britain accepted the principle, though not always enthusiastically. Britain knew that the great days of British trade would not return quickly after the war."
>
> "Before 1939 Britain had financed a large trade deficit with immense earnings from foreign investment and such "invisibles" as shipping and insurance. Britain would have to export more after the war than it ever had before, and would therefore benefit from lower trade barriers in other countries. This was true as long as no major trading nation suffered a serious depression…" [it also assumed that currencies would be valued based on GDP, and not subject to speculation and manipulation, which was not the case at the time.]
>
> "…John Maynard Keynes, [the famous economist and one of] the government's principal advisors on these matters, concluded that the successful transition to peacetime [in Britain] would have to be financed by aid from outside, obviously, from the United States…
>
> "The idea was sabotaged by President Truman's premature (and, even he later admitted, ill-advised) decision to terminate lend-lease just seven days after Japan surrendered… Less than a month after lend-lease was cancelled, a British delegation which included Keynes was in Washington in search of aid—preferably a grant, but a loan if a grant was impossible. After three months of difficult negotiations, the United States agreed to a loan of $3.75 billion, plus $650 million to help Britain pay for lend-lease and purchases of American surplus property. The terms of the loan were not generous…Britain would have to make sterling freely convertible a year after the agreement went into effect, and meet other stipulations…
>
> "Keynes's first request had been for a gift of $6 billion. It was rejected out of hand by the American negotiators…"[78]

Of course, making sterling freely convertible again also made it possible for the very basis of Britain's currency to be exported, along with the means by which Britons could own their own enterprises and grow their economy back to health. Loans to pay for US equipment merely added another layer of debt for the UK and another source of profits for wealthy Americans fortunate enough to be in a position to lend to governments. No doubt many involved in British financial circles, allied to Hawker Siddeley, had high hopes that their Canadian operation might sell product to the USA and recoup some of the losses experienced in the ongoing currency flight. The United States had also embargoed international transfers of gold out of the United States (i.e., made it unconvertible, paper international debts and US currency could no longer be redeemed by a foreigner for US Federal Reserve gold.) Roosevelt had done all this, plus had confiscated all the gold the US government could find, including from private individuals, in 1933. In short, the United States had seized all the gold the United States had acquired within her borders from the industrial and munitions profits of World War One, and during the stock market's speculative binge of the 'Roaring Twenties', and had used it to strengthen her currency. This tended to offset the power of the owners of gold, particularly the international bankers, with them retaliating by handicapping the value of the US currency to the best of their ability.[79] During the early years of the war she was able to finance a massive conversion of her industry to weaponry while observing the other nations' in their various theatres of war. By the time the United States entered the war on December 8th, 1941, there were plenty of eager customers, at any price, for weapons, or rations, stamped "Made in U.S.A."

Something else Britain suddenly found itself confronted with was the prospect of having to buy (under strict license), atomic energy, whether military or civil. With the passage of the McMahon Act in the US Congress in 1946, Britain (and Canada) were cut out of the atomic energy technology that they had helped produce—technology they had felt was promised under the Hyde-Park agreement between Churchill, Roosevelt and Mackenzie King when they formed the ABC alliance, and subsequently when they became partners in what was code named "Manhattan Engineering District": the effort to develop the atomic bomb.[80]

> "By August 1946 Britain had already clashed twice with the United States on important issues, and on both occasions the American position prevailed at Britain's expense. The subjects at hand were atomic energy and money.
>
> "When the war ended, Britain expected to begin an atomic energy program based on the information developed by the British and American scientists who built the atomic bomb. Roosevelt and Churchill had agreed in 1944 that 'full collaboration [for] military and commercial [atomic] purposes should continue after the defeat of Japan unless and until terminated by joint agreement.' But the spirit of this arrangement, known as the Hyde Park Agreement–died with Roosevelt. Two months after his death officials in Washington could not even find the American copy of the agreement...
>
> "...but it soon emerged that the United States was unwilling to allow a really complete exchange of information.
>
> "...Atlee [who replaced Churchill as British PM]...complained that Britain's contribution to the atomic project was not being fairly rewarded and that the United States was evading its commitment to help Britain establish its own atomic project.
>
> "Truman did not reply immediately because Congress was then considering the McMahon Act, which was...signed by the president on August 1, 1946. One of its provisions was that the United States could not share atomic secrets [incl. for electrical generation] with any other nation."[81]

There was to be no free trade in atomic technology or currency reserve metals. One of the end results was that Britain was as dependent as ever on coal and imported oil to keep its lights on and its industries humming. In 1952 a killer fog, resulting from reliance on coal, engulfed London and resulted in the deaths of a large number of residents. In yet another example of political expedience, the British government lied about the cause and attributed the deaths to an outbreak of influenza. Meanwhile, trade and currency issues continued to exacerbate international relations.

Due in part to Britain's financially precarious position, after the war Canada was forced to look at defense in a more North American context. Once the Cold War began to heat up in Korea and the Soviets developed long range jet bombers, nuclear weapons, and, eventually, the ICBM, the attractiveness of cozying up to the Americans seemed to grow. Canadian defense policy itself had changed dramatically for Canada from, up to the mid-1930s, an alliance with Britain against the United States, to an alliance dominated by Britain allied to the United States, and then, finally, to an alliance dominated by the United States. Some recognised that not all of America's overtures were altruistic, and that Canada was risking a great deal in deciding to be the junior partner with a nation that threw ten times its weight, compared to a junior partnership with a country only about four times bigger. In fact, it was a desire to become stronger and thus not play 'comic side-kick" to any 'big brother' that manifested itself in the Middle Power philosophy. In reality they were following nationalist economic policies much like those that had allowed first Britain, and then America, to expand their economies to the point of being the largest in the world. By maintaining first-class independent Canadian economic technical and production capability, along with a principled diplomatic policy, Canada hoped to be able to play a much more active role in keeping peace on the international playground.

77 Collier and Horowitz. The Rockefellers, An American Dynasty. Nelson and most of his brothers were involved in intelligence matters and strategic planning,with Nelson being a government advisor on Lend Lease negotiations, and advocating stripping Britain of its remaining Western Hemisphere possessions as partial payment for the weapons on which her survival depended. In fact the key brothers all had 'hemispheres of influence' with Nelson concentrating on South America, JDR IIIrd on Asia, and David busy on Army intelligence work in Africa and global banking interests with Chase Manhattan, which he would soon run. Laurance seemed to concern himself mostly with US armaments manufacturers, while Winthrop actually served in uniform, and in combat, in the Pacific Theatre.

78 Kaiser, Robt. G. Cold Winter Cold War. New York: Stein & Day, 1974 pp. 87-88

79 this is explored in Chernow, Ron. The Warburgs, The Twentieth Century Odyssey of a Remarkable Jewish Family, New York: Vintage Books, 1993

80 Kahn, David. The Codebreakers, The History of Secret Writing New York: Macmillan, 1967 p.545

81 Kaiser, Robert G.. Cold Winter Cold War. New York: Stein & Day, 1974 pp. 85-86

Chapter 12

US-CANADIAN JOINT DEFENSE

On the Canada-US front, in May 1946, under provisions of the Joint Board on Defense established at Ogdensburg, the Military Cooperative Committee (MCC) was established to look at post-war defense concerns shared by the US and Canada.

> "Two papers were drafted and approved by both sections: 'Appreciation of the Requirements for Canadian—U.S. Security' and 'Outline of Joint Canadian—U.S. Basic Security Plan.' The joint appreciation set out clearly the committee's perception of the threat against which the two countries would have to be prepared to defend. Although it was based almost exclusively on American intelligence, none of its assertions was challenged seriously by the Canadian Chiefs of Staff...Beginning in 1950 there would be the additional threat of missiles and nuclear weapons targeted against centres of 'executive, military and industrial control,' population centres, and vital concentrations of industry, transportation and communications."[82]

This reliance on US intelligence would later become a major factor in the cancellation of the Avro fighter-interceptor program. In 1947 agreements were exchanged to move towards greater integration of forces and standardization of equipment. The conclusions of its very first meeting were that the coming threats shared by the United States and Canada were against long-range bombers, and nuclear missiles.[83] If the possibilities of ICBMs, realized ten years later upon the launching of Sputnik on 4 October, 1957 [84] came as a shock to defense planners, it could only have been because they were incompetent. These documents show that the threat of nuclear missiles was being planned for ten years before Sputnik placed its tiny radio transmitter in orbit, with the development of a nuclear missile expected as early as 1950.

> "The Americans on the committee operated under the assumption that the major threat to the security of North America lay in the possibility of a massive Soviet air strike on the North American industrial heartland, coming from across the Canadian Arctic. Air deterrent must, therefore, they felt, be the principal defense priority... [T]he immediate construction of an extensive and integrated Canadian-American air defense system should be the number one priority for continental security.
>
> "...Mackenzie King and some of the Canadian military chiefs, particularly Bob Leckie, Chief of [the] Air Staff, had strong reservations. Leckie was particularly concerned that only American intelligence estimates were used in preparing the report and was not convinced that any future war with Russia would start with a polar air strike. If war was to come, reasoned Leckie, it would begin in Europe with ground and air forces, and any attack on North America would be a small operation designed to divert Allied military resources and personnel from the European Continent.
>
> "...King, as anti-military as ever, shied away from...any active joint defense effort with the United States; [he believed] it would be this above all else that would provoke [a] Soviet response... Truman was furious...and 'summoned' Mackenzie King to Washington..."[85]

On the resulting trip the Gouzenko defection was also a topic of discussion. While visiting the British Ambassador to the United States [Lord Halifax] one of the Cambridge Five spies was allowed to overhear King's discussion of the Gouzenko defection with Halifax. As we have already seen King's attitude towards integration with the United States seems to have changed from his early days when he seemed willing to cooperate fully in this abandonment of national aspirations. Perhaps King also felt that the formation of an air defense pact, indeed an integration of air forces with the United States, violated the UN proviso that members not form outside military pacts. The John Foster Dulles supported formation of NATO, SEATO (the South East Asia Treaty Organisation), the Treaty of Chapultepec (for South and Central America), were all later raised as justifications by the Soviets for the formation of the Warsaw Pact. The Cold War was well and truly on.

In another foreshadowing of the 'free trade' movement, which began to bear real fruit with the

Canadian Mulroney Conservatives in the mid-1980s:

> "King's misgivings materialized early in 1948, when the U.S. administration approached Canada and proposed negotiating a free-trade treaty. In response, King sent some of his bureaucrats, including a young Simon Reisman, down to Washington, and they negotiated an agreement entirely in secret. The Americans were proposing 'ultimate free trade', a treaty for up to twenty-five years modified only by quotas at the beginning, and they wanted the whole agreement to go to Congress by May… [When King] saw the far reaching scope of the final draft, he changed his mind, stating: 'What has been suggested to me today is almost the largest proposal, short of war, any leader of a government has been looked to to undertake."[86]

Considering that Simon Reisman negotiated for Canada on this early free trade accord, and that King considered it nothing less than an economic assault on Canada, (the same King who was bankrolled by the Rockefellers), one might consider the Conservative's choice of Reisman to negotiate free-trade in the 1980s to have been an early revelation of the Party's intentions.

But, back in the late-1940s, Canada was comparatively politically and economically unfettered, and Avro Canada's first baby was about to be delivered: the C-102 Jetliner.

Prime Minister of Canada William Lyon Mackenzie King

82 Dow: The Arrow, p.92
83 Campagna: Requiem for a Giant, p. 72
84 This was also the day of the unveiling of the Avro Arrow, at that point the most advanced long range interceptor and strike-reconnaissance aircraft the world had yet seen. This observer wonders if the timing was designed to cast doubt on the interceptor. Subsequent evidence from behind the former Iron Curtain suggests that the USSR was quite concerned by the Arrow. (ref. Palmiro Campagna: Storms of Controversy and others.
85 Stewart: Shutting Down the National Dream, pp. 57-58
86 Orchard, David. The Fight for Canada, Toronto: Stoddart Publishing, 1993 p. 95

Chapter 13

THE AVRO C-102 JETLINER

This aircraft had been undertaken as the first design project of Avro Canada, after the iconic C.D. Howe and Avro U.K.'s Sir Roy Dobson came to their "rent to own" agreement, whereby Avro took over Canada's Victory Aircraft facility. In 1945 Dobson's prospective crown jewel had, at the time of its inception, plenty of dreams and no product. Dobson had taken over the entire facility and the enormous floor space was ominously silent. The bays were still crammed with Lancaster and Lincoln parts, with equipment and tools lying where they had been at war's end. Dobson's faith and guts, and the good will of his Canadian partners were in serious need of more than the always-free verbal support and encouragement. A.V. Roe Canada Ltd. needed contracts. Discussions with Trans Canada Airlines (today Air Canada) and the RCAF had shown potential in two areas. One possible requirement was a modern indigenous fighter suitable to defend Canada's enormous territory. The other possibility seemed to come in the form of a high-speed airliner to speedily service the nation's huge landmass, while still being able to operate from rather short and undeveloped airfields. These two prospective projects were initially begun only with verbal support from the RCAF, the Canadian Government and TCA.

The Avro Jetliner was the first jet airliner to fly in North America by eight years, and the first purpose-designed medium-range jet transport in history. This promising aircraft first flew in August 1949, and, despite TCA backing away in a vivid demonstration of lack of faith, and how to break a letter of intent, it was the subject of order negotiations with US and European airlines. National tried to place an order for four, on the understanding that this would be increased to a whole fleet if the aircraft met the expectations raised by the performance of the prototype. National's main competitor, Eastern Airlines, was confidently expected to follow suit, with the remaining US carriers predictably falling like dominoes thereafter in order to compete. Even the United States Air Force tried to buy the plane, and this attempt was classified by the government until very recently. C.D. Howe used the Korean War as an excuse to order Avro to "stop work" on this aircraft and concentrate on fighters in case the Korean War expanded into a World War.[87] This reason for the "stop work" order has been given by every book on the subject, save two[88], and, of course, by C.D. Howe himself. As we shall see, this was pure subterfuge.

At the urging of the government, and in collaboration with Trans Canada Airlines (TCA, now Air Canada), Avro designed, to a TCA specification, a pure jet airliner. It didn't hurt that the crown jewel in the headdress of C.D. Howe was TCA, and he was eager to see them become a world player. In keeping with the desire of many within the government to build up a Canadian aircraft industry, the old Vickers plant in Montreal was taken over by a couple of enterprising Canadians who had a scheme to acquire surplus Douglas aircraft parts and build trans-Atlantic airliners from these parts—powered by surplus British Rolls-Royce Merlin engines. This project, which established Canadair, was likewise undertaken to supply TCA. The Avro project was to serve shorter continental and inter-city routes. In reality, the optimum choices in terms of the best routes for the engine choices would have been a propeller aircraft for the inter city routes and a jetliner for the trans-Atlantic, but somehow, between executives of the fledgling Canadair, TCA and the government, this more logical product arrangement was reversed.

Before Avro Canada came to be, engineers at Victory Aircraft began drawings for a possible commercial aircraft. At Avro's secret British plant, the underground Yeadon production facility, Stuart Davies, with Jim Floyd as his Project Engineer, had also begun investigating concepts for airliners. Concepts to emerge under Floyd's pen included a turbo-prop airliner which evolved into the Avro 700 series.[89] Upon Roy Dobson's investigations of possible aircraft programs for his prospective Canadian operation, consultations were made with the government of Canada and TCA. During the September 1945 meetings between the Hawker Siddeley experts and the government of Canada representatives, Fred Smye was busy dragging Stuart Davies to Montreal to meet with H.J. Symington, head of TCA, to discuss a possible airliner collaboration. Initially, two designs were considered. One was for a turboprop inter-city airliner, and the other a pure jet for the same market. Dobson had previously tried to interest TCA in a Canadian built Tudor, then a "Tudor II" development, but had been unsuccessful. TCA's superintendent of engineering and maintenance, Jim Bain, had previously vetoed a Victory Aircraft plan to build Avro Yorks for TCA's trans-Atlantic operations, instead favouring the North Star development at Canadair.

When the designs were shown to TCA's Chief Engineer, Jack Dyment in March of 1946, his enthusiasm was reserved for the pure jet aircraft. Previously, TCA's Bain had visited Rolls-Royce and, due to superb (but overly optimistic) salesmanship by Ernie Hives, had been sold on their Avon axial-flow engine. As Bain later acknowledged "It all started because Rolls-Royce had never had one of their engines in a civil airplane and were delighted by TCA putting Rolls engines into our North Stars. ...Hives called me into his office one day when I was in England. 'You know' he told me, 'we have a new jet-engine we have developed with what we call an axial-flow turbine... And he said that although the engine was on the SECRET list, because we had been a good customer, he was confident we could get permission from the government to install it in a civil aircraft..." How a responsible executive of a national airline could specify an untried engine in these circumstances remains to be explained. His enthusiasm for the Avon was a leading factor in TCA's decision to select a pure-jet airliner, despite representations made by the Avro people to the effect that a turboprop would probably be more economical on the shorter routes. Indeed, just this argument, later made to TCA's head by the designer of the Vickers Viscount turboprop airliner, is said to have been a leading factor in TCA's turning away from the Jetliner and purchasing Viscounts.

Nevertheless, that TCA specified an aircraft around an engine and not around economic, or for that matter thermodynamic factors is shown by a quote by Jim Bain included in *Shutting Down the National Dream:*

> "I went to Jack Dyment, Clayton Glenn, and Fred Ades and it was a question of them looking at what we would require as a domestic airplane. We had enough detail on the Avon to be able to work out what the airplane would look like. It was a matter of coming up with a specification for an airplane they thought would fit the power plants that we knew were going to be available."

The problem was, the Avon wasn't going to be available, leaving the Rolls-Royce Derwent or the similar Nene engine, as the optimum existing choice. Unfortunately TCA was determined to combine an untried aircraft with an untried, and secret, engine. Jim Bain even accuses Dobson, in *Shutting Down the National Dream*, of having moved, behind the scenes, to have the British Government refuse the Canadians the Avon engine for the Jetliner. "[Dobson] wanted a safe journey; a venturesome bold step was not for him. He lost for Canada the Avro C-102, an aircraft that could have made Canada the leader in the aircraft production industry... When one considers the outstanding success of the Avon and the reduced fuel consumption made possible by the axial flow compressor, it is clear that the C-102 could have had huge potential; a potential thrown away by Sir Roy Dobson."[90] This seems an unsupportable accusation considering he would have been working against his own company's aircraft design in the process. History shows the Avon would have been a disastrous selection for the Jetliner anyway, since Rolls encountered major aerodynamic problems in the design of the compressor, which delayed the engine's emergence for many years and well past the first flight of the Jetliner. Hawker Siddeley also, obviously, had no qualms about using the Avon in the Hawker Hunter—or the Rolls-Royce Merlin in the Lancaster for that matter. As for Dobson's reluctance to take a "venturesome bold step", clearly his record in establishing A.V. Roe Canada, and even in seeing the Lancaster into production, demonstrate, conclusively, otherwise.

With TCA's preferences in mind, Avro Canada's new engineering team refined their design with Jim Floyd and Mario Pesando visiting TCA headquarters in Winnipeg to settle on a design with Jack Dyment, Hugh Reid and Jack Grisdale from the airline. Mario Pesando later commented that:

> "TCA wanted an aircraft that could fly from coast to coast, stop at all the major cities and still beat the North Star, the DC-4, across the continent. This, unfortunately, was our undoing, but, nonetheless, they wrote the spec."[91]

The consultations resulted in the following aircraft specification, for which TCA signed a letter of intent to purchase. The letter of intent was actually written by Fred Smye, in accordance with the standard format used by the government during wartime production, and was needed to secure the financial and material requirements to begin design and development.

SPECIFICATION

> The general specification around which the aircraft was designed was basically as follows:
>
> (1) The aircraft was to be a turbojet powered short-to-medium range inter-city transport with a still air range of at least 1,200 miles.
> (2) The payload was to be at least 10,000 lb., and accommodation for not less than 30 passengers was required.
> (3) A cruising speed of over 400 mph at 30,000 ft. was specified without having to resort to the use of oxygen for the passengers or crew.
> (4) The aircraft was to be designed to operate from airports with 4,000 ft. runways under Standard Atmosphere conditions and comply with the take-off conditions of the Civil Air Regulations. A decelerated stop length of 5,000 ft. was not to be exceeded under 'hot day' conditions following an engine failure.
> (5) Controllability at low speeds was not to be sacrificed in any way, despite the high speed range required. The approach and stalling speeds were to be at least comparable with present transport aircraft.
> (6) Special attention was to be given to serviceability and maintenance problems to allow for maximum utilization and operational regularity.
> (7) The aerodynamic and structural requirements of the Civil Air Regulations were to be achieved.
> (8) The cost of operation was to be comparable with or better than existing transports.[92]

This represented a cruising speed double that of many contemporary airliners and about a third faster than the fastest planes in service. Its high-altitude performance would ensure a much smoother ride and fewer weather delays. Avro's team decided to try to exceed the requirements right from the beginning in hopes of acquiring a larger market for the plane. They increased the target cruise speed to 425-450 mph and the still-air range to 1,500 miles. Passenger capacity was expanded to 40 persons, with provision designed in to allow future increases.

87 Floyd: The Avro Canada C-102 Jetliner J.C. Floyd was the designer of the Jetliner and ran Avro's engineering from 1951 to 1959.
88 The two exceptions are: Whitcomb: Avro Aircraft & Cold War Aviation, and Campagna: Requiem for a Giant.
89 Stewart, Shutting Down the National Dream
90 Stewart, Shutting Down the National Dream, p. 97
91 Stewart, Shutting Down the National Dream, p. 68
92 Floyd, J.C.. Avro C-102 Jetliner, lecture delivered to the Society of Automotive Engineers in January, 1950

Chapter 14

DESIGN CONSIDERATIONS

The Avon powered Jetliner had used a twin-engine configuration, with the landing gear retracting inwards, into the wing. When Lord Hives announced, in the fall of 1947, that the Avon would not be available "for many years", four Derwents were selected. The plane was expected to operate at 70% of the speed of sound at cruising altitude, and so its aerodynamics were based on achieving this figure with a minimum of drag. Avro's studies suggested that, with a jet aircraft, the difference in power required between 300 and 500 mph, at cruising altitude, was not significant. In other words, if they concentrated on making the aircraft very low in drag, it would gain a great deal of speed without a big change in fuel consumption or power required. For this reason thick, pre-formed skins for the wings and fuselage were chosen for strength and smoothness. New alloys of aluminum were selected for the ultimate in strength and lightness.

The Jetliner has been posthumously criticized for its straight, rather thick, wing. It was carefully selected, however, to offer the best compromise in take-off and landing speeds, low drag at cruising altitude and speed, and to have a high strength-to-weight ratio. Since a straight, high-aspect ratio wing with a fairly high thickness-chord ratio offers the lowest drag at subsonic speeds and the greatest strength-to-weight, the Jetliner's wing was basically of this design. A few tricks were incorporated, however, to achieve more lift and lower drag than a conventional wing. First, the rear spar was arranged perpendicular to the fuselage, with the main spar being swept back 4.5 degrees, giving a moderate increase in critical Mach number (where the airflow goes supersonic and a shockwave forms). A leading edge extension was designed into the root of the wing, preventing local upwash from the fuselage from disturbing the airflow over the inner wing and perhaps causing it to stall at a lower angle of attack. Square tips were added to give better aileron effectiveness and to simplify construction. The engine nacelles were semi-submerged into the wing to lower drag, and increase lift. Avro's engineers found that, at low speeds, the proximity of the exhaust nacelles to the trailing edge "filled in" some of the turbulent area at the rear of the wing and thus lowered drag. The exhaust efflux also was found to induce airflow over the inner wing at low speeds, increasing lift and lowering the Jetliner's stall speed. When the facts are considered, it seems likely that the Jetliner's wing had lower drag at its average flight speed and altitude than a swept wing would have. As we know today, a swept wing is not even required for supersonic flight.

Control surfaces were designed to have a high aspect ratio, which meant they needed less force to operate, were less susceptible to flutter and other adverse aerodynamic effects, and created less drag for a given amount of control effect. They have the advantages of not requiring aerodynamic balance, and of reduced mass balance requirements. To lower trim drag (drag induced by deflection of control surfaces for straight and level, 'trimmed', flight) Jim Chamberlin added another innovation: double control surfaces on the tail sections. This was added to allow improved control effectiveness in adverse conditions, such as those encountered in the case of single or multiple engine failures on take-off and landing.

To handle high levels of cabin pressurization, one-piece main fuselage formers were machined using hot-oil bath techniques Avro developed. Avro designed and patented a self-centring grinder to machine the heads of the rivets flush with the aircraft skin, without weakening the skin. The fuselage was designed for a very high pressure differential compared to the outside air to allow a high level of pressurisation in the cabin:

> "To obtain the optimum operating conditions with turbojet engines, it is necessary to fly as high as possible. The reduction in engine thrust between sea level, and say, 30,000 ft. is around 40%, while the drag is reduced to less than 25%, and as the thrust from the engine is approximately constant for all speeds, the variation being usually less than 5% between 200 and 500 mph, it can be seen that flying at altitude is far more important than with conventional aircraft.
>
> In the interests of economy, it is also essential to climb the aircraft to the operating altitude as fast as possible, and to descend as rapidly as possible at the destination.
>
> Since it would not be feasible to subject the passengers to the extremely rapid changes of pressure caused by a quick descent, the pressure in the cabin has to be as constant as possible at all times…
>
> Most conventional pressurized aircraft have the cabin pressurized to 8,000 ft. conditions at any altitude, 8,000 ft. being accepted as the altitude to which the average person can climb without feeling any discomfort either from lack of oxygen or reduced air pressure.
>
> Assuming that this aircraft was pressurized to 8,000 ft. cabin conditions, at 30,000 ft. it would take 40 minutes for the aircraft to descend at the recommended rate of 200 ft./min. This is obviously not feasible with a jet aircraft, as not only would all the advantage of speed be completely lost, but the fuel consumption of four turbojet engines operating for most of the time at low altitude would be prohibitive.
>
> It was obviously necessary, therefore, to pressurize the cabin to as near sea level conditions as possible, right up to the cruising altitude to enable the aircraft to be brought down in the shortest possible time. The conditions achieved to date are as follows: a sea level cabin up to 21,250 ft., a 2,000 ft. cabin at 25,000 ft., and a 4,000 ft. cabin at 30,000 ft. The pressure differential to achieve this is 8.3 lb./sq.in., and as a safety factor of 2 is used for pressurizing, the fuselage had to be designed to withstand a pressure of 16.6 lb./sq. in. The structural problems involved with the use of these high pressures were to say the least, interesting."[93]

Another development for the Jetliner, with Montreal's Jarry Hydraulics, led to "Skydrol" fire-resistant hydraulic fluid, with this substance becoming the industry standard for several decades. Since Canada has a harsh climate, anti-icing features were designed into the plane. These included a transparent laminate in the windshields which, when electrically energised, would heat up and prevent the formation of ice. Rubberized panels, with integral electric heating elements, were designed for the wing leading edges. These were superior to the wartime rubber "boots" applied to the leading edges of some allied aircraft which were expanded with compressed air to break off ice. It was much more advantageous to prevent the formation of ice in the first place, with none of the aerodynamic penalties associated with the earlier system. Chief Design Engineer J.C. Floyd explained the system, in brief, during his presentation to the Society of Automotive Engineers in January, 1950:

> "…an electro-thermal de-icing system will be used for the wings and empennage. De-icing

power is provided by two 50 KW., 208 volt three-phase 400-700 cycle alternators situated on the engine driven gearbox.

Windscreen de-icing is provided by special 'Nesa' glass windscreen panels, which consist of a vinyl core sandwiched by two thicknesses of semi-tempered glass. On the outside surface of the vinyl between the vinyl and the outside layer of glass is a conductive 'Nesa' coating which provides approximately 5-6 watts per sq. inch power input.

The windscreen de-icing is entirely automatic and the temperature is controlled to provide the quantity of heat required for anti-icing, and at the same time, keeping the vinyl layer at a temperature which gives it the best resistance to bird impact.

The three forward panes of the aircraft are designed in this manner, and the vinyl centre layer has the additional advantage, that in the event of a windscreen being shattered by any circumstances, the vinyl will still withstand at least twice the maximum differential pressure in the fuselage by blowing out in the form of a bubble."[94]

In 1946 an alarming follow-up letter of intent was sent to Avro. This letter included so many hedges and demands that James Dow described it as "an invitation to commit financial suicide". It demanded a fixed price of $350,000.00 whether TCA ordered one, or a hundred, aircraft. It demanded a three-year monopoly on Jetliner production, and, if the plane failed to meet *any* of TCA's demands, all monies sent to Avro to that point would be refunded in full to TCA. Needless to say, this isn't how it was done in the United States, and Avro would have been foolish to acquiesce to these demands. As a result C.D. Howe and the government also began to get the jitters. When TCA asked Howe to place a stop work order on the Jetliner, Howe complied. Howe had Dobson come over and examine the program to get his opinion as to its merits. Dobson arrived in the spring of 1947 and went through the design with a fine-toothed comb. He concluded that he was "quite satisfied" with the design, but was concerned that the go-slow policy of the government would waste Avro's competitive edge in this niche. (He was proved right when the de Havilland Comet in Britain beat the Avro Jetliner into the air by a mere 13 days.) Dobson was so confident in the future of the plane that he even offered to have Hawker Siddeley chip in funds to ensure the plane was ready to fly in 1949. With reservations, Howe allowed the program to continue, in the hopes that it would make both his creations, TCA, and Avro Canada, world class players in aviation.

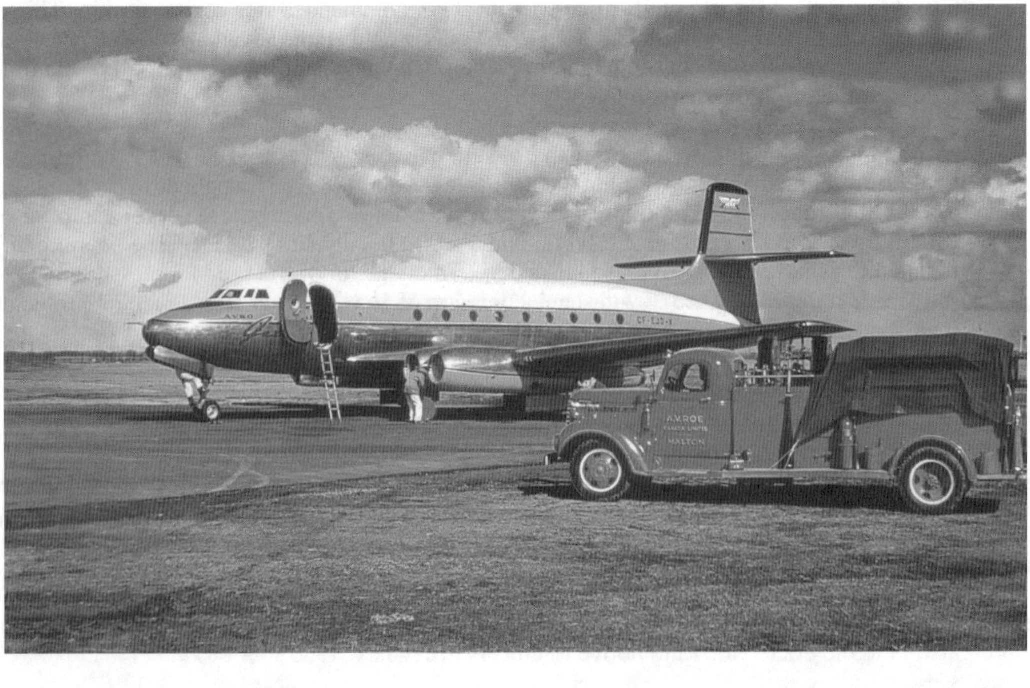

The Jetliner in its later colour scheme on the ramp at Malton Airport. (courtesy Don Rogers)

Around this time Jim Bain's over-enthusiasm for the Avon engine caught up with him. Fred Smye received a phone call from Lord Hives of Rolls informing him that the Avon was facing development problems and wouldn't be certified for military use "for many years". In something that Bain should have foreseen, the engine was also retained on Britain's secret list and was reserved for military aircraft. Paul Dilworth is on record as having been against the engine from the beginning, due to the problems axial flow engine designs were facing at the time, but his concerns were not heard at the advantageous moment. No doubt Bain faced some searching questions about the engine situation and this seemed to solidify TCA's change of heart on the plane. They didn't seem to give any credit to the possibility of changing engines when more advanced ones presented themselves. Nevertheless, Avro continued with the design, and selected the already proven, and very reliable, Rolls-Royce Derwent centrifugal-flow jet engine in a four-engine arrangement. While Jim Floyd was initially disappointed with the change from two Avons to four Derwents, once calculations were made it was realised that the drop in performance and economy was relatively mild, while design challenges related to the landing gear were alleviated which saved weight. Furthermore, four engines in place of two dramatically improved the plane's safety in case of engine failure.

By September 1947, the Avro design office had produced the revised design and performance estimates. The numbers indicated that the aircraft would still better all of TCA's letter of intent requirements, with the only possible question mark being its fuel consumption. Testing was conducted on sample assemblies at Avro and within the government research establishments. Carl Lindow, who later went to Boeing to lead several commercial aircraft programs, was involved in the stress testing of the Jetliner. He astonished his cohorts with his ability to predict precisely when an item would fail in testing, and also for wearing the same sweater nearly every day. Later in life, he would continue to amaze those around him when he became responsible for new product development at Boeing, managing, as an example, the development of the 737 airliner.

Unfortunately, with a change in leadership at TCA (from Stuart Symington to Gordon McGregor), their reluctance to acquire the design they originally specified turned to outright hostility. McGregor had been a WW II squadron mate of a leading designer at Vickers in England, and was thus easily sold on that company's Viscount airliner, despite the fact that it was several years behind the Jetliner in development, and the fact that it was a turbo-prop rather than a pure jet—TCA's initial requirement. Since the government was involved in financing the program, Howe insisted that Avro keep TCA's technical department fully informed on the engineering and progress of the design. With TCA's change of heart, this merely added a means by which TCA could attack the design in minute detail. Naturally, TCA invented problems that didn't really exist, and even attacked their own specification as being inadequate. They proposed that the delay in introducing instrument landing systems (ILS) at Canadian airports would disallow safe Jetliner operation—no matter that the Jetliner had the same, and in some cases lower, take-off, landing, approach and stall speeds as airliners that had always operated without ILS. It had a stall speed of only 78 knots! They then invented new, and absurd, reserve fuel requirements that would have totally destroyed the plane's economics.

While Avro's estimates, with standard reserves, showed a range of around 1,000 miles under normal conditions, TCA's new reserve requirements cut this to about 300 miles. On a trip that normally would have required, with reserves, 9,500 lbs of fuel, TCA now felt the plane should carry *30,000 lbs.* Obviously, carrying an extra 20,000 lbs of fuel would have made the plane very heavy, and very wasteful of fuel due to increased consumption to overcome the weight and increased drag. To top off this performance, TCA then invented new requirements for a "suitable" aircraft. With the required fuel capacity, an increase in passenger load, and an increase in cruise speed to 500 mph, the Jetliner design was, of course, then found to be unsuitable. Jim Floyd commented that "It would be easier to convert a cow to a crocodile" than to modify the Jetliner to meet these new demands. He also suspected that TCA's objections were formulated merely to discredit the program in the eyes of C.D. Howe. A secret study by the government's own Air Transport Board, which was classified and remained so until quite recently, would seem to prove Floyd's suspicions correct. (This is discussed later.)

He also felt that the plane had all kinds of potential for sales in the United States and Europe, and therefore that Avro should gracefully allow TCA to back away from their pledge to purchase it and be released of any official involvement. He has subsequently related his frustration with efforts by Avro management to try to keep TCA in the picture, and for applying some pressure to have TCA comment favourably on the plane. Avro management felt that if other airlines knew that TCA had rejected an aircraft designed for them in the first place, and flooded the industry with negative rumours about it, that its sales potential would be destroyed. This seems logical, but Floyd was so confident in his team's design they felt its merits would be obvious once the airlines examined, and flew in, the Jetliner.

That the Jetliner had excellent sales potential is beyond informed doubt. Besides its technological leap, other market factors mitigated to a good sales future. In 1947 all the major US manufacturers of commercial aircraft lost money. Several of the last generation of prop-liners, including the Boeing Stratoliner and Lockheed Constellation were facing major development problems. Some of these related to difficulties with pressurisation systems, which were becoming standard for trans and intercontinental aircraft. Their incredibly complex radial piston engines were expensive, difficult to maintain, were failing unexpectedly, and some were initially notorious for in-flight fires. Jet fuel is also cheaper than aviation gasoline.

In Canada the government had invested in two projects, the North Star by Canadair, and the Avro Jetliner. The North Star would be a good aircraft, except for two major problems. First, it was noisy as hell. Facing each side of the aircraft, with the aircraft hull resonating between them, were twelve open exhaust stacks from the potent and deafening Merlins. Passengers, like Mario Pesando, have related that, on trans-Atlantic flights in this aircraft, they were literally stunned and dizzy for days afterward. Many regular passengers refused to fly on it on long flights, given another option. High fuel consumption and high maintenance costs on the Merlin also detracted from the North Star's profitability.

With this background, one can see that Avro's fast and quiet Jetliner, appearing on the horizon in 1949, would have attracted the attention of airline executives, and, no doubt, aircraft manufacturers all over the world. Of course, the financial sector monitors trends in these industries to the best of their considerable ability, and likes to be proactive in protecting their bottom line through that of their industrial clients.

The Canadair DC-4M North Star airliner. (image by the author)

Avro Canada certainly had reason to be enthusiastic, and in a hurry, to get the world's first jet airliner into the sky. Everyone this author has spoken to who was involved in the Jetliner program at Avro describes it as the best experience of their aerospace careers. Enthusiasm and a real feeling of teamwork, under Floyd's leadership, meant that long hours and sacrificed weekends were undertaken willingly. It was a race to cross the line first. By the spring of 1949 most of the final engineering drawings had been released, and the experimental prototype XC-102 was herself nearing completion. On June 24th, while awaiting some finishing touches, the engines were lit for the first time. Tests were very encouraging until a sustained full power run damaged the rear extractor nozzles and overheated the engines. The extractor and rear nacelle skin designs were modified slightly, and new parts quickly produced.

Then, as the plane became ready for taxi-trials and first flight, one of government minister C.D. Howe's departments tore up the main runway at Malton for re-surfacing. Tests on a short alternate surface caused overheated brakes, blown tires, and further delays. Another Howe department did their bit by refusing to allow Avro to activate its new anti-skid braking feature.

> "Unfortunately the Department of Transport (D.O.T.) would not allow us to use the anti-skid system since they had yet to be approved by the U.S. flight authorities, as their application had not been recognized as critical since their propeller driven [planes] were equipped with reverse pitch propellers which were used as brakes during landing… The D.O.T. did not want us to succeed since this would have put the responsibilities on their shoulders for setting up requirements. D.O.T. had always let the British and United States air authorities do the spade work and were satisfied to ride on their coat tails."[95]

This technology is, today, standard equipment.

Then a huge let-down for Avro: the world's press announced that the world's first jet passenger plane, the British de Havilland Comet, had taken to the skies on 27th June, 1949. Temperatures in Toronto of 90-103 degrees Fahrenheit had also slowed down progress, collaborating with the short strip to complicate the safety calculations they needed to compile before the Jetliner's first flight.

First Flight of the Jetliner

> "Final engine runs having been completed over the week end, the aircraft was wheeled out of the hangar on Monday August the 8th to start taxi trails. As a special favor the temperature had gone up to 103 deg F, nevertheless, we carried out our taxi runs, braking tests, steering control tests, and towards early evening decided that it might be possible to attempt a hop, and take the aircraft a few feet off the ground.
>
> It was not a very easy decision to make in view of the fact that we had to contend with what was probably the highest temperature of the whole year, and with engines which were very much more susceptible to temperature than normal reciprocating engines. We had a very short runway, due to the alterations to the rest of the runways, and the pilot was handling a completely new type of aircraft, the performance of which could only be predicted at that time.
>
> We had calculated the distance required to take off, and the decelerated stop after the hop, and from our calculations there were only a few feet of runway left for pilot's error.
>
> The aircraft taxied down to the north east end of the runway, wasting as little space as possible, the throttles were opened up, the aircraft accelerated, and at about 90 mph, the nose wheel came off the deck. A few seconds later, there were four loud and ominous reports, the nose wheel came down, and the aircraft decelerated to a stop, just a few feet from the far end of the runway. The pilot had realized that he just could not make it and had applied the brakes a little too early before the weight of the aircraft was on the wheels, the wheels had locked, and all four tires had blown out. In spite of this, the pilot had been easily able to keep the aircraft on the runway, and there was no damage to the wheels or brakes or any other portions of the aircraft.
>
> The aircraft was wheeled back into the hangar, the tires were changed, and the next day more taxi runs were carried out to enable the pilot to feel out the brakes before making another attempt at a hop.
>
> On Wednesday morning, August the 10th, three more runs were made and a hop was attempted on the third run. This time, the two main wheels on the starboard side of the aircraft blew out, and the pilot again brought the aircraft to rest dead in the centre of the runway, and this time with quite a bit of runway to spare.
>
> The tires were quickly changed and a conference held to decide whether any more attempts at a hop would be made, as it was getting a little expensive on tires, and also on the nerves of the pilot, co-pilot, and flight engineer who had to sit in the aircraft wondering what was going to happen next.
>
> The pilot [Jimmy Orrell] decided that the next time he went down the runway he would rather take her up and "have done with it", as he expressed it. The crew took time out for lunch, and after returning, decided that in spite of a small gale that was blowing with quite a stiff cross-wind on the only available runway, and the fact that the temperature was around 103degF, the next time they went down the runway, they would just keep on going, and so just after lunch on Wednesday, August the 10th, the Jetliner came down the runway, lifted off the deck after a relatively short run, and gracefully climbed up to about 500 ft. where the pilot tried out the controls.
>
> He did a circuit of the field, and then asked for clearance to bring her over the spot where the ground crew were standing to let the boys have a look at the aircraft in the air. He then climbed away to 8,000 ft. and reported after a few minutes flying, that everything felt wonderful, and needless to say, everyone on the ground felt pretty good too.[96]

The comments of the Jetliner's flight engineer; Bill Baker, (a seasoned bush and Ferry Command pilot and flight engineer), are indicative of what an advance the Jetliner represented:

> "Fifteen years of flying had established in my mind that noise meant power, that more noise meant more power, and that power was essential for flight. The Jetliner, in first flight config-

uration, had minimal sound absorption material installed. When we gradually opened the throttles [against] the brakes, we could certainly hear those Derwents. As we gained speed, the sound level was obviously dropping. When Jimmy pulled up, the noise seemed to disappear altogether and my heart stopped at the same time. It was hard to accept the airspeed indicator winding up while the rate of climb was demonstrating fighter performance and *no noise!* What a thrill!"[97]

Obviously the Jetliner was a revelation and would be to passengers too, *particularly North Star passengers.* The Department of Transport added further restrictions, trying to prevent Avro from taking airline execs and other passengers on flights. In eventually granting permission, large "experimental" signs were required to be painted prominently inside and outside the aircraft, and all passengers were made to sign a rather frightening legal disclaimer. In the end, due to the restrictions and hostility the Jetliner faced in Canada, it was taken south of the border for demonstration to an almost-mesmerised US airline industry. US laws also made it possible to conduct flights that would prove the aircraft much more rapidly. The first, (also the world's first jet-airmail flight) from Toronto to New York City, stunned the American aviation community and captivated her media. This historic flight is the subject of the painting at the beginning of this chapter. The *Rochester Democrat* wrote:

> "This should give our nation a good healthful kick in its placidity. The fact that our massive but underpopulated neighbour to the north has a mechanical product that licks anything of ours is just what the doctor ordered for our overdeveloped ego."

In August, 1951 the headline of *Air Trails* magazine read:

> What Happened to the Great American Aircraft Industry?
>
> "[T]he Avro "Jetliner"…is the first transport plane in the Western Hemisphere to use turbo-jet engines. These are four Rolls-Royce Derwent Vs of 3,200 pounds thrust each. The Jetliner can carry 40 to 60 passengers in a large, comfortable cabin which maintains sea level altitude up to 21,500 feet in contrast to American transports which are pressurized at 8,000 feet when flying at 21,500. The Jetliner flew 450 miles from Toronto to New York City in just under 1 hour; normal transports take 1 hour, 45 minutes.
>
> "This is New York City, business capital of America. Most Americans believe that their nation has the greatest aviation industry in the world… How, then, could first honours for a jet-powered aircraft go to the Canadians instead of our own fabulous aircraft industry? In the race to get a jet transport into the air, Canada won hands down…our hat's off to the Canadians."

Nearly every single flight of the Jetliner established some kind of aviation record, usually those relating to speed and altitude. Turn-around times on the ground also set a new standard. The increase in cruising speed represented the highest single speed increase in civil aviation history, (until the Mach 2 Concorde), and the single largest speed increase ever for North American commercial aircraft. Passengers and crews alike, from most of the major American airlines and all the American military services, were astonished by its speed, ease of maintenance, reliability, smoothness, high altitude capability, and even its fuel economy when flown at the high altitudes where it excelled. Avro was looking at making a major breakthrough into the US market with their first plane, and enthusiasm was running high. And they weren't the only ones.

Most of the major US airlines sent teams of engineers, flight crew and executives to examine and fly the Jetliner. Its specifications at this time were:

C-102 JET TRANSPORT

Wing Area	1157 sq.ft.
Wing Span	98'11"
Aspect Ratio	8.31
Aerofoil	NACA230 Series
T/C Ratio at Root	16.5%

T/C Ratio at Tip	12%
Incidence of Datum Plane	2½ degrees
Dihedral on Datum Plane	6 degrees
Fuselage Length Overall	82' 9"
Fuselage Diameter	10'
Undercarriage	Tricycle
Engines: 4 Derwent 5 Turbojet Engines Total Static Thrust at Sea level (I.C.A.N.Conditions)	14,400 lb
Gross Weight (Medium range version)	65,000 lb
Gross Weight (Short range version)	60,000 lb
Maximum landing weight	52,500 lb
Still air range (Medium range version)	2,000 miles
Still air range (Short range version)	1,400 miles
Cruising speed at 30,000 ft. and 60,000 lb. gross weight	450 + mph
Payload	12,700 lb
Number of passengers	40 - 60
Payload for 1,000 mile range,with full A. T. A. allowances at 65,000 lb. T. 0. -gross weight	10,500 lb
Payload for 500 mile range with full A. T. A. allowances at 60,000 lb. T. 0. gross weight	12,000 lb
Four Engine take-off over 50 ft. obstacle at 60,000 lb. I. C. A. N. conditions sea level	3,100 ft
3 engine take-off with above conditions	3,525 ft [98]

Their reports were electrifying. They were as shocked by the lack of noise, and smooth, swift flight as Bill Baker had been. The engineers were impressed too. Pilots probably loved it most of all, though passengers were all pleasantly surprised. By June, 1950 National Airlines was seriously considering becoming the first airline in North America to deploy jet transports. G.T. Baker, National's president, wrote:

> "I send two of my most conservative men up to Canada for a couple of days to look at the C-102 Jetliner and they come back stark raving mad with enthusiasm for it!"[99]

American Airlines' chief test pilot and one of the men behind the evolution of the most successful transport plane in history; (the Douglas DC-3), Dan Beard, flew it and enthused:

> "You've got a bloody good aircraft there, I reckon it could be the DC-3 of the jets."[100]

To handle the sales effort in the United States, Dixon Speas, a promising assistant to the president of American Airlines, was enthusiastic about tackling the job after flying in the Jetliner and getting to know Fred Smye, Jim Floyd, and others from the Jetliner program. He was granted a one-year leave of absence from the airline to lead sales efforts on the Jetliner, but never ended up returning to American Airlines. A follow up letter from Speas, regarding negotiations with National, affirmed that:

> "[National is] very much interested in purchasing a limited quantity of Jetliners...In all conversations it was generally understood the limited number of aircraft would be expanded to a full fleet subject to the aircraft meeting all expectations."[101]

TCA's dropping out of the picture meant Avro was free to develop the pre-production C-102 Mk.1 to suit the tastes of the American airline executives, and to add a few things they felt would optimise the aircraft...including an even more powerful engine. To enlarge the passenger load to double the original TCA requirement, and improve the C of G situation for high capacity passenger arrangements, a standard fuselage 'plug' of 24 inches was to be installed entirely ahead of the wing. To solve a minor aerodynamic problem related to transonic speeds, where the tail reached 'critical Mach' airflow speeds before the rest of the plane (at around .78 Mach), the nose of the slab tail was extended, adding sweep-back. These small changes would have allowed an increase in cruise speed to nearly 560 mph. Fuel capacity was enlarged to accommodate more powerful engines while also increasing range. Tanks were of a specially-sealed, integral design Avro had developed. A "Thiokol based" sealant, with special plasticizers and other additives, was developed that proved superior to problematic existing systems. The split flaps were replaced by the double-slotted type, allowing the Mk.1 to meet Eastern Airlines low landing speed requirements. This feature would allow it to operate from even shorter runways, enlarging its market appeal, particularly in Europe and developing countries.

At the higher weights, calculations showed the Derwents would have to operate at too high a power setting to be economical, with increased maintenance also a likely prospect. Studies were done on all the available axial flow and centrifugal flow turbojets. A proven, certified, and unclassified axial-flow turbojet that could compete with the Derwent's over-grown twin, the Rolls-Royce Nene, remained elusive. The Nene had the added advantage that it required relatively few modifications to be made to the nacelle arrangement of the Jetliner, saving considerable expense.

National agreed to the features of the Mk.1, and the world appeared to be Avro's oyster—until C.D. Howe and the Korean War intervened.

The Jetliner at Chicago's Midway Airport

93 Floyd, J.C.: Avro C-102 Jetliner, lecture delivered to the Society of Automotive Engineers, 1950
94 ibid
95 Pesando Mario, Jetliner Flight Trials and Other Things unpublished, undated. p.7
96 Floyd, J.C.. Avro C-102 Jetliner, lecture delivered to the Society of Automotive Engineers, January, 1950
97 Baker, W.A. The Life and Times of Bill Baker, (private publication)
98 Floyd, J.C.. Avro C-102 Jetliner, Society of Automotive Engineers lecture, January, 1950
99 Floyd, J.C.. The Avro Canada Jetliner
100 ibid
101 ibid

Chapter 15

TURBULENCE OVER THE KOREAN PENINSULA

After Japan was defeated Korea was split into two, the North dominated by the Soviet Union, the other by the United States. After a bizarre series of State Department decisions, which almost made it seem like the United States wanted the communists to attack, US troops were withdrawn from South Korea. Then, in January 1950, US Secretary of State; Dean Acheson, announced in a highly publicised speech that the western defensive perimeter of the United States stopped short of Korea. In June 1950, the Communists obligingly invaded.

This, typically, seemed to shock the media and leaders of the world. In the United Nations the United States pushed for the adoption of a resolution to send UN forces, led by the United States, to repulse the aggression in a "police action". This was to ensure that the Communists knew that the United States was determined the remnants of the Japanese Empire (their Japanese Co-prosperity Sphere) would join the West. The politicians of the West, particularly the Commonwealth and United States, agreed that this conflict might very well escalate into W.W. III, and mobilised industry and the military. China and the Soviet Union foolishly boycotted the UN Security Council vote and the American action was endorsed. Orders for military planes and other equipment flooded into US industry, coincidentally curing the financial doldrums they had been experiencing. Laws were passed in the United States and Britain ensuring that all new aircraft production would have to be for the war effort—probably at the behest of the United States who would be vulnerable to commercial aircraft advances made while American industry was devoted to the Korean "police" effort.

Et voila, C.D. Howe had a 'justification' for killing the civilian Jetliner. In August, Howe told Fred Smye to stop work on the Jetliner, and shift to a 'super-priority' program to get their XC-100 fighter into mass production for the Korean War. Howe thereafter maintained that the Jetliner had to be halted to allow them to produce the CF-100 for Korea, though the CF-100 and, probably, its Orenda engine were years from full production. In fact, as of the stop-work order, the CF-100 had not flown with the Orenda engine, lacked a radar and weapons system, and had revealed a serious structural flaw in the nacelle-wing joint area. It was easily two years from production.

W.A.B. Douglas, working for the Department of National Defense under the Deputy Minister, made a note which he filed on the accuracy of the 1979 CBC documentary *There Never Was an Arrow.* Douglas was directly involved with the review of documents requested by the CBC, which were not de-classified at the time and were refused to the producers of the CBC documentary. The show had accepted Howe's reason for the Jetliner stop work order, but Douglas wrote:

> "The reason for cancelling the Avro jet liner [sic] was not convincing, *nor could it be supported by documentation.* This is a subject which requires proper historical analysis." [italics added].[102]

The reason why Douglas ventured to express the opinion that Howe's chosen reason was false is because the government held documents to disprove it. Some of these documents, which demonstrate a cover-up of sales interest, and relating to Howe's and the governments decision to order Avro to stop work on the Jetliner, have subsequently been released. Incredibly, it turns out, the United States Air Force tried to *buy Jetliners for military service early in the Korean war.*

After a stellar career in aviation, in 1994, Dixon Speas wrote to his old friend, Jim Floyd, about a mutual love. In this letter he notes one of the highlights of his employment by Avro Canada:

> "Demonstrations of the airplane to the USAF...advanced to the point, I was later told by the marketing head of GM's Allison Engine Division, that the decision had been made within the USAF to order 20 or 25 Jetliners equipped with Allison engines for high altitude navigation training."[103]

In fact, both the USAF and US Navy were interested, and Speas heard about only one aspect of the orders that were in the works. Subsequently, Canadian historians have blithely dismissed the touted orders as phantoms, after all, if the USAF had ordered Jetliners, they would have received them—right?

Wrong. In preparing *Requiem for a Giant,* author and Canadian defense scientist Palmiro Campagna was granted, through Access to Information, one of the missing documents. In a letter from the Canadian Joint Staff in Washington to the Chief of the Air Staff in Canada, dated 14 August, 1951 (barely over a year into the Korean War), the following is included.

> "1. Recently the Avro Jetliner was flown from Toronto to Washington for demonstration. The USAF and the USN are both interested in this aircraft but the only concrete proposal for purchase had come through the US AMC [Air Materiel Command] at Wright Field.
>
> 2. It is now confirmed that the USAF wish to purchase 12 Jetliners. A recommendation was made to this effect by a specially appointed committee representing all USAF Commands, to the Aircraft and Weapons Board. This Board approved the purchase of 12 aircraft.
>
> 3. The USAF intend to use the C.102 as a high-speed bombing trainer.
>
> 4. There is another application for the C.102 which is of exciting interest, this being high-speed jet fighter refuelling. It is not known, at present, whether an order has been placed but the Flight Refuelling experimental section at USAF HQ are anxious to get 4 C102s for test in this type of work."

It may be argued that this order was turned down because Avro Canada had "too much on its plate" as C.D. Howe related to Dixon Speas on one occasion, and because the CF-100 filled a more direct defense need, but these arguments do not exhibit strength. First of all, the CF-100 hadn't flown with the engines it was to be equipped with, and in fact this engine (A.V. Roe Canada Ltd.'s own TR-5 Orenda engine) hadn't flown at all as of the beginning of the Korean War. The CF-100 didn't have a radar/fire-control system. The CF-100 didn't have weapons. The CF-100 had also revealed a problem in the main-spar/engine nacelle area which required a major engineering effort to alleviate. The CF-100 also required development and equipment standardization. It was, quite clearly in this observer's opinion, at least two years away from squadron service. Meanwhile the C-102 Jetliner had revealed no flaws, with the USAF's only gripe being that they would have preferred larger cockpit windows.[104] Why would the government of Canada turn away bona fide export orders for military Jetliners (that would support the Allied effort in Korea) in favour of a fighter that was anything but a sure thing at that time?

It seems obvious that had the United States and Canada really wanted warplanes for Korea, the Avro Jetliner would have been produced either by Canada for USAF service, or under license in the United States. All defense production agreements between Canada and the United States not only allowed, but *promised* such production where it filled a unique need. Military requirements dictated it since no power on earth, at that stage, had jet cargo planes, jet bomber trainers, jet refuellers, jet med-evac aircraft, or any jets other than bombers and fighters. This, of course, makes the CF-100 production decision suspicious since the CF-100 was facing development problems, whereas the United States had plenty of jet fighters. The CF-100, of course, never served in Korea because it wasn't ready in time.[105] It is almost inconceivable that C.D. Howe would refuse the USAF an order for Jetliners in the context of the times. In fact, Dixon Speas managed to buttonhole C.D. Howe during a reunion at their mutual *alma mater*, the Massachusetts Institute of Technology (MIT). During the dinner, Speas managed to manoeuvre himself into the seat next to Howe and "chewed his ear off" over the Jetliner. On Howe's return trip to the airport, Speas also managed to insinuate himself into the seat next to Howe.

> "He got in one side of the limousine and I got in the other where I continued to chew his ear all the way to the airport… He said they had the Jetliner and the fighter and that *he had promised the U.S. government* that the fighter was going to go ahead, so the Jetliner had to go on the shelf."[106] [italics added]

One might find it odd that while the USAF wanted Jetliners as warplanes for Korea, the U.S. government was accepting promises that it would not be produced. But the reasons for that aren't difficult to conjure. In 1947 all U.S. aircraft manufacturers had lost money.[107] A Congressional committee was established to assist the American industry shortly thereafter. Sensitive issues with allies are discussed off the record in Congress.[108] During the Korean War, US industry was restricted to production of military aircraft. Production of the military Jetliner had been halted despite an attempted USAF order. An order by Howard Hughes had been stopped by first the Canadian government and then by the American. Could it be said that the Jetliner had everything going for it but partisan politics?

Something that is also ignored in the conventional telling of the Jetliner story is that at the time of Howe's decision to sacrifice the Jetliner for the CF-100, General Douglas McArthur had already retaken South Korea, right up to the 38th parallel.

> "In the early hours of September 15, [1950]...the amphibious landing at Inchon began. As promised by MacArthur,...the operation was an overwhelming success that completely turned the tables on the enemy.
>
> "By September 27, more than half the North Korean Army had been trapped in a huge pincer movement. By October 1, U.N. forces were at the 38th parallel and South Korea was in U.N. control. In two weeks, it had become an entirely different war.[109]
>
> "As things looked late in the morning of Sunday, October 15, 1950, on Wake Island, MacArthur would be winding up the war almost any day."[110]

The war, at that time, seemed already won—until the American government decided to press their advantage and invade North Korea—with the result that China intervened and turned the war into a stalemate. Once the Eisenhower Republicans replaced the Truman Democrats, the new Secretary of State, John Foster Dulles, *"expressed his wish to...postpone a settlement in Korea 'until we have shown—before all Asia—our clear superiority by giving the Chinese one hell of a licking'"*?[111] Clearly this was a questionable way to spend the human and financial capital of America, Canada, Australia and the other UN forces present. His brinkmanship almost caused a global nuclear conflagration once the Chinese made it clear that UN forces would not be allowed to take North Korea as well as South. Indeed, the hawks had been calling for a massive nuclear response virtually from the moment China got involved.

> "MacArthur called on the administration to recognize the "state of war" imposed by the Chinese, then to drop *thirty to fifty atomic bombs on Manchuria and the mainland cities of China.* The Joint Chiefs too, told Truman that mass destruction of the Chinese cities with nuclear weapons was the only way to affect the situation in Korea."[112] [italics added]

These were the leaders of the organisations with which Canada was expected to integrate its intelligence agencies and military-industrial establishment.

102 W.A.B. Douglas: Note to File: "CBC Programme on the Avro Arrow", 21 April, 1980
103 Dixon Speas in a 1994 letter to J.C. Floyd titled: "A USA Citizen's View of the Avro Jetliner"
104 Floyd: The Avro Canada C-102 Jetliner
105 Milberry: The Avro Canada CF-100
106 Speas in a 1994 letter to J.C. Floyd: "A USA Citizen's View of the Avro Jetliner", p. 15-16
107 Floyd: The Avro Canada C-102 Jetliner
108 Campagna: Requiem for a Giant. This is shown during discussions of the failing BOMARC missile where it is acknowledged, off the record, that while BOMARC should go ahead to "bail out" a struggling Boeing Aircraft Company, and because the Canadians had been persuaded to purchase this missile, thereby mitigating the waste of US funds on this controversial, and, soon after the Canadian order, abandoned missile system.
109 McCulloch, David. Truman, p. 98
110 ibid, p. 807
111 Brendon, Piers: Ike, His Life & Times, New York: Harper & Row, 1986 p. 255
112 McCulloch, David. Truman p. 832

Chapter 16

CRAWFORD GORDON JR.

Crawford Gordon Jr. came to Avro due to problems with Avro management that became evident during the development of the CF-100 long-range all-weather jet interceptor. Avro President, Walter Deisher, was inclined to delegate responsibility and authority, and Edgar Atkin, then the Chief Designer, had a tendency to monopolize information and operate in a somewhat autocratic fashion that alienated people in the production and flight test sections. This also spilled over into relationships with the government through the RCAF, the dissatisfied customer, and through the NRC and NAE in direct dealings with Avro. Diesher's distance and indecisiveness plus Atkin's tendancy towards a secretive manner and superior attitude was a dangerous combination and when the spar and other problems with the CF-100 came to light, Diesher seemed incapable of managing the situation. By contrast, Fred Smye was known to be literally running from one part of the company to another getting things done and holding the show together.[113] But he was also burning himself out. In discussions between Roy Dobson and C.D. Howe over the obviously required reorganization of the company, Dobson suggested Smye as a possible new president. Howe replied that the job would kill Smye as he was already accepting far too much responsibility, and suggested a 37-year-old who he had referred to as one of his "towers of strength" in Munitions and Supply during WW II. He suggested Crawford Gordon Jr..

As a 21-year-old, Gordon had been the comptroller of finance at Canadian General Electric. At age 28 he had been considered, among a group of outstandingly effective executives, to be C.D. Howe's "boy wonder" in Munitions and Supply. During WW II Gordon had been one of Howe's "dollar a year men" and was known for his efficiency in cutting through red tape and getting things accomplished. He held positions of Director General Organization and Assistant Co-ordinator of Production. After the war, when Howe's empire in Munitions and Supply was transformed into the Department of Reconstruction and Supply, Gordon served for a time as Director General of Industrial Reconversion; working to convert Canada's war industry to peaceful production whilst absorbing the flood of returning servicemen. By age 36 he was the Director of the Department of Defense Production and in charge of Canada's Korean War military equipment budget. He also worked in senior management positions with companies such as Inglis and sat on the boards of several industrial concerns. At 41 he became the head of A.V. Roe Canada Ltd. and presided over it as it became Canada's largest employer and presence in high technology and heavy industry. He oversaw its expansion into strategic resources, including coal and iron ore, and expanded the company's presence in strategic industry. At age 52, six-years after the cancellation of the Arrow and Iroquois programs, he died a penniless alcoholic in New York City.

Vilified today by some, Gordon's accomplishments and background are generally ignored in most discussions of the Avro story. His character and basic motivations are also generally ignored. He broke faith with his mentor and idol C.D. Howe. He preferred to not go from a reliance on Britain to dependence on the United States, but he kept an eye towards increasing Canada's freedom of action, and therefore independence, by building for Canada strategic industry and resource assets along Commonwealth, not Continental, principles. While working in Howe's department Gordon learned how to get things done in political, industrial and labour spheres—invaluable experience. One of these was to secure the basic sources of supply or face vulnerability in production. By 1957 he was turning A.V. Roe Canada into a vertically-integrated powerhouse in strategic resources and industry. Considering the accolades, Crawford Gordon Jr. must be given his fair share of the credit for the fact that Canada doubled the size of its economy in the Second World War, and, on a per-capita basis, and whilst providing the highest percentage of combat soldiers, produced the most war materiel of any nation in the conflict. He was also in charge of the Department of Defense Production when the Korean War started, and one of his biggest headaches was getting the CF-100 into production. Crawford Gordon Jr. was appointed head of A.V. Roe Canada Ltd. on 15 October, 1951.

113 Floyd: The Avro Canada C-102 Jetliner

Chapter 17

THE HOWARD HUGHES AFFAIR

In 1952 Avro was collaborating with Hughes Electronics who produced the radar/fire-control system for the CF-100 and many USAF aircraft. To assist Hughes in developing an advanced set for use in up-graded CF-100s, the XC-102 Jetliner was offered as a test and observation platform, and the aircraft was sent to Hughes' airfield in Culver City California. The docile landing speeds and handling of the Jetliner are surely evidenced by the fact that in Culver City the Jetliner operated, problem-free, from a grass airstrip. Upon viewing, and flying the airplane, Howard Hughes developed a passion for Avro's Jetliner and thereupon "kidnapped" the aircraft and some Avro employees, (including Don Rogers and Fred Matthews) for six months![114] But then, this had been Smye's plan all along.

While Hughes started out with family money from a tool company and from oil, he added RKO pictures (initially specialising in aviation movies) and soon began sponsoring his own aircraft designs. The Hughes racer and the massive Spruce Goose flying-boat, were, in ways, technical marvels but otherwise failed to meet expectations. However, Hughes wasn't afraid of high-technology, the Spruce Goose having been designed as a massive troop-lifter for WW II and made of non-strategic materials. One could say it was the first composite structure aircraft since it was mostly made from components moulded from a special wood-fibre and glue compound.

By the 1950s Hughes also owned an electronics division (within Hughes Aircraft) that quickly become the world leader in sophisticated radar/fire-control systems for military aircraft. There is no doubt that intelligence operations by various US agencies, including the NSA and CIA, had contributed to the technology that Hughes Aircraft was evolving. No doubt Hughes' knowledge of how espionage worked contributed to his secretive habits. Perhaps this and his inside knowledge of some of the more sinister events of the twentieth-century contributed to his decline in mental health. During these negotiations however, most Avro people found Hughes a little odd, but kind, likeable, and very sharp.

Hughes then owned a controlling interest in Trans World Airlines (TWA) and, after having his engineers and economists conduct a detailed examination of the aircraft, set out to secure 30 Jetliners for his airline. Don Rogers relates that "Hughes was an excellent pilot" but that the first time he flew the Jetliner he performed nine 'touch and goes' before landing to a full stop. Don mentioned that Hughes liked a very soft landing and as such came in faster than he needed to, which resulted in a long "float" and gentle touchdown. When he asked some of the Hughes entourage if nine approaches was as unusual as he thought it was, the response was that it was not at all unusual and that, in fact, Hughes had done over 30 approaches before buying his then-favourite, a Boeing Stratocruiser. This was one of many times when a Hughes' staffer would explain the boss's unusual habits as being entirely routine. Don and others described Hughes penchant for the 'cloak and dagger' in how he would materialise mysteriously after keeping people waiting for hours, and would disappear just as mysteriously in the course of meetings, sometimes to return, sometimes not. Despite these foibles, Rogers and Floyd both took a liking to Hughes, and thought he had a very engaging mind. While generous enough to move some of the key Avro families to California during the long testing and negotiations, he never carried money and was always advising people how to save a few cents. Smye and Rogers would both later write that Hughes was always borrowing dimes for the phone and dollars for the gas tank from them.

Fred Smye and other sources show that initially he, Gordon and other Avro people, fed by rumours swirling around the Hughes entourage, were not sure if Hughes was serious, or was 'leading Avro up the garden' in his negotiations. This was not an outrageous assumption considering Hughes' involvement with the intelligence agencies and with his having funded and engineered various CIA operations—one notable and expensive technical espionage effort being to raise a sunken, but intact, Soviet nuclear submarine. Robert Rummel was Hughes' personal technical advisor as well as the chief planning officer of TWA. There can be little doubt that the two shared extremely high-level knowledge in certain areas of the military, industrial, scientific, intelligence, and of course, economic and political aspects of the Cold War. In October 2006 I asked Floyd if there was any possibility of Hughes having really been involved in an intelligence effort over the Jetliner. He said : "I asked Bob Rummel one day many years ago if Hughes was playing with us. He said that Hughes was absolutely serious about buying Jetliners. He said he played with Convair on occasion, but not with us."[115]

Negotiations ensued between Hughes' people, led by the mysterious and enigmatic Hughes himself, along with Robert Rummel and appropriate specialists and a team from Avro. The Avro contingent included Avro General Manager Fred Smye, (with A.V. Roe Canada President Crawford Gordon Jr. joining the effort later), Chief Test Pilot Don Rogers, sales and service head Joe Morley, and others. The Avro people found Hughes very hard to pin down, since he was invariably thinking ahead to a myriad of options touching all the spheres of his various enterprises, while Avro was just trying to get a contract and begin production. Floyd relates meeting Hughes for a 13-hour nocturnal marathon, going over Jetliner blueprints, in the penthouse of the Beverly Hills Hotel– "practically right down to the nuts and bolts". One of Floyd's prized possessions is an autographed photo of Hughes beside the Jetliner, taken by Don Rogers, with the inscription "To J.C. Floyd with congratulations on this very good design." High-level meetings involved a certain element of Hughes' Hollywood background, with starlets and other elements of glitter and temptation present. Certainly Jim Floyd and Don Rogers kept great distance from some of the more ostentatious aspects of what was available, especially the drinking and partying, but not all management personalities resisted some of the more liberal offerings.

Hughes' demands for detailed technical and design information, including Avro studies into the effects of American replacement engines, led some to wonder if Avro wasn't being used to finance and conduct a US intelligence operation. Apparently one of those who started to manifest a reluctance to acquiesce to such possibilities was Crawford Gordon Jr. himself. Pat Kelly, hired as a part-time PR advisor for A.V. Roe (and Gordon particularly), states that one evening, towards the end of a rather alcohol-fueled day with Hughes and some of his people, Gordon finally lost his temper and left a rather obvious sign of his disaffection over Hughes' conduct. When the Avro people finally thought Hughes was ready to talk turkey on the deal, Hughes excused himself to use the bathroom. Hours went by, and Gordon finally became so upset that he asked if someone could check to make sure Hughes hadn't "disappeared down the goddamn hole"! He was promptly informed by a member of the Hughes legation that Hughes' absence was not abnormal, as Hughes had a selection of phones to different contacts in his bathroom and regularly spent hours there in consultations.

Kelly says once Hughes finally rejoined the group, an incensed Gordon walked out, but paused to urinate all over Hughes' private bathroom—including, no doubt, the multiplicity of phones he had in that room. Jim Floyd was also present however, and insists categorically that Gordon merely walked out, which was quite sufficient to get Hughes' attention. Whatever Gordon's actions, Hughes, no stranger to flamboyance, apparently shrugged them off. Smye noticed that Hughes took Avro considerably more seriously after Gordon turned negotiations over to him and returned to Malton. Crawford had, apparently, taken on a real suspicion that the whole thing was a charade whereby US interests, whoever they really were, were merely prying every bit of technical intelligence out of the proceedings that they could. Smye continued in good faith, but would write that for a time he had his own doubts about the true reason for all the technical questions (not to mention the engineering studies Avro had to produce as a result). Robert Rummel was TWA's chief planning officer and handled much of the TWA analysis of the Jetliner and became a real fan of it, and a lifelong friend to Jim Floyd.

Smye's misgivings were allayed by Hughes' decision to equip TWA with 30 Jetliners (minus at least one for himself of course). These would be powered by American engines, with TWA initially favouring a twin-engine arrangement, using (non-afterburning) Pratt & Whitney J-57 derivatives; i.e., civil versions of the engines the B-52 and KC-135/707 would employ. In 1952, this seemed to be a non-starter for reasons of US military-technological secrecy. TWA was disappointed, especially considering Hughes' involvement in secret programs. It would have made for a very economical aircraft since the axial-flow J-57 was capable of considerably higher compression (and thus efficiency) than the centrifugal flow Derwents of the prototype Jetliner.

Probably to Avro's relief (since it involved no redesign of the engine bays or landing gear), TWA was ultimately quite happy to accept what Avro was building as the second, pre-production, Jetliner. This used the split flap, 24-inch fuselage extension, double-slotted flaps, modified horizontal stabiliser (to increase the aircraft's critical Mach number) and other improvements suggested by test and evaluation of the original, CF-EJD-X.

The fuselage plug was, unusually, to be installed entirely ahead of the wing. The Jetliner has been criticized in a popular history as having a centre of gravity (CoG) problem so severe that "it mattered on which side you parted your hair". Mario Pesando; group leader on aerodynamics for the Jetliner, discussed this controversy.

> "Don Whittley had...voiced his concerns about the destabilizing effect of the air flow over the wing being entrapped downstream by the jet engines' efflux... Don based his analysis on data from the German sources and from the Gloster Meteor flight measurements. Although the wind tunnel tests conducted during the design phase gave us excellent stability data, it was not possible to simulate the effect of jet-engine inlet and outlet (exhaust) flows. Preliminary flight test data indicated that there was an adverse effect, but we had to wait until we had installed the necessary instrumentation and water ballast system to place the centre of gravity beyond both forward and aft limits allowing us to explore the more sensitive zones. The final result did establish that this phenomena did indeed exist and that we were faced with a loss of stability for the aft center of gravity situation. The generally agreed...remedy for this was quite simple, requiring the addition of a twenty four inch section to the forward...Jetliner fuselage. This would also allow us to squeeze an additional row of seats... This modification was planned for the second Jetliner along with a revised tailplane and slotted landing flaps."[116]

The entrapment of the exhaust with the wing-downwash was actually beneficial in terms of adding lift to the wing. On the prototype the problem was truly minor and only presented itself when the aircraft was loaded to demonstrate its most tail-heavy loading situation. The solution couldn't have been simpler for the company—nor more fortuitous for customers already expressing interest in higher capacity. Versions of up to 72 passengers were envisioned through the further addition of fuselage plugs. Engines for the production Mk.1 were to be the Rolls-Royce Nene engine, which was essentially a scaled-up and improved Derwent. It also fit the Jetliner's nacelles. With one-third more output than the Derwent and improved economy, the Nene was an excellent choice. In fact, until very recently the Nene was still establishing its reputation as perhaps the most reliable jet engine in history—in Canadian air force T-33 Silver Stars. As a result of these changes and expanded fuel capacity in the wings (which could have been further expanded), the Jetliner's range, with full TWA reserves, jumped from 900 nm (nautical miles) to 1500 nm. This represented twice the passenger capacity, and *three times the range,* with full fuel reserves, of the original TCA letter of intent—yet TCA, and others aligned with the Howe termination, have often attacked the Jetliner on the basis of a perceived deficiency in range. The range argument was no more valid with the Jetliner than it would be when used by the Conservatives to "justify" their cancellation of the Arrow.

Swept wing Jetliner development as proposed to TWA. (image by the author)

TWA engineering's evaluation of the Jetliner was, like that of a hushed up report by Canada's Air Transport Board (ATB), diametrically-opposed to that of TCA. They wrote:

TRANS WORLD AIRLINES ASSESSMENT OF THE AVRO C-102 JETLINER

> The direct operating cost per mile of the Jetliner compares very favorably with that of TWA's present equipment, yet reduces current trip times by as much as 30 percent between major centres of population.
>
> Although this analysis was conducted on a conventional aircraft flight plan, which puts the jet transport at a decided economic disadvantage, the Jetliner compares exceptionally well with modern propeller-driven aircraft on a cost per seat-mile basis.
>
> By making certain changes in the flight plan... the overall economic picture can be improved still further - without any sacrifice in safety.
>
> The Avro Jetliner, powered by P&W [Pratt & Whitney] J-56 [sic] engines can operate safely and efficiently over every TWA internal route except New York/Los Angeles, non-stop.
>
> The Jetliner's high cruising speed enables it to cut present scheduled operating times by as much as 30 percent. This is undoubtedly the Jetliner's major contribution to air transportation.
>
> The "Jet Power" aspect of the aircraft ensures consistently higher load factors through its passenger appeal. The absence of fatiguing propeller vibration, the smooth, swift flight and the initial novelty of jet travel collectively indicate an attractive and profitable operation.
>
> Existing runways, even at minor airports, are in most cases more than adequate for scheduled Jetliner operation. The approach speed of the aircraft is entirely normal. The simplicity of flying and handling the aircraft reduces problems in pilot training to a minimum.
>
> The numerous flights conducted to date demonstrated that the Jetliner does not present any severe traffic control problems which some anticipated for it. The fact that it can, if necessary, be operated in a conventional manner in the traffic and holding pattern and still show a profit is indicative of its versatility." [117]

Hughes tried to have Avro Canada produce the aircraft, using Pratt & Whitney's license-production version of the Nene. C.D. Howe, unfortunately, blocked this request insisting Avro must concentrate on the CF-100 all-weather fighter—thereby not ruffling feathers in the US industry or Congress. The Liberals had again bestowed Howe with virtually unlimited powers through the Defense Production Act, agreed to in the panic that ensued after the commencement of hostilities in Korea. (Howe would ask to have these powers extended after Korea, and thus during the Arrow program, and to do so without involving the normal democratic process.)[118] Hughes was also a director of Convair in the United States, and subsequently tried to have Convair license-produce his Jetliners. This too was refused, on U.S. government grounds that all new aircraft production in the United States would have to be for the Korean conflict.[119] These negotiations, according to J.C. Floyd in his authoritative book *The Avro Canada C-102 Jetliner,* involved Winthrop Rockefeller—one of the five brotherly heirs to the John. D.

Rockefeller empire and a leading executive with Convair. Eastern Airlines, which seemed to be in a position where they would be forced to acquire Jetliners if their main rival, National, did, was founded, in part, by Laurence Rockefeller.[120] Laurence Rockefeller was also involved in the formation of McDonnell aircraft—illuminating another conflict of interests between this family and Avro Canada. Another area of conflict involves the financing of American manufacturers by Chase-Manhattan and Citibank—two financial institutions with major Rockefeller financial involvement.

Avro's collaboration with the enigmatic Hughes didn't end with his purchase attempt. Hughes and Rummel worked with Avro on various advanced aircraft based on the Jetliner's fuselage technology. A swept wing plane was considered, as was a double-decker, six-engine design similar in appearance (though smaller) to the new Airbus A-380. Avro supersonic transport (SST) designs were also discussed.

Canadair was, at this time, like Convair and Electric Boat Ltd., owned by General Dynamics. Canadair's facilities had been built for war production, just like Avro's, and had been a private Canadian company when it first started making planes from surplus Douglas C-54/DC-4, C-47/DC-3, and DC-6 parts left over at war's end. This is the origin of the North Star airliner that TCA had purchased, and that, sadly, seems to have played a disproportionately large part in the cancellation of Avro's Jetliner. Records reproduced in Larry Milberry's *Canadair North Star*, show that TCA struggled to turn a profit with the North Star, partly because it had such a terrible reputation for racket.

Had TCA bought the Jetliner without some kind of government subsidy, they risked losing their capital investment in the North Star airliner. One of the demands of C.D. Howe when he established the national airline had been that it had to operate in the black. By the early fifties TCA realised it was barely breaking even, so far as they could tell, with the North Star. The airline didn't think it could afford to dump their practically new North Stars for Jetliners until they had paid for themselves. It also seems logical that they realised if they bought a few Jetliners, they'd have to buy a fleet. In fact their work in circulating their negative assessments of the plane among airline executives in the United States seems to suggest they felt that if *anybody* bought Jetliners, *everybody* would have to.[121] With the US airlines buying new Lockheed Constellations, Boeing Stratocruisers and Douglas DC-6s, it may not be a leap of logic to assume that some of them stood to lose major investments in these last piston airliners. After sampling the improved comfort, super-quietness and impressive speed advantage, the flying public would have demanded Jetliner service. It's too bad for Avro that the risk-averse types won out in this case, and probably too bad for what is now Air Canada—who lost an opportunity to lead their industry and, had the moment been seized and the advantage pursued, could have expanded its global operations.

What has been a nearly 60-year-old thorn in the sides of many close to the Jetliner program is the fact that TCA, and government executives in Howe's Department of Transportation, resorted to a campaign of negativity rather than either an honest appraisal or at least a dignified silence. Many of these Jetliner veterans will no doubt be incensed when they read the findings of the report prepared for the government by the Air Transport Board (ATB). As previously mentioned, this report, which was overwhelmingly favourable towards the Jetliner, was classified by the government, presumably in accordance with Howe's wishes.

> "Certain advantages will accrue to the airline which first employs a jet transport in domestic scheduled transport operations and these are believed sufficiently important to warrant a brief examination. Firstly, there should be an increase in traffic due to the superiority of turbine-engined aircraft over conventional types, with respect to passenger comfort. Increased speed will also be an attraction. Both these features assume greater importance as the stage length is increased. The very novelty of such a radical advance in type of equipment will also be of benefit…
>
> The study suggests that the Jetliner can be operated at a lower direct cost than the North Star for the route and schedule frequencies chosen even though the stage lengths were well below the optimum for the Jetliner...

Conclusions…

1. The service requires three Jetliners (including one as reserve) as against four North Stars (including one as reserve).

2. The direct operating cost of the Jetliner, with the present price of kerosene in tank cars at Malton, varies between 79% and 81% of the North Star direct operating cost….

3. An equal indirect cost…was applied to the Jetliner and North Star alike. On this basis, which is rather unfavourable to the Jetliner, the total operating cost of the Jetliner varies between 88% and 90% of the total North Star operating cost.

4. The introduction cost of the Jetliner in the proposed service will probably be of the order of $860,000. … [The North Stars had cost TCA $670,000 each.[122]]

6. Increased frequency of service, or an increase in stage length… either of which will result in a larger number of aircraft than specified in para. 1, will have the effect of lowering the direct operating cost of the Jetliner from the levels indicated in para. 2.

7. Due to the improved standards of comfort and speed which the Jetliner can offer, as well as the novelty of such a radically new type of transport, it is very probable that it will generate more revenue traffic than the North Star, so the difference in net revenue will be appreciably greater than that indicated by the total cost figures given in para. 4…

The application of an equal indirect cost, such as that for engine maintenance etc., for the Jetliner as compared to the piston-engined planes was probably very unfair to Avro. Turbine engines generally, and the Derwent and Nene particularly, are very reliable if operated properly. Avro had also put a great deal of thought into the layout of equipment and access panels etc. in the Jetliner to facilitate rapid maintenance.

> "The position and layout of the various accessory units which have to be serviced regularly on the ground, or which need to be accessible in flight was given a lot of thought, as this is a point, which has aroused much criticism in the past by airline operators.
>
> An accessories compartment was introduced behind the first officers bulkhead on the starboard side to carry the main aircraft accessories… The heater, refrigerating turbine, main electrical accessories such as, inverters, relays etc., and the main electrical distribution panel are all housed in this compartment, which has its own fire extinguishing system.
>
> All radio and electronic units are in a similar separate compartment on the port side behind the pilot's bulkhead, The main hydraulic units are panelized, the panels being housed in the forward wing root fillet, with easy access at ground height to all ground connections, accumulators, valves etc. The emergency power pack is also contained on these panels.
>
> Methyl-bromide engine fire protection bottles are housed in the nacelles at shoulder height and the engine starter relay panels are also in this vicinity.
>
> The extremely low static position of the aircraft ensures that practically all external servicing is done without steps or servicing ramps."[123]

Most every airline engineer and mechanic who viewed the Jetliner on her 'US Tour' commented favourably on the ease of maintenance and apparent reliability of CF-EJD-X: Canada's Jetliner. Fuel consumption was also lower than many had feared. Written in one of Don Rogers' many logbooks are the pounds of fuel used by the Jetliner on a particular airline route in the USA. The figures compared well with those of a Lockheed Constellation on a similar stage length. The ATB and other fuel calculations actually destroyed TCA's most probable excuse: that jet aircraft are harder on fuel than piston for a given weight of aircraft and distance flown. It seems quite probable that any inherent disadvantage in fuel economy for a given power output were overcome by the Jetliner's lower drag. The engines, paired, aerodynamically-cowled and semi-submerged in the wing, would provide a significant drag advantage on their own. The Jetliner's leading edge extension (LEX) also cut drag as did it's ultra-smooth fuselage, thick, pre-formed wing skins and high-tech riveting system. Even Jim Bain of TCA would be moved to write a favourable note to his superiors during the last TCA evaluation of the plane:

> "A physical examination of the aircraft showed a quality of workmanship which I have never seen surpassed on a prototype aircraft nor indeed by many production aircraft. Taken by and large, the skinning and metal work is beautiful and far surpasses the quality achieved in production North Stars. They also appear to have left very few ends untied and even in the prototype the general equipment installation design shows enough care and foresight to make the C-102 a really modern aircraft incorporating the best of present installation knowledge."[124]

The Avro Jetliner cruising over Southern Ontario. (via Jim Floyd)

As the primary source documents cited indicate:

1) Three Jetliners could replace four or more piston aircraft in routine service.
2) The Jetliner was one third faster than its competition.
3) The Jetliner was much quieter than the competition.
4) The Jetliner's high altitude performance would improve comfort and reduce weather delays.
5) The Jetliner was incredibly easy to turn around between flights and would have reduced indirect costs.
6) The Jetliner was a docile, pleasant plane to fly.
7) The Jetliner's fuel economy compared favourably to that of competing piston aircraft even while the fuel itself was cheaper.
8) Its landing and approach speeds were entirely normal compared with the competition.

Obviously, then, TCA and Canadair both had reason to feel embarrassed on behalf of their North Stars, once the Jetliner demonstrated her all-around superiority. Perhaps these facts led C.D. Howe to turn against the program he started, content in the knowledge that Avro had the CF-100 program as alternate production. If this was the case, it was probably a mistake. Why they couldn't do both is a good question—though this might have involved taking over Canadair, which lacked viable commercial production after the North Star anyway.

Convair too was rolled into General Dynamics and had been originally formed by the pairing of Consolidated Aircraft, (makers of the famous amphibious PBY and Liberator heavy bomber) and Vultee. (Vultee had produced some aircraft for the US Navy and had some radical experimental fighter designs at the end of the war which were not produced.) The resulting Convair concern won the fabulously lucrative contract to build the newly-formed Strategic Air Command's first global-reach nuclear bomber, the massive B-36 Peacemaker. As a cost-plus contract, Convair made a killing on this giant, strictly on a simple average cost per pounds of airframe calculation. It was so massive it made the Brabazon look modest by comparison. The Peacemaker was powered by six 36-cylinder turbo-compound engines (later with four auxiliary J57 jet engines added on two pylons), manned by three crews and filled with enough fuel to go around the world. The payload capacity was equally monstrous, with some being converted to experiment with releasing (no problem) and recovering (major problem—never achieved) their own on-board fighters. The wing was so thick a man could stand up in it and, indeed, a passage was included by the main spar for technicians to do exactly that.

In 1991 this author personally visited the wreckage of a Peacemaker while stationed with 103 Rescue Unit in Gander Nfld. There seemed to be acres of aluminum scattered about, with heaps of very expensive engines and other items sticking out hither and thither. It is hard to grasp the amount of materials and skilled man-hours that went into each plane, and the political thinking that led to its adoption. While it had been developed in case Britain fell and the United States had to continue the WW II air war against Germany from home, after the Nazis were defeated, and with the advent of jets, it was a questionable program. However, on reconnaissance missions the B-36s did valuable work before the advent of the Lockheed U-2.

Electric Boat, meanwhile, made the US Navy's submarines and, now as General Dynamics, still does. (General Dynamics recently acquired the Canadian GM Diesel operation which produces a successful Canadian-designed armoured personnel carrier.) With the Peacemaker and all of its other defense programs, General Dynamics became a titan in the US military-industrial complex. It has been reported that, for several years in the 1950s, up to 40% of General Dynamics' profits were generated by Canadair's license production of Silver Star jet trainers, Sabre jet fighters, and other projects.[125]

Once the Jetliner production was halted, in 1954 Boeing introduced its 367-80 (Dash 80) design, which was immediately ordered as the KC-135 for USAF air-to-air refuelling operations. The 707 airliner was produced from profits on this deal, and, on the back of that, Boeing displaced Douglas as the world's leading producer of civilian passenger aircraft.[126] Had the USAF been allowed to standardize on the Avro Jetliner, it seems apparent that Avro, and Canada, may have become the world's number one producer of jet transports. Given that possibility, one can surmise that political pressure was applied by affected US industrialists and financiers. Since the *privately owned* US Federal Reserve finances virtually all economic activity in the United States, one can see that this institution's leading shareholders would be universally opposed to competition in such an important economic sphere. With the Jetliner set to become standard equipment for US air carriers and the US military, the potential for Avro to compete with US companies is obvious, as is the probability that interested parties in the United States were able to foresee it.

Industrial concerns such as Hawker Siddeley are immense entities in terms of capital investment. Whereas the assets of financial concerns are comparatively liquid, the pillars of sophisticated technology and a skilled and creative workforce are relatively fixed, and difficult to maintain. Public (vs. private) industrial concerns' share value (and thus financial health) are dependent on the ability of the company to maintain their technical and skills modernity, and are also vulnerable to the capricious potentialities of human investors. A bad story leaked or planted in the media, no matter how incorrect, can have disastrous consequences. With a corporation dependent on defense, a loss of faith on the part of the major investor, the government, could spell the end. Such companies are, as compared to national Central Banks like the Bank of England and the US Federal Reserve, very vulnerable to a loss of financial solvency due to the loss of single large programs involving a good portion of their engineers and skilled labour. Projects of that magnitude take years of planning and design and if one is abandoned, without another in the pipeline being mature enough to replace it, bankruptcy was the frequent result. Hawker Siddeley as a financial entity, where moveable assets were concerned, was almost miniscule compared to the US banks holding direct interests in the aerospace and defense industries of that country, and money is liquid compared to machine tools and buildings. This sets up a geo-economic competition aspect, in terms of Canadian/British/American firms and their respective financial industries. But these same American banks, which hold interests in virtually all the major US companies, also comprised the central bank of the United States of America, the US Federal Reserve. And its moveable assets dwarf those of any nation on earth. This private institution is also empowered to create currency on demand—and loan it at interest, to the US government, or any other entity. The Bank of Canada and Bank of England are, to some extent, dependent on the good-will of the US Federal Reserve, and at any rate would not dare to seriously challenge it.

This makes the game more interesting because all of these entities have intelligence operations of their own, from a few people in Avro's case to thousands with the banks, the insurance companies they exchanged data with, and then the Central Banks and their governments, who of course also hold the financial data on all the citizens. Historically, a strange feedback develops where the thinking and policy making of a few powerful figures, whomever they may be at any one point in time, become self-fulfilling prophecies in terms of policies that are adopted at the national level. But then, that is the job of intelligence agencies, to manipulate people to produce those results desired by their sponsors. Logically, then, American aerospace firms, the banks that finance them, the insurance companies that protect their investors, the central bank at their head, and the federal government dependent on all of them, would be unsympathetic towards the number one foreign competitor in civil and military aerospace: Hawker Siddeley.

No matter what the mechanics of the Jetliner's demise, it is clear that American political assurances of equal treatment for foreign producers was, regardless of intent, not generating the proclaimed intended result. Worse, history shows that American political interests have regularly engaged in dubious measures designed to help American business outdo its international rivals. Today it is acknowledged that the NSA uses intelligence gathered through the Echelon and UKUSA agreements for commercial purposes.

In another act that belies US assurances of non-discrimination towards foreign product, once the Korean War ended, US Congress swiftly reinforced the Buy American Act. Originating in the Great Depression, this act forbade the purchase of foreign products for US government use. Where foreign products were deemed the only solution to important needs, duties and penalties were to be applied reducing risks and ensuring the profitability of subsequent American production. This act even contains a pugnaciously hypocritical clause stating that any foreign government that passed legislation that similarly discriminated against US products would become the object of mandatory trade sanctions. It seems clear from the above, that "free trade" in aerospace was a one-way street, whether by intent or default.

Howe's reasons for the actions described above have never been sufficiently explained. In fact, Palmiro Campagna shows in his book, *Storms of Controversy*, that C.D. Howe's files on the Jetliner were signed out and never returned to the National Archives. Subsequent investigation suggests that these documents were signed out by someone close to CD Howe, with their current disposition in some doubt.[127]

There may have also been another influence, that of Howe's devotion to TCA, commonly known to have been his proudest creation. "…Gordon McGregor told C.D. Howe that the reason TCA refused the Jetliner was that his "company would never get into the black if it purchased expensive jet airplanes." By 1959 McGregor was bragging, during his keynote speech during the celebrations of 50 years of powered flight in Canada, about the expensive new jet airplanes he had just ordered from Douglas aircraft in the United States. "I was shocked when McGregor, Chairman of T.C.A., as guest speaker on the Fiftieth Anniversary of powered flight in Canada, spent most of his speech glorifying the DC-8 which he had just ordered."[128]

Whatever the true cause, or combination of causes, the Jetliner failed due to the actions of C.D. Howe, not due to any "free market" influences or problems with being "too far ahead of its time" or being technically flawed. By allowing TCA to renege on its letter of intent, through the rock-ribbed policies of his Department of Transport, by ordering Avro to stop work not once but twice, through classifying USAF offers for purchase, by refusing production for Hughes, by classifying the favourable report on the Jetliner and other documents, Avro Canada's future in commercial transports was curtailed by the man who is credited with leading the industrialisation of Canada.[129]

Nevertheless, by 1949 Avro Canada Ltd. had already produced one of the highest thrust turbojet engines in the world, Canada's first two successful turbine engine designs, the Western Hemisphere's first jet passenger plane, and had flown what would by 1954 prove to be the most effective all-weather night fighter in the Western arsenal. As early as the time of the first Avro CF-100 Mk.2 flight in 1951, A.V. Roe Canada Ltd., a six-year-old company, was the only North American corporation even attempting to design and produce the two most difficult essentials of air defense: a long-range, all-weather, day or night transonic jet interceptor, and the cutting-edge high-thrust military engine upon which such an aircraft depends. In the mid-to-late 1950s there were many, many bad weather nights, and some bad-weather and winter days too, when Avro CF-100 interceptors of the RCAF were known to be the only aircraft reliably defending the skies of Europe.

C-102 Jetliner crew

114 ibid and personal interviews with Don Rogers, J.C. Floyd and others.
115 Interview with J.C. Floyd, Oct. 2006
116 Pesando, Mario. Jetliner Flight Trials and Other Things unpublished, undated (circa 1990) p.p. 4-5
117 Shaw, E.K. There Never Was an Arrow. Toronto: Steel Rail Educational Publishing, 1979
118 Newman, Peter C. Renegade in Power: The Diefenbaker Years. Toronto: McClelland & Stewart Ltd., 1985
119 ibid
120 Collier & Horowitz. The Rockfellers; An American Dynasty
121 Interview with J.C. Floyd, April 2002
122 Milberry, Larry. The Canadair DC-4M North Star
123 Floyd, J.C.. Avro C-102 Jetliner, Society of Automotive Engineers lecture, January, 1950
124 Campagna, Palmiro. Storms of Controversy, the Secret Avro Arrow Files Revealed. Toronto: Stoddart Publishing Co. Ltd., 1992, 1997
125 Shaw, There Never Was an Arrow
126 Mellberg, Bill: Famous Airliners
127 Interview between the author and Palmiro Campagna in 2000, and another with a private primary source individual.
128 Note to Whitcomb from Janusz Zurakowski in September, 2001:
129 Demonstrated above, and in Floyd: The Avro Canada C-102 Jetliner.

Chapter 18

GEO-ECONOMIC ISSUES AND INTELLIGENCE

Once the Truman Democrats were replaced by the Eisenhower Republicans, a nuclear Armageddon-or-nothing doctrine was proclaimed by the incoming Secretary of State; John Foster Dulles, which was termed Mutually-Assured Destruction. Yes, these were the days of the M.A.D. doctrine that proclaimed that a Soviet attack of whatever description, as solely determined by the United States government, would be responded to with an all-out thermo-nuclear war. This doctrine was also adopted, by default, by NATO and later NORAD, due to the dependence of the West on the United States for defense, and, by extension, *defense policy.* The results were very profitable (to the US manufacturers and the banks financing them) nuclear air-to-air missiles, nuclear tank rounds, nuclear artillery, nuclear surface-to-surface missiles, nuclear ground-to-air missiles, nuclear air-to-surface missiles, and soon, nuclear missiles fired from nuclear submarines; nuclear missiles capable of being launched from the other side of the planet, nuclear missiles from nuclear ships, with nuclear reactor equipped bombers being tested in the air and nuclear air and spacecraft powerplants being tested on the ground. No wonder there were so many atomic-horror B-movies in the 1950s.

Of course the Soviets had not really disbanded the Red Army as it stood, seemingly invincible, at the end of WW II. Post-war this mass of firepower loomed ominously on the old Eastern Front of Germany. The Allied air forces, however, still dwarfed the capabilities of the Soviets, particularly in strategic bombers, which the Soviets didn't develop in WW II. The short-lived US monopoly on nuclear weapons was destabilizing to any kind of strategic parity and for any Soviet sense of security. They were understandably alarmed when the Republicans integrated many Nazis into US industry and started to re-arm Germany. The American determination to monopolise atomic weapons was guaranteed to generate a reaction from the Soviets, and they quickly acquired nuclear technology through espionage. By 1947 they too had detonated an atomic bomb, and were only 18 months behind the US in unleashing the shockingly destructive power of the fusion, or hydrogen bomb. However, the US was first in the development and adoption of all nuclear weapons—other than the ICBM. When the Reds launched the first ICBM in August 1957, the CIA over-reaction included alarmist theories of Soviet missile supremacy, which replaced their previous alarmist theories about Soviet bomber supremacy.

It is interesting to note that Soviet espionage was instrumental in allowing the Russians to keep up with the West despite having an economy of perhaps half the size of that of the United States. Some involved in the Manhattan Project simply felt that it would be too destabilising to have America in sole possession of the weapon and so they shared information with the Russians. Some of them seemed to question the power of some of the financial and capitalist oligarchs and felt they needed to be restrained by an opposing philosophy. Some were very aware that similar wealthy members of the international elite had traditionally supported international Fascism and looked to socialism, and occasionally communism, as a favourable alternative. Others looked at it on a more philosophical level, and equated competition-driven capitalism with greed and envy, and cooperation-based socialism (and in some cases even communism) with teamwork and sharing.

Whatever the intellectual arguments spanning the Capitalist/Communist divide, Stalin's belligerence and suppression of human rights made it apparent, to those who decided policy, that the Soviets were a major threat to the United States and Canada's traditional friends and allies. It was noted, however, in Canadian bi-lateral discussion papers, that it was *only or primarily* due to Canada's proximity to the United States that Canada faced a direct threat of Soviet attack. While it was recognized that while the threat of Soviet aggression was the main military threat facing Canada's sovereignty, others foresaw potential problems for Canadian sovereignty becoming a by-product of military integration with the United States:

> "The fear that the United States was crossing the line from a spirit of co-operation to a strengthening desire for continental integration was on the minds of many Canadians seeking a suitable defense policy after the war."[130]

As mentioned, in 1945 the UKUSA electronic intelligence gathering system was set up with ECHELON being a system of monitoring telephone, radio and other forms of communication, ostensibly to monitor Soviet activity, find the frequencies and other secrets of their radar and communications systems, and to allow defense against them while providing intelligence on Soviet intentions.

However, it has become clear that this system had also been abused by US interests for economic purposes. Former CIA employees working on remote viewing have acknowledged on television that even their work was directed at commercial intelligence as well as more typical areas of interest. In a working paper for parliament of the European Union the misuse of intelligence for commercial purposes is also covered. The following quotations are from a poor (possibly automated) translation into English and this author has endeavoured to clean up the original for purposes of clarity.

> "Various examples could be mentioned about the abuse of privacy via global surveillance telecommunications systems (like ECHELON)… Many accounts have been published by reputable journalists citing frequent occasions on which the US government has utilised Comint [communications intelligence] for national purposes."
>
> It is interesting that some of the major violations were against European commercial aerospace projects. "On June 25, 1998 [sic. the date was 1988], in [H]absheim, an… A-320 of the European Company Airbus Industries,…crashed during a demonstration flight. The accident [was] caused by dangerous manipulations [by the pilot]. One person died and 20 were injured.
>
> "Very soon, and before the announcement of the official report, in the aerospace and transport Internet newsgroups, [there were over 240 internet newsgroups in 1988] appeared a lot of aggressive messages against the company Airbus and against the French company Aerospatiale as well, with which Airbus had close co-operation. Messages declared that the accident was [predictable] because European engineers are not so highly qualified as American engineers are. It was also clearly stated that in the future similar accidents could be expected.
>
> "Aerospatiale's agents were very [agitated by] these aggressive messages. They tried to discover the sources of the messages and they finally realised that the senders' identification data, addresses and nodes were false. The source messages came from [the] USA, from computers with [misleading] identification data and transferred through anonymous servers in Finland.
>
> "In this case Aerospatiale has arguments to insist…that American BOEING implemented one of the biggest misinform[ation] campaigns over the internet."[131]
>
> In another of six examples, the document states: "In January 1994 Edouard Balladur went to Ryad (Saudi Arabia)… certain to bring back a historical contract for more than 30 million francs in sales and weapons [involving]… especially, Airbus…
>
> "The contract went to the McDonnell-Douglas American company, rival of Airbus. Partly, according to the French, thanks to electronic listening of the Echelon system, which had given the Americans the financial conditions (and the bribes) authorised by Airbus. This information [was] collected and analysed by the batteries of hidden supercomputers behind the black panes of a cubic building that is visible… through the pines…on the motorway between Washington and Baltimore; Fort Meade (Maryland), head office of the NSA….
>
> "Fort Meade contains, according to sources familiar [with the NSA], the greatest concentration of data processing power and math student[s] in the world. They are charged to sort and analyse the flood of data [acquired] by Echelon on the networks of international telecommunications. "There is not one diplomatic event or soldier concerning the United States in which the NSA is not directly implied", recognised…the director of the agency, John McConnel, [in 1996]. "The NSA plays a very significant role as regards economic espionage", affirms John Pike…of the… Federation of American Scientists… "Echelon is the heart of its operations"…. Economic espionage justifies, in fact, the maintenance of this oversize apparatus since the end of the cold war."[132]

Not that the French are innocents in such matters—they aren't. While we are diverging from the main topic somewhat, this European Union document makes some statements that may have a bearing on the increased demands for intelligence access that accompanied the Bush administration's response to the 9-11 tragedy. During the Clinton administration a movement was formed to allow "key escrow" or "key recovery" technology as the Western standard for network security. The document mentions this system as being pushed by US interests, "solely in the context of network security arrangements". The document states that this was a deception designed to allow the United States to access information from any computer system in the Western world. This US deception was, however, clear to the senior Commission official responsible for information security. In September 1996, David Herson, head of the EU Senior Officers' Group on Information Security, stated his assessment of the US "key recovery" project:

> 'Law Enforcement' is a protective shield for all the other governmental activities... We're talking about foreign intelligence, that's what all this is about. There is no question [that] 'law enforcement' is a smoke screen..."
>
> It should be noted that technically, legally and organisationally, law enforcement requirements for communications interception differ fundamentally from communications intelligence. Law enforcement agencies (LEAs) will normally wish to intercept a specific line or group of lines, and must normally justify their requests to a judicial or administrative authority before proceeding. In contrast, Comint agencies conduct broad international communications "trawling' activities, and operate under general warrants... Such distinctions are vital to civil liberty, but risk being eroded if the boundaries between law enforcement and communications intelligence interception becomes blurred in future." [133]

9-11 certainly resulted in the blurring of those lines. One is left to wonder if the European resistance to broad COMINT demands by the US, subsequent to the terror attacks, was one reason for the belligerence of the Bush administration towards certain European governments, particularly the French, in the wake of 9-11.

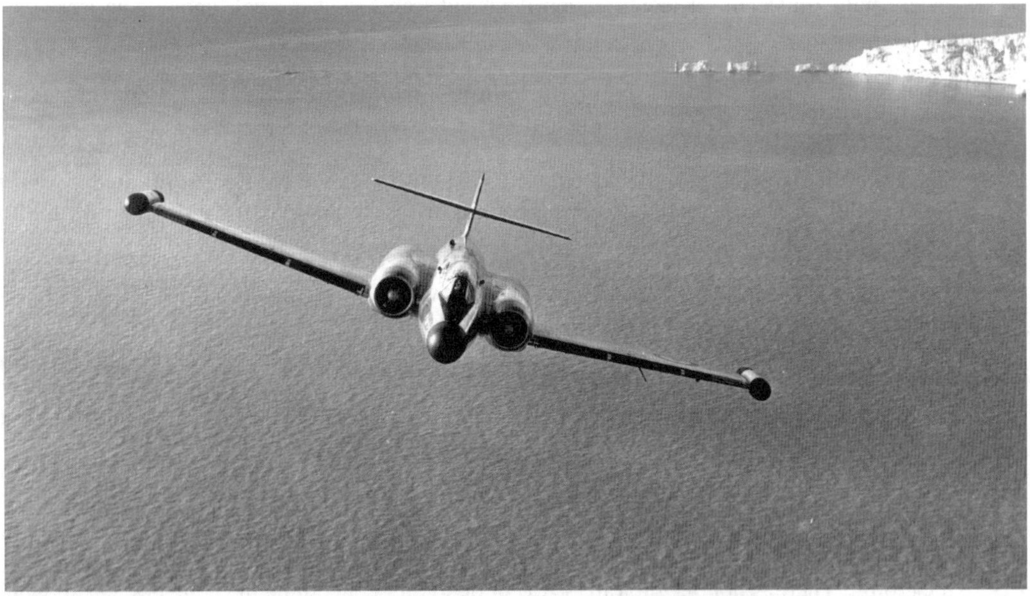

Jan Zurakowski visits Britain in the CF-100 Mk. 4

130 Dow: The Arrow.
131 From: Bogolikos, Nikos: "Development of Surveillance Tehnology and Risk of Abuse of Economic Information, Scientific and Technological Options Assessment", The European Parliament Luxembourg, October, 1999. pp.4-5
There is a disclaimer stating that this document does not necessarily represent the views of the European Parliament.
132 Ibid p.6
133 ibid, p.10

Chapter 19

THE CF-100 CANUCK ALL-WEATHER NIGHT OR DAY INTERCEPTOR

By the mid-1950s, as in wartime, Avro had shown what bilateral defense production sharing could accomplish in British/Canadian partnership. Britain purchased Canadair built Sabres, and other aircraft—including some North Star airliners. Canada benefited in the engineering and scientific expertise Hawker Siddeley and other European engineers brought to Avro and Orenda in Canada, and the sales helped offset (and justify) the government's investment in the companies.

In the 1950s the British side of Hawker Siddeley was also busy. Avro was developing the Vulcan bomber, Gloster's was producing (and modifying) its Javelin fighter, Sir Sydney Camm, Managing Director and Chief Designer of Hawker Aircraft, got the Hunter transonic day fighter contract, and many other contracts kept the Group reasonably vibrant. Avro was also designing a short range "point defense" interceptor, sort of an extension of the WW II Messerschmitt Komet tailless rocket interceptor: the turbojet/rocket hybrid-powered Avro 720 delta interceptor. It used Armstrong Siddeley's Screamer rocket engine plus a small afterburning turbojet for take-off and cruise. In 1954 Avro U.K. had also been granted a contract to design and develop a long-range Mach 3 spyplane/strike bomber; the Avro 730[134]. This was an interesting design, predating, yet similar to, the Lockheed "Skunk Works" SR-71 Blackbird—an aircraft of similar configuration, performance and intent. Glosters had won a contract for a redesigned, supersonic Javelin, the "Thin Wing Javelin" or TWJ[135], and other contracts were promising some rewards for the industrial plant. Compared to A.V. Roe Canada however, the British arm of the Group appeared somewhat anaemic.

It is generally presented that it was the inavailability of license-produced machines for RCAF needs during WW II that led RCAF and government leaders to take the monumental step of deciding to design and produce, in Canada, not just a military airplane for the RCAF, but the one that required the greatest technical and production sophistication: an all-weather, long-range, day or night interceptor. Today, even with an intervening 60 years of technical evolution and production experience, such a decision would be viewed with wonder in most nations—perhaps especially in Canada given the history. Not long after embarking on the experimental design of this fighter, the same Canadian enterprise, guided by the ethic of industrial independence in support of military and strategic independence, undertook to design Canadian engines to power this advanced fighter.

In September 1945, before A.V. Roe Canada was established, a meeting was held in Ottawa to discuss the RCAF's requirement and to assure the government of Dobson and Avro UK's commitment to establish their Canadian subsidiary. Representatives included Fred Smye, three RCAF air vice marshals including Wilf Curtis, three engineers from Turbo Research including Paul Dilworth and Winnett Boyd, and experts from the Hawker Siddeley design council. The three Hawker Siddeley Group representatives were some of the best aviation minds in Britain. Davies, now chief designer from Avro's Yorkshire plant , W.H. Lindsay from Armstrong Siddeley engines and W.W.W. Downing from Gloster Aircraft came over with Fred Smye to discuss the government and TCA's needs for a fighter, an airliner and jet engines. While Stuart Davies was concentrating his efforts on TCA and the engineering staff remaining at Malton, Lindsay was concentrating on Turbo Research, with Downing focusing on the RCAF's fighter requirements.

On viewing the RCAF plan and the specification for the light fighter, one of Hawker Siddeley's representatives, W.W.W. Downing (Gloster's chief designer), was mortified. He adamantly argued that such an aircraft might do for Britain with the short ranges involved there, but insisted such an aircraft was totally inadequate for Canada considering the size of the nation, the harsh weather and long distances between air bases. He insisted that Canada needed an aircraft with two engines of significantly higher thrust than the single one being proposed, and a crew of two to handle the chores of managing such a sophisticated aircraft over long flight durations and distances.

With Downing's words of wisdom undoubtedly ringing in their ears, A/V/M Curtis and the others threw out their specification and went back to the drawing board to devise an air defense plan that could actually defend the country. From this emerged an idea of the kind of aircraft required. They were forced to take a sober look and adopt a "best-of-the-best" approach. They needed a long-range, day-or-night, all-weather aircraft to take on and defeat alone, any likely threat coming over the top of the world from the Soviet Union. They envisaged a long-range jet interceptor using sophisticated radar and weaponry, a crew of two to handle the tasks of long-range navigation, target acquisition and the necessarily sophisticated aircraft systems which would allow it to operate semi-autonomously. Two engines were also specified for reliability during these several-hour missions. They also specified a very high rate of climb and relatively short-field take-off and landing characteristics. In short, the RCAF wanted it all! This was late 1945 and one might bear in mind that the state-of-the-art aircraft then in service which came closest to the requirement being issued was the superlative de Havilland Mosquito radar-equipped night-fighter. It didn't come close to the RCAF's very tall order, and a team left Canada in 1946 to visit all the manufacturers in the free world to see if a suitable aircraft was under development –*anywhere*. Canada was not naive enough to think that she could afford to spend this kind of money only to duplicate something that was going to happen elsewhere anyway, especially considering the rapid advances in the state-of-the-art and the risks associated with the development of such an aircraft and its propulsion and weapons systems. The team arrived home empty-handed. Curtis went on the record as asserting that such an aircraft did not exist anywhere, nor was one in the design phase or even being planned.

Thus, in 1946 the RCAF issued the revised plan under the title "Air-7-1-Issue 2." Its requirements were staggering. The specification contained a requirement for an aircraft corresponding to the following:

A two-seat all-metal aircraft powered by two gas turbine (jet) engines with a required operational combat ceiling of at least 50,000 feet requiring a highly pressurised cabin. Effective operations in Canada's climate demanded it function in temperatures from -57 to +45 degrees Celsius.

The mission profile:

- start, run-up and taxi of four minutes followed by one minute take-off,

- climb to 40,000 feet with an initial climb rate of not less than 10,000 feet per minute,

- cruise out to its combat radius of 650 nm (nautical miles, one nautical mile equalling approx. 1.15

statute miles)

- engage in combat for 15 minutes at 490 knots (nautical miles per hour) at this altitude,

- return the 650 nm, followed by a 10-minute descent and a 7-minute approach for landing.

This involved a flight time of about three and a half hours. By contrast, a combat mission of a current F-18 Hornet is just over one hour even though the average speed of the missions is, in reality, quite similar. The maximum level-flight airspeed was not to be less than 490 knots (over 560 mph). Consider this specification to the performance of the Spitfire, itself designed as an interceptor. The Spitfire Mk. 9 took over seven minutes to climb to 25,000 feet, had a combat speed of about 300 mph and a radius of action of about 150 miles.

As Chief of the Air Staff, Air Marshal Wilf Curtis was the major RCAF personality behind having the improved fighter specification approved, and in the decision to entrust A.V. Roe Canada with the job of building this very advanced aircraft. His reputation was very much on the line over this rare gamble of giving an unproven company such enormous, expensive and risky tasks. He is on record as saying he never regretted his confidence in the company. Since he worked well with both the company and the government, Curtis later took on a directorship of A.V. Roe Canada Ltd. This seemed to be viewed by the later Conservative government not as an exploitation of a talented honest-broker but as some form of bribery-after-the-fact—although it is standard practice today.

Roy Dobson's upstart Canadian company now had a very full plate. They were undertaking to build an aircraft with performance no one else in the world seemed prepared to attempt, along with the first jet passenger aircraft, *and* a revolutionary axial-flow engine of about the highest thrust anywhere—yet these were the infant company's first designs. To some A.V. Roe Canada seemed determined to fly before it had demonstrated it could crawl. At the time, other than the Avro Vulcan, the Gloster Javelin, Hawker Hunter (and derivatives) and Sapphire engine developments, the XC-100 fighter, C-102 Jetliner and TR-5 Orenda engine projects were the most prestigious undertakings going on within the Hawker Siddeley Group.

The second CF-100 prototype in flight. (courtesy Wilf Farrance)

Once the XC-100 design was crystallised, it had no major setbacks in production and the first flight date in January 1950 soon arrived. The prototype without the add-ons and modifications of the later combat-ready versions, resplendent in black with a white lightning bolt down the fuselage, had the look of a revolutionary and graceful thoroughbred. The prototype aircraft, unencumbered by armament or the large nose radar and cowl modifications to come was quite attractive. It shared basic shapes and configuration with the Jetliner and also shared the same grace and economy of line as its Avro stable-mate.

It faced development problems that seemed severe at the time, especially to powerful Canadian critics, yet history has shown its development to have been no worse than most and better than many. In the hands of Janusz Zurakowski, the CF-100 would become the first straight-winged aircraft to break the sound barrier. A little-known story about how this event came to be is worth disclosing. When "Zura" arrived at Avro Canada he was somewhat wary of designers and flight-test engineers from his experiences at Gloster Aircraft in Britain on the Meteor and Javelin fighter programs. He and engineers, such as Mario Pesando, then head of Avro flight test, became convinced that the CF-100 could exceed the sound barrier without going beyond its maximum equivalent airspeed restriction, at a certain altitude. Since the plane was 'plaquarded' at a maximum speed of Mach .85, this left a large margin for error that needed to be investigated. When flight test aerodynamicists and engineers presented this controversial finding to Avro engineering, the reception was decidely frostly. Engineering decided that the plane couldn't go supersonic and a meeting was scheduled to discuss the issue. Flight test knew it was in for heavy weather and devised an interesting scheme. Zurakowski was already in a CF-100 linked to the phone system through the company control tower. When Mario Pesando embarked for the meeting, he called Zura and advised him to take off. After hearing the objections of the heads of engineering, Pesando placed a call through the tower to advise Zurakowski that he would be addressing the meeting next. With that, Zura, circling overhead at 40,000 feet, put the CF-100 into a full-power dive, timing his rate of descent to achieve maximum equivalent airspeed at 30,000 feet, all whilst aiming his mount precisely at the windows of the Engineering boardroom. Mario's presentation being punctuated with a resounding sonic boom no doubt proved their point, but not without ruffling some feathers![136]

692 CF-100s would eventually be produced, with 58 of them being sold to Belgium, and partly paid for by the United States. RCAF CF-100s were invited to Europe by NATO in 1955 because they filled a crucial gap in European air defense for long-range, all-weather, day or night interceptors. Despite the CF-100 production fulfilling a Canadian promise to the Americans *not* to produce the C-102 Jetliner, there was a bilateral problem relating to Belgium's purchase of the CF-100. Its Hughes radar/fire-control system, having been produced in the United States, required American government approval before Belgium could acquire them. This was not forthcoming. It took direct intervention by Fred Smye, over and above lethargic Canadian government initiatives, to achieve clearance for Belgium (a NATO ally) to acquire the units.[137]

Although the CF-100 exceeded its specified speed requirement of 490 knots by more than 100 knots, it was apparent that emerging designs such as the B-52 Stratofortress and Soviet "Blinder" bombers, would require a next-generation interceptor. Within the RCAF, in late 1951, an "All-Weather Requirements Team" was set up to look into what kind of aircraft, propulsions, weapons and electronics seemed best suited to defend against such a threat.

While Floyd and Lindley managed the development and introduction into service of the CF-100, John Frost was working quietly with a small team on jet aircraft using circular and oblong planforms—flying saucers so to speak.

Superlative test pilot Janus Zurakowski

134 This was for the British Ministry of Supply's General Operational Requirement 339 for a long-range strike-reconnaissance bomber with side-looking radar and guided or even stand-off missile payload. It was designed to have a radius of about 1,500 nm, a cruise speed of Mach 2.5 to 3.0, and an operational altitude of 70,000 feet or higher.

135 The TWJ was an aerodynamic improvement of the original Javelin, benefiting from the area-rule principle as expounded by NACA Langley's Dr. Richard Whitcomb. Despite the application of this theory, the Javelin was still limited in terms of speed and effectiveness as an all weather interceptor being too "fat" in terms of total volume progression from nose to tail, to be a viable supersonic aircraft, having an essentially subsonic intake design, a tail design that compromised stability at high angles of attack that the plane's delta wing made easily achievable, and other problems. (ref. Conversations with Gloster Chief Test Pilot William Waterton in 2002-2004, and in conversations with Javelin test pilot Jan Zurakowski, 1997-2002, plus numerous other sources.) In fact, in recognition of this fact, (or perhaps for other reasons) the Eisenhower Republicans backed away from Truman's $100 million dollar Mutual Assistance Plan commitment for the Javelin in 1955, and in 1956 the RAF and MOS decided to cancel the TWJ and attempt to replace it with the Avro Canada CF-105.)

136 Letter from Mario Pesando to the author, and portions of Mr. Pesando's memoire draft.

137 Testimony of Avro sales and service manager Joe Morley included in Stewart's Shutting Down the National Dream.

Chapter 20

AVRO SPECIAL PROJECTS GROUP: Flying Saucers From Planet Earth

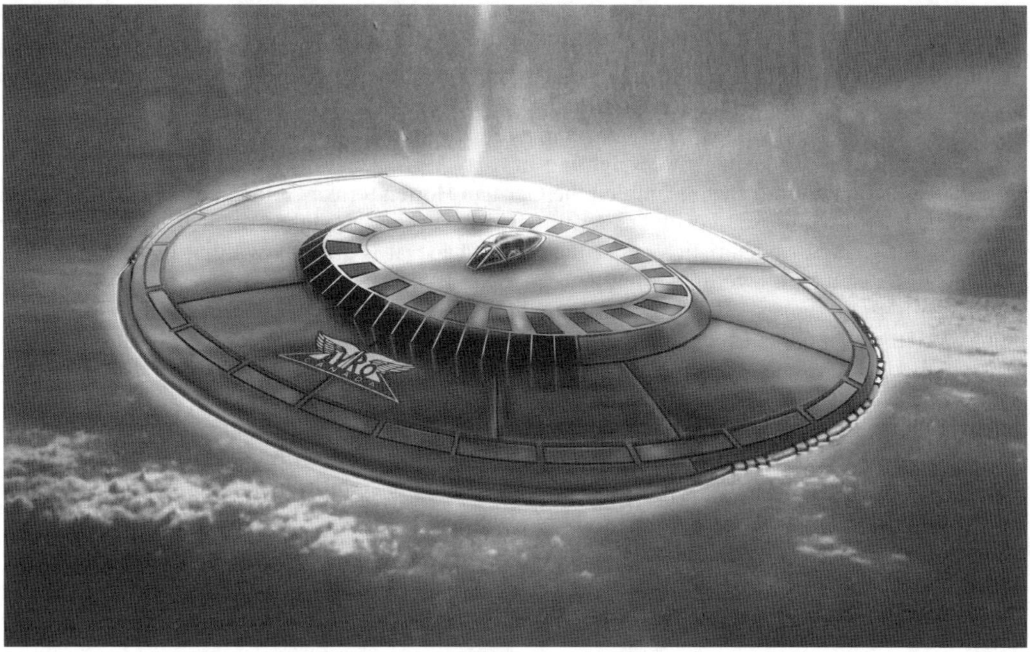

In 1945 Sir Roy Dobson said that Avro Canada would become "the centre of aircraft development and production in 10 years." Presumably he meant for the Hawker Siddeley Group or the Commonwealth not for the world. Dobson's reasoning isn't hard to fathom. Britain was bankrupt thanks to the war, and by 1952 the country was half a billion pounds in debt, although the government hid this from the British people. Dobson also believed that Canada would be in a better position to keep abreast of technical developments in the United States, and better able to sell into this huge market. Indeed A.V. Roe Canada Ltd., during the Arrow program, was responsible for 70% of all the R&D going on in Canada at the time. By 1974 however, the single Japanese electronics conglomerate, Toshiba, was conducting more R&D than Canada as a whole.

Avro conducted annual recruiting drives in the United States, Britain and elsewhere to attract the best minds in the world to the company. The flood of engineers and designers coming from the U.K. to Avro during the 1950's was known as "the British Airlift." This is, obviously, in stark contrast to the chronic 'brain drain' that many Canadians have complained about since. Avro Canada was also quietly employing several German scientists and Germany, it turns out, had been involved in flying saucer design during WW II.

Flight testing of the prototype XC-100 revealed several problems, mostly related to structure, particularly in the main spar-to-engine former area. Since C.D. Howe had sacrificed the Jetliner in favour of CF-100 production, he applied considerable pressure to Avro to perfect the aircraft and get it into production—though his hope to have it in service during the Korean War was a pipe-dream—it had too much normal development to go through, without the structural problems. As a result of unsatisfactory progress John Frost and Chief Engineer EdgarAtkin were removed from their responsibilities and J.C. Floyd and others from the Jetliner were moved to the CF-100 effort. Bob Lindley, who had left Avro in the U.K. for Canadair in Montreal, came to Avro Canada at this time and was placed in charge of a 'blitz group' tasked with speedily correcting the CF-100's most serious flaws. Jim Floyd became works manager for a nine month period helping solve production problems while Lindley concentrated on the plane's structural shortcomings. John Frost was allowed to work on his concepts for an aircraft of circular planform—a flying saucer.

GERMAN SAUCERS

But how did Frost become committed to experimentation with such an exotic concept? The answer appears to be due to lingering rumours of the Nazis involvement in the development of this type of craft, buttressed by the "UFO flaps" of 1947 and 1952. Frost had investigated over two hundred saucer sightings and came away convinced that the most credible ones had occurred in Germany. The thought no doubt crossed his mind that the Americans might have been secretly involved in perfecting German work. This is taken as being his real inspiration for their development, although he certainly seemed to believe that some of the sightings from 1947 and even during the war were genuine, and this inspired his work as well. The Kenneth Arnold sighting in early 1947 near Mt. Rainer in Washington state, involved a formation of craft that resembled the German Horten 9 (aka Gotha 229) aircraft. His sighting, ironically, is also the source of the term "flying saucer"—though Arnold used the phrase in describing their flying characteristics rather than their shape. It is also known that Dr. Solandt of the NRC was briefed at a high level regarding the American Project Sign—the U.S. response to the wave of sightings. It would appear that Frost kept any belief in an extra-terrestrial origin for the "saucer" sightings strictly to himself. Like so much to do with Avro's foray into saucer design, information is very limited. One relevant believer of the era was LCol Philip J. Corso, author of *The Day After Roswell*, who claimed to have seen alien bodies and, through his position in the U.S. Army foreign technology branch, was charged with seeding U.S. industry with alien technology. Corso worked directly under General Arthur Trudeau, who liased directly with Frost on Avro's saucer efforts. (Corso also points out that during this period the Americans acquired a significant amount of aerospace technology from the British—probably meaning via Avro Canada.) Trudeau's Foreign Technology branch issued and managed contracts with foreign producers of advanced technology. Corso's agency was, in essence, an intelligence organisation and few knowledgeable observers would accuse the Pentagon of being conservative in their collection efforts. However, in view of probable British (and Soviet?) suspicion that the United States had monopolised the German SS technology at the end of the war, the Americans weren't the only ones working the intelligence angle.

No doubt Frost, and Avro management, knew that if they started a program for a flying saucer, they'd have a good argument for being given access to American efforts in this area on a "need to know" basis. Early leaks instigated by Avro management were designed to entice American interest and support. While it may have been their intention to find out what the Americans knew, and were doing about 'flying saucers', they were also serious about cooperating with the Americans to develop a viable flying machine. Frost was intent on developing a jet propelled circular aircraft with vertical take-off and landing characteristics. It was his discovery of the radial-flow jet-engine configuration that promised the kind of power that would allow flight performance approaching that attributed to "flying saucers", which gained the interest of Avro management and the Canadian and British governments. The Americans may well have wanted Avro Canada to perfect an experimental jet powered flying saucer, to help an American effort to develop a flying test-bed on which to develop magneto-hydrodynamic and perhaps electro-gravitic propulsion techniques. Another reason suspected for why the Americans funded the Frost projects was to find out how much the British and Canadians knew about German saucer and advanced weapons research.

It is also now generally accepted that a German scientist, Viktor Schauberger, had been engaged to develop working models of flying-saucer shaped devices allegedly employing unconventional "free energy" propulsion that displayed anti-gravitation and other anomolous effects. Records available from the former Soviet bloc countries also indicate that German flying saucer research and development included several programs underway at war's end. All of this has been suppressed information until quite recently, although many leaks have emerged over the years, only to be dismissed by an incredulous establishment. Interviews with ex-Avro engineers, cleared to the highest levels on such programs and on captured German aerospace technology, insist that they only heard rumours of German flying saucer development and received no solid data. Jet information was another matter, though, with the CF-100 and Jetliner designs benefitting from its analysis.

Palmiro Campagna's book *The UFO Files* mentions RCAF headquarters being approached in 1952 by a wartime German aeronautical engineer. In his letter to the RCAF he stated:

"...I want to warn you about believing that these objects are emitted by the stars or that they are weather phenomena...In 1944 I and a group of scientists and technicians worked on a vessel that resembled the "flying saucers." In order to be safe from aerial attacks our group was transferred to Silesia. Our experiments were made with models...there was built an experimental model of 3.6 meters wing span...results were astounding...."

A purported CIA document, dated August 18th, 1952, also mentions "'Flying saucers' have been known to be an actuality since the possibility of their construction was proven in plans drawn up by German engineers toward the end of World War II." George Klein, a German engineer, stated recently that though many people believe the 'flying saucers' to be a postwar development, they were actually in the planning stage in German aircraft factories as early as 1941. Klein said that he was an engineer in the Ministry of Albert Speer…and was present in Prague on 14 February 1945, at the first experimental flight of a 'flying saucer'."[138] John Frost, already working on Project Y, was informed of this and a meeting was held where Frost debriefed the engineer in the presence of military and political intelligence agents from the ABC nations. What he heard about were reports of flight tests of saucer shaped vehicles with revolutionary performance. This was, and still apparently is, a very sensitive topic.

Nick Cook, a respected aviation editor for Jane's Information Group, has researched the topic and found good reason for its sensitivity. Allied heavy bombing and Hitler's growing dissatisfaction with German industrialists (many of whom were collaborating, to some degree, with Allied intelligence including Allen Dulles, and assisting with assassination attempts) resulted in the setting up of a "black" economy for weapons in the latter years of the war. Concentrated in Silesia, run by the SS and using slave labour, an incredibly sophisticated series of underground industrial production and scientific installations were created.

"After the abortive bomb plot against Hitler in July 1944 (a scheme hatched by anti-Hitler elements within the German Army General Staff) the control of the SS and its grip upon Germany would become absolute. But it was in August 1943, at the Wolf's Lair, that the seeds of the SS's takeover of the armaments industry were sown… The man who was to assume direct oversight of the A-4's [V-2's] manufacture, Himmler told [Albert Speer, Nazi minister of armaments] was Dr. of Engineering Hans Kammler, head of the SS's Building and Works Division—the entity that had masterminded and built the [concentration] camps. No sooner had his appointment taken effect, than he was drawing up detailed plans for the rapid expansion of the camps…[and] saw what needed to be done and requested to expand the capacity of the camps to four million; three months later, he increased this figure again to 14 million… Within a month, Kammler and Speer, the latter in his new capacity on the project as a junior partner to the SS, established the low-profile Mittelwerk GmbH (Central Works Ltd.) to run the rocket venture. By the end of the year, 10,000 Buchenwald prisoners—mostly Russians, Poles and Frenchmen—had been dispatched into the limestone cliffs of the Kohnstein, the mountainous ridge close to the village of Nordhausen into which the facility was tunneled. Their job was to bring about the impossible: the construction of the largest underground factory in the world, a facility a kilometer and a half long containing 20 kilometers of tunnels and galleries, dedicated to the construction of rockets, missiles and other top secret weapons. It was finished in a year—20,000 prisoners dying in the process."[139]

Cook makes his case that the Nazis were secretly far more advanced in many technologies than previously suspected. He states that they had indeed achieved nuclear fission and were on track to produce a bomb within a few months of the surrender. Besides beam weapon and nuclear aircraft propulsion research Cook also states that they had discovered a new energy source that displayed anti-gravity and other effects, perhaps with an unanticipated side-effect being produced—time distortion. Exploring the validity of these subjects is beyond the scope of this book, with the main point being that most of this technology, if it existed, apparently ended up in the USA, with next to nothing on these subjects being shared with their allies.

Intrepid's Last Case and Cook's *Hunt For Zero Point* discuss the allied grab for Nazi technology at the end of the war. Other sources suggest that Allen Dulles was deeply involved in discussions with German industrialists and thought he had a handle on what technology existed where, within the Reich, for exploitation after the conflict. Cook suggests that, despite agreements to share the data among the allies, particularly Britain and the United States, the American agents had a secret ace up their sleeve:

knowledge of the secret SS "black economy" centred in Silesia. This knowledge may have derived from Allen Dulles rather freelance negotiations with SS officals near war's end. Cook proposes that General Patton's brief incursion into this area of Europe, when it had been granted to the Soviets at Yalta, was actually intentional, and was done to grab the most sensitive technology and prevent it falling into the hand of the Soviets, and everyone else.

> "The rapid eastward push that had brought the Third Armored Division to Nordhausen did not stop there. Disregarding agreements signed by the exiled Czech government and the Soviet Union, troops of Patton's Third Army to the east of Nordhausen crossed the Czech frontier on May 6.
>
> "Deep into the Soviet-designated zone of occupation, a forward unit of Patton's forces entered Pilsen that morning. Records…sent..from the U.S. National Archives…showed that U.S. forces had the run of the Skoda Works for six days, until the Red Army showed up on May 12. Following protests from Moscow, the U.S. Third Army was eventually forced to withdraw.
>
> "Six days is a long time if you're retrieving something you already know to be there."[140]

It appears that the Third Army's early presence at the Skoda works was kept from the British and Soviets. The British report on CIOS Trip No. 243, describing a joint U.S.-U.K. operation, concludes that the U.S. team had only entered the complex on the 16th, rather than the 6th, under terms agreed at Yalta and elsewhere, in cooperation with the Russian authorities and that they had found nothing of particular note. Of course this gives the impression that the British were convinced that the Americans hadn't entered the complex earlier during Patton's exhuberant dash into the Soviet zone, and clearly didn't suspect the level of technical research and development going on in the Kammlerstab. Wilhelm Voss's private testimony to author Tom Agoston, who temporarily sheltered Voss during the turbulence of the surrender, demonstrates that the US indeed had sent a team of 'tech plunder' specialists to the Skoda Works before the Russians took over the area on the 12th of April. When Voss tried to surrender himself and speak to the American authorities at the Skoda Works itself on the 10th, Voss remembers the American in charge first telling him that he had orders to turn everything over to the Russians. However, when Voss exhorted on the advanced nature and strategic value of the research and development, and their potential danger in Soviet hands, the officer mentioned that an American ordnance team had already been in the complex and had secured everything it needed.[141] Cook's research also alleges that a U.S. team with nuclear expertise entered the Skoda complex and gained access to material relating to German efforts, centred around the Junkers aircraft firm, to develop nuclear propulsion for aircraft.

Both Voss and Cook's source insist nuclear aircraft propulsion, and much more, were actively being developed at Skoda and at sites throughout Silesia and the Bavarian Alps. Public history shows that two German test reactors were found at the end of the war. It is not so publicly known that a German U-boat, the U-234, had been captured enroute to Japan on May 19th, with its loading manifest indicating it was carrying Uranium oxide ore. However the storage areas (mine-laying tubes) were gold lined, suggesting it was actually carrying *enriched* Uranium, the gold was to insulate the crew and the outside world from levels of gamma radiation only enriched Uranium emits. A working reactor is required to enrich Uranium. Surviving German records also indicate that Germany was confident it would produce a working atomic bomb by the fall of 1945. The whole "mountain redoubt" scheme was based on the ability to maintain a Nazi enclave in the Harz mountains (presumably protected by flying saucers) until a bomb could be deployed, whereupon the stalemate would allow the perfection of the other secret weapons by which to re-conquer Europe… All quite mad of course.

What also appears increasingly clear is that the United States managed to pull off the intelligence coup of the war by somehow getting Kammler and the information from his secret research group at the Skoda Works, without the world becoming any the wiser for many, many years. Cook mentions that documents that should exist on these persons and events are no longer available. Kammler, one of the most notorious butchers of the Nazi regime, wasn't even registered at the Nuremberg war crimes trials, and no evidence exists to suggest anyone looked for him. Conflicting rumours of his death suggest he was around Prague (and thus the Skoda Works) in early May, when Patton's spearhead entered the area. One witness interviewed by Agoston also asserts that Kammler unexpectedly arrived in Prague in early May. No body was ever found and his failure to be tried in absentia at Nuremberg is irregular. Any record of the interrogations that Voss insists took place has never been officially acknowledged nor released.

"[SS Standartenfuhrer Wilhelm] Voss [director of the Skoda operation] described the activities of the scientists at the *Kammlerstab* as beyond any technology that had appeared by the end of the war—working on weapon systems that made the V-1 and V-2 look pedestrian. Among these were nuclear power plants for rockets and aircraft, highly advanced guided weapons and antiaircraft lasers... Voss had told the [American] CIC [Counter-Intelligence Corps] agents about the range of research activities that had been pursued by the special projects group and they informed him in no uncertain terms, that he was never to speak about the *Kammlerstab* or its programs to anyone."[142]

Thomas Townsend Brown was an American electronics expert involved in advanced research into electrogravitics and other anomalous electrical and electronic effects such as those developed with the Philadelphia Project. He was unable to interest the US government in his research. The possibility that the Americans were already well into an electro-gravitics program based on captured German data and hardware may be the reason T.T. Brown couldn't find much official support for his electro-gravitic research. As a result he took much of his research public as Project Winterhaven. An author at work producing a biography of Brown intimated to this author that Brown was also a CIA asset at times during his career—leaving the possibility that Winterhaven was also an intelligence gathering operation for the United States.

Though undoubtedly based on genuine theoretical concepts, how advanced some of these technologies were at the time is open to debate. What is no longer in any doubt, however, is that the Germans were serious about building flying saucer shaped aircraft, both manned and unmanned. The real mystery is in the propulsion systems they proposed, with some researchers assuming they had developed anti-gravity technology. The truth in at least some of the cases is probably more mundane and related to a then-secret, and exotic technology: the jet-engine. While Avro's John Frost may have come by the concept of a radial-flow jet engine on his own, it is now known that BMW's secret Silesian operation had at least prototyped an engine of this configuration in WW II to power flying saucer shaped craft.

Frost's initial work was based on a revolutionary concept for a pancake, vs. cylindrical shaped jet-engine. This concept seemed ideal for a circular-shaped flying machine, one that would have unparalleled power available. But where did Frost get the idea for a radial-flow jet-engine if not from German sources? A possible answer to this question was given by an engineer who worked on the project. He says Frost was aware of a flat, disc-shaped steam turbine used in some ships, and got his idea for a similar gas turbine engine from this source. Frost quickly produced a small flying model of a flying disc comprised of inner and outer counter-rotating vaned discs—a "turbo-disc."

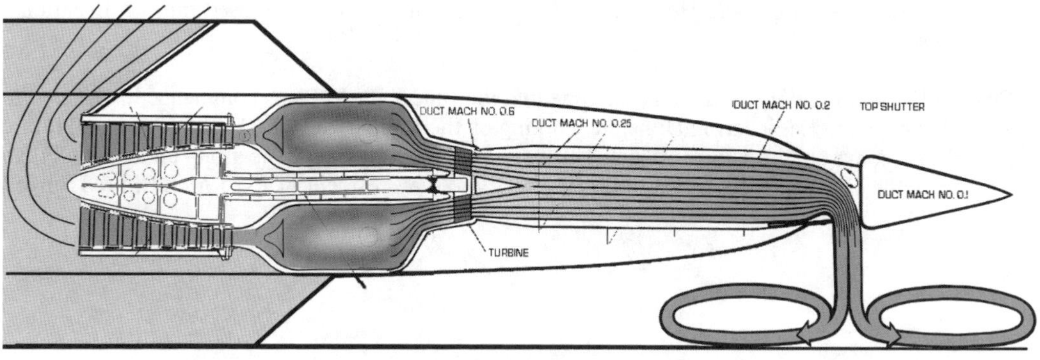

AVRO PROJECT Y-2
Radial Flow Engine - Section View-

The Radial Flow Engine

The radial flow engine shares all the same design principles of the axial (or centrifugal) flow engine; it merely exchanges a central spinning shaft for a revolving disc. A conventional axial flow engine has the disadvantage of requiring twists on the compressor and power turbine blades to compensate for the increasing speed of the blade the farther from the central axis that portion is located. An axial type engine also loses efficiency due to the centrifugal "flinging" of airflow from the shaft centre, in opposition to its ideal lengthwise flow. The radial flow design by contrast could use straight blades throughout, and would benefit from the centrifugal effect due to it coinciding with the natural flow through the engine. That being said, the radial flow engine was designed for a very modest 3-1 compression ratio, while engines to power the F-106, F-4 and Concorde were up around 12-1 compression. The engine used in the Mirage 3 was down at 5.5-1 while the original Iroquois was at 8-1. At Mach 3 or higher speeds ram-effect would increase the pressure in the intakes compensating for the low static compression figures. While this was true in the case of the Avro Arrow's straight duct intake, the efficiency of Frost's intake arrangement is unknown, but probably relatively inefficient. Nevertheless, the size of the engine meant it would have plenty of thrust to achieve take-off and high forward flight speeds.

The real challenge with the radial flow engine would have been in making the central plate, with blades affixed on both sides, function mechanically across the temperature and structural operating ranges of the airframe and intake air. Frost's team devised a system using hundreds of bleed holes in the disc connected to the last, high-pressure air stage of the compressor section. Rather than rely on oil to lubricate roller bearings, the entire disc would float on high pressure air which would make use of the centrifugal effect and pressure to prevent the disc from contacting its structural supports. For starting the engine high pressure air would have to be connected to the airframe, however this was a minor requirement considering the power-cart needs of many current aircraft.

Frost had his radial-flow engine analysed by one of the designers of the Orenda turbojet: Winnett Boyd. He had left Avro Gas Turbines division (the original name of Orenda Engines Ltd.) and cooperated with a Canadian University on an analysis of the concept.

Avro's radial flow engine comprised of a diameter of about 20 feet. Even at the low compression ratio the radial flow engine design was projected to produce about 42,000 lbs thrust. This gave it a power to weight ratio of 1.73 - 1. No known manned jet aircraft has approached this thrust to weight ratio to this day, and this was the key to its high performance potential. On February 7th, 1952, Frost distributed a paper titled Description and Thoughts on the Turbo Disc. This was followed in April 1952 by "Proposal for a Gas Turbine Propelled Aircraft of Circular Planform". This, Project Y, was the first proposal for a disc-shaped craft using a radial-flow gas-turbine engine. There were objections to the need to develop both a new propulsion system and a new aerodynamic shape at the same time. Waclaw Czerwinski, the Polish engineer responsible for the spar-nacelle structural fix for the CF-100 was a member of Frost's growing team. He developed an aerodynamic shape that used more conventional aerodynamics.

(Ed: Jim Floyd, as Chief Engineer at the time that the saucer project was commenced, wishes it to be known that his main Engineering Division working on the Jetliner, the CF100, the Arrow and future projects, played no part in the saucer project, This was carried out by a separate group under John Frost, the inventor of the saucer project. Frost reported directly to the President of Avro Aicraft, Fred Smye.)

138 Vesco, Renato. Intercept But Don't Shoot, reproduced document originally sourced from Die Dunkle Seite Des Mondes by Brad Harris (1996, Pandora Books, Germany)
139 Cook, Nick: The Hunt for Zero Point, p.p. 155-157
140 Cook, p. 174
141 Cook, p.p. 177, 178
142 Cook, p. 162

Chapter 21

TERRESTRIAL FLYING SAUCERS: Project Y-1 The Spade or Avro Omega

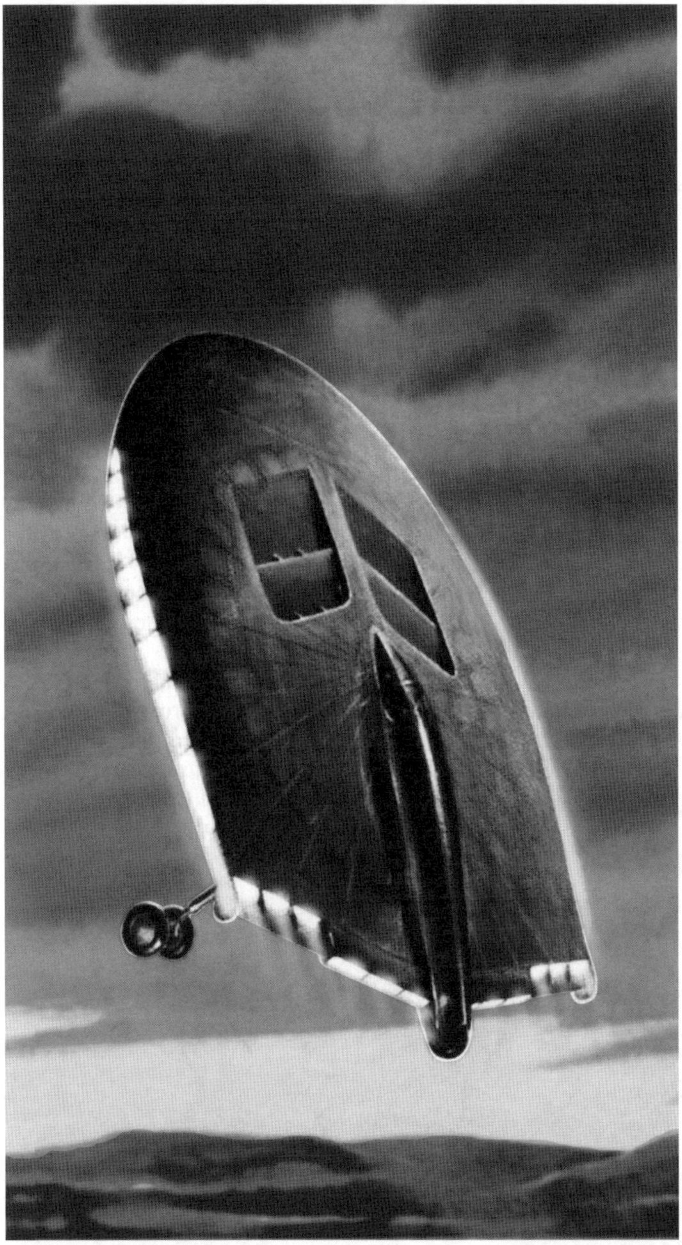

Now Avro was looking at two options for a vertical take-off (VTO) aircraft based on the radial-flow engine: the vertical riser and flat riser. The vertical riser would sit on its tail for take off while the flat riser would rise vertically with the aircraft still aligned horizontally, then transition to forward flight from the hover. The vertical riser had the problem of little visibility and control for landing again on its tail, while the flat riser would make use of ground effect (cushion) which would prevent any damaging hard landings. By this time Czerwinski had come up with a tail riser design for the radial flow engine and the designation Project Y-1 was applied to this "spade" shaped concept, with the difference being that the craft landed with some forward speed. The vertical riser and true saucer design using the same engine was then given the code name "Project Y-2."

As the illustration suggests, thrust was directed rearward, not downward, and the craft sat nearly on its tail during take-off—which was nearly vertical. Y-1 relied on "jet-flaps" along the trailing edge for roll and pitch control, and Avro developed a great deal of data on such a novel system. A great deal of new information on ducted thrust and inlets was developed by Frost's Special Projects Group.

In December, 1952 Frost and two of his engineers visited Britain and Hawker-Siddeley's wind tunnels at Woodford. There they tested four designs based on Czerwinski's Y-1 concept, with low drag being a feature of all of them. With no fin to stabilise the yaw-axis, controllability was a concern, and in early 1953, just after Frost and a nucleus of specialists were set up in an executive building previously occupied by Orenda, models of the jet-flap were tested in the Woodford facilities. It was about this time that leaks about Frost and his team's goal began to materialise in the press. A Toronto Star description of a 1,500 mph flying saucer were followed up by a hint in Avro's house organ: *Jet Age:* "The prototype being built is so revolutionary that when it flies all other types of supersonic aircraft will become obsolete." In April Field Marshal Bernard Montgomery and a delegation arrived in Canada and toured Avro and Orenda, and were briefed on the Y-1, or Omega, project. A mock-up had, by this time, been constructed and Avro was looking for development funds to develop the concept.

There were no bidders however. While intriguing and seemingly full of promise, the design proposed too many new technologies at once. The take-off and landing positions were deemed hazardous as the aircraft was well beyond the stalling angle of attack during these transitions. It was inherently unstable, and thus required an electronic stabilisation and flight control system—something not available with then-current technology. Another control problem was added by the fact that the radial flow engine, having considerable mass-inertia, would add a gyroscopic effect to the control equation. When Project Y-1 airframe was ordered to pitch using the rear control flaps, a good proportion of these would effect the airframe 90 degrees to where it was introduced (the gyroscopic effect). In other words, the pitch flaps would make the aircraft roll considerably. Thus, to effect a pitch up manoeuvre, the aircraft would need to have a "roll" input applied. While the gyroscopic effect of the engine was being exploited to add stability to an airframe which lacked the normal fins normally included for just this reason, special control parameters would have to be programed into the aircraft design compensating for different flight conditions and the gyroscopic effect—creating problems best solved with an electronic stability augmentation system. This was later achieved with the Arrow design, however the Arrow only required the system on the yaw axis and was naturally a much more stable aerodynamic design.

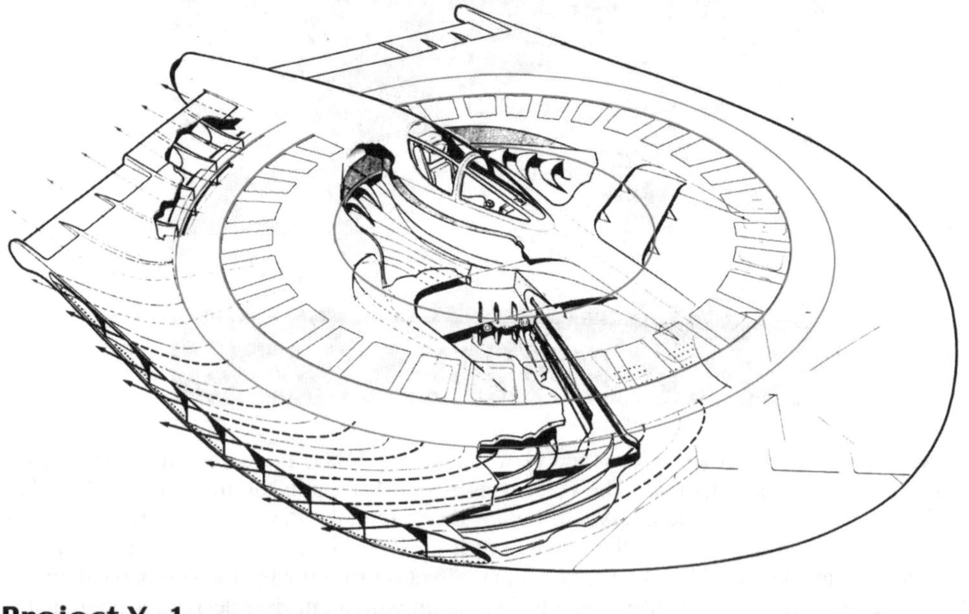

Project Y-1

Vertical Take-Off (tailriser), conventional landing, supersonic point-defence fighter. Designed to exploit John Frost's radial turbine engine concept.

Initial funding, aside from Avro, came in the form of two million dollars from the Canadian government between 1952 and 1953. In ceasing its support, C.D. Howe was quoted as saying that while the concept had merit, it required development funding beyond the limitations of the government. As hoped, the United States authorities became interested after the Toronto Star press leak. In September 1953 the New York Times described a visit by twenty-five defense experts to the Avro facility. This delegation was led by the same man who had motivated the USAF to try to order 12 Jetliners; Donald Putt—head of the USAF's Air Research and Development Command (ARDC). Perhaps in anticipation of objections to the Omega take-off, landing and taxiing positions, another flat rising vehicle of pure disc shape was proposed, only this time using conventional axial-flow jet engines. The new design was proposed as Project Y-2. Putt submitted Frost's papers and his departments analysis to the American Scientific Advisory Board (SAB) and the NACA. Jimmy Doolittle's SAB responded negatively, proposing that too many new technologies were required in a single vehicle—thus making Frost's projections meaningless, though NACA was generally favourable. Perhaps in hedging their bets the USAF purchased the development rights to the Y-2 design, as the MX-1794 project, in late 1954.

Project Y-1's design made sure each slice of intake air was directed to a specific engine combustor section. Likewise, each combuster ended in a separate exhaust nozzle. This is apparent when viewing the many sluice dividers, one per combustor, in the intake system. This was likely done simply due to insecurity over the intake mass air flow being taken from a single direction and being distributed around 360 degrees of compressor sections relative to the direction of flight. Nevertheless, all of Frost's designs proposed square ducts, which exhibit aerodynamic losses greater than tubular designs. This design would also have been somewhat vulnerable to sideslip airflow disruption at the intakes with the possibility of starving certain segments around the axis of the engine. Segments to the rear of the craft would involve longer inlet ducts which would make them provide less thrust. Construction was also complicated by the sluices and ducts having to also make-up the structure of the craft. There were also no repetitive shapes to ease manufacture. The circular flat-riser solved at least the structural problems, and with conventional turbojets replacing the radial-flow engine, the trade-off of having to develop new aerodynamics and control systems seemed less severe.

In October 1955 *Look* magazine published drawings and an article on a flying saucer that bore more than a passing resemblance to the work being done at Avro Canada. The magazine claimed the cutaways were drawn by a "British aeronautical engineer in the employ of Republic Aviation named Thomas Turner." *Look* has been described as a CIA front by Victor Marchetti (who was a former assistant to the Deputy Director CIA) in his book *The CIA and the Cult of Intelligence*. In a standard biography of the Rockefellers *Look* was mentioned as having gotten started partly due to the assistance of David Rockefeller. From *Look*:

> "...persistent and fairly credible rumors recur that a Canadian aircraft manufacturer, A. V. Roe, Canada, Ltd., has had a saucer design under development for two years...
>
> "...new air-defense problems are setting up requirements for aircraft performance that would seem to be most ideally met by a saucer craft...
>
> "Today's fighters...need extremely long runways and there are few in existence that are now long enough. These few, and the concentration of the planes using them, provide a worthwhile target for an A-bomb. With a single blow, the enemy might cripple a substantial portion of our air defense.
>
> "Planes that could take off vertically would not need long runways, which cost millions of dollars. They could be dispersed widely and safely. In this country, four vertical-rising aircraft already have been revealed. All but one, however, are modifications of conventional plane designs. None yet approaches the performance a true saucer might be capable of.
>
> "What are the requirements of an ideal defense fighter? 1) Ability to take off and land vertically; 2) high speed of over Mach 2. (more than 1500 mph); 3) high rate of climb; 4) excellent maneuverability; 5) heavy armament; 6) ability to operate at 60,000 feet.

> "These sketches indicate a highly educated guess of what a flying saucer to fulfill these requirements would look like. It provides for a one-man crew, housed in a glass bubble that would provide excellent visibility.
>
> "...Power unit is key to design. The whole success of the saucer design depends on the unusual engine. The sketched design is remarkably similar to a conventional jet engine but is many times larger. It consists of a set of combustion chambers and a large turbine. These produce blasts of propulsive air around the circumference of the saucer. Air entering the intakes around the pilots cockpit is deflected to the engine. This pressurized air is swept up by the impeller, with a subsequent rise in pressure and temperature. Next, the air goes to the combustion chamber, where fuel is added and ignited and a propulsive gas is formed. The hot gases rush through the turbine blades, in the process turning the impeller wheel. The gas then expands and exhausts at high velocity through the many-fingered jet pipes. The large turbine acts as a stabilizing gyroscope keeping the plane level even when it is hovering."

Is it coincidence that Edgar Atkin had left Avro for Republic Aviation in 1952 and, as mentioned by Jim Floyd and others, had been sold on Frost's saucer concept? "Thomas Turner," may have been an alias for Edgar Atkin. It is also suggestive of the idea that Republic had been sketching saucer designs due to Atkin's revelations regarding Frost's work. In response to Navy and Air Force requests for vertical-rising point-defense fighters, several American manufacturers produced tail-rising craft. Lockheed, Convair and Ryan produced turbo-prop and pure-jet tailsitters, but they displayed the same landing, take-off and taxi problems foreseen for Frost's Y-1 project. In June of 1954 Frost published a report on a possible solution; "Project Y-2: Flat Vertical Take-Off Gyroplane".

Avrocar Prototype

Chapter 22

PROJECT Y-2: VTO Mach 3 Saucer?

When the U.S. Air Force officers arrived in September of 1953, the Canadian government, had spent $400,000 on the project. Avro estimated $5,000,000.00 would be needed to continue work on the supersonic saucer specification until 1958. In fact $5,400,000.00 was spent up to March 1958 on the testing aspects of the craft and propulsion system. It is telling that Avro spent 2.5 million of its own money on the project. It suggests Avro management had high confidence in the program. In this case their confidence was probably excessive, and this may have worked against the best long-term interests of the company.

According to Campagna's *UFO Files* something like 1000 hrs of wind tunnel testing were done at Wright Patterson Air Force base (early home of the so-called Roswell saucer and UFO studies), at M.I.T, and other facilities. Early encouraging aerodynamic results led the USAF to up the ante from $785,000 to 2.6 million. Campagna asserts that testing had begun on the propulsion system and that some 75 models, some for aerodynamic tests, had been produced. Supersonic lift-drag ratios of around five-to-one were recorded and found admirable. (Though the Arrow was considerably better at over seven-to-one.)

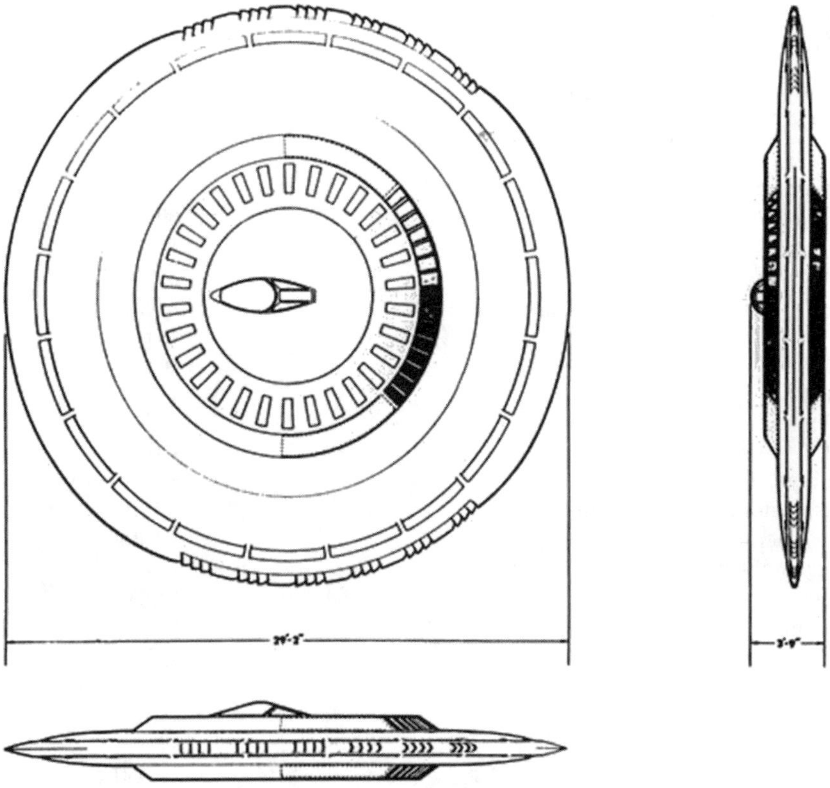

Three-view General Arrangement of research Aircraft (Radial Flow Engine)

By this time Frost had conceived a variety of possible saucer configurations using different propulsion schemes. All of these were included in a large promotional booklet for various parties, especially the USAF. Particulars released within the American system included discussion of a radial-flow pure saucer with this craft's specifications given below. USAF investigations of Avro saucer concepts took on the name "Project Silver Bug". The possibility that the American support of the Special Projects Group was being used as a cover and explanation for saucer sightings, is raised over comments in October 1955 by the U.S. Secretary of the Air Force. In a public statement Donald Quarles announced that the USAF had contracted with Avro Canada to develop an aircraft which "might give the illusion of the so-called flying saucer". Campagna, in *The UFO Files,* gives an example of one occasion where the Avro saucers were used to explain away a sighting.

TABLE I PHYSICAL CHARACTERISTICS
Radial-Flow Engine Aircraft

ParticularsValues	Weight Dimensions, etc.
Aircraft Gross Take-off Weight lb	29,000
Gross Wing Area sq ft	670
Span (" diameter) ft	29.2
Height over canopy ft	3.75
Standard mean chord ft	23.2
Aspect ratio	1.27
Mean t/c ratio excluding intake	0.06
Intake base area sq ft	20.0
Approximate jet base area in forward flight sq ft	16.0
Wing loading at mean weight of 26,000 lbs - lb/sq ft	38.8
Maximum internal fuel Imp gal/U.S. Gal	950/1,140
Take-off thrust/weight ratio	1.73
SLS thrust/frontal area lb/sq ft	900

TABLE II WEIGHT BREAKDOWN

Particulars	Lb Totals
Aircraft Main Structure	9,532
Cockpit well and fuel tank	696
Intake structure	1,341
Main structure	2,904
Outer wing and exhauster	2,990
Halo	781
Cockpit and canopy	165
Control shutters	410
Control system	245
Power plant	10,450
Rotor assembly	5,750
Stator blades, plates and attachments	2,120
Combustion system	1,180
Air bearing assembly	1,400
Extra to structure	1,068
Cockpit equipment	115
Radio and electronics	352
Fuel system	284
Air conditioning and oxygen	250
Miscellaneous	84
AIRCRAFT EMPTY WEIGHT	21,050
Disposable load	7,950
Crew	200
Fuel	7,750
AIRCRAFT GROSS TAKE-OFF WEIGHT	29,000

TABLE III CONTRACTOR ESTIMATED PERFORMANCE

Radial-Flow Engine Aircraft

Particulars		Without Reheat	With 1500 Deg K Reheat
Maximum level speed	mph	1,720	2,300
	knots	1,490	2,000
Mach No.		2.6	3.48
Ceiling (Max power at mean wt) ft		71,600	80,600
Time from hovering start to		NA	36,090 ft min 1.76
		NA	60,000 ft min 2.66
		NA	70,000 ft min 4.2
Still air range with allowance for take-off, climb, cruise-descent and landing		NA	Miles 620
Take-off and landing distances		Nil	Nil
Max hovering alt from take-off		10,000	NA
Max hovering alt at mean wt, 26,000 lbs		18,000	NA

These were certainly tantalising performance projections. The ability to take off and climb vertically and hover at 18,000 feet suggested an awesome power output. Drag figures with the projected power output also suggested it would be a Mach 2.6 aircraft—with an afterburning version promising even higher performance. This radial-flow machine would not be supported in development by the American parties. A more conventional saucer, using several small, conventional gas-turbine engines, did catch their eye.

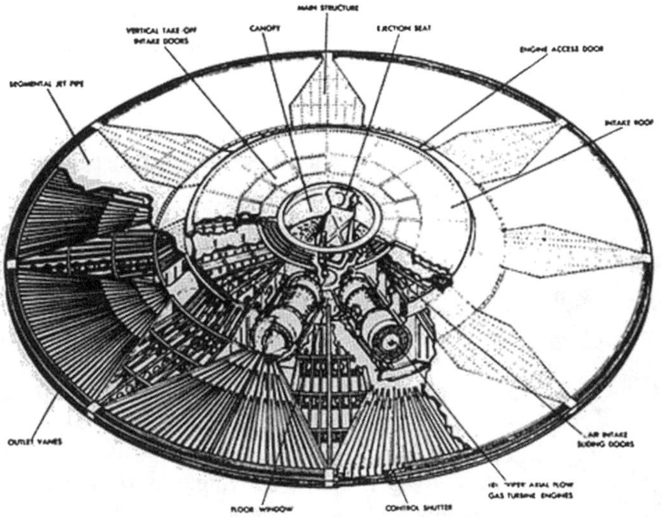

Cutaway of Research Craft

The original eight-engine Project Y-2, shown in the illustration above, made heavy use of the "Coanda" effect for vertical take-off lift. Dr. Henri Coanda, a brilliant inventor and aviator, discovered that high speed air, flowing over a smooth radius, will bend at least 90 degrees. This simply allowed the radial thrust of several engines to be deflected downward when required for vertical take off. The exhaust from each engine was directed by a fan-like arrangement of structural ribs, to the entire circumference of the disc.

Inlet air was taken in on the top and bottom of the craft in this design. A very large centre rotor contained tandem Lungstrom compressors, (similar to the impeller for a turbocharger or centrifugal-flow turbojet), and comprised the centre portion of the machine, with the cockpit being located on top. In the centre of this device was a turbine section, taking engine exhaust and using it to drive the compressors, which fed the jet engines. This turbine section turned all the engine exhaust expelled through it downward, giving part of the thrust of the vehicle. Around the circumference the rest of the exhaust air was directed down for take-off and hovering, or backwards for forward flight. The outer control shutters were also designed to provide roll, pitch and yaw control for actual flight.

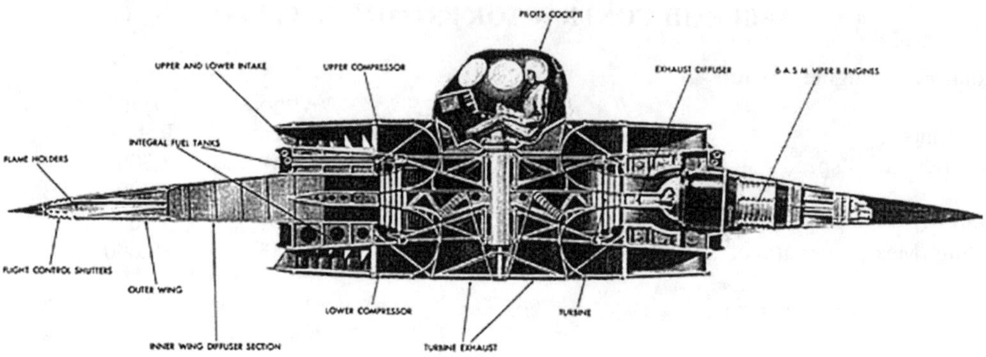

A six engine test rig was constructed on the site of the Special Projects Group, with Orenda constructing a compressor and turbine section. It was completed in October, 1956 with an enclosure to serve as a scattershield should the central section fail and then take out one or more of the Viper engines. With the compressors providing extra air to the Viper turbojets, the rig made a great deal of thrust, requiring it be bolted firmly to the concrete moorings. Noise from the unit was deafening, and vibrations with the compressor/turbine section made the prospects of sitting above the unit in flight frightening.

It is believed that another centre section was sent to the United States, under great secrecy, at the same time that the Viper test rig was built. A Toronto Star article mentioned a secret shipment to Burbank California. Alex Raeburn, a former Special Projects member, recalled a day in 1955 when the U.S. Navy came to take the prototype away for tests near Los Angeles. "We loaded it on a flatbed truck in the middle of the night. The police shut off all the traffic right down to Toronto harbour, and they put it on a U.S. tugboat. They even had one of our men sworn in to the U.S. Navy so he could go with it, along the Erie Canal, along the New York intercoastal waterway, and through the Panama Canal."

Lungstrom compressor/turbine section being lowered into saucer centre section.

While the aerodynamics for forward flight were tested in various windtunnels, with favourable results when it came to drag (and the Viper test rig proved that a great deal of thrust could be built into an experimental saucer) the controls for stability, manoeuvre, take-off and landing were still unknown. Funding was scarce, and there was still a great deal of development work needed to prove the concept. In an effort to get things moving, Avro management, including Smye and Gordon, proposed a private venture to develop the radial-flow engine version. This was designated PV 704 in January 1956. It dispensed with the Lundstrom compressor/turbine solving one problem, but re-introduced the requirement to engineer a radial-flow turbojet engine.

This was a return to the idea of a circular-planform machine with the radial-flow engine. Sources suggest it was done as something of a ploy by Avro management to accelerate American investment in Project Y-2. If so, it didn't produce dramatic results.

It dispensed with the Lundstrum turbine and impeller, that proved so loud (and frightening) on the Viper test rig, and used a donut shaped plenum, surrounding the central cabin, to provide inlet air to the radial-flow jet engine. The outer portions of the 'turbo-disc', central to the radial-flow engine, were to be suspended on jets of air directed from the structure on either side of the disc—air bearings. This was because the outer portion of the disc would be spinning so fast that conventional ball-bearings would overspeed—requiring another solution. The problems of aeroelasticity (flexing of the airframe from flight loads), gyroscopic effect and heat expansion all required a development effort, and failure in any of them would make the engine unworkable. Unlike the Lundstrom compressor of MX-1794 (and the Viper test rig), there was no turbine exhaust in the centre, meaning all the thrust was to be directed to the rim. The engine was a serious development challenge, and so were the control and stability systems. Again the mass of the engine's main disc, rotating at high speed, would mean that a proportion of control inputs would be directed 90 degrees from where the force was exerted. Pitch would cause yaw and vice-versa, while the effect at low speed would probably be much more dramatic than at high speed—posing more development hurdles. There is no record that Avro or Orenda took serious steps towards building a radial-flow gas turbine engine, and so little could be done to develop PV 704. Other than some evidence that BMW was engaged, apparently under the auspices of the SS, in prototyping a radial-flow or turbodisc engine during WW II, there is no evidence that anyone has engineered an example of this engine type.

In take-off configuration, the engine would intake evenly around the top circumference surrounding the cockpit and fuel tank centre-body, bypassing the frontal inlets on top and bottom. Around this entire centre-body was an open chamber or plenum for the intake air that would be sucked into the compressor sections above and below the main engine plate. The top sliding exhaust ducts around the circumference of the Y-2 would remain closed during take-off and the bottom ones would be open. A rounded shutter at the bottom edge of the lower exhaust ring would set up the Coanda Effect and bend the air to a downward direction for lift. Upper and lower shutters could be arranged to direct all the thrust to the rear of the craft, for forward flight, and were designed to provide control to the pilot. Again it required funding to build a radial-flow engine, and this was apparently not forthcoming. The USAF was still interested in the development though, and modest funding ensured their proprietorship of the supersonic saucer effort, though the program was not funded sufficiently to build a prototype. Nevertheless, in March 1957 the USAF extended MX-1794 through to October 1958 and provided an additional $1,815,000 dollars.

Problems inherent in each design effort had been conquered so far, but each time some of Frost's assumptions were seriously challenged. Intake and exhaust efficiencies, for example, were lower than Frost projected, reducing the attractiveness of the concept. Methods of managing the peripheral jet curtain for efficient control and thrust production were always in a state of flux as no perfect system seemed to present itself. This area in particular required development in a test craft. As a smaller effort that could solve the issues of stability and control, Frost began pondering a modest, three-engine subsonic craft.

Chapter 23

THE AVROCAR:
Success, Failure or Red Herring?

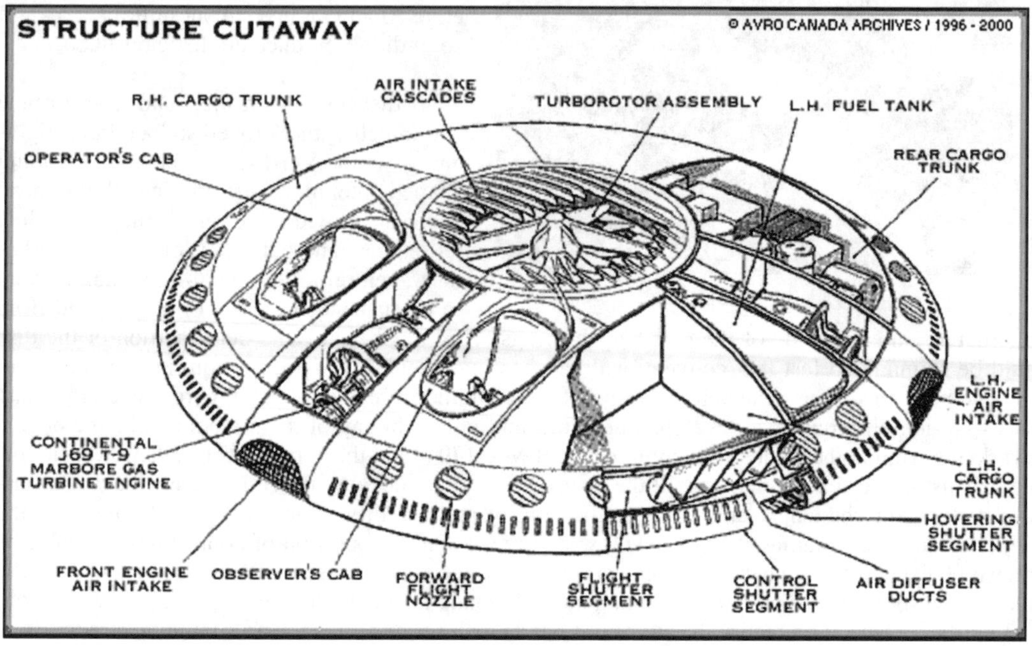

An interim development vehicle, he called the Avromobile, a sort of flying jeep, was proposed to the American authorities even while studies on the supersonic vehicle proceeded. This was described in "U.S. Army Requirement for a New Family of Air Vehicles" in November of 1957. In the spring of 1958 the Pentagon established a joint USAF/U.S. Army program with the Avro Special Projects group. With it, Avro's PV 704 was cancelled. With this project abandoned, and funding running out for the MX 1794 supersonic saucer, Avro's work on trying to directly engineer a supersonic saucer ground to a halt. According to Campagna's *UFO Files* Avro was persuaded at this time to stop work on PV 704, the supersonic saucer, and concentrate their efforts on this new contract as a "first step" towards the supersonic design. It used a turbocompessor somewhat akin to MX-1794, but it was an axial type, and was driven at the tips by engine exhaust. As the image shows, it initially was to have had three oval engine inlets at the rim of the craft, with vents on the top for forward flight—also similar to MX-1794.

In Sept 1957 a US Army requirements team visited Avro. Reportedly the Army had become interested in greater mobility for specialised operations and sought a vehicle capable of flying close to the ground with a small payload. Some have compared the requirement to an airborne Jeep. They had released development contracts in the US of almost $2,000,000 to several companies, including the helicopter manufacturers—Hiller and Piasecki—but had been disappointed with the resulting designs. Avro was then invited to brief the experts at the Pentagon in November of the same year. In early 1958 the US agreed to contract Avro through a joint USAF-US Army program. USAF-US Army Project VZ-9, or the Avrocar, was a contract for only $4,432,497.00 and was for two experimental prototypes.

During the design and construction of the Avrocars the Avro Arrow program reached its zenith, and then its nadir. The following minutes, from a February 24th meeting between Avro's Chairman Crawford Gordon Jr., Fred Smye, the Ministers of Labour, Finance, Defense, Transport and Defense Production show that the Avro executives still had high hopes of being contracted to build supersonic saucers by the USAF.

> "… Pearkes… understood that there were two types, the subsonic Avrocar or flying jeep… and the Mach 3 plane in which the United States Air Force had expressed some interest. Mr.

Gordon then asked whether or not the RCAF or the USAF could not report to the Minister regarding the advanced Mach 3 VTO strike attack bomber. To this Mr. Pearkes replied that he had as recently as last Friday received a full report on this matter from the Vice Chief of the Air Staff.

Mr. Smye then asked whether or not the government could or would make representations to the United States government… to accelerate their support on this VTO project… He pointed out that the feasibility of the project would be apparent in a very few months when the first flight was planned."

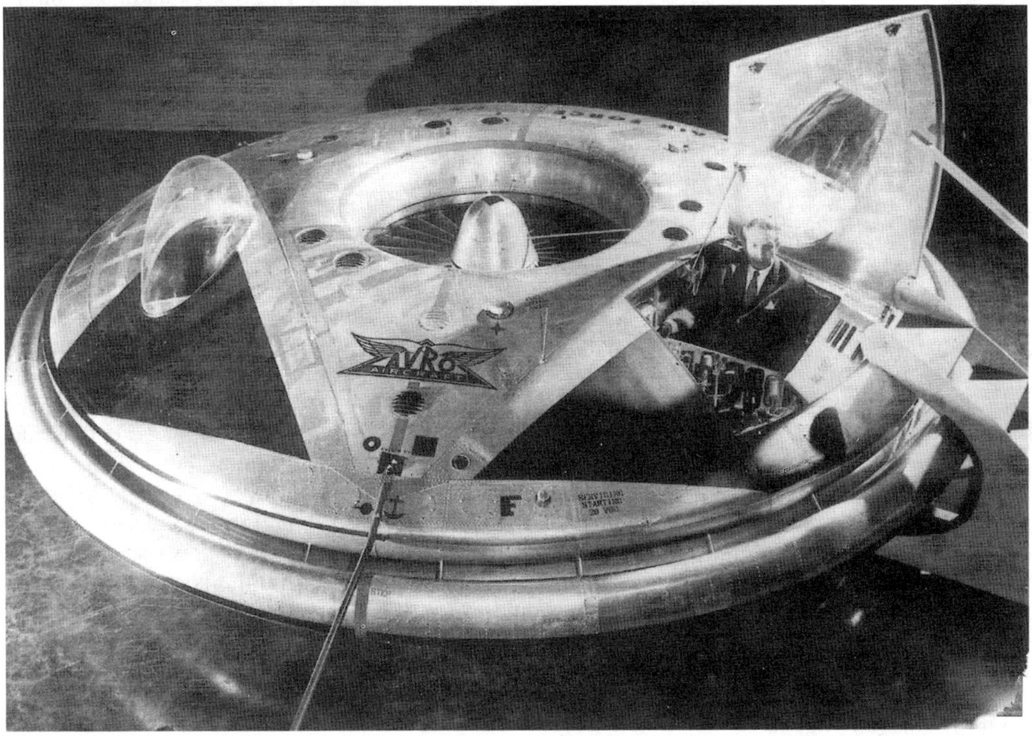

Avro test pilot Waclaw "Spud" Potocki in the Avrocar prototype.

The first prototype, with the annular intake, was rolled out in May of 1959—three months after the Arrow cancellation. It was tested for 32 hours on a static test rig at Malton and was then sent to NASA's Ames research facility where it completed its first wind tunnel tests in April 1960. During shipping, security was as tight as it had been during the 1955 shipment—of whatever it was—to Burbank.

The Avrocar, at 18 feet diameter, was 11 feet smaller than the PV 704 design and used three small conventional turbojets, Continental J69s of 925 lbs thrust each. As such, it had about a sixth of the thrust of the Y-2. Empty it weighed about 2,600 lbs and specified a payload of almost as much—meaning, unlike Project Y-1 or Y-2, it would not have greater than one-to-one thrust. To provide additional lift a five foot "turbo-rotor" was located in the centre of the craft. This fan was driven through a 'tip drive' concept where the exhaust from the engines was ducted to pass by an outer ring of turbine blades attached to the rotor and isolated from the intake air. The duct would then combine both these flows and direct it out toward the rim of the aircraft for lift and control thrust. Unfortunately the exhaust pressure caused the fan to lose some efficiency, thus diminishing thrust.

On November 12, 1959 the second prototype underwent free flight tests. These revealed some serious problems. The single turbo-rotor proved to be only a moderately effective method of making lift, and intake efficiencies were lower than projected. On the prototype the original oval inlets were abandoned in favour of an annular ring around the rim of the craft. It was probably done to try to move air over the upper surface of the Avrocar and thus make more lift (and less drag by encouraging laminar flow in forward flight). This led to a problem in the hover and at low speed. The close proximity of the exhaust and intakes, separated by a nicely rounded surface, caused the engines to ingest exhaust gases (and any blown up dust and debris), reducing thrust. Another shortcoming of this arrangement was that it aggravated a phenomenon common to helicopters known as the "annular ring vortex" which, as demonstrated with some unfortunate helicopters, can make the rotors suddenly lose lift. The hover requires undisturbed air to be pulled downward as "mass airflow" towards the ground in order to support the aircraft. Recirculating air in a ring vortex from the exhaust to the inlets created a situation where the craft lost lift as some helicopters will do on a windless day if held in a stationary hover too long. While the Avrocar concept seemed to be designed to encourage flow from the centre of the craft to the edges, creating lift in the process, instead, it produced the annular ring vortex and hurt both lift and thrust. The inlets were quickly redesigned to open in three round holes on the top surface of the vehicle.

Another problem came from the fact that the peripheral exhaust jet, or curtain, of gases used for thrust and flight control, proved inefficient. Experimentation and testing revealed that for best results a focused core of gases at the centre, not a narrow band at the edge, was needed for control and aerodynamic reasons. Both the intake and exhaust systems would have to be redesigned and improved. Frost and others later remarked that they had almost created the hovercraft, with the Avrocar lacking only the rubber skirt to become a very high-performance machine. Even so, John Frost is credited with discovering the ground cushion effect, which is described in one of his relevant patents. Perhaps what it really needed was to have the turborotor and exhaust flows separated, with the cooler turborotor air being directed to the edges, while the engines would exhaust in the bottom centre. Special Projects group members mention that the system had once been conceived to work that way, but that Frost had changed the design to have exhaust and inlet air both directed to the rim. In some of his later design sketches, he showed vehicles using both a jet curtain at the edges with a central core of separate air taken in by a large rotor.

Setting up partial or total annular ring vortices around the early Avrocar without doubt contributed to its famous instability. The initial version was shown to display an instability which made the Avrocar dip an edge unpredictably. While ground cushion generally prevented the edge from striking the ground, it gave a wobbly impression when moved over the ground. According to John Frost himself, writing for the Oct 1961 Canadian Aeronautical Journal, the aircraft was unstable both statically and dynamically. This was also due in part to the fact that the centre of lift on a saucer shape is in front of the centre of gravity, causing a tendency to pitch-up during forward flight—but speeds for forward flight hadn't even been achieved. In the ground cushion stability would be enhanced provided the ring-vortex did not rear its ugly head. The cures were repositioning the intakes and redesigning the exhaust ring to focus the gases towards the centre. Of course, within this arrangement the nozzle flaps had to be movable for control purposes. It required a considerable redesign.

Due to these problems, the Avrocar went through at least three major design changes. The second design, (shown in the publicity photo at the beginning of this section) of the most complete looking Avrocar has the annular inlet arranged around the circumference of the saucer. The diagram below shows the initial elements of the prototype. Intake air is in blue, J-69 exhaust is in yellow, and mixed gases for thrust and control are in red.

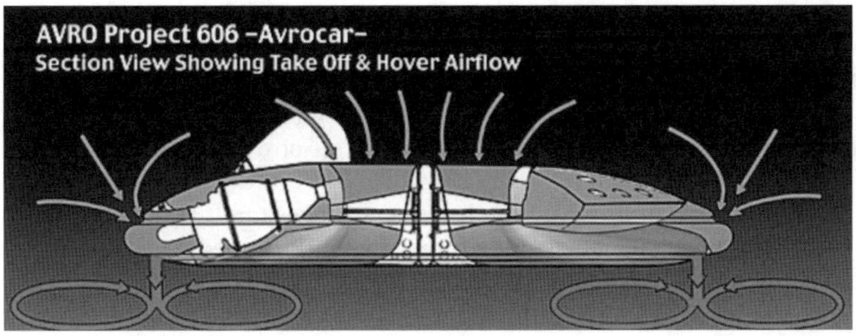

Finally, in August 1960 the Avrocar was displayed to the press for the first time. Speeds of up to 35 mph were attained yet it clearly still had a wobble problem. The Air Force Flight Test Centre at Edwards Air Force Base concluded that the design was lacking in performance, stability and controllability resulting in the Avrocar's inability to transition to forward flight. Testing revealed that if the craft could make 35 to 40 knots airspeed, it would achieve free flight and could then accelerate to about 100 knots maximum. This was well below the original estimated airspeed of 300 knots. Hover altitude was also much lower—only in ground effect in fact. Its instability resulted in NASA Ames building a T-tail assembly for it, in an effort to provide some directional (yaw) stability and pitch control. The tail wasn't a success. And Frost was committed to his pure saucer shape. Revisions commenced on both prototypes.

Modifications were complete by April 1961 with Frost and others stating that testing suggested full forward flight was finally within reach and that full scale flight tests were slated as the next phase. According to *The UFO Files*, Arnold Rose, an Avro engineer, stated that the design had indeed been fixed and was ready for forward flight. Witnesses claim that one flight of the completed saucer was made, for the benefit of its key builders, but only within the hangar. The claim is made that it was taken off and hovered well above the ground. The next day, USAF security forces moved in, Avro employees were moved out, and the project was shipped south. All that was required was funding for this final test flight stage from its sponsors, the USAF. This money was not forthcoming and the two development saucers were taken to the US for testing. They were found unsuitable for further development and one was sent to the Smithsonian, whilst the other was later put on a pedestal at an Army base.

But is this all there is to the story? During an enjoyable meal with J.C. Floyd in October 2006, he asked me what I made of the whole flying saucer thing at Avro. I said I'd spent years looking at it from every angle I could and that I had to conclude that American involvement in the program had several purposes related to intelligence. First they wanted Avro to cheaply develop and experiment with methods of ducted and vectored thrust and flight controls for a vertical take off aircraft of circular planform. This Frost and his team succeeded in doing, although the final proving vehicle was admittedly marginal in performance. We agreed that aircraft like the Arrow had a much better aerodynamic performance, and were adaptable to Frost's thrust schemes and stealth-shaping. Avro and U.S. assessments of the Avrocar mention that the vehicle still needed thrust to be directed rearward for high speed flight, and that this wasn't efficient with the focusing ring design. I suggested the only logical reason for focusing on a saucer shape was due to its being ideal for electro-gravitic research and stealth, though there is nothing to suggest Frost was trying to design anything other than a turbojet-powered craft.

Thomas Townsend Brown was an American involved in electrical sciences (and, at one time, with intelligence). He had been developing devices which seemed to defy gravity for years and, failing to have his concepts developed by the US government spent most of the 1950s *publicly* advocating and demonstrating electrogravitics through his Project Winterhaven. His studies used and promoted saucer shapes as being the ideal shape for aircraft using this principle. In 2003 I spoke to Mario Pesando, head of Avro's Project Research Group in 1957-59 and asked what state Avro's electro-gravitic research had reached during the period in question. While he wasn't associated with Frost's project, he did recall that Bill Barratt, an electronics genius, had been essentially conducting an intelligence operation to acquire data on that subject at the time, but that Avro's work hadn't progressed very far in terms of experimentation or independent successful results. He mentioned having heard at the time that someone (possibly T.T. Brown) in the United States had managed to levitate a metallic object, perhaps a ball, electrically, but that they found "much smoke but little fire". In the end the facts seem to suggest the Avro saucer programs were multi-faceted. They were overt intelligence operations, in developing certain aerospace sciences, and they were exploited for other reasons, including deniability for sightings. Were they also efforts to convince Avro management that they had an ace-in-the-hole in case of Arrow cancellation? Clearly, as late as the Arrow cancellation, Gordon and Smye were still hoping for a big saucer contract. One thing is certain, in most circles the fact that Avro management was pursuing flying saucer designs in the 1950s has been seen as grounds for criticism—or even ridicule. No doubt there were serious detractors within the government and its research organs at the time—for the same reason.

Avro Special Projects P.450 STOL aircraft design.

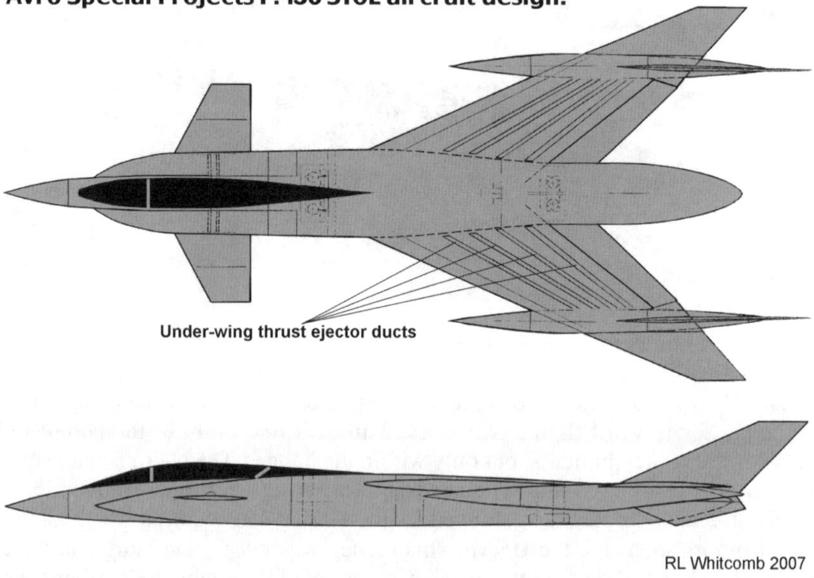

It appears that even John Frost eventually became convinced that the circular planform was not the ideal configuration for aircraft. No prior mention has been made of it, but at the end of the Special Projects operations, Frost devised a supersonic short take-off aircraft benefiting from his group's research into ducted thrust. Designated P.450, the aircraft adopted a canard layout, with sponsons at about two-thirds span serving as mounts for the twin tail arrangement. For circa 1961 this was a bold configuration. Thrust could be ducted for take-off, landing and slow speed operation, through four slots under each wing. A reflection plane wind tunnel model was made of P.450, but no further information on this intriguing design has come forth. The design was, obviously, not taken up by Canada or the United States.

Chapter 24
THE ARROW WEAPONS SYSTEM

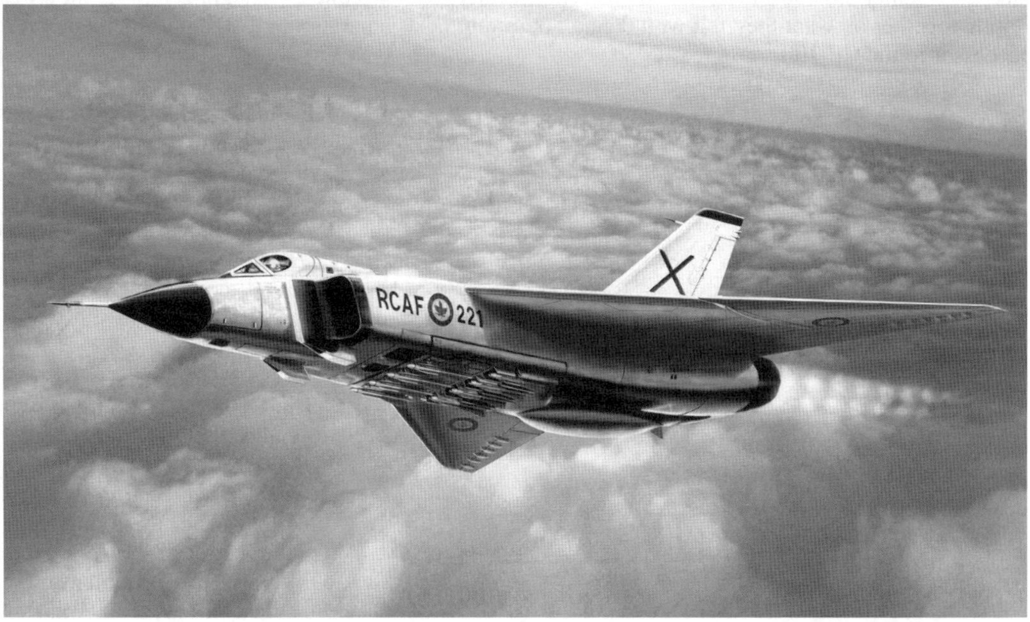

An Arrow Mk. 2 displaying its Falcon missiles and belly tank. (image by the author)

Avro's designers, like most active design teams, were constantly working on possible future adaptations of existing designs, and proposing altogether new ones. As soon as John Frost had arrived at Avro Canada, he put to paper a swept wing version of the CF-100 that also featured a much narrower engine installation. It is probably unfortunate that the existing XC-100 design was so far along in terms of design, engineering, and the bureaucratic process, since Frost's design would, quite probably, have been supersonic.

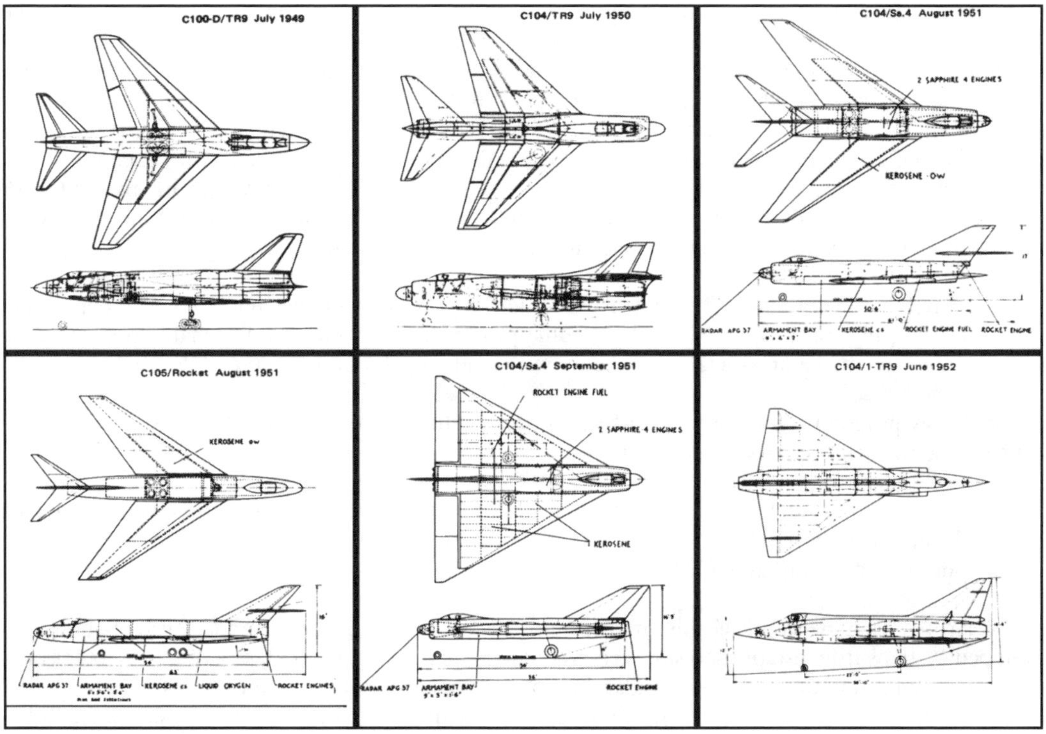

Once Frost was allowed to establish his Special Projects Group and begin work on his disc-aircraft concepts, Chamberlin and Floyd took over responsibility for new concept design. By 1952, they were working together on what they felt would be an optimum next-generation, all-weather interceptor; i.e., a successor to the CF-100.

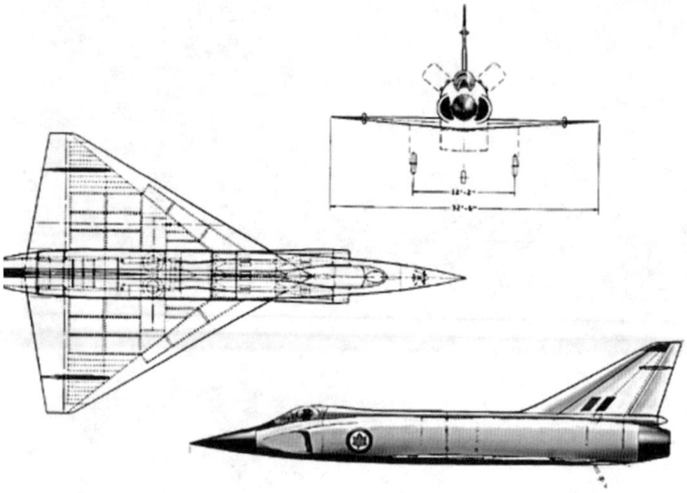

> "In June we submitted two possible designs, both with delta wings. The C104/1 was a single seat, single engine, low wing, tailless delta weighing 28,200 lb., with a wing area of 617 sq. ft., and powered by one TR9 engine (under study by Orenda)."
>
> "The C104/2 was a larger, twin-engined, high-wing, tailless delta with a wing area of 1,189 sq. ft., powered by two TR9 engines…The main advantage of the larger C/104/2 was the very large armament bay, designed to stow internally a wide variety of weapons, resulting in the potential for using the aircraft in many roles, such as long-range interceptor, advanced trainer, bomber or photo-reconnaissance aircraft."

This inherent flexibility inspired confidence on the part of the government and Avro executives since it could undertake many foreseeable missions for the RCAF, and, indeed, for most of the air forces of the West.

By this time Bob Lindley had circuitously re-joined Jim Floyd from Avro U.K.. After being involved in early concept work for the Vulcan bomber, he had asked to come to Canada and join the Canadian effort. He was advised he was needed more at Avro Manchester and so quit his job and took one with Canadair in Montreal, before being hired by the Canadian division. He, one of the "British Airlift" of engineers and other specialists to Canada in this period, was appointed to head a "Blitz Group" of engineers to go through the entire CF-100 design, and to fix it. Which they did. He was later appointed Chief Engineer on the Arrow program. In a documentary interview, Lindley mentioned that he had been responsible for the large Lancaster-like weapons bay on the Arrow. Apparently the RCAF team was having a difficult time deciding on what kind of weapons their next-generation aircraft should have. On the quick-change weapons pack feature of the Arrow, Lindley said:

> "I put that feature in there because we couldn't figure out what weapon we were supposed to be carrying. So I said, 'OK, I'll solve the problem…we'll make a detachable portion. Take your time, make up your mind, when you're ready, we'll put it in there."[143]

The Arrow program commenced in 1953 as a project study to meet the RCAF's expected requirements for their next-generation interceptor:

> "[T]he Cabinet Defense Committee, at its 97th Meeting of 2 December, 1953, had approved a development programme for the CF105 and the building of two prototype aircraft as the first phase of this programme."[144]

The Arrow, as Avro saw it at this time, would use weapons, engine and radar systems based on developed systems from established suppliers. In view of their being, in 1953, practically no other likely options, Avro felt the MX-1179 radar being developed by Hughes for the American "1954 Interceptor" and their Falcon missiles would probably be acquired for the Arrow. They chose the Rolls-Royce RB106 engine for the plane, and hoped the use of these suppliers would save a great deal of expense and headaches. This was not to be since the RB-106 was cancelled early in the program.

Requirements were an expansion of a USAF specification let in 1949 for what was termed the "1954 Interceptor", 1954 being the date of intended service. The expansions added by the RCAF were in its range, manoeuvre capability at high altitude and speed, and the requirements for a two-man crew and two engines for safety. A delegation, led by G/C Foottit of the RCAF, investigated all programs in the Western alliance to see if an interceptor corresponding roughly to the RCAF requirement was in design or production anywhere. They concluded one was not, and the American F-102 Delta Dagger, F-106 Delta Dart, and F-101 Voodoo were examined.

The requirements for the CF-100 and Arrow were also based on US (primarily CIA) intelligence, since Canada, and indeed Britain were (and remain) dependent on a dominant US intelligence apparatus. In fact, with the UKUSA agreement, British and Canadian intelligence assets were subsumed within it. An additional influence was Canadian knowledge of US and British bomber programs and their expected progress, coupled with the generally-correct assumption that the Soviets would match the Americans in all weapons systems.

In 1955 Avro was granted a contract to begin design and production of the CF-105 interceptor, now with the Iroquois engine following a stop work order and technical reappraisal wrought by the Canadian National Aeronautical Establishment (NAE) in late 1954. Prices at that time were quoted as 270 million for 40 pre-production aircraft and 70 million for the development and production of fourteen Iroquois engines. The airframe expenses were to range from 1954-60 and the engine's from 1954-58.[145] We will return to those figures when the legends of Avro's cost over-runs are examined.

Under the Liberal St. Laurent government, including C.D. Howe and Minister of Defense Brooke Claxton, the Arrow program continued in tandem with plans to adopt the Bomarc missile once it emerged from its troubled development, along with a nuclear air-to-air missile. It was felt that a vast expansion of the ground control and radar installations were required to make these systems supportive of the Bomarc, the Arrow and USAF interceptors which were expected to operate over Canada in time of war. In efforts to standardize systems to US preferences, Canada was soon convinced to adopt the American Semi-Automatic Ground Environment (SAGE) system, a 'ground-controlled intercept' (GCI) technology, using the emerging 'real time', or at the speed of light, computing technology then code-named WHIRLWIND.[146] SAGE was then being designed to work with Hughes' emerging fighter radar/fire control system, called MX-1179. All of these systems were under crash development in the United States for the 1954 Interceptor. In reality program delays meant none of these American systems were deployed until 1960. Avro found itself in a leadership position in real-time computing, telemetry and other exotic electronic specialties.

Unfortunately, the Arrow faced difficulties right from the beginning. First, its intended engine, the Rolls Royce RB-106, was cancelled in 1953 just as the design was being crystallised. Avro then specified the Curtiss-Wright J-67.

143 There Never Was An Arrow, CBC Documentary, produced by George Robertson ©1979
144 Memorandum to the Cabinet Defence Committee, 3 October, 1955
145 Memorandum to the Cabinet Defence Committee, 3 Oct., 1955.
146 Gainor, Chris: Arrows to the Moon. Toronto: Apogee Books

Chapter 25

ENGINES FOR THE ARROW: RB-106 to J.67 to PS-13 Iroquois

In the 1940s and early 1950s the British were far ahead of the Americans in jet-engine design. Armstrong Siddeley Motors, a member of the Hawker Siddeley Group like Avro Canada, produced several axial-flow jet engines which were license-produced by US manufacturers. This soon changed as America felt that it was unwise to depend on a foreign country for military technology—even as they were working to make the Western nations dependent on the USA for just that.

The Bristol aircraft company was also, like Hawker Siddeley and Avro Canada, one of the few manufacturers producing both engines and aircraft. Bristol was later forced, by the British government, to abandon aircraft production while Hawker Siddeley was similarly forced to abandon engine production through their Armstrong Siddeley motors subsidiary. Charles Grinyer, who later came to Avro Gas Turbines/Orenda Engines Ltd. to lead the effort on the Iroquois, was responsible for the successful type-test certification of 10 engines at Bristol, all on the first attempt.[147] One of the engines he certified was the Bristol Olympus, a large capacity turbojet engine which, in this author's statistical analysis, was the second-best engine in the world after the Iroquois, and after Iroquois cancellation, probably the best high-thrust turbojet in the world until about 1980.[148] Not a bad run for an engine that first ran in the early 1950s. This engine was selected in Britain for the Vulcan bomber and others, and through the use of Iroquois engine technology (along with one running engine) was developed with an afterburner, for the TSR.2 supersonic low-level strike-recce aircraft. This engine was further developed for the Concorde and became the only engine ever certified to take civilian air travellers across the Atlantic at the far side of the sound barrier. An impressive feat, one might add that it gave many people wonderful jobs and flying experiences, while helping defend Britain.

Based on the promise shown by this engine, right from the beginning, American defense planners initially seemed determined to develop this engine in collaboration with the British, and had Curtiss Wright embark on developing an afterburning license-built version of the Olympus, designated the J67. It was slated to go into the next generation of America's most powerful fighters, including the F-106 Delta Dart, the XF-103, and the F-108 Rapier.[149] However, the J67 was cancelled, and in some cases was replaced by the Pratt & Whitney J75, which bore more than a superficial resemblance to the J67.

It is 'rumoured' that the J75 was simply Pratt & Whitney's old J57 from behind the compressor to the nozzle, and copied, essentially, the J67's (i.e., Olympus's) impressive compressor section.[150] Photos of the J57 and J75 seem to confirm this. The compressor configurations were virtually identical, as was the compressor ratio. It seems reasonable to assume that, if not the original intent, "acquiring" Olympus technology for American manufacturers was the probable end result of this bi-lateral defense production sharing arrangement. It also adds more shade to the history of defense cooperation between the United States and its allies.

Sources state that the J-67 version of the Olympus was abandoned in late 1955. Yet development of the Republic XF-103, which used the J-67 and an intriguing bypass ramjet design, was continued until 1957, when the North American F-108 Rapier was selected as the USAF Long Range Interceptor Experimental (LRIX).[151] As an illustration of how optimistic US manufacturers' performance estimates were at the time, Republic Aviation estimated their XF-103 design to be capable of Mach 4, although, unbeknownst to their allies or the general public, the USAF secretly thought it would be good for about Mach 2.7.[152] Secrecy relating to genuine US performance figures served some American interests quite well, while inflated manufacturers' estimates certainly assisted the political movement to cancel the Arrow program. In a review written by Bill Gunston of the Arrow's first flight, he mentioned the projected performance, as an example, of the F-108 (an Arrow competitor) as being Mach 5. "[A] hardly credible figure" he sagely acknowledged even then.

147 Stewart: Shutting Down the National Dream.

148 Whitcomb: Avro Aircraft & Cold War Aviation based on a statistical analysis of engines with figures from: Wilkinson: Aircraft Engines of the World, (various years) and Richardson: "Burning Desire for Power." [review of current and future turbofans and turbojets] Air International Vol.47, No.2. Stamford: Key Publishing, 1994

149 ibid.

150 general arrangements of the compressors are identical according to Wilkinson's Aircraft Engines of the World, and photos of the aft sections of the J-57 and J-75 also support this theory. The personal testimony is private.

151 XF-103! Airpower, Jan 2004

152 ibid

Chapter 26

INTER SQUAD RIVALRY AND INTERFERENCE

Stemming from involvement in the Second World War, Canada had several research and development agencies monitoring and contributing to the Arrow Weapons System. These included the NAE (National Aeronautical Establishment), the DRB (Defense Research Board), the RCAF's various technical branches, and CARDE, the Canadian Armament Research and Development Establishment. Several works and primary sources point out that the NAE, particularly, felt that they were the government's proper aircraft design organization, and that there was considerable jealousy within this organization towards Avro's having been granted design authority for the CF-100 and Arrow.[153] In the NAE's original 1953 review of the CF-105 design proposal, their criticisms of the Arrow design were mild:

> "...we consider that the tests were well done and that, within their range, they bear out the A.V. Roe estimates of most of the Aerodynamic parameters effecting the aircraft performance." [154]

However, an event which exacerbated the government research arms' opinions of Avro involved the government decision to install a large quantity of test and scientific equipment at Avro, *not* in the research agencies. They were in danger of losing their *raison d'etre* and Parkin, head of the NRC, really turned on Avro after this, as did Jack Templin of the NAE, DL Thompson of the DDP and others.[155] This is one reason so many derogatory reports from various government "experts" exist and poison the attitudes of many in establishment circles today. Another reason is that various governments have released negative information, however erroneous, about Avro and the Arrow while supportive documentation appears to remain classified. Buck passing and secrecy in administratively embarrassing situations appears to be a characteristic of politicians and others in positions of influence and power.

An added dimension to the NRC's obstructionism *vis a vis* Avro is suggested by information derived through the defection of the Soviet cipher and communications expert, Igor Gouzenko, in Ottawa in 1945:

> "What was alarming was the degree of penetration into Canadian government offices, naval and air intelligence, [C.D. Howe's] ministry of munitions and supply, (covering atomic research and all military developments) external affairs and Parliament."[156]

As was also revealed, *not one* of these spies was ever convicted, and, since the vast majority were in the civil service (and not elected) most of them retained their positions for many years. Gouzenko's revelations, which were later confirmed by other Soviet defections, indicated that the NRC and its organs, the DRB, NAE, CARDE, (etc.) were particularly well penetrated by Soviet intelligence. Stevenson, in *Intrepid's Last Case,* discloses that, regarding these espionage cases, large quantities of government of Canada files simply disappeared, including one of Mackenzie King's closely-guarded diaries. "Mountains of stuff were missing" in the words of Canadian professor and historian J.L. Granatstein.

Former MI-5 agent Peter Wright also points out a more typical example of document destruction when he describes in *Spycatcher* how intelligence files are routinely destroyed to prevent future embarrassment—as does Chapman Pincher:

> "[S]candal could be safely concealed from the public because should investigative writers, [like himself] for example, seek out such information they could always be threatened with prosecution under the Official Secrets Acts, which were passed to deter and punish spies, but have been monstrously misused to prevent the disclosure of official information of all kinds."
>
> ...The truth had to be kept from the public by every means, from misinformation when total silence could no longer be maintained, to blatant lies. That policy of cover-up concerning disasters has been maintained to the present time."[157]

Other primary sources indicate that fights between Avro's brilliant aerodynamicist, Jim

Chamberlin, and the NAE really polarised the two groups. In fact, the government scientists became so frustrated with the inflexibility of Chamberlin over the Arrow's aerodynamics that Avro was asked to fire Chamberlin. J.C. Floyd wrote: "I was fiercely supportive of Jim [Chamberlin] in the 'dark days' of the NRC [via the NAE] criticism of our aerodynamics when they even suggested that Jim should be taken off the project. I told them that I would resign myself rather than do that!"[158] Chamberlin stayed. But so did the NAE. At the time, Julius Lukaseiwicz, a Polish ex-patriot, was the NAE's high-speed aerodynamicist and the man most at odds with Avro's engineering and design staff. Later in life, without disclosing his involvement in the program, Lukaseiwicz was interviewed by the CBC and was highly critical of the Arrow program, to the point of ridicule. In late 1954 disagreements over the Arrow's aerodynamic design came to a head.

NASA portrait of Jim Chamberlin

153 Floyd, letter to this author, 26 March, 2002
154 NAE letter to AVM D.M. Smith, 28 September, 1953.
155 telecon with J.C. Floyd, 9 February, 2004, surviving Avro engineering files and government records plus primary source anecdotal information all reveal the negativity, even hostility, of the various government research establishments towards Avro.
156 Stevenson, William: Intrepid's Last Case, p. 98
157 Pincher, Chapman: Too Secret, Too Long, p.p. 156 (He is referring to the Cambridge Five spies and similar events)
158 letter from J.C. Floyd, 9 February, 2004

Chapter 27

NACA INVOLVEMENT

In mid-November, 1954, the NAE, DRB and RCAF (without inviting Avro) descended on NACA Langley to "Discuss Aerodynamic Problems of Avro CF-105 Aircraft." Fed by NAE criticisms, NACA was convinced to issue an extremely critical report on the Arrow design. Their negativity would, no doubt, have been enhanced by their knowledge of the incredible difficulties the delta-winged Convair F-102 Delta Dagger project was experiencing. Their report on those meetings suggested that:

1) The Arrow probably had at least twice the aerodynamic drag Avro was projecting and therefore probably wouldn't be supersonic. (It eventually proved to have lower drag than even Avro estimated.)

2) The plane should be area ruled. (Area rule was formalized by Dr. Richard Whitcomb at NACA in 1953 and the USAF endeavoured to keep the theory secret according to Bill Gunston.)

3) The intake wouldn't work. (It turned out to have one of the best intakes ever designed, with a pressure recovery factor of 96% at Mach 1.8 dropping to 88% at Mach 2.)

4) The delta wing was a poor choice for range. (then why did the SR-71 Blackbird, B-58 Hustler, Concorde, XB-70 Valkyrie, F-108 Rapier, the Shuttle and the current {undisclosed}

hypersonic spyplane adopt it?)

5) The delta wing was a poor choice for induced drag. (see above note)

6) The delta wing was a poor choice due to serious pitch-up problems. (Avro cured them, and telemetry 'phugoid' graphs from flight test prove this.[159])

7) The Arrow would be directionally unstable, more so than any aircraft in the USA and that it shouldn't rely on electronic stability augmentation. (This was not true, as a secret document from Avro Engineering on Zurakowski and Potocki's visit to the USA to fly the F-102 reveals. Zura pointed out that the F-102 was *unflyable* due to directional (yaw) instability at low speeds and absolutely *required* a stability augmentation system. Zura pointed out that the 102 had a tube-technology non-redundant stability augmentation system, whereas the Arrow had a solid-state system that included redundancy for reliability and safety.[160] Of course, electronic stability augmentation and flight controls are now the standard practice, even for commercial airliners.)

8) The Arrow would probably benefit from using elevons rather than separate elevators and ailerons. (Avro didn't want to do this because the Arrow wing had negative camber in the inboard sections changing to positive camber at the tips (with leading edge droop building in washout–to prevent tip stalling and aileron reversal) and planned to use aileron trimming along with elevator trimming to achieve the lowest possible drag at all heights and speeds. Manual aileron trimming was installed in the Mark 1s [161], and automatic aileron trimming was applied in the Mark 2.[162])

9) The Arrow shouldn't use negative camber on the wing because it would hurt drag and thus range, and would result in higher trim drag. (Chamberlin had added the negative camber to improve longitudinal stability, prevent aileron-reversal and tip-stalling {which caused pitch-up}, and *reduce* trim drag. They also programed the fuel consumption to move the centre of gravity during the mission to match the changing centre of lift position to reduce trim drag, an idea that was expanded upon with the Concorde program.)[163]

This internal bureaucratic opposition spread (along with the rumours) and did the program serious harm. They were also proven wrong by the Arrow itself, and by subsequent design history. The result was that the Arrow program was put on hold in Canada until the controversy was concluded.

Avro, naturally, protested this harsh condemnation and asked to be allowed to confront their accusers. There were subsequent meetings at NACA Langley, with the NAE and other Canadian critics in attendance, with Jim Floyd, Jim Chamberlin, Fred Smye and others from Avro present. Recollections suggest that Chamberlin in particular dazzled the NACA crowd, giving them insights into more empirical and computer-intensive methods of design and evaluation. The resultant paper, penned by NACA, was much more favourable to the Arrow, yet still raised a couple of flags.[164] These may have been included as a concession to the Canadian critics present. A letter written by Iroquois design engineer, Harry Keast , insists that after the Avro presentation, the NACA engineers themselves felt that Avro's performance projections were actually conservative, which they proved to be once flight tests of the Arrow commenced.

> "As Chief Engineer of the Orenda Iroquois program at the time of the Arrow/Iroquois cancellation, I am tired of standing by and let [sic] counterpart and admired friend at Avro, Jim Floyd, fight alone the anti-Arrow conspiracy… After over 30 years it is time that the real facts were made available from Government sources, but let me put the cards on the table.
>
> "Jim Floyd has been hesitant in relating the true role that [Julius] Lukasiewicz played at the time the Arrow was designed. Lukaseiwicz was at that time with the National Research Council in Ottawa and Canada's expert in supersonic aerodynamics. So he reviewed the design and produced a report that was scathingly critical of the aerodynamic design, to the extent that there was no point in continuing with such a flawed aircraft. It was decided to approach the U.S.A. for an expert opinion. Hugh Dryden, a renowned aerodynamicist at The National Advisory Committee on Aeronautics, forerunner of NASA, gathered a team of his top men in the field of supersonics. Their verdict was that Avro had an excellent design and if anything they were being conservative in their estimates of performance. Lukasiewicz has never forgotten his humiliation and, despite the fact that the Arrow behaved perfectly and achieved a speed of 1.98 times the speed of sound while still climbing and with the lower powered J-75 engines, never ceased to twist the facts."[165]

Keast was responding to a disparaging editorial on Avro and the Arrow by professor Michael Bliss in the *Globe & Mail* newspaper titled "The Legend That Wasn't". The *Globe & Mail* unfortunately failed to print the rebuttal, despite Keast's vastly superior credentials.

NACA's Dr. Hugh Dryden chaired the meetings on the Arrow, with Jack Ames and Dr. Richard Whitcomb present. Dr. Whitcomb was NACA's transonic and supersonic aerodynamics genius. By that time Ames already had a research centre named after him, whereas the NACA facility at Edwards Air Force Base (AFB) was later renamed after Dryden. Robert Gilruth ran the NACA Langley centre and later ran the space program once NACA morphed into NASA. Gilruth would hire over twenty-eight Avro engineers from the Arrow program, including Jim Chamberlin and Bob Lindley, both of whom were present at the NACA meeting. Chamberlin, in fact, assumed responsibility for *all* of the engineering involved in Project Mercury and Project Gemini and had major responsibilities for Apollo.[166] Lindley, at McDonnell Aircraft after the Arrow program, was in charge of the design work on the Gemini spacecraft, and, in fact, designed it in cooperation with his old colleague, Jim Chamberlin. At one point Chamberlin moved into an office within McDonnell Aircraft to collaborate with Lindley on the Gemini spacecraft design. Lindley was also influential in changing NASA's spacecraft designer, Maxime Faget's original, straight-winged space shuttle design into a delta-winged craft and would later run NASAs Goddard research centre.[167]

There are other rather ironic (in view of later criticisms by self-professed experts) reasons for believing the Arrow as aerodynamically advanced. In 1955 the Canadian Chiefs of Staff Committee (CSC) wrote to the Cabinet Defense Committee (CDC): "It is significant that, four years after our concentration on this particular aircraft… the U.S. and Britain have both recently drawn up requirements for a supersonic all-weather 2 seater fighter closely similar to the Canadian CF-105. This would appear to substantiate the wisdom of our course of action."[168] Unfortunately, both of the aircraft produced to these specifications, while essentially copying the Arrow design, would be used by their respective nations of origin as excuses not to buy into the Arrow program. Needless to say, in elite circles there is an unfortunate tendency to place issues of prestige above technological and military merit. As the famed Canadian-born US diplomat, author and economist John Kenneth Galbraith wrote: "Men of high position are allowed, by a special act of grace, to accommodate their reasoning to the answer they need. Logic is only required in those of lesser rank." [169] Equally unfortunate is the lack of resolve and ability shown by Canada's politicians in convincing their allies that their reluctance to purchase the superior Arrow went against the concept of joint defense, and that they could save design and development costs by adopting the Arrow – thereby also saving Canada money that might be spent in their countries for other items. After all, Canada was using British tanks and naval technology and plenty of American weapons.

Hugh Dryden

159 J.C. Floyd: "The Canadian Approach to All-Weather Interceptor Development – The Fourteenth British
160 J.C. Floyd papers.
161 telecon with Arrow test pilot, Peter Cope, fall 2002.
162 discussions with J.C. Floyd, fall 2002
163 Joint report on an RCAF-DRB-NAE visit to N.A.C.A. Langley laboratories to discuss "Aerodynamic Problems of Avro CF-105 Aircraft", 19 November, 1954 Criticisms are from the joint report, commentary is by the author and is expanded upon in Avro Aircraft & Cold War Aviation.
164 NACA: Meeting to Discuss CF-105 Problems held December 20 and 21…, 1954. Fred Smye, Avro's general manager at the time, was present and wrote in his unpublished manuscript The Avro Arrow and Canadian Aviation, that NACA was actually very impressed with Avro and came to the conclusion that Avro's estimates were conservative.
165 Keast, Harry: Letter to the Editor of the Globe & Mail newspaper. This letter is available as part of a CD Rom from www.avroarrow.org
166 Brooks, Courtney G., James M. Grimwood and Loyd S. Swenson Jr. Chariots for Apollo: A History of Manned Lunar Spacecraft. Washington: NASA Science and Technology Information Division, 1979 Hacker, Barton C. and James M. Grimwood. On the Shoulders of Titans: A History of Project Gemini. Washington: NASA Science and Technology Information Division, 1977 Hallion, Richard. On The Frontier [part of NASA history series] Washington: US Government Printing Office, no date.
167 Gainor: Arrows to the Moon
168 CSC: Memorandum to the Cabinet Defence Committee: CF 105 Development Programme. 3 October, 1955
169 Stevenson, Intrepid's Last Case

Chapter 28

THE PS-13 IROQUOIS ENGINE

In April of 1952 Charles Grinyer, another of the 'British Airlift' of engineers to Canada, joined Orenda Engines Ltd. Grinyer had worked on early jet and turboprop powerplants for Bristol in the UK and was renowned for having seen ten engines through their type-test certification runs without a failure. Orenda had been considering a future engine design called the Wakunda, which was a single spool engine with afterburner. It was eventually decided that the engine didn't offer enough of an advance over competing engines. In the fall of 1953 Grinyer, Harry Keast and Burt Avery presented an engine design called Project Study 13 (or PS-13) to the Hawker Siddeley Design Council.

It was a bold advance over competing designs using two spools and a three-stage turbine in a mostly titanium engine. It was designed to use a transonic compressor to increase efficiency for high speed operation while using fewer compressor stages to do the same amount of work. With its air cooling and two bearing design, it was a very ambitious and technically challenging design. On January 13th 1954 the board of A.V. Roe Canada Ltd., with the concurrence of Hawker Siddeley, allocated 3.5 million dollars of company money in a private venture to construct three prototype PS-13 Iroquois Mark 1 engines. Authorisation was also given for the company to purchase three expensive ingots of titanium to use as the main material for the engines. This posed fabrication, forming and welding problems, with Orenda and Avro learning enough about the material to become industry leaders in its use. Orenda audaciously planned to have a running prototype in one year's time. They beat their own estimate by over a month.

The first self-sustained run of the Iroquois took place as a nervous Charles Grinyer was deplaning in Ottawa on his way to give a presentation on the engine to the government officials in charge of the pursestrings. It was his job to sell the engine and have the government and/or RCAF take over its funding. Being able to report that the engine was running certainly assisted his sales effort.

> "The RCAF has completed a careful study of this engine... This study indicates that the engine is more advanced in design concept than any engine being developed in the U.K. or U.S.A. The engine was supersonic in concept from the beginning. The design incorporates, a transonic first-stage compressor producing an exceptionally high mass flow. Design emphasis on mechanical simplicity coupled with the extensive use of titanium has produced engines which are about 1000 pounds lighter than other engines in the same power class. [In terms of thrust to weight]...the PS13 at its 20,000 lb. [thrust] rating exceeds the [de Havilland] Gyron by 22% and the [Curtiss Wright] J-67, [the Pratt & Whitney] J75 and [the Rolls Royce] RB 106[170] by over 50%. These comparative figures are of great importance, particularly with respect to the increased performance at high altitudes of a supersonic craft such as the CF-105.
>
> " Studies...indicate that there is little or no advantage either in time or money in building an engine under license as opposed to Canadian design."[171]

The study which indicated that the Canadians could produce their own engine in a competitive time frame and at a competitive price was done on A.V. Roe Canada's impressive TR-5 Orenda engine. This engine took less time and less money to develop than the competing J-47 by General Electric. An analysis of the CF-100, despite its development troubles, against similar programs in the United States yielded a similar conclusion.[172]

At the time the RCAF selected the Iroquois however, its future was anything but assured. While few of the engine's features hadn't been previously proposed, or used in other engines, it was a radical design because it incorporated virtually every emerging engine design concept in a single engine. It therefore was a somewhat risky effort. Tony Buttler has mentioned in one of his books that the PS-13 Iroquois design owed much of its technology to the Rolls-Royce RB-106, the first engine proposed for the Arrow. There is probably some truth to this, though the RB-106 had a much lower specified thrust than the Iroquois making the latter a considerable technical advance over the Rolls-Royce product.

In 1956 a new propulsion research centre, named after Hawker Siddeley Chairman Sir Thomas Sopwith, was opened. A new complex, housing high altitude test cells capable of testing engines up to 40,000 pounds thrust, was built. A great design and engineering team was established for the design and production of what was then the most advanced turbojet engine in the world.

In June of 1956 the Iroquois underwent its first official test, the 50 hour Pre-Flight Rating Test (PFRT). During this test the engine beat every known record for thrust output at 19,350 lbt (pounds thrust) without afterburner. Its throttle response was also world-beating. It took only 2.8 seconds to go from idle to full military thrust and only 4.5 seconds to go from idle to full afterburning thrust. It was an impressive performance but there were problems. Vibrations and flexing of the central drums in opposition to the case caused rubbing of compressor discs with potentially catastrophic consequences. The air-cooled turbine blade feature of the Mk. 1 engine was discarded as new materials and the already designed-in air cooling made them unnecessary. Titanium compressor blades were changed to stainless steel when it was found they could catch fire. Tips of the compressor blades were "feathered", with a portion of their outer trailing edge cut away to alleviate interference with adjoining discs when the assembly flexed. Many other changes were made to the structure of the engine and a new prototype, the Iroquois Mk. 2 was produced.

Orenda Iroquois publicity photo (courtesy Aerospace Heritage Foundation of Canada)

During the program at least five running engines were sent to the United States for test and evaluation. Iroquois engineer Colin Campbell relates that the engine was tested at up to 25,000 pounds dry thrust in Canada, and at up to 27,000 pounds in the Cornell Institute in the United States. These are phenomenal outputs for an engine of this size even today. The rating they were aiming for was 20,000 pounds dry thrust and 30,000 pounds with afterburner. Clearly they had reason to hope for even more powerful versions once they addressed the reliability and longevity issues.

In 1957 the USAF allowed the Canadian government to borrow a B-47 bomber to serve as a test-bed for the Iroquois. A nacelle was constructed by Canadair on the rear fuselage to house the engine. Unfortunately this nacelle was not aligned with the thrust line of the aircraft and this caused serious controllability issues when the engine was tested. Mike Cooper Slipper was the Orenda chief test pilot who underwent the standard USAF B-47 pilot training and flew the aircraft during these tests. On the first test the engine was spooled up to maximum RPM during a run over Georgian Bay near North Bay Ontario. A compressor blade let go and punctured a hole through the engine case and through the side of the bomber. Smoke and noise alerted the pilot. Chris Cooper Slipper, son of the test pilot, stated that this was the most frightening flight of his father's life—quite a statement considering Mike intentionally rammed a Dornier in his Hurricane during the Battle of Britain. Restrictions were placed on the RPM of the early Mk. 2 versions until they devised ways to overcome the problems.

June Callwood spent a great deal of time with the Iroquois engineers and other staff writing a piece for *Saturday Night* magazine. Her resulting story is replete with a discussion of how the main engineers, Keast, Avery and Grinyer, had worked themselves to exhaustion and near nervous breakdowns perfecting the engine. It is true that the delays in producing a reliable engine caused delays in the Arrow program. It had been hoped that the engine would be ready for unrestricted flight in late 1957 or early 1958.

Even so, on 27th July 1957 Grinyer felt the engine was ready for its 100 hour PFRT—though at a reduced thrust of 18,750 lbt dry. It passed the test but some problems still remained. After many improvements were made, by early 1959 only one seemed to remain—a propensity for the engine to throw seventh-stage compressor blades. Ironically, the Orenda engine had also been slightly delayed in its introduction for precisely the same reason. Grinyer postponed the final 150 hour type test and certification run until August, 1959. The thrust specified for the engine was 19,350 lbs dry, and 26,000 with afterburner. Considering its size and weight, these figures promised to make it the most advanced engine in the world for at least a generation. Over 7,000 hours running was accumulated on 13 engines before cancellation though at least 18 were eventually built. There are questions as to the disposition of some of the engines, particularly the five that went to the United States. 147 million dollars were spent on the Iroquois up to cancellation, about half of what had been spent to bring the American J-75 engine to its pre-flight rating test (PFRT).

Even while they were perfecting the Iroquois 2, Orenda's engineers were already looking to future versions. To overcome limitations imposed by less efficient intake designs on some US aircraft and also to provide a lower-altitude and speed version for possible commercial use, a higher compressor ratio version was planned. This added another stage to the compressor of the engine and would have resulted in a very efficient and comparatively lightweight engine to compete with the engines that powered the B-52 and Boeing 707 (and others). This version was proposed for a version of the Republic F-105 Thunderchief that was a contender for the RCAF NATO strike-reconnaissance aircraft contract that followed Black Friday.

For Mach 3+ versions of the Arrow or other aircraft an Iroquois Mk. 3 was proposed on 27 October, 1958. This engine was to use a larger diameter inlet and exhaust and narrower turbine sections. While Orenda engineers claim they hoped to eventually get 30,000 lbs dry thrust and 40,000 pounds with afterburner from this engine, by Black Friday they were only projecting that it would produce about 600 pounds more, wet or dry, than the Iroquois 2. The Orenda engineers wanted to ensure their estimates would be seen as conservative and not challenged or ridiculed.

The Iroquois was seen as a very attractive engine by interested parties throughout the western world. The USAF was watching it as a potential powerplant for many of its aircraft, including the B-52 Stratofortress bomber. It was sized to replace the J-57, J-67, J-75, Olympus and other high-capacity turbojets and thus would suit any aircraft relying on any of those powerplants. Since it produced double the power of French engines in its size class, it was looked at to power their Mirage 5 bomber. The French negotiated for a supply of 300 engines pending its successful certification. However, in late 1958, hearing rumours of cancellation, the French backed out, citing their belief that the government of Canada was going to cancel the engine. When this happened Charles Grinyer tabled his resignation. A direct call to the Minister of Defense Production, Raymond O'Hurley, where O'Hurley reassured Grinyer that the engine would not be terminated, convinced Grinyer to stay. It was a reassurance that wasn't warranted.

Others deride A.V. Roe Canada for not seeing the engine through to its certification. This blame is misplaced since the government of Canada owned the engine through their funding of the program and they had placed a stop work order on it. It would have been illegal for Orenda to continue the development in view of this order.

There is also some controvery between the engine side of A.V. Roe Canada Ltd. and the airframe side as to whether the Iroquois was ready for production and service by the cancellation date. Those on the engine side say it was, those on the airframe side and Mike Cooper Slipper claimed that it wasn't. Colin Campbell, an Orenda engineer assigned to the Iroquois claims that there was only one example in existence of the production engine by cancellation, and it was slated to go into the first Mk. 2 Arrow—RL 206. He states that the design was frozen in the configuration of this engine and that all the Orenda personnel were confident it was ready for reliable service. A post-cancellation analysis by the RCAF echoes this view and notes the honesty of the Orenda engineers in discussing the problems and solutions.

My own analysis indicates that the Iroquois Mk. 2 would have become the top afterburning turbojet engine throughout the 1960s and 70s, without *any* subsequent development. Below are the technical advances my analysis indicates the Iroquois introduced:

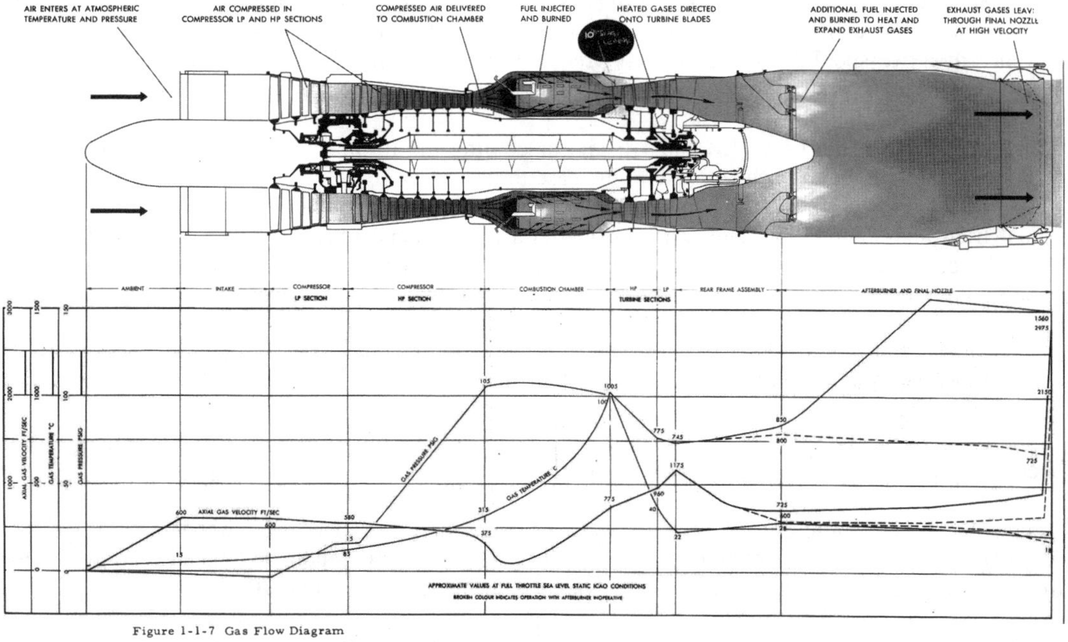

Figure 1-1-7 Gas Flow Diagram

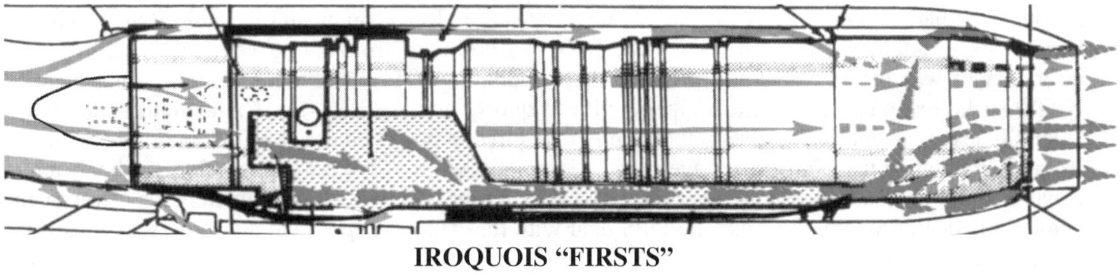

IROQUOIS "FIRSTS"

- First overhung-stator two-shaft design using two (vs. three or more) bearing assemblies thus dispensing with a central casting, and replacing the two shafts with an inner and outer drum, making the entire centre core of the engine turn. The combustors were overhung with the floor comprising the spinning outer drum which connected the high-pressure (HP) turbine to the HP compressor section. The drum connecting the low-pressure (LP) compressor to the LP turbine was smaller and rotated inside the HP drum.
- First to make extensive use of Titanium for reasons of high-strength, high-temperature tolerance and low weight.

- First to house a high proportion of its machinery (pumps, gearbox drives etc.) internally to lower installed size. This meant a smaller, lighter aircraft stucture, and improved over-all aerodynamics and efficiency.

- First to concentrate on a constant gas speed throughout the core to maximize aerodynamic efficiency and allow a higher average speed of flow through the engine. (Rather than varying gas temperature, pressure *and speed,* through the core, they designed it in such a way as to keep the gas speed relatively constant and vary only gas temperature and pressure.)

- First to try air-cooled turbine blades with comparatively cool compressor air ducted to the blades through the core structure of the engine, and through pressurized, annular ducts formed by the outer case of the engine. The Iroquois 1 used this but the Orenda designers dispensed with air-cooled blades in the Iroquois 2 due to otherwise excellent air-cooling after the combustors and improved metallurgy (availability of Inconel X). The Pratt & Whitney J-58 for the A-12/YF-12A/SR-71 used a similar arrangement on a single-spool design.

- First (with the General Electric J-79 of the B-58 Hustler and F-4 Phantom) variable pitch stator design. (Variable pitch stators allowed improved throttle handling and resistance to compressor surges, stalls, and engine flame-outs. On the J-79 variable stators allowed the designers to produce a single-spool engine with handling qualities usually associated with two-spool designs, on the Iroquois, which was already a two-spool design, it allowed Orenda to design it with 40 to 60% fewer compressor and stator sections, compared to contemporary and most later designs, greatly lightening the engine.)

- First "bypass" engine using LP and HP air for cooling the turbine section and machinery while exhausting through the extractor nozzle to increase thrust.

- First transonic compressor. This was considered a radical concept at the time, however, the later Rolls-Royce RB-211 turbofan for large airliners and the Pegasus II of the later Hawker Harriers also incorporate transonic compressors validating Orenda's leadership in this technology.

- "Hot-Streak" ignition for the afterburner. A streak of hot combustion gases was piped directly back to the afterburner fuel spray zone as an ultra-reliable afterburner ignitor and sustainer.

- First oxygen-injection relight system in case of engine flame-out at altitude. This technology was licensed by Orenda at the time, providing income for the company.

- First fully variable afterburner. Previous systems came on all at once or in two or more stages. A fully-variable system in an engine of the low weight, high thrust and good fuel economy of the Iroquois would have been a major tactical advantage during the 1960s and '70s.

Before cancellation and in keeping with the government's efforts towards securing Defense Production Sharing (DPS) deals with the United States A.V. Roe Canada and Republic Aviation in the United States attempted to form their own DPS deal separate from the government's efforts. The arrangement was that Avro would produce the Republic F-105 Thunderchief aircraft for Canada's NATO strike-reconnaissance role equipped with Iroquois engines. Since the Thunderchief had a considerably less efficient intake system than the Arrow, Orenda proposed using a higher compressor-ratio Iroquois adaptation using an extra stage in the compressor section. This engine would have been applicable to many lower altitude and lower performance aircraft worldwide. Unfortunately the government vetoed this deal, probably because the DPS deal with the American political authorities such as John Foster Dulles hinged on the production of US aircraft by American-owned Canadair rather than British-aligned Avro Canada.

During the cancellation fiasco Leslie Frost, Premier of Ontario, tried to have the government chip in three million dollars to see the Iroquois through its final PFRT and certify it for military or commercial use. Had this been done he (and Orenda) were confident the engine would be purchased by other nations for their aircraft. Some have questioned why Orenda didn't spend the money themselves. The answer is that the development was owned by the Government of Canada through the RCAF and the owners wouldn't allow the engine to be completed and placed in production.

Iroquois versus turbojets from the 1960s

Note: All figures taken from Paul Wilkinson's *Aircraft Engines of the World* periodical.

	PS-13 Mk 2	Olympus 320	J-93	J-58	TF-30
Dry Thrust	23,000 lbs	23,000 lbs	24,000lbs	24,000 lbs	11,500
Wet Thrust	30,000 lbs	34,000 lbs	32,000 lbs	32,000 lbs	19,000
Wet-Dry Ratio	1.43-1	1.48-1	1.33-1	1.33-1	1.65-1
Diameter/length	45"/231"	42"/320"	52.5"/237"	50"/180"	38"/178"
Frontal Area (FA)	9.6 sq. ft.	9.6 sq. ft.	15 sq.ft.	13.1sq.ft.	7.9 sq. ft.
Dry Thrust to FA	2400 lbt/sq ft	2400 lbt/sq ft	1750 lbt/sq ft	1740lbt/sq ft	1456lbt/sq ft
Wet Thrust to FA	3125 lbt/sq ft	3541 lbt/sq ft	2133 lbt/sq ft	2443 lbt/sq ft	2405 lbt/sq ft
Weight	4,300 lbs	6,000 lbs	5,200 lbs	6,500 lbs	3200 lbs
Compression Ratio	8-1	12-1 est.	8-1	6-1	2-1 (turbofan)
Shaft Number	2	2	2	1	2
Compressor Rotors	3+7	8+7	5+3	8	3+7+7
Turbine Rotors	3	2	2	2	4
Thrust -Weight Dry	5.35 lbt/lb	3.8 lbt/lb	4.6 lbt/lb	3.7-1	3.6-1
Thust-Weight Wet	6.97 lbt/lb	5.7 lbt/lb	6.15 lbt/lb	4.9 lbt/lb	5.93-1
Year of figures	1961 est.	1965	1964	1964	1965?
Fuel Consumption Dry	.75 lb/lbt/hr	.75lbs/lbt/hr	.86 lb/lbt/hr	.8 lb/lbt/hr	.85 lb/lbt/hr
Fuel Consumption Wet	1.8 lb/lbt/hr	2.0 lb/lbt/hr	1.94 lb/lbt/hr	1.9 lb/lbt/hr	2.0 lb/lbt/hr
Aircraft	CF-105 Mk 2	TSR.2	F-108/XB-70	Blackbird	F-111/F-14A

Iroquois versus turbojets from the 1970s

	PS-13 Mk 2	Olympus 593	PW F-100	GE F-110	GE F-404
Dry Thrust	23,000 lbs	30,000 lbs	14,590	lbs	17,260 lbs
10,500 lbs					
Wet Thrust	30,000 lbs	35,000 lbs	23,770 lbs	28,980 lbs	16,000 lbs
Wet-Dry Ratio	1.43-1	1.17-1	1.62-1	1.68-1	1.52-1
Diameter/length	42"/231"	47.8"/138"	40" (est)/208"	40" (est)/182"	30" (est)/159"
Frontal Area (FA)	9.6 sq. ft.	12.5 sq. ft.	8.7 sq. ft.	8.7 sq. ft.	4.3 sq. ft.
Mass Flow	350 lb/sec	440 lb/sec	225 lb/sec est.	250 lb/sec est	150 lb/sec est
Dry Thrust to FA	2400 lbt/sq ft	2400 lbt/sq ft	1670 lbt/sq ft	1983lbt/sq ft	2441 lbt/sq ft
Wet Thrust to FA	3125 lbt/sq ft	2,800 lbt/sq ft	2732 lbt/sq ft	3330 lbt/sq ft	3720 lbt/sq ft
Weight	4,300 lbs	5,000 lbs	3,700 lbs	4,000 lbs	2,200 lbs
Compression Ratio	8-1	12-1	25-1	25-1 est.	N/A
Shaft Number	2	2	2	2	2
Compressor Rotors	3+7	8+7	3+10	3+9	3+7
Turbine Rotors	3	2	4	3	2
Thrust -Weight Dry	5.23 lbt/lb	6.0 lbt/lb	3.94-1	4.31-1	4.77-1
Thust-Weight Wet	6.81 lbt/lb	7.0 lbt/lb	6.42-1	7.14-1	7.27-1
Year of figures	1961 est.	1969	1972	1975?	1974
Fuel Consumption Dry	.75 lb/lbt/hr	.75lbs/lbt/hr	.75lbs/lbt/hr est.	75lbs/lbt/hr est.	N/A
Fuel Consumption Wet	1.8 lb/lbt/hr	2.0 lb/lbt/hr	2.0 lb/lbt/hr	2.0 lb/lbt/hr	N/A
Aircraft	CF-105	Concorde	F-15/F-16	F-15/F-16	F-18

Notes: Iroquois and Olympus figures taken from *Aircraft Engines of the World*, figures for the F-100, F-110 and F-404 from *Air International* Vol 47, No 2 Aug. 1994. Figures for the Iroquois are for a fully developed engine while the initial PFRT rating was 19,250 lbt dry and 26,000 lbt with after-burning. One change from these published figures being the weight for the Olympus 593 as used in Concorde. 500 lbs has been added to the weight of the engine since the figures quoted in the reference did not include the variable/thrust reversing nozzle and rear duct section since these were made separately (by Dassault) and were considered part of the airframe. This weight handicap is probably quite conservative. Inlet diameter and frontal area calculations of the US engines are estimates since only the maximum diameters of the engines were available during research.

170 Tony Buttler, in British Secret Projects, Jet Fighters Since 1950, insinuates that the Orenda Iroquois was based on the Rolls Royce RB 106, however, the difference in thrust-to-weight shown here debases that claim. Certainly, the Iroquois included nearly every advanced engine technology being contemplated at the time.

171 CSC: Memorandum to the Cabinet Defence Committee, date unknown, but sometime in early 1955.

172 Shaw: There Never Was an Arrow

Chapter 29

ARROW ARMAMENT: Velvet Glove to Falcon to Sparrow 2D missiles

The Velvet Glove Missile

Up until around 1955 the RCAF and Avro had been assuming that the Arrow would be equipped with the Canadian Velvet Glove missile.[173] At the Canadian Armament Research and Development Establishment (CARDE), Gerald Bull and cohorts were designing and testing a radar-guided missile equivalent in guidance concept and size to the US Navy's Sparrow 1 and Sparrow 3 radar guided missiles. This was aptly named the Velvet Glove missile. Official sources state that every launch of this weapon was a success. Yet for some reason it was cancelled in 1956 to make way for the presumed-superior Sparrow 2D. The official history of the Defense Research Board (DRB) states that the Velvet Glove had only been conceived from the beginning as a research tool to acquire guided missile expertise.

Dr. Julius Lukaseiwicz, however, a then-colleague of DRB head Dr. Solandt working in the National Aeronautical Establishment (NAE), (he later became professor of aerodynamics at Carleton University), shows that the reason the RCAF decided to cancel Velvet Glove is because they became convinced that it didn't have the range and speed to catch a Soviet jet bomber. "It was designed to meet the threat of World War II vintage. It began in 1951 and by 1955 involved several companies, including Canadair, Canadian Westinghouse, and Computing Devices of Canada. Some 300 missiles were built and test fired. By the mid-1950s however, it had become apparent that the Velvet Glove and CF-100 were inadequate to cope with jet bombers. In July 1956 the Minister of National Defense announced the cancellation of the Velvet Glove and stated that that U.S. Sparrow missile would be produced in Canada instead. The project had cost $24 million; the Sparrow was cancelled in September 1958."[174] The range and speed of this type of weapon is determined by the rocket portion of the missile, and this, compared to the guidance package, was easily upgraded. In fact, since Velvet Glove and the Sparrow family were virtually identical in size, it could have merely used the Sparrow's rocket section—presuming it actually was superior. Why Canada would, in 1951, after the revelation of Soviet jet bombers, with the Boeing B-47 Stratojet bomber being in service, embark on the design of a missile to intercept WW II bombers was not explained.

Sparrow 3 didn't become an effective weapon until well into the Vietnam War as Randall Cunningham makes crystal clear in his book *Fox Two*.[175] Sources agree that Velvet Glove technology was turned over to the Americans, free of charge, to help them perfect their passive-guidance missile technology used in the Sparrow 1 and 3. The reason for this generosity? Canada would reap the rewards in the resultant Sparrow missile.[176]

The Sparrow 2D Missile

Unfortunately there was roughly a zero percent chance of those rewards materializing because the Sparrow 2D missile the RCAF Chief of Operational Requirements (COR) Jack Easton selected, in June 1956 (three years after the Arrow program launch) was not, like Velvet Glove, or Sparrows 1 or 3, a passive-guidance missile. Rather, this weapon used active guidance, and was therefore the orphan of the Sparrow family.[177] In reality, today's AMRAAM is identical in concept to the Sparrow 2D – and is even based on the same missile airframe, yet the Pentagon's scientists and suppliers presumably weren't able to make it a viable weapon until around 1990 and it was used on a trial basis in the first Gulf War.[178] Even then it was touted as a technological triumph.

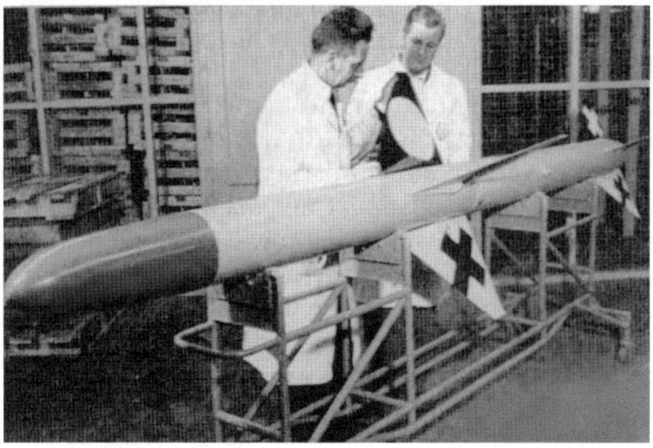

Technicians at work on a Sparrow 2D missile.

One should understand that there were actually three Sparrow missiles in development at the time. In the mid-1950s Raytheon was working on the Sparrow 1 with Sperry concentrating on the Sparrow 3, both of which used passive homing, while Douglas was working on the Sparrow 2, which was an ambitious active-guidance weapon. All these missiles were based on the same airframe but used different guidance technology. Douglas was also, according to Avro documents, working on the Sparrow X, which had a nuclear warhead for air-to-air combat.[179] The advantage of an active-guidance missile is that the launching aircraft can immediately turn away from the target, i.e., "fire and forget" the weapon, whereas passive-guidance missiles required the launching aircraft to keep illuminating the target with its own onboard radar whereupon the missile would home in on the signal reflected off the target. This generally results in the interceptor closing on the target and potentially exposing itself to the target's own defensive weapons. The miniaturization of the active weapon's radar transmitter and guidance system, and processor speed, were major hurdles in the development of the active-guidance weapon. In today's jargon, the RCAF had selected a "fire and forget" missile thirty years before the technology was ready. Nevertheless, the RCAF also specified that the Arrow be compatible with the passive Sparrow 3—until 1957 when it was cut to save money and allow, at US urging, nuclear air-to-air weapons to replace it.[180]

Several months after Air Vice Marshal (AVM) Easton of the RCAF decided to specify that the Arrow use the Sparrow 2D with its entirely different guidance concept, the US Navy, who had been developing it with Douglas, cancelled the missile, perhaps because they realised the technology just wasn't ready.[181]

As a result, rather than settling for a missile the US Navy was continuing to develop (and thereby saving development money with the attendant benefit of US orders allowing a lower unit price), AVM Easton took over the Sparrow 2 program, and brought it to Canada—to Avro's unmitigated horror. The technology however, was to be owned by the United States.[182] In fact, once the US Navy cancelled the weapon, Fred Smye of Avro flew to the United States to discuss the implications of the missile cancellation and its potential impact on the Astra radar/fire control system if the Canadian institutions taking over the missile design were overwhelmed by the technology requirements. RCA told Smye that a substitution of the Sparrow 3 would not entail any major problems as a modification to the Astra system.[183] For their 20-20 foresight, Avro received a double-barrelled blast from the Department of Defense Production's (DDP's) head of the aircraft division: D.L. Thompson. Despite their official responsibilities as program coordinators, Avro was accused of meddling in the affairs of the D.D.P. and RCAF, even though it was obvious they were trying to ensure that the Arrow received a functional and compatible weapon on time and within the budget.[184] Bob Lindley subsequently discussed missiles with Raytheon and was told that the development of the Sparrow 2D missile would be exceptionally expensive, and would cost Canada at least 100 million dollars, based on Raytheon's experience in developing their less sophisticated version of the Sparrow. It is interesting to note that G/C Foottit, in response to these points as Avro had raised them, admitted in 1957 "that they had themselves come to the conclusion that the Sparrow 2 would probably not be available for operational use until about 1965".[185] Why the program, then, survived until late-1958 is a good question.

In J.C. Floyd's files, in discussing the RCAF choice of weapon, it is noted that the US had encouraged Canada to take over development of the Sparrow 2, and that the RCAF seemed to view this as an indication that the project was feasible. In a confidential letter to Fred Smye, J.C. Floyd wrote: "[G/C Foottit] confessed that he was not clear himself on some of the reasons for the CAS's decision[186] to continue with the Sparrow 2 and abandon the Sparrow 3 [and nuclear Sparrow X version which had up to then been included in the capabilities of the ASTRA 1 system], however, he said that this move had been made after many checks, including a visit to BuAeR [The US Navy Bureau of Aeronautical Research] by the Vice Chief, and that there had also been a strong recommendation from the U.S. Navy that Canada should not switch from Sparrow 2 to 3 at this time." Floyd continued: *"This is probably because Buaer feel that it would be in their own interest to have Canada complete the development of the Sparrow 2 missile, at Canada's expense, as a back-up for their Sparrow 3 development program."*[187]

It is interesting that Canada should have received a "strong recommendation" to continue with a missile the US Navy was abandoning. It is even more interesting that the RCAF would continue with that missile when the cost projections Avro was hearing, very credibly as it turns out, were as high as what would be spent in developing the Iroquois engine up to cancellation. Compounding this lunacy is the suggestion that the RCAF itself had come to the conclusion that the Sparrow 2 wouldn't be ready for service until about 1965. CAS Campbell displayed his scepticism in remarks recorded by the RCAF Air Council: "Even if little brother, the RCAF, is so much smarter than big brother, the USAF, in choosing a superior weapon—an orphan Sp.II, is it worth the price?"[188] It would seem that AVM Easton getting beyond-the-state-of-the-art avionics, electronics and weapons for the Arrow was the price of his support for the Arrow program, and this is perhaps why CAS Campbell reluctantly went along with the Sparrow 2 program.

Avro's sales and service manager Joe Morley stated:

> "John Easton must hold himself as one of those more than somewhat responsible for the death of the Arrow. He was responsible for the armament spec, and this was way, way beyond the state of the art. The cost of his program was about one-third of the total cost of the program. Even in the dying days, when I implored him to let off and go with a less sophisticated system, he wouldn't relent. It took Wilf Curtis to break him down, and both went to Wright Field to negotiate a supply of USAF systems for a limited number of aircraft, but it was too late." [189]

It should be mentioned that some Army generals to occupy chairs on the Chiefs of Staff Committee (CSC) and thus also on the Cabinet Defense Committee (CDC) were opposed to the Arrow program from the beginning. At the time, and due to German V-2 short-range missiles having impacted London during WW II, there was a debate, (or perhaps it is more accurately called an argument), regarding the perceived superiority of missiles for offence and defense. In the USA and other countries, this was aggravated by typical inter-service sibling rivalry. The US Army was in a competition with the USAF to be the primary holders of anti-aircraft missiles, and the Army was lobbying fiercely against fighter planes as a result. In Canada, General Guy Simonds, one of Canada's D-Day Generals, was dead set against the Arrow program, even penning an article for McLean's titled "We're Wasting Millions on an Obsolete Air Force". Simonds dislike of the air force, *any air force*, may have been due to his being 'short rounded', (bombed), by the RAF, RCAF and US Army Air Force in WW II. So right from the beginning the Arrow had powerful enemies, and a competing operational doctrine working against it. Simonds would even state that he retired from his Chairman Chiefs of Staff (CCSC) position as a protest against the Arrow program.

The Sparrow 2D missile program was not the only development effort undertaken by Canada for the Arrow that would result in a product owned by the US government. The Arrow weapons system was about to have another expensive and risky development added to the airframe and engine.

173 Floyd: The Avro Canada C-102 Jetliner, and The Arrowheads: The Avro Arrow: The Story of the Avro Arrow from its Evolution to its Extinction. Both sources reproduce design studies showing Avro proposals using the Velvet Glove missile as primary armament.
174 Lukaseiwicz: Canada's Encounter with High-Speed Aeronautics, first published in Technology and Culture, Vol. 27, No. 2, April 1986.
175 Cunningham, Randall: Fox Two, Cunningham was the top US fighter ace in Vietnam and throughout his book he points out universal frustrations with the ineffective Sparrow 3 missile throughout most of the Viet Nam war. "Fox Two" is actually airmens' jargon for the Sidewinder missile, which Cunningham found very effective, in contrast to the "Fox One"—the Sparrow 3 missile.
176 Godspeed, D.J.: A History of the Defence Research Board of Canada. Ottawa; Queen's Printer, 1958
177 author's air force training in 1993
178 Aviation Week & Space Technology, various issues.
179 J.C. Floyd, letter to AVM Hendricks, 30 August, 1957
180 ibid.
181 Campagna, Requiem for a Giant, p.135-38
182 Dow: The Arrow
183 Floyd in a memo to Bob Lindley, 19 June, 1957
184 Floyd, confidential memo to Fred Smye: "Complaint from D.L. Thompson on Avro's Over-Enthusiasm on Sparrow Program". 28 June, 1957 p.1
185 ibid.
186 RCAF Air Council: Notes on Air Council Meeting…"Comparison of Air Defence Weapons Combination". During this meeting a paper by Chief of Operational Requirements, AVM Easton, was discussed. This paper suggested, through arithmetic that was doubted openly during the meeting, that the Sparrow 2D missile would have double the kill probability of the Hughes Falcon armament.
187 Floyd, confidential letter to Fred Smye titled: Notes on Discussions with G/C Foottit
188 RCAF Air Council: Notes on Air Council Meeting…Comparison of Air Defence Weapons Combination. 27 August, 1957
189 Stewart: Shutting Down the National Dream, p.247

The Avro C-102 Jetliner

Canadair DC-4

The Avro 730

Avro Jetliner in TWA colours

Project Y-2 Supersonic Disc

Project Y-1 "Omega" - The Flying Spade

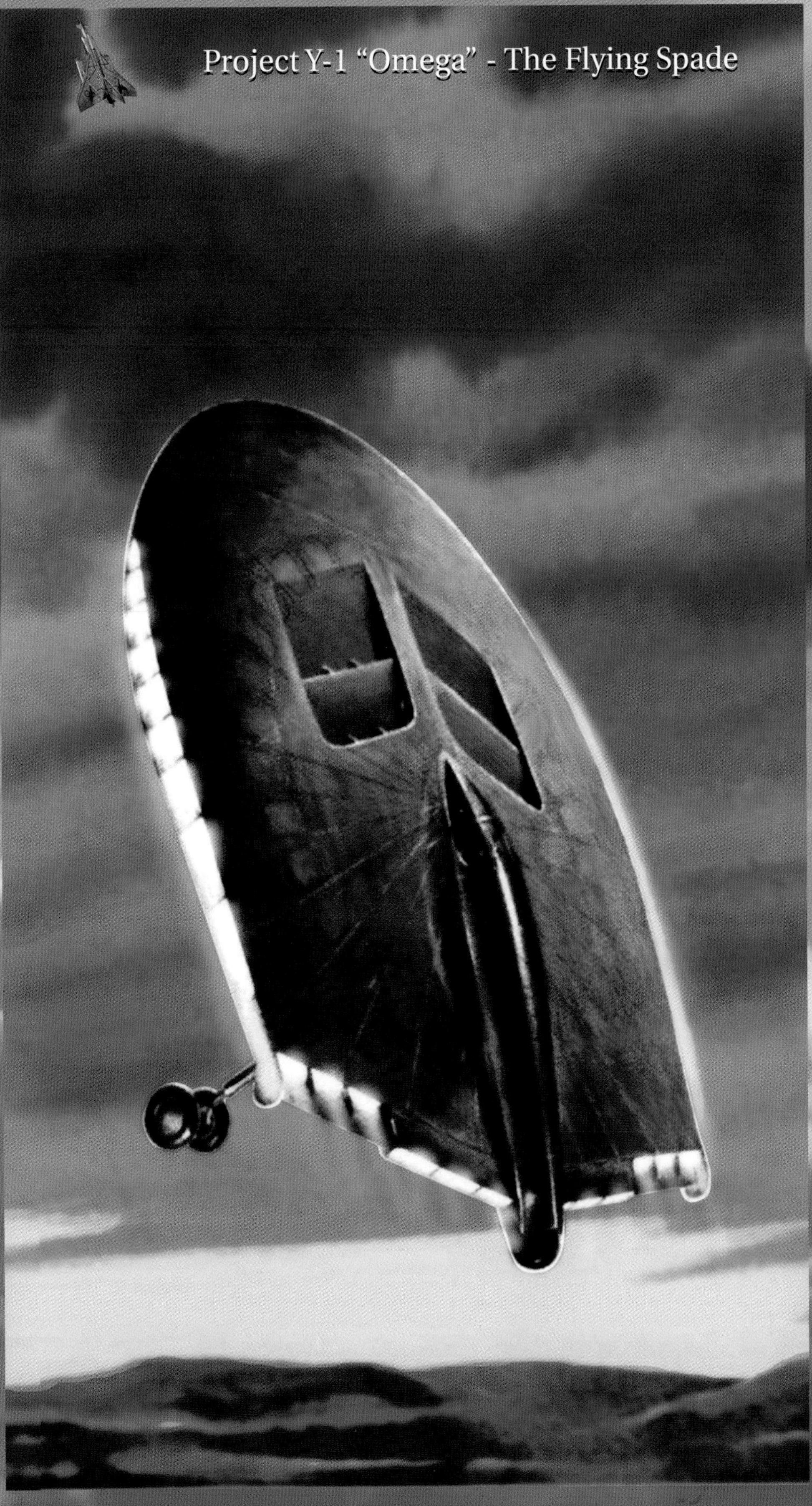

The McDonnell F101 Voodoo

The Long Range Avro Arrow

RAF Long Range Arrow

Avro USAF Experimental VTOL X-Wing

The Orenda PS-13 Iroquois
IN THE EXPANDING MARKETS OF CANADA AND THE WORLD ORENDA ENGINES LIMITED IS IN THE FOREFRONT PROVIDING HIGH QUALITY PRODUCTS AND SERVICES
Associated with the rapid advancement of industrial technology is the growing requirement for products of special design. Ideally suited to fulfill this requirement, Orenda, in addition to satisfying the advanced propulsion commitments for the defence of Canada, offers unique engineering potential for the design, development and manufacture of lightweight gas turbines, pumps, compressors, combustion systems special purpose machinery and equipment.

Orenda Advertisement

Avro HSA-1000 SST

Avro HSA-1011 SST

Avro HSA SST

Anti-Satellite Arrow

Avro STV Space Threshold Vehicle

Chapter 30

THE ASTRA RADAR/FIRE-CONTROL SYSTEM

In the beginning, Avro quite logically specified the Hughes MX-1179 radar/fire-control system for the Arrow, and once the Velvet Glove was cancelled went along with the Hughes Falcon missile, both items being designed to work well together. It was a logical choice and it seemed reasonable to assume that both Hughes' products would be ready and well developed by the time the Arrow needed them. It was also slated to enter service on an aircraft that was certain to equip the USAF, and therefore its price would be reasonable based on a larger production run. The Falcon missile had the added advantage of being built in radar-guided and heat-seeking versions, giving added insurance and operational flexibility. What the Avro engineers were really waiting for, however, were the larger, more powerful and longer-range air-launched missiles anticipated in the coming years—weapons well-suited to the Arrow's massive weapons bay. The AA-10 Eagle missile in the US was a promising early candidate.

The RCAF seemed to go along with these choices in radar and weapons until 1956 when RCAF Chief of Operational Requirements (COR) Easton went shopping in the United States. Being aware (and overly-sold) on the emerging digital and real-time technology, A/V/M Easton returned with a determination to acquire not only an active guidance missile, but also the most powerful, flexible and sophisticated new radar/fire-control system conceived to that date. Easton decided that the Arrow should have an extremely sophisticated, fully transistorised, all-can-do radar that would be integrated with the navigation and flight control systems. Astra 1 was to incorporate ground-mapping capabilities, home-on-jamming, angle-off-jamming, electronic countermeasures (ECM), *and* integrate the world's first infra-red detection and tracking system.[190] It was also to incorporate twin, coupled radar altimeters, which would have allowed terrain following and would, with the ground-mapping capability, have given the Arrow highly advanced bombing capabilities. The problem was finding somebody willing to take on such risky and early development work.

An Astra 1 development set, circa 1958.

With the award of the MX-1179 contract for the '1954 Interceptor' project, Hughes emerged as the world leader in radar/fire-control systems for fighter aircraft. The RCAF, not illogically, wanted them to develop a very powerful, multi-mode radar for the Arrow. The helpful authorities in the USAF suggested they contract RCA to develop it, partly because, as they said, *they* wanted a second source for this kind of equipment to reduce their dependency on Hughes. It is bizarre to realise that they certainly could have secured a second source by picking up the phone and calling Westinghouse who made most of the US Navy's radar/fire-control systems. This was, perhaps, a symptom of the era's elevated inter-service rivalry, something that had been encouraged in Washington as a means of encouraging the military services to generate public support for their funding.[191] AVM Easton of the RCAF dutifully complied.

On reading the ASTRA progress reports, it becomes clear that there were to be *two* ASTRA versions. A fully transistorised, but analogue Mk.1 set, and a fully transistorised, fully *digital, pulse-Doppler* version; ASTRA 2.[192] This meant it would have become the first 'look-down, shoot-down' radar in the world. Most people think the F-14 Tomcat had the first 'look-down, shoot-down' radar in the world. Yet it's radar, the AWG-9 by Hughes, was not fully transistorised, and was not digital.

Avro documents reveal that at this time RCA was building, under license from Hughes, several radars, including the MG-3 which was used in the late Avro CF-100s and early Convair F-102s. The MG-13, however, was marketed as an RCA design for the later F-102s, and RCA considered it their proprietary technology. Hughes apparently disagreed, feeling it was only a development of their MG-3 system, and a lawsuit was either threatened or actually carried out over patent infringement.

Floyd's documents describe a meeting he had with the head of RCA, a Mr. Hertzberg. He told Floyd that the ASTRA system was going to be, essentially, a development of the MG-13 radar. Floyd was quite worried that it would never come to be because of Hughes' technology, and the reassurances of the RCA chief, as described in the note to file, are not convincing to this observer. From this it appears that the ASTRA 1 system was not to be an extreme leap in technology, but was to incorporate many more functions that had formerly been specialized in various radars, into one "all-can-do" system. RCA had a brilliant R&D section, working with very advanced technology for defense and other purposes. It is plausible that RCA merely used their MG-13 as the skeleton of a system that, through replacement of each subsystem, they would radically upgrade into a much more advanced system. Whatever the origin, it was to be the most powerful and flexible system envisioned to that date, and this required advanced data processing capability. ASTRA, in either form, was to introduce "real time" computation to airborne operations in a multi-role installation along with the replacement of vacuum tube technology with transistors. This was, to say the least, a real leap in technology, flexibility and operational philosophy.

Avro engineering documents also reveal that RCA's president, Hertzberg, revealed to J.C. Floyd that RCA had won, with the ASTRA 2 system, the contract to produce the radar/fire-control system for the LRIX, aka the F-108, which was being funded by the USAF.[193] Upon learning this, Smye proposed a way for Canada to equip the Arrow with a fire-control system and missile that would have saved all the unnecessary development costs. He proposed that the RCAF wait for RCA's ASTRA 2 system and adopt the system in the F-106 or F-101, along with the Sparrow 3, all of which were already essentially finished development. That way Canada wouldn't have to pay *any* development costs, and would, after a few years, end up with a radar/fire-control that was superior to ASTRA 1 anyway by purchasing a USAF-developed ASTRA 2. Furthermore, since Canada was being pushed to adopt nuclear weapons, it was pointed out that the Sparrow 3 was being developed into a nuclear version, the Sparrow X.[194] These suggestions were, unfortunately, ignored. Actually, these suggestions resulted in Avro getting a bloody nose from the DDP for sticking it where they felt it didn't belong. More bad rumours about Avro reverberated through the halls of power as a result.

It is known that, once the F-108 (aka LRIX) was cancelled, the radar and avionics from it went directly into the YF-12A interceptor version of what became the SR-71 Blackbird.[195] Yet the YF-12A's radar is recorded as having been built by Hughes, and was called the ASG-18. Avro engineering documents from 1957 also reveal that Hughes had also begun work on a pulse-Doppler radar at that time. It emerges that Hughes was actually developing *two* pulse-Doppler radars as of the early 1960s, the AWG-9 for the F-111B, and the ASG-18 for the YF-12A. Tests of the ASG-18 in the YF-12A credit it with the *amazing* detection range of 500 miles. This radar, like both Astra versions, also provided launch computation for an active-guidance missile, and used a large 38-inch dish. Since RCA got out of the fighter radar/fire-control business about this time it may be that Hughes inherited Astra 2 and renamed it the ASG-18.

Originally ASTRA was projected to cost 72 million dollars to develop. By 1958 that projection had leaped to 208 million dollars.[196] That is roughly as much as was spent developing and building the Arrow up to first flight *with* developing the Iroquois up to cancellation. No wonder Fred Smye railed against ASTRA and predicted it would result in the end of an independent RCAF, and the end of the Arrow program, and probably the end of Avro itself.[197] After all, once a design team like that assembled for the Arrow and Iroquois disperses, no amount of industrial infrastructure and equipment can replace them without a massive amount of money being spent, and even then risks are astronomical. With the signing of NORAD and with Black Friday, Smye was proven prophetic.

ASTRA 1 and the APQ-72 of the F-4 Phantom bear incredible similarities, right down to the "switchology" (military jargon for the arrangement of switches, gauges and controls etc.). US documents I received from Westinghouse's Historical Electronics Museum in Linthicum Maryland state it cost them merely *one million dollars* and a *single year* to develop the APQ-72. Canada dumped at *least* 40 million into ASTRA over a two year period, and RCA had been designing aspects of it before it was specified for the Arrow. The APQ-72 radar is listed as the "second" radar in the West to incorporate infra-red detection and tracking, and the first one to use a shock-isolated, retractable, rack mounted system. In reality ASTRA 1 was first on both counts. Westinghouse was, of course, a subcontractor on ASTRA/Sparrow. Westinghouse brochures state that the APQ-72 was developed from their APQ-50 used in the US Navy's Douglas Demon, yet they share only two common operational abilities, and used different methods (electric vs. hydraulic) of slewing the emitter/receiver dish. ASTRA 1 and APQ-72 had virtually everything in common, and that is a long list indeed and includes the arrangements and connections for the ground power cart.[198] Westinghouse service documents state that the APQ-72 used miniature vacuum tubes and "discreet components" meaning transistors and perhaps even early integrated circuits. However, ASTRA 1 was specified to be entirely transistorised according to RCA progress reports, and Jim Floyd says that the Arrow made use of early integrated circuits.

In an uncorroborated testament, a gentleman who worked on ASTRA at CARDE describes how, at the end, he was personally responsible for dismantling six completed ASTRA 1 pre-production sets, and that they appeared to him to be good, functional sets.[199] CARDE conducted a technical analysis of the Arrow with ASTRA 1 and commented in early 1958 that the combination appeared "very promising". This evaluation was classified and it was not released to *anyone* until 1960, when it was too late.[200] The ex-CARDE official also told me that the infra-red detection and tracking feature of ASTRA was proprietary Canadian technology, and that the United States was so desperate to acquire this technology for ICBM launch detection that they started jacking the price of ASTRA through the roof to get it. As mentioned, the USAF owned the system Canada was paying for, and thus had great leverage on its development, production and use. In September of 1958 Diefenbaker cancelled Canadian involvement in ASTRA and Sparrow, signing off on any technology or production interests.

So what happened? I believe ASTRA 1 was repackaged and 'dumbed-down' slightly in concept and technology to become the APQ-72. To accommodate this powerful, multi-mode radar the nose of the F-4H1 Phantom had to be cosmetically-altered in a counter-intuitive direction. I suspect that ASTRA 2 was given to Hughes to perfect, and evolved into the ASG-18 system of the YF-12A. RCA, busy with missile and space technology, seems to have been encouraged to get out of the fighter radar/fire-control business—with Hughes patent infringement being a possible additional motivator. Mario Pesando, who was a senior engineer at Victory Aircraft and Avro Canada, later ran some of RCA's space efforts, including PROJECT SAINT, which was for a space-based SAtellite INTerceptor.[201] He mentioned that "if anybody could have pulled off ASTRA, it was the RCA division where it was designed." He added that it wasn't designed at RCA Camden (New Jersey), as most people believe, but at a secret advanced research facility in up-state New York and that the people there were simply brilliant and were developing extremely advanced technology.[202]

190 According to Fred Hotson's The De Havilland Canada Story, the infra-red technology came from de Havilland's Special Projects Group. It would be interesting to know how much of this Canadian leadership in infra-red technology came from Britain since de Havilland in Britain was, by this time, heavily into the missile business.
191 This is mentioned in both Truman, and Ike: His Life and Times
192 1957 RCA progress reports for Astra 1 and 2.
193 Floyd: Private & Confidential memo to Bob Lindley, 12 June, 1957
194 Floyd: Confidential memo to Fred Smye titled: Notes on Discussions with G/C Foottit, 28 June, 1957
195 Interview with US defence engineer Evan Mayerle. Mayerle worked with Boeing Rocketdyne on missiles and collaborates with authors on American defence history pieces. He claims North American Aviation veterans insist on this, and also claims there are photos in the public domain which prove this assertion. It is not felt to be a big secret.
196 Campagna: Requiem for a Giant
197 Canadian Aviation and the Avro Arrow; Frederick T. Smye, Pg. 69: "A last futile attempt was made to change the decision on grounds which seemed obvious and with a concluding warning that this decision would certainly threaten the Arrow program and, hence, the very independence of the RCAF if, indeed, it would not kill both... The date of this meeting was July 1958."
198 APQ-72 introductory service training manual by Westinghouse, 1960, and ASTRA progress reports by RCA, plus photos included in Arrow Scrapbook and Avro Arrow.
199 Interview in North Bay Ontario, September 2002
200 Campagna: Storms of Controversy
201 Interview with Mario Pesando, fall 2002 and US Dept. of Defense.
202 Interview with Mario Pesando, fall 2002

Chapter 31

ELECTRONICS, COMPUTERISATION AND TELEMETRY

Avro was clearly leading the industry in the application of 'at the speed of light' computing. Even the scale Arrow test models that were launched on NIKE boosters and their corresponding ground telemetry truck shared real time computational capability, and were, in fact, the first examples of the practical application of this technology in the world.[203] What Avro launched off Point Petre Ontario, and at NACA Langley Virginia, were similar in core technology to NASA's Project Gemini, and superior to the technology of Mercury.

An Arrow telemetry model launch at Wallops Island Virginia. (via Jim Floyd)

To develop the 'fully powered' flight controls, Avro modified a CF-100 to incorporate this technology, terming the resulting airframe 'the Iron Bird'. One Avro technician informs the author that during the last phase of testing of this unit, while trying to ascertain the effects of feedback and other phenomena, the powered-up airframe started to shake and buck violently, ultimately severely damaging itself. A great many lessons were learned in this program and were incorporated into the Arrow.

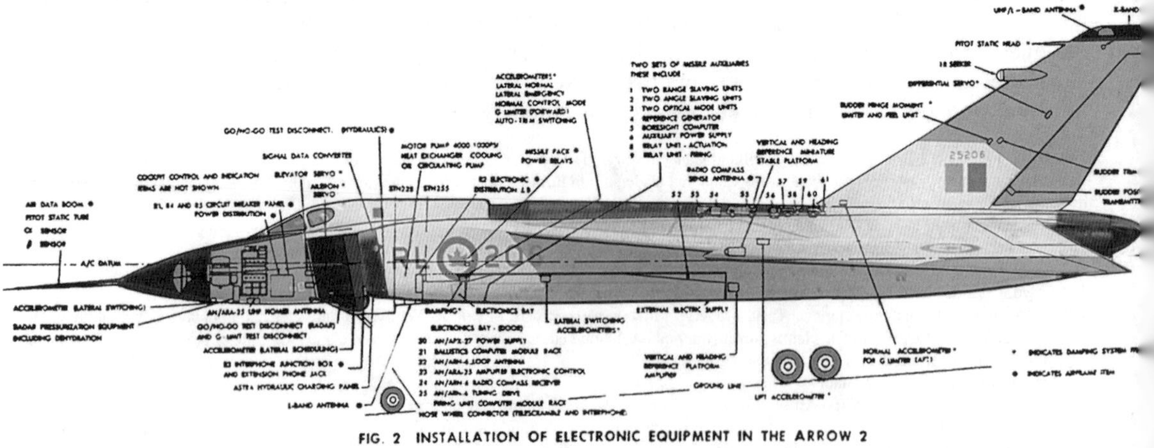

FIG. 2 INSTALLATION OF ELECTRONIC EQUIPMENT IN THE ARROW 2

With the Arrow, signals were transmitted and received at the speed of light and were used to report on the functions of the craft on data downlink, and respond to real time commands transmitted at real time on data uplink. This used the same key processors as Whirlwind, which is what the NORAD detection, tracking and ground control were based on, and they used it in the mid-1950s, almost a decade early considering Project Gemini was the next machine to use the same level of technology. As Chris Gainor's *Arrows to the Moon* shows, the same people (from Avro) were involved in both programs.

The Arrow engineers took these components and concepts and developed them in the Arrow itself, resulting in the first aircraft in the world designed to ultimately be able to take off itself, fly itself, navigate itself, fight, and even land, without pilot input. Spud Potocki, an Arrow test pilot, documented that he achieved several automatic take-offs and landings with the Arrow. The basic processor for this function was made by Honeywell, also the prime contractor for later electronic flight control systems in NASA's Mercury and Gemini projects, the X-15 hypersonic rocket-plane, and the SR-71 Blackbird. On the Arrow, the main component was installed and functional in all the Arrows, located just behind the air conditioning exhaust. This and other electronic packages (then called "black boxes") were orange because Avro, in another example of advanced thinking, decided to colour code basic subsystems to ease maintenance.

A section of Avro's analogue computer facilities. (via Jim Floyd)

Avro made early use of computers in the design process, and, initially, relied on an NCR 102A analogue system, plus a Ferranti which Avro England had developed for analysis of their delta winged aircraft and had provided to their Canadian sister company. They were analogue, vacuum tube machines. Once it became available to them in 1957, Avro acquired the largest real-time, solid state mainframe in the world (the now-famous IBM 704) with the highest capacity of what would probably now be termed "flash memory". These were, rather than micro-processors, magnetic amplifiers, with magnetic tape drives and punch tape being used for data storage and software. It was on the restricted list in 1957 but Avro rented one for the then astronomical price of one million dollars a year.

A corner of the IBM 704 computer room at Avro. (via Jim Floyd)

The heart of the 'real time', or 'at-the-speed-of-light' computation Avro had built into the rocket launched models, and as employed by the IBM 704, was "magnetic amplifier" technology. It was also at the heart of the WHIRLWIND system then being developed for NORAD. Before the development of the microprocessor, this technology bridged the analogue and digital ages. Avro was developing expertise in telemetry, guidance and other exotic electronics technologies years ahead of any organised competition. They had already developed methods of employing their analogue computers to do the mundane calculations of many design aspects, and the IBM 704 allowed Avro to really begin to exploit the number crunching capacity of this new-technology mainframe. It was used to model various flight parameters and test the effects of aerodynamic and centre of gravity changes to the Arrow. Stability, vibration and flutter modes, control effects and other work was done on the computers to allow them to refine the design and make accurate performance projections. Important, indeed pioneering work in the transonic and supersonic performance areas was done on the IBM 704. Avro probably deserves to be credited with having taken the first steps towards what is now termed 3-Dimensional, Computational Fluid Dynamics (CFD). Structural matrix work was also done on this computer, and it was even used to run the Arrow flight simulator, which was also connected to every actual flight control component in the aircraft under full power, and was used to develop the Arrow's redundant, dispersed, solid state, real time, flight control and automatic stabilisation system. Clearly Avro was making every effort to justify the IBM 704's annual million dollar rental fee.

For the main air data computer's reference data, the Arrow had a miniature high-speed gyroscope, working as the aircraft's inertial reference, located at the aircraft's centre of mass. Redundant systems attempted to keep this early inertial unit properly 'caged'. Components were dispersed near where they were required to reduce cable runs and reduce the potential consequences of localised battle damage, facilitate maintenance, and reduce development risks, while easing future modification or improvement.

In the Arrow, for the first time in aviation history, the stick did not control the hydraulics for the flight control surfaces. The computer checked the aircraft's performance state and the pilot (or data-link) inputs, and then decided what control surface movements were required. Pilot inputs were measured by the first 'stick force transducer' and calculated how much change to make based on performance data, and then moved a servo a calculated amount to let the first flying 4,000 psi hydraulic system move the hydraulic actuators in the wing and fin. Only then would the stick or rudder pedals move, however, it all happened so fast that it felt completely normal.

A big advantage of the computerised flight control system was that it allowed the Arrow's designers to design into the plane marginal or even negative stability factors, another first (by many years). The Arrow was intentionally designed to accept marginal stability, going from moderately positive to neutral on the pitch axis, and from slightly positive to moderately negative on the yaw axis. Because of the extra instability in the yaw axis, every aspect of it was at least double redundant, except the single redundant hydraulic actuator itself. Perhaps now you can appreciate how truly advanced the Arrow was. We weren't able to really compare it to anything until today because there was nothing to compare it to until today. They wrote the book in terms of the modern method, yet the book had to be written all over again once Avro was killed and the engineers dispersed.

The following are the technologies introduced on the Arrow from analysis done for the author's first book *Avro Aircraft & Cold War Aviation.*

ARROW BENCHMARKS:

1) The first fly-by-wire flight control system.
2) The first fly-by-wire flight control system using solid-state components, operating in 'real time'.
3) The first fly-by-wire flight control system with at least single redundancy.
4) The first fly-by-wire flight control system designed to be coupled with the computerised navigation and automatic search and track radar (ASTRA).
5) The first fly-by-wire flight control system providing artificial feedback, or feel, to the pilot.
6) The first fly-by-wire flight control system that was flyable from ground installations through data uplink, with data downlink systems reporting. (This, along with its designers, became the basis of the data-link fly-by-wire systems for Mercury, Gemini and Apollo.)
7) The first aircraft to have its aerodynamic design aided by solid-state (real time) computers. Avro thus appears to be the company that evolved the technique now referred to as Computational Fluid Dynamics.
8) The first aircraft to have its structural design aided by solid-state computers.
9) The first aircraft to have complete hydraulic and electronic systems development rigs (simulators), generally using actual aircraft components whenever possible, coupled to their computers to produce a realistic computerized flight simulator.
10) The first aircraft to have a pulse-Doppler, "look-down, shoot-down" radar designed for it. (The second was the F-14 Tomcat, although ASTRA II was to be fully digital, while the Tomcat's AWG-9 was not digital. In fact, the first aircraft in service to have radar/fire control systems integrated with a flight control system of equal conceptual technology to the ASTRA-Arrow was the F-18 Hornet.)
11) The first aircraft designed with marginal, or negative, static stability factors. This was done to

ensure good manoeuvrability across its very wide flight envelope while keeping trim drag to a minimum thus allowing a larger flight envelope.

12) The first aircraft to have an advanced, integrated, bleed-bypass system from its self-adjusting intakes to its extractor-nozzle exhaust. (The F-104 is credited with being the first to introduce bleed-bypass integration but it was comparatively rudimentary and probably of similar sophistication to that introduced on the Jetliner years earlier.)

13) The first aircraft to have a by-pass turbojet designed for it and the first to integrate the bleed-by-pass and cooling systems of the engine, intakes and extractor nozzle.

14) The first aircraft to have its engines located at the extreme rear of the aircraft. In fact it was about the first jet fighter to have what might be termed "longitudinal spacing" of all its major systems. Previous to the Arrow most aircraft designers had tried to locate fuel tanks, weaponry and engines as close to the centre of gravity and centre of lift as possible. This contributed to their being "fat" in aerodynamic terms, which is why so many of them ran into 'area rule' problems.

15) The first aircraft to have major components machined using Computer Numeric Control (CNC) equipment. (The second is believed to be the F-111 Aardvark)

16) The first aircraft to have major components and fasteners made of Titanium.

17) The first aircraft to use a 4,000 psi hydraulic system. (The second was the B-1 bomber)

18) The first supersonic aircraft designed to have better than one-to-one thrust-to-weight ratio at close to combat weight (allowing it to accelerate while climbing vertically) The "Reaper" ground-attack version of the Gloster Meteor was around 1-1 thrust, but was not supersonic. The first supersonic aircraft to compete in this area was the F-15A Eagle.

19) The Arrow combined the lowest thickness-chord ratio (thickness of the wing compared to the length {not span}) wing with the lowest wing-loading (surface area of the wing divided by the weight of the aircraft) of any high-capacity service design. Both are crucial to low supersonic drag, good manoeuvrability and high speed at altitude.

The Arrow 2 design included provision for "chaff and flare" (chaff being radar jamming filaments with flare being heat-seeking missile confusing pyrotechnic flares), active countermeasures, while ASTRA 1 and 2 radar/fire-control systems were to incorporate its own passive and active electronic counter-measures (ECM), including Infra-Red detection, tracking and launch computation (the world's first), home-on-jamming (helping the plane to navigate to the jamming aircraft), radar warning (telling the aircraft when it was being tracked or targeted), etc. It was a fully modern compliment and introduced sophistication which is today *de rigeur* to the world of multi-role and air-superiority fighters.

The Arrow was designed to out-fly, out-think, and out-fight, with its own on board missiles, any expected threat until about 1970. Unlike any aircraft save the heavy bombers, the Arrow was capable of carrying several *guided* missiles capable of nuclear armament, considerable 'stand off' range and high supersonic speeds. This high performance, even when heavily loaded, combined with the capability of the kinds of weapons it could carry, gave the Arrow more potential flexibility than most aircraft built to this day. Also unlike missiles, the Arrow could be dispatched to visually-identify intruders, it could also be dispatched to do tactical reconnaissance (it has been said that the reason the Arrow was feared by American interests was because it could "shoot down the U-2". While it could certainly have done so, a more likely cause for concern would be the emerging probability that the Arrow might be able to match the flight performance of the CIA's next-generation spyplane. The top secret Project SUNTAN (for a Mach 2.5, 70,000 feet spyplane) was in the works at the famed 'Skunk Works' at Lockheed's Burbank California complex, and at a secret location in Florida, under the project designation CL-400. US calculations of the Arrow's true performance capability through wind tunnel data, plus intelligence on the Mach 3+, 70,000 ft. +, Arrow Mk. 3 design may well have had a heavy influence on the cancellation of the CL-400 Suntan aircraft. These Arrow projections may also have been critical in the development of the A-12 specification, which culminated in the SR-71 Blackbird program—still the fastest piloted turbojet aircraft ever built. It seems unreasonable in today's world to imagine an upstart bunch of British and Canadian engineers making the mighty US military-industrial complex nervous, or at least that part of it devoted to producing fighters and jet engines. However, flight performance envelope graphs, accumulated and transposed by your's truly for *Avro Aircraft & Cold War Aviation,* show that no medium or long-range armed fighter—to this day—could match the Arrow's 1G combat weight performance curve, except the F-22 Raptor, now entering service in the USAF.

203 Personal testimony from J.C. Floyd and other primary sources, plus Gainor's Arrows to the Moon.

Chapter 32

FIRST SALES EFFORTS

From 1951 to 1953 the Arrow was only a project study. During the RCAF investigation into US and British manufacturers, both nations were told that Canada would buy a plane from either country if they produced something comparable to the RCAF specification, even after the Arrow program was started.[204] The Arrow studies were cancelled in 1954 [205], after the scathing assessment by the NAE and NACA, then re-started in 1955—but only after receiving encouragement from NACA (after a presentation by Avro) *and* the USAF. By this time all the aircraft then under development as interceptors in the United States had been rejected by the RCAF as unsuitable for Canadian requirements.

In 1955, before the NORAD agreement was signed, and before the Arrow program left the paper phase and became a genuine production program, the RCAF approached the USAF and asked them to give their appraisal of the technical and military merits of the Arrow, and to state whether they would be willing to purchase any. Their view was that the CF-105 and Iroquois engine projects were technically sound (they could hardly have said otherwise since the British, and other western nations were also investigating it and commenting favourably). They pointed out that with its superior range and speed that the Arrow would be a good aircraft for the first line of defense of North America and that the program should go ahead as planned. They added that the fact it used a different missile than the USAF aircraft provided a measure of insurance should one or another missile prove ineffective due to jamming or some other unforeseen problem. They also added, however, that the USAF would not be interested in buying Arrows.

The US reasons for declining on the Arrow were:

a) They had in progress the F-106 and F-101, which they stated would be available one to one and a half years earlier than the CF-105.

b) The CF-105 had a combat altitude at least 6,000 feet higher than the F-106 but this advantage would be irrelevant since the F-106's Falcon missiles could climb an additional 13,000 feet to intercept any foreseeable bomber threat.

c) The CF-105 would weigh twice as much as the F-106 and thus the price was expected to be approximately double. [In the final analysis it turned out to be priced about the same.]

d) The F-101B would be inferior to the Arrow by 12,000 feet in combat altitude, by .5 Mach in speed, and about 80 miles in range.

e) The LRIX 1 [the F-108 Rapier] would be operational about three years after the CF-105 and would exceed the combat radius of the Arrow by 600 miles, but would have "about the same speed and altitude capabilities as the CF-105". [206]

204 AMTS report titled: Notes of a Meeting to Review a USAF appraisal of the CF-105 Held at Avro Aircraft, Malton at 0900hrs, 1 Nov.1955 "It was further pointed out that from the commencement of the CF105 programme, the Defence Department had carefully scrutinized all aircraft and guided missile projects under development in the United States and the United Kingdom, with the object of modifying or discontinuing the CF105 programme if such action appeared by virtue of the project being overtaken or duplicated by the efforts of our Allies."
205 According to Jim Floyd in telecon on 9 February, 2004, there was a stop work order placed on the Arrow programme after this devastating assessment by NACA, the DRB, NAE et al.
206 AMTS report titled: "Notes of a Meeting to Review a USAF appraisal of the CF-105 Held at Avro Aircraft, Malton at 0900hrs, 1 Nov.1955"

Chapter 33

ARROWS FOR THE RAF

In late 1955, a month after the USAF appraisal, Jim Floyd was found in Britain consulting with officials within the Hawker Siddeley Group, the RAF, the Royal Aeronautical Society and the Ministry of Supply. At this time the British were concentrating on the Gloster Javelin as their (subsonic) all weather fighter and the English Electric P.1B Lightning as a short-range, Mach 1.5+ day fighter. Due to their analysis of the Soviet threat, they too had let a request for proposals (GOR 329) for a long-range, missile-armed, supersonic, all weather interceptor, quite similar in performance to the Avro Arrow. When Floyd revealed the Arrow design he also invited the British to send a team of experts to Malton in the spring of 1956. The RAF and other British authorities were so interested that a team arrived about a week after Floyd's return from Britain. Their evaluation of the Arrow was very favourable, though they had misgivings about whether the currency issues at home would allow them to buy in Canada. They also felt Avro was underestimating the aircraft's drag by about ten percent. (They were wrong on this count and even Avro overestimated the drag of the Arrow.)

Of course, there was a strong element of national pride at play within Whitehall and British industrial cliques, and even British elements of Hawker Siddeley were competing with Avro Canada for the GOR 329 contract. Sir Sydney Camm penned several elegant designs, none of which would have matched the Arrow in range, payload, flexibility, or all-round performance. In fact, I think it is safe to say that the GOR 329 design studies turned into an effort to produce a British design that could beat the Arrow. Floyd, in discussion with British military and government research scientists, found them quite surprised by the performance promised by the Arrow and they began considering it for their GOR 329 specification. In a letter to Sir Roy Dobson describing this trip, Floyd wrote:

> "With regard to the trip itself, I believe that it was well worthwhile for a number of reasons, one of the most important to me being that the discussions with Roy Ewans and the boys at Woodford, and also with Nicholson and his experts at the R.A.E., made me more sure than ever that we are really on the right track on the CF-105, especially with regard to the aerodynamics side… I spent a day with Nicholson, Chief of the Supersonic Aerodynamics Group at the R.A.E., Mr. Newby, and Dr. Kuchemann, and a number of other people, and asked them point blank whether they felt there was anything on the CF-105 which would cause them to lose any sleep,… Mr. Nicholson said emphatically that there was not, and that he still believed the CF-105 is more advanced than any contemporary aircraft on this side of the Iron Curtain. He indicated that the R.A.E. put in good reports to the Ministry of Supply from time to time.
>
> "I believe I was encouraged most of all by a visit to my old friend, Bob Lickley, [They had both worked under Sydney Camm at Hawkers for a time during the war] Chief Designer of Fairey's, since they have been having a lot of success with their delta…and is considered by Farnborough to be far superior, performance wise, than the calculations would have indicated… The Fairey delta is closer to the CF-105 than anything else that is flying at the moment…which is certainly encouraging to me personally, and in the absence of our extensive supersonic wind tunnel tests, should give us a great deal of satisfaction.
>
> "I had an excellent discussion with A/V/M Satterley and his people, and also with Sir Thomas Pike and Mr. Handel Davies, Scientific Advisor to the Air Ministry. I also visited Sir John Baker and A/V/M Silyn Roberts, and Mr. Woodward-Nutt, the Principle Director of Aircraft Research and Development in the Ministry of Supply.
>
> "They were *all* very keen technically on the CF-105 and considered it to be the most potent weapon in its time scale… There is no question that there is genuine interest in the aircraft in the U.K., and especially in its collision course armament, and I believe a lot of the spade work has now been done, and it is now a matter of follow-up and keeping the interest of the people concerned, which we will endeavour to do."[207] [italics added]

Floyd suggested that the RAF and MOS send a team to Avro to look at the Arrow in the spring of 1956. Sir Reginald Maudling, the British Minister of Supply, asked for special secrecy during this visit. The British evaluation was very positive, although they assumed, probably for reasons of caution, that the Arrow would have 10-15% higher drag than Avro assumed, and would probably face some schedule slippage—very common on an aircraft of this sophistication, both then and now. As such it was presumed that the plane would not quite meet the GOR 329 specification in terms of speed and altitude capabilities, although it was acknowledged it would have a vastly superior radar and tracking system to anything available in Europe. They also found Avro's intake design "particularly laudable". As a result of this assessment the RAF's stop-gap interceptor program, Hawker Siddeley's own so-called "Thin Wing Javelin (TWJ)" development was cancelled, and, according to Tony Buttler in *British Secret Projects: Jet Fighters since 1950,* the Arrow was selected by the RAF to fill their need for a supersonic all weather fighter. Derek Wood, an exceptionally accomplished British aviation writer, wrote of the impact the Arrow design had on the British RAF, government, and thus, industry—that news of this "super fighter" upset all the designs in the works in Britain, and this included the Supermarine Swift, the Supersonic Hunter, the TWJ, and a host of emerging designs, including a number of advanced design studies. In the end, Britain, more from pride than logic, selected the Fairey Delta III design, which was a rather inferior copy of the Arrow 3. It too was never built. All of these designs competed for the British GOR 329 specification, which the Arrow 2 design suited almost perfectly. Had the British not been padding the Arrow's drag coefficient, they would perhaps have realised this in time to prevent the disruption of their industry and air force.

There has been a great deal of conjecture, much of it derogatory, about why Britain failed to produce a serious supersonic fighter throughout the 1950s and '60s. Part of the reason is that the British 'establishment' experts decided in 1946 that supersonic flight was impractical and dangerous to human life. As a result, Britain fell a generation behind in aircraft design, and had an exceedingly difficult time making up for lost time. (This might suggest one reason American manufacturers and other powers were so disinclined to purchase the Arrow. It may have resulted in them permanently losing technological leadership in this area to Canada and Hawker Siddeley.) By the mid-1950s, however, British designers were producing viable supersonic designs, but none of them combined the simplicity, performance, technology and adaptability of the Arrow. As a result, one could say that the British did design an excellent supersonic interceptor, however it was done in Canada. Wood's *Project Cancelled* and Buttler's *British Secret Projects* both show the myriad of designs and variations that British designers produced in the mid-1950s for the GOR 329 specification. None of them were nearly as elegant in terms of design as the Arrow, so none of them were produced. Wilf Farrance, a design section head at Avro, has mentioned that the American evaluation of the Arrow concluded it was a 'near optimum' design. Surviving documentation shows that the British were also very interested in the radar and electronics of the Arrow, since they had nothing to compare. In fact, the British were very impressed with even the CF-100's 'collision course' capability, and had nothing to match it. For these reasons, J.C. Floyd has written that "there was no doubt in my mind that Britain would have eventually bought the Arrow". This author's examination of Floyd's original documentation from this period, and the few public resources on genuine Arrow performance, along with British design efforts and political/financial wrangling over GOR 329, (not to mention Arrow pricing vs. projected costs for British designs) suggest very strongly that Floyd's evaluation was correct.

While the RAF may have wanted the Arrow, the politicians had other plans. Duncan Sandys was then Defense Minister in the UK and shared the belief that missiles had rendered manned aircraft obsolete. His decision to cancel virtually all manned military aircraft programs in Britain came as an especially rude shock to the British industry since Sandys, while Air Minister, had previously been instrumental in granting government approval for the concurrent production of *three* long-range jet bomber designs. While he was responsible for the funding of three concurrent bomber programs which would soon be vulnerable to SAMs, he was also responsible for the abandonment of high-performance fighters which weren't and wouldn't be for many years. This may have been due to his work during WW II studying possible defenses against the V-1 and V-2 missiles which the Nazis unleashed on Britain after D-Day 1944. It may also have been due to consultation with American experts—particularly the CIA—which then began lobbying against fighters and for missiles (to foreign countries at least). All the vociferous Arrow critics neglect to discuss the Arrow's ability to carry, *internally,* long-range missiles that were *seventeen feet long,* with the aircraft's mobility granting a major advantage in survivability of the deterrent.

Not that some British experts weren't enthusiastic participants in the destruction of the British aerospace industry. Sir Solly Zuckerman, then the chief defense scientist in Britain, stated once that "there is more technology in the little finger of a single American designer than in all of Britain."[208] One would imagine Sir Barnes Wallis was insulted. Of course, such a view could hardly have better represented the interests of the US military-industrial complex. In April 1957, Sandys brought down his notorious White Paper on defense. Sandys appears to have succumbed to the CIA's super-secret intelligence, which was diametrically opposed to that of the rest of the Western intelligence community, and sounded the false alarm of the 'missile gap'. Of course, the CIA became famous for, in order of appearance, the 'intelligence gap', the 'bomber gap' the 'missile gap', and even a psychic spy gap.[209] All of which, some would say, seem to have contributed to closing a gap that military industrialists, financiers, and intelligence agencies felt existed in their funding. Whatever the motivations, the result of Sandys' White Paper called for the cancellation of all manned military aircraft programs in Britain with a priority shift to an independent British strategic nuclear missile: Blue Streak. When it too was cancelled in favour of US systems—due to dubious politics—Sandys developed a solid streak of economic and technical nationalism and thereafter worked very hard to ensure the Concorde was produced.

The Avro Arrow was in contention for GOR 329 by the time of Sandys' White Paper, (having seen off the Group's own 'Thin Wing' Javelin) and was still beating all the continuing British design proposals, especially on timing, simplicity, price and particularly in radar and avionics. But with the 1957 British White Paper on defense, it suddenly had its requirement disappear. Avro UK was also affected.

GOR 330 had also been released in 1954 and called for a Mach 2.5, long-range, strike-reconnaissance aircraft. After a number of design changes Avro was contracted to produce a mock-up, which was almost complete when Sandy's White Paper also abolished this requirement. A few books describe this aircraft and note a design progression from four afterburning engines in two wing-tip pods to one using two afterburning turbojets on each wing. Prior to this work, no public sources mention the Iroquois as having been considered for the Avro 730, yet towards the end of the program it was; as surviving Avro Canada documents show. It would have been an ideal engine for the Avro 730 since it was considerably smaller and lighter than the few emerging contemporary engines capable of similar levels of thrust. Though these terminations hurt Hawker Siddeley particularly badly, they were only two of a number of cancelled aircraft programs that really pulled the proverbial rug from beneath the entire British aircraft industry. Similar cancellations of promising jet airliners also helped decimate a justifiably proud industry. The net benefactors of these policies were, by default, American manufacturers and financial institutions, with a corresponding increase in American political, military and economic dominance of the West.

Artist's conception of the Avro 730 long-range strike-reconnaissance aircraft. (image by the author)

Perhaps it is timely to compare the competing American aircraft programs with the Arrow.

207 Confidential letter from J.C. Floyd to Sir Roy Dobson, December, 1955.
208 Wood, Derek. Project Cancelled. The disaster of Britain's abandoned aircraft projects. London: Jane's Publishing Limited, 1986
209 This resulted in their Project MK-Ultra

Chapter 34

VOODOOS, DARTS, PHANTOMS AND ARROWS: THE CONVAIR DELTAS

Convair became privy to the research on delta-winged jets undertaken in Nazi Germany by Dr. Alexander Lippisch and established an experimental fighter program to exploit this technology. The resulting XF-92 experimental plane failed to even approach its expectations, and revealed a tendency to pitch up without pilot input in manoeuvres. As a result of poor speed and altitude performance, the project for a fighter version; the F-92, was cancelled.

In 1947, at the annual Toshino Airshow in Moscow, several new Soviet jet fighters and bombers were revealed. This airshow was a strong factor in establishing the myth of the "bomber gap" and gave urgency to American plans to produce a supersonic fighter. The defense analysts in the US were projecting that the Soviets could have a jet bomber force capable of striking North America by 1954, and so a requirement for a supersonic jet interceptor was created, to be in service by that year. Thus was born the appropriately named "1954 Interceptor" project in the United States Air Force. It was anticipated to require an advanced radar, missile weaponry, and advanced jet engines, all of which were given separate project designations.

The airframe portion of the weapons system was designated MX-1554 and American manufacturers were invited to submit proposals in June of 1950. Nine aircraft designs by six manufacturers were submitted. Ironically, the two designs chosen were the two worst in the eyes of the USAF scientists and planners. The lucky winners were Republic Aviation with their AP-57 (XF-103) concept, and Convair with a delta design based on knowledge acquired in the XF-92 program. The Republic design, however, required variable turbojet/ramjet propulsion and very advanced materials and production technology, and was given a much lower priority than the Convair XF-102.

> "The Convair entry in the MX-1554 project was closely related to the experimental XF-92A which Convair had built in 1948 to provide data for the proposed F-92 Mach 1.5 fighter designed in consultation with Dr. Alexander Lippisch. Dr. Lippisch had done pioneering work on delta-winged aircraft in Germany during the war, and Convair had become convinced that the delta configuration provided a viable solution to the problems of supersonic flight. The XF-92A had been the first powered delta-winged aircraft to fly, but the F-92 project had itself been cancelled before any prototype could be built.
>
> On September 11, 1951, Convair received a contract for its delta winged design which was designated F-102."[210]

The YF-102 prototype. Really limited to transonic flight, it could not achieve supersonic speeds in level flight. (USAF Museum)

The initial version of the XF-102 was to be powered by the Westinghouse J40 turbojet, but production aircraft were to receive the Curtiss Wright J67—the license built Bristol Olympus. In an example of vastly inflated performance projections on the part of some manufacturers, the J40 version was projected to achieve Mach 1.88. After the more powerful Pratt & Whitney (P&W) J57 was substituted in the XF-102, it still failed to even break the sound barrier, let alone reach nearly twice that speed in level flight.

"A severe problem cropped up early in 1953, one which was potentially fatal for the entire program. At that time, wind tunnel testing discovered that the initial drag estimates of the YF-102 had been way off, and that the F-102 would be unable to exceed Mach 1. In addition, the maximum altitude would be only 52,400 feet, versus the predicted 57,600 feet, while the combat radius would be reduced from 350 to 200 nautical miles.

Even though early wind tunnel tests had indicated that there would be a problem with excessive drag, it took a long time to convince the Convair engineering staff that there was a problem with their basic design. It was not until August of 1953, that Convair engineers reluctantly agreed to redesign their aircraft. By that time, it was too late to incorporate the required changes in the first ten YF-102 aircraft that had been ordered.

In the meantime, work on the first YF-102s was proceeding at a rapid pace. The first YF-102 was finally completed in the autumn of 1953. It was powered by a J57-P-11, rated at 10,900 lb.s.t. dry and 14,500 lb.s.t. with afterburning. It was trucked from San Diego out to Edwards AFB. It took off at Edwards on its maiden flight on October 24, 1953, with Richard L. Johnson at the controls. In initial tests, severe buffeting was encountered at Mach 0.9. Even more serious, the aircraft proved to be incapable of exceeding the speed of sound in level flight, fully confirming the results of the wind tunnel testing. Additional problems were encountered with the main landing gear, and the fuel system operated erratically. To make matters even worse, the J57-P-11 engine did not develop its full rated power.

The first YF-102 was written off on November 2 in a forced landing following an engine failure. Test pilot Johnson was seriously injured. The cause of the accident was traced to a failure in the Bendix fuel control system. The second YF-102 flew on January 11, 1954. This aircraft was limited to Mach 0.99 in level flight. Dives at higher speeds resulted in severe yaw oscillations. Even in a 30-degree dive, the YF-102 was only able to reach Mach 1.24. Even though an altitude of 47,000 feet could be reached, handling difficulties limited the practical ceiling to only 40,000 feet.

The F-102 program was in BIG trouble. In fact, the performance of the YF-102 was not all that much better than the F-86D Sabre [or Avro's CF-100], which was already in production. If no cure could be found, the whole program would undoubtedly be cancelled."[211]

Work on ten aircraft on the line at Convair was halted, and a major modification program was undertaken to reduce the transonic drag of the Delta Dagger, and to alleviate tip-stalling and pitch-up problems. This was an expensive prospect since the Dagger was the first aircraft produced, from the beginning, on hard tooling—according to the Cook-Craigie Plan.

The F-102A, stretched, with a new canopy, tail blisters, and wing modifications from the YF-102 prototype. Designed for over Mach 1.5, the plane was still barely supersonic.

The wind tunnel tests which so suddenly revealed the Convair engineers' serious under-estimation of drag took place once the first transonic wind tunnel was activated at NACA Langley. Here Dr. Richard Whitcomb perfected the "area rule" principle, and published a paper in 1953 outlining his findings, which the USAF endeavoured to keep secret.[212] The aerodynamic refinements required involved a major program to stretch the design significantly, thereby improving its aerodynamic 'fineness ratio', and reduce cross section according to the 'area rule' concept. The fuselage was lengthened several feet, tail blisters were added, and the wing underwent several design evolutions. Avro's designers already incorporated close to the ideal in terms of area (volume actually) distribution and were in the happy position of being able to check the design in the NACA high speed tunnel and against the "area rule" mathematically, before the design was finalised.

The J67 version was initially just supposed to be an engine installation modification to the F-102 design, and was called the F-102B. But with the F-102A requiring a redesign, the program for the F-102B had become distorted out of recognition. The engine for the F-102B, the J67, was also cancelled and the P&W J75 took its place. With the problems of the prototype starkly revealed on the first flights, a major re-think was called for among the chieftains of the US defense establishment.

To hedge their bets, the USAF decided to have McDonnell develop an interceptor version of their XF-88. It would beat the F-106 into service, and would ultimately be selected by Canada to replace the Arrow. The F-102 did enter production, however, yet missed the 1954 service date by three years. It was also good for no more than Mach 1.2, far below the 1954 interceptor requirement, underscoring the wisdom of the USAF decision to fund the McDonnell interceptor, designated the F-101 Voodoo. It was also decided to change the designation of the F-102B to that of a new aircraft, the F-106 Delta Dart, mostly in reflection of the fact that it was no longer a modified F-102, but, in fact, a different aircraft.

Problems with the missile armament (Falcon missiles), the ground control radar program (SAGE), and the onboard radar (MX-1179) resulted in the substitution of existing systems for the first F-102s with deployment of the MA-1 radar and weapons system, and the whole SAGE concept, being delayed until the F-102B was ready (which was also being delayed to allow for a thorough redesign.) In the same month that a USAF delegation arrived at Avro to evaluate the Arrow, they ordered 17 F-106s—a month before the mock-up was ready. In April 1956, this contract was finalized with the air force, with all 17 aircraft being earmarked for test and development work. On December 26th, 1956, the YF-106 first took to the air. The flight was aborted due to ram-air turbine vibrations, and the fact that the speed brakes would not close. After a myriad of changes were made to the F-102 design, it became apparent that Convair would have to go through much of it again with the F-106, despite area-rule features being designed into it. Performance was considerably below expectations in level flight speed and altitude capabilities, and acceleration was notably poor much above Mach 1.

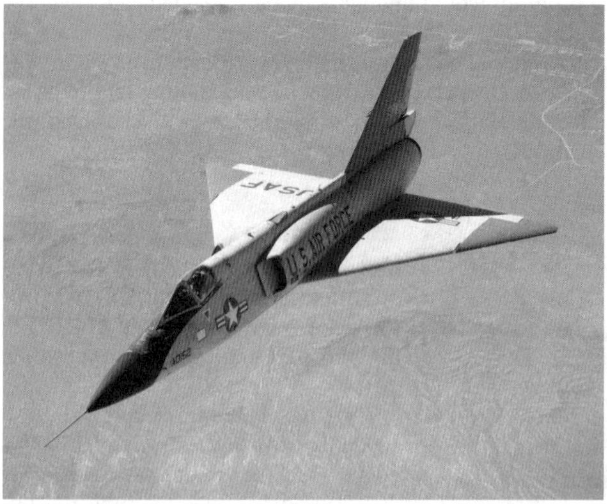

An F-106A Delta Dart flying in the service of NASA's Dryden flight research centre. Notice the longer, slimmer fuselage, compared to the F-102A, with the extra pinch where the wings' volume is greatest. This is done to lessen and smooth the rate of volume expansion of the total aircraft body measured from its nose, which prevents the formation of early, and/or additional, shockwaves in the transonic and supersonic speed ranges. Shockwaves dramatically increase drag, and can cause vibrations, flutter, and even loss of aircraft control. (NASA Dryden)

Convair set about making changes to the design and tooling to accomplish what Avro had done before cutting metal. They thinned the intake lips, altered the intake design and made other improvements to improve engine pressure recovery and reduce drag. Problems were legion. MA-1 and SAGE were still having problems. The side-stick controller was placed back in the centre of the cockpit to meet pilot demands. This was given a rather odd yoke at the top of the control column containing radar controls and other items requiring two-handed operation during an intercept. This too was not popular with many pilots, because it takes the pilot's hand off the throttle during combat.

The wing still had nasty pitch-up problems, and equipment problems were causing nightmares. By September 1958, and with the relative success of the F-101 providing some insurance, the ultimate F-106 order was cut down to a third of the original number originally specified. Considering that this was done in the middle of negotiations with Canada over air defense and the future of the Arrow, it must have reassured the Canadians to know the US was, apparently, cutting back production of interceptors, in line with CIA assurances about their redundancy. The Pentagon also had an ace in the hole regarding future interceptors, the McDonnell F-4 Phantom. As of 1955 this plane was being designed to specialise as an interceptor, and flew—with satisfying results—four months before the F-106 program was cutback. Only 260 additional F-106s were ordered aside from the 35 development aircraft and two prototypes. Shortly after the Arrows and their production line ceased to exist, it was decided to refurbish the 35 development aircraft and issue them to the air defense squadrons. The first squadron F-106s were delivered in May, 1959, but continuing problems meant that the Delta Dart was not declared operational until October 31, 1959.

Problems continued. Engine problems, canopies jettisoning in flight, fire control problems and upgrades, fuel starvation, and other maladies afflicted the plane's entry to service. MA-1 was upgraded no less than 60 times. Flight testing continued into 1961, with each phase revealing a long list of defects. Incorporating them into the design was exascerbated throughout the program because there were so many changes to be made to hard tooling devised to suit the Cooke-Craigie plan. In the case of the F-106, the Cooke-Craigie plan was a disaster. Convair spent more on changing the F-102 airframe (they used the same wings) into that of the F-106 than Avro had spent on developing the entire Arrow Mk.1 and 2 designs, tooling and seven complete airframes, five of them flying. 67 changes to the airframe alone were required to produce the service F-106A from the prototype, and many changes were made in the field.

To underscore the post-Arrow cancellation resurgence of the interceptor in the defense picture of the United States, in 1961 US Secretary of Defense, Robert McNamara, proposed to re-open the F-106 line to produce another 36 aircraft. Since the F-4 Phantom was promising such impressive performance and flexibility, and was already being supported by the USAF, it was decided to pit the Phantom and Delta Dart against one another to assuage their relative merits. Project High Speed produced results 180 degrees out of phase with expectations. The F-4 Phantom proved to have the superior radar for air defense purposes, yet was also a multi-mode system capable of ground attack. Its APQ-72 had longer search, tracking and missile-lock ranges compared to the MX-1179 system. The Delta Dart however, was king of the dogfight. No new F-106s were ordered.

Project Broad Jump was initiated to make long-term solutions to the F-106s chronic problems. It lasted from 1960 to 1963. During this period the 106 received infra-red detection and tracking capability, something that had been designed into the ASTRA system. The F-101B's MG-13 radar system would be similarly upgraded in the early 1960s, in the process removing flight refuelling capability from the Voodoo. In late 1961 the 106 was grounded due to crashes caused by fuel starvation to the engine. The early ejection system, a complex Convair design, was also replaced due to fatalities and pilot dissatisfaction. In 1967 the first Darts were modified to incorporate aerial refuelling capability. In 1969 a Vulcan rotary-breech cannon was installed inside the missile bay, replacing the nuclear Genie missile. In 1968 new "supersonic" tanks were added, bringing the combat radius of the F-106 to 325 nautical miles, about half of that of the Arrow 2.

Once the Delta Dart was flying reasonably safely, the Air Force exploited its propaganda potential to the hilt. Three years after its first flight, Major Joseph Rogers established a new world absolute speed record at 1443.83 mph or Mach 2.18, over a closed course. Also on this December 1959 flight Rogers coaxed the specially-prepared F-106 to a speed of 1,225 mph, or Mach 2.31. This figure has always been quoted as the maximum speed of the F-106, but is no reflection of what a service aircraft could achieve with half internal fuel, a full armament load and a typical engine. The numbers quoted in the first flights are probably more indicative, with a top, practical level flight speed of about Mach 1.9, and a ceiling of 57,000 ft. The test Arrow 1, with 44% less thrust and more weight than the Arrow 2, exceeded both these figures.

In a statistical comparison of the Delta Dart and Arrow, they display some similarities, particularly in wing loading, however, the Arrow has a serious advantage in terms of thrust-to-weight performance. While the Delta Dart, by virtue of its thicker wing, probably has a drag coefficient 15% higher than the Arrow, it has about 30% lower thrust-to-weight performance at military power. This would result in a great advantage to the Arrow in terms of acceleration and fuel economy. At combat weight the Arrow had nearly 40% more military thrust per pound of aircraft than the F-106, and had a third more thrust with afterburner. The Arrow being able to cruise at transonic and supersonic speed without afterburner use is one reason it had superior range to the competition. Compounding this advantage, at combat weight the Arrow actually had a higher proportion of its total weight in the form of fuel. This and the power advantage mean the Arrow would have been able to outfight and outlast the F-106 in a combat engagement, pilot skill and luck notwithstanding. At combat weight the Arrow had about a 6% advantage in wing loading, and its thinner wing meant it would have had lower wave drag at supersonic speeds. With all of these advantages, it is remarkable that the Arrow, with two, superior engines, was actually priced about the same as the F-106.[213] The USAF museum lists the average price of the F-106s it received at 3.3 million dollars each: Arrow 2's as of September, 1958 being priced at 3.5 million each for the first hundred, and 2.6 million for the next hundred. The price for the F-106A in offers to Canada is unknown, however it is clear from other evidence that the US government was dramatically subsidising the price of their military aircraft to secure sales in competing industrialised countries. These subsidies would be publicly disavowed during the Kennedy administration by Defense Secretary Robert McNamara when he stated that the United States needed to not only stop the subsidies, but to sell to foreign nations much more military equipment than it had been doing during the Eisenhower years.

Nevertheless, 340 Delta Darts were produced, and it was remembered, by pre-F-22 Raptor pilots in the USAF, as having been the best air superiority fighter (interceptor) the United States has deployed. This means, of course, that pilots felt the Delta Dart had better flight performance than the F-15 Eagle which replaced it. Considering even the USAF acknowledged that the Avro Arrow would considerably outperform the Delta Dart, conclusions as to its performance vs. the F-15 are obvious.

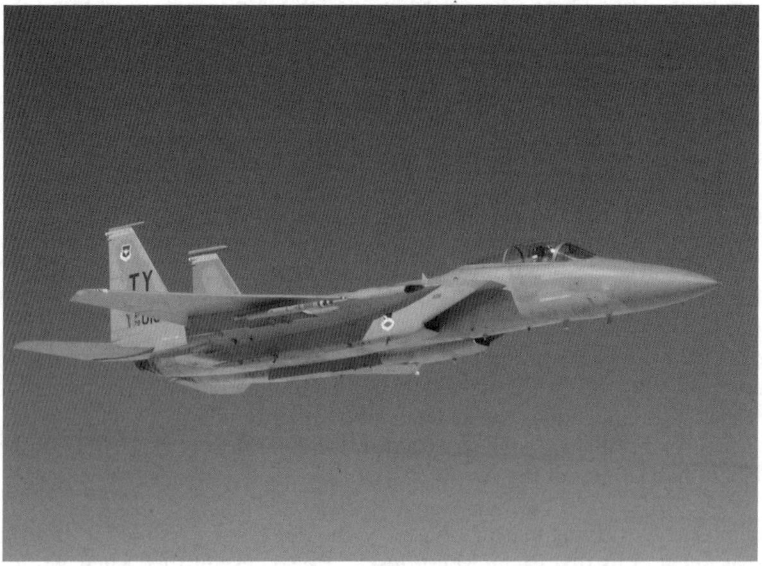

The F-15 Eagle

210 Baugher, Joseph. Convair YF-102: http://home.att.net/~jbaugher1/f102_7.html 1999.

211 ibid

212 Gunston, Bill Faster Than Sound. Somerset: Patrick Stephens Limited, 1992

213 As an example, before Arrow cancellation the F-101 Voodoo was quoted to Canada as being worth about 2.2 million dollars each. After the Kennedy Democrats replaced the Eisenhower Republicans, this price leaped to about 5.6 million dollars a copy.

Chapter 35

THE McDONNELL F-101 VOODOO

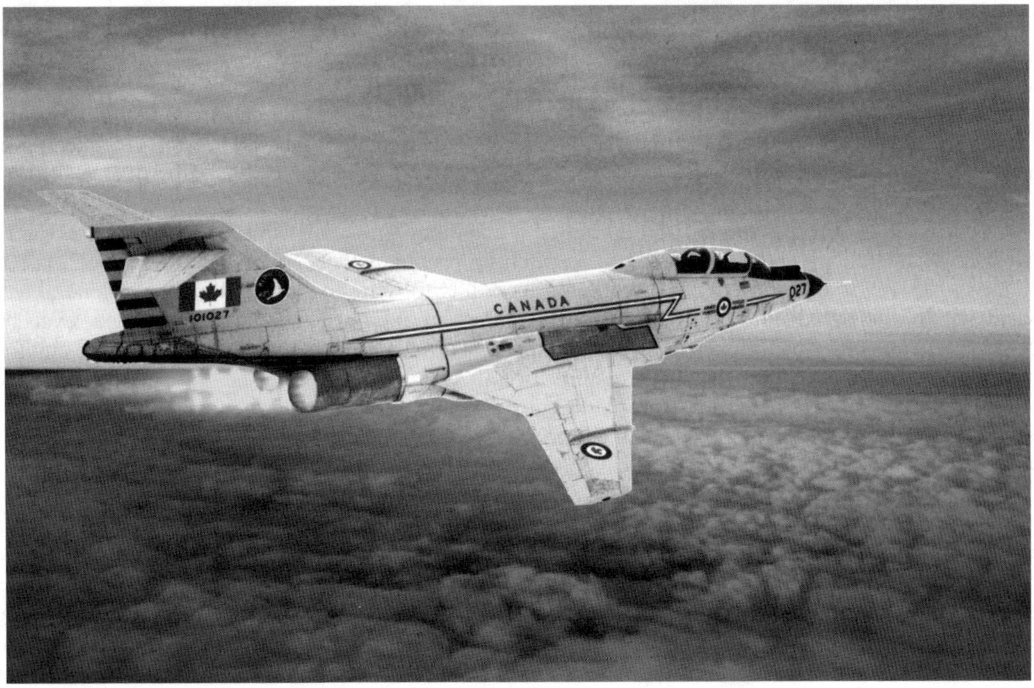

An F-101B Voodoo in the service of 425 Alouette Squadron in Canada. (image by the author)

The project that became the F-101 Voodoo, like the F-106, began in the 1940s. McDonnell had developed a twin-jet fighter, the XF-88, intended as a long-range fighter escort for SAC bombers. Its performance was inspiring, being handily supersonic while the XF-92 was failing to even break the sound barrier. So inspiring, in fact, that when the F-102, like the XF-92, stumbled badly, the Air Force decided to develop an interceptor version of the XF-88. It was considered in 1952 and 1953, but rejected in favour of the Convair program. However, when it was realised that the F-102's problems were crippling, the USAF produced the WS-217A requirement for a "stop-gap" fighter. Northrop and North American Aviation (NAA) submitted proposals based on existing airframes, and the more promising McDonnell design was given the thumbs up. Engines considered for the Voodoo once again included the J67 afterburning version of the Olympus, but also ranged to include the General Electric J79 and the P&W J57 and J75. The J75 and J79 were still in development at this time so, probably for reasons of prudence, the older J57 was chosen. The MG13 radar/fire control was selected for the Voodoo, and, although it is always listed as a Hughes system, was at this time in the hands of RCA, and RCA considered it their proprietary design. This too was likely selected to hedge USAF bets, and at this time the USAF was encouraging Canada to select another supplier other than Hughes, because, as they said, *they* wanted a second source to reduce reliance on Hughes Aircraft.

The final production decision was taken on February 25th, 1955. First flight was to take place in mid-1956 with the expected entry into service being slated for early 1957. The initial development batch numbered 28 aircraft. In September of 1955 the mock-up was ready for inspection. The Voodoo actually had an internal fuel capacity not too much under that of the Arrow, at nearly 16,000 lbs, though it had higher drag, a much lower thrust-to-weight ratio and less fuel efficient engines (and thus shorter range). Despite being a redesign from the F/RF-101A which was in service, the first flight of the F-101B was a year late. On March 27th, 1957, the plane took to the skies for the first time, and broke the sound barrier on its first flight.

Two years of flight testing and development work ensued on 50 airframes. The MG-13 was found wanting, and bore too close a resemblance in technology and (poor) capability to the E-6 system RCA was building under license from Hughes. A plan to replace the system with the Hughes MA-1 system was turned down and the MG-13 was developed with a better central air data computer.

As should be expected of a design that had been flying for nearly 10 years, the F-101B proved to have few serious problems during development. Late production Voodoos were modified to accept a pair of Genie air-to-air nuclear rockets and a field retrofit was applied to older airframes to allow them to carry this weapon. The Voodoo also was equipped with infra-red search and track features starting in 1963, with its refuelling probe being deleted to accept the scanner. Some 480 F-101Bs had been produced when production ceased in March 1961.

Avro test pilots flew the Voodoo and discussed it and other American fighter designs such as the F-104 Starfighter. It, apparently, shared the same pitch-up problems that had plagued the XF-92, F-102 and the F-106. It also had roll-coupling problems according to Avro documentation, but in general was considered by the USAF to be a good performer. Interestingly, the F-104 was considered, even by USAF experts, to suffer badly from roll-coupling, and was considered to have too short a range and too small a payload to be a very tactically useful aircraft. Starting in 1964, the Voodoo began to be equipped with an automatic feature to force the nose of the aircraft down when it approached speeds and angles of attack where pitch-up became a problem. This limited the aircraft's manoeuvre capability.

So how did the Voodoo compare to the Arrow? Not very well it turns out. The Voodoo had double the wing loading at combat weight compared to the Arrow and this would have seriously increased the Voodoo's induced drag, thereby reducing its altitude and manoeuvre capability. The F-101's wing was also nearly twice as thick, in terms of thickness-chord ratio, as that of the Arrow, suffering a wave-drag penalty. The Arrow also had at least 30 percent better dry thrust-to-weight ratios than the Voodoo, and was about 25% better with afterburner. In short, the Arrow would have been able to fly much higher and faster, and would have been able to turn and accelerate better, than the Voodoo. It was capable of carrying much higher capacity and range missiles. In short, the Arrow would have embarrassed the Voodoo, and as of circa 1960 was priced about a third lower.

As mentioned in the section describing the F-106, the US was subsidising aircraft to certain western nations during the Eisenhower years. This form of corporate welfare resulted, of course, in the cancellation of foreign competing programs and the destruction of a good portion of the advanced aerospace industries in countries like Canada and Britain. Was this the intention of those guiding US foreign policy? Larry Milberry researched the genuine price of the McDonnell Voodoo at the time of Canada's negotiations for it in 1960, about a year after the Arrow cancellation. He quotes the genuine price, *sans* subsidy, as being about 5.6 million dollars a copy. This was more than the Arrow was quoted at, even before the cancellation of ASTRA and Sparrow.

This author has aquired an annex used in discussing American planes under consideration, two months after Black Friday (in April 1959), for Canada's new strike-recce role in Europe. Interestingly, the F-101 Voodoo, in a ground attack version, is priced at less than two-million dollars each. Imagine the consternation of the Diefenbaker Conservatives at the price difference between offers before the Arrow was cancelled and those after. The difference a year and a program cancellation made, despite the existence of a new defense-production sharing treaty, was nearly triple! To hide this glaring evidence of political ineptitude, it is said, the Conservatives embarked on a convoluted deal involving cost-sharing and Canadian acceptance of costs for more NORAD installations. They also bought *used* Voodoos in the process—though one Canadian aviation writer wrongly insists they were "brand new, beautiful birds". Photos of these worn aircraft displayed to air force candidates such as this author during their air force indoctrination course in 1991 certainly put the lie to this idea.

McDonnell wasn't banking its future on the Voodoo however. Their F3H Demon had been a hit in the US Navy, and a faster, more potent version was desired soon after the Demon hit the carrier decks.

Chapter 36

THE McDONNELL DOUGLAS F-4 PHANTOM II

An F-4 Phantom in service of the German Luftwaffe circa 1994. (image by the author)

In August, 1953 design work on what would eventually emerge as the F-4 Phantom began at McDonnell aircraft under Herman Barkley. Initially, the goal was not to produce a new airplane, but to modify and extend the life of the USN's F3H Demon. The first proposal was for an F3H-C "Super Demon" powered by a single J67 built by Curtiss Wright, but based on Bristol's Olympus design. This was expected to reach Mach 1.69.

This design was followed by the F3H-G project, which called for a version using two J65 engines, also built under license by Curtiss Wright, but based on Armstrong Siddeley's Sapphire engine, which was already in production. Speed projection for this version was Mach 1.52 and generous provision was designed in to allow a wide range of external stores.

McDonnell was encouraged to submit a version using the General Electric J79 turbojet with this variant being termed the F3H-H. In 1954 this engine was unproven, but promised up to Mach 1.97 if it met expectations. On December 14th, the Navy decided to delete the design's multi-role requirements and concentrate on improving its capabilities as an all-weather interceptor. The design's cannon armament and several hardpoints were removed. The fuselage was modified to accept 4 Sparrow missiles in a conformal arrangement. The APQ-50 radar with a 24-inch dish replaced the earlier arrangement. (This would soon be followed by the APQ-72 which required a major enlargement of the nose of the plane.) Following a letter from the Navy's Bureau of Aeronautics (BuAer) to the Commander of Naval Operations on April 15, 1955, the Sapphire powered version was dropped in favour of the General Electric engine. In May the Navy officially ordered that the development concentrate on all-weather interception using an all-missile armament. On June 24th, a contract for 18 pre-production planes incorporating the above changes was awarded, plus the last minute addition of compatibility with the Sidewinder heat-seeking missile, with the plane now designated the F4H-1.

The plane also had some aerodynamic changes made. It initially had a swept wing with a straight leading edge. This changed with the outer sections of the wing, beyond where it folded for carrier storage, being swept upwards, giving 12 degrees of dihedral. The horizontal stabilizers, formerly arranged horizontally, were swept downward 23 degrees, to help solve stability problems (by giving more vertical surface area behind the centre of gravity of the plane). A sawtooth was added, and the intake was redesigned to add features included in that of the Arrow. The outer wing sections had no control surfaces. This feature eliminated any requirement to deal with aileron reversal and, to a lesser extent, tip stalling. A combination flaperon/spoiler arrangement on the inboard sections of the wing were responsible for roll inputs, and the downward-raked horizontal stabilizers were responsible for pitch control. A poor rate of roll, in most performance and load states, would be overlooked by the Navy when the otherwise high-performance and superb flexibility were considered. In fact, to generate taxpayer enthusiasm for the Navy, the second of the two pre-production Phantoms was modified repeatedly to win various world records for speed and altitude. In fighting for its funding, the Phantom's success proved a propaganda bonanza for the Navy. McDonnell and other corporations involved in the Phantom program saw their fortunes rise, quite literally, with each record the "phabulous Phantom" assaulted.

An early mockup of the F-4 Phantom II.

On May, 27, two months after the first flight of the Arrow, the F4H-1 took to the air in St. Louis Missouri, for the first time. The flight was marred by problems with the engines, the hydraulic system, and a nose gear door that didn't want to close. On its third flight it was flown to Mach 1.3, and reached Mach 1.7 on its fourth. A year and a half later, on its 296th flight, an engine access door failed and set up a structural chain reaction ending with the prototype crashing—taking the life of test pilot Gerald Huelsbeck in the process. The second prototype went on to set some very tantalizing performance records during a Navy publicity campaign. Alcohol and water injection boosting the specially-prepared J79s, this aircraft achieved ballistic climb altitudes of 98,560 feet, and a sustained altitude of 66,444 feet.

During testing the intake ramp angle was increased twice, to a number beyond what NACA had earlier criticised as excessive in the case of the Arrow. From changes to the Phantom intake, one would imagine McDonnell received some of the Arrow intake design information from, or through, NACA. When flight crews complained about poor visibility from the cockpit, McDonnell raised the seating positions 23 inches and designed a new canopy and nose section. This extra room also helped accommodate the electronics of the new radar/fire-control, the Westinghouse APQ-72, which had a much larger dish than had the APQ-50 which it replaced at this time.

In Viet Nam, the Phantom was credited with 277 air-to-air victories, and would score 116 in Israeli hands. In a production run of over 5,000 airframes, it served the air forces of eleven nations. With a production run spanning 21 years, from 1958 to 1979, it retains the record for the longest production run of a supersonic fighter. Boeing states that Phantom production produced over 1 million man-years of employment.

The Phantom first flew only two months after the Arrow and was about a third smaller, and behind the Arrow in performance (wing loading and power-to-weight ratios) by about 20% at its best fighting weight. Even with a centreline tank, it had less fuel per pound of airframe and less fuel per pound of thrust than the Arrow. Despite the comparative limitations, the Phantom was priced at nearly double Avro's final price guarantee on the Arrow 2. In hindsight, the Arrow suddenly appears quite saleable on the world market, considering it had better range, lower wing loading, an equivalent *internal* weapons load, a higher thrust-to-weight ratio, and a lower price. It should have, frankly, equipped the USAF, given the political freedom to perform.

Considering it was ordered by the USAF primarily as a strike-attack aircraft, it is interesting that the Pentagon directed McDonnell to specialise the F-4 as an all-weather interceptor in 1957. It is interesting that the USAF had so many programs in place, as of 1955, to ensure the US could meet its fighter-interceptor requirement with domestic production.

1960 Fighter–Interceptor Evaluation

Convair F-106A Delta Dart

Thrust–

16,000 lbs dry,
24,000 lbs w/afterburning

McDonnell F-4 Phantom II

21,000 lbs dry,
33,000 lbs w/afterburning

Avro CF-105 Arrow 2

38,500 lbs dry,
52,000 lbs w/afterburning

Radius of Action–

F-106A
F-4E
CF-105 Mk 2
CF-105 Mk 2a

☐ Internal fuel ☐ with two tanks

Wing Loading @ Combat Wt.
(Pounds per Square Foot Area)

F-106A 44 (no tanks)
F-4E 72 (no tanks)
CF-105 Mk 2a 46
CF-105 Mk 2 44

Thrust to Weight Ratio
(Combat Weight)

F-106A .73
F-4E .85
CF-105 Mk 2 .98
CF-105 Mk 2a .9

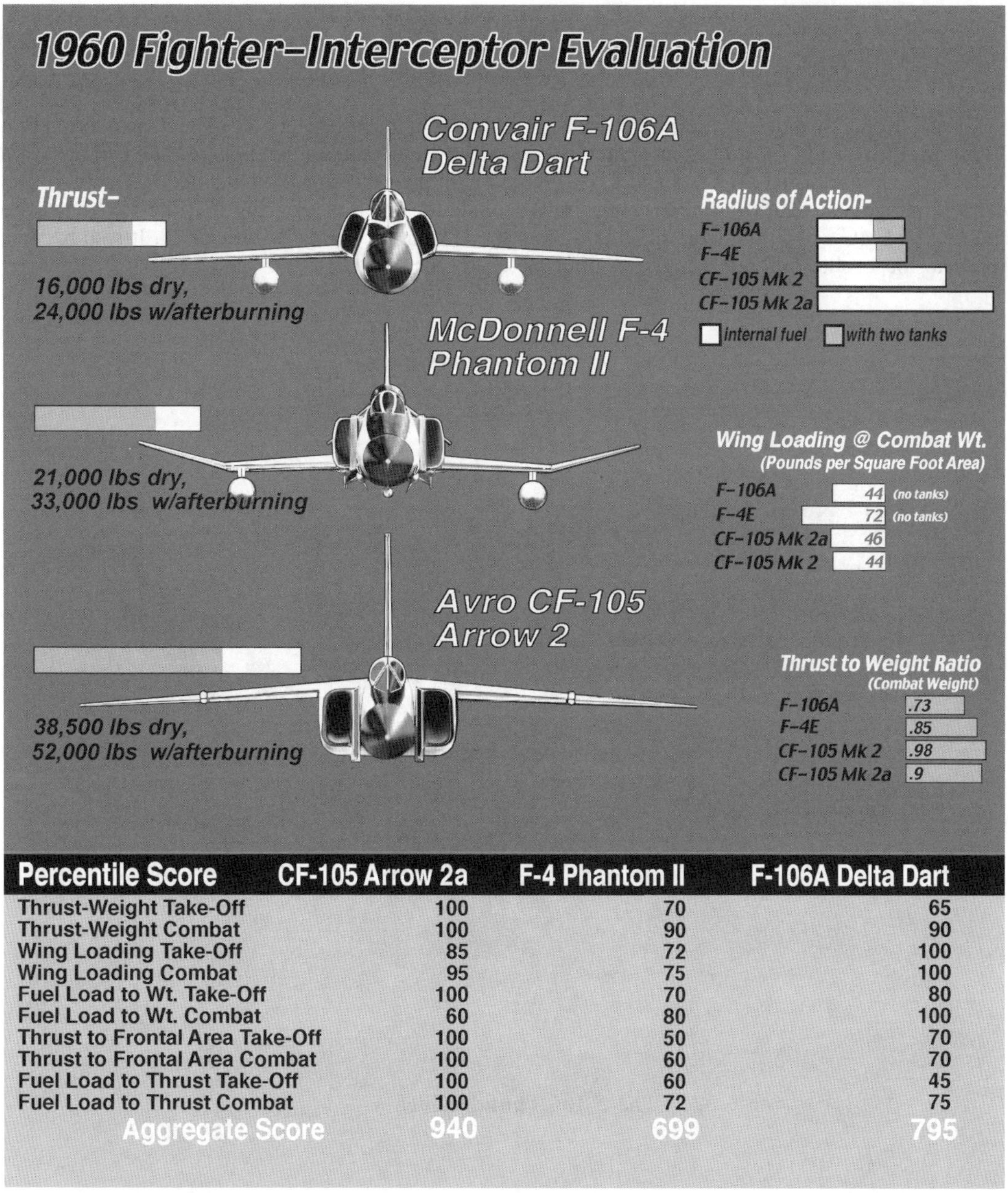

Percentile Score	CF-105 Arrow 2a	F-4 Phantom II	F-106A Delta Dart
Thrust-Weight Take-Off	100	70	65
Thrust-Weight Combat	100	90	90
Wing Loading Take-Off	85	72	100
Wing Loading Combat	95	75	100
Fuel Load to Wt. Take-Off	100	70	80
Fuel Load to Wt. Combat	60	80	100
Thrust to Frontal Area Take-Off	100	50	70
Thrust to Frontal Area Combat	100	60	70
Fuel Load to Thrust Take-Off	100	60	45
Fuel Load to Thrust Combat	100	72	75
Aggregate Score	**940**	**699**	**795**

"The impressive performance of the Navy F4H Phantom immediately caught the attention of the USAF, which ordinarily would have been quite reluctant even to consider any aircraft that had originally been designed for the Navy.

"A comparative evaluation between the F4H-1 and the F-106A took place under the code name *Operation Highspeed*. The F4H-1 had better overall speed, altitude and range performance than the F-106A. In addition, it could carry heavier loads than the F-106A over longer distances and had a 25 percent greater radar range. Later, the Air Force also looked into the possibility of using the Phantom as a tactical fighter and as a tactical reconnaissance aircraft. The F4H-1 was much more versatile than the Air Force's F-105 Thunderchief, since it could not only carry similar external loads but was also potentially a much better air superiority fighter due to its more favorable wing and power loadings. In the reconnaissance role, the Phantom offered a much better performance than the RF-101A/C, and unlike the Voodoo, could be fitted for night photographic missions."

> Since the Phantom had so much going for it, in January of 1962, President Kennedy requested Congressional approval for the procurement of F4H-1 derivatives for the Air Force under the designation F-110. [This was soon changed to F-4C.][214]

Clearly Kennedy didn't believe that missiles had made manned fighters obsolete. Considering that Dulles, McElroy, and CIA studies were then suggesting to Pearkes, Fleming, Foulkes and perhaps even Diefenbaker himself, that the USA and USAF would both probably abandon manned interceptors and bombers altogether, with the F-108 being the last of the breed, it is amazing that the USAF was to acquire 583 F-4C's by 1966, from the 5,000 or so the US military actually purchased. It also became America's best seller to foreign countries until the F-16 Falcon.

The F-105 Thunderchief

214 Baugher, Joseph. McDonnell F-110 Spectre/F-4C Phantom II: http://home.att.net/~jbaugher1/f4_7.html

Chapter 37

THE LONG RANGE INTERCEPTOR EXPERIMENTAL (LRIX)

Mockup of the North American Aviation F-108 Rapier, selected as the USAF LRIXl.

The Hyde Park Agreement, Truman's Statement of Economic Principles, assurances in the Mutual Assistance Plan, and other US pronouncements promised the Allied nations, especially those of the British Commonwealth, that the US would buy any weapons made by an ally if they were the best available. It was implied that this willingness to purchase was irregardless of price, since it would relieve the US of expensive public-funded programs and contribute to overall Western security and economic development. Once it became clear that the Arrow was shaping up to be better than anything else available in its time scale, it seems obvious that the only way the US could reasonably refuse to purchase the Arrow was if they had a plausibly superior aircraft in the pipeline. The North American F-108 Rapier filled this need precisely.

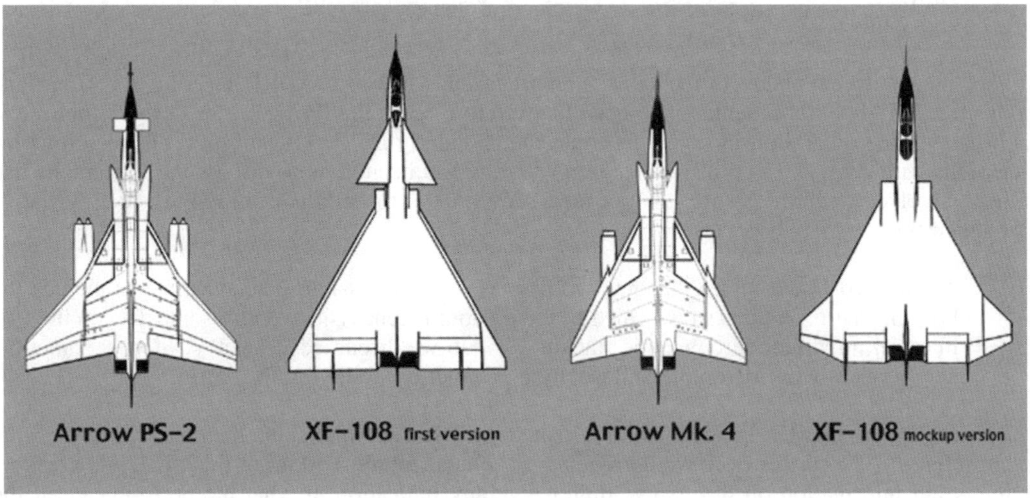

On October 6th, 1955, a mere three-weeks before the USAF delegation arrived in Malton to deliver their conclusions on the Arrow, North American Aviation was given a government contract to do a design study for the LRIX, which they designated the F-108 Rapier.[215] Earlier in the year, the USAF had tentatively ordered the F-101B Voodoo with this order being solidified shortly before the arrival at Avro of the USAF evaluation team. Both the Rapier and Voodoo had previously been conceived as long-range escort fighters to accompany SAC strategic bombers and both orders filled possible sales avenues for the Arrow. (The supersonic long-range bomber design was resuscitated in 1959 and flew in the mid-1960s as the XB-70 Valkyrie. At the same time American politicians and intelligence agents were telling the Canadians that the United States and the Soviet Union were abandoning manned bombers and would soon abandon manned fighters.) The F-108's projected performance seemed to change in tandem with the performance that Avro projected for advanced versions of the Arrow. Clearly the date on which the USAF delegation arrived at Avro was very close indeed to the date that North American Aviation were given a contract to put their former escort fighter onto paper as an interceptor. The Pentagon's concurrent order for the F-101B also rounded out the USAF interceptor force, closing another door to American purchase of Arrows.

ARROW LRIX

On March 7th and 8th, 1957, J.C. Floyd visited the DRB and RCAF in Ottawa. Apparently the expectations for performance of the next generation interceptor had changed again. Perhaps it is not surprising that the requirements were US-generated, and reflected the hoped-for performance of the F-108 Rapier. In a resulting letter that Floyd sent to Smye on the 12th, he states;

> "In our conversations with Dr. Watson [of the DRB], he indicated that the recent study which D.R.B. had carried out on the defense of Canada from 1960 to 1970 showed a definite requirement for a manned interceptor in addition to guided missiles.
>
> "The report favours the idea of taking the battle North and intercepting the threat as far North as possible, primarily because of the hazards of exploding atomic warhead defensive missiles close to populated areas…" [Why the BOMARC missile was adopted in view of this policy is a very good question.]
>
> "The general picture then…was as follows:—
>
> Range: As close to 1,000 miles as possible.
>
> Speed: Mach 3 for as long a period as possible…
>
> Altitude: Around 60,000 feet (it is expected that the weapon will climb to 15 to 20,000 feet above this altitude."

Very interesting numbers. In the same month and days before the DRB meeting, Dr. Courtland Perkins, the USAF Chief Scientist, had been to Avro to discuss the flying saucer designs John Frost had been working on. Palmiro Campagna contacted an elderly Dr. Perkins in the 1980s regarding his discussions with Avro and Perkins replied that while he had been there to discuss the saucers, he had not been involved with the Arrow "then or now". Yet a letter to Perkins from Floyd, dated 6 March, 1957 suggests otherwise. It begins:

> "I know you want to see the enclosed data as soon as possible. The attachments include the briefing charts on the Arrow, which I used on your recent visit, and also some data on the L/D max [an important aerodynamic statistic], which we discussed… I will send you, sometime next week, a write-up on the philosophy of synthetic stability on the Arrow."[216]

It would appear that Dr. Perkins had also visited the DRB and had given them new input on what the air defense of North America would require in the near future. Perkins at this time, while asking for important information on the Arrow, didn't give any indication of what the performance of the LRIX was specified to be, beyond the 1955 estimates. It is also of interest that the DRB report on this new requirement wasn't given to anyone in the RCAF except AVM Easton, who was then a lukewarm supporter of the Arrow and held a strong attraction for advanced electronics and the missile technology it seemed to promise.

Then, on 18 July 1957, after receiving all the data on the Arrow's electronic stabilisation system, fly-by-wire controls, and L/D max, Dr. Perkins came to Avro for another visit. Floyd pointed out to the author that Perkins expressed interest in the Arrow for the LRIX requirement and that he was reluctant to state the specifications for this aircraft. Floyd told him that it would be difficult to quote to a specification if they didn't know what the requirement was, and admitted to this author that, as a result, he and Fred Smye took Perkins aside and "pumped" him for the specification, which he divulged. The specification was virtually identical to the DRB report of over four months earlier, which had coincided with Perkins' earlier visit to Canada. Floyd's subsequent note to file on the visit stated:

> "Dr. Perkins said that his interest and feelings on the Arrow at present ran something like this. U.S.A.F. have let out a contract for a design study on a L.R.I. [long range interceptor] with North American, and are embarking on a complete and major weapon system program with associated engine, missiles, fire control system, etc., in much the same manner as the R.C.A.F.

embarked on the Arrow complete weapon system.

"In view, however, of the figures which are coming out of the design study, both in aircraft weight, which is around 110,000 lbs., and the situation on dollars for defense, the project appears to be losing a great deal of support, and he went so far as to say that he felt it might be discarded in the not too distant future. Since the Arrow comes closer to the requirement than anything they have seen at the present time, he felt that we should keep the U.S.A.F. constantly aware of our progress on the aircraft so that in the event of a cancellation of the L.R.I., there would be a good chance that they would become vitally interested in the Arrow, especially around that time. The L.R.I. basic requirement is for the interceptor to be scrambled on the receipt of DEW Line information, fly out to 250 nautical miles radius, loiter for one hour with very high search capability, and then be able to proceed at Mach 3 for a distance of another 325 nautical miles. On encountering the target, 10 minutes combat is required, at 1.2 'g', at 70,000', at Mach 3.

"On the basis of the previous visit to Dr. Perkins by Messrs Lindley and Chamberlin [John Frost, involved in the Mach 3 flying saucer design for the Pentagon, was also along for this visit] we had a look at the Arrow in this role and, while it is not possible to stretch the aircraft in its present configuration to meet this requirement, if re-fuelling was permissible during the loiter period, we could achieve the complete mission, provided that we made certain modifications to the aircraft, such as variable intakes, insulated skins, optimised Iroquois, etc. Dr. Perkins mentioned that there was no mention of re-fuelling in the requirement, and North American had done all their studies assuming that this would not be permissible. However, he felt that it was well worth talking about and asked us to write up a note for him on our philosophy on the possibilities of using the Arrow with re-fuelling for this particular mission."[217]

Few American aircraft then had this capability, the ones that did were bombers. All front-line USAF fighters and reconnaissance aircraft designed after this time would use in-flight re-fuelling and *many* aircraft in the US and Britain would be retrofitted to include it. As of the date of the Avro communication with Perkins on aerial re-fuelling, the concept was still experimental as far as high-performance jet aircraft went. Of course it was the Englishman Sir Alan Cobham who had invented and proven the technique, with Avro Lancasters, during the Berlin Airlift.

"The weapons specified are two Falcon "Z" type missiles weighing approximately 750 lb. each, with 25 miles range[218] and 40,000 foot differential altitude. He suggested that we keep very close to Messrs Horner and Putt to try to keep the Arrow in the picture, without appearing to be on a sales campaign. He particularly suggested that we do not approach the U.S.A.F. with a new type of airplane to meet this mission and said that our studies should be confined to outlining what the Arrow will do and showing the effect of certain modifications."[219]

In reality, the Falcon Z, aka GAR-9, aka AIM-47 missile had a range of about 100 miles, as later tested on the YF-12A. It was a large, advanced, long-range air-to-air missile of the performance Avro had been awaiting. It would have suited the Arrow's large internal weapons bay while competing aircraft could not have carried it internally—resulting in a huge performance advantage to an Arrow so equipped.

Was Perkins planting seeds at the DRB, and with A/V/M Easton of the RCAF, to suggest the Arrow wasn't worth developing? Was he working to get Avro's aerodynamic and flight control technology for the United States? A possible answer is provided by the actual progress of the F-108 design. Up to 1957 the design drawings show a plain delta-winged aircraft with a rather bizarre looking canard attached right behind the navigator's canopy, with plain intakes, and three fins. In 1957 it changed to a configuration virtually identical to the Arrow.

We can see, therefore, that the F-108 design study contract was given at the time the RCAF approached the USAF with the original Arrow Mk. 2 projections from Avro. Once the wind tunnel and major design work had been done on the Arrow, Perkins and the USAF had been given the Mk. 3 specifications which indicated a Mach 2.5 combat speed. The DRB appears to have then been immediately advised that the USAF had developed a new requirement, for range exceeding the Arrow 3, with a superior speed requirement as well. Any aviation buff with modest knowledge will acknowledge that the F-108's original intake design would not have allowed a speed above Mach 2. While the DRB was formulating their Mach 3 requirements Perkins was at Avro "pumping" them for design information on the Arrow. On 6 June, 1957, North American Aviation was given a contract to produce two F-108 prototypes, but now with a configuration nearly identical to the Arrow. In July Perkins was back at Avro telling them the F-108 was probably going to be cancelled, so therefore Avro should keep the USAF "constantly aware" of the progress of the Arrow. He also said Avro should *not* propose a new aircraft, but should provide progress reports on the Arrow, and advise the USAF of the effect of any modifications Avro felt it would be worthwhile to help it meet the LRIX specification. These had inflated dramatically from the USAF's first statements about the aircraft's specification back in 1955, when they used it as an excuse not to buy into the Arrow program. Oh yes, and would Avro please provide information on their proposed air-to-air refuelling and fly-by-wire system! Canada, however, got nothing in terms of genuine data and performance figures on this aircraft and didn't even get flight test numbers on the F-106, a plane that the US acknowledged would be inferior to the Arrow.[220]

At Avro Mario Pesando was placed in charge of the Project Research Group in early 1957 and was in charge of the design studies for an Arrow to supercede the Mk.3, and provide a possible aircraft to fill the LRIX and DRB advanced interceptor roles.

Avro began by doing two project studies, to see how the basic Arrow might be adapted, with the first brochure being released in September 1957. The first concept (PS-1 shown in the diagram at left with PS-2 at right) had large ramjets at the wingtips and a trimming canard above the fuselage and just behind the navigator's station, this latter feature being the same as on NAA's first XF-108 proposals. Avro determined that the aircraft would have problems with gear strength, centre-of-lift variation and other things. PS-2 was found to be much more promising.

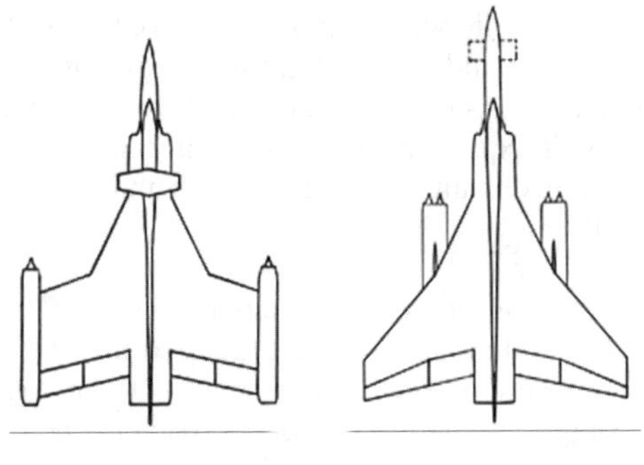

His study led to the proposal of a radical Arrow version for hypersonic, sub-orbital interception using a new "cranked arrow" outer wing extension, a nose extension housing a retractable canard, two extra finlets on the wing to compensate for the destabilizing effect of the nose extension, and four large auxiliary ramjets on wing pylons. Avro estimated that this aircraft would be capable of sustaining Mach 3 at 95,000 feet, with a climb rate from 40,000 feet of over 130,000 feet per minute: Mach 2.5 straight up! It would have had a thrust to weight ratio double that of the F-108 and over double that of the SR-71 Blackbird, the fastest jet-powered aircraft ever to fly. The following is from Pesando's initial investigation.

"BASIC MODIFICATIONS OF LONG RANGE ARROW

"UNDERCARRIAGE

"It has been established that the take-off weight of a Long Range Arrow is of the order of 105,000 lb. and it is very unlikely that the present main undercarriage scheme can be developed to cope with these loads. Further the redesign should be capable of a potential take-off weight of much more than the immediate 105,000 lb. requirement.

A plausible solution would be to:

Remove the existing undercarriage and utilize the space for fuel storage.

Integrate the main undercarriage with the pylons which support twin ramjets and are located at the transport joints of the inner and outer wing. The bulk of the increased weight would be concentrated at the undercarriage thus keeping the other structural changes to a minimum.

"MIXED POWER

"A high supersonic performance may be achieved without sacrifice of subsonic capability by the utilization of mixed power plants. This principle when applied to the Avro Arrow results in increased performance at altitude. It is therefore recommended that;

A pair of 36" [diameter] ramjets straddle each pylon-undercarriage structure.

"INCREASED FUEL

"Additional fuel can be carried in: (1) Ramjet pods 29,200 lb.

(2) Outer wings 6,000 lb.

(3) Former wheel well 2,000 lb.

thus increasing the fuel load to at least 19,438 + 37,200 = 56,638 lb. It is noteworthy that the Long Range Arrow mission profiles to be shown later are based on a 54,600 lb. fuel load and a 105,000 lb take-off weight.

"DRAG REDUCTION

"A drag estimate of the Avro Arrow 2 showed that at M 2.4, 90,000 ft. altitude and W/P = 250,000 sq. in. the drag components to be:

Profile Drag – 4,080 lb.

Induced Drag – 11,080 lb.

Trim Drag – 6,960 lb., totalling 22,120 lb.

"Profile drag is relatively a 'fixed item' and any large improvement of it was unlikely. Therefore the reduction is more probable in the induced and trim drags. Consequently it is recommended that:

A canard be added to provide supersonic trim, 32 sq.ft., L.E. at station O.

The wing area be increased from 1225 to 1410 sq.ft. (outer wing increased).

The aspect ratio be increased from 2.04 to 2.55.

"The preceding three basic modifications would in effect reduce the drag at M 2.5, 90,000 ft. altitude to:

Profile Drag – 4900 lb.

Induced Drag – 6950 lb.

Trim Drag – 1230 lb., totalling 13,080 lb. and reduction of over 9,000 lb.

"It should be noted, however, that the subsonic drag, at M = .92, 40,000 ft. and W/P = 22,000, increases approximately from 6,660 to 7,000 lb., a small subsonic penalty to pay for attainment of a 90,000 ft. ceiling.

CANARD

It is intended that the canard be used as an additional trim control at supersonic speeds only.

At subsonic speeds it would be retracted into the 4 ft. nose extension. The aircraft controls in all other respects would function essentially the same. It is felt that the additional canard air loads induced into the fuselage can be adequately catered for by increasing the skin thickness.

WING AREA

The increased wing area may be obtained by utilizing an entirely new outer wing of a lesser sweep-back angle. The resulting increased tip chord (from 52.085 to 102 in.) also provides for a much stiffer wing. It is however anticipated that some re-vamping of the aileron and aileron control may be necessary.

The addition of 10 ft. to the existing span increases the aspect ratio from 2.04 to 2.55 thereby resulting in a substantial reduction in induced drag."[221]

The performance figures were based on drag projections before the Arrow Mk. 1 flew and revealed that they had significantly overestimated the aircraft's drag coefficient. In the case of the Mk. 3 Arrow, that difference in drag resulted in a combat speed increase from Mach 2.5 to Mach 3. Even so, Avro was estimating that the PS-2 version would be capable of *sustaining* Mach 3 at 85,000 feet while pulling the USAF standard 1.2 G. Its 500 fpm climb ceiling was estimated to be at least 90,000 feet.

LONG RANGE ARROW - Mission # 3 - Low Altitude Toss-Bomb

SUBSONIC CRUISE OUT

INTERNAL FUEL 25,400 LBS, PLUS 29,200 IN RAMJET PODS

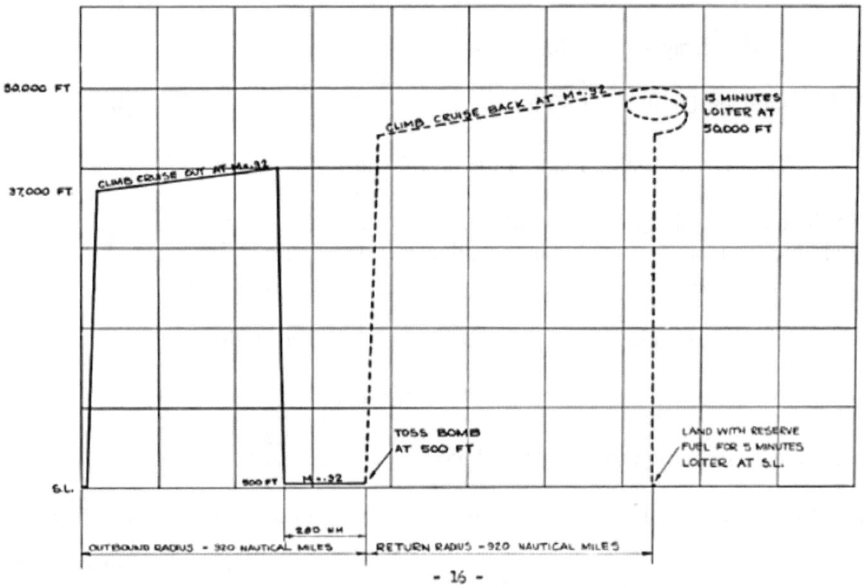

That the Arrow was always looked at as a potentially offensive weapon, and also would have been adaptable to the British TSR.2's role is suggested by the "mission # 3" graph from Pesando's 1957 Long Range Arrow document. (via Jim Floyd)

215 Whitcomb, Randall: Avro Aircraft & Cold War Aviation. St. Catherines: Vanwell Publishing, 2002 The date of the USAF-NAA design study contract was 6 October, 1955 with the USAF delegation arriving at Avro on the 30th of that month.
216 Floyd to Smye, Private and Very Confidential letter titled Some Highlights of Visit to Ottawa, March 6-7-8th /57 "A/V/M Hendrick agreed to provide us with a copy of Dr. Watson's report. Incidentally, he had not seen the D.R.B. report, which had apparently gone straight to A/C Easton."
217 Floyd: Memorandum toFile Re: Note on Visit of Dr. Courtland Perkins, Chief Scientist, U.S.A.F., July 18/57
218 They actually had a range of around 100 nm, as shown later in tests.
219 Floyd: Memorandum to File Re: Note on Visit of Dr. Courtland Perkins, Chief Scientist, U.S.A.F., July 18/57
220 Footitt letter Feb. 18 1959
221 Mid-1957 design study by Mario Pesando on the development potential of the Arrow.

Chapter 38

THE ARROW MK.4

Artist's conception of an Arrow Mk. 4—aka the Long Range Arrow. (image by the author)

It would seem that Perkins felt that this PS-2 Arrow was too radical a redesign of the basic Arrow airframe and requested a less modified version. Accordingly, Avro developed a less-modified design and this became the Mk.4 version.

Mario Pesando, then head of the Avro Project Research Group, discussed this less-modified long-range Arrow in a document to Jim Floyd dated 7 November 1957:

> "In view of the still apparent interest in a longer range version of the Arrow, we have undertaken to simplify the original proposal that we made. You will see that the canard has now been eliminated with a resultant loss of 10,000-15,000 ft. in operating altitude. In other words the aeroplane should be good up to 70,000 – 75,000 ft. The ramjets have been reduced in size with the corresponding slight reduction in performance which really does not show up because we should limit the aircraft within the Mach 3 and 75,000 ft. boundary. The [only] piece to be added consists of an insert that is placed at the joint between the inner and outer wing panels and it consists of the pylon, undercarriage and ramjets.
>
> "We have carried out a check on the longitudinal balance, which appears to be in order. The missions of this particular proposal are fairly close to the original one [described above relating to the PS-2] so that in this brochure we have merely substituted pages of the original one with the necessary weight changes. However, I would like to suggest that for practical discussion purposes, a factor of 95% should be used in all of these figures. [Again, Avro was being conservative, and again these numbers were too low since they were still overestimating the Arrow's drag.]
>
> "During one of the [Hawker Siddeley] Design Council meetings, it was mentioned that Perkins of the USAF was alleged to have said that the aircraft to meet the LRI specification

should be under 100,000 lb. We obviously cannot do this without resorting to gimmicks such as flight re-fuelling, high energy fuels [Zip fuel] and buddy systems, etc., and I do not think anyone else can do it either, within the present state-of-the-art. In other words there is no royal road to achieving this unless there are some major technical break-throughs, and I doubt whether the project can be postponed until these occur."

This version of the Arrow is shown at the beginning of this section. Jim Floyd stated that this aircraft version differed from the basic Mk. 3 airframe by being skinned in titanium. From the arrangement we can see it relied on a slightly more advanced ramjet installation than the PS-2.

Mario Pesando while with Avro Canada. (via Jim Floyd)

Curtiss-Wright seemed to have a genuine respect for British engineering as evidenced by their licence-production of the Sapphire and attempted licence-production of the Olympus as the J-67 (and others). They always seemed prepared to work with Avro Canada, and tried to secure rights to licence-produce the Orenda Iroquois. This author suspects that many of that company's problems were brought about by their attitude which did not conform to the attitude of the American establishment, as delineated by the Buy American Act.

Curtiss-Wright had also developed ramjets in the United States for the promising (but cancelled) North American Navaho missile project. They had also developed the propulsion system for the XF-103 which included the J-67 and also ramjets, making the XF-103 a mixed propulsion aircraft. Mario Pesando addressed a letter to Jim Floyd and Bob Lindley on 12 December 1957 which referred to a visit by Curtiss-Wright representatives:

"Two Curtiss-Wright representatives, W.J. Mann and B. Nierenberg, visited Avro on Nov. 29, 1957, to discuss the possibility of using their ramjets on the Long Range Arrow. During the course of the meeting it was revealed that Curtiss-Wright have some 34" ramjets, which were produced for the ill-fated Navaho project, available as off-the-shelf items. These units have been paid for by the USAF and, if satisfactory, may be obtained for our use. The meeting was somewhat restricted by Security, i.e. Curtiss-Wright was not cleared to reveal the ramjet information necessary for a detailed design and performance study."

The most interesting thing about the ramjets, other than the fact that the 35-inch version Avro finally settled on produced 16,164 lbt at Mach 2.5 and 40,000 feet, was the fuel carrying system they employed. In short, when they weren't running they were entirely immersed in fuel which the Arrow's main engines would consume before the ramjets were started. From Pesando's letter to Floyd on the subject:

Ramjet/Tank scheme for Arrow Mk.4 (the Long Range Arrow)

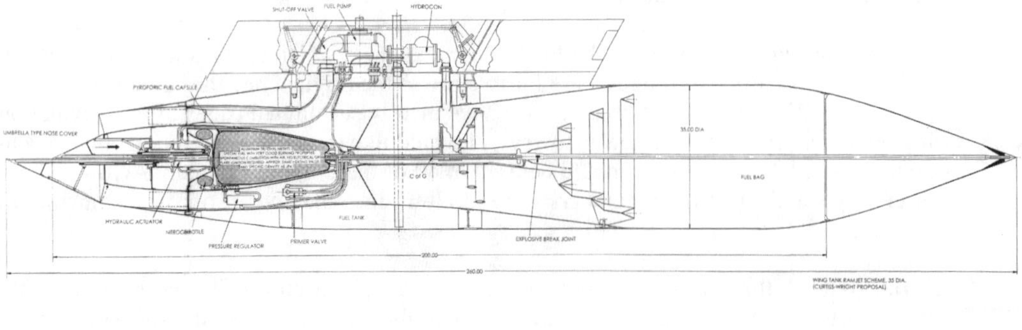

Ramjet Features and Performance

"Mr. Nierenberg was able to give some leading particulars of a 35 inch diameter ramjet equipped to carry 1000 lb. of fuel in a collapsible bag in the duct aft of the flameholders. A further supply of about 650 lb. of fuel of which 600 lb. is JP4 is carried in an annular skin tank and in the centrebody, to be burned in the ramjet. The fuel contained in the centrebody is aluminum-tri-ethyl and is pyroforic, i.e. it will spontaneously ignite in a quite tenuous oxygen-containing atmosphere. Its excellent burning characteristics have made possible the burning of a mixture of 15% by weight of this fuel in JP4 at pressures down to 1/4 lb. per square inch …

"While being used as a fuel tank the intake [of the ramjet] is closed off by an umbrella of meshing plates and the exit is plugged by a conical body which is fixed to the centrebody of the ramjet by a long rod. The rear fairing is jettisoned when the tank fuel has been used through breaking the rod by an explosive charge. Presumably the empty bag is either jettisoned before or burned on light up …" The letter went on to describe what the representatives did disclose, and mentioned Avro having supplied Curtiss-Wright with enough information on the Long Range Arrow's specified missions etc. to allow the visitors to compile data that Avro could use for a detailed performance study. On 31 January 1958 Pesando, Rolf Marshall and two other Avro representatives were at Curtiss-Wright's facilities to see what the Americans had come up with. They came away impressed with their ramjet test facilities (capable of simulating Mach 4 at 85,000 feet) and with a source of a new teflon-related seal material called Viton A.

"Arrow Mk. 4 -Long Range- Mission NO.7 USAF Long Range Intercept Mission

"This mission consists of an economical climb cruise for 250 nautical miles followed by a 60 minute loiter at 38-41,000 ft. The aircraft is then accelerated to Mach 2.5 and climbed to 80,000 ft. at which altitude an approximately 280 nautical miles, Mach 2.5 dash is executed, bringing the out-bound radius to 575 nautical miles. This is followed by 10 minutes combat at 80,000 ft., Mach 3 and sustained 1.5G manoeuvre. The return radius consists of a descent to 48,000 ft. altitude, a Mach .92 climb cruise followed by 15 minutes loiter at 40,000 ft., and a landing with reserve fuel for 5 minutes loiter at sea level. The operational radius of this mission is 575 nautical miles. The deviation of this mission from the [USAF] requirement is dash at Mach 2.5 in lieu of Mach 3, and combat at 80,000 ft. in lieu of 70,000 ft. altitude."

LONG RANGE ARROW - Mission # 7

SUPERSONIC DASH AT MACH 2.5 - COMBAT AT MACH 3

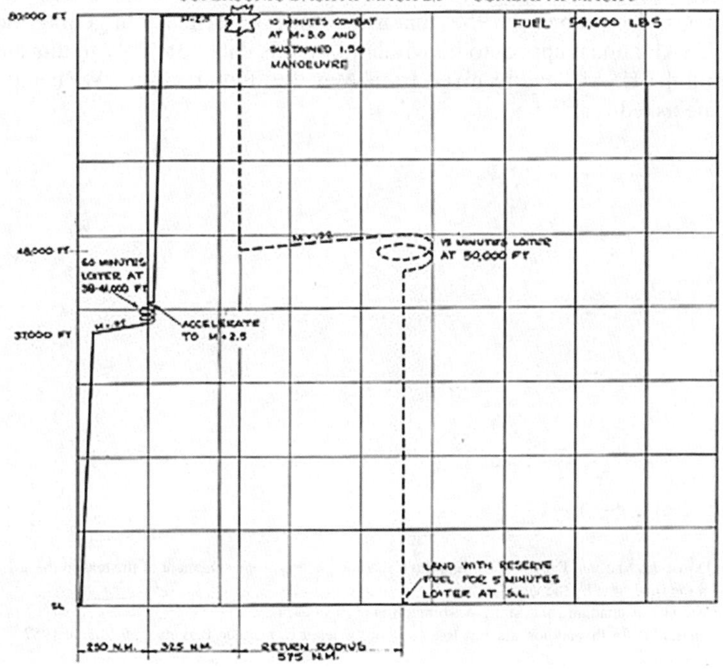

As we can see from the mission 7 information, the Arrow 4 was largely capable of meeting the LRIX specification and was being proposed for just that. (Whether the F-108 was as well, is a valid question.) This is from 1957 so again we know the estimate is conservative. Avro projected the ferry range of this aircraft to be 2,540 nm (over 2900 statute miles). This is comparable to the range of the SR-71 Blackbird spyplane. The ramjet-augmented Mk. 4 would have had double the thrust-to-weight performance of the Blackbird. We also know that John Foster Dulles told MND Pearkes in mid-1958 that the US would never buy Arrows. Not even to save American taxpayers the expense of developing the F-108 and SR-71 and in the process endearing the US government to the people of Canada and Britain. But then, the United States does not buy primary weapons systems from foreign countries, no matter how friendly, for economic, military and political reasons.

It is interesting to note that one of the later reasons given for the Arrow cancellation by the politicians was that the Arrow "couldn't maintain supersonic speed long enough".[222] Some have assumed that this was a reference to the Mk. 2, and that this meant it didn't meet the RCAF requirement. Yet what was really being referred to was the Canadian attempt to sell an *advanced Arrow* to the USAF for the LRIX mission. This deficiency of the Arrow 3 and 4 designs was true according to the LRIX specification, yet it is absurd to believe that the F-108 could have met this specification either, considering it had more weight, more frontal area, half the thrust and no aerial refuelling provision. It probably wouldn't have met the performance of the Arrow 3, and Perkins admitted it didn't have the Arrow 3's in-flight refuelling capability. But then, the actual performance projections of the F-108 were not shared with the Canadians. In fact, the genuine performance figures for even the F-106 were not shared with the Canadians. Had they been, the Arrow would have appeared much more attractive to the RCAF and government. As of two days before the Arrow cancellation G/C Foottit was writing:

> "The matter of obtaining F-106 data from Convair was discussed with the F-106 WSPO [Weapons System Project Office] at WADC [Wright Air Development Centre] on 5 Dec 58 by representatives of this Headquarters. The F-106 WSPO stated that they required authority from USAFHQ to release Convair F106 flight test data and analysis to the Canadian government and contractors. Further, the F106 WSPO stated that, upon obtaining USAFHQ authority, they would hold a meeting, with representatives from HAC [Hughes Aircraft], Convair, AVRO and the RCAF to define Canadian data and analysis requirements."[223]

This effort to secure F-106 flight test data was generated by a RCAFHQ letter to DCINC NORAD A/M Roy Slemon, in December of 1958, that asked for his assistance in getting the information, and noted that the "USAF almost appear to be withholding this data." In reply to this author's question on what Perkins (and the USAF) had received from Avro Jim Floyd wrote: "We bared our soul and gave him everything he asked for!"[224]

222 Stewart: Shutting Down the National Dream. regarding the Canadian government's statement of the reason the Arrow was turned down the final time by the USAF.
223 G/C Foottit to Air Member, Canadian Joint Staff, Washington D.C., 18 February, 1959
224 Floyd in a hand written note for this author attached to a copy of the letter he sent Dr. Perkins on 6 March, 1957.

Chapter 39

ANTI-ICBM ARROWS

Concept of a PS-2 Arrow launching an ABM weapon from suborbital altitude.

It is interesting in the government discussions on ABM weapons that the Arrow was never considered as capable of undertaking this role. Certainly Avro had been suggesting it do just that:

> "It might be supposed, for example, that in every aspect of employment the anti-missile missile would prove to be very far removed from the manned fighting aeroplane. Yet the possibility is already seen that, in order to achieve its maximum kill potential, the "anti" missile may actually form an alliance with the manned fighter.
>
> "The feasibility of this…has been expounded by Jim Floyd, Avro Aircraft's vice-president engineering... 'whereas the launching of the Russian sputnik satellites was a very significant event in the annals of aviation, its effect on the Arrow programme should be singularly positive… If you think about it for a minute," he says, "the normal launching platforms for anti-missile missiles are stationary. The Russians can find out where they are and destroy them. On the other hand, an airborne missile mothership (which could be the Arrow) can be rapidly moved from one place to another carrying an anti-ICBM missile…'
>
> "It might be imagined that a missile suitable for carrying an anti-missile warhead would prove a formidable load even for the mighty Arrow; but Mr. Floyd had looked into the matter with a 'quick specific calculation' on an ICBM approaching at Mach 10 at 200 miles above the earth. He finds that if an "anti" is launched from an aircraft flying at Mach 1.5 at 60,000 ft, its thrust need only be about one-third of that required for ground-launched weapons carrying the same size of warhead to a given point in approximately the same time. And dividends would accrue in range and accuracy."[225]

In other words, any Arrow could carry the ABM weapon Avro was considering. The British technical journal *Engineering* also discussed the possibilities of an Arrow carrying an ABM weapon in their 17 October, 1958 edition. Jim Floyd has subsequently related that Avro was working with Douglas to adapt a version of the Nike-Zeus system for use on the Arrow. The first stage of the ground launched version could be abandoned, with datalink modifications made to the remaining upper stage to accept targeting information from the Arrow's onboard radar system. Of course, nothing came of this plan, perhaps in part because it wasn't mentioned to the right decision makers. There is no evidence available suggesting that the Chiefs of Staff or the Conservative Cabinet were aware of Avro's plan to carry ABMs on the Arrow nor the fact that the system they were proposing was based on the American first choice for their ABM system, the Nike weapons.

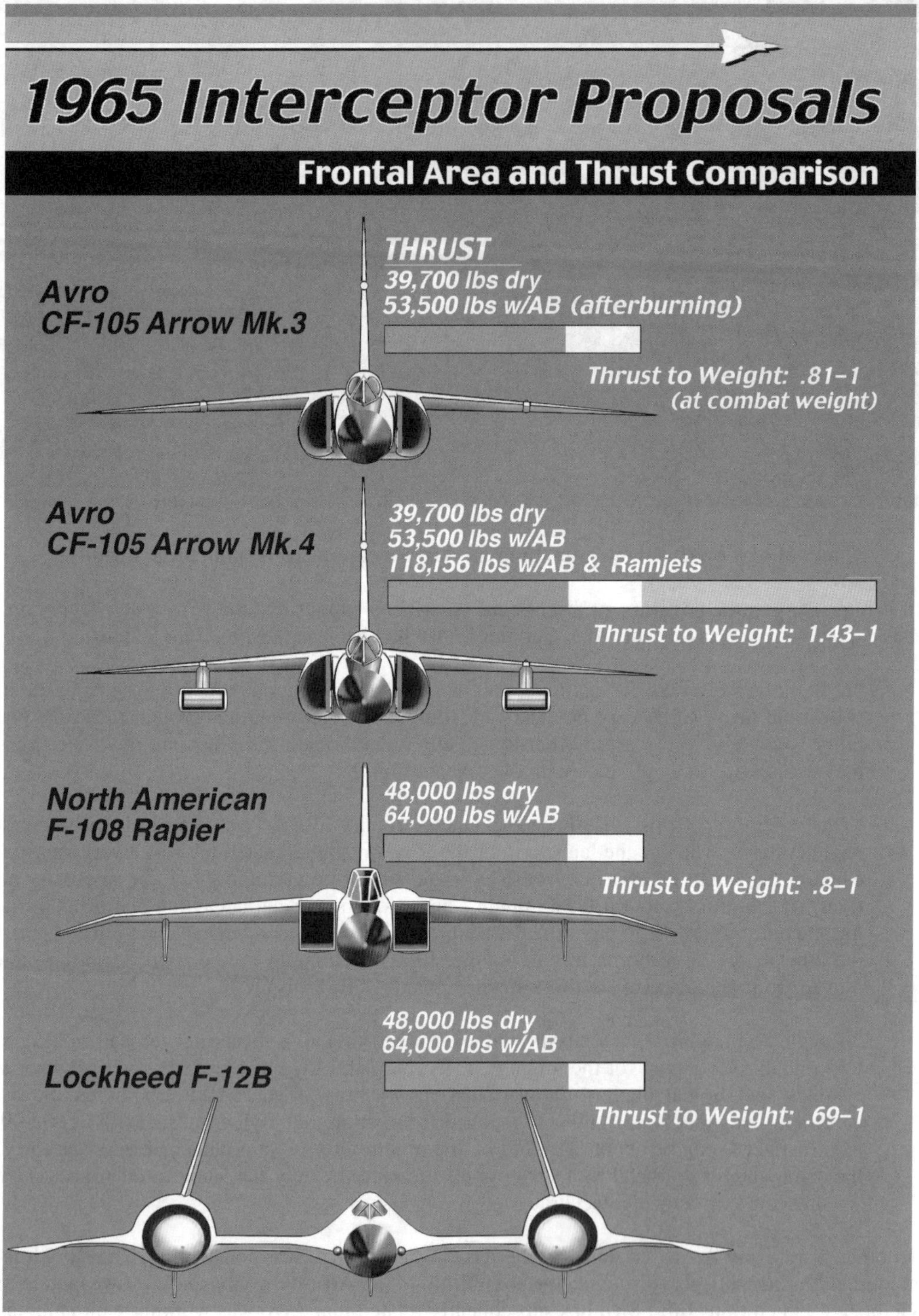

225 Flight and Aircraft Engineer, "Ironclads and Arrows" 14 February, 1958

Chapter 40

INTELLIGENCE AND THE POWER ELITE

We now know that the Arrow Weapons System comprised efforts to develop:

1) The highest performance interceptor in the world.

2) The highest technology interceptor in the world.

3) The worlds first fly-by-wire flight control system.

4) The highest technology radar/fire control system in the world.

5) The highest technology air-to-air missile in the world.

6) The highest technology afterburning turbojet engine in the world.

7) The most powerful afterburning turbojet engine in the world.

8) The most advanced, real time, computerized flight control, navigation, airborne search and ground mapping radar/electronics package in the world.

For those reasons alone there can be no doubt that intelligence agents from any industrial power would be exceptionally interested in the Arrow program. Competing industrial and financial concerns would also be very interested. Campagna relates meeting a former East German military officer who related that the East Germans received weekly reports on the progress of the Avro Arrow. There can be no doubt that the CIA was also heavily involved, but to understand what is really involved it is perhaps best to have a look at some of the Western intelligence services to learn about how they work, but perhaps more importantly, *who they work for.*

Reinhard Gehlen (of German intelligence fame) wrote: "We received much financial assistance…from wealthy industrial circles, partly in the shape of loans and partly in the form of valuable goods; and in due course I established…a 'special connections' section whose responsibility it was to maintain touch with government and industry." [226] Considering Gehlen's lack of difficulty working for Hitler earlier, and this testimony, it is fairly safe to assume that West German intelligence was quite right-wing. The *raison d'etre* of the rejuvenated Gehlen organisation was to integrate the remnants of his Nazi intelligence system with the CIA's global efforts.

Peter Wright, in *Spycatcher,* describes how MI-5 and the CIA collaborated to try to discredit the Labour party of Harold Wilson in an effort to keep him from being democratically-elected. Even after he was elected, dirty tricks continued. Obviously, this demonstrates that these two agencies were also quite right wing, and, in the case of MI-5, at least after Wilson was elected, would even work against the government which it was supposed to be working *for.*

In the book *A Man Called Intrepid*, Canadian WW II spymaster Sir William Stephenson, Intrepid himself, proclaims that Churchill mused to him, regarding the requirement to secretly fund the secret war: "We need Rothschilds and Rockefellers. We need Gold. Did you know Britain has *none?"* The Rothschilds were the Jewish banking dynasty, established in five European powers, that were known to finance both sides in wars, and, according to author/historian Niall Ferguson, had been the principle financial agents for most of the aristocracies of Europe in the 19th century—during the period of their demise, he adds. This banking family had gotten their start from their father Meyer's success in the court of the Landgrave of Hesse, a German branch of one of the oldest families in Christendom, traceable back to Charlemagne. The Bush family is also traceable to this lineage, as is Prince Bernhard of the Netherlands and the British royal family. Bernhard was a regular visitor to Avro, had been an intelligence officer with I.G. Farben, and was a member of the German SS before moving to Holland and marrying the Dutch crown princess. He also founded the Bilderberg Group in 1954, an annual assemblage of the world's leading industrialists and financiers, leading owners of global media, and powerful serving politicians. The demographic served by the institution can be discerned by the fact that politicians are generally only invited to the conferences while they are in power, while the owners of major media, industry and financial powers are more permanent. The Rothschilds, Rockefellers, Agnellis, for example, have all been long-term attendees.

According to Stevenson, the Rothschilds financed British espionage in Europe, while the Rockefellers did the same in the United States. Stevenson points out that the Rockefellers received, in compensation for their financial support, access to the intelligence gathered. How the Rothschilds were rewarded is not mentioned, but a similar arrangement is probable. Peter Wright mentions Victor Rothschild's involvement in British intelligence work:

> "[Rothschild was] a brilliant scientist, a Fellow of the Royal Society, with expertise in botany and zoology, and a fascination for the structure of spermatozoa. But he has been much, much more than a scientist. His contacts, in politics, in intelligence, in banking, in the Civil Service, and abroad are legendary. There are few threads in the seamless robe of the British Establishment which have not at some time or other passed through the eye of the Rothschild needle."[227]

Victor Rothschild also became a member of the British government's Central Policy Review Committee, a secret and totally undemocratic body charged with approving anything the government proposed. It did the Concorde program, for example, no favours.

Intrepid's headquarters were in the Rockefeller Centre. It is interesting to read Intrepid's own remarks from the foreword, where he describes his reasons for disclosing some of the events of his secret war:

> "After all these years, why tell about them now? In my view, there are compelling reasons for disclosure... Prophetic as he was, Churchill did not foresee the awesome extremes to which [the follies of democracy, once victorious] would extend: diplomacy negotiated within a balance of nuclear terror; resistance tactics translated into guidelines for fanatics and terrorists; intelligence agencies evolving technologically to a level where they could threaten the very principles of the nations they were created to defend... Were crucial events being manoeuvred by elite secret power groups? Were self-aggrandizing careerists cynically displacing principle among those entrusted with the stewardship of intelligence? ...What had happened over three decades to an altruistic force that had played so pivotal a role in saving a free world from annihilation or slavery? In the name of sanity, the past now had to be seen clearly."[228]

Perhaps it is now timely to point out that Ian Fleming's character, James Bond, was always fighting renegade industrialists and financiers, not national governments, just as Fleming had in WW II. The above was also, obviously, in Intrepid's masterfully qualified opinion, a warning that something was very wrong with how the intelligence community had changed since WW II.

John Foster Dulles was, at the time of Arrow cancellation, the American Secretary of State while his brother, Allen, ran the CIA. The Dulles brothers were far from innocents in the high-stakes world of finance, intelligence and government. John Kenneth Galbraith, the noted American economist and former diplomat pointed out Dulles' involvement in the Crash of 1929:

> "The most famous example of this leverage [which helped cause and exacerbate the crash] was created by Goldman, Sachs and Company, which, in late 1928, organized the Goldman Sachs Trading Corporation. Its only reason for being was to own stock in other companies; to do this, it issued securities amounting to $100 million, around a billion dollars in today's prices. There were no bonds or preferred stock; leverage was not yet involved. [In other words, it was wholly owned by Goldman Sachs and Company.] That oversight was, however quickly corrected. The Trading Corporation organized the Shenandoah Corporation with common stock and preferred stock, the latter with a fixed return. [In other words, the return on investment of the "preferred" wealthy who provided the money to begin the rise in price of the stock, i.e., who provided the money to get the speculative cycle started, was guaranteed.] The initial issue was 102.5 million, and it was said to have been oversubscribed by some sevenfold."

Goldman, Sachs had sponsored the Trading Corporation with an investment of $10,000,000. The Trading Corporation, in turn, sponsored an even larger firm, the Blue Ridge Corporation with capital of $142 million. Speculation in Blue Ridge increased the value of its stocks, which profited the Shenandoah Corporation, increasing the price of their stocks, which profited the Trading Corporation and also increased the value of their stocks. The Goldman Sachs investors profited from the inflation of all levels of this speculative bubble. One of the directors was John Foster Dulles. After the Crash, the value of, as an example, the Goldman Sachs Trading Corporation, went from 104 to 1.75, a loss of nearly 6,000%.[229] At the top of this grand pyramid scheme were those who pocketed much of the difference. It is interesting that *A Man Called INTREPID* records that it was Alexander Sachs who acquired Einstein's appraisal of the dangers of the Nazis perfecting an atomic bomb. This letter was crucial to Roosevelt's decision to undertake the Manhattan Project in cooperation with Britain and Canada.

Both Dulles brothers, and several of the Rockefellers, and many other 20th Century icons linked to the banking and industrial powers, were involved in intelligence in the Second World War. John Foster circulated with diplomats and politicians in various advisory roles under Roosevelt and Truman, despite being a Republican, whereas in 1942, his brother Allen arrived in Berne, Switzerland, to become an OSS station chief. Allen is credited with the coup of receiving a great many high-level German wartime documents from Fritz Kolbe, who had turned while working in the Nazi Foreign Office. While this "walk in" was a stunning success, there remains controversy on less coincidental aspects of Dulles' work in Berne, involving German industrialists and aristocrats, transfers of gold and securities, particularly those linked to American investment in the pre-war years. More controversy surrounds Allen's negotiations with Germany and the SS for an armistice, despite unconditional surrender being the official policy of the United States and Britain.

One of the companies most implicated in attempts to integrate into a global consortium with a key industrial unit of the Nazis, I.G. Farben, was the Rockefeller's own Standard Oil. (John D. Rockefeller is also known to have consulted with the Rothschilds at a time when they were worried about mutual competition in oil in Europe and America.)[230] Both companies were also clients of the Dulles brothers' Wall Street law firm; Sullivan Cromwell.[231] *A Man Called INTREPID* spells out some of the damning documentation relating to what the participant corporations called a "marriage' between the interests of I.G. Farben and Standard Oil. The basic proposal was for the Rockefellers to grant I.G. Farben, through subsidiaries, a monopoly on the chemical industries of North America if Farben granted Standard Oil (Exxon-Mobil and so many others) a monopoly on petroleum in Europe. Farben comprised the main chemical company of Germany, and held a controlling interest in many German companies, such as Siemens, Bayer, and others. Standard Oil, of course, was part of the Rockefeller empire.

John Foster Dulles was accused by members of his own law firm of being too reluctant, for too long, to repudiate aspects of his, and the firm's, involvement in Nazi Germany. The main American organ of isolationist pressures against Roosevelt crystallized into the 'America First' movement. John Foster, never a friend of Britain's, is shown to have shared sympathies with this movement, although he denies having helped finance them. Money from Nazi sources, through various fronts, along with money from American collaborationist finance and industry, helped the America Firsters gain considerable media coverage and influence. In fact, the power of this group and those behind it might have been what motivated Roosevelt, Marshall and others to, apparently, *allow the Pearl Harbour attack* [232]. Churchill became so concerned by the involvement of Americans in supporting Hitler and keeping America neutral that he proposed an intelligence operation, somewhat outside the traditional British and American intelligence establishments, to root out the worst offenders.

An appreciation of the threat was given in 1937 by historian William E. Dodd, who served as US Ambassador to Germany:

> "A clique of US industrialists is hell-bent to bring a fascist state to supplant our democratic government and is working closely with the fascist regime in Germany and Italy. I have had plenty of opportunity in my post in Berlin to witness how close some of our American ruling families are to the Nazi regime...
>
> Certain American industrialists had a great deal to do with bringing fascist regimes into being

> in both Germany and Italy. They extended aid to help Fascism occupy the seat of power, and they are helping to keep it there."

They were also helping to keep America out of the war, and to keep profits from lending money and selling arms, oil and supplies to the belligerents coming in.

The British sponsored Project Ultra was approved by Roosevelt and run by Stephenson (Intrepid). The participants had their work cut out for them. The program was international, but had a major concentration in the New York financial district, since this was where collaborationist commerce and trade was concentrated. Several floors of the Rockefeller building were set up as dummy offices with wire-taps and other forms of surveillance running throughout this, the RCA building, various clubs, shipping firms, and other "hot-spots". Ian Fleming was a British Naval Intelligence officer who was occasionally loaned to Stephenson. He was granted a 'license to kill' at least one American collaborator, who he shot through his open office window. Fleming ran the idea for his first Bond novel past British intelligence and was told to make it more abstract, since it was obvious to them that he had composed a tale to which actual events and persons at large could be linked. (Have you seen Casino Royale? It was really about Nazi gold in Martinique during WW II.) Is it surprising, in light of these realities, that James Bond's fictional adversaries are almost never nations, but usually renegade industrialists and financiers?

Under British and Intrepid's guidance, a US intelligence agency took form under "Wild" Bill Donovan known as the Office of Strategic Services (OSS) which would later form the basis of the CIA. However, Donovan himself had worked for the Rockefeller Foundation, ostensibly distributing aid to starving Poles, Germans and others after World War I. The OSS, however, was much more elitist and right-wing than Intrepid's organisation. The joke of the day was that OSS stood for 'Oh so social".

In the fall of 1942:

> "…the still-continuing German reading of coded American dispatches endangered the work of Allen W. Dulles, nominally a [US] diplomat attached to the Bern legation [in Switzerland], but actually chief American spymaster in Europe. Dulles…had recently begun to plot with the anti-Nazis in Germany to overthrow Hitler… Gisevius, an official in the German consulate at Zurich, told Dulles that Germany had broken one of the American codes. [Dulles later wrote] 'Fortunately, it was not my own code and I had not used it for sending any operational messages… The Germans never succeeded in deciphering any of the messages I sent, and I had the satisfaction of knowing that no one who worked with me was ever jeopardized through deciphered telegrams.'

But this self-promoted and commonly-held view of American diplomatic security under Allen Dulles proves unfounded:

> "For although the Germans may have not solved his cryptograms, the Hungarian Army…had. It fed its information to the R.S.H.A. [*Reichssicherheitshauptam*, Nazi diplomatic intelligence organization] through Wilhelm Hottl…" [233]

No official damage assessment or consideration of Dulles' over-all activities relating to wealthy German and American interests is known to have been conducted. But then, it is hard to analyse a subject for which the primary source material has either been destroyed or remains classified. Today, however, with the ability of the web to bring together diverse facts from around the world, and with access to materials formerly hidden behind the Iron Curtain, more and more of the picture is emerging.

Dulles had extensive connections in the Vatican, Swiss Banking circles, and many governments. Recent international news stories have brought into the public domain knowledge of the at best "blind eye," and at worst, active collaboration, of many financial institutions (particularly Swiss, Dutch and American) with Nazi schemes. According to *Power Inc.* and other sources, Cardinal Eugenio Pacelli, then the papal representative in Munich Germany, secured for a superficially-Catholic Hitler a large sum of Church funds immediately before the war. Pacelli also helped negotiate the notorious papal Concordat with Hitler's Germany. Pacelli became Pope Pius XII in 1939 and has recently been nominated for sainthood, over the understandable outcry of the Jewish people. Franco's fascist revolution in Spain was also approved by the Vatican, due to the Vatican's anti-Communist stance.

Once the impending Nazi defeat became obvious to the German industrialists and their American and foreign colleagues, much of the money was smuggled out of the Reich through paper-changes, and physical movement of Nazi gold through the Swiss Banking system, routes through Argentina, and directly through the Vatican. The OSS representative in the Vatican was a hand-picked crony of Allen Dulles: Hugh Angleton, who had volunteered for duty when his personal interests in Germany, through his company National Cash Register (NCR), were endangered by the Nazi regime. It is alleged that Hugh Angleton's secret job was to make sure the money and profits stayed in "friendly" hands, his family's included. His son, James Jesus Angleton, also worked in intelligence in WW II and later became head of CIA counter-intelligence.

The activities of the Dulles brothers and Rockefellers (and others) relating to their involvements in Germany with financiers, industrialists and Nazis, before, during and after WW II, suggests a more accommodating policy than that of the Roosevelt administration (at least!) towards aiding and abetting a hostile power and ideology. For example the Dulles' law firm represented the Warburg's, Kuhn Loeb's, and Rothschild's International Acceptance Bank, specialising in financing German-American trade, and also represented an off-shoot of the IAB, the American Continental Corporation, which specialised in the American financing of German corporations.[234] There are many questions remaining to be answered about negotiations and accommodations made with the Nazis by the Dulles brothers and others in this circle.

Peter Wright, himself quite right wing and not above apologising for the excesses of elements of the elite, describes Angleton's penchant for "conspiracy," and points out that the CIA's worst excesses occurred under Angleton and Dulles's watch. That is far from a revolutionary opinion.

John Foster Dulles, despite these striking links to Wall Street bankers and industrialists on both sides of the ocean with investments in the Nazi regime, would become Secretary of State when Eisenhower and the Republicans took over from the Roosevelt/Truman Democrats.

> "Dulles had not been Eisenhower's first choice for Secretary of State however, [t]hat had been John J. McCloy, but Senator Robert Taft had vetoed him as being too close to the "international bankers" and "Roosevelt New Dealers" and, by implication, to the Rockefellers. "Every Republican candidate for President since 1936," Taft charged bitterly after his defeat in the 1953 convention, "has been nominated by the [Rockefeller's] Chase Bank."

The Rockefellers were also powerful shareholders in the National City Bank, through the rarely heard-of brother of John D. Rockefeller; William, who was also treasurer of Standard Oil. Despite his anonymity, the Stillman-Rockefellers would rival the (John D.) Spellman-Rockefellers, and *two* monster US banks and partial owners of the US Federal Reserve would fall within this family's sphere of influence. Today CitiGroup and Morgan/Chase are two of the most powerful financial entities on the planet, and today even own part of Russia's Central Bank. The Federal Reserve and its component banks have the power to crush any currency on Earth.

McCloy and the bankers interests would be well represented in the Eisenhower administration, and in Kennedy's as well, where McCloy was Special Presidential Advisor on Disarmament—continuing the absurd upward spiral in spending on redundant weapons of mass destruction. While Taft made a rather modest charge against the candidate selection process of the Republican Party, others were making more dramatic charges against The Council on Foreign Relations (CFR). FBI agent and former Administrative Assistant to J. Edgar Hoover, Dan Smoot, wrote:

> "...since 1944, all candidates for President, both Republican and Democrat, have been CFR members, except Truman who became President by "accident". Every Secretary of State since Cordell Hull [and James Byrnes] has been a CFR member. Over 40 CFR members comprised the American delegation to the UN Organizing Conference in San Francisco including Alger Hiss, Nelson Rockefeller, Adlai Stevenson, Ralph Bunche, John Foster Dulles, and the Secretary of State Edward Stettinius. CFR affiliates have controlled an unusual number of

> cabinet posts and top Presidential advisory positions."[235]

The origin of the CFR also involved the Dulles brothers.

> "In May 1919, a group of young intellectuals who had helped draft the League of Nations Charter during WW I met at the Majestic Hotel in Paris. They were bitterly disappointed. The U.S. Senate…had rejected the concept of a world governing body…This group included Christian Herter [who married the daughter of a Standard Oil magnate and replaced John Foster Dulles as Secretary of State on the latter's death] and John Foster Dulles. They came home and incorporated the Council on Foreign Relations. The influence achieved by Herter and Dulles twenty five years later as secretaries of state under Dwight Eisenhower, and Allen Dulles, as head of the powerful and controversial C.I.A., is one indication of the power obtained by this group.
>
> "Extremely selective in its membership, the Council has never been a "mass" organisation. However, according to the C.F.R.'s 1960 membership roster, its 1400 members control the U.S. State Department, many top Cabinet posts, the major newspapers, magazine[s], and radio and T.V. networks, most of the large tax-exempt foundations, a host of other opinion moulding groups and organizations, and the nation's largest companies including U.S. Steel, AT&T, GM, duPont, IBM and others."[236]

The FBI's intelligence efficiency was always a matter of irritation to some elements of the American ruling class, not to mention the CIA. On at least one occasion, however, it withheld information that would have cleared a Canadian diplomat fatally involved in one of Angleton's witch-hunts.[237] It should not be lost on the reader that most of the men to hold positions in the US National Security Council (NSC) had been indoctrinated at the Council of Foreign Relations, which, like other supposedly 'non-partisan' right-wing think tanks, such as the Brookings and Hudson Institutes, had been founded and subsidised by the Rockefellers and/or other American 'High Capitalists' with interests in US multinational corporations.

> "[T]he corporate money behind Brookings reads like a who's who of blue chip companies. A brief sampling of some 138 corporate supporters: Bell Atlantic, Citibank, J.P. Morgan, Goldman Sachs, NationsBank, Exxon, Chevron, Microsoft, HP, Toyota, Pfizer, Johnson & Johnson, Dupont, Mobil and Lockheed Martin, and the foundations of companies like American Express, Travelers, AT&T, GM, ADM and McDonnell Douglas. A few media conglomerates, like Time Warner and the Washington Post Co., are among the donors.[238]

It is clear from Nelson Rockefeller's statements and policies in South America that a major goal of the American Power Elite was to eliminate any remaining British influence in the Western Hemisphere. Rockefeller gave his reasons for American "involvement" in South America as being to secure South American strategic resources and industries under the ownership of American-based multinationals. Surely this policy extended (and still extends) to Canada. An example of the effects of Nelson's own IBEC company is provided by Collier and Horowitz:

> " Once committed to making 'normal' Latin American profits, the next logical step was to maximize these profits by building a chain of supermarkets throughout the country, selling goods of U.S. producers, and driving small business to the wall. [Is the Wal-Mart phenomenon, then, really something new?] Rather than building up a native Venezuelan economy, therefore, his enterprises—working under the guise of American-Venezuelan cooperation—actually helped to make the country more dependent than before on U.S. corporations and the goods they offered… In fact, far from being a semi-philanthropy altering the fundamental realities of Latin American dependence, IBEC was an avatar of a new business form—the U.S. multinational with subsidiaries and markets flung across the globe…"[239]

Of course, the above anecdote neglects to elucidate the 'other means' employed by American interests to preserve Yankee-Capitalist-friendly dictators in power in South America, as opposed to liberal or social democrats, no matter how democratically elected were the latter. The interests of the Rockefellers and corporations such as ITT, United Fruit (UFCO) and others in South America were also adopted by the Dulles' State Department and the other Dulles' CIA.

Most serious appraisals of American policy in the 1950s suggest that the clandestine activities and influence on the government of the military-industrialists became excessive in those years. In fact, the very lack of oversight and political control over clandestine US activities and the more hawkish aspects of US foreign policy were ironically caused by the same President who would later, in his farewell address, warn of the dangers of the "military-industrial complex".

> "According to Dillon Anderson [who would succeed Nelson in the Cold War Strategy post]... the post was necessary because when Congress had established the CIA it had been placed under the jurisdiction of the National Security Council, since, for constitutional [or secrecy and accountability?] reasons, Eisenhower had decided it should be under the President's jurisdiction. At the same time, however, he preferred not to know about clandestine operations such as the recent overthrow of the democratically elected Arbenz regime in Guatemala because of the difficulty he experienced in presenting the cover story at press conferences. To resolve the difficulty, he appointed a group [the Planning Coordination Group] to oversee these operations; it included the Deputy Secretary of Defense, the Undersecretary of State [Herbert Hoover Jr.], and his own Special Assistant [for Cold War Strategy]."[240]

These three men were responsible for all the "black arts" employed by the United States in those years, including espionage and subversion in foreign nations, and they originated the "plausible deniability" precedent, where not even Presidents were informed of the undertakings going on during their watch. Eisenhower added the unfortunate innovations of removing the CIA from congressional oversight and placing it in the Executive (his) domain, and then proceeding to ask *not* to be informed of its dirty tricks. Whilst historians argue about how much Eisenhower knew, it now seems safe to assume he approved most CIA and other operations in principle, if not in detail. The Planning Coordination Group, a triumvirate consisting of the Special Assistant for Cold War Strategy, the Deputy Secretary of Defense, and the Undersecretary of State, ran the 'security' apparatus of the United States during the Eisenhower years.

Nelson Rockefeller was promoted to something approaching his dream job in October, 1954, around the time the Arrow program was began in earnest.

> "Eighteen months after his appointment to the [Health, Education and Welfare] position, which he had never regarded as more than a holding pattern, Nelson finally got his chance in international affairs when C.D. Jackson resigned his post as Special Assistant to the President and Nelson was named his successor. Jackson's full title had been Special Assistant for Psychological Strategy; Nelson's would be Special Assistant for Cold War Strategy. The odd designations reflected the peculiar nature of the post itself, which officially was to give "advice and assistance in the development of increased understanding and cooperation among all peoples," but was in fact that of Presidential Coordinator for the CIA." [241]

This position allowed Rockefeller to attend meetings of

> "...the Cabinet, the Council on Foreign Economic Policy, and the National Security Council, the highest policy-making body in the government. He also functioned as the head of a secret unit called the Planning Coordination Group, consisting of himself, the Deputy Secretary of Defense, and the head of the CIA." [242]

Nearly every member of the nearly omnipotent NSC has been an inductee of the Council on Foreign Relations, as have practically every 20th century US Secretary of State, US President, and member of the State Department. The Council on Foreign Relations being one of a plethora of 'opinion factories' spawned by the Rockefellers and their fellow travellers.

The members of the even more secretive Planning Coordination Group in this case were all involved in the US-Canadian negotiations on air defense, negotiations that killed the Arrow, initiated an ill-fated free-trade pact on defense, and cut the Arrow out of a European NATO role. They also essentially ran the US "military-industrial complex", the armed services, and the intelligence apparatus of the United States. A clue as to where Cold War Strategy adviser Nelson Rockefeller's sympathies lay regarding British global interests had been demonstrated by his involvement in the formulation of the lend-lease act which was so vital to arming and saving Britain from the Nazis. He advised the government to drive a hard bargain with Britain, especially regarding her remaining territorial and economic interests and influence in the Western hemisphere, which he felt the U.S. should strip from Britain in exchange for armaments and strategic supplies in the fight against Hitler.[243] His views of the ideal relationship with Canada can be deduced from other sources.

> "By the mid-1950s, the United States was locked into its global crusade and the Rockefeller family was established as an important resource in the life of the nation. If it was not quite the 'Rockefeller conspiracy' some charged, it did have the appearance of careful organization. Through its connections with the Chase Bank and the Standard Oil companies, and its associations with such great Wall Street investment and law firms as Kuhn, Loeb; Lazard Freres; Debevoise, Plimpton; and Milbank, Tweed, the family had its fingers on the pulse of the country's industrial and financial heartlines. Through the Rockefeller Foundation, the Council on Foreign Relations, and the Republican party, it was connected to the highest directorates of national policy. Whenever members of the power elite were gathered to make the crucial decisions of the postwar period, one or two of the key individuals would inevitably be drawn from the executive levels of the institutions with which the family was deeply involved. Men like John. J. McCloy, C. Douglas Dillon, James Forrestal,…the Dulles brothers, and Winthrop Aldrich [*all* Wall Street alumnists] were never elected to office, but wielded a power that was in many ways greater and more sustained than that of the elected officials they served. While they shaped the contours of America's postwar strategy, the policy technicians who would succeed them—individuals like W.W. Rostow, Zbigniew Brzezinski, and Henry Kissinger—were busily working their way up through the think tanks the Rockefeller Foundation had played such a key role in creating."[244]

These comments, it should be pointed out, are from a generally quite friendly, even apologetic book on the family. It should perhaps be clear, then, that these various institutes, with their members drawn from politics and corporate boardrooms, have relentlessly waged a continuous campaign to have the public adopt attitudes favourable to their interests. These include un-regulated global capitalism, currencies regulated and created (even for national governments) by borrowing from private bankers, and rule by an administration largely comprised of members drawn from and/or sponsored by, a wealthy elite. Genuine democracy, in the media and in governments has not been part of this agenda. It can be argued that most successful politicians are well aware that they must conform to this model if they have hopes of acquiring the vast sums of money and sympathetic media coverage required for election.

226 Gehlen, Reinhard: The Service p.p. 140-41
227 Wright, Peter: Spycatcher, p.p. 117-18
228 ibid, p. xii-xiii
229 Stock Exchange Practices, Hearings, April-June 1932, Part 2, pp. 566-67, quoted from Galbraith, A Journey Through Economic Time, pg. 65
230 Collier and Horowitz, The Rockefellers, An American Dynasty
231 Mosley, Leonard, Dulles, Ch. 11 pp. 166-188
232 For a compelling exposé of this conspiracy, read Day of Deceit by Robert Stinnett.
233 Kahn, The Codebreakers, p.p. 498-99
234 Chernow, Ron. The Warburgs, The Twentieth Century Odyssey of a Remarkable Jewish Family, New York: Vintage Books, 1993, p. 350
235 Stormer: None Dare Call It Treason, p. 210, quotation is from: Smoot, The Invisible Government, based on Dan Smoot report, Vol. 7, Nos. 24-31
236 Stormer, None Dare Call it Treason, p. 209
237 Adams, Ian. Agent of Influence. Toronto: Stoddart Publishing, 1999 pp. 230-232 According to Adams, the diplomat concerned was John Watkins whose cause of death, while under RCMP interrogation due largely to the CIA's efforts, was falsified by the government of Canada.
238 www.fair.org/extra/9811/brookings.html
239 Coller & Horowitz, The Rockefellers, p. 265
240 ibid, footnote, p.273
241 ibid.
242 Collier & Horowitz, The Rockefellers. p. 273
243 ibid,
244 ibid, p. 277

Chapter 41

OPEN SKIES

> "On May 10, 1955, Soviet negotiators had reversed nine years of disarmament history and accepted the Western plan for manpower ceilings, reduction in conventional armaments, and the Western timetable and technique for the abolition of nuclear stocks and for the reduction of all armed forces. Most unexpected of all, the Soviets agreed for the first time to Western plans for inspections, including on-site inspections with permanent international control posts behind the Iron Curtain."[245]

This appeared to be part of the dramatic softening in the Soviet camp due to the de-Stalinization plans of his replacement, Nikita Khrushchev.

> "Historians would later see it as perhaps the first and last opportunity to stop the escalation of the nuclear arms race. But at the Pentagon and in CIA headquarters at Langley Field, Virginia, the news of the Russian turnabout was greeted with suspicion. Determined to preserve the U.S. advantage in the arms race, yet apprehensive that a simple rejection of apparent Soviet concessions would give the Kremlin an immense advantage in its current 'peace offensive,' they agreed that the problem before them was recapturing the political initiative. It was a task that appealed to the Special Assistant for Cold War Strategy."[246]

As a response, the Open Skies proposal was concocted for the 1955 Geneva Summit and was *promoted* as a means for each side in the Cold War to conduct aerial reconnaissance over the other's territory and thereby re-assure one another of their armament production and intentions. Its real intent was less altruistic. Rockefeller pulled together a group of thinkers who were secreted away at the Marine base in Quantico. In a few days they came up with the "Open Skies" proposal, which proposed allowing reconnaissance flights from each country over the other as a confidence-building measure. *It was designed to be rejected!*

> "It was a plan world opinion would regard as bold and generous, but which the Russians were equally bound to resist as a retreat from the concrete disarmament measures already agreed to and as a scheme that would trade away their most important [strategic] asset, secrecy, for no palpable return… A few days before the President was due to leave for the Summit, Nelson presented the Open Skies idea in a terse, one-page memo. The President agreed it was a good proposal and called Rockefeller to a meeting with Secretary of State Dulles the night before they were scheduled to depart…
>
> "Nelson was called to Geneva, where Eisenhower…stood in the magnificent Palais des Nations, looking down at the expectant faces. Staring squarely at the Russian delegation, he summoned up all his Kansas sincerity and began, "The time has come to end the Cold War," and went on to outline the Open Skies plan. Its [propaganda] success was instantaneous and complete, and Eisenhower became the hero of the conference. A month later, Harold Stassen, U.S. delegate to the disarmament conference, was able quietly to withdraw all the disarmament proposals that the United States had made over the previous ten years, and which had been substantially accepted by the Soviet Union."[247]

Even Dulles would say of this Summit in a message to all State Department mission chiefs: "For eight years [the Western alliance had] been held together largely by a cement compounded of fear and a sense of moral superiority. Now the fear is diminished and the moral demarcation is somewhat blurred." The fear didn't subside for long however, and certainly the failure of the Summit to achieve real arms control assisted the profits of US arms makers, and the banks which financed them.

It seems clear, when it is finally appreciated that the Arrow program represented cutting edge technology in *every* aspect, that the company and country would thereafter be serious competition to American arms manufacturers. What is generally not appreciated is that Canada and the Commonwealth would also possess the means to defend themselves with little or no reliance on the United States. This would potentially place them in technical, military, diplomatic and commercial competition with the United States. This would also have meant, during the Cold War, that the

Commonwealth could have become a viable alternative in the Superpower confrontation. Nations uncomfortable with the extreme polarities offered by the US and USSR might have had a more moderate alternative, providing a third option in the Cold War.

There is a growing body of evidence that the United States ruling elite, at the time, used the Cold War to advance their political and perhaps especially, their economic interests world-wide. In view of the above it seems increasingly evident that they actually exacerbated the Cold War and acted to ensure there were only two options in it, the American side, and the Soviet. This is one reason the United States viewed the British Commonwealth as intelligence, technical and economic competitors as much as allies. Commercial and military-technical security concerns usually trumped joint efforts to restrain the Soviets. In fact John Foster Dulles, when interviewed by *Time* when he won their "Man of the Year" accolade, said that he had four main goals as Secretary of State of the United States of America. One of these was to expand, prolong and intensify the Cold War. Such a statement today seems almost insane. But then, it was John Foster Dulles who came up with the nuclear doctrine of Mutually Assured Destruction, or M.A.D. Why hold a nuclear gun to the head of the entire planet unless fear and dependence on America for defense were the agenda? Dependence on America for defense also involved making sure that the leading defense technology was in the United States, not elsewhere, and thus involved making the "allies" dependent for technology as well. This obviously had great economic benefits in terms of patents, production, technological superiority, and balance of payments and balance of trade. Today, aerospace [248] and weapons are two of the only areas in which the United States has a positive balance of trade. In fact, the United States sells more weapons than the other top five competitors combined.[249]

In 1956 the US government authorised the Rockefeller brothers to fund a panel on U.S. foreign policy involving fourteen Rockefeller-selected panellists, nine of whom were members of the CFR, including one of its directors, and Dean Rusk, a future Secretary of State under Kennedy. The panel's report: *Prospects for America,* included the admission that, to achieve the goals the panel supported for America, "…it has been necessary to drum up support for U.S. policy by stressing the imminent threats and crisis and by harping on the less attractive features of communism." McCarthyism, heightened paranoia and fear were, under Eisenhower, officially-sanctioned tools by which to manipulate society, indeed, democracy at large. This was no news to the Democrats under Truman and through the 1950s. "What [Truman's Secretary of State] Dean Acheson referred to as 'the Attack of the Primitives' had been raging for several years in Washington. Senator Joe McCarthy of Wisconsin and other Red hunters were waving phony lists of subversives and hounding government agencies to cut loose their 'security risks,' no matter how trivial their 'leftist' associations. The State Department under John Foster Dulles was particularly craven; Dulles had hired one of McCarthy's henchmen to help him sweep out subversives."[250] Dulles may have also found it an opportune way to dispose of some of the social democrats that had caused him and his German-collaborating clients such trouble before and during WW II.

It was in response to Prospects for America—also known as the Rockefeller Panel—that some of St. Laurent's Liberals in Ottawa agitated for an economic inquiry of their own: a Royal Commission on the Economic Prospects for Canada, undertaken against the wishes of a pro-American cadre in the Cabinet, including C.D. Howe. Under Walter Lockhart Gordon, this commission looked particulary hard at American economic involvement in Canada with an eye to discerning its goals and long-term effects.

245 Ibid, p. 274
246 Ibid.
247 Collier & Horowitz, The Rockefellers, p. 275
248 United States General Accounting Office, Report to the Chairman, Committee on Science, Space, and Technology, House of Representatives, July, 1991 report titled: Aerospace Plane Techology, Research and Development Efforts in Europe.
249 Scowen, Peter: Rogue Nation: The America the Rest of the World Knows. Toronto: McClelland and Stewart Ltd., 2003
250 Thomas: The Very Best Men, p. 99

Chapter 42

SECOND THOUGHTS ON BI-LATERAL INTEGRATION

In Canada in the mid-1950s there was growing concern about US direct investment (ownership), of an increasingly dominant character, in the Canadian economy. Elements of the Liberal party, *not* assisted by Mitchell Sharp and during the absence of C.D. Howe, had agreed to let Walter Lockhart Gordon head up a study on the Canadian economy in terms of strategic interests and long term effects. Wrote Gordon: "For some time during the late 1940s and early 1950s, I had been worrying about the government's economic policies, and particularly the complacency with which Canadians were witnessing the sell-out of our resources and business enterprises to Americans and other enterprising foreigners."[251] On 17 June, 1955, the Royal Commission on the Economic Prospects for Canada was established.

Another Gordon, of the Crawford variety, testified to the Gordon Commission and his words are quoted in the December 1956 interim report of the Commission:

> " The foundation of the aircraft industry in this and all countries has been, is and always will be predicated on the needs of national defense and military requirements. If it is accepted that an efficient air force is needed, it must follow that an efficient aircraft industry must also be maintained. An aircraft industry is an essential part of an air force.
>
> "And because an air force must be free to choose its own weapons, the industry must be technically competent to design and develop and produce whatever is required. If the Canadian aircraft industry is to fulfil this role as the industrial arm of the RCAF, and keep it supplied with up-to-date equipment, then it follows that it can only be done with products of our own design and development."

Also in December of 1956, after re-investing every dollar earned into building up the infrastructure of Avro Aircraft and Orenda Engines in Malton Ontario, old Sir Thomas (T.O.M.) Sopwith himself, at this time Chairman of the Hawker Siddeley Group, invited Canadians to take a stake in the company's expansion. A half million shares were offered to Canadians in that month, comprising 17% of the value of A.V. Roe Canada Ltd. Orenda engines was also unveiling a spanking-new high-tech jet propulsion laboratory in Sopwith's name, an important tool in the design and improvement of the Iroquois and the hoped-for subsequent engines. Sopwith, while taking A.V. Roe Canada Ltd. public on the Toronto Stock Exchange through Wood Gundy, proclaimed:

> "Our Canadian group has now become a vital part of the Canadian economy, in which every Canadian citizen is interested. At the same time, it has become a matter of concern to the Canadian people that so much of their industrial activity is in the hands of non-resident owners and, whilst they welcome the assistance which is given in developing their vast potential resources, there is a growing feeling that they should be allowed to share in the ownership, as well as the operation, of these activities." [252]

It is perhaps worthwhile to consider where American interests lay in the 1957 election. It was in response to this growing concern, in some quarters in Canada, about the alarming growth of American ownership in the Canadian economy, that the previous Liberal administration had started a Royal Commission in the first place. It seemed tailor made to rebuff the Rockefeller panel's overt economic imperialism. This commission pointed out the negative impact this increasing ownership was going to have on Canada's future. Some of the problems foreseen were:

1) The decline of research and development in Canada due to this work being concentrated in the home offices of the American companies then buying Canadian production facilities.

2) The inability of Canada to look after its strategic needs, including defense, if Canadian strategic resources were allowed to be bought out by American interests.

3) An exodus of Canadian administrative, scientific and technical talent to the United States as a result of the above.

4) A decline in Canadian economic, military and political independence brought about by the above, with the probable result of Canada losing any real sovereignty and thus becoming a satellite of the United States.[253]

One of the recommendations of the Gordon Commission, as it was informally known, was that foreign-owned businesses operating in Canada and doing the majority of their business in Canada might have to be compelled to sell a minority stake (20-25%) to Canadian shareholders. It was suggested that this be accomplished in small increments, at fair market prices. This policy was anathema to the ruling American financiers, industrialists and aligned politicians. The CIA had, in fact, in their first successfully engineered "regime change", deposed Iran's democratically elected premier: Mossadegh, for policies similar in intent to those advocated by the Gordon Commission.

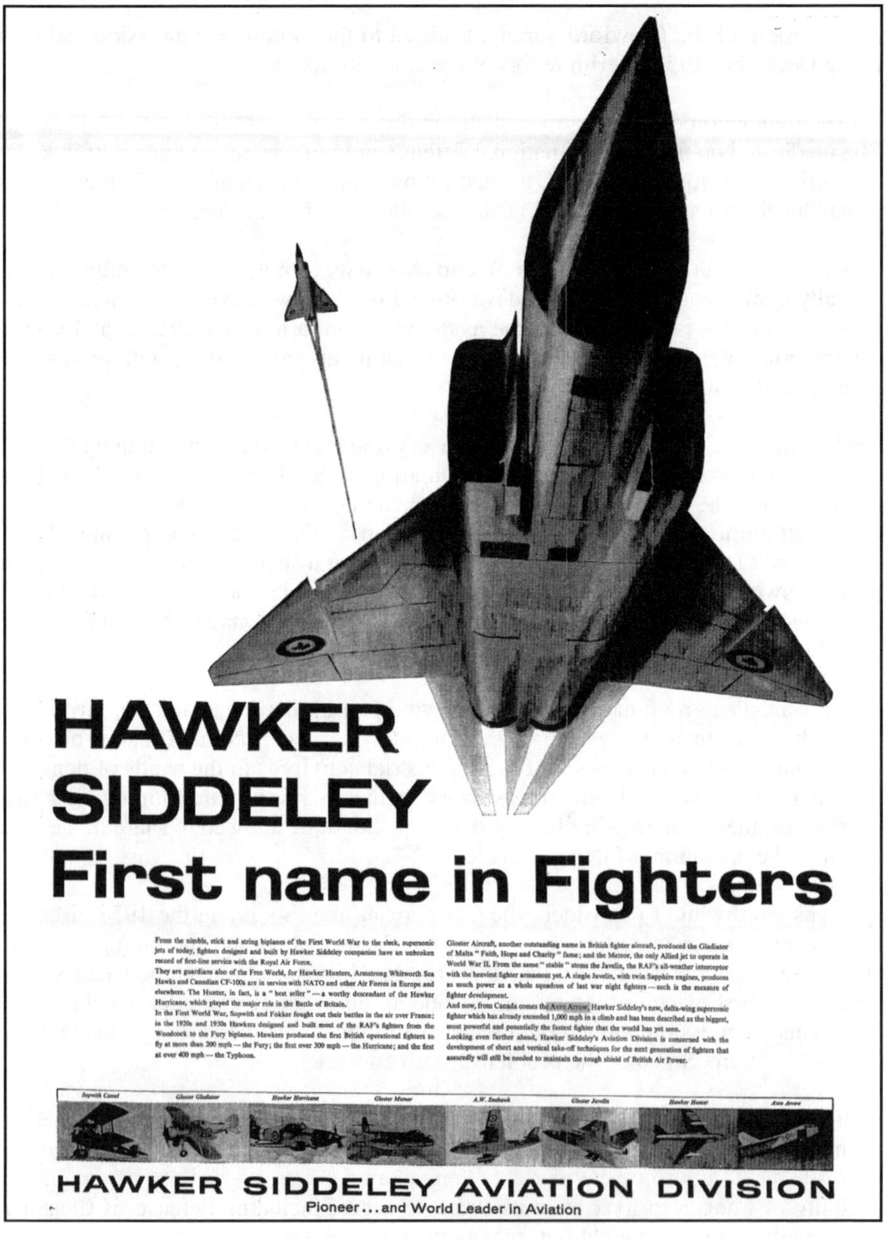

251 Gordon, Walter L. A Political Memoir. Toronto: McClelland & Stewart, 1977 p. 59
252 Financial Post, 6 October, 1956, p.5.
253 Gordon, Walter L.: A Choice for Canada, based in part on the Gordon Commission.

Chapter 43

A PERSIAN DIVERSION

It is well known that Britain and/or the United States used covert and military means to prevent unfavourable governments in the Middle East, in Italy, and in other countries, from gaining power, ultimately resulting in the overthrow of the democratically elected Mossadegh regime in Iran in favour of the Shah. This adventure was touted by the CIA as its first successful regime change, yet the ultimate reaction to this meddling was Ayatollah Khomeini and the Islamic fundamentalism that it caused, and is still causing.

> "The plot begins in 1952 with Britain, under an aging Prime Minister Winston Churchill, going to the Americans with the idea of overthrowing the Iranian government of Premier Mohammed Mossadegh. The British government controlled the country's oil production after the Second World War through the Anglo-Iranian Oil Company. [This partly British government-owned company was started through Churchill when, as First Lord of the Admiralty, he had ordered conversion of the Royal Navy from coal fuelled steamships to oil. The oil company was promoted as being required for national security.] Mossadegh was a militant nationalist who came to power in 1951 after the assassination of a pro-Western leader. Mossadegh despised the West, and especially Britain, for the way it exploited his country's oil resources… 'The Premier, whose mind runs in a deep single track, was committed to nationalization—and much to the surprise of the British, he went through with it…'" Rather than negotiate to get its oil back,…the British turned to the CIA for help. The Americans were at first reluctant to arrange a coup… They changed their minds after President Dwight D. Eisenhower was inaugurated… The joint British intelligence (SIS) and CIA plan, code-named TPAJAX, quickly gained steam… Pressure to get the timid shah to sign the [necessary decrees] was applied by his twin sister…and by U.S. General H. Norman Schwarzkopf, the father of "Stormin'" Norman Schwarzkopf, the leader of the United States forces in the Gulf War… The British agreed to hammer home the communist threat and play down the true motivation for the coup, Britain's oil interests.
>
> "Also by this time, the CIA's propaganda machine was busily building support for Zahedi [the American choice for Premier] and opposition to Mossadegh. The Agency's "Art Group" prepared realistic protest posters and flyers that appeared to be the work of legitimate protest groups… As well, the United States government began to destabilize Mossadegh's regime through statements planted on the lips of members of Eisenhower's cabinet by the CIA; on July 28, the secretary of state of the day, John Foster Dulles, told a press conference that, 'The growing activities of the illegal Communist Party in Iran and the toleration of them by the Iranian Government has caused our government concern. These developments make it more difficult to grant aid to Iran.'" [254] [Is this not remarkably similar to the second Iraq War and the constant harping on the terrorist threat?]

One wonders who had the authority, moral or legal, to decide for Iran that the Communist party was illegal, or even that the nationalist Mossadegh was communist. But then, the statement was given at the suggestion of the CIA.

One of the reasons that the Americans were concerned about nationalization measures in resource rich countries was given by Nelson Rockefeller to the US House Committee on Foreign Affairs, then considering the Mutual Security Act, which established the Mutual Assistance Plan.

> "[Nelson then] launched into a prepared statement, which he called *A New Approach to International Security:* 'As a nation, we have six percent of the population of the world, and seven percent of the land area. Just before the last war we produced about thirty-three and a third percent, a third of the world's manufactured goods, and a third of the raw materials in the world. The two have been in balance.' Then Nelson turned to the array of statistical charts his aides had set up to illustrate the comparative growth of industrial goods and raw materials from 1899 to 1951. These showed that U.S. industrial production had now increased to 50 percent of the world's total, while raw materials production was still only one-third. 'Thus,' Nelson explained, 'to supply more than one-third of the raw material requirement for our fac-

tories…The question is from where do we get the raw materials we import. *The answer is that seventy-three percent of our needs for strategic and critical materials come from the underdeveloped areas. We face the blunt fact that the United States no longer finds the base of its own security within its own borders.* That is a pretty startling fact in view of our own history of complete, as we thought, independence." [255] [italics added]

Canada is, for the United States, the single most important source of strategic resources. In light of this it is interesting to note that the Mutual Assistance Plan, whereby the US funnelled money into some allied nations for armament purchases, was seen, among many, as an altruistic measure on the part of the United States. The above suggests it had other intentions, such as to encourage the allies to purchase "superior" US weapons, and let their own industries and research and development efforts languish—which is what happened. In the case of Canada, it is obvious how Rockefeller and those of like mind would have viewed a foreign company that went from nothing in 1945 to one of the top 80 North American corporations in thirteen short years.

During the Gordon Commission, A.V. Roe Canada Ltd. was called to testify and during their testimony the comparative costs of production of the CF-100 and its Orenda engines (both A.V. Roe Canada Ltd. products), were analysed. It turned out that the Orenda and CF-100, despite its development problems, had cost Canada less than similar programs had cost the United States.[256] By this time A.V. Roe Canada Ltd., until then a wholly-owned subsidiary of the British Hawker Siddeley Group, had begun selling shares to Canadians. By 1958 the company was 43% Canadian owned, whereas its chief rival, Canadair in Montreal, was 100% owned by the American General Dynamics corporation, as was Avro Canada's number one competitor in interceptor design and production: Convair. No wonder there was so much passion exhibited during the annual Canadair vs. Avro hockey tournaments.

It seems apparent enough that the United States would have viewed such an economically-nationalistic policy, as advocated by Gordon and his supporters, with alarm. The Mossadegh precedent suggests they would have acted to support the Diefenbaker campaign as a result, and this charge was laid in Kay Shaw's book, *There Never Was an Arrow.*

C.D. Howe obviously came to regret having established Avro. Could it be because they broke the "Continentalist" mould he had crafted, and were expanding the British Commonwealth weight in strategic industry and resources through the diversification that his old underling, Crawford Gordon Jr., had undertaken? Certainly among Avro's staunchest supporters were those economic nationalists most vocal in denouncing C.D. Howe and the Liberals' integrationist policies. One clue to Howe's thinking is reflected in his response to Walter Lockhart Gordon's Royal Commission on the Economic Prospects for Canada:

> "Most of the commission's proposals were expressed in very general terms. Nevertheless, they provoked a great deal of attention and considerable controversy. C.D. Howe was furious. He had been away when it was decided to set up the commission and had always been opposed to the idea. Now he interpreted its findings as a criticism of policies for which he had been responsible, and to some extent this was quite true."[257]

Diefenbaker raged against the national-economic policy recommendations of Gordon, later calling Gordon "The Toronto taxidermist who fills Mr. Pearson with flossy economic ideas."[258] —although he later admitted in Cabinet that, due to independence lost to the United States through his own government's cancellation of the Arrow program, that they might have to adopt some of the measures Gordon had advocated:

> "As regards the point that cancellation would mean that Canada would be still further "under the wing of the U.S.", it should be remembered that maintaining freedom from U.S. control was a continuous struggle. It might appear that the present decision was a retrograde step. But there would be other opportunities to assert Canadian sovereignty and independence. For example, *it might be necessary in the near future to introduce legislation to ensure the independence of Canadian companies…* It would be unwise to blame the U.S. for the outcome of the Arrow contract." [259]

Note that while Diefenbaker suggested it would be unwise to blame the US for the cancellation of the Arrow, he didn't say it would be *untrue* to do so.

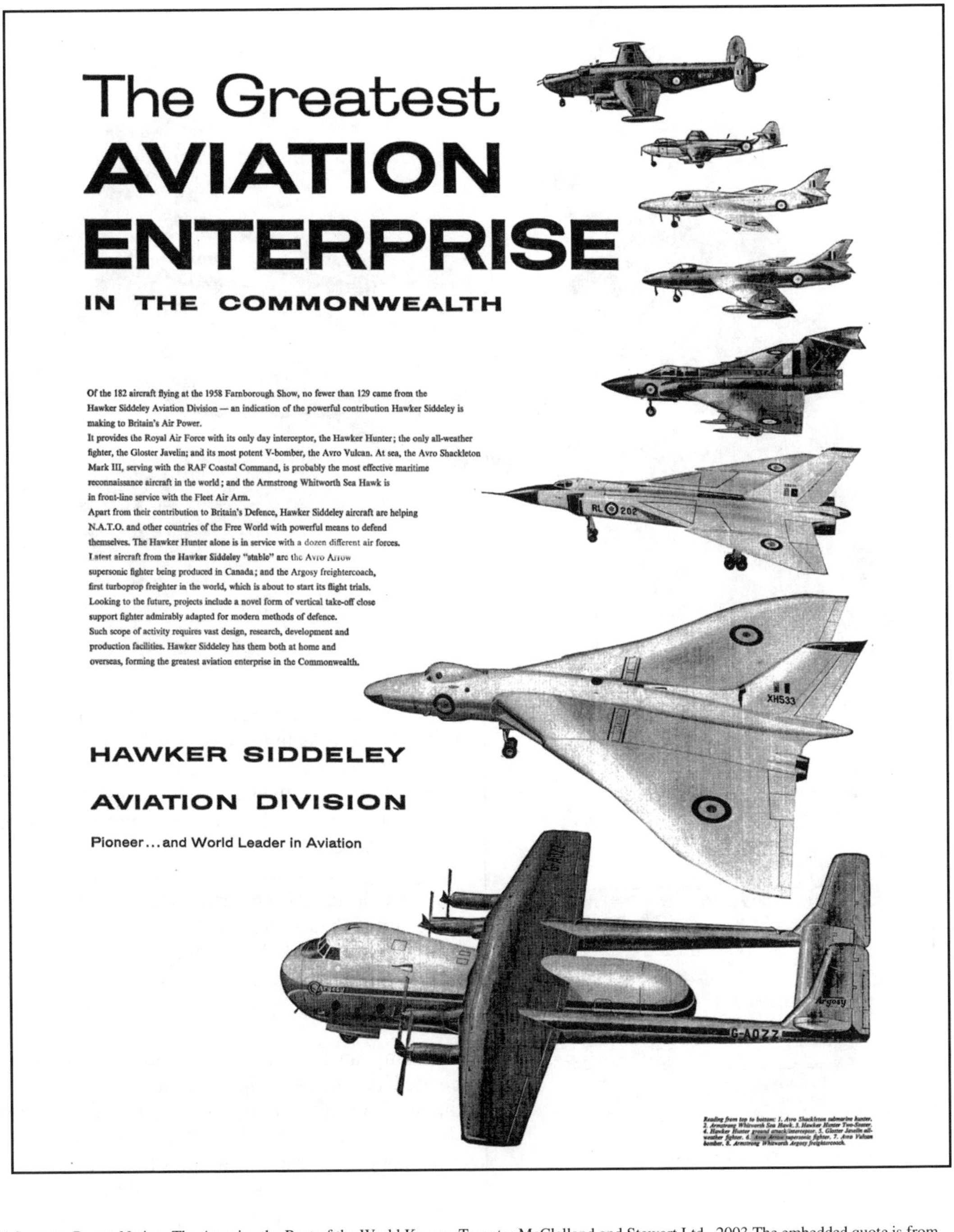

254 Scowen: Rogue Nation: The America the Rest of the World Knows. Toronto: McClelland and Stewart Ltd., 2003 The embedded quote is from Time magazine, in an article titled "Mohammed Mossadegh: Challenge of the East", January 7, 1952

255 ibid. p.p. 268-69

256 Shaw: There Never Was an Arrow. This study concluded that the programs had cost between 80 and 90% of similar programs in the United States, and that the prices of the products were correspondingly lower.

257 Gordon: A Political Memoire, p.64

258 Newman: Renegade in Power, p.427

259 Cabinet minutes, 23 February, 1959, p.4

Chapter 44

AVRO'S X-WING FIGHTER

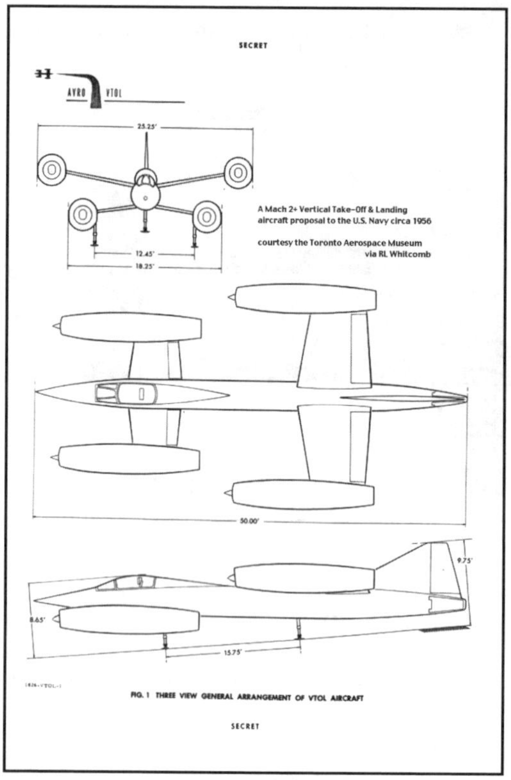

After the Arrow was analysed by the United States in 1955, and rejected, Avro was allowed to bid on a specification for a supersonic vertical take off (VTO) fighter for the US Navy. Many US manufacturers also bid on this contract, and even Avro's Special Projects Group, with their 'flying saucer' designs, were allowed to compete. Since the preliminary design of the Arrow was essentially complete, Jim Floyd's engineering group found time to prepare a remarkably original and functional design. The result was almost without question the most feasible and high-performance design offered.

Using an X-wing configuration with engines podded on the wingtips, this aircraft promised a thrust-to-weight ratio of over one-to-one at take-off weight. A speed of Mach 2 was promised, with armament consisting of missiles housed in the central fuselage. Since the aircraft could land and take off vertically, a simple landing gear without wheels was incorporated saving weight and other design problems.

Performance and other statistics are reproduced below from a page of the proposal given to the US Navy.

Simple eyelid shutters housed in the rear of the engine nacelles would rotate 90 degrees to deflect engine thrust downwards. Forward flight would be achieved by the pilot pitching the aircraft forward to gain speed, once the aircraft was a safe distance above the take-off area. Fly-by-wire controls would be used to provide stability and engine thrust balance, and the pilot could roll or pitch the aircraft to compensate for any winds across the take-off area. Once aerodynamic flight speed was achieved, the eyelids would be rotated to their forward flight position, with the jet exhaust then being directed rearward. While the aircraft would be vulnerable to engine failure on take-off, the fact is that all vertical take-off aircraft are; even the vast majority of helicopters. Unlike the Hawker Harrier and new Joint Strike Fighter, the Avro VTO fighter would have been highly supersonic, and once forward flight was achieved, could fly great distances with an engine out. All in all, it was an elegant and relatively simple solution to complex problems—Avro design hallmarks. Like all Avro designs after the CF-100, it was, obviously, not produced.

SECRET

AVRO VTOL

6. 3. PERFORMANCE SUMMARY

TABLE 6

LOADING AND PERFORMANCE

(I. C. A. O. Standard Atmosphere except where otherwise stated)

WEIGHT:

Take-off gross weight	16, 250 lb.
Operational weight empty	11, 250 lb.
Combat weight (40% fuel gone)	14, 250 lb.
Landing weight (with reserve fuel and armament)	12, 384 lb.
T/W ratio; sea level at 89. 6°F and T. O. gross weight	1. 1

SPEED:

Maximum level speed at combat weight:

(a) At sea level	635 Kts.
(b) At 60, 000 ft.	1146 Kts.

CEILING:

Combat ceiling, (rate of climb 500 ft/min), at combat weight at 1. 75 M. N.	62, 000 ft.

RATE OF CLIMB:

Steady rate of climb at combat weight:

(a) At sea level at 0. 9 M. N.	55, 600 ft/min.
(b) At 45, 000 ft. at 1. 75 M. N.	13, 200 ft/min.

TIME TO HEIGHT:

Time to attain 60, 000 ft. and 1. 75 M. N. from T. O.	7. 94 mins.

ACCELERATION:

Time to accelerate in level flight at 40, 000 ft. from M = 1. 0 to M = 1. 75 at combat weight	3. 21 mins.

MANOEUVRABILITY:

Combat load factor at combat weight at 45, 000 feet and 1. 75 M. N.	2. 34

MISSION:

For a 100 N. M. combat radius of action with initial climb at 0. 9 M. N., cruise out at 0. 9 M. N. at 45, 000 feet, accelerate to 1. 75 M. N., climb to 60, 000 feet at 1. 75 M. N., combat at 60, 000 feet at 1. 75 M. N. for 5 Min., cruise back at 0. 9 M. N. at 45, 000 feet, requisite fuel reserve on landing, then loiter time over station	16 Mins.

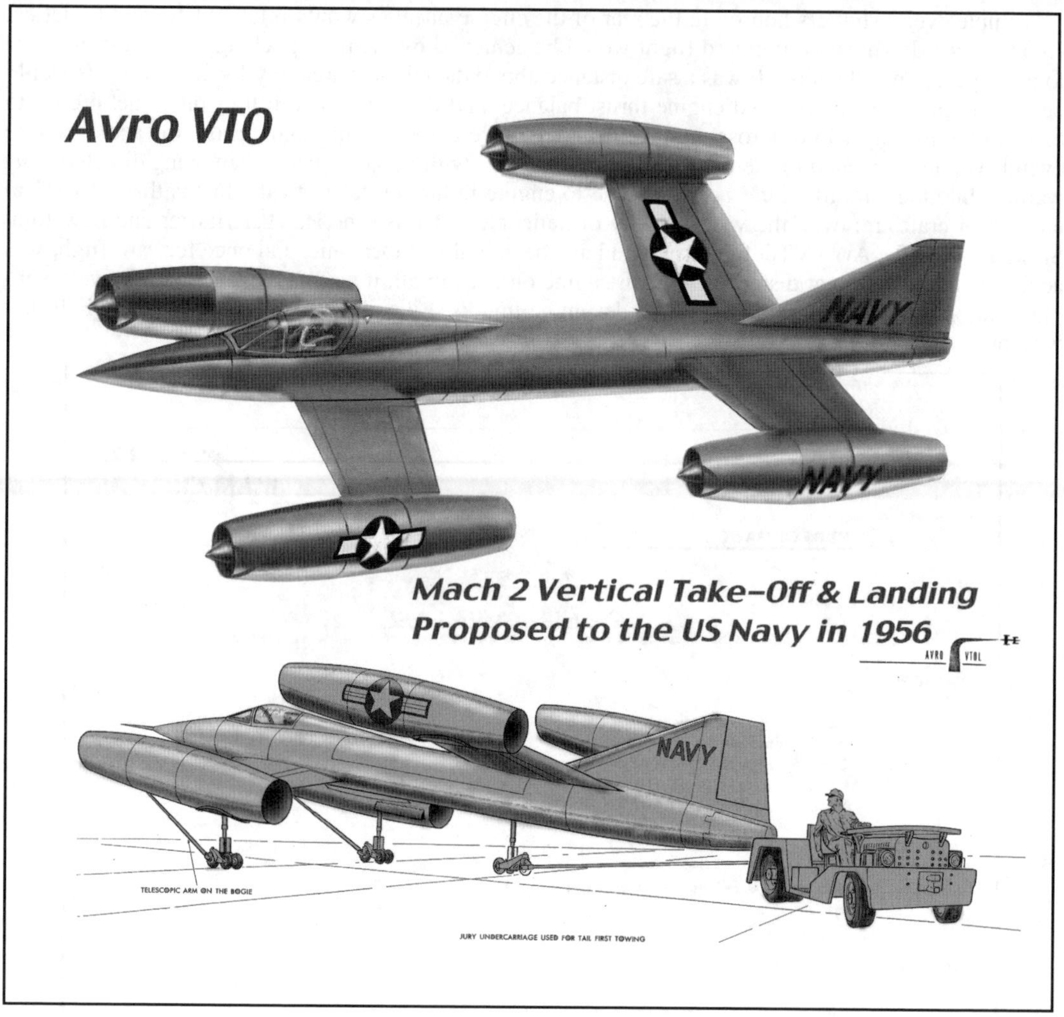
Avro VTO
NAVY
NAVY
NAVY
Mach 2 Vertical Take-Off & Landing
Proposed to the US Navy in 1956
AVRO VTOL
TELESCOPIC ARM ON THE BOGIE
JURY UNDERCARRIAGE USED FOR TAIL FIRST TOWING

Chapter 45

POLITICS AS USUAL
A CHANGING OF THE GUARD

On 21 June, 1957, despite the virtually unanimous predictions of the media, the Conservatives under John George Diefenbaker squeaked into power with a minority government. Somehow they had even made a major breakthrough in the province of Quebec—traditionally a Liberal bastion. Actually, this was no mystery, since the autocratic and corrupt Quebec government of Maurice Duplessis had turned their party election machinery over to the Conservatives…for promises unknown. Could it have had something to do with the Quebec aerospace industry? As Peter C. Newman notes, a young Brian Mulroney, then a corporate lawyer in Montreal serving American corporations operating in Canada, helped swing Quebec to the Diefenbaker Conservatives.

After 22 years of Liberal rule, not everyone in the civil service, military and industry were happy to see the Conservatives take power.

> "The new deputy minister of Trade and Commerce, Gordon Churchill, was steered away from his offices by the deputy minister, Mitchell Sharp,[260] while his old files were moved out. 'Then,' he later recalled, ' I moved down with a small staff of four or five to the coldest reception that I have ever received in my life."[261]

Avro found no improvement in the atmosphere with Ottawa once the Diefenbaker Conservatives took office. Diefenbaker and the party had campaigned against government industrial investment in central Canada and his new defense minister, retired Major General George R. Pearkes, V.C., of Kamloops BC, was a former colleague of two high-ranking Army generals who were dead set against the Arrow. Pearkes had worked with the Chairman of the Chiefs of Staff Committee (CCSC), General Charles Foulkes at a high level for years before entering politics. None of this boded well for Avro.

Defense Minister George R. Pearkes V.C.

Pearkes had also worked with the General who preceded Foulkes as the CCSC, General Guy Simonds. There can be no doubt Simonds, considered by many a heroic Canadian Army general from WW II, hated the Arrow program from the beginning, and said so publicly anytime he was asked. Foulkes was more discreet, and, I'm sure most would agree, more cloak and dagger, but was also opposed to the Arrow. Under Foulkes on the Chiefs of Staff Committee (CSC) the Chief of Staff of the Canadian Army was also opposed to the Arrow. Indeed, when Simonds resigned as CCSC, the job should have gone to RCAF Air Marshal Roy Slemon. Slemon was considered, by parties favourable to Canada's defensive military-industrial program, to be a highly capable, motivated and articulate voice favouring both an independent RCAF *and* industry to sustain it specialising in air defense (i.e., fighters.) All of this was, of course, designed to bolster an image of Canada as a friendly, advanced and generous nation working to defend those threatened by regimes holding more selfish motives. That another Army General was chosen to replace Simonds might be indicative of which way the wind was blowing by the old guard of the Liberal party before the election: Slemon was not chosen to replace the Army CCSC. Rather, Slemon was posted far from the political morass of Ottawa to Colorado Springs as Canada's first Deputy Commander in Chief NORAD (DCINC NORAD), with this seemingly exalted new position being sufficient to justify another Canadian Army representative in the seat of the CCSC. This time it was General Charles Foulkes.

It is interesting to note an official opinion of Foulkes included in Granatstein's *The Generals.* In an American appraisal, designed to guide US officers in dealing with the British commanders in the field post-D-Day, Foulkes was considered:

> "...pleasant but unimpressive, restrained and thin-skinned. He is not a forceful leader nor is he endowed with any great brains. He appears to think highly of US military leaders and enjoys associating with them. In dealing with him a little flattery and personal attention on a "first name" basis would be helpful."[262]

Granatstein also seemed to support Foulkes controversial tactics of the period when he seemingly congratulates Foulkes for "masterminding the scrapping of the Arrow". He has also written, in *Who Killed the Canadian Military,* that the Arrow was a boondoggle because it cost at least 10 million a copy whilst there were roughly comparable aircraft offered by the United States for $250,000 each! This, by the way, was about the price of a Spitfire before WW II, and the United States did *not* have comparable aircraft at the time–at any price.

As a result, throughout most of the Arrow program, half the members of the CSC were opposed to the Arrow program. They had been, up to cancellation, going along with the emphatic recommendations of the RCAF—the responsible experts—with the agreement of the key politicians who at the time provided the funds.

One is forced to then ask *why* the Army Generals were opposed to the Arrow, with the Navy Admiral remaining largely neutral. The answer given by Simonds, and also given by his successor Foulkes, was that ground-to-air missiles (which the army could deploy rather than the air force), were better and cheaper. (At the time there were similar, vehement arguments between the USAF and US Army over who would deploy anti-aircraft missiles and other items.) *(In fact historical precedent would show that the same argument existed in the Soviet Union and even previously in Nazi Germany. This remark by Mr Whitcomb cuts to the heart of this whole issue. The US Air Force fought a prolonged battle to wrest control of America's missiles away from the US Army, they ultimately succeeded and therefore after 1960 no voice was raised in America comparing fighters to missiles. The battle for funding one over the other ended when Wernher von Braun's Army missile team was handed over on a plate to the newly formed NASA and the US Air Force took control of both fighters and missiles. Ed.)* It is interesting that when pressed, the Army couldn't name any particular missile system they thought would do the job of the long-range interceptor with its independent radar and its own missiles. During a meeting of the CSC, Air Vice Marshal Hendricks, in charge of RCAF Technical Services, in his archived diary of that day, asked which missile system the army had in mind. The response to this question was that they didn't know which missile to recommend, and that they were basing their judgement on *"a feeling"* that ground-to-air missiles had rendered manned aircraft obsolete. No doubt much of that 'feeling" came from the US Army and missile manufacturers. Of course, money has an influence and the RCAF was then getting half the defense budget, and therefore the toys for the Army were more scarce than they would have preferred.

260 Mitchell Sharp would go on to head the Bilderberg Group after its founder, Prince Bernhard, was forced to resign over his complicity in the famous Lockheed Scandal, where the French Atlantique anti-submarine warfare plane, a European NATO project, was abandoned in favour of Lockheed P-3 Orions.

261 Stursberg, Peter, Diefenbaker, Leadership Gained, 1956-62, Toronto: University of Toronto Press, 1975, p. 73 (quoted from Dow: The Arrow, p. 163)

262 Granatstein, J.L.: The Generals: The Canadian Army's Senior Commanders in the Second World War, Toronto: Stoddart, 1993

Chapter 46

BOMBER GAP TO MISSILE GAP

In 1957 there was a change in US intelligence assessments and projections that had serious repercussions for Avro Canada and the British aerospace sector. The CIA, based upon a few U-2 overflights of the Soviet Union, proposed, to various suitably-approved authorities, that the Soviet bomber threat had been vastly over-estimated, and that their true strength, in terms of intercontinental bombers capable of hitting Canada, or the United States, lay between about 100 and 200 bombers. This quantity refers to Soviet bombers capable of flying from the Soviet Union to North America and then back to the Soviet Union. The Soviets also had, however, about 800 Tu-4 Bull bombers (their copy of the B-29), which was capable of flying from the Soviet Union to North America, but not all the way back again—unless they were refuelled in flight. Those who pretend the Arrow was designed for a nearly non-existent threat also ignore the existence of 1,000 to 1,500 Soviet tactical bombers threatening Britain and continental Europe—also an area of Canadian responsibility. It was also an area in which allies who might be convinced to buy Arrows resided. Naturally these minimised threat assumptions, particularly a CIA projection that the Soviet Union *and* the United States were going to give up their aeroplanes for missiles, were contested by leading Western air defense experts. Duncan Sandys, then British Minister of Defense, having already developed an over-appreciation for missile technology in WW II, was quite prepared to accept this advice and issued his aviation industry devastating White Paper of 1957. This white paper cancelled many development programs in the U.K., including the entire GOR 329 fighter requirement which the RAF had decided would have been best filled by the Avro Arrow.[263]

Adding to the urgency for a change in Western defense strategy were CIA projections relating to Soviet progress and intentions regarding Intercontinental Ballistic Missiles (ICBMs), with this appreciation becoming the foundation on which NORAD, and thus Canadian air defense, was planned. Alarmist National Intelligence Estimates of December 10, 1957—just after Sputnik—estimated that the Soviets might have 100 operational ICBMs as early as 1959 and perhaps 500 by 1960. Up to 2,000 Soviet ICBMs were projected for as early as 1966.[264] The intelligence on these matters given to Canada and Britain by the CIA was restricted to the very highest levels, which meant only a few politicians having a 'need to know', and, perhaps, the CCSC. While this was done purportedly out of fear of Soviet espionage, it also added the factor of unaccountability to service specialists, since they didn't know of, and thus couldn't argue, the dispensed wisdom granted to the higher-ups. All of these missile estimates, like the bomber gap, proved absurd. By 1960 the Soviets may have had ten ICBMs and, throughout most of the 1960s, many of their 'warheads' were filled with radioactive dust, not atomic fission or fusion devices. By about 1968, when the Soviets achieved near-parity with American ICBM forces, the United States began putting multiple warheads on their ICBMs—each with its own target.

Apparently unswayed by the American intelligence, and even their own WW II missile experience, in February 1957 a team from the German Luftwaffe, led by its head (the legendary General Kammhuber), arrived in Malton. They spent a day at Avro mostly investigating the Arrow program, and the evening at Briarcrest, the company's corporate retreat.

> "They were apparently very impressed and told Air Marshal Slemon that they were really impressed with everything that they had seen in Canada, and particularly at Avro, whom they considered comparable with anything on this continent, both technically and manufacturing-wise.
>
> "Our assessment of the situation is that they are not particularly interested in the CF-100, but are extremely interested in the CF-105 because of its versatility, and even with my elementary smattering of German, I noticed considerable discussion among themselves about its use as a light bomber. I only hope that the Jerries never go in for that game again!!"[265]

The CIA's new (as of 1957) intelligence on Soviet bomber strength was purportedly based on overflights of the Soviet Union by Lockheed U-2 spyplanes. As Larry Milberry asserts; "U-2 flights quickly revealed that the long-argued Soviet bomber threat, represented by the Myasishchev MYA-4 Bison and Tupolev TU-95 Bear, was relatively small." These aircraft were challenging CF-100 targets, and the Arrow was designed to counter these and follow-up designs (one of which was then in testing in the Soviet Union) or fulfil the interception and other roles in Europe and other allied countries, such as Australia.

Well researched books on intelligence point out that the launch schedules and targets of the U-2s were known, in advance, to the Russians through espionage. Furthermore, the Americans had been conducting flights within Soviet airspace for years prior to the appearance of the U-2, with the massive Convair RB-36 Peacemakers, B-47 Stratojets and other aircraft—leading one to question why the sudden 'new' intelligence on Soviet bomber strength. In fact, overflights had occurred in the late 1940s by the British, equipped with US planes, and directly by the US as soon as the Republicans took office in 1953. While most historians suggest that American overflights and aerial reconnaissance of the Soviet Union began under Eisenhower, and that the Francis Gary Powers shootdown was the first example of the Soviets shooting down Western spyplanes, the facts suggest otherwise:

> "In April 1950, a Navy patrol bomber [equipped for intelligence work] with a crew of ten was attacked and destroyed by Soviet fighters while flying over the Baltic. A year and a half later another Navy bomber was shot down, with the loss of all ten on board. That year an Air Force Superfortress…on another reconnaissance flight met the same fate over the Sea of Japan…
>
> "One of the luckier missions took place on March 15, 1953, when a four-engine American reconnaissance plane flying twenty-five miles off the Soviet coast…was set on by two MIGs.
>
> "Six months later there was still another attack. This time the ferret was protected by sixteen Sabrejets while it collected signals over the Yellow Sea… By September 1954, American luck again began running out. On the fourth day of that month a Navy bomber on a reconnaissance flight from Atsugi, Japan, was shot down by two Soviet jets forty miles off the coast of Siberia with the loss of one flier. Only two months later another was shot down near the northern Japanese island of Hokkaido… The men aboard a Navy ferret attacked by Soviet aircraft over the Bering Sea on June 22, 1955…managed to crash-land on St. Lawrence Island with no loss of life.
>
> "In 1958, little more than two months apart, two American aircraft were shot down after crossing the Soviet border into Armenia. Several months later two more attacks occurred, one over the Baltic and one over the Sea of Japan."[266]

Considering the long, secret history of US spying on the Soviet Union, would it be too inflammatory to suggest that US hawks were deliberately 'whipsawing' the intelligence agencies of the Western nations to invoke policy changes that disrupted national military-technical programs? Many US commentators have also revealed how the Soviets would hide their planes and missiles when later satellites were known to be in range, and it seems no stretch to assume that they would do the same when knowledge of spyplane overflights was in hand. In short, the U-2 was not even close to being the first American reconnaissance aircraft to fly over Soviet territory, and any assumption that a few flights by U-2s had produced conclusive proof of Soviet production is subject to question. In reality, they had little to go on aside from the facts that they had several development programs underway, and had always matched the US weapon for weapon.

Meanwhile, the Soviets had thousands of fighter-bombers menacing Western Europe, all of them being perfect interdiction targets for the Arrow. The Russians have still not abandoned their long-range bomber fleet and the fact remains that, throughout the Arrow program and for some time afterward, the West really didn't know how many bombers the Soviets had—despite the hindsight exhortations of various 'experts'. It turns out that in the late-1950s the Soviets were designing a Mach 2.5, high-altitude, long-range strike-reconnaissance aircraft, called the RSR, but this was later abandoned due to technical and financial problems. The potent Backfire bomber would present another relevant Soviet threat as of 1969. A B-1 equivalent, the Tu-160 is today in the Russian inventory and penetrations of North American territory recommenced under Putin.

In reality it appears that the Soviet Union didn't build that many intercontinental bombers for two reasons: First of all, they were pre-occupied with Europe. Soviet Cold War military plans generally called for an overwhelming armoured 'blitzkrieg' through Western Europe, (with massive tactical air support) to the English Channel. This made sense because then Soviet territory would be one contiguous, defensible landmass. They stood to more than double their industrial (and thus military) capacity by doing what Hitler showed could be done, only with an infinitely larger force than the Nazis had at their disposal. They certainly didn't plan on a nuclear war, since this would render the value of the conquered territory at, approximately, zero. Prevailing Westerly winds at this latitude would also have sent the fallout from nuclear war in Europe directly back over the Soviet Union. They hoped to grab Europe at some opportune time, and present it as a *fait accompli,* before the West could politically bring itself around for a nuclear battle. With this in mind it might appear reasonable that the Soviets, through their infiltrators, (etc.) were working to disarm the West in *conventional arms,* content to see the US mitigate for just that whilst building up a nuclear force they would be exceedingly reluctant to use.

The second reason the Soviets did not build a force to match the US Strategic Air Command's complement of intercontinental Boeing B-52 Stratofortresses may have been because the designs intended to fulfil this mission were either deficient in speed (the Bear), or in range (the Bison). The West did not really know the range of the Bison however, and by this time Allied intelligence had learned that the Soviets were designing and building the Bounder, which was hoped to be an intercontinental jet-bomber with a speed of Mach 1.5 or more. (This would have made it something like a long-range B-58 Hustler in terms of performance.) This resulting plane was, however, a flop and was not ordered into mass production for this reason, not necessarily because the Kremlin really wanted to abandon strategic bombers.

A crisis of confidence among some experts led to a growing belief that high-altitude aircraft, no matter what their speed or manoeuvrability, were becoming easy targets for surface-to-air missiles. The Francis Gary Powers shootdown in the subsonic U-2 spyplane by a Soviet SA-2 *Guideline* missile is itself in some question as to the real cause of the downing (he is rumoured to have been flying about 10,000 feet lower and somewhat slower than he should have been). This shootdown convinced many that even supersonic or Mach 2+ aircraft were easy targets. In reality an evading aircraft at that speed and altitude with countermeasures, in the hands of an aware and trained pilot, remains a very difficult target for any nation's missiles. The US Navy's top ace of the Viet Nam war, Randall Cunningham, describes in his book *Fox Two,* how, even at significantly lower altitudes and subsonic speeds, he routinely evaded Soviet SAMs—SA.2s included.

By 1959, when the Conservatives decided to cancel the Arrow, new National Intelligence Estimates were issued that continued to suggest fantastic Soviet superiority in ICBM technology and production, when significant evidence exists to suggest that the CIA and American intelligence (on which the NIEs were based) knew by that time that the so-called missile-gap was a fraud. *Time* magazine let the cat out of the bag in 1980: "Three years later [1959], the overhead view (from the U-2 spyplane overflights) of the Tyuratam site gave the US some needed reassurance. Determining that the rocket booster aperture at the base of the launch pad was 15 meters in diameter, photo interpreters concluded that the Soviets were still using missiles boosted by auxiliary rockets strapped around the circumference of the main rocket. Because they could not be practically deployed, the U.S. strategic planners concluded that the missile gap did not exist either."[267] For our purposes, it would be nice to know exactly when the CIA really decided that there was no missile gap. According to Chris Pocock, an authority on the U-2's history, during a five week period starting on 5th August, 1957, nine overflights of the Soviet Union were completed by a U-2 detachment operating out of Pakistan. According to Pockock's 2006 lecture to the Allied Museum conference, "A large number of high-priority targets were successfully photographed, including Kapustin Yar; the newly-discovered ICBM test launch site at Tyuratam; and nuclear weapons development facilities as far north as Tomsk." What the U-2s had failed to detect were, again according to Pocock, any Bison or Bear bombers, yet they certainly existed. The evidence, as it was, suggested that there was neither a bomber nor a missile gap. Yet Kennedy, during his election campaign, blamed the Republicans for allowing the Soviets to secure a commanding lead over the United States in ICBMs. This politicization of intelligence certainly promised a huge dividend to American aerospace corporations. Convair was well into development of the Atlas ICBM, and Kennedy won the 1960 election.

In reality the Soviets were well behind the United States in missile technology. While Werhner Von Braun's team of German rocket scientists developed new rocket engines of increasing power, sophistication and safety, the Soviets' German rocket scientists, led by the Ukrainian Korolev, basically concentrated on developing German wartime technology. The result was a requirement to cluster groups of small engines on their rockets as opposed to the American approach which resulted in more reliable, accurate and easily controlled systems. The booster system as mentioned was difficult to deploy, meaning the Soviets would only have a few, vulnerable, launching sites. Their guidance and computation technology was rudimentary compared to that of the West, meaning their missiles would be relatively inaccurate.

Apparently Von Braun had offered to orbit a satellite before the Soviets, but was turned down. "Long before the Soviet Union launched the first satellite…von Braun said his team had the capability to orbit a payload by putting an upper stage on the Redstone. But President Dwight D. Eisenhower turned him down."[268] This may have been because the first stage was to be a politically-unacceptable adaptation of the WW II German V-2 rocket. Considering this and the earlier Navaho missile program it seems the missile gap was mostly an illusion—certainly on the technology side of the argument.

The Lockheed U-2 spy plane

263 Buttler, Tony. British Secret Projects, Jet Fighters Since 1950. Specialty Publishers & Wholesalers, 2000

264 Campagna, Palmiro: Requiem for a Giant, based on primary source (government of Canada) documents.

265 J.C. Floyd to Mr. J. McCulloch, G.M. Avro Aircraft (U.K.) 22 February, 1957

266 Bamford: The Puzzle Palace, p. 181-82

267 Time, April 7, 1980. quoted from: Epperson, Ralph: The Unseen Hand, p.p. 76,77.

268 "Rocket Pioneer Von Braun Dies" Arizona Daily Star, June 18, 1977. Quoted from: Epperson, Ralph: The Unseen Hand, p. 335

Chapter 47

THE RED MENACE

While there may be debate over which Americans were for and against the Arrow program, we can be sure that the Soviets would almost universally have wanted to see it dead. It was a conventional tactical weapon that could be used as a strategic theatre weapon if employed in Europe in the nuclear strike-reconnaissance role. It was a major tactical defensive threat to their 'blitzkrieg' strategy, should it be stationed in Europe, which seemed likely if it went into production. It would be a dominant air superiority (combat air patrol or CAP) fighter meaning any Soviet aircraft flying to support the land armies (in accordance with their war doctrine) would be vulnerable. The Arrow would be similarly difficult to counter if used for tactical reconnaissance. Employed with suitable weapons, such as glide or toss-bombs or guided stand-off missiles, the Arrow could be used for attack and reconnaissance during the same mission. It could be used for tactical or theatre-sized nuclear weapons, and could probably deliver them with minimal error considering ASTRA's incorporation of twin radar altimeters and ground-mapping radar features which were integrated with the aircraft's flight control system. An aircraft of the Arrow's flexibility, performance, and sophistication, set to appear in 1960, would have been seen as a real threat by responsible parties in the USSR.

The Soviets also had many well-connected spies—as Gouzenko showed in 1945—with many being native to the victim countries, in place in the West. Britain was, it is assumed, especially well infiltrated. It appears that the secrecy of the RCMP on their counterintelligence activities may have made Canada less well penetrated than popularly believed. However, a read of the *Mitrokin Archive* shows that virtually every country was heavily penetrated by the KGB and GRU, the United States being no exception. Kim Philby was posing as a British diplomat in Washington, but was really employed by MI-6 as their CIA liaison up to the early 1950s. This would have made him privy to planned US overflights of the USSR. He was also a top Soviet spy and blew the whistle to the Soviets about Gouzenko's Ottawa defection almost as soon as the Canadian authorities became aware of the event—and well before Gouzenko and family were given refuge by a reluctant and blundering Mackenzie King it should be added. Apparently King had been a lot busier than Gouzenko's bureaucratic difficulties in defecting would lead one to believe. He was in consultations with the British and American government's immediately, with the RCMP, MI-6, CIA, and the various foreign ministries involved from the beginning. He even visited Truman (to belatedly report the situation) who suggested that King also visit Lord Halifax, then Britain's Ambassador to the United States. In the room during the latter meeting was one of the notorious Cambridge Five spies, Donald Maclean. Also privy to the revelations made about a vast web of KGB (party intelligence) and GRU (army intelligence) agents throughout the West, and particularly inside the Manhattan Project, was Kim Philby. Included in Gouzenko's revelations was the fact that Canada's civil service was well infiltrated, including the government military research and development establishments. Gouzenko fingered Dr. Alan Nunn May, one of the atom spies, and provided evidence of at least twenty others in the Canadian civil service, and of links to an American network, including an assistant to the US Secretary of State (probably Alger Hiss).[269]

After leaving Cambridge in 1935, Maclean was accepted by the British Foreign Office and, in the spring of 1944, was posted to Washington to work in the British Embassy. He soon rose to First Secretary, and became involved in the atom bomb project and virtually every other important aspect of the ABC wartime alliance.[270] By the time he was posted to Cairo, and became less directly involved in matters pertaining to Canada, Kim Philby was nearly in place in the Washington embassy. Philby worked as the head of MI-6's Secret Intelligence Service Section IX, dealing with analysis of Soviet espionage throughout the world, aside from inside Britain, beginning in 1944.[271] In October, 1949, he left for America, posing as a diplomat, but was really SIS Head of Station for counter-intelligence in America, also with responsibilities for liaison with the CIA and RCMP.[272] As such, both had been privy to the Gouzenko information and much more, and were in positions to influence policy from 1944 until Philby left Washington under suspicion in 1956.

John Cairncross, who had been working at MI-5's Bletchley Park cryptanalysis establishment during the war, was subsequently even more directly involved with aerospace activities. According to British Treasury colleague G.A. Robinson, Cairncross:

> "...knew not just about atomic weapons developments, but also plans for guided missiles,

microbiological, chemical, underwater, and all other types of weapons. He also needed to know, inter alia, about projected spending on aeronautical and radar research and anti-submarine detection, research by the Post Office and other bodies into signals intelligence, eavesdropping techniques, etc.. He…could legitimately ask for further details thought necessary to give Treasury approval to the spending of money."[273]

Cairncross worked as a re-activated Soviet agent in the British Treasury until 1952 when he was posted to Canada, then the United States, and finally, in 1958, to the Food and Agriculture Organisation of the United Nations.[274] During his re-activation in the Treasury, he had particular influence on defense spending.

Even more relevant to the Avro story is the case of the Canadian-born economist, Hugh Hambleton. He had been recruited into the KGB in 1950, and, from 1956 until 1961, had been…

"…a highly productive spy at N.A.T.O. headquarters…where he was cleared for access to 'cosmic top secret' documents which he could claim he needed to consult for his work in the Economic Directorate. [After leaving NATO headquarters in 1961,] Hambleton remained at the London School of Economics until 1964, when he…took an academic post at Laval University in Quebec."

He too would have been able to ask for any details on any program he wished, for the same reasons as in the case of Cairncross' work in the Treasury. Even more directly involved, though probably on a very low level, was an agent codenamed LIND by the KGB. He…

"…was an Irish-Canadian Communist employee of A.V.Roe aircraft [sic] company…resident in Toronto… The intelligence supplied by LIND included plans for the CF-105 Arrow, then among the most advanced jet fighter aircraft in the world."[275]

Many who know of LIND seem to think that he must have betrayed the entire Arrow design, in detail, to the Soviets. This doesn't appear to be the case, since LIND had been betrayed by Yevgeni Brik (codenamed HART) after Brik had gone to the RCMP in 1953. The Soviets did not learn of LIND's betrayal until 1955, which might suggest that LIND had been kept in place and fed misleading data by the RCMP until this time. At any rate, in 1953 the Arrow's plans were decidedly basic, and subject to alteration. Much more than line drawings are required anyway, particularly materials specifications, and fabrication information. Anyone who thinks a fighter can be replicated by copying captured plans should read Ken Follett's book *Mirage.* This entertaining book discloses how Israeli Mossad agents stole the design plans, materials specifications and fabrication data of the French Mirage fighter for their Kfir program.

Among the twenty or so in the political establishment of Canada was an alleged spy of particular interest where this work is concerned. In a subsequent chapter, Canadian government Cabinet minutes are quoted at length, in order to deduce the facts regarding the cancellation. In addition to being Cabinet secretary and recording those facts, Robert Bryce was Chairman of the Canadian Government Security Panel. If the testimony of the notorious Elizabeth Bentley is accurate, during the critical phases of the Arrow program Canada's political security head, and Cabinet secretary, was a Soviet spy. Bryce had also apparently been involved with a notorious Communist cell in China, and had introduced the Canadian diplomat, Herbert Norman (also implicated by Bentley), to a Japanese Marxist of note.[276]

It is interesting that the Canadian government, besides showing a marked reluctance to prosecute, did more witting things to promote Soviet knowledge of the Avro Arrow. When discussing the spy issue, Jim Floyd has reported his surprise when the government asked Avro to host a team of Russian designers and aerospace experts, and to take them through the Arrow and Iroquois programs. In a second interview on this subject in October 2006, Floyd reiterated that he had questioned Fred Smye on the advisability of giving a full engineering briefing, as ordered, to the Russians. Crawford Gordon Jr. was particularly against this and the government was again asked if they thought a tour of the facilities and provision of full engineering briefings on the airframe and engine were really advisable. They were again directed to comply. Floyd said "I still wouldn't do it. I said I'd answer any questions they had, in full, which I did, but I wasn't going to give a briefing." A full briefing was given on the Iroquois, however, which Floyd feels was their primary interest anyway. Perhaps LIND's supply of information (or disinformation) on the Arrow is the real reason for their relative lack of interest on the Arrow. After all the accusations levelled over the years as to the security of the Avro and Orenda programs, *it is clear that the Conservatives were quite willing to provide the information directly.*

RCMP Counter-Intelligence had a file, FEATHERBED, on investigations of suspected Soviet Agents, active at the time of the Arrow cancellation. It was only really staffed, however, beginning in the early 1960s. When it wound up, it concluded

> "...that the public services were riddled with Soviet sympathizers, naming twelve in the Canadian hierarchy, four deputy ministers, 245 secret members of the Communist Party International in government employ."[277]

Not much had changed since the Gouzenko defection, and none of the spies were ever convicted—at least not in Canada. Even now, the Canadian government is exceedingly sparing of information on this subject—not, apparently, due to any lingering threat from the non-existent Soviet Union, but to protect the confidence of the Canadian people in the competence, loyalty and soundness of the government.

It seems obvious that it would have served Soviet interests to use whatever means they had at their disposal to convince Western governments to drop planes like the Arrow. In keeping with their desire to develop crushing superiority in conventional weapons, they worked tirelessly to convince the Allies to drop, particularly, their air superiority fighters. In promoting the Soviets' emerging arsenal of surface-to-air missiles (SAMs), Khrushchev loudly propagandised that the "manned bomber is dead". It is more likely that he was merely trying to convince the Americans and British that their fleets of over 1,500 bombers capable of striking Moscow were obsolete than an honest admission that the Soviets were abandoning manned bombers. They were also aware of American supersonic bomber programs, and their discouragement was also a priority. Some, for various reasons, took the emergence of SAMs to mean that fighters were also rendered dinosaurs by this technology. Certainly some of those were sympathetic to the Soviet desire to see the West abandon its planes. Some in the West standing to profit from missile production and deployment were also, through self interest, inclined to promote these concepts. In promoting the concept of the obsolescence of manned bombers, and even fighters, to Canada and Britain it seems odd that the CIA and Soviets were strange bedfellows. There is no question technologically that the Soviets were being left behind in aerospace technology, even by the late 1940s. Emphasising the missile threat and downplaying aircraft would be an obvious way to encourage the abandonment of military fighters. Promoting the fallacy of Soviet missile supremacy was also designed to discourage the United States from attempting a first strike. Was it *really* a total coincidence, then, that Sputnik went into orbit on the same day as the curtain was parting to reveal to the world the first Arrow, a plane that promised to become the highest performance, longest-range, missile-armed, *multi-role* combat aircraft the world had yet seen?

Some of the fear felt by the Soviets was generated by their perception that the American oligarchs and Republicans were aligning themselves with the right wing in Germany, at whose hands the Russians had suffered so grievously in the Second World War. "The United States must understand that the Russians genuinely look upon the United States as an aggressor... The Soviets fear the U.S. because it is allying itself with the Germans who attacked Russia during World War Two.[278] Part of that fear, no doubt, relates to their knowledge of the integration into the American military industrial complex of the SS's "black" weapons programs, centred around Prague and in Silesia. The magnitude of this secret event, which was the real reason for General Patton's "unauthorised" exuberance in taking this area in early May 1945, in violation of the Yalta and other agreements between the United States, Britain and the USSR, is explored in Nick Cook's *The Hunt for Zero Point.* Nick Cook's credentials are impressive, having been, among other things, an aviation editor for Jane's publications—probably the most trusted source of information on aircraft and naval vessels. What the Americans found was secret, even from the rest of the German Wehrmacht and industry, advanced research and development into beam weapons, mature atomic technology, long-range missile programs, and the other exotic technology mentioned earlier. Wernher von Braun and the V-2 rocket team's integration into the American system was only the public side of what Cook believes evolved into a sinister element in right-wing American politics and industry—not only a black economy, but something of a black ruling elite. What Cook postulates they found on anti-gravity, electro-gravitics and exotic beam weapons, particularly relating to SS "flying saucer" programs, would appear to be very relevant to the interest of the USAF Foreign Technology branch in the flying saucer programs undertaken by Avro Canada, under John Frost, circa 1951.

One of the most interesting of the 'new facts' to emerge after the fall of the Iron Curtain relates to Soviet perceptions of the Cold War situation during the years of the Arrow program. The *Mitrokhin Archive* illuminates the fact that a large part of the Soviet leadership, during the late 1950s and early '60s, became convinced that the United States intended a crippling, preventative nuclear attack on the USSR. Some influential voices have suggested that the Soviet belief in a United States' planned nuclear first strike was evidence of how paranoid and dangerous the Reds really were. However, an analysis of the secret statements of Strategic Air Command (SAC) CINC Gen. Curtis LeMay, General McArthur, John Foster Dulles and many others at the top of the Eisenhower administration shows that there was a strong lobby to do just that: strike the USSR decisively with nuclear weapons before she gained the ability to do the reverse. Dr. John Von Neuman, another German ex-patriot and a brilliant mathematician, had invented the "mini-max" theory and was a major consultant of Eisenhower and senior members of his administration. His theory essentially stated that the only way to minimize the probability of being destroyed by the Soviet Union was to destroy it first, with nuclear weapons, while America had the advantage. He is portrayed, by Peter Sellers, in Kubrick's classic movie *Dr. Strangelove* as the title character.[279] He also became quite insane. But then, isn't the mini-max theory, expressed as it was, itself insane? Isn't the logical extension of it a consideration that the only way to prevent crime, murders and war would be to exterminate all human beings? It is now known conclusively that the Soviets had cracked enough of the codes of the West to know what was being said by those who counted in these matters. They also had *plenty* of high-level agents in place to discern potential American intentions.

As a result of this knowledge, the USSR apparently panicked around the time of Arrow termination and began making feelers to the West to show that Russia had no plans whatsoever to employ nuclear weapons first, and that their ICBM program had been seriously overestimated by Western organizations. Both of which were true; the Soviets lagged behind the USA until about 1968, when the USA began to put multiple warheads on each missile, and again left them far behind in terms of destructive power. It also seems clear that the Soviets also undertook to expand their 'strategic rocket force' at this time, in order to develop a force to deter any first strike thoughts on the part of SAC, with its thousand or so B-47s and B-52s, its theatre nuclear missiles (stationed in Okinawa Japan as early as the Korean War), and emerging ICBMs and nuclear submarine missile-boats etc.). While the Soviets always maintained a quantitative advantage in conventional arms, the USA led the way in every conceivable nuclear weapon—other than the first ICBMs. As mentioned earlier, it turns out that the Soviets were able to field the first ICBM because, rather than develop one large, sophisticated main rocket engine for a missile, a cluster of smaller, less-sophisticated rockets could be arranged to do the same thing. With that strategy and a group of German rocket scientists the Soviets produced the first orbit-capable heavy-lift rocket. In the process, they narrowly beat the American team in creating nuclear missiles that could threaten the whole planet. But by concentrating on large, high-performance and high-reliability rocket engines, Von Braun's team created engines capable of lifting men into space with relative safety—surely the most positive by-product of this aspect of the arms race.

Another reason for Soviet paranoia was the fact that the CIA integrated the formerly Nazi Eastern intelligence operation, run by the notorious General Reinhard Gehlen, into the American intelligence apparatus. A great deal of men and arms were smuggled into the Soviet zones as a result, and considerable blood was shed by these *agents provocateur,* with no real success and a litany of failures. The Gehlen Org also generated a steady stream of phantom threats to ensure themselves a continual supply of money from their friends in the CIA.

269 Stevenson, William Intrepid's Last Case

270 Andrew, Christopher; and Mitrokhin, Vasili: The Mitrokhin Archive, Middlesex : Penguin Books, 2000. p. 166

271 ibid.

272 Pincher, Chapman: Too Secret, Too Long, p. 104

273 Andrew and Mitrokhin, The Mitrokhin Archive, p.p. 184-85

274 Pincher: Too Secret, Too Long, p.p. 394-95

275 Andrew and Mitrokhin, The Mitrokhin Archive, p. 219

276 Stevenson: Intrepid's Last Case, p.p. 262-63

277 Stevenson: Intrepid's Last Case, p. 259

278 Congressional Record, Feb. 22 1963, Dr. Ralph K. White, head of the Soviet division, U.S. Information Agency, speaking to the American Psychological association in Sept. 1961.

279 Strangelove's Game

Chapter 48

FOULKES' NORAD STAMPEDE

In the recommendations of the 1947 paper by the joint Military Cooperative Committee (MCC), it was agreed that a combined Canada-US Air Defense Headquarters was desirable for coordination and control over the North American air defense system in its entirety.[280] This was the seed that sprouted into the North American Air Defense Command, or NORAD.

> "In 1956, a committee of Canadian and American officers, working under the auspices of the MSG [Military Study Group], an MCC subgroup, developed a study designed to determine how to make a joint command politically acceptable to Canada... author Ann Denholm Crosby notes that Canadian Chief of Staff General Charles Foulkes had asked that this study be conducted in secrecy."

Foulkes certainly behaved in line with American interests while he was Chairman of the Chiefs of Staff Committee (CCSC). A study on NORAD was produced in December 1956 and approved in principle in February 1957 by the militaries of both countries and the US Secretary of Defense. The Canadian government, in the throes of preparing for an election, had not yet had any input to any of the report's recommendations."[281] This may not have been completely accurate however. There are rumours that the RCAF had major reservations about the American stipulation, that because they had the lion's share of the defense hardware, they should have permanent command of NORAD.[282] It seems logical that the RCAF leaders would have reservations about handing over their responsibilities to American officers, thereby making themselves somewhat redundant and reducing the RCAF to an arm of American air defense.

> "When external affairs asked Ralph Campney, then the minister of National Defense, for a joint appreciation on the implications for Canada of the advent of nuclear weapons and missiles, Foulkes advised against it, claiming it would only impair his relations with the American chiefs of staff [283]... The study was never done."

> [After the 1957 election] "General Foulkes approached the newly elected Minister of National Defense, [his former army colleague] MGen George R. Pearkes, in the hopes of gaining early acceptance for [NORAD]... Minister Pearkes approached Diefenbaker on July 24, and the latter accepted the report without consulting the Cabinet or External Affairs...The report was later accepted by the Canadian Cabinet on July 31."[284]

This isn't quite comprehensive either, however. There was direct American input to this as well.

> "The more complicated chain of events that eventually led to the acquisition of nuclear equipment...for the domestic defense of Canada, began on July 27, 1957, when John Foster Dulles came to Canada... Instead of reviewing the terms of the NORAD agreement when he came to office, John Diefenbaker, who was then acting as his own Secretary of State for External Affairs, merely gave his verbal approval of the scheme to John Foster Dulles. In a Commons debate ten months later, Sidney Smith admitted that neither he nor his department had been aware of the NORAD compact's details."[285]

Diefenbaker's compliance is surely a sign of John Foster Dulles' skill in manipulating people. No doubt playing on the Republican affinity for Conservative governments in Canada Diefenbaker was reassured of the benefits of NORAD verbally, and was sold on a non-democratic acceptance, without review by responsible experts, of a package that Diefenbaker surely didn't understand. Why did Diefenbaker wait ten months to introduce his NORAD agreement to the House of Commons? Had Diefenbaker been stampeded into NORAD? The answer is given below.

> "General Charles Foulkes testified, in October 1963, before the House of Commons Special Committee on Defense, that, as Chairman of the Chiefs of Staff Committee in 1957, he had "stampeded" the new Conservative government into accepting the North American Air Defense (NORAD) Agreement."[286]

From the above it is clear that Foulkes was capable of circumventing the democratic process when it suited his aims. In this regard, at least, his aims coincided well with those of the American military-industrial-financial establishment.

NORAD was a major victory for the Americans in several areas. First of all, it placed the RCAF's Air Defense Command under USAF command. Secondly, it called for the construction of new radar lines and control centres in several lines across Canada, providing the US with early warning of attack. Thirdly, it called for US interceptors and bombers to move forward onto Canadian fields in event of hostilities. It wasn't permanent US basing in Canada, but it was a step in that direction. It also called for the acceptance of nuclear weapons for defense in Canada, something that apparently escaped the Conservatives when they agreed to the plan.[287] This should have been no surprise to the Conservatives since nuclear air defense weapons had been in the planning stages for Canada at least as early as 1956, as we have seen. What is perhaps the worst tactical error in this *carte blanche* acceptance of NORAD is that it gave away the single most powerful lever the Canadians had for convincing the Americans to equip with the Avro Arrow. As Dow wrote in his well researched but early book titled *The Arrow,*

> "No one suggested, however, that Canada try to get American support for the CF-105 before conceding to NORAD. In the light of what later happened, it was a tragic oversight."

It is obvious from documentation that the US air defense experts saw Canada as a very important "top cover" to the United States and were determined to establish defense with in-depth installations, including radars, ground control stations, fighters and ground-to-air missiles on Canadian soil. The Canadian politicians and Army experts, and the influential people at the NAE, NRC and DRB, and even within the RCAF, all had reasons to oppose the Arrow, and were quite content to accept promises and advice that reduced, rather than justified, any faith in the Arrow.

As for Diefenbaker's thoughts on the effects of NORAD on the sovereignty of Canada, the following is indicative of the man's way of distorting the English language for political purposes. In fact his memoirs are a troubling read due to his inability to restrain himself from settling old, illusory political scores.

> "[W]e had accepted the view that NORAD was an "effective" part of NATO... We did not see the relationship as hinging on the fact the CINC NORAD ws not responsible to the NATO Standing Group and derived no authority from the North Atlantic Council....External Affairs, I was to discover, had no sympathy for the perception of the NORAD-NATO relationship advanced by our military advisors; they sided with the views expressed by the Opposition in the House and took comfort in the fact that Mr. Pearson's old friend, as he described him, Paul-Henri Spaak, NATO Secretary-General, saw fit, during his visit to Ottawa in late May 1958, to question the NORAD-NATO link. The hard fact that NORAD was advancing Canadian interests and making Canadian sovereignty more, not less, secure seemed to escape some paragons of diplomatic virtue."[288]

As the last line shows, Diefenbaker was very confident in the correctness of his path, even in the face of such esteemed experts expressing contrary opinions in their professional capacities, and he could carry a grudge. His politicisation of virtually every issue is also clear, as if not being a Conservative, or a fan of his policies automatically rendered one not credible. Of course, NORAD has absolutely nothing to do with NATO and was designed primarily for the defense of the United States.

CCSC General Charles Foulkes also testified to the Commons committee that the Liberals had resolved to cancel the Arrow after the 1957 election—had they won it. There is no evidence to support this other than the fact that Howe was now opposed to Avro on all terms, and was at the zenith of his power, while the Minister of Defense Brooke Claxton, who had not been cowed by Howe over the Arrow, had retired in favour of Ralph Campney, thought to be a less confident and forceful individual. In a personal interview with Paul Hellyer, Liberal defense critic at the time of Arrow cancellation and an associate minister of national defense in the prior Liberal government, he stated that he was unaware of any such decision having been taken, but that the program was certainly going to be reviewed, as it had been on a year-by-year basis.

Further evidence is available from Lester Pearson's diary, which points out that Canada had a compelling bargaining chip to convince the US to adopt Arrows for USAF service, and that it was the duty of the government of Canada to use it. At variance with Pearson and the new leadership of the Liberals, C.D. Howe would cast his ghost over the Liberal response to the Arrow cancellation. In a post-cancellation letter to Pearson he advised that the Liberals should attack the manner of the cancellation, with no warning etc. to Avro, but stated that the Arrow should have been cancelled. Today Howe gets a very easy ride by historians as purportedly having been the man who industrialized Canada when in reality it was inevitable in light of the need to fight WW II. He has certainly always been considered a "continentalist," meaning he preferred to align Canada with his native United States rather than with the British Commonwealth.

A small fraction of the people laid off when the Avro Arrow program was cancelled. This picture was taken on October 4th 1957, the day of the first roll-out of the Arrow.

280 Campaga: Requiem for a Giant, p. 72
281 ibid. p.75
282 Shaw: There Never Was an Arrow
283 Dow, The Arrow, p.167, from an interview with George Ignatieff in 1979.
284 Campagna: Requiem for a Giant
285 Newman: Renegade in Power, pp. 444-45
286 Diefenbaker, John George: One Canada, Vol.III, Ch. 2 (Annex 18: FoulkesStampede.jpg)
287 Crosby, Ann Denholm: Dilemmas in Defence Decision-Making, New York: St. Martin's press, 1998
288 Diefenbaker: One Canada, Vol. III, Ch. 2 (as reproduced in DND document R-PD-050-006/PG-600)

Chapter 49

BOMARC: DIEFENBAKER'S FOLLY

> "With the emergence of the soviet [sic] thermonuclear weapons and long range jet bombers an Air Defense Planning Group of the U.S. Continental Air Defense and RCAF Air Defense Command were actively participating in plans for the air defense of this continent. This Air Defense Planning Group proposed to introduce a line of Bomarc guided missile bases from coast to coast crossing the U.S. and Eastern Canada at roughly the 48th parallel of latitude."[289]

It is a myth that the Diefenbaker Conservatives adopted the Bomarc nuclear surface-to-air missile (SAM), or integrated into NORAD, on their own initiative. Both had been proposed well before the 1957 election. The Conservatives would claim, in defense of their decision to cancel the Arrow, that the Bomarc and SAGE systems were a new panacea for air defense that would replace the interceptor and even form the basis of an anti-missile defense system. This had never been the intention. In fact Canada was planning on adopting the Bomarc and nuclear weapons at least as early as 1956, long before the Conservatives came to power to augment a primary defense consisting of interceptors. It was also planning on integrating into NORAD, and introducing nuclear air-to-air missiles for its interceptors once they were ready.[290] They clearly saw interceptors as the first line of defense, with SAMs like Bomarc providing last-ditch point defense for important installations (primarily USAF Strategic Air Command bases) to hopefully take care of any bombers that made it past the interceptors. Bomarc was never intended to replace interceptors, but to augment them. Protection of SAC's deterrent power and the American industrial heartland established the need for Bomarc, additional radars and ground control installations, and the re-equipment of nine squadrons of interceptors as the primary air defense system with a supersonic machine capable of carrying the Hughes MB-1 Genie air-to-air nuclear rocket…all according to agreed NORAD doctrine. Previous to the NORAD agreement the RCAF was primarily concerned with defending Canadian territory.

It is interesting that a 1957 RCAF document to the Canadian Joint Staff in Washington mentioned: "…present US regulations preclude Canada from having sole custody of atomic and other sensitive equipment."[291] While Soviet espionage was touted as the reason for such stringent security, there is no question that commercial patent security was a major factor as well—perhaps the leading factor when the history of US defense "sharing" initiatives and their results are considered. Whatever the case, during the Arrow program and afterwards, Canadian officials have sometimes been guilty of assuming the availability of US defense technology that wasn't.[292]

In fact, in discussions of the Bomarc acquisition "…the Canadian Army raised several issues in April of 1958 that garnered responses from the air staff. According to the latter, it was true that the Bomarc could not intercept low-flying targets. This was a limitation of the radar network, but no other system could do so either."[293] This wasn't entirely true. Low flying interceptors could intercept low level targets, provided the target was above the interceptor's radar horizon, or if the target was acquired visually, or if it was tracked by infra-red—a capability the Astra system incorporated. There was other expert opinion to the contrary as well.

> "The considered opinion of the responsible people with whom I talked in the United Kingdom is that, as a result of recent deliberations, and from the results of Operation Sunbeam, recently carried out as a U.K. defensive exercise, the manned interceptor is the best means of dealing with both high level and low level threats, and in the face of carcinatron jamming, which the Russians are known to possess, the two-man interceptor is considered to be the only means of reasonable defense available for some time to come, since it is considered that the enemy can completely jam out range information for the operation of a close controlled guided mis-

sile, including Bomarc. The people responsible for carrying out the defense of the U.K. (not the politicians), are now apparently convinced that the manned interceptor is an essential element in the defense of the U.K., and this decision was reached within the last two months.

"We personally saw a demonstration of a new interception technique which had been studied at the Central Fighter Establishment in the U.K., and which was used in Operation Sunbeam with great success, even against low level attacks, assuming all ground radar was jammed, i.e., conditions under which a defensive ground to air missile would be out of action."[294]

It was acknowledged that range rate information was easily jammed on radar-guided missiles—a characteristic of pulse-Doppler type radars. It was also acknowledged that the missile's poor performance at low-level was due to ground clutter degrading the missile's mid-course guidance (which was transmitted from ground radars—not the missile's radar). Pulse-Doppler can look down and is not nearly as vulnerable to ground clutter, yet it is highly debatable if the computer technology of the day would have allowed a successful interception. Pulse-Doppler is also blind to targets travelling perpendicular to the radar beam. The record of Bomarc test failures suggests the technology, especially when automated, was not ready. Considering the ability of a strategic bomber to blot out a powerful ground radar's return over a huge area, it is no wonder Avro felt that Bomarc, with its tiny radar for terminal guidance, was "unworkable" in the face of jamming. It relied on the ground radar, already vulnerable to jamming, to transmit a radio signal, also vulnerable to jamming, to get the missile close enough for its active seeker, also vulnerable to jamming, to home onto the target. During this period the weapon's onboard computer had to process the image, and eliminate what it perceived to be jamming, steer the weapon, and time the detonation. In reality the only hope the Bomarcs had was to get within a few miles and hope the shock wave from its nuclear warhead would knock the intruder from the sky. Collateral damage was, well, a secondary consideration.

Avro had also produced an in-house study on the Bomarc, probably when they acquired Bomarc data during their bid to produce the missile—which was not granted to a Canadian contractor on the absurd Government of Canada pretext that all Canadian manufacturers lacked the technological ability to produce it. In reality Canada was precluded by US legislation from possession of many American defense technologies, particulary nuclear armaments. In short this report concluded that the Bomarc was so vulnerable to jamming that it would be a useless, if not dangerous, alternative to interceptors.[295] A page from Avro's prescient evaluation is reproduced here.

By 1958-'59 the US Congress was also starting to hold their noses over the Bomarc system.

"In 1959, a House of Representatives Appropriations Committee actually voted to terminate the Bomarc because the system was not yet proven... On May 26, 1959, the first Bomarc B was test-fired unsuccessfully, an ominous sign of their future effectiveness..."[296]

So why did the Canadian politicians decide to adopt the Bomarc? It would, again, appear to be American pressure [297], with the cooperation of a pliable CCSC, Gen. Charles Foulkes.

But the American authorities didn't just recommend adoption of Bomarc:

"Writing in the April 1962 edition of *Foreign Affairs,* a U.S. quarterly review, [and the house organ of the Council on Foreign Relations], writer Melvin Connant observed that the USAF urged the Canadian government to accept the Bomarc and to consider the phasing out of the interceptor aircraft force."[298]

Author Palmiro Campagna discovered one reason why the US defense planners were pushing a useless system onto the Canadians. In Congressional hearings on Defense appropriations for 1961, held 24 March, 1960, the following quote is quite interesting:

"Insofar as the moment is concerned, other than General White's...high hopes...there is no proof before this committee that BOMARC has ever proved itself to any great degree... so you scale back, but keep enough on order to maintain [the] appearance of defense, and bail out Boeing...[299]

S E C R E T 72/TACTICS/18

COMPARISON OF ARROW 2 AND BOMARC IN

THE AIR DEFENSE OF EASTERN CANADA

	ARROW 2	BOMARC
1. PHYSICAL DATA		
Length	77.8 ft.	47 ft.
Wing Span	50.0 ft.	18 ft.
Planform	Delta	Cropped Delta
A.U.W.	70,000 lb.	15,000 lb.
Power Plant	2 X Orenda Iroquois 2	2 X 25" Marquardt Ramjets + Rocket Boosters
Armament	2 Genie Rockets	H.E. or nuclear warhead
Radar Search Pattern	Various modes, from narrow band with central positioning from ground control, to wide angle search between antenna limits	±15° in azimuth and elevation centred about expected bearing of target
Antenna Traverse Limits	±70° Azimuth +75° -45° Elevation	±70° in azimuth and elevation (?)
2. PERFORMANCE		
Cruise altitude (Subsonic	35,000 ft.	-
(Supersonic	50,000 ft.	65,000 ft.
Combat speed and altitude	M = 2.0, 50,000 ft.	M = 2.5, 60,000 ft.
* Manoeuvrability at combat condition	3.6 g	7.0 g
** Radius of action (Subsonic Cruise	(600 n.m. combat at M = 1.5 (500 n.m. combat at M = 2.0	- -
(Supersonic Cruise	300 n.m. Cruise and combat M = 2.0	280 n.m. at M = 2.5
A.I. Radar Range	25 n.m.	8 n.m.
3. GROUND ENVIRONMENT		
SAGE	Can be used:Not essential	Essential
Close control,manual operation	Can be used:Not essential	Marginally Adequate
Broadcast control	Adequate	Completely Inadequate
Data Link	Might be used. Not preferred	Essential
Voice Link	Adequate and preferred	Completely Inadequate
Condition for launch or take-off	Any time a possible target appears	Close control target track established

* In both cases the limitation is aerodynamic and not thrust.

** Preliminary investigation of the aircraft configuration when carrying 2 Genies indicates that the additional fuel capacity required to give these radii is available.

And that is what they did immediately thereafter. Apparently, Boeing was in trouble, just as they had been when the Jetliner was revealed, and a Canadian purchase would help bail-out them out, reducing the cost of such corporate welfare to the US Treasury. Campagna makes the case that this reason for Bomarc adoption was always downplayed and kept off the record because Canada's subsidy of a dubious weapon, which was used to kill an entire Canadian industrial unit, would be politically explosive. But this was by no means the only reason the Bomarcs were pushed on Canada. There can be little doubt that various parties, with allegiances elsewhere, were using the Bomarc, the non-existent missile-gap, and the USAF LRIX projects (and others) as levers against Canadian arguments for the Arrow and its requirement. As we shall see, once the Arrow and its production lines were destroyed, the interceptor requirement re-emerged at US insistence.

ARROW vs. BOMARC COVERAGE

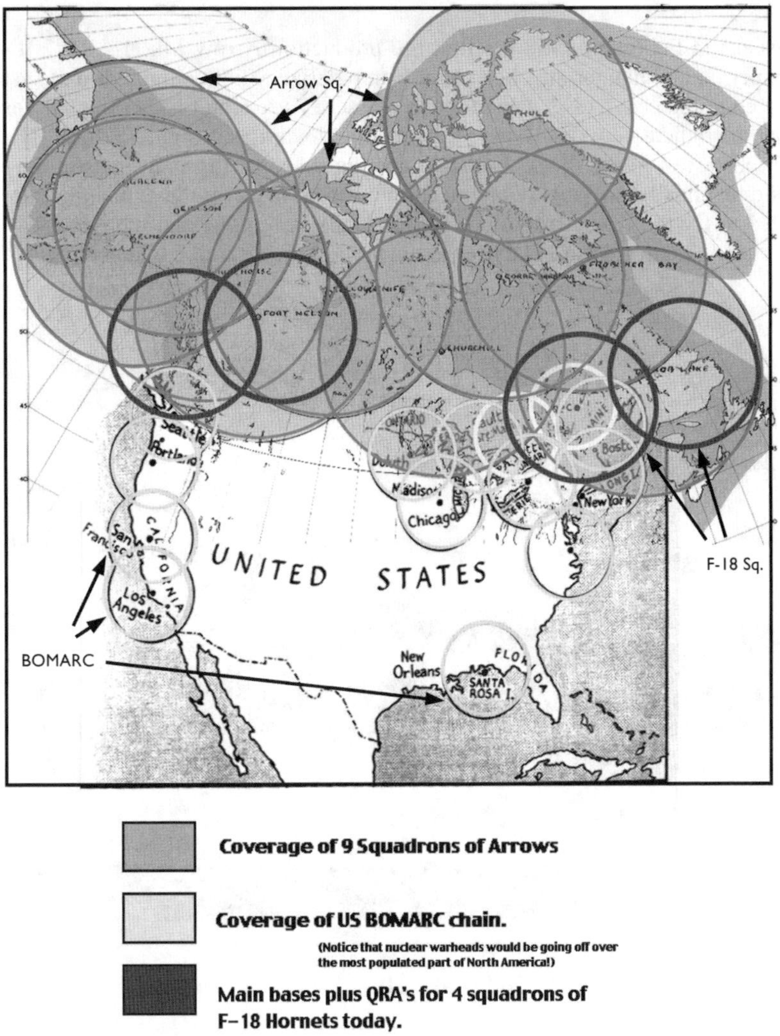

A final comparison of the utility of the Arrow as compared to the Bomarc, is given by the following map, which points out the range of the Bomarc installations, both Canadian and American, against the range of the Arrow Mk. 2. The range of Canada's current F-18 Hornets, without aerial refuelling, is also indicated.

289 Campagna: Requiem for a Giant, pp.105-06

290 CDC minutes 13 June, 1956: "The Development of the Introduction of the BOMARC Ground to Air Guided Missile and the MB-1 Air to Air Guided Missile on Canadian Manned Interceptors for the RCAF for the Defence of Canada."

291 Letter to Air Member, Canadian Joint Staff, Washington, D.C. 29 Apr 57 This document shows that the Canadians made arrangements to allow US personnel on Canadian bases to retain custody of nuclear weapons and other sensitive equipment.

292 A more recent example being the Mulroney government's initial desire to acquire US nuclear subs for Canadian avy use in patrolling the Canadian Arctic (the sovereignty of which is disputed by the US). Canada was told, diplomatically, that this was protected technology and would involve major security concessions to the United States. The matter was dropped with the White Paper shortly thereafter.

293 Campagna: Requiem for a Giant, p.98

294 Floyd: Strictly confidential memo to J.L. Plant (then Avro's president), titled: "The Arrow Controversy", 7 November, 1958.

295 Cohen, J.: Secret Avro Technical Department document:"Comparison of Arrow 2 and Bomarc in the Air Defense of Eastern Canada", 29 September, 1958

296 Campagna: Requiem for a Giant, pp.105-06

297 CDC minutes 13 June, 1956: "The Development of the Introduction of the BOMARC Ground to Air Guided Missile and the MB-1 Air to Air Guided Missile on Canadian Manned Interceptors for the RCAF for the Defence of Canada".

298 Campagna: Requiem for a Giant, p.115

299 Hearings Before the Subcommittee on Appropriations, House of Representatives, Eighty-sixth Congress Second Session, Re: "Appraisal of Air Defense Program Revisions in 1960 and 1961 Air Force Programs".

Chapter 50

ARROW FIRST FLIGHT AND PERFORMANCE

For three weeks in February, 1958 the first pre-production Arrow Mk. 1—RL 201—was on jack stands in the experimental hanger attached to the computerized flight simulator and systems development rig. These comprehensive tests were done to reassure Avro Chief Experimental Test Pilot Janusz Zurakowski that the radical new fly-by-wire system would work as designed. While flying the simulator "Zura" and fellow test pilot "Spud" Potocki experienced short survival times in the regions where the Arrow was dynamically unstable. Convinced that the systems on the actual aircraft worked properly Zura elected to fly the first Arrow due to confidence in himself and the aircraft's designers and their belief that the simulator wasn't truly representative of the aircraft's characteristics.

First flight take-off. (Avro Canada)

March 25th the plane and pilot were ready to fly. Once everything was ready to go the plant loudspeaker blared an invitation for employees not involved in essential activities to leave their posts and witness the making of history. The plant emptied in seconds. Zura's diminutive form marched smartly around the gleaming Arrow as he conducted his pre-flight inspection. He then climbed the ladder, completed his strap-in and helmet connections and began the cockpit check. Seconds later the switches were flicked, throttles set and the big J-75 engines began their slow moan, ignitors snapping, as they spooled up to light-off rpm. After a brief roar they were throttled back to idle rpm. Zura scanned the instruments for rpm, exhaust gas temperatures, hydraulic pressures and other signs of life while working the controls and checking for correct flight control surface actuation. "RL-201 taxi 3-2" was the characteristically succinct request for taxi clearance. On reply the brakes were released, throttles quickly cycled to about 75% then back to idle as the big delta eagerly sprang forward. A quick stab at the rudder pedals indicated proper nose-wheel steering function but Zura apparently found differential braking to be more accurate with the Arrow's wide track main landing gear as he swung the nose around and entered the taxiway. Final checks were mouthed along the route to Malton's longest stretch, runway 3-2. The glistening white wedge paused serenely at the entrance to the runway as Avro's chase planes, a CF-100 and a CF-86 Sabre clambered down the runway and took off. Film of the event makes the leisurely turn of the Arrow onto the runway, after the chase planes roared by, look like an act of almost arrogant confidence. Zura moved the throttles to full military thrust. The engines responded to the command by howling their eagerness while the test pilot flicked experienced eyes across the panels and the engine note went from a low moan to a hissing bellow. Zura's mind considered wind speed, crosswind component, engine rpm, exhaust gas temperature, magnetic versus gyro-compass alignment and a score of other factors. As a sign of his approval two small flight-booted feet relented on the brakes and Zura's body was snapped to attention by the force of 25,000 pounds of unrestrained thrust. Small corrections were made with the brakes to keep the plane's course centred on the runway. As the indicated speed passed 100 knots the control stick was progressively pulled back. The nose began to rise as control authority increased with speed. At 120 knots the nosewheel left the tarmac. By 170 knots the main gear legs completely extended and the wheels left terra firma—the Arrow was flying! Once airborne Zura selected gear up and the chaseplanes closed in to look over the aircraft.

Performance Curves – ***Arrow versus Modern Fighters***

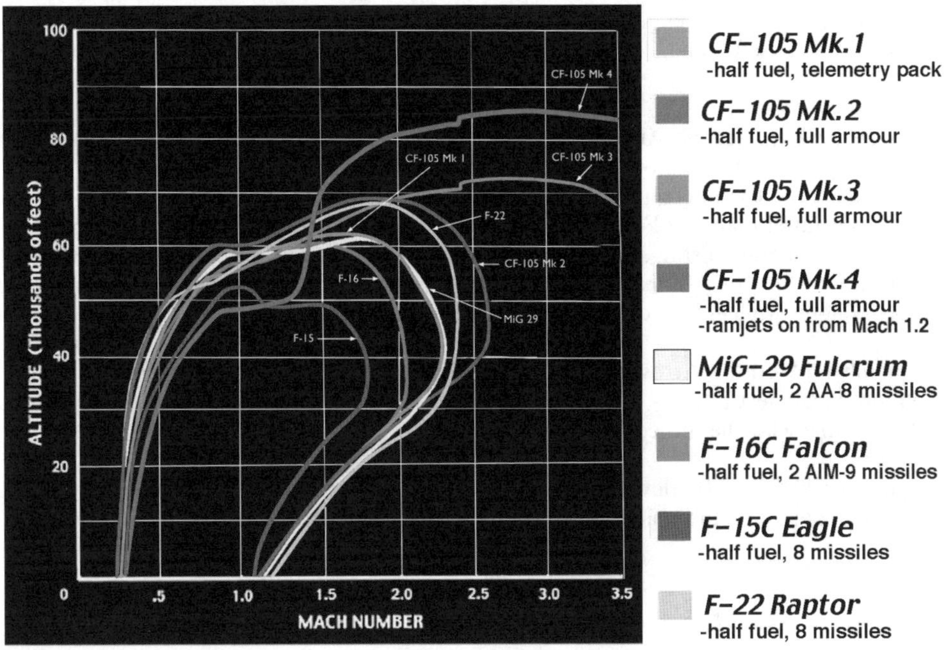

Externally all appeared as it should have, despite Zura's cockpit indication of incomplete nose gear closure. The throttles were nudged forward to give an indicated airspeed of 250 knots. At 11,000 feet a general handling assessment was conducted with the fly-by-wire system in emergency mode. A slight amount of pitch oscillation is barely apparent in the flight footage until Zura started to finesse the controls and not over-control the aircraft. The plane was apparently very sensitive to pitch inputs meaning it would have excellent manoeuvrability. A half-hour of flight time passed and the plane was returned to the landing circuit. A faster than necessary approach was made for the sake of safety and the jet touched down, tires leaving a smoke trail, right on the threshold. The drag chute streamed "as advertised" and the plane only required light braking to slow to taxi speed about half way down the runway length available. Flight audio tape records chaseplane pilot Spud Potocki (a WW II Polish Spitfire ace and comrade of Zura's) exultantly shout "WONDERFUL stuff!"

Once the plane was returned to the ramp and shut down Zurakowski climbed out and was immediately accosted by a jubilant horde of his fellow Avroites, hoisted shoulder high and paraded around the tarmac. The first flight snag sheet was framed since it only showed the malfunction of a microswitch designed to indicate proper nose gear door closure. Zura's laconic comment regarding this history-making flight was that the plane performed "within expectations". His only complaint was the lack of a cockpit clock by which to tell the time.

Statistically speaking, the second flight of the Arrow, conducted less than a week later, roughly doubled the performance of the first flight. Speeds of up to 400 knots were demonstrated at altitudes up to 30,000 feet. The aircraft was banked past 60 degrees and 2.5 G were pulled during the turn. Again the nose gear door closure microswitches weren't adjusted properly and indicated incorrect door closure.

Two short days later the Arrow spread its supersonic wings and exceeded Mach 1.1 at 40,000 feet before Zura throttled back. On its third flight the Arrow had, for all intents and purposes, matched the top performance of the Convair F-102 Delta Dagger without even breaking a sweat. On the return from this flight Zura began something that would become his trademark during Arrow testing. Thundering over the runway at low level he pulled the nose up…higher…higher still then impossibly high to the vertical with full afterburning thrust ripping attentive eardrums. The glittering delta pulled up into a vertical climb and almost disappeared from sight. This manoeuvre became a symbol of the confidence of the company and pilot in their product. It was certainly an analogy of what they expected the project's future to bring not only to Avro and Orenda, but to the people of Canada and perhaps even the people of the free world. (In the fall of 1958 the British magazine *Aviation Studies* stated that "Canada owes it to the free world to put into production the Arrow aircraft, the most advanced interceptor in the Western world.") The Iroquois engined Mk. 2 would have been able to accelerate while climbing vertically and carrying a useful load. The developed Iroquois promised this performance at close to gross take-off weight.

By August, 1958 the second Arrow prototype was flying and broke the sound barrier on only its second flight. RL-202 flew twice on August 26th and once on August 27th and again two flights were completed on the 28th. The interceptor reached speeds of between Mach 1.5 and Mach 1.7 on each of these flights—far faster than any F-102 ever flew. This performance was an outstanding achievement for an aircraft just entering testing, particularly considering the history of the Convair deltas—the F-102 and F-106. Five Mach 1.5 flights in three days on one airframe is an excellent serviceability record for modern developed fighters in squadron service.

On September 14th, 1958 Arrow RL-202 reached Mach 1.86—the highest speed reached by Zura before he retired from test flying—thereby somewhat belatedly fulfilling a promise to his wife to quit the dangerous game when he turned 40.

On September 22nd RL-203 flew for the first time and "went super" on its maiden voyage. RL-204 first flew on the 27th of October and the fifth pre-production Arrow, RL-205, flew only once on 11 January 1959.

During the test flying two landing accidents occurred. The first one was caused by a flaw in the design of the landing gear where the mechanism responsible for turning the wheel bogies into alignment with the aircraft centreline jammed. Engineering had already redesigned the landing gear due to minor increases in aircraft weight before first flight and now it was redesigned again to prevent a similar mishap. The second landing accident was probably due to pilot error. Spud Potocki had taken RL-

202 on a long-range high-speed flight from Malton to Lake Superior, conducted a supersonic run over Ottawa (on Remembrance Day!) and returned the plane to Malton. He was very low on fuel and his approach was too fast to be able to land properly on the runway available. Fearing running out of fuel he tried to force the plane down against ground effect and locked the main wheels before there was sufficient weight on them to brake properly. This resulted in the aircraft swinging off the runway and tearing off one of the main landing gear legs and otherwise damaging the aircraft. As a result of this accident the Mk.1 gear was banned from flight and replaced by the stronger and improved Mk. 2 landing gear—even though the Mk. 2 was significantly lighter than the Mk. 1. This was also the fastest recorded flight of the Arrow with a speed of Mach 1.98 being reached. Jim Floyd has related that they didn't really know the correct atmospheric correction factor to apply to this flight and as such the flight could have been Mach 2 or slightly higher. They apparently decided to state the speed as Mach 1.98 in order not to record a new world speed record and agitate their peers in the rest of the industry, and their enemies in government. Others have said that A.V. Roe Canada president Crawford Gordon Jr. absolutely forbade a speed record attempt in the Mark 1 Arrows, wishing to preserve this accolade for an Iroquois engined Mk. 2.

In a little-known anecdote, RL-202 was moved into the experimental hangar for repairs. Engineering decided that since the plane would be out of action for some time that they could save the government and themselves time and money by converting RL-202 to accept Iroquois engines and the MA-1 fire-control system. This would yield, essentially, a Mk.2 Arrow. This has been corroborated by Jim Floyd and one of the experimental shop workers. For those who suspect that "one got away" (like June Callwood and others) RL-202 seems the most likely candidate. RL-207, the second Mk. 2 on the assembly line, also seems like a candidate for preservation and this author has seen a government document ordering that one complete Arrow Mk. 2 with two Iroquois engines be dismantled, properly preserved and stored…somewhere. There are persistent rumours that one flying Arrow went to the United States, probably Groom Lake (aka Dreamland or Area-51) for American testing. An examination of the salvage records by Scott McArthur of Arrow Recovery Canada (involved in trying to retrieve an Arrow telemetry model from the floor of Lake Ontario) reveals an ambiguity in the records that could have allowed two planes to escape. The question is this: where on the line did they consider the planes to be essentially complete and where were they considered just components?

In late 1957 government agency criticism of the Arrow and Avro became somewhat universal. G/C Footit has written in period documentation that some of the criticism was due to professional jealousy in organisations like the National Aeronautical Establishment who felt they should be the ones charged with design and testing of aircraft like the Arrow. Some of the criticism was also centred around the terrible legacy of the American F-102 Delta Dagger, which some thought, due to its sharing the delta-wing arrangement, indicated what the performance of the Arrow would be like. Chief of Operational Requirements Jack Easton actually penned a paper calling the mathematical application of the F-102s characteristics to the Arrow "a dangerous assumption." Due to professional criticism of the performance projections by peers in NACA, the USAF and British agencies during their evaluations, Avro chose to temper their performance projections in late-1957.

In 1955 Avro had projected the performance of the Mk.2 Iroquois powered Arrow to be:

Maximum speed of Mach 1.9 at 50,000 feet altitude.

Combat speed of Mach 1.5 at 50,000 feet while sustaining a 1.84 G turn without bleeding energy.

Time to 50,000 feet of 4.1 minutes.

500 foot per minute (fpm) climb ceiling of 62,000 feet. (i.e., able to climb at 500 fpm from this height)

400 nm (nautical mile) radius of action on a high-speed mission.

630 nm radius of action on a low-speed (including 5 minutes supersonic combat) mission.

Ferry range is not given but estimated at 1,500 nm.

These figures were impressive enough to gain Avro the government contract to produce the aircraft, and also resulted in the British RAF attempting to buy 200 Arrows for the defense of Britain even though they had applied a handicap to Avro's performance projections. By December, 1957 Avro had released Performance Report 12 which indicated a reduction in performance, in line with the consensus outside Avro that they had underestimated the aircraft's aerodynamic drag. The figures from this report indicated:

Maximum speed unchanged at Mach 1.9.

Combat speed of Mach 1.5 at 50,000 feet while sustaining about 1.6 G in a turn.

500 fpm climb ceiling of 58,000 feet.

264 nm combat radius on a high-speed mission.

408 nm combat radius on a low-speed mission.

Ferry range of 1254 nm.

An enormous amount of bad ink was generated among the government "experts" by these lowered performance projections. Footit for one accused Avro engineering of mismanagement and repeatedly insisted that Avro was mismanaging the program. In one of Footit's letters he accuses Avro of having covered up various facts, but later had to admit that Avro had properly informed the RCAF but that he simply hadn't seen the documentation. One can see that by this time Avro was in a difficult position. If they stuck to their original projections they would be universally condemned by all the outside agencies who insisted that their drag projections were too low. If they lowered them they would be accused of incompetence and of producing an aircraft that wouldn't meet the specification—thereby endangering the program.

However, and to the elation of the Arrow designers and company in general, the Arrow Mk. 1, with about 40% less thrust than the Mk. 2 and more weight, actually exceeded Avro's own higher 1955 estimates for the Arrow 2 by exceeding Mach 1.9. By October of 1958 due to test flying Avro was able to refine the drag estimates, feed them into the IBM 704 computer, and produce accurate projections that indicated 20% lower supersonic drag at maximum performance than even they themselves had projected. Performance Report 15 included the empirically refined performance projections and the figures in this document indicate that the Arrow 2 would have remained the top-performing fighter-interceptor in virtually all categories until the advent of the Lockheed Martin F-22 Raptor, now entering service in the USAF. Unfortunately by this time the Conservative government was committed to program cancellation in favour of nebulous and ultimately unfulfilled promises from the American Republican politicians and their cronies.

RCAF Arrow test pilot Jack Woodman later related the success of Avro's designers in dealing with aerodynamics and stability concerns for the transonic to supersonic transition. "I reported the transition from subsonic to supersonic speed to be very smooth, compressibility effects negligible and the sensitive control problems experienced at lower speeds and altitudes eliminated." In his first flight, he had felt the controls too sensitive in pitch (Zurakowski's recommendations had already resulted in control sensitivity being reduced on the roll axis) and this was altered by programming a gradient into the control system whereby it was made less sensitive at the first stages of stick movement. This demonstrates the advantages of a 'fly-by-wire' system and also of the Arrow's natural control sensitivity–meaning the Arrow would have been very manoeuvrable.

In fact, an enormous amount of verbiage has been expended in claims that the Arrow would not have been manoeuvrable, based merely on perceptions of it being such a large aircraft. In reality, it was not much bigger than an F-101 Voodoo or an F-15 Eagle, neither of which would have seriously challenged an Arrow 2 in a combat air patrol, "top cover" or "air superiority" mission. Furthermore, size means nothing in determining an aircraft's manoeuvrability. A plane's manoeuvrability potential *can*, however, be calculated based on five factors. In comparison with any of the aircraft built at the time and since in similar roles, from virtually any country, the Arrow appears to have had attributes which would have given it superior manoeuvrability to virtually any plane to this date—save the F-22 Raptor, which has reverted to internal weapons carriage and a relatively low wing loading. The five critical attributes are: wing loading, thrust-to-weight ratio, control effectiveness, critical alpha (or stalling angle of attack) and, finally, the amount of 'G' loading the aircraft structure can absorb. The Arrow had the lowest wing loading of any supersonic interceptor to ever enter service, its only competition being the F-106 Delta Dart and, to a lesser extent, the F-22 Raptor. In terms of thrust-to-weight ratio at combat weight, the Arrow was superior to everything up to the F-15 Eagle. The Arrow's allowable manoeuvring 'G' at combat weight is equal, and in most cases superior to, virtually anything to fly then or since. Control effectiveness is difficult to estimate, especially with a supersonic delta design since the "moment arm" changes with control actuation and also with speed since the centre of lift moves aft (back) at supersonic speeds. Designing a tailless aircraft with good manoeuvrability *and* stability characteristics across a wide speed range requires exacting engineering.

Chamberlin's unique features on the Arrow wing, such as negative camber inboard, leading edge droop, the sawtooth/notches were responsible for the Arrow's good characteristics at subsonic *and* supersonic speeds. Avro's inclusion of a Honeywell Controls engineered automated fuel management system also allowed them to tailor the aircraft's centre of gravity to be very close to the aircraft's centre of lift at each point (and thus expected speed) in its mission. The simple secret of making a delta craft very manoeuvrable is to have the centre of lift and centre of gravity at nearly the same place, sufficient control surfaces will do the rest. In interviews with Jan Zurakowski and Peter Cope, both said the Arrow had awesome natural control sensitivity. Zura mentioned the roll rate was reduced at high subsonic speeds because he felt it was excessive. It was limited to one complete roll, or 360 degrees, in a second. Cope mentioned that the Arrow handled very well, was *very* stable on approach if flown correctly (contrary to some third party sources). Jack Woodman mentioned that a mere one-fifth of an inch of stick movement would result in a .5 'G' loading on the aircraft, which he felt was excessive. In other words, the Arrow had very good control effectiveness, better than any of the USAF and British jets these experienced test pilots flew.

The simple fact is that the Arrow had an awesome power of manoeuvre as anyone who studies such things empirically will readily acknowledge. When 1 G performance curves for even the Arrow Mk. 1, with early, de-rated J-75 engines, are compared to contemporary and even current fighters, it emerges that the Arrow really was a *world-beating* design. It had the attributes in terms of low drag, low wing loading and high thrust-to-weight to defeat virtually any fighter at low altitude in a dog fight scenario. While its delta wing is argued, by some, to result in high drag during turns, the Arrow's internal weapons and higher thrust-to-weight would compensate. The Arrow 1, at higher than combat weight, displayed a larger flight envelope than a late production F-16 Fighting Falcon that carried only two tiny heat seeking missiles.[300] France's Mirage 2000, an updated version of their 1950's Mirage III delta fighter is also known to embarrass the F-16 at medium and high altitude in turning fights, despite the F-16's better thrust-to-weight ratio. Nevertheless, the Mirage III was never considered a competitor to the Arrow in any performance measure or military role. The performance of the Russian MiG 29 Fulcrum, under equally light loading conditions to the F-16C mentioned above, is equal to that of an overloaded Arrow Mk. 1. An F-15C Eagle, with up-rated engines, but at a true combat weight (no tanks, half internal fuel and eight missiles) displays a vastly smaller performance envelope to even an Arrow Mk. 1 with at least 40% less thrust than a service Arrow 2 would have had. The Arrow 2, as specified by Avro for the 21st Arrow, would have been able to sustain a nearly 2G turn at about Mach 1.8 and 50,000 feet. An F-15C could, at combat weight, sustain the same 'G' loading at about Mach 1.2 and 35,000 feet—hardly competitive. The F-15C was felt, subsequent to the retirement of the F-106 Delta Dart, to exhibit the highest performance in the Western world on such an air superiority mission. Clearly, then, the Arrow had vast "power of manoeuvre". It had the ability to utterly humiliate anything flying, particularly at medium and high altitude. In a supersonic turning fight at altitude, the Arrow would remain unmatched by anything save the F-22 Raptor due to the F-22's higher thrust-to-weight ratio. The Arrow still had lower wing loading and, with a drag coefficient probably under .0185 and a lift-drag ratio of over 7-1 would therefore still not be a push-over for the Raptor—all other things being equal, which, of course, 45 intervening years of progress in electronics have ensured are not. Still, the Arrow 2 was proclaimed capable of an instantaneous 6 'G' at 50,000 feet. The F-106 was also a high performer at altitude, capable of about 4 'G' at 45,000 feet whereas the Raptor is estimated to achieve 5 'G' at 50,000 feet.[301]

The Arrow would have been a dominant aircraft for many, many years and therefore could be expected to sell well to allied nations. That American authorities would not purchase any, and recommended that Canada not produce them, tells its own story. A Canadian civil servant involved in a review of the CBC documentary "There Never Was An Arrow" noted the following regarding the documentary's conclusion that American interests were not involved in the Arrow cancellation: "The programme concluded that no American interests were involved in the decision. On the face of it this seems a remarkably innocent point of view. Previous accounts have suggested with some reason that the American aviation industry would not have been comfortable with the Arrow as competition and therefore was not likely to give the Canadian firm much opportunity to compete."[302]

SPECIFICATION	**F-106A**	**CF-105Mk2a**	**F-4E Phantom**	**F-101B Voodoo**	**F-15A**
Length	70.8'	80'	63'	71'	63.8'
Span	38.3'	50'	38.5'	39.6'	42.8'
T/C	**4%**	**2.6%**	5.5%	6%	5%
Empty Wt	24,000 lbs	42,000 lbs	28,500 lbs	29,000 lbs	27,000 lbs
Combat Wt	33,500 lbs	55,000 lbs	39,400 lbs	40,853 lbs	40,000 lbs
Combat Take-off Wt.	38,700 lbs	67,250 lbs	46,900 lbs	45,664 lbs	58,000 lbs
Max Take-off Wt.	41,831 lbs	72,250 lbs	58,000 lbs	52,400 lbs	66,000 lbs
Fuel Load					
Internal	11,000 lbs	19,700 lbs	15,100 lbs	15,600 lbs	13,600 lbs
Svc. Tanks	4,200 lbs/5,475 lbs	3,900 lbs	4,600 lbs	6,850 lbs	4,550 lbs
Normal Svc.	15,200/16,475 lbs	23,600 lbs	19,700 lbs	15,600 lbs	18,200 lbs
Max Fuel	16,475 lbs	24,600 lbs	25,150 lbs	22,450 lbs	27,500 lbs
Wing Area	697 sq. ft	1225 sq. ft	530 sq. ft.	368 sq. ft.	608 sq. ft
Wing Load (empty)	**33.81 lbs/sq. ft.**	**34.28 lbs/sq. ft.**	54 lbs/sq. ft.	78.7 lbs/sq. ft.	44.4 lbs/sq. ft.
Wing Load (combat wt)	**48 lbs/sq. ft.**	**45 lbs/sq.ft**	74 lbs/sq. ft.	111 lbs/sq. ft.	66 lbs/sq. ft
Wing Load (Com t/o)	**55.44 lbs/sq. ft.**	**54.9 lbs/sq. ft.**	88.5 lbs/sq. ft.	124 lbs/sq. ft.	95 lbs/sq. ft.
Wing Load (Max t/o)	**59.9 lbs/sq. ft.**	**58.9 lbs/sq. ft.**	109.4 lbs/sq. ft	143.4 lbs/sq. ft	108.5 lbs/sq. ft.
Average	**49.3 lbs/sq. ft.**	**48.3 lbs/sq. ft.**	81.4 lbs/sq. ft	114.4 lbs/sq. ft.	78.5 lbs/sq. .ft.
Dry Thrust	17,000 lbs	38,500 lbs	21,000 lbs	20,400 lbs	29,250 lbs
A/B Thrust	24,000 lbs	52,000 lbs	33,000 lbs	32,000 lbs	47,750 lbs
Fuel to Thrust ratio					
Internal	11,000 lbs fuel	19,700 lbs fuel	15,100 lbs fuel	15,600 lbs fuel	13,600 lbs fuel
Dry	.64 lbs fuel/lbt	.51 lbs fuel/lbt	**.71 lbs fuel/lbt**	**.76 lbs fuel/lbt**	.46 lbs fuel/lbt
W/afterburning	**.46 lbs fuel/lbt**	.38 lbs fuel/lbt	.46 lbs fuel/lbt	**.48 lbs fuel/lbt**	.28 lbs fuel/lbt
Combat Weight					
Dry	.35 lbs fuel/lbt	.25 lbs fuel/lbt	**.36 lbs fuel/lbt**	**.38 lbs fuel/lbt**	.23 lbs fuel/lbt
Afterburning	**.23 lbs /lbt**	.19 lbs fuel/lbt	.23 lbs fuel/lbt	**.24 lbs fuel/lbt**	.14 lbs fuel/lbt
Tanks:	(2@ 2,100 lbs ea.)	(1& 3,900 lbs)			(1@ 4,550 lbs)
Dry	**.89 lbs fuel/lbt**	.61 lbs fuel/lbt	**.94 lbs fuel/lbt**	.38 lbs fuel/lbt	.62 lbs fuel/lbt
Afterburning	**.63 lbs fuel/lbt**	.45 lbs fuel/lbt	**.59 lbs fuel/lbt**	.24 lbs fuel/lbt	.38 lbs fuel/lbt
Max fuel	(2@ 2,750 lbs. ea)	(1& 3,900 +1,000 intl.)			(3@4,550 lbs ea.)
Dry	.97 lbs fuel/lbt	.64 lbs fuel/lbt	**1.2 lbs fuel/lbt**	**1.1 lbs fuel/lbt**	.94 lbs fuel/lbt
Afterburning	.68 lbs fuel/lbt	.47 lbs fuel/lbt	**.76 lbs fuel/lbt**	**1.1 lbs fuel/lbt**	.57 lbs fuel/lbt
Average fuel-thrust	**.6 lbs fuel/lbt**	.44 lbs fuel/lbt	**.65 lbs fuel/lbt**	.58 lbs fuel/lbt	.45 lbs fuel/lbt
Weight-fuel Ratio					
Combat Wt.	6.9 lbs/lb fuel	5.58 lbs/lb fuel	**5.1 lbs/lb fuel**	**5.23 lbs/lb fuel**	5.88 lbs/lb fuel
Combat T/o Wt.	3.51 lbs/lb fuel	**2.84 lbs/lb fuel**	**2.38 lbs/lb fuel**	2.92 lbs/lb fuel	2.94 lbs/lb fuel
Max Fuel	2.53 lbs/lb fuel	2.93 lbs/lb fuel	**2.3 lbs/lb fuel**	**2.3 lbs/lb fuel**	2.4 lbs/lb fuel
Power Loading dry thrust					
Empty Wt.	1.41 lbs/lbt	**1.1 lbs/lbt**	1.35 lbs/lbt	1.41 lbs/lbt	**.92 lbs/lbt**
Combat T/o Wt.	2.27 lbs/lbt	**1.74 lbs/lbt**	2.23 lbs/lbt	2.23 lbs/lbt	**1.64 lbs/lbt**
Combat Wt.	1.97 lbs/lbt	**1.43 lbs/lbt**	1.87 lbs/lbt	2.0 lbs/lbt	**1.36 lbs/lbt**
Max T/o Wt.	2.46 lbs/lbt	**1.88 lbs/lbt**	2.76 lbs/lbt	2.56 lbs/lbt	**2.25 lbs/lbt**
Average:	2.0 lbs/lbt	**1.53 lbs/lbt**	2.05 lbs/lbt	2.05 lbs/lbt	**1.54 lbs/lbt**
Power Loading w/AB					
Empty Wt.	1 lb/lbt	**.8 lb/lbt**	.86 lbs/lbt	.89 lbs/lbt	**.56 lb/lbt**
Combat T/o Wt.	1.61 lb/lbt	**1.3 lb/lbt**	1.5 lbs/lbt	**1.42 lbs/lbt**	1.5 lb/lbt
Combat Wt.	1.27lb/lbt	**1.0 lb/lbt**	1.19 lbs/lbt	1.26 lbs/lbt	**.83 lb/lbt**
Max T/o Wt.	1.74 lb/lbt	**1.39 lb/lbt**	1.76 lbs/lbt	1.59 lbs/lbt	**1.38 lb/lbt**
Average:	1.4 lb/lbt	**1.1 lb/lbt**	1.32 lbs/lbt	1.29 lbs/lbt	**1.06 lb/lbt**
Initial Climb	42,500 fpm	**44,500 fpm**	**40,500 fpm**	**40,000 fpm**	

300 Braybook, Roy. "Fighting Falcon V Fulcrum." Air International Vol.47, No.2. Stamford: Key Publishing, 1994
301 Sweetman, Bill. The F-22 Raptor
302 Douglas, W.A.B., Note to File "CBC Programme on the Avro Arrow", 21 April, 1980

Chapter 51

ARROW MARK 3

As early as 1956, before the Arrow Mk. 1 was flying, Avro was considering a future version of the Arrow designated, naturally, the Mk. 3. Since the Arrow 2 was expected to only be capable of Mach 1.9, Avro hoped that an improved Iroquois, new variable nozzles for the engine and other changes would allow an increase in combat speed to Mach 2.5. By the time the Arrow Mk.1 was into flight test, and, despite having about 40% less thrust than the Mk. 2, the Mk. 1 proved capable of Mach 1.98. Due to this exceptional performance Avro knew the Mk. 3 would be capable of considerably more than Mach 2.5. With improved materials and a new intake design that would be efficient at Mach 2.2 and above, Avro knew they would have an Arrow capable of at least Mach 3. This was nearly ten years before the SR-71 Blackbird or MiG 25 Foxbat flew, suggesting Avro had an excellent advantage over the competition—given the freedom to exploit it.

The Arrow Mk. 3, at take-off weight, was projected to weigh almost 17,000 pounds more than the Mk. 2. An extra 10,000 pounds of internal fuel was responsible for the majority of this weight gain with a total fuel load of 28,738 pounds being specified. This extra fuel was carried by using more of the empty wing structure, filling some of the fin with fuel, and in a redesigned central fuselage sub-assembly. The construction technology of these and some other sections was an impressive technological advance Avro termed "sculptured skins". These "skins" were made from billets of a new high-temperature aluminum alloy that were machined to include the structural members (integral formers) with them being "sculpted" out of the billet and joined to the similarly sculpted formers beneath. Again, Avro's ground-breaking use of computerised production equipment (CNC machining) made this possible and efficient. The central fuselage area, over the armament bay and surrounding the intake ducts, was to be completely filled with fuel by application of these new fabrication techniques and Avro's advanced sealant technologies. This fuel would also act as a heat sink to help cool the airframe at high supersonic speeds, while helping the aircraft's range.

Interesting high-temperature aluminum alloys were looked at with Avro proposing X2020-T6 alloy for the structure instead of the 75ST used for the Arrow 2. This appeared to promise acceptable characteristics up to about 350 degrees F. This is about 100 degrees higher than aluminum alloy specifications for normal light-alloys and would have, by itself, allowed a sustained speed of around Mach 2.4. Avro's metallurgical department had done comprehensive testing on two promising aluminium alloys, X2020-T6, and 2024-T81, finding the former superior by over 10 percent. North American, at this time into the development of the X-15 hypersonic rocket plane, (designed for up to Mach 7, which it never reached) had chosen 2024-T6 for cooler areas of the structure. In areas facing extreme kinetic heating, such as the leading edges, stainless steel and/or titanium were specified, while other surfaces would employ a combination of any of these materials and/or an advanced honeycomb-composite insulation Avro was developing. This insulation scheme had things in common with the evolving ablative "paints" used on missile nose-cones, and with the heat shields for Mercury and Gemini. In fact, the technology for the heat shields for Mercury and Gemini appear to have come from the Arrow program, with Brian Erb being Avro's thermodynamics specialist and later taking a similar position within NASA. A carbon fibre, or fibreglass honeycomb matrix was to be filled with either an epoxy or vulcanising compound that would suspend glass "microballoons". This was to be applied over the Arrow

3's aluminum skins in some areas to provide an ablative insulation to the structure. Erb was largely responsible for NASA's rejection of their original beryllium heat shield and adoption of the Arrow 3's honeycomb matrix composite insulation scheme. For some reason (perhaps commercial patent infringement) this heat shield system was the most highly classified part of the Mercury/Gemini systems.

It is interesting to note that the Space Shuttle uses a conventional light-alloy structure and relies on external insulation to keep the *extreme* structural temperatures under control on re-entry. The SR-71, as most aviation enthusiasts are aware, uses mostly titanium for structure and skin and represents the opposite approach to that of the shuttle. Lockheed's uncompromising approach was commendable perhaps, but it was heavy and was probably not required for components far from the engines and leading-edges and around the fuel tanks. Gunston's *Faster Than Sound,* published in 1992, shows diagrams of presumably modern external insulation for spaceplanes that can in no way be considered as advanced as Avro's evolving method as it stood in 1958. Avro's thinking for the Mk.3 was a hybrid approach with the subsequent success of the Shuttle and Blackbird, and of course Mercury and Gemini, suggesting the Arrow 3 was feasible.

Propulsion for the Mk. 3 Arrow was to be the Iroquois Mk. 3. Changes from the Mk. 2 version of the engine included a new combustion section, six inches shorter than that of the Iroquois 2, a new turbine section with much narrower blades (thereby allowing a much shorter turbine section overall) yet with a larger bell-mouth size with correspondingly larger diameter compressor rotors and stator blade sets and structure. To handle the increased mass-flow a larger diameter and slightly longer afterburner section and nozzle assembly was specified. Orenda was also designing a variable, convergent-divergent nozzle for the Mk. 3, which would have increased its efficiency at less than full power settings. A larger final nozzle also promised more thrust due to it being able to allow nearly full expansion of the exhaust gases before they exited the nozzle. For reasons of conservatism and prudence, Avro, as of mid-1958, only specified a thrust gain of about 600 pounds, wet or dry, for the Iroquois 3. Based on a linear comparison by compressor diameter with the Iroquois 2, with development the Iroquois 3's thrust would have been *much* higher. Considering the smaller "hole size" Iroquois 2 had produced 27,000 lbs thrust, *without afterburner*, on the test stand at Cornell laboratories in the United States. A developed Iroquois 3 should have been able to reliably generate at least this amount of thrust dry, and nearly 40,000 lbs thrust in afterburner. Orenda was specifying the lower figures to ensure that the projections were conservative and thus could be realistically achieved. Primary sources from Orenda state that they were expecting up to 30,000 lbt dry and nearly 40,000 lbt with afterburner. Therefore, developed, the Mk. 3 Arrow would have been capable of a lot more than Mach 3—given the materials and insulation technology to allow the airframe and engine to withstand kinetic heating at those speeds. Performance curves even at the low thrust projections indicate speeds well above Mach 3.

An advanced feature of the Arrow 3 was the provision for "probe and drogue" aerial refuelling. This feature seemed to come as a shock to the chief scientist of the USAF. As of 1957 it was an experimental feature being tried on the North American F-100 Super Sabre, although it was being designed into the F-101B Voodoo. The poor stability of early swept wing supersonic designs seemed to preclude the early adoption of this system. Of course, Avro's real-time fly-by-wire and stability augmentation systems would have eliminated this problem.

The intake for the Mark 3 (and later higher-performance Arrow design studies) is especially interesting. The intake Avro proposed was a four-ramp, three-dimensional, variable concept and was designed to give *no* shock-induced airflow separation on either the ramp surface or the fuselage diverter plate at all supersonic speeds. This was, and is, very advanced thinking and once again Avro's massive computer installations allowed them to design, with confidence, to this radical ideal. This was achieved by very careful computer modelling of the strengths of the triple shock waves produced on the variable ramps at different speeds, while designing the intake to benefit from the bow shock from the aircraft nose. The only speeds at which Avro found shock-induced separation *at all* with this intake design were between Mach 1.4 and Mach 1.6, where the disturbed airflow was "bounced" against the fuselage with this turbulent air being bled off between the diverter plate and the fuselage side and spilled over-board. A very narrow "slit" of boundary-layer air was removed on the inside of the intake at the rear of the diverter plate by a knife-edge "razor" bleed and this was supplied to the air-conditioning heat exchangers. Those exchangers, as on all Arrows, exhausted nearly axially (rearward) which is "nearly" perfect. The intake was designed to run at up to 45 psi and thus boosted the compressor ratio of the engine considerably. This explains why the SR-71's engine was designed to give only 6-1 compression and why the Iroquois was also low, at only 8-1.

The most astounding aspect of the intake, however, was the fact that it was designed to *swallow* the normal shock wave coming off the nose and use this to both increase thrust and also reduce drag. This was radical thinking. Getting rid of large portions of the normal shock wave would decrease the drag of the airframe somewhat since the normal shock "plows" air. Swallowing it actually increased the compression of the air inside the intakes resulting in a boost in performance in some regions of the performance envelope, as the reproduced performance curve shows. As such it was a "supercritical" intake and was the first of its kind to the author's knowledge. The first to enter service was that used on the SR-71. For an indication of the drag and efficiency advantages of swallowing the normal shock, one should look to the D-21 reconnaissance drone piggy-backed on the SR-71 for a time. This device swallowed the normal shock with its 3-D intake being at the nose of the drone. In Sweetman's book *Aurora, The Pentagon's Secret Hypersonic Spyplane*, the D-21 is proclaimed to possess an incredible range of 10-15,000 miles! The official USAF Museum site, however, lists this range as being "3,500+ miles."

While still using inflated drag numbers, Avro quoted the combat ceiling at combat weight to be at least 70,500 feet at Mach 3 while still allowing a margin for a 500 feet per minute (fpm) climb. Maximum attainable speed was in the neighbourhood of Mach 3.4. An *anticipated* limitation of the Arrow 2, as pointed out in Avro's Performance Report 13 (before the Arrow flew and revealed her much lower drag coefficient), was due to nearly full up-deflection of the elevators at maximum altitude. The resulting trim-drag was in the order of 5,000 pounds. Evidence that Avro was already thinking of cross-programming the "fly by wire" system to reduce trim drag and allow more pitch authority at maximum altitude, by allowing the ailerons to operate as elevators in tandem with the latter, is found in the Mk. 3 proposal. Above 45,000 feet they specified that the Mk. 3's ailerons would be programed for 5 degrees up deflection. Subsequent discussions with Jim Floyd and Peter Cope also indicate that the Arrow 2 had a similar system designed into it. It also had fuel consumption programed to move the aircraft's centre of gravity in the appropriate direction as speed and altitude increased, with this feature, and the aileron trimming, being designed to reduce trim drag at high altitudes and speeds thereby improving manoeuvrability and maximum attainable altitude and speed.

SPECIFICATION	CF-105M3	F-111A	TSR.2
Length	85.5'	73.5'	89'
Span	50'	63/31 swing	37'
T/C	2.6%	4.2%-6.5% est	4.5%
Empty Wt	52,000 lbs	46,172 lbs	44,750 lbs
Combat Wt	70,000 lbs	63,050 lbs	63,000 lbs (est)
Fuel Load			
Internal	28,738 lbs		
Svc. Tanks	3,900 lbs		4,600 lbs
Total	32,650 lbs		
Wing Area	1225 sq. ft	525 sq. ft	695 sq. ft
Wing Load (combat wt)	**52lbs/sq. ft**	120 lbs/sq. ft	**90.6 lbs/sq.ft**
Dry Thrust	**42,000 lbt**	24,000 lbt	**40,000 lbt**
A/B Thrust	**60,000 lbt**	37,000 lbt	**60,000 lbt**
Power Loading	**.945 lb/lbt**	1.7 lb/lbt	**1.05 lb/lbt**
Initial Climb	**30,000 fpm**	25,550 fpm (clean)	**42,000 fpm**
VMax	**3.0+Mach@60,000 ft**	2.35M@56,000 ft	**(???) 2.5M@36,000ft**
Combat Spec	**70,500ft@3.0M 1.5G**	25,000 ft@1.5M@1.5G?	**35,000 ft M1.8 2G**
Service Ceil	**76,000 ft.?**	**56,650 M1.8 1.2G**	50,000 ft 2.0M 1.2G
PwrLtd Ceil	**83,000 ft ?**	47,000 ft	**57,000 ft**
Zoom Ceil	**120,000 ft. ?**	66,000 ft	**90,000 ft?**
Service date (projected)	1963-1965	1967 (1973 actual)	1967

Chapter 52

ARROW DECISIONS:
A Tangled Web, Woven to Deceive.

Most commentators on the subject of the Avro Arrow have concluded that it was in mid-1958 that the Conservative government became convinced that the Arrow was too costly, and that projections indicated that it would require an increase in the defense budget, and that this was unacceptable to the Conservatives for good reason. Most of them also conclude that this was the genuine advice of the CSC, and that the government acted on this sincere recommendation. Yet it was always known that during the production of the Arrow the defense budget would have to be increased.

> "The program initially called for the re-equipping of the nine squadrons from a production run of 169 aircraft, and still does. It was clear that this number of aircraft would substantially increase the Defense Budget." [303]

Something else which debases the assumption that the Conservatives genuinely supported the program at first is shown by a secret Air Council meeting on 22 August 1957. The Chief of the Air Staff AM Hugh Campbell stated:

> "Things are moving quickly in an alarming way. [The] Gov't has told us, this week, to cut back expenditures in 58/59 and not to expect any increase in following years.... Whether or not we stay with the 105 depends largely on getting the US to come in with us during the next two months—before November when we go to the Gov't."[304]

This resulted in the second attempt by the RCAF to sell the Arrow to the USAF, although the events which followed made this sales attempt unnecessary in terms of saving the Arrow program—temporarily. Now, if it was well known that Arrow production would significantly increase the budget, but Pearkes ruled out an expansion of the budget "in following years", does this indicate support for the program or predict that they were going to go ahead with it? The Treasury Board had done a study showing a contraction in the economy followed by tight government money and this generated a review of all the government's programs. The Ministry of Finance was thus compelled to initiate program analysis to see where they could save some money. This Treasury Board document of the Winter/Spring 1957-'58 was the real impetus that eventually resulted in the cancellation of the Arrow. This prophecy became a self-fulfilling one once the Arrow (and Avro and Orenda and A.V. Roe Canada) were cut down. One wonders who provided the crystal ball used by the Treasury Board. A book on banking in Canada, *The Money Spinners,* states that the directors of the Bank of Canada—all senior chartered bank executives—really run Canadian economic policy and essentially only limited meddling by politicians. Diefenbaker had also always campaigned against the Bay Street monopolies, and most commentators have linked Avro to this perceived entity, whereas that is not really the right way to describe Avro at all. To Diefenbaker's possible credit, (although, like Eisenhower, it was almost always impossible to tell what he really thought, unless he lost his temper that is) he at least urged caution and initially considered giving Avro a license-build contract for a much simpler aircraft to replace the RCAF's Sabres in Europe. This however, may have been a sop to satisfy those in his Cabinet who were arguing about cancellation. Pearkes also, until July 1958, appeared reluctant to cancel the Arrow and had, before winning their majority, recommended the expansion of the Arrow program from the 11 already on order to 37 pre-production samples. He had single-handedly, in fact, short circuited the normal CSC to Cabinet Defense Committee (CDC) to Cabinet process, and had written his own paper and got it passed by Diefenbaker the next day. This decision was influenced by representations made by himself and the Minister of Finance, Donald Fleming, and others, in Cabinet discussions, that the program should continue as "no announced layoffs could possibly occur" until the Spring. Considering his earlier assertions about budget restrictions in August 1957, one must wonder if Pearkes rather unexpected expansion of the Arrow program wasn't done for political reasons. After all, they had demanded reductions in defense spending while knowing that Arrow production would, rather, increase the defense budget significantly. While the mere presence of interceptors in the arsenals of all the major industrial countries demonstrates that two of the assumptions about the wisdom of the Arrow cancellation have not stood the test of time, there is now evidence to show that the persons involved in the decision to terminate the Arrow interceptor program did not believe the reasons they themselves gave.

303 CAS Hugh Campbell to MND Pearkes, 21 August, 1958

304 RCAF Air Council: Notes on Air Council Meeting "Comparison of Air Defence Weapons Combination" 27 August, 1957 During this meeting a paper by Chief of Operational Requirements, AVM Easton, was discussed. This paper suggested, through arithmetic that was doubted openly during the meeting, that the Sparrow 2D missile would have double the kill probability of the Hughes Falcon armament.

Chapter 53

DEPARTMENT STORE ARROWS

Once the USAF had been informed of Avro's advanced Arrow proposals, there was a very interesting meeting held between the Canadian Ambassador, Mr. Robertson, and USAF Secretary James H. Douglas, on 30 January, 1958. This meeting is promoted, with considerable fanfare, by Peter Zuuring in his book *Arrow Scrapbook* as an indication of USAF support for the Arrow program, and that a strictly *personal* musing of the Secretary, that the USAF might be willing to buy Canada two squadrons of Arrows, was the golden, missed opportunity of the Conservatives to save the Arrow program. This seems an exceptionally naïve opinion. In a summary of the meeting reproduced in Zuuring's book, it would appear this meeting was really all about convincing the Canadian ambassador that the Arrow was obsolete, and that the USAF was going missiles, and that if the Canadians really wanted the USAF to buy them a couple of squadrons of obsolete, "department store" airplanes, they might do so. To quote a summary of this meeting by N.R. Chappell:

> "He [US Secretary of the Air Force James Douglas] led into what was obviously the purpose of the get-together by enquiring concerning the progress of the Canadian CF-105 program…The Secretary said that they had been looking over their manned interceptor programs and that the possibilities of the utilization of the CF-105 in a continental defense role had not escaped them. [Remember, by this time they had seen the Arrow 3, 4 and PS-2 proposals for Mach 3+ long range versions of the Arrow.] The U.S.A.F. problem in its simplest terms, with respect to the CF-105, is that they have in production the F-101B and F-106 manned interceptors, which they considered pretty good and to which he alluded as being more or less in the CF-105 class as to performance. The decision had been taken within the parameters of the FY59 budget for a decrease in both tactical air squadrons and interceptor strength in favour of emphasising other programs… [This didn't turn out to be the case, since they purchased a great many F-4 Phantoms for both interception and tactical duties.] There was no place in the U.S.A.F. system that he could see for the CF-105. He mentioned the F-108 and stated very firmly that they were going ahead with it, and that its cost would make the CF-105 'look like something which might be picked up in a department store'. Quite clearly, the Secretary and his advisors view the F-108 as being of a much more advanced design and capability than the CF-105."[305]

Hardly words to inspire confidence in the CF-105 with the Canadian ambassador. While we have already seen that any consideration that the F-108 would have been truly superior to the CF-105 Mk.3 or 4 is dubious at best, they also cancelled this aircraft once the Arrow and its production line were scrap. Not only that, but we have also seen that Dr. Courtland Perkins, the USAF Chief Scientist, was telling Avro within a month of the F-108 prototype contract award that he felt the program might be cancelled. It seems clear this meeting was designed to inform the Ambassador that interceptors were obsolete, the Arrow was un-sellable, and that it would be a waste at any rate with the so-much-superior F-108 lurking right around the corner. Even if the personal musing about charitably buying Canada a couple of squadrons of Arrows was sincere, the Americans told the Canadians during the later summer exchanges that the US would never buy Arrows.[306]

In the spring of 1958 the Diefenbaker Conservatives won an overwhelming majority due to a golden opportunity provided on a silver platter by the Liberal's new leader, the Nobel Peace Prize-winning Lester Pearson. Pearson stood up in the House and shouted out that the government was so inept that they should just resign and turn the government over to the Liberals *without an election!* An incredible gaffe. Diefenbaker called his bluff, shook hands with the Governor General, and Canada marched to the polls. Even the RCAF and Avro workforce were voting Tory in droves, and no wonder, the Conservatives had expanded the preproduction order for Arrows to 37—providing a tantalising vision of the RCAF and industry's future. However the change of guard in the Liberal party wrought by the Diefenbaker minority victory of June 1957 also brought a change in thinking towards a more independent strategy for Canada in economic and military matters. C.D. Howe lost his seat, in part due to growing frustrations with his autocratic and unaccountable style, exacerbated by the trans-Canada pipeline scandal. That scandal was a worthy one as well. Financed in part by North Eastern United States investors (read Wall Street) who would gain the profits from the gas directed into the US industrial heartland, the pipeline itself was built using Canadian taxpayers' money.[307] Pearson's variance with

C.D. Howe underscores the change in the thinking of the party leadership, and hardly suggests that Pearson would have cancelled it:

> "If we are to continue to have with the United States a continental system of air defense on a cooperative basis, it is clearly the responsibility of the U.S. government to buy the CF-105 to meet its own requirements and it was the duty of the Canadian government to use all possible ways and means to so convince our American friends."[308]

Avro and government documents show that the true price of the Arrow, even before the reduced price offers made by Avro, was lower than the closest US interceptor. This plane, the F-106C, was proposed by the US Secretary of State John Foster Dulles and Defense Secretary Neil McElroy, as a cheaper and equally effective interceptor. Prices used in Pearkes' briefing document for these meetings in July 1958 were lower in terms of direct aircraft cost than the F-106C, (at 5.58 million a copy) and this was known to members of the Conservative Cabinet before the decision to cancel the Arrow was taken. The F-106C failed to meet the RCAF specification in a number of ways, two obvious deficiencies were its being single-engined and single-crewed. It was also comparatively deficient in range and payload, and would not realistically be available until years after the Arrow 2.

After using the 5 million dollar fly away cost of the Arrow in his July discussions with Secretary of State Dulles and Defense Secretary McElroy, Pearkes then quoted $12.5 million a copy for the Arrow to his own Cabinet, as the *production* cost of an individual Arrow interceptor *after* completion of development. As we shall see, this figure was entirely disingenuous.

On hearing cancellation rumours, Fred Smye stepped up to the plate and met the government. He suggested that, if the government were to cancel the Astra and Sparrow systems, Avro could offer the aircraft for $3.5 million a copy, including the Hughes MX-1179 radar/fire-control. He also flew to the United States and secured a (probably spurious) US promise to provide free radar/fire-control systems, which would further reduce the price of the Arrow. This radar/fire-control system offer was not revealed to the Diefenbaker Cabinet at any time, according to several sources, including the CBC, but has subsequently been proven to exist, again according to several sources, including the CBC. In other words, senior members of the Diefenbaker Cabinet were intentionally misleading their peers. This final offer was also described in Fred Smye's book *Canadian Aviation and the Avro Arrow.* Smye was the man who delivered it to Minister of Defense Production, Raymond O'Hurley. $3.5 million each was much less than even the comparatively pathetic F-101 Voodoo which, according to Larry Milberry's research, was genuinely priced at over $5.5 million dollars a copy.[309]

In begging for its survival Avro was reduced to offering its products, the best in the world, for no profit at all, and a probable loss if they ran into development snags. Obviously they were willing to cannibalise part of the A.V. Roe conglomerate in order to remain in business.

As usual, there is an odd financial incident that coincided with the Conservative's negotiations with the United States authorities—negotiations that secretly doomed the Arrow, Iroquois, and Canada's number one employer. In July of 1958 the Conservatives introduced the Conversion Loan, a complicated financial manoeuvre that was essentially a second mortgage on the due-to-be-retired Victory Bonds of WWII. One can be sure that in making their representations to the bankers and investors they were asked why the government of Canada needed all that money. They were also likely told that they needed to tighten up their spending, and the "luxury" of the Arrow weapons system would have stood out like a sore thumb, considering the concession of needing such an enormous loan. This argument would have more force if "cheap" American interceptors were sitting in the shop window, and intelligence debasing the requirement for interceptors was available. As Peter C. Newman makes clear in *Renegade in Power*, Diefenbaker wasted on average 400 million a year on unbudgeted, short-term vote buying. This amount would have covered the annual projected expenses of the Arrow Weapons System with plenty to spare. His other policies ensured that the Liberal surplus was consumed in no time and, by early 1958, they were already going deeply in debt. Something needed to be done to "buy" time for them to right their fiscal ship.

As the Shaw's report said of the Conversion Loan:

"Mr. Diefenbaker had a serious political problem. In a short time, he had gone through the Liberal surplus, and gone deeply into debt. A large addition to this debt was the huge gift paid off to the investment houses, insurance companies and banks, through the conversion loan – a totally unnecessary burden loaded onto the taxpayer. (It has been suggested in the press that this was a return for campaign funds donated for two expensive campaigns; that we have had to pay for being persuaded to vote Conservative. McKim's fees are probably high.)"

McKim and another advertising company were paid handsomely, with public funds, to convince the Canadian public to buy bonds that weren't a good deal for the nation, and which put the government of Canada even more at the mercy of the financial elite.

In September and November 1958, Avro had offered the Arrow at a reduced price, contingent on the government cancelling Astra and Sparrow. This price, 3.5 million before direct taxes, was first inflated to 7.8 to 9 million dollars by CCSC Foulkes. The inflated figure was based on figures provided by DDP Minister Raymond O'Hurley, and were quoted by Defense Minister Pearkes, in Cabinet, to influence them to terminate the program. (O'Hurley, a timber grader in civilian life, had lied on his resumé to the Conservative Party, and was rumoured to have been a 'bag man' for the Duplessis government of Quebec.)[310] Research material indicates that Cabinet was not informed about much at the end of the Arrow program other than the opinions of Pearkes, Foulkes and finance minister Fleming—which were negative. Once Pearkes and Diefenbaker had cancelled the Arrow and Iroquois programs, they then set about cutting Avro out of consideration for the NATO strike-recce aircraft contract, and otherwise made it their policy to see Avro fail. The natural question is, was this their intent as of the meetings with the Americans? If so it would explain the feebleness of their purported sales efforts if, in fact, they really tried to sell the Arrow at all.

305 Message from the Canadian Ambassador to External Affairs, January 1958 (reproduced in: Zuuring: Arrow Scrapbook)
306 Cabinet minutes of 25 August, 1958
307 Newman: Renegade in Power.
308 Quoted from Campagna: Requiem for a Giant, p.117
309 www.canavbooks.com See the "The Great Arrow Debate" under the "Editorials" banner.
310 Newman: Renegade in Power, and Shaw: There Never Was an Arrow

Chapter 54

NATO ROLE CHANGE

In 1957, once the Arrow design was finalized, NATO, under American commander General Norstad, wanted Canada and Britain to add a low-level nuclear strike-reconnaissance role to their missions. "When General Pearkes took office, he was generally familiar with the Arrow project but probably unaware that [USAF] General Norstad, Commander in Chief of the NATO forces, had been pressing for the re-equipping of the RCAF Air Division. Furthermore, Norstad wanted the traditional defensive role of the RCAF changed to an offensive-attack role with nuclear weapons. This request would presumably have been rejected out of hand by the previous Liberal Government since the cornerstone of its policy was that Canada's role would always be defensive."[311] At this point Canada's NATO roles involved specializing in air *defense*, not offence, with CF-100s being recognized as easily the best, if not only, effective all-weather and night fighter. The CF-86s, using A.V. Roe Canada's Orenda engine, were recognized as being the best day fighters in Europe.[312]

At some point in their cancellation campaign the government, not the RCAF, Chiefs of Staff Committee or Cabinet Defense Committee, decided that the Arrow should *not* be the plane for Canada's NATO roles. It was decided that they wanted a small aircraft for reasons of economy—in line with their desire to do the absolute minimum to satisfy Canada's military obligations. In the subsequent competition they dismissed aircraft such as the Arrow, F-105 Thunderchief and F-4 Phantom as being too expensive and concentrated on small, less-capable, and much shorter-range alternatives like the Grumman Tiger and Lockheed Starfighter. Anecdotal evidence suggests that this was due in part to the RCAF's fighter pilots preferring the single-set F-86 Sabre over the CF-100. Unfortunately, this preference had nothing to do with operational capabilities as a weapon, but in the freedom from responsibilities associated with a backseater, and because the technical challenges of managing a radar-less, guns only, day fighter were considerably less. In other words, the Sabre was one heck of a lot more fun to fly. Cabinet minutes, however, make it clear that the role change and aircraft selection process were managed at the political level—not by RCAF pilots nor even the RCAF leadership.

At this time American authorities began telling their allied counterparts that high and medium altitude missions were more dangerous than low-altitude missions. Considering the capabilities of the Arrow in anything but a low-level supersonic mission, the decision to adopt this US-inspired role change was a foolish move indeed. The presumed relative safety of low-altitude missions has been accepted as operational philosophy among some of the allies ever since, until, of course, they actually had to go to war in this role. In the Gulf War it was shown that the low-altitude aircraft suffered the highest losses, and Iraq had plenty of Soviet surface-to-air missiles. The European Tornado fighter-bomber's low-level role was subsequently changed to medium-altitude bombing. Due to high wing loading and other limitations the Tornado is not suited for high-altitude bombing. Simple physics also debases the low altitude concept, where planes are vulnerable to trees, birds, thrown stones, shoulder-launched missiles, small arms fire, anti-aircraft artillery, power lines and, particularly, pilot error. History has shown that few missiles can achieve the altitudes the Arrow was capable of, and not a single SR-71 was ever shot down although over 1,000 missiles had been fired at them.

The Arrow was also being looked at by a NATO ally, for interception and strike-reconnaissance work. During Floyd's fall 1958 trip to the U.K., the Arrow was looked at to fill the new RAF General Operational Requirement (GOR) 339—eventually almost filled, but for cancellation, by the TSR-2 aircraft. Jim Floyd's letter to his boss spells out his thoughts on the Arrow's adaptability:[313]

> Dear Sir Roy:
>
> The following is a preliminary shot at looking at the ARROW with reference to G.O.R. 339.
>
> Basically, of course, the requirements for the ARROW and G.O.R. 339 are different. The ARROW being designed for high speed, high altitude, high G capability and G.O.R. 339 being designed towards a tactical role, with low altitude capability, short runway length, etc., being the prime requirements. However, I certainly agree with you that if we could show that the ARROW would go even part way to meeting the G.O.R. 339 requirement, we should do so on the chance that its existence as an aeroplane at the time that G.O.R. 339 is required,

could make a lot of difference.

In the two days that we have had since your phone call we have obviously only been able to do a very cursory check but these are my conclusions based on this:

1. The present MK.2 aircraft is very limited in range at low altitude, but with the addition of about 8,500 lbs. of fuel carried in the armament bay and a drop tank, assuming that the drop tank is jettisoned after climb and the bomb is semi-submerged, we can increase the range [radius] to about 450 n.m. including the 200 n.m. at low level (1,500 ft.). While G.O.R. 339 asked for a supersonic capability at low altitude, we have shown on chart 1 a speed of Mach .9, since we could only get to M = 1.09 at sea level, due to structural limitations, and this is an almost un-usable transonic area, and we would have a penalty on range of about 100 miles.

The all-up weight would be around 71,000 lbs. and the runway length required would be somewhere in the order of 7,000 ft. which is, of course, much longer than the 3,000 ft. quoted in the spec. and it is not too easy to do anything about this on the ARROW since jet flap, etc., would involve considerable redesign and the benefit in any case would only be small.

2. We have had a very preliminary look at what we would have to do with the ARROW to come as close as we possibly can to G.O.R. 339 which, basically, would involve the following:

a) We would have to add approximately 38,000 lbs. of fuel. This would be achieved by installing two large fuel tanks at semi-span on each wing, also filling up every bit of available space in the aircraft such as the space between the intakes and fuselage, most of the armament bay, and also installing the long range belly tank.

b) To accommodate this increased weight we would have to completely redesign our undercarriage arrangement and would probably retract the undercarriage (which would obviously be much larger than the present one) fore and aft into the wing pods.

c) We would have to do quite a bit of beefing up on the structure, increasing the outer wing skin thickness and the inner wing joint and do some fuselage strengthening where extra fuel is carried in the fuselage.

d) We would install the high pressure ratio Iroquois engine to give us better fuel consumption at low altitude. [Along with the Iroquois 3, Orenda was also developing a version for lower altitude and lower speed use incorporating an additional compressor stage. This engine was proposed, after Arrow cancellation, to equip RCAF F-105 Thunderchiefs for the NATO strike-recce role.]

With the above basic changes we could probably get close to the 1,000 n.m. that is called for in the spec. provided that we carried out the low level portion at Mach .9 and operated at around 3,000 ft. altitude. The gross weight of this version would be around 110,000 lbs. It would have a very high stalling speed, somewhere in the order of 230 miles per hour at maximum gross take-off. [This is still a lower stall speed than the current F-15E Strike Eagle.] We have estimated very roughly that without JATO the take-off run would be over 13,000 ft. With JATO this would be reduced to around 7,000 ft. which is, of course, still way above the requirement."

Leaders in the U.K. were impressed that the Arrow could undertake this strike reconnaissance role, whilst at the same time providing a superb, long-range, supersonic, all-weather interceptor. Floyd tried to have some of the British experts visit Canada and consult with the government over their re-established requirements for manned fighters and the growing consensus on the vulnerability of both missiles like Bomarc and ground controlled intercept schemes like SAGE. However, the government of Canada was exceptionally sensitive to anything they could construe as salesmanship or pressure brought about in favour of Avro or the Arrow. Aware of this hostility, J.L. Plant had Floyd politely revoke his invitations to several British defense authorities.

In the summer of 1958 Pearkes and finance Minister Donald Fleming made a trip to NORAD headquarters in Colorado Springs. Apparently the US Undersecretary of Defense spent a great deal of time on this flight speaking to Pearkes about air defense, expense, and the Arrow.

In a series of *recently released* taped interviews with Dr. Reginald Roy at the University of Victoria in 1967, Pearkes had the following to say about that chat:

> "…I had the assurance that the Americans at this time had lots of fighters. That was when I was talking to [the] Undersecretary of Defense. I flew out from Washington to Colorado Springs *the first time I went to see NORAD. On that aircraft he told me, "We have got lots of fighters."* [Pearkes pounds the table with each word, for emphasis]. We were sitting together like this talking. He said to me, *and we can't quote this* [his voice goes soft here], *'If I was you I wouldn't put all that money into that aircraft. If you don't want to buy aircraft from us you may rest assured that we have got lots of them [emphasis in voice here] which we can use to help in the defense of the North American continent if a crisis comes.' That's what convinced me more than anything else."*[314] [italics added]

What the Americans were really after is also clear from an earlier portion of the interview where Pearkes admits:

> "I took chances. We were defenseless against the high power bomber where we had the old CF-100. It couldn't compete with the modern Russian bombers. We had no supersonic fighter but the Americans emphasised the fact that they had lots of them. Now…one thing I had to face was, if you scrap the Arrow you've got nothing. What will you do? Will you buy American aircraft to fill this gap?… Or say, 'Here, you can rely on American aircraft', not having bought them, but putting your pride in your pocket and saying, 'Here, we will give facilities [to] American fighter squadrons to come and be stationed in Canada', so that they can get the advantage there, or, if not actually stationed in there, when the situation deteriorates they can move forward and operate from Canadian airfields… *I said let us make full arrangements for these American fighter squadrons to come in*, practice from our airfields. Let them store equipment and aircraft if they want to, at places such as Cold Lake and various other points all across Canada, and they came there and then carried out training exercis-

es, moving a squadron up at short notice to one of these airfields. Now, that was how I filled this defenseless gap during those times. He [name of an author which is not clear on the tapes, probably Peter C. Newman or J.B. McLin] doesn't bring that out and I don't know how he would have known...

[Dr. Roy then interjects:] "No, he probably wouldn't. It certainly wouldn't be something that would be advertised. [Peakes responds:] *"It was not anything which was advertised at all."* [italics added]

Apparently not to the RCAF either.

So there we have it, as of the summer of 1958, due to consultations with the Republican politicians Pearkes resolved to cancel the Arrow program and rely on the United States for the primary air defense of Canada. This would explain why Dulles and Eisenhower *immediately* came to Canada for secret negotiations on air defense, and apparently a deal was struck, tentatively, and then officially during a Presidential visit to Canada on July 9th through 11th, 1958. Curiously, while these meetings were about air defense, the President was not accompanied by the Secretary of Defense or Secretary of the Air Force, but by the Secretary of State, John Foster Dulles.

Pearkes' briefing notes read more like begging for a hand out than a negotiating position:

"Pearkes explained that if Canada had not been a "northern outpost" of the United States but rather an island, air defense requirements would be significantly reduced. However, by virtue of our geographic location, Canada was compelled to spend nearly half the defense budget on air requirements. He complained that despite close cooperation between the two countries, the United States had never accepted a Canadian aircraft, nor had there been any success at a joint development. He then addressed the problem of...the Arrow:[315]

"...we have had under development in Canada a supersonic aircraft known as the CF-105... The development of this aircraft to date has cost $250 million, and its development will be continued for the next two or three years, to cost about $530 million, making a total of $780 million. Our requirements for this aircraft will be relatively small, somewhere around 100, [the RCAF requirement was at least 169!] and therefore the individual cost of the aircraft will be about $5 million, plus the cost of development. If this were the only requirement for our air defense, we could perhaps make provision for it in our succeeding defense budgets; but in order that aircraft of this type and the type to be used by the United States can operate in Canadian airspace we will be required to introduce SAGE into Canada. The introduction of SAGE into Canada will cost in the neighbourhood of $107 million..." [316]

At the time, in Canada, there was alarm among the Navy and Army staffs due to the fact that the budget of the RCAF was approaching half of the defense budget. Yet at the time the US was spending two-thirds of its defense budget on its air forces, and was also spending double what Canada was on defense as a whole, taken as a percentage of Gross National Product. It would appear that those facts weren't mentioned to Pearkes and Diefenbaker when they complained about the air defense component of the military budget to Dulles and McElroy.

From Eisenhower's briefing notes for the meeting, it seems his perspective of the issue may have been as simple as "Canada is having a bit of trouble financing her air defense and has cooperated significantly in integrating and improving North American defense. Should we, or can we, establish a way to help them in this regard, including maybe subsidizing their purchases of NORAD standardized equipment, and could we maybe negotiate to allocate some defense production to them too?" This is far from the wording used in the document, but captures the flavour in my opinion. Campagna also notes that it is unclear if Diefenbaker and Eisenhower themselves even really discussed the details of the agreements they were about to authorize. On the other hand, the ambiguity was quite possibly included to provide the leaders with plausible deniability.

Another section of this Canadian government record of the summer Summit, a DDP commentary, states:

> "...the Americans now are interested in terms of their own defense in the installation on Canadian soil of not only Warning Lines and communications, but also actual weapons, such as Bomarcs, to bring down enemy bombers. However, the concept of area defense in depth, combined with the fact that the whole complex of radars, computers, communications, aircraft and missiles are part of a single defense system indicates that no division can be made between air defense of Canada and air defense of the United States."[317]

Simplifying this sententiousness gives: "The Americans are interested in the installation of the whole complex of radars, computers, communications, aircraft and missiles on Canadian soil and consider it necessary for their own defense." Describing this document, Campagna continues: "The document reasons that to build the sophisticated radar and support centres required would unduly strain the Canadian defense budget, and that the only solution would be to enter into defense sharing 'whereby Canada has allotted to it the production of certain components of weapons systems for the joint use of the two countries.'"[318] It would seem the Diefenbaker Conservatives were convinced that the American government was going to ensure Canada received a share of US production. Hardly an adherence to the Conservative/Republican holy grail: the free market system.

The Eisenhower Library provides evidence that any Canadian expectations of being allocated stakes in an American ABM development scheme were highly premature. Two months after Black Friday Eisenhower's Cabinet papers included the following conclusions:

> "The Air Force has consistently opposed any agreement to assure Canada a given share of the production... If Canadian competence can be demonstrated and reasonable decisions agreed to on individual items, it is our position that the end result will be a reasonable share for the Canadians. From the recent statement by the Prime Minister to Parliament *it is assumed that the Canadians have accepted the U.S. position* on this matter." [319]

311 Smye: Canadian Aviation and the Avro Arrow, p.p. 77-78

312 Floyd: confidential report on his November, 14-December, 9th, 1955 visit to England and France: "Report on Visit to England & France, 15 December, 1955": "[AVM Campbell] said that the Orenda Sabre had made such an impression in Europe that the Canadians were being treated with a great deal of respect these days." p.8

313 J.C. Floyd to Sir Roy Dobson, 19 February, 1958

314 1967 interviews with Dr. Reginald Roy of the University of Victoria in 1967.

315 This portion is Campagna's interpretation of the document he had released (referenced immediately below), as published in Storms of Controversy, 2nd Edition, pp. 90-91

316 Aide Memoire for MND Pearkes in discussions with Dulles and McElroy in July 1958. It is believed to have been written by CCSC Gen. Foulkes.

317 RG 49, Vol. 427, File 159-44-B, part 1.

318 Campagna: Storms of Controversy, pp. 108-109 inside quote is from ibid.

319 Eisenhower Library, secret Cabinet Paper, dated 3 April, 1959, p.4

Chapter 55

NIKE ZEUS BAIT

Canada decided there was no way they could afford to pay for what the US considered essential to their defense, which obviously included the weaponization of Canada, in a nuclear sense, and thus sought any assistance the Americans would grant. The necessity to do so was leaked to Pearkes on 3 July, 1958:

> "The answer may lie in a letter sent to Charles Foulkes from CINCNORAD, General Partridge, dated July 3, 1958. In that letter *General Partridge stressed that his views were to be treated as private and not for general consumption by the Canadian government. He explained that the U.S. had under development the Nike Zeus anti-ballistic missile...* General Partridge had been asked by the U.S. Joint Chiefs of Staff to study the feasibility of siting Nike Zeus batteries in the U.S. and Canada.... Shortly thereafter work began on the development of both short and long-range NORAD planning documents for continental air defense. These were the North American Defense Objective Plan (NADOP) 1959-1963, a five-year plan, and the North American Defense Objectives (NADO) 1959-1969, a ten-year forecast. Draft documents were prepared in August 1958, and completed documents were presented to Canada in December 1958.
>
> "The first priority listed in the ten-year NADO 59-69 was establishment of an anti-ICBM capability. Second on the list was for an improved anti-ICBM. The document projected that the Soviets would have up to two thousand ICBMs by 1966, and this number was repeated when the Canadian Chiefs of Staff were briefed on the subject in January 1959, one month prior to termination of the Arrow....
>
> "NADO 59-69 made reference to the need for the detection of incoming bombers as only its third priority and interceptors as a fourth. In the latter category, the plan made no mention of specific aircraft types but instead placed emphasis on long-range interceptors and shorter-range surface-to-air missiles. The long-range aircraft required a cruise speed of Mach 3 with a Mach 3.5 to 4 dash capability. They had to operate at all altitudes and have a range of two thousand nautical miles, and there was a stipulation for nuclear armament... The plan also required all interceptors to carry nuclear weapons.
>
> "Specific aircraft types were mentioned in the NADOP 59-63. The document itself remains classified, but this author was able to have the following paragraph de-classified. It reads:
>
> "Existing and programed interceptors include F4D, F-86, F-89, CF-100, F-101, F-102, F-104, CF-105, and F-106 aircraft... The F-102, F-104, CF-105 and F4D aircraft should be improved by the incorporation of nuclear armament in the normal operational role."[320]

From the list above it is clear they were pointing out that they had lots of fighters, even though many of them were obsolete and some of them were not designed as interceptors. But how many of them were compatible with NORAD and how many operated in Canada? It seems clear they were promoting the idea that the Arrow wasn't saleable and was redundant. That its all-weather interception role was outmoded, or that the Americans at least *truly* thought so, are proven false by their promotion of a Mach 3 long-range fighter role, and the aircraft they were developing to fill it, the F-108 Rapier.

Another twist involves a glamorous artifact of the Cold War, the anti-ICBM missile (ABM) system. It could be thought of as Reagan's Star Wars plan, and can be compared to George W. Bush's new ABM system. Considering the difficulties of the modern system, one can see that such technology would pose a stern challenge, even with a tactical nuclear warhead on the ABM, in the late-1950s. Nevertheless, Diefenbaker became convinced that the United States government was going to ensure that Canada got a decent slice of the development and production of the system that NORAD (i.e., Canada and the United States) decided to standardise on. The twist is that Diefenbaker may not have known—because CINC NORAD General Partridge cautioned Foulkes not to disclose it to politicians—that the USAF had decided on Douglas' Nike-Zeus ABM, which would, naturally, be built by Douglas in the US.

Were the politicians kept in the dark in order to promote Bomarc over the Nike family of missiles and debase the Arrow requirement? Or was it done to allow American politicians to suggest to the Canadians that they would get contracts for development and production of ABMs in Canada? Or all of the above? Since Canada had been precluded from Bomarc production due to American security regulations it is valid to question how they became convinced they would gain production rights to even more advanced technology inherent in an ABM system. Perhaps it was further assurances by John Foster Dulles, though we will not know for sure unless the government of Canada decides to release all the related Arrow decision making documentation…assuming it hasn't been destroyed.

The surviving documentation indicates that Pearkes and Diefenbaker thought that the United States was going to "allocate" Canada a significant share of the ABM design, development and production work, plus some kind of trade in US fighters for Canada with Canadair transports, cost sharing on the radar and SAGE network USAF permanent basing in Canada, and related stuff. According to Diefenbaker's memoirs the Bomarc system was only the first step in long-range anti-aircraft missiles, a step leading, so thought Diefenbaker, with SAGE, to an effective ABM system. But the Nike missiles were from an entirely different family and manufacturer. How could Bomarc evolve into an ABM, and how could Canada participate in the design of such a system, if the Nike-Zeus system had already been chosen, was already well into design at Douglas, and while Canada was precluded from sensitive US defense technology anyway? It was quite a package and it appeared to be wrapped by none other than… John Foster Dulles. Diefenbaker acknowledged in his memoires that he had been convinced SAGE was going to be an integral part of future missile defense systems:

> "…the Canadian government was asked to approve the expenditure, exclusive of new interceptor costs, of from $120 million to $190 million (depending on cost-sharing arrangements) to modernize control and data handling, to extend radar coverage in certain areas, and to introduce more effective anti-bomber weapons… The United States had recently completed the development of an impressively effective, and expensive, electronic control system…known as SAGE, which stood for semi-automatic ground environment… On 23 September, 1958, I announced that the Canadian government had approved the introduction of SAGE to Canada… We now had acquired a system with the capacity to handle mass bomber attacks, and to control high speed aircraft, like the CF-105, or surface-to-air missiles, like the Bomarc. Further, *our technical advisors considered that, with improvements, SAGE could be adapted for anti-missile defense."*[321]

The improved SAGE system was termed CAGE, for Completely Automatic Ground Environment, and was one of the systems the Americans unilaterally dumped after the Arrow cancellation.[322] One problem with the above statement is that as of a year after his decision on SAGE and Bomarc, there was still only one SAGE development site in the United States, and the Bomarc had begun failing its first launch tests. Another problem is that the Arrow was designed to work within the SAGE (or another kind of ground control) system, *or beyond its range.* One should always remember that the SAGE system was built around the Pinetree line, which wasn't very far above the Canada US border. Another problem is, once the Arrow was cancelled, virtually all of the commitments the US made in terms of anti-missile systems and SAGE and Bomarc development and acquisition were unilaterally dropped by the United States. Another problem was that the entire SAGE network was vulnerable to jamming.[323]

320 Campagna: Requiem for a Giant, p.103 quote of NADOP 59-63 is from DND Directorate of History, File 113.014 D1, NADOP 59-63
321 Diefenbaker: One Canada, Vol II, Ch. 2, p. 294.
322 See Campagna: Storms of Controversy
323 Campagna: Requiem for a Giant, according to a SAGE designer, it was "a peacetime only" system.

Chapter 56

THE SERVILE PRESS: Media Manipulation

As General Reinhard Gehlen, the former Nazi intelligence chief and head of West Germany's intelligence service for many years after the war wrote:

> "It has always been the custom of hostile propaganda agencies (and not just intelligence services) to arrange for the publication of either spurious or genuine allegations about inconvenient adversaries...and then to follow this up with additional material themselves, referring to the original disclosures."[324]

In their April 1959 report to Avro management on the factors behind the Arrow cancellation, Kay and George Shaw suggested that Canada had suffered a new kind of political attack from the United States. What they meant by the "type of attack", is suggested by the following:

> "In Chapter 10 of Donald Wilber's case study [into the CIA overthrow of Mossadegh], he laments that the CIA [then] lacked contacts capable of placing material so that the American publisher is unwitting as to its source, as well as being able to see that no changes in theme or emphasis were made. In contrast to this relatively ineffective venture, the Iran desk of the State Department was able to place a CIA study in Newsweek, using the normal channel of desk officer to journalist. Recognizing the fact that the Agency is not able to employ such a channel as just described, it does appear that some improvement of capabilities might be desirable. Either these contacts used to secure the unwitting publication of material should be expanded and improved, or else there should be provision made for passing material directly to cleared editors and owners of press media."[325]

Wilber also wrote in his analysis:

> "At [the] same time, the psychological campaign against Mossadeg [sic] was reaching its climax. The controllable press was going all out against Mossadeq, while [a newspaper whose name had been blacked out] under station direction was printing material which the station considered to be helpful."[326]

One might bear these things in mind the next time they read neo-conservative opinion from institutions like the Council on Foreign Relations, (such as their house organ *Foreign Affairs*), the Hudson Institute, the Brookings Institute and a plethora of other American right-wing opinion factories. Not that Canada is without its own right wing economic and political lobbyist organisations. Two that spring instantly to mind are the Fraser Institute, and the C.D. Howe Institute.

Of course, there are other examples of CIA manipulation of media and governments during the Eisenhower (and virtually every other) administration. The democratically-elected and semi-socialistic Arbenz government of Guatemala is another prime example:

> "[Arbenz] aimed, it has been said, at a 'green revolution', not a Red one. UFCO [the United Fruit Company], a rapacious, racist giant of the robber baron era, and almost a state within the state of Guatemala, was determined that the country should remain, quite literally, a banana republic. [Its] tentacles extended into the highest echelons of Ike's administration. Both the Dulles brothers, [Walter] Bedell Smith [another one-time CIA director], Robert Cutler, [Henry Cabot] Lodge, and several others had such close relations with the company that [John] Foster Dulles evidently found it embarrassing.
>
> "Ike needed no convincing and he was directly responsible for the operation which toppled Arbenz's regime. It was given special top-secret classification, but by January 1954 Guatemala broadcast evidence of the plot and the State Department was obliged to issue an official denial. 'The charge is ridiculous and untrue. It is the policy of the United States not to intervene in the internal affairs of other nations.' [How many times has the world heard that one?] Actually, the CIA was employing a remarkable range of 'dirty tricks' against

> Guatemala. It placed anonymous articles in the Chilean newspapers naming Guatemalan officials as Communists and then reprinted them elsewhere with a Chilean attribution. It blackened Arbenz's character, taking full advantage of its connections with the American press... *It parachuted Russian-made arms into Guatemala in order to be able to claim that the Soviet Union was supplying Arbenz...* It also organized a tiny 'army' of Guatemalan mercenaries, led by a puppet called Castillo Armas and supported by the [US-supported] dictators in Nicaragua and Honduras. When Arbenz tried to arm a peasant militia with Czech weapons, Ike isolated Guatemala diplomatically and ordered that the coup should proceed.
>
> "He also imposed a unilateral naval blockade on Guatemala, an action that...outraged international opinion [and violated the UN Charter]. Britain and France, who had not been consulted, were particularly upset. To Ike's horror and rage, they proposed to support Guatemala's appeal to the United Nations... Luckily for Ike, he was able to prevail on his colonialist allies to abstain, threatening that 'if they take an independent line backing the Guatemala move...we would feel entirely free to oppose them in Egypt [which they did anyway during the Suez Crisis], Cyprus, Algeria, and so on.'
>
> "His intervention had disastrous long-term effects. It inspired future presidents, [no doubt including George W. Bush] to pursue hidden and sometimes iniquitous policies abroad from which Congress was excluded and the press and the people were kept in ignorance or deceived."[327]

CIA media manipulation played a crucial role in Arbenz's ouster. "The American press played along with this charade. They simply ignored Arbenz's cry that the CIA was plotting against him. Most reporters accepted uncritically whatever American officials told them, and if they didn't, their editors did. Dispatches from *Time* magazine reporters in Guatemala, generally sympathetic to Arbenz, were rewritten at the magazine's editorial offices in New York to take a hard line against the Guatemalan government. The editor in chief of Time Inc., Henry Luce, was a friend of Allen Dulles... The most naked—and successful—attempt to control the press came at the *New York Times*. The dispatches of Sydney Gruson, the *Times* man in Mexico City, seemed overly influenced by the Guatemalan foreign minister. ...Wisner suggested to Dulles that the CIA try to silence Gruson. As a 'left-leaning' émigré who travelled on a British passport issued in Warsaw, Gruson was a 'security risk,' Wisner argued. The necessary phone calls were made, and as a patriotic gesture *New York Times* publisher Arthur Hays Sulzberger ordered Gruson to stay out of Guatemala—just as Gruson was about to launch an investigation of Armas's [spurious] army."[328]

Evan Thomas, assistant managing editor of *Newsweek,* (also commonly held to have fronted CIA articles), notes that the Schroder Banking Corporation was United Fruit's partner in Guatemala operations.[329] *A Man Called INTREPID* notes that, earlier, "[t]he German banker, Kurt von Schroeder joined the directors of ITT subsidiaries... Schroeder was on his way to becoming Gestapo treasurer and a general in the SS security service."[330] ITT was a notorious Nazi-collaborationist company run by Sosthenes Behn. "ITT was becoming involved in German arms manufacture, after talks with Hitler in 1933."[331] Allen Dulles also met Hitler in 1933 and remarked later about how Hitler constantly condemned the Jews' alleged financial manipulations. This couldn't have much bothered either of the Dulles brothers since their law firm, Sullivan Cromwell, worked hand in glove with the Nazis and American Nazi collaborators well into WW II. According to many sources ITT owned 25% of Focke Wulf during the Nazi era. Focke Wulf's Condor maritime patrol bombers and their FW.190 'butcher bird' fighter—both powered by license-built Pratt & Whitney engines, were to prove scourges to the allied forces in WW II.

Even in the middle of the 20th Century the ownership of the American media was highly concentrated, and generally owned by businessmen with right-wing Republican affiliations. Some activists today complain about how meetings of the Bilderberg Group, which includes many owners of major global media, are secret—not even the media comments on these meetings of the owners of global wealth. A pro-corporate global form of capitalism has been promoted through other institutions comprising large numbers of media owners:

Stormer writes in his book *None Dare Call it Treason*:

"How can so much power be concentrated in the membership of such a small organization [the Council on Foreign Relations] without public attention? ...Among the 1,400 CFR members are:

Henry Luce, editor-in-chief of *Time, Life* and *Fortune;* David Lawrence, *U.S. News and World Report;* the late Philip Graham, publisher of *Newsweek* and the *Washington Post;* Gardner and John Cowles, who publish *Look* [often used by the CIA] and own several influential newspapers and broadcasting companies; Arthur Hayes Sulzberger, chairman of the board, *New York Times,* Mark Ethridge, publisher, *Louisville Courier Journal;* syndicated columnists Marquis Childs, James Reston, Ernest K. Lindley, [the legendary and Republican] Walter Lippmann and Hanson Balwin, plus dozens of other lesser known writers, editors and publishers... Other CFR members who hold important posts in other opinion-making media are: William S. Paley, chairman of the board, CBS; David Sarnoff, chairman of the board, Radio Corporation of America [then operators of NBC]; broadcasters Edward R. Murrow, Charles Collingwood, William L. Shirer [who wrote the standard history, from within Germany, titled *The Rise and Fall of the Third Reich,* which omits the subject of U.S. investment in Nazi Germany and banking issues], and Irving R. Levine; Harry Scherman, founder and chairman of the Book-of-the-month Club; Joseph Barnes, editor in chief, Simon & Schuster, ...opinion pollsters George Gallup and Elmo Roper and others."[332]

Niall Ferguson points out in his study of the Rothschilds how this banking family became something of a sacred cow among the leading newspapers of the Great Powers in the 19th and early 20th Century. In America in the early 20th Century the J.P. Morgan banking colossus, part owner of the US Federal Reserve, was busy consolidating whole sectors of the American economy under the ownership of his primary investors. This reduced competition and with the overall power of the bank and its investors, was often able to forge monopolies with the blessing and protection of various levels of government. Legal monopolies are always reliably profitable, and a decisive proportion of politicians, reporters and lawyers can also be purchased with these profits, as John D. Rockefeller also demonstrated. The corporate media, being responsible to their wealthy directors, naturally presents a view sympathetic to the interests of wealthy capitalists rather than to the ethics of democracy.

One Congressman, Oscar Calloway, mentioned a direct effort by the wealthy clique represented by Morgan's bank to acquire general control of the editorial policy of American newspapers: "In March 1915, the J.P. Morgan interests...got together twelve men high up in the newspaper world and employed them to select the most influential newspapers in the United States and sufficient number of them to control generally the policy of the daily press of the United States... They found it was only necessary to purchase control of twenty-five of the greatest papers.

"An editor was furnished for each paper to properly supervise and edit information regarding issues of preparedness, militarism, financial policies and other things of national and international nature considered vital to the interests of the purchasers."[333] The CIA had many organs by which to have the public hear its tune. "[Deputy Director Plans, Frank Wisner] considered [popular columnists and] his friends Joe and Stewart Alsop to be reliable purveyors of the company line in their columns, and he would not hesitate to call Cyrus Sulzberger, the brother of the publisher of the *New York Times*."[334]

Right after the air defense meetings between McElroy, Dulles, Eisenhower, Pearkes and Diefenbaker, many close to the story noticed a radical change in the treatment of the Arrow in the national press. As Jack Woodman related in his paper to the Canadian Aeronautics & Space Institute of 1978:

"The decision to cancel the Arrow program was, in my opinion, very poorly founded. Nothing has happened since 1959 to support that decision as being correct. In fact, just the opposite happened.

"Several months before the cancellation announcement, there was a lot of bad publicity in Toronto newspapers about the Arrow. It was like an anti-Arrow campaign was being waged. Retired Army officers and self-proclaimed experts and others, were implying that the day of the manned interceptor was over."

Smye wrote:

> "The Arrow became of more than usual interest with the press which gave rise to a great deal of speculation and increased public interest… Experts sprang up from everywhere, particularly from behind the desks of editorial writers. There were many self-appointed experts advising on defense policy and particularly on the airplane-missile debate."[335]

Peter C. Newman referred to the media during the first years of Diefenbaker rule as

> "the servile press".[336]

Avro employees Kay and George Shaw wrote in their 30 April, 1959 analysis of the reasons for Arrow termination:

> "Since September, a howling lobby has swept the country from coast to coast. It has included, with few exceptions, every newspaper and magazine in the country, and TV and radio programs. The type of attack, and reasons behind it are unprecedented in this country…"

What they meant by attack is from American financial, industrial and (thus) political interests. What is clear is that, in Canada, contrary to the interests of the nation's largest employer and arguably the interests even of the Canadian financial community, the media was selling the "missiles over interceptors" argument being used by US intelligence, Secretary of State Dulles and Secretary of Defense McElroy in their deliberations with Pearkes, Fleming and, perhaps, Diefenbaker. This is probably a reflection of the fact that even then, the majority of economic activity, and thus advertising, was directed by American interests. There were a few exceptions to the general media negativity though, with a very good question being fruitlessly posed:

> "Other editors have made wonderfully pat statements about the missile making the manned interceptor obsolete. Who says the manned interceptor is obsolete? What military authority – in a position to have intimate knowledge of the problems of modern air defense…claims that the manned interceptor is obsolete? They do not believe it in the U.S."[337]

It turns out, contrary to 50 years of prognostications to the contrary, that *no* responsible *military* authority responsible for air defense was suggesting that the manned interceptor was obsolete when the Arrow cancellation decisions were being made. In testimony to the 1960 Defense Expenditure Committee Pearkes was questioned by Liberal defense critic Paul Hellyer:

> "A number of military advisors made public statements to the effect that manned interceptors would be required as far ahead as they could determine – at least through the greater part of the 1960's. Statements along this line were made by General Partridge, Air Marshal Slemon, General Kuter, General Thomas White, Commander in Chief USAF, General Pearkes, General Taylor, General Twining, and others… Can the Minister give the Committee any public statement of any senior military person during the same period in which the contrary opinion was expressed?" Mr. Pearkes replied: " No, I do not know of any serving officer of either the army or the air force who made a *public* statement to the contrary effect. *That is any Canadian serving officer, I cannot say anything about the American serving officers."*[italics added]

324 Gehlen, Reinhard: The Service, p.167
325 Wilber, Dr. Donald: Overthrow of Premier Mossadeq [sic] of Iran, November 1952—August 1953, Chapter 10.
Dr. Wilber was a CIA analyst and the document referenced was produced for the Agency.
326 Scowen: Rogue Nation, p.144
327 Brendan: Ike, His Life & Times, p.p. 284-86
328 Thomas: The Very Best Men, p. 117
329 Ibid, p. 111
330 Stephenson: A Man Called INTREPID, p. 25
331 Ibid.
332 Stormer: None Dare Call It Treason, pp. 211-212
333 Oscar Calloway, Congressional Record, February 9, 1917, Vol. 54 p. 2947
334 Thomas: The Very Best Men, p. 63
335 Smye: Canadian Aviation and the Avro Arrow, p. 78
336 Newman: Renegade in Power, This is the title of chapter 13.
337 Canadian Aviation Industries, October, 1958. quoted from the Shaw report of April, 1959.

Chapter 57

MANIPULATING THE DECISION MAKERS

Unfortunately, it was Dulles, McElroy and US intelligence that were stating these things secretly to very highly placed politicians, and therefore unaccountably.

Campagna alleges that the Arrow, which was made to protect the perimeter of North America, was rendered superfluous by the American concept of defense in depth, that is, *nuclear* defense in depth. From all the government documents, it is clear that the Canadian politicians had no stomach whatsoever with regards to resisting this American rush to cover Canada with nuclear air defense weapons, and it appears quite reasonable to assume that to make this American defense plan appear to be Canadian for political reasons, they had to assume at least some of the cost of the radar nets and BOMARC sites. But to pay for it they had to kill the Arrow. What is particularly offensive about this is that the US abandoned the entire concept of heavy BOMARC and SAGE deployment in Canada *and* in the United States *almost immediately* after the Arrows were cut up. They also de-activated their own BOMARC sites within a year of when Canada's were finally installed and activated. But then, John Foster Dulles was known for heavy tactics and colossal nerve. The Canadian Army was already against the Arrow and was only too happy to receive information justifying the abandonment of the Arrow. One motive is suggested by the following quote of Fred Smye:

> *"[Air Marshal Wilf] Curtis had built the post-war air force. He had fought tooth and nail for the lion's share of the defense budget...Those donkey's in the Chiefs of Staff Committee were anti-Air Force and were all former colleagues of Pearkes. Curtis had ridden all over them."*[338]

The NAE, NRC and DRB were also no friends of Avro because they (especially the NAE) felt they should be the primary design houses for Canadian defense, rather than having a private company entrusted with those tasks. Indeed, the NAE had been invited to submit a design for Canada's first jet fighter program, filled by the CF-100. They produced what looked like a rather ugly version of the Gloster Meteor—obsolete even then. This resentment was exacerbated by Avro's proving them wrong on many occasions, and sometimes not being very delicate while doing it. Had anyone been involved in a disinformation program against Avro, they would have found fertile soil in many quarters in Canada, all too often because Avro had demonstrated the lack of leadership of the parties concerned, and this was responded to vindictively.

Another government of Canada document, this time from the Department of Defense Production, stated, regarding the Eisenhower/Dulles meetings on 9th and 10th July, 1958,: "A study of the financial implications of continuing this program [the Arrow Weapons System], and its impact on the overall defense program, and the necessity of giving consideration to future requirements such as defense against the intercontinental ballistic missiles have necessitated a study of alternative plans." This document then describes the thrust of the bilateral meetings as being directed at defense production sharing agreements. It also mentions that, to this end, the Canada-United States Committee on Joint Defense was established.[339] This is one half of the proverbial "smoking gun" which proves that Pearkes and presumably Diefenbaker agreed, during these meetings, to cancel the Arrow for nothing more tangible than US goodwill in defense production sharing negotiations. The other half follows and relates the failure of defense production sharing. It was printed on the letterhead of the Deputy Secretary of Defense of the United States of America and was dated 1 June, 1960. It reads:

> "MEMORANDUM ON PRODUCTION SHARING PROGRAM — UNITED STATES AND CANADA
>
> *"The current program dates back to at least 1941 and the Hyde Park Agreement.* This agreement provided generally that each would produce in areas of greatest capability. In 1950 a Statement of Principles of Economic Cooperation was issued by the Truman Administration. It advocated, among other things, a coordinated program of requirements, production and procurement; the exchange of technical knowledge and productive skill; the removal of barriers impeding the flow of essential defense goods. In 1950 a DOD Directive on Defense Economic Cooperation with Canada was issued. *A Presidentially approved NSC paper, 5822/1, dated 30*

December 58, reaffirmed the Statement of Economic Principles and provided for equal consideration to be accorded the business communities of both countries.

"Prior to the NSC paper, and following a visit of the President to Canada in July 1958, Canada took the following actions with the understanding that her defense industry depended largely upon the U.S. channeling defense business into Canada: cancelled the CF 105 and related systems contracts; decided to make maximum use of U.S. developed weapons, integrated into NORAD; worked with the U.S. toward a fully integrated continental air defense.

"The U.S. in turn established a Production/Development Sharing Program with Canada with the first quarterly meeting in October 1958. Since then, policy obstacles impeding a free flow of business have been modified in a number of areas such as: Buy American Act; duty free entry of defense goods; security requirement; etc.. Also, working groups have been set up on programs of mutual interest (for example, BOMARC); cost sharing agreements have been worked out; and possible joint development programs are being explored.

"The last quarterly meeting of the Production Sharing Policy Group was held on 25 May, Despite all efforts, *over the period 1 January 59 through 31 March 60, Canadian defense business in the United States almost doubled that placed in Canada.* Canada is not satisfied with these results, nor do they appear acceptable from our view.

"We must: re-emphasize the program of development sharing activities; encourage American industry to subcontract in Canada; and seek out other legitimate techniques to stimulate the program. Canada should be encouraged to energize her industry which has not displayed the necessary aggressiveness." [italics and underline added]

Now, if Canada agreed to cancel the Arrow program on the understanding that her defense industry depended on US business *prior* to the NSC paper, then that means *prior to 30 December, 1958.* If the US *in turn* established a joint Production/Development Sharing Program working group with its first meeting in *October, 1958,* then Canada had agreed to kill the Arrow program *before October, 1958.* In fact, if the United States agreed to this working group, as the DDP document above states, in *July, 1958,* then obviously, *Pearkes and/or Diefenbaker agreed to kill the Arrow in July, 1958!* In other words, Pearkes had resolved, in conversation with the US Secretary of Defense during his first visit to NORAD headquarters, to kill the Arrow when he was supposed to have been trying to sell it to the USAF! It is also interesting that this document points out previous defense production sharing agreements, meaning that any new one was nothing new at all. Of course, the 1954 Buy American Act put the lie to all the preceding agreements. It seems plausible that the Buy American Act was reinvigorated to help kill the Avro Jetliner, and that Canada was given an exemption to it in 1958 to kill the Avro Arrow!

It is clear, from other documents, that Pearkes agreed to this disastrous decision because American authorities, working through similar working groups in the RCAF, the DRB and others, convinced Pearkes that missiles had rendered interceptors obsolete, that the Arrow was not a particularly great design, that bombers were a much lower threat than the RCAF, NORAD, NATO, and Britain believed, that the USSR ICBM force was expanding *much* more rapidly than it did, and that the first and second priorities of NORAD had to be, firstly, an anti-ballistic missile weapon, and secondly, an improved ABM. Interceptors were only a fourth priority in these summaries, while their own F-108 had such incredibly superior performance to *any* Arrow version, that to acquire Arrows would be a waste of money. Oh yes, and that the USA would allocate a large part of ABM and other defense development and production to Canada, and that Canada would get more production out of producing parts of US systems than they would out of their own programs for defense.

How convinced Pearkes was of the disappearance of the Soviet bomber threat by Dulles and Dulles is indicated by this remark:

"...on April 1 [1960] his [Diefenbaker's] Defense Minister indicated privately to Defense Secretary [Thomas] Gates that Canada would probably abandon interceptors unless the United States regards their retention as really important..."[340]

Yet in his presentation to the July Committee on Estimates Pearkes had said: "There are important factors necessitating the use of manned interceptors in the air defense system for many years, indeed, as far into the future as we can forsee."[341]

Campagna received a summary of the discussions during the Eisenhower and Dulles visit from the Eisenhower Presidential Library. They suggest the origin of Pearkes' professed change of heart concerning air defense and aerospace industrial policy.

> "The Secretary [Dulles] concluded his remarks by pointing out that missiles which were now becoming available would be obsolete in a few years and that they were merely a stop-gap until much improved missiles were available. He also thought it might be well for the military people on both sides to exchange views on Soviet bomber capabilities, as one way of assessing the need for a fighter plane production effort which Mr. Pearkes had discussed."[342]

Frank Lowe, associate editor of *Weekend Magazine*, in an article titled "Is the RCAF Obsolete", wrote:

> "Pearkes told me that the decision to cancel the Arrow) was non-political, merely something based on U.S. intelligence reports…"[343]

The Shaw report on the cancellation raises an important point regarding the limitations of a missile air defense:

> "The U.S. which developed the Bomarc and other ground-to-air guided missiles, knows them for what they are – short range, area defense weapons, incapable of performing the first essential of identifying incoming aircraft. They are merely a backstop for the long-range interceptors – an inflexible, last ditch defense, - and there is no certainty that their guidance system will not be jammed by attacking forces. There is no substitute for human intelligence and the missile cannot carry it into battle. The matter of identification is primary…[t]he RCAF is scrambled frequently, perhaps several times a day – to identify 'unidentified flying objects' which appear on the radarscopes. So far, none has been hostile.

It also seems probable the Canadians were told that Avro, being a British company, would not be allowed any US defense production sharing contracts because of it being a subsidiary of a British company, and therefore a security risk in terms of technology, and in terms of US commercial patents. The problem became how to make it appear as though the cancellation of the Arrow was done for military, not political reasons.

> "If Diefenbaker had finally settled on a decision to cancel the Arrow, a flat announcement to that effect could have destroyed his government. His instinct for political survival would have told him there was a need to prepare his ground. On the one hand he would have to portray Avro in the worst possible light by vilifying the company and pulling every possible dollar into the costs of the program he would show the public. He would also have to throw out some propaganda to show that Canadian defense would not be compromised by termination. This would mean downplaying the bomber threat and introducing Bomarc missiles in a way that would overplay their performance. He would not, for obvious reasons, agree to seek interceptors in the United States, at least not for the time being."[344]

Was Diefenbaker really the architect of this strategy? Or did he have a little public relations assistance from his friends?

Cabinet, the Chiefs of Staff Committee (CSC) and the Cabinet Defense Committee (CDC) were manipulated—with varying degrees of success—in part by imposing terms of reference on the deliberations of the CSC forcing them to make recommendations that the government could then use to "justify" the cancellation, thereby escaping responsibility. In reality, it appears that they didn't want to have the recommendation to cancel the Arrow coupled to a decision to purchase a US interceptor for political reasons, as the following Cabinet quotes indicate:

> "The minister [Pearkes]... himself recommended cancelling the CF-105 program in its entirety and deferring for a year any decision to order interceptor aircraft from the U.S."[345]

Also from Conservative Cabinet minutes:

> "On military or financial grounds, it seemed clear that there was no reason to continue the program... However, to abandon the CF-105 now and undertake to produce the U.S. F-106C, which was physically quite possible, would be a serious political mistake."[346]

In an unpublished summary of the Arrow project by former CCSC General Charles Foulkes, he wrote:

> "In late 1958, the Chiefs of Staff were advised that the government was ready to deal with the final stage of the Arrow program and required a proposal from the Chiefs of Staff Committee.
> "It was indicated that the Prime Minister did not want to combine the straightforward decision to cancel the project with the contentious issue of substituting a United States aircraft. The question of augmenting the present air defenses was a separate matter that could be dealt with later."[347]

Obviously the air defense needs of Canada took a backseat to political considerations with the Diefenbaker Conservatives.

The real reason that the Chiefs of Staff Committee didn't recommend the adoption of US aircraft was because they didn't agree with the idea. What followed indicates that Foulkes and Pearkes, ably assisted by Finance Minister Donald Fleming and probably Minister of Defense Production Raymond O'Hurley *engineered* the cancellation by imposing terms of reference that the Chiefs of Staff could not ignore. When they are "authorized" to consider alternative interceptors, that means they were *ordered* to provide options including that possibility for the Cabinet Defense Committee and then Cabinet to consider. This becomes quite clear when the related documentation is reviewed. When this partly failed, they resorted to outright deception and finally resorted to a straight political decision imposed by the Prime Minister and his Minister of Defense.

On 21 August, 1958 there was a meeting of the Cabinet Defense Committee which included the Chiefs of Staff, some of the government ministers, and representatives from various defense related government establishments. The minutes of this meeting included references to no less than five documents that had been discussed as a basis on which the recommendations of the committee were based. One was by Minister of Defense Production Raymond O'Hurley, another was by the Secretary of State for External Affairs, a third was from the Minister of National Defense, George Pearkes, and a fourth was from the Minister of Finance, Donald Fleming. They were all anti-Arrow, meaning the meetings terms of reference were already biased. There are three main points to the document. First, the...

> "Committee *agreed to recommend to Cabinet,-*
>
> (a) that approval in principle be given to:
>
> > (i) the installation of two BOMARC bases in the Ottawa-North Bay area; and
> >
> > (ii) the installation of two additional heavy radars in Northern Ontario and Quebec and the installation of the associated gap filler radars.
>
> (b) that authority be granted to commence negotiations with the United States for cost-sharing and production on the installation of two BOMARC bases for the Ottawa-North Bay area, the two heavy radars in Northern Ontario and Quebec and the associated gap filler radars;
>
> (c) that *consideration* be given to:
>
> > (i) abandoning the CF-105 (Arrow) program and the associated fire control and weapons projects; and

(ii) authorizing the Chiefs of Staff to *investigate and submit proposals* for any additional missile installations required and/or any additional interceptor aircraft of a proven, developed type that might be required in place of the CF-105.[348]

We have already seen that Foulkes and Pearkes were quite capable of short-circuiting the normal, democratic process. In an unpublished summary of the Arrow project written by (by this time former) CCSC General Foulkes:

> "In the latter part of 1958, the Chiefs of Staff were asked again to submit a proposal to the Government. Apparently, the PM indicated that he would not entertain a proposal that involved the cancellation of the Arrow with the procurement of a U.S. substitute. Accordingly, a submission was prepared to provide for the cancellation of the Arrow leaving for further study the matter of the interceptor replacement. The Chief of the Air Staff refused to go along with this decision. In order to cover up dissention among the Chiefs of Staff, the Minister decided to put forth the submission without any recommendation from the Chiefs of Staff."[349]

CAS Campbell did object, immediately, to the attempt to force him to recommend things with which he, and presumably the majority of the leaders of the RCAF, disagreed as his memo to Pearkes indicates:

> "The Air Defense submissions, and in particular the CF-105, now being discussed by you with your Cabinet colleagues at Cabinet Defense Committee are of such a nature and import that I feel I should *again* make clear my recommendations, in order that there may be no misunderstanding.
>
> "The Chiefs of Staff have considered at great length and over a long period of time the future of the 105 and associated air defense programs. The program initially called for the re-equipping of the nine squadrons from a production run of 169 aircraft, *and still does*. It was clear that this number of aircraft, if ordered, would substantially increase the Defense Budget, if we went into production while at the same time maintaining the present overall pattern of Canadian forces.
>
> "As a consequence *the Chairman, Chiefs of Staff, attempted to get agreement on a program of 60 front-line aircraft* to keep the budget within two billion dollars. More recently, *on your return from Washington,* you announced your decision to recommend to Cabinet the cancellation of the 105 program in its entirety…
>
> "It is *clearly not my responsibility to comment on the Budget or its size.*
>
> "It is, however, my responsibility to recommend to you the military requirement as I see it in order that the Royal Canadian Air Force may be capable of carrying out its responsibilities… I cannot, however, associate myself with your decision to cancel the 105 program but must recommend that it proceed as now planned, or, alternatively, to couple the cancellation of the 105 with the procurement of a supersonic interceptor to fill the gap…
>
> "I could go on at some length and re-reason the requirement pointing out the threat as I understand it from various Intelligence Agencies. I would, however, be covering ground which we have previously discussed on many occasions during the review of this problem… Consequently, the Royal Canadian Air Force needs the 105, or, alternatively, another supersonic manned interceptor of comparable performance within the time scale in order to continue to assume its responsibilities, and so I recommend."[350] [italics added]

It is apparent that Pearkes and his fellow politicians were trying to get the CSC to recommend that the CF-105 be abandoned altogether to take the heat off the politicians for such a decision, but were refused. This possibility too becomes more credible as we investigate the surviving documentation.

> "Because the recommendation was not unanimous, Pearkes, in an attempt to cover up what

might be interpreted as dissention among the Chiefs, decided to put forward the submission to cabinet without any recommendation. In this way the government could make a decision *without* the advice of the CSC rather than risk having to admit that a decision on Canada's air defense was being made by politicians, in direct defiance of the advice of the Chief of Air Staff. 'The formal submission,' said Campbell, 'was made by Pearkes and Foulkes. We had rejected it so the government acted alone.'"[351]

The formal submission included CSCC Foulkes' interpretation of the advantages and disadvantages of cancelling the Arrow program, but appear to have been presented to Cabinet as the recommendations of the CSC. Some of the amazing assumptions which were included are:

"…it will be realized that even if the CF105 is allowed to proceed, these plants will all have to close down by 1962. [Despite this, Orenda engines is still around today, though in much diminished form.]

"There is no alternative production that could be put into A.V. Roe and the Orenda engine plants." [Why not? What about the NATO strike-recce aircraft, or any of a number of options that Avro was already discussing with the government, with the British, with TWA (for supersonic airliners) and with a myriad of other potential customers?]

"The production of the CF105s would meet the minimum foreseeable military requirements for interceptor aircraft but it is not expected that any other interceptor aircraft will be produced in Canada, and our whole reliance is expected to be placed on ground-to-air missiles in the future. [Nobody except Foulkes, John Foster Dulles and other American authorities had ever said that, as we shall see shortly. If the Arrow, which was acknowledged by everyone—except *certain* Americans—to be superior to any available US aircraft, could only meet the minimum requirement against bombers, then why were they then considering the inferior F-106C?]

"…missiles such as Bomarc will provide a cheaper and more effective type of defense against the manned bomber." [ridiculous, as we have seen. Bomarc was a total failure and we're still using interceptors.]

"A further disadvantage is financial… It is quite clear that this aircraft will require almost $500 million to complete development *and then* it will cost between $10 and $12 million a copy *for production.*" [wildly and deliberately inflated, as we shall see. In fact, in his briefing notes for his meetings with Dulles, Pearkes had been advised that the "individual cost of the aircraft will be about $5 million, plus the cost of development, before the expensive Astra and Sparrow programs were cancelled.[352]]

"On the other hand, Appendix A shows very clearly that a program involving 100 aircraft purchased from the United States could be obtained at much less cost…" [The flyaway cost for an inferior single engine, short range, Convair F-106C was quoted in Cabinet at $5.59 million each. Furthermore, it would take many more than 100 F-106Cs to equal 100 Arrows as they had vastly shorter range and carried less armament—as was also pointed out by the RCAF.]

"It should be realized, in purchasing a fully developed U.S. aircraft, that the development has been completed and our orders would be tacked onto the end of the U.S. production run." [This obviously fails to recognize that the producers worked for *profit* and also sought to recover their development expenses in any sales, especially outside the USA. This would be why the F-106s cost the USAF 3.3 million each, while they were offering F-106Cs to Canada for 5.58 million each, a higher price than the Arrow. Furthermore, the F-106C hadn't been built and therefore wasn't even fully developed.]

"Furthermore the United States produce a series of aircraft…from 600 to 1000 aircraft, and therefore the prices can be much lower." [Perhaps, but not always. Only around 100 B-58 Hustlers were produced, and only about 300 F-106s were produced. This imagined lower cost of US production had also been demonstrated not to be the case with the CF-100 and Orenda engine as compared to the American F-89 Scorpion and General Electric J.47 turbojet.[353]

> Furthermore, Canadian aircraft programs were known to require 15% less man-hours for production than the identical planes in the USA and Britain.[354]]
>
> "There is some concern in the Defense Department that a continuation of the CF105 program would not leave the program flexible enough to allow for other urgent projects. A careful study which was made last autumn shows very clearly that there is no room in the present defense program for major economies which would be required to carry out this program. Therefore an increased defense budget must be anticipated if this development and production of the CF-105 is to continue."
>
> "The abandonment or limitation of manned aircraft in the air defense system and more reliance being placed on ground-to-air missiles would bring about a necessity for arrangements to be made for the use of nuclear warheads for air defense. It is not possible to put a nuclear warhead on the Sparrow missile, and therefore the CF-105 with Sparrow cannot be said to be the most modern air defense weapon available."

The conclusions clearly demonstrate that this was the work of Foulkes, *not* the CSC.

> "Therefore *I conclude* that the disadvantages far outweigh the advantages of continuing the CF105 program…I am convinced that the missile will provide more defense per dollar than the manned interceptor, and now that the range of the missile is reaching the range of the manned interceptor, the advantage appears to be all with the missile. The use of missiles will also save manpower and allow us to take over more U.S. establishments in Canada." [italics added This last line is particularly offensive. Adoption of nuclear warheads, which the US would *not* place in the custody of foreign nationals, caused *more* US installations and personnel to come to Canada. In fact, while undertaking the Air Force Indoctrination Course at CFB Comox in 1991, students—such as this author—were informed that Diefenbaker had ceded the missile storage areas of Canadian air bases to the United States in order to make true his claim that there were no nuclear weapons on Canadian soil!]
>
> "The Minister of Finance has stated that the strain which would be placed on the national budget by continuing this program would be intolerable, which indicates that a $2 billion budget may mean increased taxes."[355]

CAS Campbell's memo shows that it was *always* known that the defense budget would have to increase for about three years if the Arrow was ordered into production. But not even this turned out to be entirely true. The first year's Arrow production, once Astra and Sparrow were cancelled, required about 250 million dollars. After the close of the Department of National Defense's fiscal year in 1958 it was discovered that there was an unspent $262 million which was returned to the Treasury by the Department. This was enough to continue the program for the *next year.* In other words, no increase in the defense budget was required to acquire one year's production of Arrows.

> "The exchange took place between Minister of National Defense George Pearkes and Paul Hellyer, defense critic in the opposition cabinet of Lester B. Pearson. Pearkes had just stated that in 1958/59, the Department of National Defense underspent its funding to the tune of $262 million… Naturally, one might expect this under-expenditure to have resulted from the cancellation of the Avro Arrow. This was not the case."[356]

Why did Foulkes (or anyone) consider it desirable to abandon a non-nuclear aircraft for nuclear missiles that would have a good probability of exploding over, or upwind of major Canadian cities? The answer is that the Americans were insisting on them. The Arrow was also quite capable of carrying nuclear air-to-air missiles such as the MB-1 Genie which had been planned for since 1956. Furthermore, Raytheon, the producers of the Sparrow 1, were working at developing a nuclear Sparrow version, the Sparrow X, as of mid-1957, and its adoption had been recommended to the RCAF by Avro in August, 1957.[357]

The whole plan was shifting to allowing US nuclear surface-to-air and air-to-air missiles into the air defense system of Canada, along with their radar warning and computerized ground control and relay installations. Boy! They sure seemed to be in a panic to cover Canada with the most devastating and expensive air defense imaginable if they really believed that the Soviet bomber threat was the only use for the Arrow, and that the Soviet bomber force, in totality, existed of about 160 aircraft.[358] These CIA estimates were about one tenth of what had been previously assumed by the intelligence communities of the armed services of the Western Alliance and neglected the existence of about 800 TU-4 Bull bombers. They also suggested the Soviets wouldn't likely build any more but would turn entirely to missiles, and this was clearly the thinking guiding Pearkes at the time. *What is really remarkable about the document is that they said the Soviets lacked the industrial ability to produce many bombers!*

By the fall of 1958 Pearkes also knew about the Bounder design being in test flying. It was a supersonic bomber but didn't carry the fuel to be a long-range threat—though the West didn't know that. It was a threat to Europe though. In reality the Soviets were tooling up to build more intercontinental bombers and by 1968 would have the Backfire, a Mach 2 capable long-range (using air-to-air refuelling) jet bomber using supersonic, guided, stand-off weapons, and some fly-by-wire technology—a potent machine. Nevertheless, the Soviet Strategic Air Force never approached the numbers of intercontinental aircraft of the USAF—because they were preoccupied with Eurasia. Ironically, the earlier high bomber number figures had been built up on faulty CIA projections made in overreaction to the revelation of Soviet intercontinental jet bombers in 1949. But if Europe, also an area of Canadian responsibility, is considered, then the figure of about 1,500 Soviet bombers was a credible figure. One must again ask why the Conservatives and Republicans were insisting on seeing the Arrow as only applicable to the air defense of North America. By 1959 the US had over 1,500 intercontinental jet bombers with nuclear payloads. [359] In 1959 the CIA was debunking their old theory and hyping the sudden missile threat, with estimates suggesting the Soviets would have 2,000 ICBMs by 1969.[360]

James Dow, in the conclusions from his book *The Arrow,* provides a breath of fresh air:

> "The need for manned interceptors was not disappearing in 1959 because bombers were not disappearing. The Russians had more bombers in their strategic arsenals than ever before and they had no more intention of abandoning this component of military force than the Americans had of setting aside their Strategic Air Command".

338 Stewart: Shutting Down the National Dream, p.181, Quoting Fred Smye.
339 RG 49 Interim 135 Volume 67 File 151-9-1, part 3
340 quoted from ibid, p. 120, reference document is: Eisenhower Library, "Memorandum For Meeting With Prime Minister Diefenbaker"
341 Dow: The Arrow, conclusions, p.1
342 Eisenhower Library, July 6-11 memcoms USA re: DDE trip to Canada (Annex 13)
343 Campagna: Requiem for a Giant, pp.120-21
344 Dow: The Arrow, p. 178
345 Cabinet minutes, 25 August, 1958
346 Cabinet minutes for 28 August, 1958. (Cabnt28Aug58.jpg)
347 Stewart: Shutting Down the National Dream, p. 250, quoting James G. Eayrs, and Gen. Charles Foulkes. "To Set the Record Straight" Unpublished paper written in 1967
348 CDC: Record of Cabinet Defence Committee Decision, 21 August, 1958
349 Smye: Canadian Aviation and the Avro Arrow, p. 114
350 CAS A/M Campbell: Confidential memo to MND Pearkes: "CF-105 – Supersonic Interceptor", 21 August, 1958
351 Smye: Canadian Aviation and the Avro Arrow, p. 251 embedded quotation is CAS Campbell
352 RG 49, Vol. 427, File 159-44-B, part 1.
353 Campagna: Storms of Controversy, p.85 "In a memo dated March 28, 1958, the Chief Aeronautica Engineer for the RCAF compared the costs of the Arrow to those of the F-106, F-102, and F-101 in order to determine if these American aircraft were less expensive... Conclusions from the memo indicated: 'Arrow costs compare favourably with the somewhat less sophisticated aircraft in the U.S.A.... It has been interesting to learn that RCAF fly-away costs for the CF-100 from production were less than for the comparable F-89 Scorpion. Similarly, quantity production of the F-86 and T-33 was undertaken in Canada at a lower per aircraft cost than from U.S.A. production.]
354 Air Industries Association of Canada studies, shown in Requiem for a Giant.
355 All quoted sections from Foulkes: :Aide Memoire for the Minister; Advantages and Disadvantages of Continuing Production of the CF105", 25 August, 1958
356 Campagna: Requiem for a Giant, pp.143-44
357 Floyd: memo to AVM Hendrick, 30 August, 1957, pp.1-2: "It appears to us that the Raytheon family of missiles, staring with the Sparrow III and developing to the Sparrow X, which has a provision for either a high yield TNT or an atomic warhead, gives this continuity of development."
358 CIA estimates released in 1957, right around the time Duncan Sandy's released his White Paper on Defence which cancelled every manned military aircraft programme in Britain, including one that was being considered for the Arrow in the RAF.
359 Coldicott: Missile Envy
360 NADOP 1959-1963

Chapter 58

PRICE DECEPTION

Foulkes later left evidence on the record demonstrating his "erroneous" conclusions above regarding the price of the Arrow. Above he wrote:

> "It is quite clear that this aircraft will require almost $500 million to complete development and *then* it will cost between $10 and $12 million a copy for production."

So, according to Foulkes' spurious CSC recommendations to Pearkes, the 10 to 12 million figure obviously was for costs for production *not including design and development.* However, in an unpublished article on the Arrow debacle Foulkes later wrote:

> "The Defense Production Department advised that approximately $300,000,000 had been spent on the Arrow project and that an additional $871,000,000 would be required to complete it. This resulted in the $12,500,000 figure."[361]

Foulkes was obviously capable of considerable modification of statements when embarrassed.

Dow wrote:

> "$12,500,000. This was the cost per aircraft cited by the prime minister for 100 Arrows equipped with Astra and Sparrow… To arrive at these figures it was necessary to total the cost of all components of the weapons system: airframe, engine, missile and fire control. This included agreements for design and development, tooling, spares, ground handling equipment, test assemblies and overhaul. To make these figures appear even more outrageous, the cost of the 37 aircraft on contract was considered as a development expenditure for the proposed program to build 100 Arrows. In effect, the cost of 137 was divided by 100 to inflate the price per unit even more."[362]

It was worse than this in fact. Foulkes and Pearkes, before a Commons investigation into their air defense decisions, and before Arrow cancellation were stating this as the price *not including development to date.*[363] Private anecdotal testimony from former RCAF staffers state that this price even included construction and improvement of runways and quick reaction hangars, expenses that were later incurred anyway— primarily for USAF interceptor, bomber and tanker operations in Canada. Clearly DDP, who was compiling the numbers, was involved, with Foulkes and Pearkes, in the deception of Cabinet. This price deception has been used, apparently without much research, by Diefenbaker supporters and supporters of the cancellation ever since.

Smye would later view some of the government cost figures, and even using their own admitted math, would come out with an average price for 100 operational Arrows, including all design and development to operational standard and engines and fire control, of $5.62 million dollars. The government said it came to $7.8 million a copy. This was because they were writing off the entire 37 preproduction run and were including design and development expenses incurred to date, missiles, lifetime spares, ground support and test equipment and more. It was a very deceptive way to influence the thinking of Cabinet, the press and the public. Of course, in comparing figures, the fact that payroll, income, and other taxes would be immediately recouped from Canadian production was, inexplicably, ignored.

The USAF would estimate that a similar number of F-106As cost them, after development expenses which dwarfed those of the Arrow, an average fly away cost of 3.3 million dollars each.[364] This was an aircraft with about a third of the range, half the engines and half the crew and much lower strategic value especially in a multi-role capacity. Literally, in terms of tactical value, this represented half the aircraft for 76% of the price, development not included! It cost Pratt & Whitney as much to bring the F-106's J75 engine to its 50 hour P.F.R.T. as it did A.V. Roe Canada to bring the Iroquois *and* the Arrow to equivalent states of readiness. It cost Convair more (150 million dollars) to turn the F-102, which used the same wings and many other components, into the F-106 as it did Avro to build the first 5 Arrow Mk.1s and fly them, and have Mk.2s on the production line.[365] Development of the MA-1 system, comprising the SAGE system, the Falcon missiles, the Genie missile and the MX-1179 radar/fire-control, certainly weren't quoted in the US figures either.

After Astra and Sparrow systems were cancelled Fred Smye flew to the United States and met with an Assistant Secretary of the Air Force. During these meetings Smye was offered the MA-1 radar/fire-control system for free, but was cautioned by the American authority that the offer would only officially be made upon a request by the Canadian government. Why weren't the government figures on the Arrow showing the offer of the USAF of these systems for nothing? Obviously because the government of Canada didn't pursue it—probably because they knew the US government believed the Arrow was dead as of July 1958 and would therefore be astonished by a request for those highly-classified systems on a charity basis! Indeed DDP Minister O'Hurley stated to the July 1960 Committee of Defense Expenditures:

> "The United States, at no time, would consider the purchase or make any contribution towards the development of this aircraft. They were quite prepared to sell us any parts that we needed—and, of course, some parts were obtained from the United States—but there was no indication at any time that they made a financial or other contribution..."[366]

It also appears that Avro's final offer was not brought to the attention of Cabinet, nor anyone else, for many years—until Fred Smye made it public in his unpublished manuscript: *Canadian Aviation and the Avro Arrow.* So what was Avro's final offer on the Arrow? It was 3.5 million dollars each for the first 100 Arrows and 2.6 million dollars each for the next 100.

> "In light of these circumstances, Avro and Orenda undertook detailed reviews of the costs, on the assumption that the number of aircraft involved was one hundred, in addition to the thirty-seven on order. The unions were appraised of the situation and reacted magnificently in the joint effort to cut and hold costs. In order to eliminate any uncertainty, it was decided voluntarily to submit a fixed price for the complete operational airplane, including the fire control system. This involved the Company in unprecedented risk, but it was considered that it was better to run the risk of breaking the company in this fashion than to stand by and see it die by other means. The price submitted to the minister was $3,500,000... This price would have been $500,000 less had the U.S. supplied the fire control system [free as mentioned earlier]."[367]

Or, as Dow put it:

> "Details of Avro's offer to the government were given in a letter from the company to D.L. Thompson, director of the aircraft branch of DDP, on 30 December. The letter confirmed a *fixed price* offer of $346,282,015 for 100 aircraft (25221 to 25320), including Iroquois engines and the Hughes MA-1C electronics systems. Adding applicable sales tax of $28,717,985 brought the price per aircraft to an even $3.75 million. The contract proposals attached to the letter covered design and development, tooling and tool maintenance, manufacture of 20 development and 100 squadron aircraft...and technical support for the squadron aircraft."[368]

In other words Avro was offering the Arrow for 3 million dollars each for the first 100 and 2.6 million for the next hundred. In reality they were quoting 3.5 million for the 100 aircraft to follow the pre-production run of 37 aircraft already on contract if they had to purchase the MA-1 system. The 37 had been proposed to cost an additional 229 million dollars in FY 59-60 to complete to Mk.2 standard with missiles and the MA-1C system but did not include development flying and improvement to service standard. The final offer included development to service standard of 20 aircraft from this first 37, at a total price of 295,000,000. If the first 17 are considered unfit for service, then the RCAF would receive 120 Mk.2 Arrows for an average price of 5.375 million per service aircraft. If these figures were to include the MA-1C system at no cost, as was oddly offered to Smye, the price drops to $4.875 million a copy. If all 37 aircraft are considered in the equation, the price drops further to $4.1 million an aircraft. Had another 120 been considered for NATO service in Europe, the price per plane, with radar purchased for all service aircraft, the price to equip the RCAF with Arrows would have been an average of $3.99 million an aircraft, fly away cost. These final prices even included Avro Orenda technical support to the squadrons, but didn't include lifetime spares and ground handling equipment and the myriad things the government tacked on to the Arrow prices.

CAS Campbell, after retirement, was interviewed by Greig Stewart:

> "Pearkes had a high code of ethics but had gone entirely missile. DeWolf and Graham [Chiefs of Staff for the Navy and Army respectively] had agreed on a replacement aircraft [the F-106C]—I did not. I had tried to reconfirm the original CF-105 requirement and had confidence we were going to have a supersonic interceptor almost to the very end.[369]

One must question whether Pearkes really had a high code of ethics or was merely capable of simulating it. Armed with Foulkes' false conclusions, Pearkes presented them to Cabinet on August 28th, and stated that they were the recommendations of the CSC. At this point he was still trying to substitute the F-106C for the Arrow to satisfy the RCAF insistence on a supersonic interceptor:

> "The Minister of National Defense said that the Cabinet Defense Committee had reviewed the air defense requirements for rounding out the air defense weapons system against the manned bomber...The committee had *referred to Cabinet* for consideration *proposals to cancel the CF-105 program* and to investigate additional missile installations and a possible alternative interceptor to the CF-105" [Italics added. The wording is misleading. This makes it sound like the CDC had developed proposals to cancel the CF-105, and had sent them to Cabinet for consideration. This is not true. They referred the *consideration* of the cancellation of the CF-105 to Cabinet.]
>
> "The RCAF now had nine all-weather squadrons and the present program called for their re-equipment with the CF-105, requiring a production order of 169 in number. These, together with aircraft recovered from the development and pre-production order for 37, would provide sufficient aircraft for nine squadrons. The total cost would be $2 billion spread from 1959-60 to 1963-64." [If this is so, then why did Foulkes state in his Aide Memoire, that the plants involved in production of the CF-105 would *all* have to close by 1962? Why did Pearkes inflate the number of aircraft that the RCAF had stated they required from 169, to 169 *plus* those recovered from the 37 pre-production aircraft (estimated at 20 giving a total of 189 for service)? It seems apparent that this was a means of inflating the total program cost to $2 billion. This figure certainly appears to also include development costs already spent. As the final audit figures showed, the program for 120 Arrows, with everything conceivably included, including all monies spent in design and development, would have cost $1.1 billion.[370] Using the audit figures, 169 Arrows would have cost 1.391 billion, everything from 1953 onwards included.]
>
> "A study of the implications of continuing this program, its impact on the whole defense program... [etc.] had necessitated a review of the air defense program. *The Chiefs of Staff had undertaken such a review.* [again these were really Foulkes' opinions] The main points that were considered were...ground-to-air missiles had now reached the point where they were at least as effective as a manned fighter, and cheaper. The original requirements in 1953 for between 500 and 600 aircraft had been drastically reduced. Subsequently, thought had been given to reducing it still further now that the BOMARC missile would probably be introduced into the Canadian air defense system. [This was something new, the RCAF's requirement for 169 Arrows had included Bomarc in their requirements. Pearkes is seemingly trying to reduce the order so that unit costs would be prohibitive.]
>
> "Finally, the cost of the CF-105 program as a whole was such that *the Chiefs of Staff* felt that, to meet the modest requirement of manned aircraft presently considered advisable, it would be more economical to procure a fully developed interceptor of comparable performance in the U.S. [This simply wasn't true. The Army and Navy Chiefs wanted the Arrow program kept alive for at least a year as we have seen in Foulkes Aide Memoire, and the RCAF had not consented to a reduction in the requirement for 169 aircraft, and wanted the production order given forthwith.]
>
> "...He also described the U.S. intentions on BOMARC and how they related to Canada." [This could only be a reference to the assertions of Dulles and/or McElroy that if Canada didn't pur-

chase the BOMARC, the US would site them just south of the border near major Canadian cities.] "There were considerable advantages in adopting BOMARC. It was cheaper than the CF-105…and just as effective… As regards aircraft, the U.S. authorities had made it quite clear that they did not intend to buy any CF-105s. Their own F-106C was comparable in performance to the CF-105, it would be available several months earlier, and it cost less than half as much." [It wasn't cheaper if Canada paid for the whole cost of Canadian Bomarc sites and it was shortly thereafter proven ineffective if not dangerous (as Avro *and* AVM Hendrick predicted in 1957), there was no way the "paper" F-106C would have been ready sooner.]

A long Cabinet debate ensued with points being made back and forth. The party line was now clear and would be reiterated thereafter, as it was by Diefenbaker in his memoires:

"In the end, although we tried hard to secure orders for it in the United States and among our NATO allies in Europe, we had no success. The attitude of the military authorities in those countries paralleled a view that was becoming dominant in our own Chiefs of Staff Committee: the CF-105 was a fine example of what could be done technologically, but that it was altogether too costly, had too short a range, and would be out of date by the time it got into production. The CF-105 would be able to do nothing but intercept, and that within a very sophisticated ground environment and only within a range of 150 to 200 miles from its base."

Of course that statement has serious defects on all points. Pearkes briefing notes, before his visits with Dulles in August 1958, showed that they knew the production cost of the Arrow would be about 5 million each (with Astra/Sparrow), not 12.5 million as they stated after these meetings, and this was below the price of an inferior American intercepter then touted as a cheaper alternative. If it had an inferior range, why was it twice or three times that of US, British and French aircraft in the interceptor role? As for it being suited only for interception, this was also rather far fetched.

"…the concept of a multi-role combat aircraft clearly intrigued the RCAF for the C104/2 design closely resembled the CF-105 in size, appearance and capability. The key to its flexibility lay in its massive armament bay. Install six Hughes Falcon missiles and twenty-four rockets and it was an interceptor. Not satisfactory? Try four [Velvet Glove] missiles or four thirty-millimeter cannons with 200 rounds each and fifty-six folding fin rockets. Need a tactical bomber? Four 1,000-pound general purpose bombs would do the job. Put in a camera pack and the aircraft was transformed into a photo-reconnaissance model. Add more fuel and it became a long-range fighter. Carry a second pilot on any of these and it could be used as an operational trainer. The possibilities were too numerous to resist."[371]

It was clearly an argument between those who had already agreed with the Americans to cancel the Arrow and those who thought it would be a horrible mistake:

<u>"During the long discussion the following points emerged:</u>

(a) It was doubtful if the BOMARC missile or components could be manufactured in Canada. [Yet Avro had been asked by the preceding Liberal government to submit a proposal on BOMARC production. They were clearly technically competent, therefore the only reason it couldn't be produced in Canada was because the US would not allow the technology transfer.]

"The CF-105 would be of no use against ballistic missiles. [Six months earlier, in *Flight and Aircraft Engineer,* Jim Floyd is quoted as revealing his plan to incorporate an anti-ICBM missile into *any* Arrow version. They already knew about Douglas Aircraft's emerging Nike-Zeus ABM and were planning on deleting a stage from the booster rocket sections and carrying them on the Arrow.][372]

"The Sparrow…could not be fitted with an atomic warhead." [see earlier regarding the nuclear Sparrow X.]

"Although it would be most helpful if the facilities presently used on the CF-105 could be converted for the development of missiles, this was highly unlikely. [Why?] The best possibility for the future was a production program of partnership with the U.S. *The U.S. authorities had indicated they would be willing to allocate a significant share of future missile development to Canada...*"

The U.S. had not yet reached a decision on the type of anti-missile missile they would require." [While this is the advice the Canadian politicians were receiving, we know that the USAF had, as shown earlier, selected the Nike-Zeus system for development as an ABM. We also know that this was not supposed to be mentioned in political circles. We know that Avro's P-13 air-launched ABM was to be based on technology developed for the NIKE ZEUS ground-launched ABM. Avro's ABM scheme for the Arrow was never mentioned to cabinet, nor, apparently, to the CDC and perhaps not even to the CSC.]

"The United Kingdom would not buy the CF-105 and it was most unlikely that any other N.A.T.O. country would either."[373]

This last remark on British disinterest in the Arrow was exceptionally debateable as we have seen. The leaders of the RAF and similar British bodies certainly wanted them. Jim Floyd is on the record as stating:

"There was never a moment's doubt in my mind that Britain would have eventually bought the Arrow..." [374]

This author's research suggests they would have been foolish not to, especially after Duncan Sandys had ensured that there were no military aircraft in development in England when the UK defense planners changed their minds on the requirement for manned fighters, and even on the requirement for manned aircraft.

Jim Floyd had also been back to England to consult with his peers in the Hawker Siddeley Group, with officials in the British Ministry of Supply, in the RAF and with British defense scientists. This visit, much like the similar one two years earlier, resulted in the British air defense authorities and scientists once again looking very hard at the Arrow. By this time Floyd had the aerodynamic drag figures that mirrored what Robert Lickley's team had achieved with the Fairey Delta 2—it had proved to have lower drag than even the designers had projected, and they had projected less than anyone else. The Arrow was suddenly shaping up to be an exceptionally powerful defensive, or offensive weapon, and one with superior range providing a much longer list of possible targets and thus roles for the aircraft.

Here is what Sir Thomas Pike's organization had to say about the Arrow Mk. 2 as it stood at this time:

"...when we were at C.F.E. [RAF Central Fighter Establishment] and Bomber Command, they both expressed a great desire to get their hands on a quantity of Arrows, and C.F.E. in fact said that they believed they could adequately defend the United Kingdom with 200 Arrows, and they knew of nothing else that would be just as good..." [375]

361 Smye: Canadian Aviation and the Avro Arrow, p. 113
362 Dow: The Arrow, p. 180
363 Foulkes: "Aide Memoire for the Minister" August, 1958 and August 28th Cabinet minutes.
364 USAF museum website.
365 Shaw: There Never Was an Arrow, and others. Engine development of the J-75 cost $279,000,000 up to its 50 hr. PFRT. Arrow and Iroquois program costs to Sept. 1958 were actually less than this, at about $242,000,000.
366 From Smye: Canadian Aviation and the Avro Arrow, p. 88
367 ibid, pp. 89-90
368 Dow: The Arrow, p. 186
369 ibid, p. 250
370 Campagna: Requiem for a Giant, pp.142-43: "Audit reports produced after the cancellation show that the program was for the production of the thirty-seven aircraft discussed plus an additional eighty-three. Added to this...would be spares and...missiles. The total program, from start to finish with all work complete, would cost $1.1 billion for 120 aircraft."
371 Dow: The Arrow, p.126
372 Flight and Aircraft Engineer, No. 2560, Vol. 73, 14 February, 1958, in an article titled "Ironclads and Arrows...": "...the possibility is already seen that, in order to achieve its maximum kill potential, the "anti" missile may actually form an alliance with the manned fighter."
373 Foukes: "Aide Memoire for the Minister" August, 1958
374 CBC documentary: There Never Was an Arrow, 1979 and interviews with the author,
375 Floyd: strictly confidential memo to Avro Canada President J.L. Plant: "The Arrow Controversy", 7 November, 1958

Chapter 59

AVRO STV:
THE SPACE THRESHOLD VEHICLE

While the Conservative political machine was engaged in their cancellation machinations Avro was looking to the future. Along with ramjet research for the Arrow 4, Mario Pesando's Project Research Group was also looking into the "next big step" in interceptor evolution. Avro apparently felt the next air defense frontier wasn't down in the weeds with low-level roles but lay at even higher altitudes—space. In the Engineering Division report of June 5th 1958 the Space Threshold Vehicle is described:

> "It became obvious to us some three or four months ago that it was possible to put a winged vehicle into orbit, and that there was a corridor where normal winged flight was possible between the minimum speed curve, above[sic] which it was impossible to sustain lift, and the maximum temperature curve, below [sic] which the structure gets too hot. This opens up the possibilities of hypersonic flight with a relatively conventional aircraft of low wing loading (about 20 lb. per square foot.), which appears to us to be the easiest way to get a man into the threshold of space and recover him, flying back through the corridor.
>
> "We are at present carrying out a study to ascertain the relative merits of the winged vehicle versus boost glide or ballistic techniques. We hope to shortly give a briefing on this and later determine where we should go from there.
>
> "The concept has been discussed with John Orr [Director of Engineering at the D.R.B.] and Gord Watson, who expressed a great deal of interest in it, and suggested that they may like to have a joint study carried out between ourselves and DRB." [italics added]

From other Avro documents [see *Avro Aircraft & Cold War Aviation*] it is apparent that Avro was well aware of the three types of re-entry vehicles that the United States defense and NASA researchers were working on. Project Mercury, the panic operation of the newly formed NASA to get a man into orbit is a "drag re-entry" approach to the problem. NASA and military documentation regarding Project Mercury show that everyone knew this was the simplest "quick and dirty" method of lobbing a man into orbit and recovering him, especially with limited rocket boosters. Avro did not like this approach since it promised dangerous re-entry temperatures.

The boost-glide concept was actually proposed in 1938 by Sanger and Bredt in Germany and was pondered by the Nazi's. The idea was to loft a winged vehicle with low-wing loading via rocket into a ballistic trajectory at extreme altitude. It was felt that the speed of re-entry would allow the glider type vehicle to "skip" off the atmosphere in slowly descending steps and thus be capable of deploying a weapon anywhere on the globe.

Of course the Americans latched onto this concept, along with many of the German scientists, at the close of WWII through *Operation Paperclip.* Army Major General Walter Dornberger had been the commandant of the Peenemunde facility where Von Braun and the others had worked on the V-2 and other advanced weaponry. Dornberger was soon running Bell Aerospace in the United States while Von Braun made a name for himself in US Army rocket facilities in Alabama. According to Gunston in *Faster Than Sound,* while at Bell Dornberger and Ehricke worked out a two-stage to orbit system using two delta-configured craft, one serving as a mothership, the other being the manned spaceplane. This project, called BoMi (for bomber-missile) went from 1951 to 1955, apparently without bearing fruit. *(An anecdote I was not able to relate to Randall Whitcomb was that one of the chief aerodynamicists for the Bell Bo-Mi program was Wilfred Dukes, an ex-Avro Canada alumni. He was fondly remembered by one ex-Bell employee I met in Buffalo as "the best engineer I ever saw." Wilfred went on to be on the Presidential committee to investigate why so many tiles fell off the Space Shuttle Enterprise during its first cross country jaunt aboard NASA's converted Boeing 747. Ed.)* What seemed to replace it was the X-20 Dyna-Soar, a collaboration between Bell Aerospace, Boeing and Martin. It was less demanding using Martin's Titan II missile as the primary launch vehicle. Dyna-Soar was also to be basically un-powered, having only thrusters for station-keeping and limited manoeuvring, but no main engine. After Project Mercury got going and promised results, Dyna-Soar, or X-20, was cancelled. *(Dyna-Soar may well be the American equivalent to the Avro Arrow. Hundreds of millions were spent on its development and the factory floor at Boeing was tooled up and ready to produce it in quantity when it was cancelled by Defense Secretary Robert McNamara, just days after President Kennedy was assassinated. Ed.)* It has always seemed odd to the author that the United States persisted with the drag-re-entry concepts for Gemini and Apollo and then made the big leap to an aerospace plane, the Shuttle. On the other hand, one never knows, considering the secrecy surrounding CIA and Black projects. Dornberger's "Bo-Mi" for example, used the same concepts as Germany's modern-day aerospace-plane concepts, not surprisingly named Sanger and Sanger D.

From the above it is clear that some believed winged aerospace-planes "flying" out of the atmosphere and into space were viable, and at a very early date. Avro documents show that engineering was looking down the road for a project to replace the Arrow once production ended. In those days, the idea of a Commonwealth space program, competitive with American efforts as a means of ensuring the Commonwealth possessed all key technologies and could thus compete economically, was seen as a distinct possibility.

A concept was under study at Avro for a hypersonic-plus sub-orbital space-plane design called the Space Threshold Vehicle. This document explored all the main variables and limiting technologies and graphically presented the findings. One of the key findings was that the state-of-the-art presented a corridor into space using a winged vehicle which employed hybrid-propulsion techniques.

STV Aerodynamic Configuration

It has been related how Avro was forced to develop a sort of integrated, or "lifting-body" method of aerodynamic modelling for the Arrow. Using Avro's computer facilities, Chamberlin, Pesando, Floyd and other brains allowed Avro to develop aerodynamic theories and methods of problem solving which essentially corresponded to today's three-dimensional fluid dynamic modelling, then used it to develop the structural design, using testing at various times in the development to refine the design.

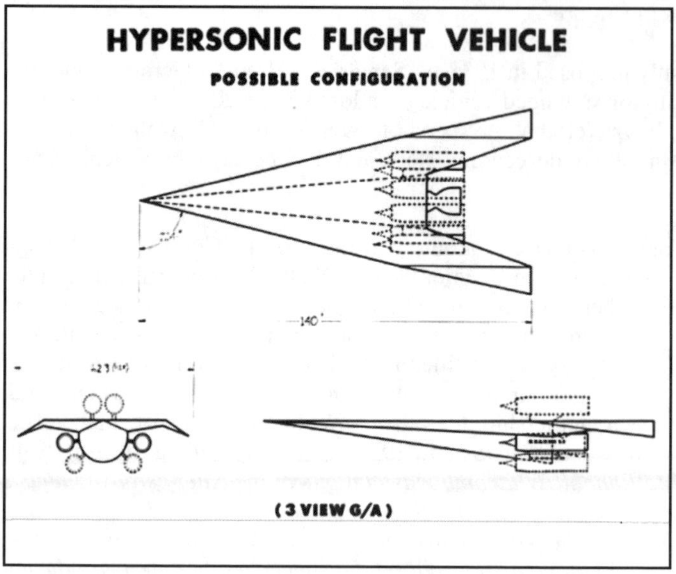

Pesando's STV configuration from the study dated June 1958. The wedge shape on the underside would produce shockwave compression which the winglets would convert to lift. (via Jim Floyd)

NACA and various other American government agencies, the military ones especially, were looking hard at a means of overcoming the contradictions between space flight and aerodynamic flight in hopes of eventually producing a more efficient means of getting into orbit. The reasons for wanting such a hypersonic vehicle were described as late as 1993 in the House of Representatives Appropriations Committee Energy and Water Development Subcommittee during the 102nd Congress, 2nd Session, Part 6, pages 1669-1670:

> "The need for a Hypervelocity Aircraft-Delivered Weapon derives from the ability of such a system to rapidly deliver, or threaten to deliver, nuclear weapons into a theatre, while maintaining the launch platform well outside potential defenses. Hypersonic velocities enhance defense penetrability and survivability of the weapon and the delivery aircraft against state-of-the-art defenses, while precision guidance can lead to reduced yield requirements, and consequently, collateral damage."

It seems that Avro Canada and a few others certainly felt that Canada and the Commonwealth should have their own independent systems and capacities in these regards, *and* the ability to defend against them, up to about 1959. Like the Arrow, this was to be a primarily defensive weapon, but it would retain the ability to be more than slightly offensive as well.

The US saw the same potential and the *Aerospace Daily* issue of March 1985 includes the article *DARPA Chief Notes Potential of Supersonic Combustion Ramjet:*

> "[The hypersonic aerospace-plane could] fly up to maybe 150,000 to 200,000 feet, sustain mach 15 plus for a while, slow down and engage an intercontinental bomber or cruise missile carrier at ranges of 1000 nautical miles…"

The range mentioned by the DARPA (Defense Advanced Research and Development Agency) seems more than slightly sanitised for public consumption considering Avro's STV and the American Bo-Mi and Dyna-Soar vehicles were designed for ranges of at least half the circumference of the earth (about 12,500 nautical miles).

The problem with developing an aircraft that would fly most or all of the way from take-off to re-entry under its own power has proven daunting. On the purely aerodynamic side, it was obvious that a means of getting a high L/D (lift to drag ratio) in a vehicle suitable for hypersonic speeds (and this of narrow wingspan) was a crucial requirement. A gentleman named Alfred J. Eggers Jr., then an assistant director at NACA's Ames Aeronautical Laboratory, had been pondering methods of improving the L/D performance of hypersonic aircraft. Apparently he was mowing his lawn one day in 1957 and the drone of the machine allowed his mind to wander. He postulated that at high-speed, a conical body could be shaped in such a way as to benefit from the shockwave produced by the basic shape to create lift. This was the origin of the famous USAF/NASA lifting bodies, well known from the crash-sequence at the beginning of the TV series, *The Six-Million Dollar Man.* His compression lift theories were the basis of the NAA XB-70 Valkyrie Mach 3 bomber design.

Egger's compression-lift and lifting-body theories and research, and proposals relating blunt-body re-entry shapes as a means of reducing re-entry temperatures of ballistic-launch vehicles, were mentioned in the 21st Wright Brothers Lecture in early 1958. This lecture would appear to have been more of a catalyst for the space race by far than President Kennedy's 1961 challenge to be the first to land a man on the moon. Apparently Avro had some talent present at that lecture taking notes. Interestingly, Egger's-lifting body showed a modified inverted airfoil as the ideal shape; –this corresponding crudely to Avro's highly criticised airfoil shape for the Arrow, as well as Whitcomb's later "supercritical" airfoil.

It was compression-lift that the Valkyrie's designers and Avro's Mario Pesando found especially brilliant. Pesando grasped the concept immediately and did research suggesting Avro could achieve an L/D max of around 7:1 using a delta-shaped vehicle that employed Egger's theories. This L/D max is very high, and exceeds that of the Boeing B-52 which uses swept high-aspect ratio wings to achieve it. Interestingly, NASA-Ames later lifting body work, with Eggers heavily involved, produced the blunt-bodies that only had L/D ratios in the neighbourhood of 1.5-1 while Pesando was looking at 7-1. If the Canadian NAE and DRB had problems following Avro's aerodynamics with the Arrow, they would have been even more at a loss with the STV design. An interesting NASA-Langley discussion of "integrated" versus "waverider" shapes for precisely an STV-type craft are at http://larcpubs.larc.nasa.gov and is titled *Aerodynamic Performance of Realistic Waverider-Derived Hypersonic Cruise Vehicles.* It concludes that a smoothly blended, integrated design would suffer in terms of potential L/D ratios, and that a waverider style design could provide an L/D max of about 7, with its L/D ratio at a lift coefficient of .05 would be about 6. Pesando quoted exactly those figures for the STV design, which he acknowledged was essentially an "Egger's body."

Materials were proposed from the same selection as envisioned for the Arrow Mk.3. The insulation scheme proposed for the Arrow 3 would have been acceptable for this vehicle, especially considering it was essentially the same as the heat shields used on Mercury and Gemini. Being fibreglass honeycomb with resin filled by microballoons meant it was reasonably light. The structure of the STV was to be mainly high-temperature steels with titanium alloys in the skin and structure where required. Pesando felt that Avro could produce a vehicle with a take-off weight to landing weight ratio of 4-1. In other words, that 75 percent of the vehicle weight would be devoted to fuel, consumables (oxygen etc) and payload using mostly known materials and construction techniques.

Some will no-doubt be thinking that a blunt-body is the best shape for a vehicle of this type, perhaps due to representations made in other books and articles. Today however, NASA's Dryden Flight Research Centre website (http://www.dfrc.nasa.gov) shows an interesting graph which plots L/D ratios against range for several configurations of hypersonic and ballistic re-entry shapes. It shows the L/D ratio of the blunt-bodies coinciding with that of the Space Shuttle at a relatively poor 1.0-1.5 range. This restricted their re-entry glide ranges to the order of 600-1,500 miles. The ballistic "capsule" shapes were even less, which is why they heat so much on re-entry. This also explains why the shuttle needs such a heavy tile insulation scheme; the steeper the descent, the higher the heating penalty. The shape shown with the best range performance however, is the X-24B, which was the X-24A blunt-body redesigned as a sharp body like the STV. This shape is shown to have an L/D max of about 2.5-3.0 which shows it is about one half the L/D ratio of 7 which is what Pesando thought the STV could achieve. This low L/D ratio for the X-24B would be for two reasons, the most important was that it didn't employ Egger's compression lift, and the second being it was an adaptation of a design intended for another purpose. As mentioned above, NASA is now of the same opinion regarding a similar waverider hypersonic body and perhaps have been all along. On the other hand, research facilities have been known to disagree within NASA, and the Ames Research Centre was the leading proponent of lifting-body hypersonics throughout this period and the 1960's, at least (Avro aside). It is interesting to remember that Ames himself was one of the NACA consultants invited to hear Avro's Chamberlin, Floyd and Lindley's rebuttal of NACA Langley and the RCAF, DRB and NAE's condemnation of the Arrow's aerodynamics. That two-day conference was chaired by Hugh Dryden, –another NACA leader who would have a research facility named after him. (At this time Ames already did.)

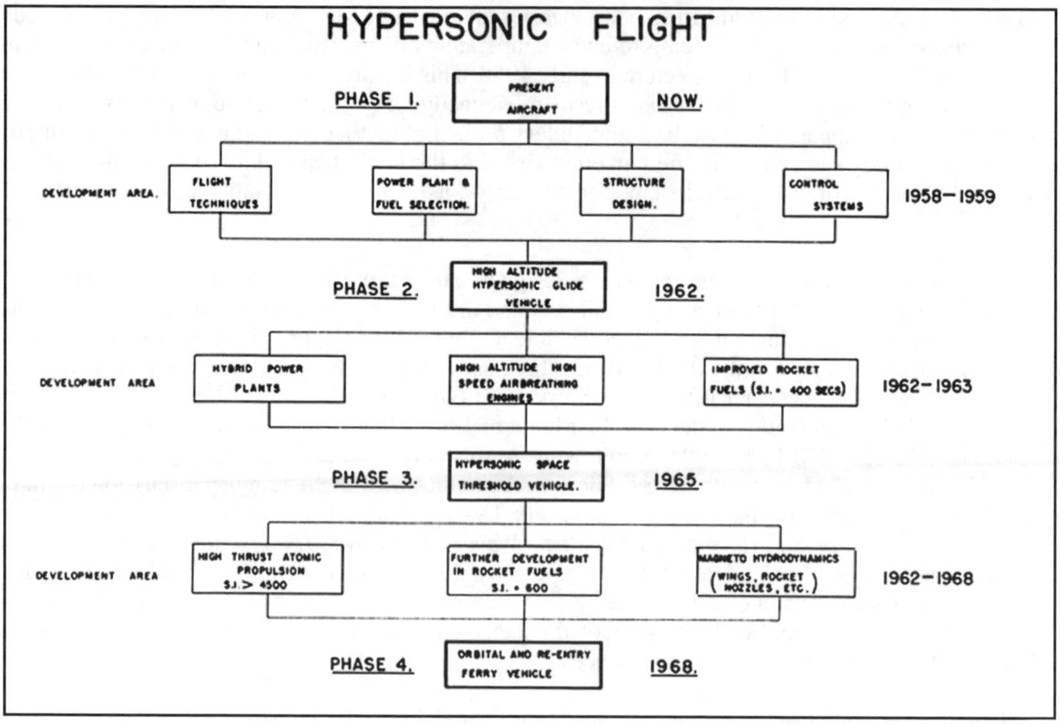

This page from Avro's study postulates a development plan and timeline to produce a winged sub-orbital aerospace-plane and have it ready by 1965.
Nuclear/hydrogen-plasma was one of several propulsion technologies proposed for the later orbital version of vehicle proposed for 1968. (via Jim Floyd)

Pesando's STV document discusses this plan and it is clear that the "present aircraft" in the chart above is the Arrow. When the Mk.4 Arrow, with the high-temperature materials and ramjets, is considered, this consideration of the Arrow as phase one becomes even more striking considering this aircraft could have zoomed to somewhere around 150,000 feet. In discussing this schedule, Pesando wrote:

> "Considering a possible time table, it is believed, as shown on the accompanying chart, that using known data and techniques within one year it should be possible to finalize engineering of an interim hypersonic glide vehicle with burn out speeds in excess of 10,000 ft. per second [about 6,000 mph]. Such a vehicle could possibly be built by 1962 and would be considered a research vehicle.
>
> "Further development in the areas indicated could, by 1963 at the latest, increase our knowledge and techniques sufficiently to enable us to extend our vehicle concept to velocities approaching orbital speeds. We have, therefore, shown this vehicle as operating by 1965, this vehicle would constitute the long range operational vehicle with ranges of 12,500 miles or greater.
>
> "Having this vehicle completed would enable us to immediately begin the utilization of further advances in propulsion methods and magneto-hydrodynamics expected by 1968, to provide us with a winged orbital and re-entry ferry vehicle by the late 1960's.
>
> "The importance of phase 3 and 4 vehicles in the military field is of course obvious and this could be one of the objectives expected of such a development program."

Pesando's STV was envisioned as being a single-stage to orbit (SSTO) vehicle (or perhaps, considering the aerial refuelling provision, a stage and a half to orbit). SSTO was a concept the Lockheed Skunk Works proposed for the cancelled X-30, and one that some of the Europeans have been exploring –the British HOTOL design being one of the best. From Pesando's STV study:

> "The hypersonic vehicle postulated, takes off on rocket power alone with a full load of oxidizer and sufficient ramjet fuel to enable it to climb to an altitude in excess of 40,000 ft. and maintain flight during airborne fuelling proceedings. [The STV concept] is for a hypersonic vehicle which is really an extension of the conventional supersonic airplane. When airborne fuelling operations have been completed the aircraft is accelerated to ramjet light up speed and begins its climb and acceleration to higher speeds."

Flight refuelling is a rather novel approach to the SSTO problem, one that appears to be entirely original and has only recently been suggested again.

NUCLEAR HYDROGEN PLASMA AND ELECTRICAL PROPULSION

The final stage of Avro's STV development scheme was to produce an orbital ferry or shuttle. This would have employed new propulsion schemes including nuclear power and magneto-hydrodynamics. Documents from Floyd show that the specific nuclear propulsion system Pesando was considering was a nuclear-hydrogen plasma drive while ionisation and magneto-hydrodynamic effects, similar in concept to those said to be secretly used by the B-2 Spirit bomber, were being investigated.

Ion, plasma and electrical propulsion methods have been discussed for a very long time and are still being discussed although they are limited to small vehicles and for thrusters. Although ion plasma engines actually cover a fairly wide range of possible engines, the concept has been around since Robert Goddard postulated briefly on the possibility of electric propulsion in 1906. Nikola Tesla is rumoured to have done work to this end, including discussing a flying saucer design that employed anti-gravity techniques. Hermann Oberth, the father of German rocketry and a flying-saucer theorist also discussed electric propulsion in a chapter of his 1928 book *Wege zur Raumschiffahrt.* Sanger also contributed some theories as did Ernst Stuhlinger who, in 1954, introduced the concept of specific impulse. In 1958 the American Rocketdyne Corporation operated the first ion-engine demonstrator. By 1964 the Russians had the first plasma thrusters in space aboard their Zond-2 satellite. *(Soviet research in this field began in the 1930's courtesy of Soviet engine wizard Valentin Glushko. Ed.)*

Pesando had been proposing the eventual development of a nuclear-hydrogen plasma drive for the STV's final development phase. This seems to be considered a NTR (Nuclear Thermal Rocket) today although Pesando was looking at various methods of modifying the engine with electrical means. NTRs were projected with specific impulses of about 900 seconds at the time, but Pesando seemed to feel that with hydrogen plasma and electrical techniques, the specific impulse could be raised to about 4,500 seconds. The heat of a reactor would superheat hydrogen into plasma. Electrical techniques would be used at the nozzle to ensure the plasma beam detached from the ship and provided propulsion. Pesando was also eyeing ducted-rockets, which are now called ram-rockets. This ducted or ram-rocket concept appears to be very promising for hybrid propulsion techniques, combining possibilities for chemical, air breathing, rocket and electric propulsion, even nuclear techniques, into one multi-function design.

Of course nuclear propulsion for aerospace-planes or any other type of aircraft has been taboo for many years despite the fact that many satellites went up with reactors on board. The Americans and Soviets were also never afraid to simply not tell the populations what they were doing. *Popular Mechanics* ran an interesting article in late 2000 postulating that a lifting-body nearly saucer-like military shuttle has been in operation for years, using nuclear propulsion, and designed to either remain in orbit with nuclear weapons, or drop nuclear missiles off in orbit for later use.

During the February 24th meeting between Avro management and the ministers, Avro tried to promote the spaceplane concept as a means of putting satellites in orbit. They were trying to interest the Canadian government in pursuing a joint space program development program with Britain and other members of the Commonwealth.

People might scoff at the possibility of Avro having pulled off such a coup. One might suggest that Chamberlin, Lindley and about 28 other ex-Avro engineers *did* prove they could have built such a craft, when they took so much responsibility for Project Mercury, Project Gemini and Apollo. For an excellent reference on this subject see Chris Gainor's *Arrows to the Moon.*

Chapter 60

AVRO FIGHTS BACK

Perhaps naturally, since Avro wasn't friendless, the company began hearing rumours that the government had resolved to cancel the Arrow program in the fall of 1958. As a result Fred Smye made arrangements to speak to the government to find out if this was true. As Smye stated in an interview to the CBC in the documentary *There Never Was an Arrow;*

> "We approached the government on the one hand and the Air Force on the other, and got two completely different answers."

No doubt the word had quietly gone out through CAS Campbell that Pearkes had decided to cancel the Arrow—with Campbell leaving the documentary evidence that Pearkes had made up his mind *after* meeting with the Americans.

> "During the summer of 1958, the company got the first inklings that something was going drastically wrong. Jan Zurakowski and John Plant got the first clues... In early August, he and Plant were part of a contingent from Avro Aircraft making a presentation at RCAF headquarters in Ottawa..."[376]

To quote Jan Zurakowski on this matter:

> "There were about fifty air force officers present and when Plant asked if there were any questions, there was silence until one of the officers said he was under strict instructions not to ask anything about the Arrow. Now this was a very, very unpleasant moment for me. It was then I realized something was wrong."[377]

Avro couldn't get a straight answer.

> "As Mr. Gordon, president of the parent company [A.V. Roe Canada Ltd.] was in England, Mr. Tory, a director of the parent company, its legal counsel, and a leading Conservative acquainted with Mr. Diefenbaker, undertook this assignment in early September.
>
> "In his meeting with the PM, Mr. Tory was indeed informed that the Arrow project was in some jeopardy. The PM arranged for meetings with the Ministers of Finance, Defense, and Defense Production. [These were all anti-Arrow and were already, it seems clear, party to the arrangements made in the United States earlier.] I accompanied Mr. Tory to these further meetings which took place the same day. To the remark by me that it would appear that Canada might be about to decide that it could not afford to defend itself, the Minister reacted sharply, while delivering a fierce denial. To the question as to whether or not the Government would be interested in a $350,000,000 reduction in the program's cost of 100 aircraft, Mr. Fleming replied that he would be interested in a reduction of 350 cents. Mr. Fleming was then advised that this $350,000,000 saving could be affected by replacing the Astra system and Sparrow missiles with the Hughes MX-1179 and the Falcon missiles, which ought to have been chosen in the first place. Mr. Fleming demonstrated serious interest in the idea and asked that the suggestion be made to the two ministers we were about to meet."[378]

How serious Mr. Fleming's interest was is suggested by the Cabinet minutes detailing this offer:

> "...Mr. Tory and Mr. Smye...stated that the R.C.A.F. made a major mistake three years ago by recommending the adoption of SPARROW and ASTRA. A great deal of money could be saved by using the FALCON and the Hughes fire control system. [Notice he neglected to tell the cabinet how *much* money Avro had suggested could be saved.] Mr. Fleming had pointed out to Messrs. Tory and Smye that their arguments, that the Falcon missile and Hughes fire control system should be good enough for Canada, could also be used against them in regard to the airframe and engines which they wanted produced in Canada by their own firm."[379]

Apparently, as shown below, Fleming was taking 'credit' for statements he didn't make. Surely this points to his enthusiasm for slagging Avro before his Cabinet colleagues rather than transmitting facts about potential savings.

Returning to Smye's version of events:

> "The [subsequent] meeting with Mr. Pearkes...was as brief as it was futile. The suggested change of the fire control system and missile was received with utter disdain."[380]

Smye's version seems clear enough from the Cabinet minutes of 3 September:

> "The Minister of National Defense...said that the figures on savings mentioned by Mr. Smye should be treated with reserve. The latter had not been aware, for example, that there were a number of types of FALCON."[381]

This last comment was absurd. The Arrow had been designed from day one around the infra-red and radar-guided versions of the Falcon missile, (with ASTRA/Sparrow being added in 1956) and this author has Avro documents between Fred Smye and J.C. Floyd that indicate that Smye was deeply involved in issues relating to every missile considered for the Arrow, which were many.

Returning to Smye's written remarks:

> "...the [following] meeting with Mr. O'Hurley, with his deputy Mr. Golden in attendance, was full of surprises and very productive. Apparently of all the various proposals placed before the Government, none had contained the possibility of a switch in the fire control system and the missile, and the minister *asked his deputy* why this was so. Mr. Golden remarked that the company was proposing the junking of the electronics and missile systems, which were the technologies of the future, in order to preserve their own products and technologies of the past. He also wondered why the company did not propose the scrapping of the Iroquois in favour of the J-75. I advised him that the company had already investigated this possibility but had rejected it, as it would involve delay and little saving, if any, but were prepared to explore it again, which it did, with the same results. In the end, *the minister asked his deputy to examine the effect of the change of the fire control and missile immediately to advise what savings could be effected"*[382] [italics added]

Whereas Fleming took "credit" for this exchange in Cabinet he neglected to mention Smye's response regarding the engine substitution. This author has documents showing that Avro had proposed a J-75 Arrow in 1956, and has further documents showing that Smye did have Engineering develop another J-75 version (that could take either the Iroquois or the J-75) and related proposal, involving a removable extension to the rail mounting the Iroquois, for use if the J-75 was substituted. From O'Hurley's reaction, it appears that it was Davie Golden, who was responsible for the cost estimates on the Arrow proposals, he was very anti-Arrow and was sold on missiles over aircraft. The opening remarks of the Minister of National Defense in this meeting are interesting in terms of Smye's contention that the meeting with O'Hurley and Golden, with Fleming obviously in attendance, was "very productive":

> "The Minister of National Defense said that, since this subject had last been discussed, Mr. John Tory, one of the directors of A.V. Roe, and Mr. F.T. Smye, Vice-President of Avro Aircraft Ltd., had discussed the future of the CF-105 with the Prime Minister, the Minister of Finance, and himself. [He left out O'Hurley and Golden.] These men recommended that the airframe and Iroquois engine elements of the program be continued but that the fire control system (ASTRA) and the weapon (SPARROW) projects be dropped, and substitutes obtained in the United States. Instead of ASTRA and SPARROW, they had suggested the U.S. Hughes MA-1 system and the FALCON, respectively. He had cost estimates prepared on this suggestion and comparisons made with other alternatives. These were as follows:
>
> "Expenditures for 100 aircraft, *from September 1st, 1958:*
>
> 105/Astra-Sparrow $1,261.5 million, or $12.61 million each
> 105/Hughes MA-1-Falcon $ 896 million, or $ 8.91 million each
> U.S. 106 $ 559 million, or $ 5.59 million each
> BOMARC, (to provide roughly equivalent defensive strength)
> $ 520.3 million
> 4 batteries of 60 missiles each (no cost sharing with the U.S.)[383]

Notice, with ancilliary costs, disposable Bomarcs were worth over two million dollars apiece. Notice that somehow the RCAF requirement for 169 aircraft has been reduced to 100. Somehow 100 F-106s, with roughly one-third the range of the CF-105 and lower performance, are, by implication, considered equal to 100 Arrows. Notice how 240 one-shot BOMARCs, despite all their disadvantages already revealed, are somehow considered equal to 100 Arrows, with eight missiles each—an aircraft that could be re-used, refuelled, rearmed and re-launched in *ten* minutes. Notice how the costs projected are said to be from *that day forward,* whereas we have already seen that those figures included *all* monies spent to date in developing Astra, Sparrow, the Arrow airframe, the Iroquois engine and all the test and ground handling equipment, lifetime spares, missiles, simulators etc. and yet were still inflated. It is believed that all the Arrow figures quoted also included runway lengthening and strengthening, quick reaction hangars and other things which had to be done later, for US interceptors in Canada, anyway.[384]

This is clearly a *very* deceptive document and, in fact, the Arrow quotes provided by DDP are proven to be fallacious in the 1960 parliamentary Special (all-party) Committee on Air Defense. It would appear that cost calculation was Davie Golden's work—although it is questionable if he did this "work" on his own initiative. It was Davie Golden's comments that resulted in the title of the CBC documentary, *There Never Was an Arrow:*

> "If you mean the Arrow as a fighting instrument of war, which must therefore include an airframe, an engine and a sophisticated fire control system, then of course, *there never was an Arrow.*"

These comments so enraged Kay Shaw that she also titled her stunning book, based on her and her husband's analysis of what was behind Arrow cancellation, *There Never Was an Arrow.* Cabinet refused to accede to the requests of Fleming and Pearkes to cancel the Arrow program on that day, and continued to refuse to cancel it until February 1959.

Two days later, the Arrow was again discussed in Cabinet:

> "The Prime Minister opened the further discussion of the proposal of the Minister of National Defense to cancel the CF-105 program by stating that although ministers were relatively well agreed on the defense aspects, the serious problem still requiring consideration was the effect on employment and the general economic situation.
>
> "The Minister of Finance said that in considering matters of defense he naturally put the safety of the country ahead of finance. When it had been recommended a year ago that the CF-105 program be continued, he supported the recommendation. Now, however, the military view was that the program should be cancelled. In these circumstances, he did not see how the government could decide not to discontinue it… other things being equal or nearly so, military equipment should be produced in Canada. But in this case the cost per aircraft was twice as much as the cost of a comparable unit which could be obtained in the U.S., and, more important, the military authorities had now decided that the aircraft was not necessary…There was no time that was the right time for a decision like this one. He was sure, however, that it would be better to cancel now than be faced with a final shut down of the plants three or four years hence. Another factor to be kept in mind was that, by deferring cancellation, the program, in effect, become [sic] the present government's program, whereas in cancelling now it could be said that the government had considered all aspects of the project started by the previous administration and had come to the conclusion that the best course was to abandon it… In short, cancelling the program would be of much greater help to the economy as a whole than continuing it."[385]

At no time did Fleming mention the balance of trade or balance of payments problem affixed to the replacement of the indigenous Arrow with American missiles and/or fighters. At no time did he refer to the 600+ subcontractors affected in terms of employment, technical ability and production. At no time did he mention the importance of the high technology sector, built at such expense over many years, and the effects the destruction of those jobs would have on the long-term competitiveness of Canadian industry and exports. At no time did he mention the effects of exporting hundreds of millions of dollars and thousands of high-tech jobs to the United States. There were those in Cabinet who disagreed with his appraisal that cancelling would be a "much greater help to the economy as a whole than continuing it":

> "Cancelling now, apart from the effect on the employees concerned, might be the one psychological factor which would result in a break in the economy and lead to a drastic down-turn from which recovery would be extremely difficult. The program should be allowed to continue over the winter and a decision taken then as to its future. During that period, management could consider what their plants might do in the future." Someone else remarked: "...while cancellation might be sound in theory, it might result in a recession. If employment prospects were better, the project could be dropped quickly. Continuing, even for only a few months, involved insignificant amounts compared with what would have to be spent during a real depression."[386] During the 1962 election campaign currency devaluation crisis they found out exactly what this prescient individual meant.[387]

An American contact of this author mentioned a US Public Broadcasting Service documentary on Kennedy and Diefenbaker which alleged that the "Diefenbuck" currency crisis was caused by the CIA and sympathetic financial powers due to Kennedy's consternation over Diefenbaker's failure to stay in line with American foreign policy during the Cuban Missile Crisis.

Unfortunately, the government actively conspired to ensure Avro would *not* know the program would be cancelled until they made it official on 20 February 1959, as we shall soon see. Further interesting logic in these Cabinet discussions is evidenced by this incredible remark:

> "The U.S.S.R. had always said that the western economies would ultimately collapse. Carrying on a project like this...was surely only playing into Russian hands."[388]

Someone else, probably Pearkes, then mentioned other US offers and comments on air defense, which included the push towards adoption of nuclear air-to-air missiles, which, due to US insistence on them, some defense authorities, especially Foulkes and Pearkes, equated with modernity. Meanwhile, Avro engineering documents and surviving records of AVM Hendrick, point out the "kill probability", as calculated for the Sparrow 2 and a nuclear, passive guidance version of it, were about the same anyway; in other words, they calculated that they didn't need nuclear weapons on purely military grounds, never mind any considerations of the after effects. This is something else that is *glaringly* absent in any of the surviving discussions of Canada's decisions to adopt nuclear weapons for use over our own territory. The effects of radiation poisoning, nuclear fallout, and other long term effects of nuclear war were never even mentioned as something they thought at all about in the various meetings deciding these policies, and conversely, the policy of Arrow weapons system cancellation.

> "If the project were abandoned, arrangements could quite probably be made with the U.S. to purchase 106Cs and also secure atomic heads for the weapon with which they would be equipped. The U.S. authorities had also indicated in the last few days that they would be prepared to consider seriously cost-sharing and production sharing of defense equipment. They had also said *they would be prepared to relocate northwards some of their proposed Bomarc installations.* These Bomarc bases hardly seemed to cover Canada at all. [The Bomarc option was reneged upon by the US right after the Arrow was cancelled] They were most concerned at the moment over improvements to the warning system... Surely the Canadian public would give credit to the government in the long run for good housekeeping and it appeared that on defense and on economic grounds it was good housekeeping to discontinue the program *now.* "The Cabinet deferred decision on the recommendations of the Cabinet Defense Committee regarding air defense requirements, including the future of the CF-105 program." [389] [italics added]

The United States also reneged on their offer to move Bomarcs into Western Canada after Arrow termination. So far we can see that the advice and promises the Canadians were receiving from the US government included:

1) Relocation of US Bomarcs north to cover Canada.
2) They would be happy to sell them F-106C's that were promoted as being just as good and half the price.
3) Nuclear missiles were the future, aircraft were the past.
4) Bomarc and SAGE were the foundation of a comprehensive future missile defense system.
5) They would allocate a good deal of missile development and production into Canada.
6) They would be happy to have their fighters in Canada for the protection of Canada permanently, or, failing that,
7) They would be happy to forward deploy their fighters into Canada for Canadian protection in times of crisis.
8) They would be happy to send other defense business into Canada.

Various documents cited in this work show that CCSC Foulkes and some key members of the Diefenbaker Cabinet became convinced that Canada would receive more defense production, and therefore economic development, through the United States channelling defense business into Canada. The exact source of this amazing belief is unknown, but it appears to be part of the sales job done by John Foster Dulles and other American politicians, probably including Secretary of Defense Neil McElroy. What is not in doubt, any longer at least, is what happened in Canada as a result. From September 10th Cabinet minutes:

> " Government purchasing policy; purchase for defense program (previous reference Sept. 7)
>
> "The Minister of finance said he now had a chance to discuss the implications of the new government purchasing policy directive, which had been approved by Cabinet, with the Minister of Defense Production who had not been able to be present when it was considered. The Deputy Minister of Defense Production [David Golden] would be in Washington shortly to carry out negotiations...
>
> "He hoped to be able to say something on this subject privately to the United Kingdom and to ask them not to press the Canadian government on this matter. The British had expressed some concern about the "buy in America" policy of the United States. He thought it preferable to soft-pedal the purchasing directive rather than jeopardize negotiations with the United States. Mr. O'Hurley was also of this opinion.
>
> "The Cabinet noted the report of the Minister of Finance on the recent government purchasing policy directive and agreed that it be withheld for some time."[390]

This directive actually appears to have been withheld ever since. From the above it seems apparent that to secure American defense production in Canada they had ordered the Department of National Defense to review all programs underway and to consider American equipment over British. Equally clear is that they undertook to "soft-pedal" the implications of this policy change to the British, and that they were privately, without a paper trail, asking the British not to publicly embarrass the Canadian government over this change. It is also clear from this document that the British had genuine concerns over American reciprocity in purchasing foreign product. Finally, they made the policy secret, no doubt in part to prevent Avro and much of the military from finding out that they had sold British interests in defense production, indeed Britain's largest collaborative industrial effort in Canada, "down the river for American interests." [391]

To the best of this writer's knowledge no minutes of Golden's negotiations in Washington following the Diefenbaker-Eisenhower Summit of August 1958 have been made available to researchers. It becomes clear that US knowledge that Canada had already secretly ordered a "buy American" policy would, indeed, jeopardize Golden's negotiating position. It is has been mentioned in print on at least one previous occasion that someone had overheard a meeting of the American negotiating team just after the conclusion of the meetings. If the report is to be believed, what transpired was a general back-slapping and round of self-congratulation on the part of American negotiators for having turned Golden's sales attempt into a successful sale on their part instead. If so, it was a sale which included a mortal wound to their leading North American competitor in aerospace, heavy industry and resources: A.V. Roe Canada Ltd. Included in the bargain was another setback for America's number one competitor in aerospace and propulsion: the Hawker Siddeley Group of companies.

Official Use Only

MR. DOUGLAS

THE DEPUTY SECRETARY OF DEFENSE
WASHINGTON 25, D. C.

June 1, 1960

5

MEMORANDUM ON PRODUCTION SHARING PROGRAM -- UNITED STATES AND CANADA

The current program dates back at least to 1941 and the Hyde Park Agreement. This agreement provided generally that Canada and the U. S. should attempt to coordinate activities so that each would produce in areas of greatest capability. In 1950 a Statement of Principles of Economic Cooperation was issued by the Truman Administration. It advocated, among other things, a coordinated program of requirements, production and procurement; the exchange of technical knowledge and productive skills; the removal of barriers impeding the flow of essential defense goods. In 1950 a DCD Directive on Defense Economic Cooperation with Canada was issued. A Presidentially approved NSC paper, 5822/1, dated 30 December 58, reaffirmed the Statement of Economic Principles and provided for equal consideration to be accorded the business communities of both countries.

Prior to the NSC paper, and following a visit of the President to Canada in July 1958, Canada took the following actions with the understanding that her defense industry depended largely upon the U. S. channeling defense business into Canada: Cancelled the CF 105 and related systems contracts; decided to make maximum use of U. S. developed weapons, integrated into NORAD; worked with the U. S. toward a fully integrated continental air defense.

The U. S. in turn established a Production/Development Sharing Program with Canada with the first quarterly meeting in October 1958. Since then, policy obstacles impeding a free flow of business have been modified in a number of areas such as: Buy American Act; duty free entry of defense goods; security requirements; etc. Also, working groups have been set up on programs of mutual interest (for example, BOMARC); cost sharing agreements have been worked out; and possible joint development programs are being explored.

The last quarterly meeting of the Production Sharing Policy Group was held on 25 May. Despite all efforts, over the period 1 January 59 through 31 March 60, Canadian defense business in the United States almost doubled that placed in Canada. Canada is not satisfied with these results, nor do they appear acceptable from our view.

We must: re-emphasise the program of development sharing activities; encourage American industry to subcontract in Canada; and seek out other legitimate techniques to stimulate the program. Canada should be encouraged to energize her industry which has not displayed the necessary aggressiveness.

376 Smye: Canadian Aviation and the Avro Arrow, pp. 80-81
377 Stewart: Shutting Down the National Dream, p. 239 Zurakowski repeated this statement to Whitcomb in 2001
378 Smye: Canadian Aviation and the Avro Arrow, pp. 80-81
379 Cabinet minutes, 3 September. 1958
380 Smye: Canadian Aviation and the Avro Arrow, p.81
381 Cabinet minutes, 3 September, 1958, p.5
382 Smye: Canadian Aviation and the Avro Arrow, p.81
383 Cabinet minutes, 3 September, 1958, p.2
384 Private testimony from ex-RCAF officers.
385 Cabinet minutes for 5 September, 1958
386 ibid
387 See: Newman: Renegade in Power
388 Cabinet minutes, 5 September, 1958
389 Cabinet minutes, 21 August, 1958
390 Cabinet minutes for 10 September, 1958
391 Words of unidentified ex-Avroite on Black Friday as he was leaving the plant, having been dismissed moments before, to a CBC reporter. Included in the CBC documentary There Never Was an Arrow, 1979

Chapter 61

DIEFENBAKER MEETS GORDON

> "Upon his return from the UK, Mr. Gordon submitted a brief to the PM to outline the economics of the Arrow-Iroquois programs. This brief indicated that the projected Arrow-Iroquois five-year program did not exceed the annual costs of the comparable program of the CF-100 and Orenda. The brief also endeavoured to portray the real net costs of the project to Canada by estimating the direct and indirect taxes which would flow back to the Government. For example, [all estimates] were of necessity inflated by a 10% sales tax, which was merely a transfer from one Government department to another."[392]

This was presented during the "infamous" meeting between Crawford Gordon Jr. and Prime Minister John George Diefenbaker on 17 September, 1958. Contrary to the strange assertions of Pat Kelly, which were repeated in the CBC mini-series *The Arrow,* it appears that this brief was not left on the train:

> "Armed with a detailed brief on why we should continue the Arrow program, he met me on 17 September [for the first time]. To clear away a misrepresentation of what happened at our meeting, in no sense could it be described as a nasty personal confrontation."[393]

Although we have already seen that Diefenbaker was hardly a credible source when it came to these subjects, in this case he had no reason to lie, and every reason to portray Gordon in the worst light possible. There are many conflicting versions of what transpired in this meeting, with Pat Kelly, who worked somewhat intimately with Crawford Gordon, giving very damning testimony about this meeting and other things. Myself, Jim Floyd, and author Chris Gainor have not been able to find anything to support his claims as put forth in Stewart's *Shutting Down the National Dream.* Floyd doesn't believe that Gordon could possibly have been so foolish considering his vast experience in dealing with government and in war production. Gordon's history and experience in the DDP would suggest Floyd is correct, but who knows. However, an examination of this issue is beyond the scope of this piece. It is known though, that Diefenbaker accompanied Gordon to subsequent meetings with Pearkes and Fleming, making Kelly's statement that Gordon was thrown out of Diefenbaker's office somewhat questionable. James Dow states in his book:

> "No one else was there, b ut Grattan O'Leary of the Ottawa Journal was outside when Gordon emerged "white as a sheet."[394]

Perhaps Smye, in describing this meeting, is correct when he mentioned the "personality clash":

> "But, whether or not Diefenbaker and Gordon had a personality clash… they only met on this one occasion… what does this have to do with the air defense policy of Canada, or anything else?"[395]

Avro then stepped up to the plate with a reduced price offer:

> "In order to get the costs down and to cut out the chatter about escalating costs and so on, we voluntarily stepped up an offer for a fixed price for one hundred airplanes. That involved gigantic risk, believe me, and in the price—which was $350 million, three million five hundred thousand dollars,—in that price was $500,000 for the [Hughes] fire control system, not the missile. So we could knock half a million off the price right there, which gets you down to $3 million for a fly-away operational airplane including fire control system, the whole thing."[396]

What Smye was referring to in his statement—that half a million dollars could be dropped off the price of the plane—is that he had secured a verbal offer from the Assistant Secretary of the Air Force in the United States government for the provision of the MA-1 radar/fire-control system for free:

> "The next mission [after meeting with the government in late September 1958] took me and my assistant, a former Assistant Secretary of the USAF for Research and Development, to

> Washington to endeavour to ascertain the outcome of Mr. Pearke's visit there in August. Meetings took place with an Assistant Secretary of the USAF. In an effort to reduce costs and to have some U.S. participation, I asked if the USAF would supply, free, the fire control system and missiles and if they would allow the free use of their flight test centre at Muroc Lake in California. [Edwards Air Force Base] They said they would be happy to grant this request. *They said it would be improper for them to volunteer this offer to the Canadian government but the company was free to advise the Government* that any request of this nature would be looked upon favourably by the Secretary of the USAF."[397] [italics added]

It seems, in light of the documents which have recently surfaced, that this was an empty gesture on the part of the US government, since they, by then, already knew the Arrow was dead. It was obviously up to the government of Canada to make the request, and this request was apparently never made. It certainly would have helped prevent Smye and Gordon from accusing the US of being behind the cancellation once it occurred. While Smye pointed out that the United States was the big winner in the Arrow cancellation and subsequent policy direction, neither he nor Gordon, nor J.L. Plant ever publicly stated that they thought powerful US authorities had a hand in the cancellation. But then, no matter the American influence, the responsibility lay with the government of Canada.

> "Mr. Gordon put particular emphasis on the question of cost and suggested a more realistic public appraisal of what it would be. He said: 'The change in the fire control system and armament has resulted in substantial reductions in the overall cost of the program as indicated in the Prime Minister's statement', and added that analysis of the implication of these changes had 'reflected further savings in the program.' In addition, Mr. Gordon said the figure previously mentioned for 100 aircraft ($9 million each) included the whole basic development and tooling costs. These expenditures, he said, should be eliminated from a realistic appraisal of the possibility of continuing the program…
>
> "By considering only those costs which would be incurred from this point on in the actual production of Arrows for combat use and including new savings, it is now estimated that 'we can produce 100 Arrows, complete in every respect, including the cost of the engines and fire control system, and excluding the missile armament, for a cost of approximately $3,500,000 each.'" [398]

Four days later Prime Minister Diefenbaker referred to his meeting with Crawford Gordon Jr., President of A.V. Roe Canada Ltd.

> "[Diefenbaker] reported that he had seen Mr. Crawford Gordon, President of A.V. Roe Company, who had also interviewed Mr. Pearkes and Mr. Fleming. Mr. Gordon had recommended that production of the Arrow aircraft and the Iroquois engine be undertaken but the programs for the Astra fire control equipment and the Sparrow missile be cancelled. There was nothing essentially new in his proposal.
>
> "The Minister of National Defense and the Minister of Finance reported on their conversation with Mr. Gordon and noted that he made certain assertions in regard to the willingness of the U.S. government to provide fire control and missiles that would be suitable for the Arrow aircraft. He had mentioned some large figures of possible savings that might be made by obtaining such equipment from the United States, but had been unable to be precise about these, and the figures appeared to be exaggerated. [In the course of an ensuing "long discussion", wherein the "Cabinet was clearly divided", another comment was made revealing more of what was discussed between Pearkes and Dulles:] If production of the Arrow and its associated equipment went forward, it was likely to become *publicly known that this was done contrary to military advice…*" [399]

Whose "military" advice? Or was it American political and CIA advice? The advice given was American, and Pearkes was breaking with Western intelligence and all military air defense experts in accepting the advice of the CIA and American politicians. Perhaps aware of the break with reality espoused by Pearkes an undisclosed minister caused the following to be recorded:

"There was some question as to just what the views of the Chiefs of Staff really were on this issue and how much reliance should be placed upon them. Their recommendation for termination of the program now appeared to be at variance with their views earlier..."

In reality the only thing that had changed in terms of the views of the Chiefs of Staff was that CCSC Gen. Charles Foulkes had taken his opposition to the Arrow from officially correct neutrality to an official condemnation that was somewhat outside his official responsibilities. From the available documentation, it appears that of the three heads of service in Canada, the Army had always been opposed, the Navy went along with the RCAF plan or was neutral, and the RCAF always insisted on it, as Fred Smye wrote many years later, as their primary requirement.

Another objection to cancellation followed:

"The current international tension would make it appear foolhardy to cancel an important development program such as that of the Arrow and Iroquois, although it was noted that, if in fact war broke out, it would be necessary to use current types of aircraft and possibly to concentrate on the CF-100 rather than proceed with the CF-105."

It was further noted, perhaps by the Minister of Finance: "To carry on the development of the Arrow aircraft and the Iroquois engine until March would cost in the neighbourhood of $86 million; the economy might be better able to stand the shock of the cancellation of the program in March than at present and the international situation might be less tense at that time." 400

General Charles Foulkes

392 Smye: Canadian Aviation and the Avro Arrow, p.81
393 Diefenbaker, John: One Canada (passage reproduced in Smye's Canadian Aviation and the Avro Arrow, p.82
394 Dow: The Arrow, p.176
395 CBC documentary: There Never Was an Arrow, 1979
396 Quote of Fred Smye in Stewart: Shutting Down the National Dream, p.247
397 Smye: Canadian Aviation and the Avro Arrow, p. 88
398 Orenda News, October, 1958
399 Cabinet minutes, 21 September, 1958
400 Ibid.

Chapter 62

SEPTEMBER COMPROMISE

> "The Prime Minister suggested that a compromise should be considered on which possibly the Cabinet could agree. He thought such a compromise might involve carrying on the development program until March, but not beginning the production program on the Arrow or the Iroquois at this time. This continuation of development might be regarded as a form of insurance in the present tense situation." This, essentially, the Cabinet did, adding that "a careful and comprehensive review of the requirements for the Arrow aircraft and Iroquois engine should be made before March 31st, 1959, in order to reach a decision…as to whether *development should be continued or production ordered.*"[401]

The meeting continued after lunch and DDP Minister Raymond O'Hurley, rarely heard from in other cabinet minutes,

> "noted…that if development of the Arrow aircraft were to be carried on, there was great advantage in deciding forthwith about the future of the Astra [system]. He noted that one alternative was to stop development of both Astra and Sparrow and switch to the American counterparts already developed, making the necessary modifications in the air-frame development." MND Pearkes then added his views: [Pearkes] expressed the view that if, as seemed likely, the development of the Arrow would be terminated at the end of March, the sensible thing to do would be to terminate the development of the Astra and Sparrow at the present time. Even if it were decided to continue with the production of a small number of Arrow aircraft, it would still appear sensible to terminate the highly expensive Astra development. The electronic engineers and other technical personnel would be better employed to get to work on missiles and receive special training rather than continue the expensive work on the Astra and Sparrow…"[402] [Pearkes then moved that these items] "should be terminated forthwith, and that this decision should be announced the following day along with those decisions on the [Arrow development continuing until at least 31 March]."[403]

From this passage it seems clear he was counting on getting missile programs "allocated" out of the US and into Canada.

On the 23rd of September Diefenbaker made a long, winding statement where he revealed permutations of his thinking and those of his cohorts. He went on at length about his view of the promise of missiles and the purported changing emphasis away from manned aircraft, then cancelled Astra and Sparrow, and allowed the Arrow and Iroquois programs to survive until Judgement Day: 31 March, 1959.

Now, due to the simple fact that as a whole the Cabinet would not vote to cancel the Arrow and Iroquois programs, those opposed to the Arrow were facing a winter during which the Arrow was being worked on to reduce cost, and also flown to prove itself. To add to the confusion, Diefenbaker embarked on a two-month-long tour of Europe. During this time period Avro recorded at least six attempts to have meetings with government officials to either find out if the Arrow was likely to be cancelled, to explore replacement projects Avro had been developing, and, of course, demonstrate the value of the company and its products to Canada. Shaw and Smye agree that senior Avro executives could not get direct meetings with any responsible member of the government in this period. They either wouldn't see him or anyone with authority from A.V. Roe Canada Ltd., or the meetings were delegated to powerless mandarins. Later, in justifying indelicate handling of Avro by the Prime Minister, it was expounded in Cabinet and publicly that Avro imploded because it had made no attempts to find alternatives when they knew, or should have known, that the project was going to be cancelled by 31 March, 1959. These Conservatives were certainly conservative with one commodity: truth!

Avro's Hugh McKenzie stated to Greig Stewart:

> "About September [1958] I took an advance party of engineers down to Hughes Aircraft with the intention of bringing an Arrow out of Canada and down to Los Angelas to introduce the Hughes fire-control system into the aircraft on site [as had been done with the CF-100]…But for reasons which I can't even now understand, the aircraft wasn't allowed out of the country…"[404]

This certainly suggests that the die was cast by September and explains Smye's efforts to find out what was happening. The Department of Defense Production (DDP), who had been compiling the greatly exaggerated prices on the Arrow, also added something at this time that boded very poorly for the future of the Arrow program.

> "In September, for example. Orenda noticed that the language had been changed on the letters of authorization for the PS 13 [Iroquois]. Since the end of August the year before, the limit of liability paragraph had been altered in the manner shown in italics: 'The liability of Her Majesty shall in no event exceed the last mentioned amount unless an increase is authorized in writing by or on behalf of the Minister *regardless of the work performed and expenditure incurred by your company'*. What alarmed Orenda was the fact that this clever addition, in the event of cancellation of the Iroquois, could leave the company wholly liable for termination costs."[405]

Considering David Golden's role in all of this it is small wonder that he worked so hard in later years to denigrate the Arrow and Avro. His reward for political loyalty was a position as head of Telesat Canada.

President Eisenhower and Prime Minister Diefenbaker

401 Cabinet minutes for 21 September, 1958.
402 Cabinet minutes for 22 September, 1958
403 Ibid.
404 Stewart: Shutting Down the National Dream, p.246
405 Dow: The Arrow, p. 184

Chapter 63

NOVEMBER SECRETS: Keeping Avro in the Dark

REMEMBRANCE DAY MACH RUN

On Remembrance Day 1958 Avro's new Chief Experimental Test Pilot "Spud" Potocki was scheduled to take the second Arrow, RL 202, up for high-speed flight control development work and aircraft clearance for higher Mach number tests. In a flight of an hour and a quarter Potocki later spoke:

> "I remember I took the aircraft up around Lake Superior in order to get a good stabilized run for my 1.96 Mach run. This run was from about Lake Superior to Ottawa. I mentioned Lake Superior and I am sure it was fairly close to there that the high speed run was started. I recall I had climbed to something like 46,000 feet to get cleared to the 1.96 Mach number…"

This exhilarating experience was followed by an even more exhilarating one! Potocki had a landing accident, blew all four mainwheels, left the runway, and tore off one main landing gear leg. As explained earlier, it is known he landed hot and long (fast and well past the beginning of the touchdown portion of the runway).

> "Having used a lot of fuel, I gave little or no thought to going around again, I just made the best of conditions as they seemed to be and attempted to complete a normal landing. In the meantime my brakes were still locked and I suppose I kept them that way not knowing that they were already burning into the drums… The heat generated by locked brakes burnt through the brake drums and the tires exploded. I lost control of the aircraft, which swung to the right off the runway." [406]

It was proposed by Avro that a flight control system malfunction might have contributed to this accident. At this time they were in the process of fully-enabling the computerized damping (and more fly-by-wire functions) into the pitch (or longitudinal) axis. In fact in the beginning flights this feature was not active and resulted in the Arrow then landing about 20 knots faster than had been projected. By the end of the program, with the longitudinal damping fully activated, landings at speeds of 140 knots were accomplished—right on original projections. Zura noticed, when he approached the stricken Arrow, that the elevators were deflected downwards 20 degrees. He thought this suggested that a flight control system malfunction had caused the braking problems and blown tires. Later photos, which had been confiscated from teenage trespassers, seem to debase the theory of a flight control glitch.

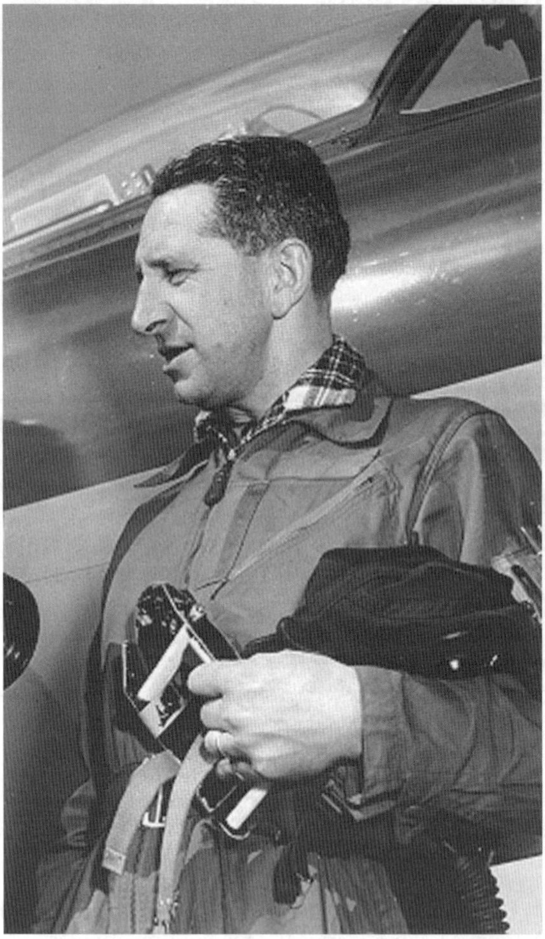

Waclaw "Spud" Potocki, a Battle of Britain Spitfire veteran, post-war British test pilot. Shown here standing beside a CF-100 while with Avro Canada. After Arrow cancellation he went to North American Aviation. (Avro photo)

One must wonder about this flight. On Remembrance Day Spud Potocki, a Polish Spitfire ace from the Battle of Britain, (with three other wartime ace fighter veterans also being Avro test pilots) on a long range mission from Toronto to Lake Superior, turned around, lit the afterburners, and ran an Arrow at nearly Mach 2 over the national Cenotaph in Ottawa, (when there was a high probability of politicians being present) and returned to base. Was it to perhaps make a point? Whatever the impact of the point was, it appears that he also ran the Arrow out of gas and made an approach that was too "safe" in terms of speed, and not safe enough in terms of distance.

And yet Avro and the RCAF were elated with what this flight proved. First of all it showed that all the previous criticisms and negative predictions of the NAE, NRC, NACA and even the mostly congratulatory 1955 appraisal by the British, were wrong. The Arrow 1, with 40% less ultimate thrust and 25% more weight in its engines than the Mark 2 version, had exceeded *Avro's own 1955 estimates.* In 1955 the Arrow *2* was only predicted capable of a maximum speed of Mach 1.9, yet a Mark 1 machine had just exceeded that! With this performance proven, Avro was able to refine the drag estimates with their computer modelling systems and produce more accurate projections for the Mark 2 and subsequent versions.

Because lower drag performance meant that the Arrow would easily exceed its Mach 1.5 requirement, Avro had wisely optimised the Iroquois engine for Mach 2 operation (thereby making it more saleable in the process), and was severely chastised by some in the RCAF, DND and government research institutions for having done it. It is interesting they were criticizing Avro for having exceeded their specifications. It is even more interesting to realize that the original request for tenders, to which Avro originally submitted the CF-105, encouraged the manufacturers to exceed the specifications which were to be considered minimum requirements only. Of course, the government should then have realised that Avro's Arrow 3 Mach 3+ version was credible, but this was never discussed. In fact, no Arrow version past the Mark 2 was discussed in Cabinet, not even a Mk. 2a version, with even more fuel, which Avro was suggesting as a relatively inexpensive improvement for the service aircraft. Yet these were the aircraft that the US had been rejecting, and which would, by extension, be known to senior DND and ministerial executives because they were part of the bargaining process. It is a rather glaring omission. It is an omission that puts the entire decision making process in a somewhat different light

Since September Avro had been pouring its own money into converting the Mark 2s on the line from the ASTRA system over to the Hughes MA-1 system, and reworking their old Falcon missile weapons pack to accept these missiles, plus the Genie nuclear air-to-air missile. (This latter satisfied the "modernity" question posed by the US through the CCSC and others for nuclear air-to-air missiles.) This system was entering service in the USAF in the F-106 Delta Darts and, in modified form, in the F-101B Voodoos. In other words, it was operational and would ease Arrow development, which was ready for weapon's and radar integration by that stage.

RCAF Arrow evaluation test pilot Jack Woodman later stated that when it came to Avro's flight test plan he "didn't understand it then, and don't understand it now". As of September 23rd, the plan was for engineering to run the test program in the cheapest way possible to get the very maximum effect in terms of clearing the basic aircraft for its full flight envelope and getting it towards being a serviceable aircraft that the RCAF could use with confidence. They were also employing a new development system whereby recordings of all the flight parameters were analysed by computer in many cases, with refinements being incorporated into each flight. This system, which is current today, involved a great deal of work to be done between flights. The USAF flight test system at the time consisted of flying their test aircraft until they broke something—not the most visionary nor safe way to go about things. Test flying of the F-22 Raptor, by comparison, has taken over ten years.

Avro test pilots

Chapter 64

POLITICAL DECEPTION

Also in November of 1958 the Conservatives secretly killed the Arrow, while also committing themselves to a contract to convert it to the MA-1 radar/fire-control system, apparently in an effort to prevent Avro from learning the program was going to be terminated: "The Minister of National Defense noted that there was a problem, in making up his main estimates for 1959-60, as to what assumption should be made about the decision to be taken…in regard to the Arrow aircraft and Iroquois engine. He proposed to assume that the contract would be cancelled and to include only the cancellation costs." In fact, in September, they had taken steps to ensure that Avro and Orenda would have to bear most of the cancellation expenses.

Avro was dumping their own money into the conversion from ASTRA/Sparrow to MA-1/Falcon/Genie.

> "In the past, it was the Government's practice to appropriate funds for each fiscal year ending March 31. These amounts were established as ceilings in the contracts from year to year… In January, 1959 it became apparent that some of the contract limits were about to be exceeded. The amount was estimated to be approximately $20,000,000 by the end of March. There would be an additional amount of some $40,000,000 [for long lead time items already ordered] in outstanding commitments…in the past the company would carry the over run with the concurrence of the Government.
>
> "The situation was now very different. The officers of the Department of Defense Production would not or could not discuss the matter as all matters concerning the Arrow were in the hands of the politicians. I was unable to contact the acting Minister of that Department, Mr. Green, as he refused to see me."[407]

As mentioned earlier, after Diefenbaker's September, 23rd announcement, he had disappeared, and nobody was talking to Avro. The handling suggests that the government actually intended for the company to be in the weakest possible position when cancellation came. This also suggests that the company itself was the ultimate target of some of the forces working for Arrow termination. This charge was laid by Kay Shaw, and subsequent investigation does nothing to diminish the strength of the allegation. Quite the contrary. After all, it is apparent that the Arrow was decided against in terms of the understanding and subsequent offers of the United States, as of the meetings in July and August 1958 between Dulles and McElroy and Pearkes and Fleming etc.. That they were working to keep the company in the dark is obvious from the documentation and the fact that in November of 1958, while deleting the Arrow from the FY 59-60 budget, they added conversion of the Mk. 2 Arrows to MA-1 standard to the FY 58-59 budget.

In Cabinet minutes from November 1958, on discussing the future of the Arrow program, MND Pearkes moved that since, in his opinion, Cabinet was relatively united on cancelling the Arrow, that it should be removed from DND budget projections for fiscal year '59-60. This was done, and, to the Treasury board and anyone in their circle, it would then be known that the program was dead. Nevertheless, and apparently in an effort to keep Avro misinformed, a budget amendment was later made in the same month to grant Avro money to convert the Mk. 2 Arrows from the Astra/Sparrow systems to the Hughes MA-1 system.

407 Smye: Canadian Aviation and the Avro Arrow

Chapter 65

FRENCH IROQUOIS ORDER

Minister of Defense Production Raymond O'Hurley's promises to Orenda V.P. Charles Grinyer are another November surprise. At that time the French government was negotiating for 300 Iroquois 2 engines to power their Mirage IVB bomber development. Through the (probably financial) grapevine they had heard that the Arrow and Iroquois projects were going to be cancelled by the Canadian government and informed Grinyer that they were withdrawing from the negotiation due to this belief. Grinyer's conviction was partly the result of a presumptuous article 'What led the Government to Junk the Arrow" in the *Financial Post* by Blair Fraser. As a result, Grinyer tendered his resignation from Orenda Engines Ltd. Avro was officially in the dark and sought assurances from the government that the decision had not been made. Fred Smye even flew to Ottawa to interview Fraser to find out if he had any inside information but was convinced that the journalist was merely surmising and offering plausible reasons.

> "I went to Ottawa to meet Blair Fraser of the *Financial Post* and Michael Barkway of the *Financial Times...* They were positive in their opinion...that the Arrow project was finished... When asked why they were so certain, they said it was reflected in the attitude of the PM during the press conference. Furthermore, this advice had been leaked by one or more of the Ministers. Apparently, the Ministers would talk more freely with the press than they would with the company.
>
> "The next meeting was with Howard Green, Minister of Public Works and acting P.M.. Mr. Diefenbaker was away on a European tour. He said, in effect, that he was unable to add anything to the PM's statement, which spoke for itself. Other meetings were held with Messrs Pearkes, O'Hurley and Hees...they all vehemently denied that the Arrow was in effect cancelled. The impression gained from this series of meetings and others which followed was that the RCAF had not stated a requirement for the Arrow and if a requirement...was established and if costs could be reduced, there was every likelihood that the airplane would be produced."[408]

Raymond O'Hurley was telephoned and he personally provided assurance to Grinyer that the program would not, in fact, be cancelled and that while there were concerns over cost and other matters, the current contract for 37 aircraft was not in any real danger. He was successful in convincing Grinyer to reverse his decision. This happened in November, when the government had secretly decided to cancel the whole program. Other sources sum up the information Avro and the RCAF were given as consisting of "get the price down and plane ready, and we'll probably order it into production." One must wonder, then, why the government wanted Avro kept deliberately in the dark about its future or lack thereof. Smye also referred to the company being forced by the government's secrecy to exceed its financial obligations in order to keep the program going:

> "There is also another small item which has never been mentioned and that is, that the company had technically exceeded its financial authority by some $50,000,000. The Government had forced the company into this position, the alternative to the company being to stop all work and discharge the staff of its own volition. In the strictest sense, had it wanted to, *and I personally believe it intended to, the Government could have bankrupt the entire A.V. Roe organization*"[409] [italics added]

As Kay Shaw wrote in the April 30th study:

> "It becomes quite clear, in the light of overwhelming evidence, that the Government was deliberately deceiving not only the public, but the Company, and deliberately putting it into an impossible position, in which it could take no action to save itself; so that, whatever course it took could be used against it. This, of course, has been done with great success since February. However, to create the necessary public opinion to allow this to be done, it was necessary for the Government and press to grossly deceive and mis-inform the public. If they had had a good case for cancelling the Arrow, they could certainly have allowed the public to be told the facts, and to listen to the evidence of informed authorities. That they could not do so,

tells its own story. The normal processes of democracy would have prevented them from carrying out this vindictive and costly blunder.

"The contradictory, false and inexcusable statements which Mr. Diefenbaker and Mr. Pearkes have given to the public as justification for this action imply that they are merely excuses to cover up the real reasons.

"In the face of all evidence to the contrary, the people of Canada were told the Arrow was obsolete, a costly failure, and money down the drain. They were told that we couldn't sell it, implying that no one wanted it, and suppressed evidence to the contrary." [410] [italics added]

Unfortunately, this author has found nothing to suggest that Edith Kay Shaw was wrong on any of these counts. A letter from Jim Floyd to the new President of Avro Aircraft, J.L. Plant shows how those who actually worked in air defense in Britain, Canada and the US felt, while adding some insights into the Arrow. Of course, it makes perfect sense.

7 November 1958

Mr. J.L. Plant

J.C. Floyd

THE ARROW CONTROVERSY

In view of the fact that on return from my recent trip to the United Kingdom I was shocked by the air of despondency and gloom which had settled on the program in Canada, I feel that it might be worthwhile to put on paper a summary of my own thoughts on the subject, since, from 3,000 miles away, I was able to take a more distant, and, I think, a clearer look at the overall situation.

My only reason for doing this is the hope that it might help to shake a few people out of the coma into which they appear to have lapsed at the moment.

In reading some of the press reports, I believe that too much emphasis is being put on the unemployment aspects of the decisions to come, and there is no doubt in my mind that if the Arrow was a "dud", or not required for the defense of Canada, we should not wish to proceed with it soley on the basis of "keeping people busy", since they would obviously be better employed on some other program that was of more significance.

My points, therefore, will be based on the facts as I now see them, from the military standpoint, and the defense of our country.

1. It is an established fact that for some time to come the manned bomber will be a major threat. There are, at the present time, over 4500 SAC type bombers in service in the world capable of carrying a nuclear offensive weapon, and the U.S.S.R. possesses more than half of this total.

2. Russia is known to be developing a new delta wing bomber (the Bounder).

3. Intelligent estimates put the ICBM as a real threat in 1964-65, with bombers still the maximum threat at that time.

CONCLUSION NO.1:

There is general agreement that the manned bomber will be the major threat for the next 5 to 6 years at least, and will continue to be a threat even after that time.

4. The considered opinion of the responsible people with whom I talked in the United Kingdom is that, as a result of recent deliberations, and from the results of Operation Sunbeam recently carried out as a U.K. defensive exercise, the manned interceptor is the best means of dealing with both high level and low level threats, and in the face of carcinatron jamming, which the Russians are known to possess, the two-man interceptor is considered to be the only means of reasonable defense available for some time to come, since it is considered that the enemy can completely jam out range information for the operation of a close controlled guided missile, including Bomarc. The people responsible for carrying out the defense of the U.K. (not the politicians), are now apparently convinced that the manned interceptor is an essential element in the defense of the U.K., and this decision was reached within the last two months.

5. We personally saw a demonstration of a new interception technique which has been studied at the Central Fighter Establishment in the U.K., and which was used in Operation Sunbeam with great success, even against low level attacks, assuming that all ground radar was jammed, i.e., conditions under which a defensive ground to air missile would be out of action.

It might be argued that the defense of the U.K. is somewhat different to that of Canada. However, the manned interceptor philosophy is obviously also being followed in the United States, where the F.108 long range interceptor is now being developed as another generation.

CONCLUSION No.2:

There now appears to be complete agreement, at least at the military level, that a manned interceptor is required for defense against the manned bomber threat, especially in the face of electronic jamming, which the Russians are known to possess at the present time, and the adoption of the Bomarc by the R.C.A.F., which is obviously to fill in some gaps in the eastern Bomarc cluster defending the United States, cannot be considered as an alternative to a manned interceptor.

---

6. Assuming then that everybody is in agreement with the first two conclusions, the question now arises as to which manned interceptor should Canada adopt. It may be argued that, despite the 1953 requirements at that time, which launched the Arrow into being, the threat and general defense picture has changed to the extent that, say, the F.106, which is available in the United States, while inferior to the Arrow, might now be adequate. However, I believe that the following points will show this not to be the case, although in the final analysis of course, the R.C.A.F. must decide what, in fact, is adequate for the defense of Canada.

1. The Arrow with the presently conceived armament pack containing MB-1 [Genie] and Falcon missiles plus fuel, has a subsonic radius of action, based on indications of drag from flight test, of around 500 N.M., with a supersonic combat and all allowances, which is considerably higher than any other aircraft in its class.

Whilst our Air Force have said they do not have any stated requirement for increased range, I believe that operating under jammed conditions without close control, which is the environment now assumed by all the experts in the U.K., range will be particularly important on this loiter type of mission suggested by C.F.E. as being the optimum defense, and as demonstrated in Operation Sunbeam.

2. The Arrow has more military payload capacity than any other contemporary bomber-destroyer, and this will be particularly useful when other versions of the aircraft are considered. For instance, we are carrying out a study to check whether an anti-ICBM missile can be carried and launched from the large armament bay, and this looks very promising.

In a country such as Canada, which can only afford one major aircraft project per generation, this flexibility has always been assumed to be very important.

3. At the price per aircraft quoted by Mr. Gordon, the Arrow in production appears to be approximately the same cost as the F.106 with the advantage that, in the case of the Arrow, the money stays in Canada.

7. The continuation of the Arrow program retains technical skills which have been collected together with great difficulty, and provides continuity in the aeronautical research and development programs in Canada which, if properly exploited, should give our country a firm foundation to participate in an active way in the future technical progress in astronautics, space research, etc.

The case, then, for the manned interceptor, and for the Arrow in particular, is ironclad to even the most unbiased Canadian, and this philosophy is also understood and agreed in the United Kingdom (without solicitation!).

How then can we account for the statements made by the Prime Minister and, more recently, by the Minister of Defense, who said the other day that nobody wanted the Arrow? (Incidentally, when we were at C.F.E. [Central Fighter Establishment] and Bomber Command, they both expressed a great desire to get their hands on a quantity of Arrows, and *C.F.E. in fact said that they believed they could adequately defend the United Kingdom with 200 Arrows, and they knew of nothing else that would be just as good.*)

We can only assume that the policy makers in Ottawa have not been provided with the facts (since they are obviously sincere and honest people), otherwise, they could only have come to the same conclusion as did the people who have the facts, assuming of course that their prime concern is the defense of Canada, rather than political expediency, which point we would not question.

Whatever the reason, the results have been the most confused and ridiculous situation ever to come up for a major decision by any Government, and Gilbert and Sullivan could not have done any better! The Ruskies must be almost falling off their chairs in amusement at the present situation, since Mr. Khruschchev could not have done a better job himself of creating such a ridiculous situation…"[411] [italics added]

Despite all the noise of super-technologies and rapidly emerging and ebbing threats, J.C. Floyd, and thus Avro Engineering, seemed to take a historically-supportable view of events on a number of still controversial yet highly technical topics—while still retaining a modicum of English grace and Canadian(?) humour. The current adoption by the largest military-industrial-financial complex on earth (the USA) of a high-altitude, twin-afterburning turbojet-powered long-range interceptor with internal weapons, low wing-loading and a high thrust-to-weight ratio (the F-22 Raptor), suggests Floyd & Co. were a pretty sage bunch. So why forty years of controversy? The answer appears to be that many people allied with the Canadian political system, particularly Conservatives, wish to protect the legacy of John Diefenbaker and the Conservative Party of Canada, if not the less-than-universal opinion that our politicians and leading civil servants have integrity and wisdom. Others sympathetic to American economic and foreign policy, and the idea that the United States is a technical leader in all spheres, protest against Avro for their own reasons.

408 Smye, The Arrow, unpublished, p. 87
409 Attachment, p. 13, of a letter dated 13 May, 1968, to Dr. J.J. Brown from Fred T. Smye
410 Report done on a freelance basis by Avroites George and E.K. (Kay) Shaw, released within Avro 30th April, 1959, quoted from Whitcomb: Avro Aircraft & Cold War Aviation
411 J.C. Floyd "Strictly Confidential" letter to J.L. Plant, President and GM of Avro Aircraft, dated 7 November, 1958.

Chapter 66

AIR FORCE TURBULENCE

Avro weren't the only ones fighting back. So were the RCAF and some leaders in the USAF and RAF.

> "In comments published in the October 1958 issue of Canadian Aviation Industries, DCINC NORAD A/M Roy Slemon, RCAF, stated: "Both Britain and the U.S. are developing new advanced interceptors against the 'manned bomber'. They know that Russia is developing very high altitude supersonic bombers and that the first line of defense against the bombers is, and will continue to be, the manned interceptor. The U.S. ...are bringing along the F108 to cope with even faster, heavier bomber threats anticipated years hence."

Slemon also stated there would be nothing to equal the Arrow for several years. He made those statements at NORAD HQ in Colorado Springs with NORAD CINC Earle Partridge standing beside him in a press scrum. It is apparent that the air chiefs were speaking publicly against the policies and intelligence being pushed, at Canada and Britain at least, by John Foster Dulles as Secretary of State, and Allen Welsh Dulles, as Director of the CIA.

Once Diefenbaker learned of these events, his anger at Slemon's response and general attitude to the Arrow are shown by an outburst he made in Cabinet on 22 December, 1958:

> "The Prime Minister said he had been shocked at the statement Air Marshal Slemon had made about the Arrow. It was not a question of whether Slemon's remarks had been misinterpreted or not but whether he should have made such a statement of that kind at all. Avro had put on a tremendous publicity campaign and this played right into their hands. If the government decided to continue development it would be accused of giving in to a powerful lobby. *Even if he thought the decision reached last September was wrong, he was determined, because of what had happened since, to adhere firmly to it.*"[412] [italics added]

That he would do, despite having receiving Performance Report 15 weeks earlier, along with a *fixed price* bid that only a fool could have refused.

In November there were other PR problems for the Conservatives set on cancellation. *Aviation News* for 10 November, 1958 said;

> "Arrow is bettering its performance predictions... Estimates are that the Orenda Iroquois engines...will give the Arrow a top speed of better than 2000 miles per hour, or in excess of Mach 3.0 at 40,000 ft. and above. The price will be 3.6 million per aircraft, for 100 Arrows as of now. Speculation is that it will be difficult for foreign governments as well as that of Canada to turn down a Mach 3 aircraft that is flying in early 1959. This would be several years before other Mach 3 aircraft now in development, and would give Canadian industry an achievement that could not be ignored."[413]

The writer was referring to projections for the Arrow Mk. 3 based on established Iroquois thrust. It wouldn't have been a 3.6 million dollar aircraft but even so, having the engine and basic aircraft flying in 1959 at that price did made the aircraft very attractive, but it was too late for anyone interested.

On 22 December, 1958, to satisfy Cabinet that they had exhausted all sales avenues (a point normally reached after an aircraft has been adopted by its country of origin and the production line is closing down), Pearkes mentioned:

> "...it was still his understanding that development would be terminated by March 31st. In Paris, the U.S. Secretary of Defense had made it quite clear that the US was not interested in the CF-105, even if it were equipped with the MA1 fire control system and the Falcon missile. *The U.S. had now decided not to proceed with the development of any new interceptor aircraft except the F-108 which was years in the future.* This was a long range aircraft of advanced design to be employed from bases in Alaska and Greenland. *This U.S. decision would strengthen the government's position in deciding to abandon the CF-105.*" [414]

How production of an Arrow clone as a next generation interceptor debased the Arrow requirement is, obviously, questionable. However Dulles, in cooperation with the CIA, convinced Pearkes to break with this NORAD plan and the intelligence on which it was based, which was that of NATO in general, and go with his plan for shared missile-defense technology and production with Canada, with Bomarc and SAGE being phase one of this new system. Presumably, the politicians, or some of them, believed the air forces would eventually accede to the wisdom of dropping their aircraft. In this cabinet meeting the Cabinet again deferred decision on the CF-105.

In early 1960 the US would be found having done a *volte face* and was telling Canada the maximum new contribution the country could make to the air defense of North America was the adoption of 66 F-101 Voodoos! In the words of the relevant Acting Secretary of the [US] Air Force in May, 1960:

> "As we have previously discussed, we have under very serious consideration an arrangement…which should prove to be of maximum benefit to both the United States and Canada. I believe that our defense position can be greatly enhanced…
>
> From our point of view, modern interceptor aircraft will be deployed as far north as practicable with very significant gains to North American defense as an immediate benefit."[415]
>
> Clearly then, no matter what US intelligence and John Foster Dulles had told the Canadians before the Arrow was cancelled, in early 1960 they still believed very much in the value of fighter-interceptors and their deployment in Northern Canada. Whether the Soviets had 100 or 1000 bombers, having long-range fighter-interceptors in Northern Canada were believed by the Republicans to afford "very significant gains to North American defense".

On 28 January, 1959 there was another Cabinet meeting held to try and get agreement to officially kill the program. Once again, fear of the budget estimates being made public and revealing that they had intended to kill the Arrow from at least as early as November was a factor in the discussion: "The Minister of Finance said that almost as soon as he tabled the main estimates for 1959-60 it would become known that there was no provision for expenditures on the Arrow beyond April 1st, except cancellation costs." [416]

> "The Prime Minister said he had received suggestions that Avro might be given a contract to produce, under licence, a Blackburn aircraft of United Kingdom design." This last passage suggests that perhaps Avro wasn't favoured for US licence contracts.
>
> "The Minister of National Defense said that the Blackburn aircraft was not in existence…and could not be available for three years. It had been studied as a…replacement for the F-86…in Europe. The N.A.T.O. military authorities had in mind two roles for the Air Division, all weather reconnaissance and strike… They had suggested, however, that the F 86…be replaced with an aircraft with a strike capability."[417]

Of course, the NATO authorities consisted of the US faction, led by CINC NATO General Norstad. As we have seen, European NATO authorities were primarily interested in all-weather, day or night interceptors like the CF-100 and its intended successor, the Arrow. As for the existence of the Blackburn aircraft, it was slightly more extant than the F-106C version. At least a prototype was eventually built of the Blackburn NA.39 though it was not ordered into production. Unfortunately the Arrow embarrassed it in, really, any role.

In this meeting it was also proposed that Canada might adopt the Grumman Tiger for the new NATO strike-recce role, and have Avro produce it. This option never materialised once the F-104 was selected in its place, whereas, of course, the RCAF, once the Arrow was disallowed, wanted something along the lines of the F-105 Thunderchief or the F-4 Phantom, which, for the money, would have made the Arrow an attractive all-purpose machine for all required roles. The US subsequently sold over 4,000 Phantoms, and certainly, had it been produced, the Arrow Mk. 2 would have taken a considerable portion of this market. Cabinet again deferred decision on the Arrow.

412 Cabinet minutes for 22 December, 1958
413 Aviation News, 10 November, 1958, quoted from Shaw report of April 30, 1959
414 Cabinet minutes, 22 December, 1958
415 Charyk, Joseph V.: "Memorandum for the Deputy Secretary of Defense", May 27, 1960
416 Cabinet minutes for 28 January, 1959
417 ibid

Chapter 67

RUMBLES IN THE CABINET

February 3rd found the Prime Minister being attributed with saying

> "...when the estimates for 1959-60 were tabled, questions would probably be asked about production of the Arrow aircraft. In the circumstances, it might be advisable to make a final decision now, and announce it when the estimates were tabled. He had discussed the Arrow and other defense matters with the Chiefs of Staff a few days ago, and they had said that no new military factors regarding either the manned bomber threat or developments to meet the threat had emerged since September which would have any bearing on the Arrow decision. He had raised with the Chiefs the possibility of the United Kingdom "Blackburn" replacing existing equipment in the Air Division. If this were a suitable aircraft, the work might be given to AVRO. However, they [the RCAF] favoured U.S. equipment."[418]

Meanwhile, didn't the joint defense agreements with the United States for integrated and interoperable systems already preclude UK equipment and wasn't this made official by the September 7th, 1958 purchasing policy directive they were keeping secret? Again it also seems possible that Avro was not favoured for US defense contracts. There ensued another argument about the cancellation with the Cabinet obstinately still refusing to recommend termination.

The next day, however, it seems Pearkes had had enough.

> "The Minister of National Defense reported again on the present state of the CF-105 Arrow program... The average cost per weapons system for a program of 100 operational aircraft was now estimated to be $7.81 million... Although the cost had been reduced from $12.5 million to this figure, he still considered that the production of 100 such aircraft could not be justified at this price..."

Unfortunately, Avro's last cost proposal wasn't mentioned, and it, in fact, reduced the price to about 5 million dollars a plane, even by the government's skewed method of costing. Pearkes was frustrated, and indicated his desire to cabinet to see the Arrow cancelled, and revealed his intention to essentially order the Chiefs of Staff Committee to recommend cancellation:

> *"He recommended that development of the CF-105 be discontinued and that the Chiefs of Staff present at an early date the recommendation they had been requested to make."*[419]

This certainly implies that he was making his earlier request at the CSC and CDC meetings into something more like an order. It wouldn't be the last time either, as we shall see in the NATO strike-recce aircraft selection process. In the ensuing discussion, Pearkes also mentioned the US offer made during the summer '58 meetings, when he mentions that the "Chiefs of Staff were considering the possibility of having some Bomarc squadrons moved from south of the border in the central U.S. to areas in western Canada. If it were felt that the manned bomber threat was decreasing, then it was obviously preferable to concentrate on defensive missiles rather than continue with the production of interceptors."[420]

He was obviously choosing his words carefully for equally obvious reasons. Dulles and McElroy had made these statements privately, as part of package US defense offers, and Pearkes had secretly taken them as his own line in Cabinet... in the process deceiving Cabinet into believing that the CSC was of the same opinion. While he and Diefenbaker were suggesting no military factors existed to support the production of the Arrow in the minds of the Chiefs of Staff, in fact the situation hadn't changed since August of 1958. The RCAF still wanted 169 to 178 Arrows for nine air defense squadrons, and there was a NATO aircraft replacement needing a decision too. The cut to 100 aircraft was made unilaterally by Diefenbaker in his 23rd September address apparently in line with American political advise.

Also in the 4 February meeting, it was noted that if:

> "...a question on the future of the Arrow were tabled, it should be answered in a way which would show that a decision on the program would be taken before March 31st. There was sufficient money in the estimates to pay for cancellation charges or to continue development for a while."

In reality, there was nothing but a small amount added for termination and to cover the MA-1C conversion. Pearson charged in the house that he had found no budget allocations in the estimates for cancellation charges or continuation. The above statement was really nothing more than a "response to questions" briefing by either the Prime Minister or Minister of Defense—and a non-factual one at that.

The discussion raged on. In response to the defenselessness of Canada in event of Arrow termination, more of the US offers of July were put forth:

> "If the Arrow development were cancelled and no alternative interceptors were produced in Canada...in the event of a war... Canada might have to rely on the U.S. to provide manned fighter defense."

Probably Pearkes replied:

> "Under the terms of the NORAD agreement, U.S. squadrons could be stationed temporarily on Canadian airfields."

Someone else must have wondered why the Arrow wasn't considered for Europe:

> "The re-equipping of the Air Division in Europe was a separate problem... The Cabinet Defense Committee would be considering this problem and would make recommendations in the near future to the Cabinet about it. Replacing the Sabres overseas would cost at least $350 million."

This price rose to over $420 million when all was said and done.

> "Cabinet agreed that the matter should be put before the Cabinet Defense Committee the following day."[421]

How the CDC responded to the increasing pressure is noted in minutes from 10 February, 1959. They didn't seem any more prepared to take the wrap for recommending Arrow cancellation than they had been earlier:

> "At the meeting of the Cabinet Defense Committee, the Chief of the Air Staff stated that the R.C.A.F. would need 100 to 115 interceptor aircraft for several years ahead. [Apparently Campbell's position was softening in view of his earlier insistence that Canada needed at least 169 Arrows.] These would have to be bought in the U.S. or, failing that, presumably U.S. squadrons would provide interceptor defense for Canada. This would be particularly awkward when, at the same time the 1st Canadian Air Division might be in the process of having its F-86 aircraft replaced...at a cost of $400 million to $500 million. *In effect, Canada would be defending Europe, and the U.S. would be defending Canada.*"

Obviously A/M Campbell didn't know that this is exactly what Pearkes had secretly agreed to do. It would also seem that he was resisting the rush to separate the Arrow from consideration for Canada's *traditional* NATO role. Someone countered in the meeting that

> "The proposal now being considered was to assign the Air Division a strike-attack role and equip it with aircraft suitable for the purpose."
>
> Pearkes had opened the discussion to state what the recommendations of the CDC had been.
>
> "The Minister of National Defense reported that the Cabinet Defense Committee had considered the recommendations *he had made* to the Cabinet that further development of the CF-105

be now discontinued and that the Chiefs of Staff be asked to present soon their recommendations on what requirements, if any, there were for additional air defense missile installations in Canada, and for interceptor aircraft of the nature of the CF-105 or alternate types."[422]

This seems to make the terms of reference clear for the CDC. The Minister was putting the cancellation to cabinet and the CDC was asked to provide alternatives, if any, for the Arrow. In other words, Pearkes, despite all his attempts at dodging and weaving, was, in the end, forced to accept responsibility for the cancellation of the Arrow program.

"During the meeting, *the Chairman of the Chiefs of Staff Committee* reported that the Chiefs of Staff had reviewed the position concerning the production of the CF-105, and were still of the opinion that the changing threat and the rapid advances in technology, particularly in the missile field, along with the diminishing requirements for manned interceptors in Canada, created grave doubts as to whether a limited number of aircraft of such extremely high cost would provide defense returns commensurate with the expenditures."[423]

That was it. CCSC Foulkes related that the Chiefs would only sign off on "grave doubts", they did not recommend cancellation of the Arrow. Again this showed the Chiefs were not in agreement on cancellation and was again his own opinion. While they mentioned that such a small number might not make economic sense in the strictly military sense, they didn't mention the common sense continuation would make, in terms of value to the overall Canadian economy, because this was not their responsibility. Of course the RCAF was fighting like crazy to save the program by this point, but too late.

And despite all of this, even the Cabinet refused to cancel the Arrow that day. The noose had been tightening bit by bit since they blindly signed off on NORAD only to learn its full nuclear implications, and the program was still on the books.

Things came to a head on February 14th. Due to Avro having received no reply to their inquiries on whether the government was seriously going to cancel even the 37 on contract, and being convinced otherwise, had exceeded their financial authority from the government's FY 58-59 authorizations. As Smye mentioned, the company was pouring in its own money.

"Mr. Green, as Acting Minister of Defense Production, stated that it was necessary to reach a decision as to whether or not a clear undertaking should be given to the Avro Aircraft Company that the government would meet the expenses involved in continuing development until notice of termination of the contract was given. The company noted that the costs of this development were, in fact, likely to exceed the financial limitations that had been previously set on the program, and that, unless these financial limitations were increased, it would be necessary for them now to begin laying off personnel until such time as the contract was extended or terminated. The Minister proposed to reply that the company would be paid reasonable and proper costs incurred under the development contract until it was terminated." [424]

Don Fleming wasn't having any of that however, and his response proves that nothing was set aside for Avro in case of cancellation other than what was in FY 58-59 estimates:

"The Minister of Finance said the Treasury Board had withheld approval of proposals of this kind in recent weeks and should not be over-ridden in this matter but should be allowed to consider it again.

"In the discussion of this proposal, the opinion was expressed that, if this undertaking were now given to Avro, it would increase the government's expenditure undesirably on this contract; no such undertaking should be given but, instead, a decision should be taken forthwith on the termination of the development contract. On this latter proposal it was noted that the Cabinet was clearly of one mind that work on the Arrow should be discontinued. A decision on the matter had practically been taken some weeks ago, but it was thought that the Cabinet Defense Committee should meet and discuss it again… This had now been done and the committee had recommended termination."[425]

Of course, this was a gross distortion, Foulkes had related only that the Chiefs had "grave doubts" about such a high cost for so few airplanes. The last meeting of the CDC was also supposed to discuss Arrows for the NATO role but this was deflected.

Even then, Cabinet was not of one mind.

> "It was pointed out that the government faced a serious decision in regard to the equipment of the Air Division of the R.C.A.F. in Europe. The replacement for the F-86 in the Air Division might cost over $500 million… It was also pointed out that the government faced the possibility that the RCAF might be using interceptor aircraft to defend Europe but not to defend Canada itself, which would be defended by American interceptors."

This argument was deflected by statements to the effect that the NATO purchase had no bearing on the decision for or against Arrows for NORAD, although it should have because it effected the price of the aircraft dramatically. Even so, Cabinet again deferred the cancellation, but agreed that the deed would be done on 17 February, 1959. By this time Avro Aircraft was technically insolvent, and was dragging A.V. Roe Canada down too.

> "The Prime Minister said a draft announcement on the termination of the development contract for the Arrow had been prepared. It included a section on arrangements with the United States for production sharing and a section on the acquisition by Canada of nuclear weapons for defense…
>
> "The Minister without Portofolio (Mr. Macdonnell) reported that, the previous day in Toronto, the Premier of Ontario had spoken to him in strong terms about the effects of terminating the Arrow contract upon the municipalities in the vicinity of Malton.
>
> "The Minister of Finance said Mr. Frost had also spoken to him in pungent language about work on the Arrow being stopped. Mr. Frost had complained about so little notice being given to Avro, and had asked why other contracts could not be given to the company."

Despite this, Cabinet finally

> "… agreed that the development of the Arrow aircraft and Iroquois engine be discontinued, effective as of the time of announcement; that this announcement be accompanied by one on defense production-sharing arrangements with the United States, and that notes already prepared on Bomarc, SAGE and radar cost-sharing plans be exchanged with the US government." [426]

From the progress of cost-sharing offers as detailed in *Avro Aircraft & Cold War Aviation,* it seems apparent those notes couldn't be exchanged because US cost-sharing was tied to Arrow cancellation, as is suggested in the US Memorandum on Defense Production Sharing (DPS) already cited. In fact the DPS deal wouldn't be announced until after the Arrow cancellation, many months after it had been negotiated, (similar to the NORAD agreement) probably because they had no concrete defense production "allocations" from the United States to show for it. From the Eisenhower Library a privileged cabinet document was preserved and eventually found its way to Palmiro Campagna. It reads, in part:

"The decision to terminate the CF-105 was predicated in part on the agreements to provide Canada with better chances to share in production of defense items of mutual interest. The Deputy Minister of Defense Production has stated in effect that if production sharing does not work, Canada has no alternative but to use her limited defense budget for whatever items she is able to produce, whether or not it makes a maximum contribution to North American defense."[427]

The last sentence shows Deputy Minister David Golden's negotiation position with the Americans to secure DPS contracts from the United States. One wonders how many teeth Golden's bark presented considering that the Americans almost certainly knew that the Arrow was dead as of July 1958, or as of the Cabinet Purchasing Directive of September, or when it was deleted in November from Defense Department budget estimates for 1959.

Finally, on 19 February, 1959, Diefenbaker was moved to set the final date.

> "The Prime Minister said that he would make a statement announcing the termination of the Arrow contracts in the house the following day. The C.B.C. Television Service would present a program on the following Sunday or Monday on the development of the Arrow. It would be well to make the statement before the broadcast."[428]

So the CBC was in a way the final prompt in the Arrow cancellation, for bizarre reasons. It shows that publicity is a powerful motivator in government circles. It is a situation that all too often breeds secrecy.

Finally, on 20th February, 1959, Diefenbaker rose in the House and cancelled the Arrow with no notice being given to Avro. Due to the abrupt cancellation, Avro was forced to lay off all its employees and sort out union seniorities going back to WW II. 14,900 people walked when the government failed to respond to a 4:00 deadline to either provide Avro with some kind of alternative, or monies to allow an orderly shutdown. No reply came. In fact Avro first got word of the cancellation from radio reports and a stock broker. One of the points made by the Conservatives was that the Arrow wasn't saleable, despite their best efforts. A secret message from the Royal Air Force soon arrived suggesting otherwise:

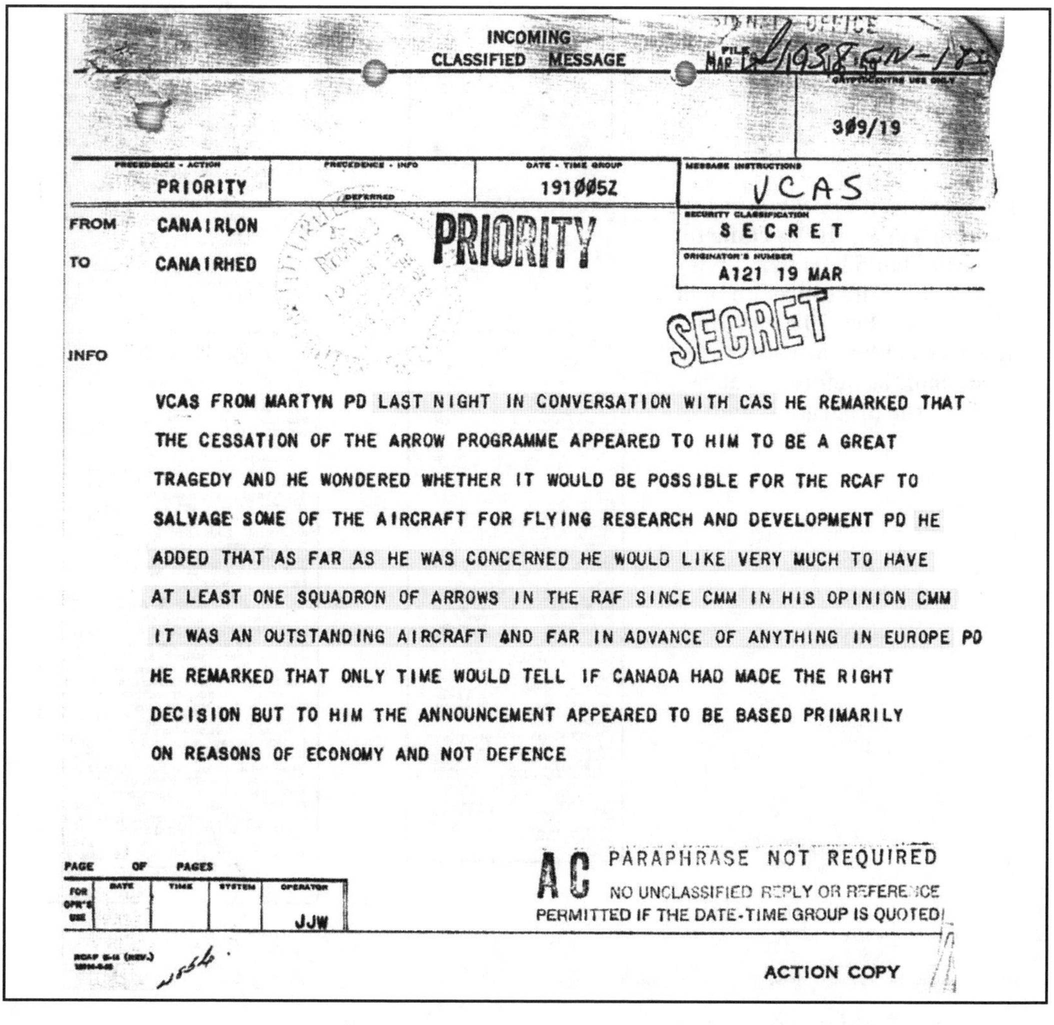

INCOMING CLASSIFIED MESSAGE

S1938-CN-180

309/19

PRECEDENCE - ACTION: PRIORITY

DATE - TIME GROUP: 191005Z

MESSAGE INSTRUCTIONS: VCAS

FROM CANAIRLON

TO CANAIRHED

INFO

PRIORITY

SECURITY CLASSIFICATION: SECRET

ORIGINATOR'S NUMBER: A121 19 MAR

SECRET

VCAS FROM MARTYN PD LAST NIGHT IN CONVERSATION WITH CAS HE REMARKED THAT THE CESSATION OF THE ARROW PROGRAMME APPEARED TO HIM TO BE A GREAT TRAGEDY AND HE WONDERED WHETHER IT WOULD BE POSSIBLE FOR THE RCAF TO SALVAGE SOME OF THE AIRCRAFT FOR FLYING RESEARCH AND DEVELOPMENT PD HE ADDED THAT AS FAR AS HE WAS CONCERNED HE WOULD LIKE VERY MUCH TO HAVE AT LEAST ONE SQUADRON OF ARROWS IN THE RAF SINCE CMM IN HIS OPINION CMM IT WAS AN OUTSTANDING AIRCRAFT AND FAR IN ADVANCE OF ANYTHING IN EUROPE PD HE REMARKED THAT ONLY TIME WOULD TELL IF CANADA HAD MADE THE RIGHT DECISION BUT TO HIM THE ANNOUNCEMENT APPEARED TO BE BASED PRIMARILY ON REASONS OF ECONOMY AND NOT DEFENCE

PAGE OF PAGES

OPERATOR: JJW

AC PARAPHRASE NOT REQUIRED

NO UNCLASSIFIED REPLY OR REFERENCE PERMITTED IF THE DATE-TIME GROUP IS QUOTED

ACTION COPY

On February 23rd the Cabinet met to discuss political defense strategy. It was also mentioned in the discussion that there "had been a prospect of Canadair obtaining a large U.S. contract for radar picket aircraft but, unfortunately, this seemed to be less and less hopeful in view of the pressure from the aircraft industry in the U.S."

So much for defense production sharing! The tack taken by Diefenbaker also showed that he thought the Avro layoffs could be used to justify harsher treatment, in the House and in the media, of the company in the wake of the cancellation.

A few years later, Arthur Sylvester, then Assistant Secretary of Defense for Public Information (i.e., propaganda) in the United States, crystallized a tactic used to one extent or another by not only governments, but most large, centrally-organised corporate entities: "…it would seem basic; all through history, that it's an inherent government-right to lie, if necessary, to save itself." It is one thing to lie to adversaries however, and quite another to deceive the public—in anything claiming to be a democracy at least. An ill-informed citizenry is the greatest enemy of a functional democracy, as Thomas Jefferson observed: "Yes, we did create a near perfect Republic. But will they keep it, or will they, in the enjoyment of plenty, lose the memory of freedom. Material abundance without character is the surest way to destruction."

The story as it appeared in the London Times. Dulles came to Ottawa (Jan 5 left) just a few weeks before the cancellation of the Arrow, (Feb 20 right) but the decision had already been made months before to cancel the program.

MR. DULLES DUE IN OTTAWA TO-DAY

STRONG TEAMS FOR ECONOMIC TALKS

FROM OUR OWN CORRESPONDENT

OTTAWA, JAN. 4

Two meetings designed to promote greater understanding between Canada and the United States are due to take place in the next few days. To-morrow Mr. Dulles, accompanied by a strong team of Ministers and officials, is due here for two days' discussions with the Diefenbaker Administration. Next weekend a parliamentary delegation led by the Speakers of the Senate and Commons is to meet Congress leaders in Washington.

Among those with Mr. Dulles will be Mr. Benson, the United States Secretary of Agriculture, Mr. Anderson, Secretary of the Treasury, Mr. Lewis Strauss, Secretary of Commerce, and Mr. Seaton, Secretary of the Interior. Although the Canadian-American economic committee was formed five years ago, this will be only the fourth time it has met. From certain strains and difficulties that have arisen between the two neighbours in recent years over trade, it might be asked what purpose it has achieved, but it must be realized that while Canadian Cabinet Ministers are in a much better position to commit the Government to various policies, the American members have to answer not only to the President but also to Congress.

DOMINATING FIGURE

At to-morrow's talks Canada will be represented by Mr. Churchill, the Minister of Trade, Mr. Fleming, Minister of Finance, Mr. Harkness, Minister of Agriculture, and Mr. Sidney Smith, Minister of External Affairs; behind the scenes will be the dominating figure of the Prime Minister.

Although on the surface there may seem sometimes to be an atmosphere of discord between the two countries, some believe here that relationships between the Diefenbaker Administration and Washington have noticeably improved in recent months. Cooperation on continental defence and future strategy is remarkably close; more difficult is the question of what contribution Canada can make towards North American defence production Canada has the Avro Arrow, a fine though costly supersonic interceptor aircraft, and a decision on whether to put it into production will be made by the Government at the end of March. The Americans seem to prefer their own manned interceptors for first-line defence, and unless other western countries are prepared to buy the Arrow, its future looks gloomy.

There is some conjecture whether the United States Navy might not look favourably on the Canadian Argus, an aircraft developed for anti-submarine patrolling. Certainly if the United States were to share with Canada some of its contracts for the defence of North America, political embarrassments in Canada in this field might be overcome.

DISCUSSION ON QUOTAS

Among the subiects expected to be discussed are American quotas on oil, lead, and zinc, and the current agitation in the United States on the need for restrictions on Canadian fish, aluminium, and food products. The Americans, on the other hand, may well have some searching questions to ask about the anti-dumping legislation passed by the Government during the last session of Parliament.

CANADA DROPS JET INTERCEPTOR

PURPOSE "OVERTAKEN BY EVENTS"

FROM OUR CORRESPONDENT

OTTAWA, FEB. 20

The Canadian Prime Minister, Mr. Diefenbaker, to-day announced the Government's decision to terminate now the development of the Avro Arrow CF105 jet interceptor aircraft and the Iroquois engine, on which $303m. (£108m.) has been spent. The decision not to proceed with production had been announced last September, but at that time the final decision on development was deferred.

Mr. Diefenbaker said that the development of the aircraft and the engine was successful, but construction of the CF105 had been overtaken by events. The bomber threat that it was to counter had diminished, and alternative means of meeting this had developed earlier than was expected. Potential aggressors were now more likely to put their effort into missile development. The CF105 could not be fully operational before the middle sixties, and it seemed likely that by then the missile would be the major threat.

He also said that Canada would assume financial responsibility for one-third of the cost of introducing the American Bomarc guided missile and Sage electronic system and computing equipment into Canada's air defence, and of extending the Pinetree radar control system by adding stations. The Canadian share was to cover the construction of bases and unit equipment, the United States share covering the technical equipment. Both countries recognized the need for Canada to share in the production of technical equipment, and it was expected that Canadian industry would have a fair share of the work.

CONTROL OF WARHEADS

"Under the irresistible dictates of geography, the defence of North America has become a joint enterprise of Canada and the United States," Mr. Diefenbaker added. The two Governments were examining questions associated with the acquisition of nuclear warheads for the Bomarc and other weapons, but it was Canadian Government policy not to undertake the production of nuclear weapons in Canada. It was considered expedient that the ownership and custody of nuclear warheads should remain with the United States.

Mr. Lester Pearson, leader of the Opposition, welcomed the announcement that nuclear weapons were not to be manufactured in Canada, but thought it would be intolerable to have United States squadrons with nuclear weapons on the same airfield as Canadian aircraft without such weapons.

418 Cabinet minutes, 3 February, 1959
419 Cabinet minutes for 4 February, 1959
420 ibid.
421 all quotes from Cabinet minutes for 4 February, 1959.
422 Cabinet minutes February 10, 1959
423 Ibid.
424 Cabinet minutes 14 February, 1959.
425 Ibid.
426 Cabinet minutes, 17 February, 1959
427 Campagna, Requiem For a Giant, Appendix: White House Cabinet Paper-privileged-secret, 3 April, 1959
428 Cabinet minutes, 19 February, 1959

Chapter 68

DISSENSION AMONG THE CHIEFS

In April 1959 there were hearings on air defense in the US Congress. CINC NORAD and other heads of the Air Forces of the United States were called upon to testify. Some of their statements are recorded below:

General Twining USAF AMC:

> "The Russians are now building a new bomber far beyond the capabilities of the Bear and Bison long-range bombers. We do not know what it is yet, but it is an advanced heavy bomber. [It was the Bounder, and the air forces of the West had known about it for a long time.]

General White, CAS USAF:

> "The advantage of the bomber over the ICBM is – it can carry multiple nuclear weapons – a much bigger yield and variety, and can be deployed. It has greater potential for use in limited war."[429]

General Earle Partridge, CINC NORAD:

> "At the present time the Soviets can attack us only with bombers. Our intelligence estimates reveal that they will improve the quality of their bombers and, in a few years, will have a supersonic bomber force. This means that we must not only maintain the defenses,…but must also improve them, so we can counteract a supersonic attacking force. The aim of the North American Defense command is to hit an attacker as far away as possible, i.e., over the Arctic. Bomarcs are useless for this function and are intended only as 'defense in depth' to give the SAC 'time to get away' and to provide limited 'point defense'.

Partridge also said that they needed

> "The fastest, highest flying, longest-range interceptor available for as long as we can foresee," adding that there was "unfortunately" nothing in the inventory to suit this threat "except the F-101."

Contrast this statement to the advice Pearkes received, including powerful statements that the USA "has lots of aircraft" and memos to that effect during the July and August 1958 negotiations:

> "Existing and programed interceptors include F4D, F-86, F-89, CF-100, F-101, F-102, F-104, CF-105, and F-106 aircraft…

From Partridge's words, one would assume the CINC NORAD didn't consider even the F-106 to be a suitable first line of defense for North America, and obviously not the Bomarc either. All of the above mentioned aircraft were subsonic except for the F-101, F-102 (which was barely supersonic), F-106 and the CF-105 Arrow.

Once the Arrow was dead and Canada had committed to purchasing Bomarcs, with American monetary support, the United States unilaterally cancelled their plans to adopt the Bomarc, and the CAGE (Completely Automatic Ground Environment) system that had been counted on for missile defense, in anything like the strength that the United States had proposed during the run-up to Arrow cancellation. As Acting Secretary of the USAF, Joseph Charyk wrote to his Deputy Secretary of Defense on 27, May, 1960:

> "As I have mentioned previously, a sensitive political situation has arisen in Canada due to a series of events involving the CF-105 cancellation in favour of BOMARC and SAGE joint procurement with the U.S., followed by [unilateral US] reduction in BOMARC and SAGE super combat centres."[430]

Yet 5 September, 1958 Cabinet minutes show Pearkes proposing:

> "[The US authorities] had also said they would be prepared to relocate northwards some of their proposed BOMARC installations."

The Conservatives finally developed a sense of outrage with their erstwhile Republican friends and political counterparts. In formerly Top Secret minutes from the meetings which were held with the US relating to the issues described above,

> "Mr. Green stated that they were told two years ago that the manned bomber was on its way out and that is why they cancelled the Arrow. Now they have to go back and say that both are still needed. Mr. Fleming referred to the fact they tried to interest the Americans in buying the Arrow at the Paris Conference but had been turned down flat by Mr. McElroy. Mr. Pearkes...said perhaps the expectation of two years ago that the bomber threat was lessening has not been fulfilled. At the same time he said we expected Bomarcs to cover the whole country. These had been reduced, and therefore some more protection to the western part must be made in those areas which were to be protected by Bomarc. *It wasn't fair*, he said, *for Canada to fill this western gap created by the Americans all by themselves."* [431]

Mr. Gates, leading the US negotiating team continued to press the Canadians to accept an F-101 Voodoo for Canadair transport's defense production sharing deal, to both improve US defense and to solve the "sensitive political situation," but the Canadians demurred. Once bitten twice shy.

While Dulles, McElroy and cohorts had previously convinced Canada's Conservatives that the manned interceptor was obsolete as of mid-1958, further negotiations to introduce the F-101B into the Canadian air defense system belie the true opinions of those who counted in American air defense...but only after the Arrow was finished:

> "Mr. Gates [new US Secretary of the Air Force and head of a US air defense delegation,] said [to Deputy Minister DDP; David Golden, Howard Green; Minister for External Affairs, and Minister of Finance; Donald Fleming] you must decide the policy first. Do you want the fighters [the last 66 McDonnell F-101Bs off the McDonnell production line in St. Louis), and then we can argue about price. Mr. Green stated that *they were told two years ago that the manned bomber was on its way out and that is why they cancelled the Arrow.* Now they have to go back and say that both are still needed. Mr. Fleming referred to the fact that they tried to interest the Americans in buying the Arrow at the Paris Conference but had been turned down flat by Mr. McElroy...
>
> "Mr. Pearkes...said that [at the same time] we expected Bomarcs to cover the whole country. These had been [unilaterally, by the US,] reduced, and therefore some protection to the western part [of Canada] must be made in those areas which were to be protected by Bomarc. It wasn't fair, he said, for Canada to fill this western gap which had been created by the Americans by themselves."[432] [italics added]

A haste for resolution, perhaps borne of embarrassment, surfaced in Gates's subsequently recorded response:

"Mr. Gates referred once again that we must get this aircraft deal settled if at all possible because they [presumably the American politicians] could not afford to stand up to the political pressures at home too long."[433]

This changing of the subject was interrupted by an adjournment, and, upon the recommencement of ceremonies on the following day, the record shows further efforts by Gates to force the issue to a favourable result for America: "Mr. Gates suggested that the matter [Canada buying American F-101s] has already been discussed in the press and therefore it would be wise if it could be settled as soon as possible, especially at this meeting."[434]

Further to these discussions of interceptors, which the Americans obviously viewed as primary to the first line of defense of North America, a public relations ploy regarding missile defense was proposed. It was to be euphemistically-termed “Sky Shield”, and was, logically, to include Bomarc as the first in a series of defensive *nuclear* missiles using an upgradeable SAGE system, both of which would eventually furnish a comprehensive defense against bombers, and, later, missiles too. All Canada had to do was sign on the line, committing itself to perpetually helping finance this technologically-unlikely security blanket.

“Referring to “SKY SHIELD”, Mr. Green said that he would have to take back the proposed *public relations policy* to the Prime Minister. As to the question that the first [public] announcement [of a bi-lateral policy to evolve such a system] had been agreed to, the reply [from the responsible Canadians] was yes.”[435]

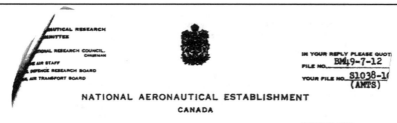

UTICAL RESEARCH
MITTEE
ONAL RESEARCH COUNCIL
CHAIRMAN
E AIR STAFF
DEFENCE RESEARCH BOARD
AIR TRANSPORT BOARD

IN YOUR REPLY PLEASE QUOTE
FILE NO. BM19-7-12
YOUR FILE NO. S1038-1((AMTS)

NATIONAL AERONAUTICAL ESTABLISHMENT
CANADA

E OF THE DIRECTOR

MONTREAL ROAD
OTTAWA, ONT.

SECRET

28 September, 1953

Air Vice Marshal D.M. Smith,
Air Member for Technical Services,
Royal Canadian Air Force Headquarters,
Ottawa, Ontario.

Dear Air Vice Marshal Smith:

A.V. Roe C/105 Design Study

In reply to your letters of 15 July and 18 September, 1953, and Group Captain Foottit's request on Thursday, September 22, we have not yet finished our assessment of the C/105 design proposal, but our preliminary comments on the Cornell wind tunnel tests are:

Although the measurements extended only to a Mach number of 1.2, and although we disagree with the claim that shock wave reflections are entirely cancelled at the wind tunnel walls, we consider that the tests were well done and that, within their range, they bear out the A.V. Roe estimates of most of the Aerodynamic parameters affecting the aircraft performance. It is important that wind tunnel measurements be extended to higher Mach numbers as soon as possible.

For Mach numbers above 1.2, we have extrapolated the Cornell data using the A.V. Roe estimates as a guide. With RB-106 engines, the attainable sustained load factor at M = 1.5 and 50,000 ft. altitude under combat conditions with half fuel gone is found to be very close to the required value of 2.0. (Actually it was found to be 2.05 using the A.V. Roe estimate for minimum drag coefficient and 1.85 for the corresponding NAE estimate, which was 20 percent higher at this Mach number). The calculations show that the load factor is extremely sensitive to the elevator effectiveness

429 This and the preceding quote are from the Shaw report of 30 April, 1959
430 Charyk, Joseph V.: Memorandum for Deputy Secretary of Defense, 27 May, 1960
431 Directorate of History, minutes of bilateral air defence representatives, 1960 (Annex 39)
432 Formerly TOP SECRET May 1960 summary of US/Canadian bi-lateral negotiations on air defence, Canadian Directorate of History, originally sourced from Campagna, Storms of Controversy, Appendices.
433 ibid.
434 ibid.
435 ibid.

[redacted] 4.

CABINET PAPER—PRIVILEGED

Property of the White House—For Authorized Persons Only

CURRENT SITUATION

The present strong interest of Canada in production sharing is the result of the decision made by the Canadian government in September to curtail drastically the CF 105 supersonic interceptor aircraft program, and to introduce into the Canadian air defense system the U.S. produced BOMARC missile and SAGE control equipment. This decision recognized the rapid strides being made in missiles by both the U. S. and Russia and the high cost of the CF 105 in relation to its potential contribution to North American defense.

The specially developed Astra fire control and Sparrow missile systems for the CF 105 were terminated in September, with the subsequent cancellation of the complete program 20 February. Reaction to this decision from the press and the opposition has been most unfavorable, and will greatly increase the strong pressures which have existed on production sharing.

With over $300 million already expended in the development of this sytem and a potential production program of another $1.25 billion for 100 aircraft, this was a heavy blow to Canadian industry and the pride of their people. The implications on the Canadian economy can be measured in terms of their defense budget, which is in the order of $1 billion annually.

The decision to terminate the CF 105 was predicated in part on the agreements to provide Canada with better chances to share in production of defense items of mutual interest. The Deputy Minister of Defense Production has stated in effect that if production sharing does not work, Canada has no alternative but to use her limited defense budget for whatever items she is able to produce, whether or not it makes a maximum contribution to North American defense.

Since September negotiations have been underway on the basis of Canada paying one-third of the cost of two 30 missile BOMARC sites, one SAGE super combat center and a radar improvement program. The Canadian share of $125 million would be associated with site construction and unit equipment, with the United States share of about $250 million applied to the procurement of BOMARC and SAGE technical equipment. It has been agreed that this is the only practical way to make the split, however, the Canadians fear it will not give them any assurance of sharing in the production of the electronic and missile hardware. Since construction on Canadian soil is normally done by Canadian contract, Canadians are assured that substantially all of their $125 million will be spent in Canada in any event. However, they do not want to become a "brick and mortar" economy.

The Air Force has consistently opposed any agreement to assure Canada a given share of the production, based on the conviction that technical competence, costand delivery considerations must be the deciding criteria. If Canadian competence can be demonstrated and reasonable decisions agreed to on individual items, it is our position that the end result will be a reasonable share for the Canadians.

From the recent statement by the Prime Minister to Parliament it is assumed that the Canadians have accepted the U. S. position on this matter.

Dated April 3, 1959

CABINET PAPER CJ-59-54

For Information 3-5-59

[redacted]

US document showing that the Arrow had been slated for cancellation months before the actual cancellation. The US government knew but no one told Avro.

Chapter 69

THE NATO STRIKE RECCE AIRCRAFT

During deliberations on the aircraft required to assume Canada's new offensive NATO role, we have already seen that the government forced the Arrow out of consideration and then forced out a British aircraft that Avro could have built, and also aircraft that the RCAF preferred. They then ignored Avro's lower bid for the aircraft that was politically chosen for the role:

> "Ideally, requesting three companies to bid on a fair price basis was the best approach. But firm price bidding was unrealistic in the present circumstances.
>
> As for the engines, there were two possibilities for production: Canadian Pratt Whitney [sic] or Orenda Engines Limited. It would, however, be an incompatible situation if a subsidiary of Pratt Whitney were chosen to manufacture a General Electric engine as the two firms are direct competitors in the United States. [But it was fine for Canadair, owned by a direct competitor of the F-104's producer—Lockheed—to build the F-104 Starfighter.]
>
> "The Minister recommended,-
>
> a) that the Lockheed F-104G [Starfighter] be selected as the replacement for the Sabre squadrons in Europe;
>
> b) that the airframe contract be allocated to Canadair…
>
> c) that the engine contract be allocated to Orenda Engines on a firm price basis.
>
> "The Minister without Portfolio (Mr. Macdonnell) said that it was the Minister of Finance's understanding that this matter would not be considered in his absence.
>
> "The Minister of National Defense said it would be very embarrassing to him when his estimates were before the House on Thursday next, to announce that the Air Division was being re-equipped but not to be able to say with what aircraft…
>
> "Mr. Pearkes added that the Cabinet Defense Committee had had the report of the Minister of Defense Production before it at its last meeting. Since then the Chiefs of Staff had discussed the matter further with Defense Production Officials, and had stated that they would be willing to go along with…the Lockheed F-104G."[436]

Besides it being one of the cheapest aircraft the RCAF would accept, another reason it was chosen was because of a DDP report mentioning Canadair would get an additional order to build parts of German Starfighters. It was this, and Pearkes' pressure, that caused the RCAF to select the F-104, not military considerations. The RCAF, once it had been forced to change from an all-weather interceptor role, had stated a preference for an aircraft in the class of the F-105 Thunderchief or the F-4 Phantom.

The Republic F-105 Thunderchief also was the subject of a defense production sharing offer between Republic and Avro. The RCAF Thunderchief would use the Iroquois engine and be built by Avro, and Republic would sell some Iroquois-engined Thunderchiefs to the USAF. This deal was struck between Mundy Peale of Republic and Fred Smye and was promoted to the Premier of Ontario. Peale himself went to Ottawa to discuss the venture but came away with nothing.[437] One wonders what the concerned American politicians thought of Mundy Peale's independent negotiations with Avro.

Once again, Pearkes' unilateralism invoked an argument.

> "It was undesirable for Canadair to be given most of the work in view of the fact that it was fairly busy now and in the light of Avro's position following the cancellation of the Arrow. The Minister of National Defense, in his opening statement on his estimates, should make it quite clear that the Arrow could not have been used for the strike attack role in Europe.

"The implication of the views of the Chiefs of Staff was that they would prefer a better aircraft than the F-104G if more money were available. It would be highly embarrassing if…it became known that the Chiefs of Staff were, on military grounds, in favour of a different and presumably more efficient type of aircraft. *The Chiefs of Staff should be asked to submit a firm recommendation on the F-104G…before the Cabinet reached a decision.*

"The Cabinet approved the choice of the F-104G to re-equip 8 squadrons of the Air Division in Europe, subject to receiving a firm recommendation from the Chiefs of Staff for it…"[438]

As we see above, it was the politicians, not the RCAF, who selected the F-104. On the 13th August Cabinet met again:

"The Minister of Defense Production reported that tenders for the manufacture of the Lockheed F-104G had been received from de Havilland, Canadair and Avro aircraft. The bid of de Havilland was almost 50% higher than the other two who had provided almost identical tenders… The figure from Avro was slightly lower than that of Canadair but did not appear realistic.

"*It was the view of the Department of Defense Production that it would not be possible to support three major aircraft firms in Canada.*"

"The Minister of Finance said…the Treasury Board…had recommended that Canadair be offered the first opportunity to make its proposal a firm bid..." [italics added]

Someone else noted during the discussion:

"By awarding the contract to Canadair, the government would, of course, find itself in a position of having to defend the award to the second lowest bid. *The Defense Production Department had added $3.3 million to the Canadair bid on the assumption that labour costs might rise. However…by removing this amount the difference between Avro and Canadair had been reduced to $1.3 million.*"[439] [italics added]

This of course, means that Avro's bid on the airframe was 4.6 million less than Canadair's, but, as we have already seen, Pearkes was determined to award the contract to Canadair and so was the DDP and Ministry of Finance. This must, surely, prove that the government made it their official policy to kill Avro.

The next day strategy, in the form of a discussion of some responses to questions were proposed by Diefenbaker. A couple of interesting points emerge:

"The fundamental question was whether Canada could afford to maintain three major aircraft plants. The industry was overexpanded… The Canadair plant, though owned by a U.S. parent company, could reasonably be regarded as a Canadian establishment. It received no orders from the parent company…Even if A.V. Roe received the contract, it would merely postpone the evil day."[440]

Profoundly interesting logic. In other cabinet discussions it is mentioned that the Treasury Board had also determined that "a rebuilding of Avro was not in the national interest." And to think had Arrows been purchased for the NATO role, they would have been priced at 2.6 million each. The F-104 came in at 3.5 million each in the final analysis. Half the plane for more money! But when the F-104 was originally offered, the price was quoted as two million dollars each.[441]

436 Cabinet minutes, 30 June, 1959
437 Dow, and Smye books.
438 Cabinet minutes, 30 June, 1959
439 Cabinet minutes, 14 August, 1959
440 ibid
441 Annex to government of Canada documents describing the price and characteristics of the aircraft considered for the NATO strike-recce role, provided by J.C. Floyd.

Chapter 70

THE SST SAGA: Canadian roots exposed

THE AVRO STAT: SUPERSONIC TRANS-ATLANTIC TRANSPORT

Avro's STAT: Supersonic Trans-Atlantic Transport. Perhaps the first credible SST design by a major manufacturer. (image by the author)

Little known in popular aviation circles, Avro Canada produced a number of jet passenger plane designs after the Jetliner flew in August, 1949. Some of these were very advanced using swept wings and podded engines similar to those of the Boeing 707. It is generally not known that Avro was also conducting parametric studies to determine if a supersonic airliner could be economically and technically feasible. In the process they produced several SST designs optimised for slightly different route and economic "niches".

Jim Chamberlin in the Initial Projects Office had been working with Jim Floyd and other designers and engineers on parametric studies for supersonic transports, exploring configurations over a wide variety of stage lengths, altitude considerations and maximum supersonic cruise speeds and analysing them against various market models. Avro's leadership in supersonics and SST design did not go unnoticed, according to Jim Floyd, by the rest of the western aviation fraternity and related parties. Jim had been discussing supersonic technologies and airline needs for years with RAeE, Hawker-Siddeley Design Council and British ministry officials, plus his American contacts from the Jetliner experience. He pointed out that Avro Canada's SST designs were actually produced due to the interest of Howard Hughes and Trans World Airlines. In the book "Howard Hughes and TWA," TWA's Chief Engineer and Mr. Hughes' personal technical advisor, Robert Rummel, acknowledges that the SST designs produced by Avro for TWA were the first credible SST designs he was aware of in the world.

> "I never doubted that Jim Floyd and his team could have produced excellent jet transports well tailored to satisfy TWA's operational requirements, not withstanding the shadow of possible government interference cast by Minister C.D. Howe's untoward actions in the Jetliner affair. The design of AVRO's Jetliner was superb, and given the freedom to perform, comparable results seemed likely."

> "During 1958-59, Jim Floyd proposed several supersonic transports for TWA's transatlantic

operations-as far as I know, the first supersonic proposal by a responsible, major manufacturer. The first was designed to operate at 900 mph supersonic speeds, the final one was an attractive, extremely sleek, 1,200 mph jet with a double-ogee wing plan-form. It would have been years ahead of anything else."[442]

Avro's "Configuration 6" SST

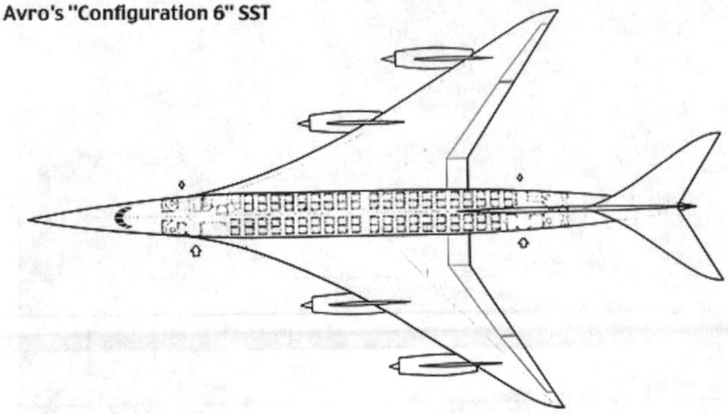

Avro's Configuration 6 in their in-house studies was the "900 mph" aircraft referred to by Rummel. Floyd has mentioned that Rummel initially had some concerns about the tailless delta configuration, so this design was produced using a separate tail and four podded engines. With the crisis in the Arrow program revealing itself in the fall of 1958, the attention of management and staff was directed towards the Arrow, and efforts to develop and sell the SST concept, and much else, were put on the back burner. Not long after the axe finally fell in February, 1959, Crawford Gordon Jr. was found in the office of "Sir Roy" when he placed a call to Jim Floyd at Malton. Dobson and Hawker Siddeley Aviation's Technical Director, Stuart Davies, wanted him on the earliest available plane to discuss the possibility of his leading Hawker Siddeley Aviation's most prestigious design effort; to produce a winning design for the British SST competition.

Floyd refused to go over right away since he was travelling around the United States for a couple of months trying to "loan" his top engineers to US firms until the future, or lack thereof, of Avro was decided. He and others were also somewhat suspicious that the whole SST project could be another political disaster in the making and never get off the ground. Davies reassured Floyd in a personal letter in which he gave the effort a better than 50/50 chance of production if the design was good and Hawker Siddeley behaved as a fully integrated company to satisfy the "establishment". Davies also pointed out to Floyd that he would occupy the most important and prestigious position in the rapidly integrating Hawker Siddeley Aviation concern and be entrusted with their most important projects. It was something akin to his dream job, that of being recognised in the ranks of the Chief Designers such as Sir Sydney Camm and the like. Of course in those harried days Floyd and most senior engineers and managers from Avro Canada were being bombarded by lucrative offers from the United States as well. They were, and are, also keenly aware that they were comparatively lucky, considering the fates of thousands of others after the cancellation. He hoped to salvage some of his engineering team and the data and expertise accumulated from the Arrow program, plus their growing body of work on supersonic transports while merging this nucleus of talent with the best of the Hawker-Siddeley engineers in Britain. Their number one task, out of about a dozen, was the design of the Group's entry into the British SST competition.

By this time British studies into supersonic travel had been ongoing at the Supersonic Transport Advisory Committeee (STAC) since 1956 and nothing suitable had been presented by a British manufacturer. At the time that Avro was submitting their advanced SST designs to Howard Hughes' TWA and their competitor Pan Am, Convair in the United States was proposing an SST version of their B-58 Hustler bomber. The limited passenger load would have made the expense of operation of such a transformation prohibitive. At the time there was a technical competition developing between Britain and the United States over who would deploy the first SST aircraft. After apparently losing the initiative in supersonic fighter and missile design to the United States, Britain was hoping to salvage something of her former technical reputation, and with it to stimulate trade and her economy. Studies had shown the market was relatively small due to higher fuel consumption at supersonic speeds, therefore the first company or nation to build a trans-Atlantic SST that was reasonably economical stood a good chance of dominating the market. After so many politically-wrought technological disasters in Britain, and the change of heart regarding industrial nationalism taken by Duncan Sandys and others, Britain steeled herself and set out to produce the world's first SST. The arrival of the Avro team, with voluminous data from the Arrow project and their own SST studies in hand, provided a needed kick-start to Britain's SST effort. As Jim Floyd pointed out in a 1990 paper:

> "I know that the small team that went with me to the Advanced Projects Group in the UK were highly respected and acknowledged to be among 'the best in the business'.
>
> "Five of the senior ex-Avro Canada engineers who had worked with me on the Arrow were in the group, John McCulloch, who had been our UK liaison man on the Arrow, was brought in as chief of administration, Pat McKenzie, structural engineer on the Arrow as our chief of structural design, Colin Marshall, systems designer on the Arrow, was chief of systems design at APG, Ken Cooke, landing gear specialist on the Arrow was put in charge of landing gear design at APG, and Joe Farbridge, also an engineer on the Arrow, was in our tactical analysis team in APG. John Morris, who had been chief of performance on the Arrow, later joined APG in the same capacity."[443]

Peter Sutcliffe was Jim Floyd's "number two" at the APG however and had formerly been Avro Manchester's chief aerodynamicist. They all reported to Stuart Davies, the same man that had persuaded Jim Floyd to go to Canada for the Jetliner program and who had persuaded him to come back from Canada as well. But first Floyd spent a couple of months trying to place his engineering team into decent jobs in the United States and Britain. Most major US manufacturers took on the Avro engineers, North American Aviation, taking the most into their F-108 and XB-70 Valkyrie programs, at around 100.[444] Once Jim Chamberlin and Bob Lindley led a group making the transition to NASA (with Lindley going to McDonnell), Frank Brame, Chamberlin's former assistant, took over as Chief Technician. [445] Brame would later join Boeing and would play a major role in Boeing's design evolution, rising to head a renewed SST effort in the 1980s. Jim Floyd wrote to me in 2005:

> "...the final SST design discussed with Rummel, which he [erroneously] describes in his book as 'a 1,200 mph jet with a double-ogee wing'...was, in fact, the result of work done at both Avro Canada and HSA/APG [Hawker Siddeley Aviation Advanced Projects Group]. "
>
> After accepting Stuart Davies' offer to set up the APG in April 1959, I returned to Malton with some of the UK bods who were to be with me at APG and between them and some of my old Avro team who were still left at Malton, we cooked up a number of parametric studies on SSTs. We returned to the UK in June '59 to formally set up the 'think tank group' at Kingston and pushed on with a number of parametric studies of SST configurations."
>
> In August '59 I returned to Canada...[and] took that opportunity to visit both Pan Am and TWA to discuss our SST designs with them, since Bob Rummel and Sanford Kaufmann of Pan Am were old friends, and I valued their input. The design to which Rummel refers in his book...was an 'integrated' design with six engines on top of the wing. [Floyd has mentioned that had the Iroquois, or the later versions of the Olympus engine been available, a four-engined version would have been feasible.] The intakes were 'squared off' similar to those on the Arrow, but with variable geometry for cruise efficiency. "

A July, 1959 Avro Canada Technical Department document describes analysis of a British Royal Aeronautical Establishment study on a 120 passenger slender delta SST concept weighing nearly half a million pounds. This design represented the best British guess at what technology could practically produce in terms of a delta-winged trans-Atlantic SST. It was also a gauntlet thrown down to industry—"Here's what we think can be engineered, can you do it or beat it?" Avro's IBM 704 computer was used for number crunching on these studies to great effect to see how their experience on the Arrow and their own SST studies compared.

> "Mainly on the basis of the RAE report TM No Aero 33 dated March 1959 on "An Assessment of Slender Shapes for Supersonic Transport Aircraft," a supersonic transport design was selected and its range performance analysed in detail. This design was denoted Model "B" and had a design cruising Mach number of 1.8 with 79 degrees leading edge sweep

and had leading edge extensions permitting landing speeds of the order of 140 knots. All up weight was 470,000 lbs., wing area 8400 square feet, aspect ratio 0.775, root t/c =5.76, fuel weight 248,000 lbs. and a passenger loading of 120 @ 220 lbs. each…

"Engine performance was based on Orenda Engines Limited upscaled Iroquois 2 turbojet data which closely approximated N.G.T.E. [Next Generation Technology Engine, a benchmark established by committee] engine type "C"…

"Original data gave cruise S.F.C. [specific fuel consumption] too high but when all information was resolved a final cruise S.F.C. of 1.22 [pounds of fuel per pound of thrust per hour] at M=1.8 above 36,089' [altitude] and this appeared realistic and desireable…

"…intake pressure recovery…varies from

.93 at M = 0 [or 93%]
to .98 at M = .35

.98 at M = .9
and .915 at M = 2.0

Lift drag ratios and coefficient of lift was calculated three times, resolving the data each time. Lift/Drag ratios varied between 8.39-1, 8.77-1, and 9.00-1. These numbers included vortex and wave drag due to lift yet are very high and haven't really been exceeded in a practical design even today. Compared to the Royal Aeronautical Society's study for a slender delta, Avro noted that the Iroquois engine thrust-to-weight ratio was better than that proposed for the N.G.T.E. engine, that their design had lower drag due to lift, and lower wave drag than those given in the R.Ae.S. study. Avro calculated that 40,300 lbs of aircraft weight could be saved through using an enlarged engine of the Iroquois 2 class in terms of thrust-to-weight. Since the initial study was with an aircraft using eight Iroquois 2s, seemingly small reductions in weight and drag resulted in a magnified effect when it came to how many engines and how much fuel were required for a supersonic, trans-Atlantic flight. The study also indicated that, like with the Jetliner, minor reductions in drag could allow a higher cruise speed of Mach 2, and this would result in a significant increase in range.

With this study in hand, Jim Floyd in Britain asked Frank Brame to optimize the design based on improvements indicated by the initial study and their experience from the Arrow program. An early response from Brame notes:

"3.0 SUPERSONIC TRANSPORT

The design studies summarized in this report have concentrated on an aircraft to carry 120 passengers on the North Atlantic route at about M=2. The configuration has been assumed to be a slender delta-type wing with integrated fuselage. This configuration seems to have great promise and is also a logical extension of the company's experience on the Arrow…"

3.1 PERFORMANCE ANALYSIS

Available engine data was combined with drag estimates of a selected supersonic transport aircraft design, to determine the range performance in detail…for various cruising Mach numbers. From this an appreciation was gained of the fuel used for various stages throughout the flight… Drag estimates were then refined… A total of 8 range flights were calculated, in which the first four gave a pessimistic result and the last four showed what was achievable under realistically refined conditions. The latter gave more than the desired performance, which should cover any off-design conditions or any over optimistic assumptions."

AERODYNAMIC DESIGN OF SUPERSONIC TRANSPORT

Since the configuration is very slender…the design of the aerodynamic shape is based on Adams and Sears "not-so-slender body theory"…[and] its simplicity enables the shape to be optimized directly for minimum drag…"

The area distribution and cross-section shapes have been computed to give minimum wave drag consistent with the restrictions of internal space required for passengers, fuel, undercarriage, etc. It has been found that considerable drag reductions seem to be possible by a spanwise redistribution of area near the trailing edge, so that the area is concentrated further outboard toward the tips. It is proposed that this drag reduction be checked by a supersonic area rule analysis on the IBM 704. This programme will also be used to check the range of Mach numbers in which the "not-so-slender body theory" is valid."[446]

Avro Canada's integrated SST concept design. (image by the author)

This design became the foundation of Hawker Siddeley Aviation's first submission to STAC and was the first industry-produced SST proposal in Britain, yet had been developed mostly in Canada. It featured six engines above the wing, seeming to follow an R.A.E. idea that airflow induced over the wing by the intakes would decrease the landing and take-off distances, and lower landing speeds.

STAC responded to the Hawker Siddeley submission by calling for a joint study, to be conducted by two rival factions in British aviation: The Hawker Siddeley Group, and everybody else. The British government was then, and had been for years, trying to restructure not only the aviation industry, but all their industries into larger conglomerates, presumably to avoid duplication, pool talent and compete with large American firms. Around this time, Armstrong Siddeley Motors, with official encouragement, was getting out of the car business. Now all the independent British manufacturers were being encouraged to join Bristol Aerospace, and form a rival to Hawker Siddeley. One of the 'levers' used to pressure smaller firms to join the intended company: British Aircraft Corporation or BAC, was the SST contract. (Another was the contract for the TSR.2.) No small firm would be considered for either. Earlier, MetroVick engines had been encouraged to join Armstrong Siddeley, thereby giving the Group leading jet-engine technology. Later, in the 1960s, Armstrong Siddeley would be merged with Bristol, forming Bristol-Siddeley, and later, with Rolls-Royce. Eventually Britain's dynamic and diverse aircraft and aero-engine manufacturers were united in two British monopolies: British Aerospace and Rolls-Royce. The government had come to believe that economy of scale was more important than competition in establishing a competitive position vis-à-vis the United States.

442 Rummel, Robert. Howard Hughes and TWA, Smithsonian Inst. Press, p. 267
443 Floyd, J.C., Arrow to SST to Concorde unpublished personal aide-memoire, 1990
444 J.C. Floyd interviews
445 Frank Brame is an example of both Avro's progressive employment policies and of the triumph of the human spirit against personal disability. Brame was born with a serious physical birth defect related to an improperly tested drug that was marketed for years. Brame was a brilliant engineer and even became a glider pilot—still flying as of 2002!
446 Brame, Frank Avro Technical Department report to J.C. Floyd, 9 July, 1959 p.8

Chapter 71

THE HSA.1000 SUPERSONIC TRANSPORT

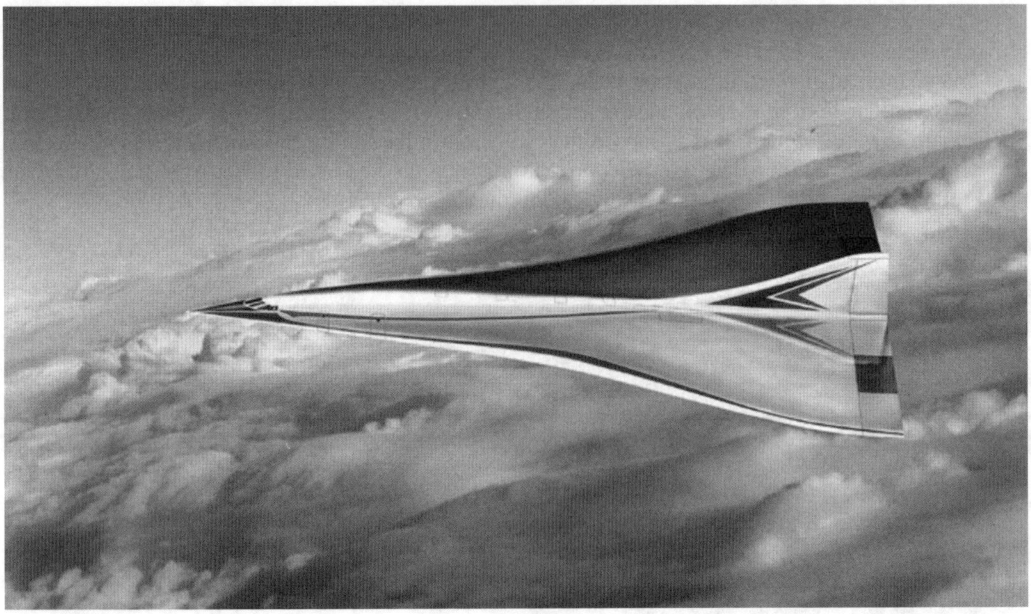

The HSA.1000 Supersonic Transport design produced by Jim Floyd's Advanced Projects Group at Hawker Siddeley in the U.K. It was submitted in December of 1959, only 10 months after Black Friday. It featured an integrated or blended wing and fuselage. Mach 2.2 and Mach 2.7 and military versions were proposed. (image by the author)

One can only imagine the misgivings experienced by those from the Arrow program to be told that they had to share their data and design with a competitor that was being formed to provide an alternative to the Hawker Siddeley Group. In latter day representations, Jim Floyd displays an inability to graph this strategy, and responded that since neither group wanted to reveal their hands, they 'agreed' to submit separate proposals.

Originally Hawker Siddeley Aviation had hoped to design to Mach 3 since they understood that Kelly Johnson's "Skunkworks" was working to this specification. The powers at Britain's "Supersonic Transport Aircraft Committee" or "STAC", working since 1956, had settled on a cruise speed requirement for the SST of only Mach 2.2. Perhaps this is as good a sign as any that they were desperate to beat the United States in this field after unhappy collaborative ventures in missiles, and the destruction wrought to the British industry by US intelligence.

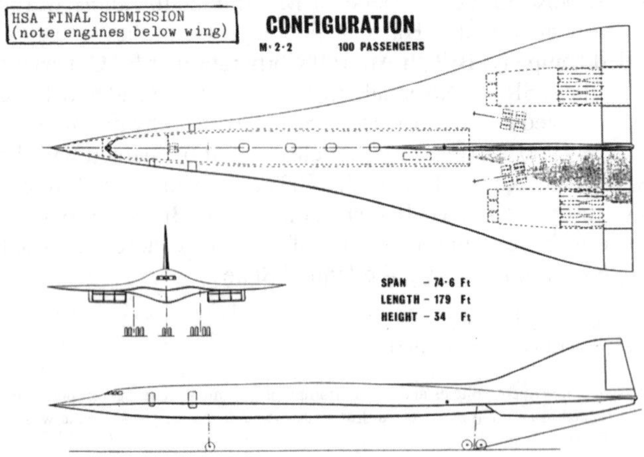

At the beginning of the joint study HSA's team began with the basic integrated design from Avro Canada. The Royal Aeronautical Establishment had been consulting with many leaders in the aerospace field on the SST problem during the 1950's and had also discussed it at length on more than one occasion with Jim Floyd well before Black Friday. They had proposed three concepts they thought promising, the gothic delta, the slender delta, and a bizarre M-shaped design. Avro Canada's concept was similar to the slender delta, while Bristol chose to develop the gothic delta concept. In keeping with Jim Floyd's inherited requirement to ensure designs were expandable and adaptable, the basic HSA SST design was modified to allow a cruise speed of Mach 2.7 and was co-submitted with the Mach 2.2 cruiser. The most important re-engineering was simply in materials substitution with the light-alloy structure of the Mach 2.2 vehicle being replaced by high-temperature and strength steel alloys for much of the Mach 2.7 aircraft. By the end of the study wind tunnel tests on scale models had allowed the shape to be refined, and the engines were moved to the underside of the aircraft. They were also separated and spaced as far out on the wing as possible, perhaps realising more of the advantages of "spanwise distribution" at the rear of the craft noted in Brame's report. In December 1959, the HSA.1000 Mach 2+ airliner was submitted to the Ministry of Supply, along with a secret military version for speeds up to Mach 2.7.

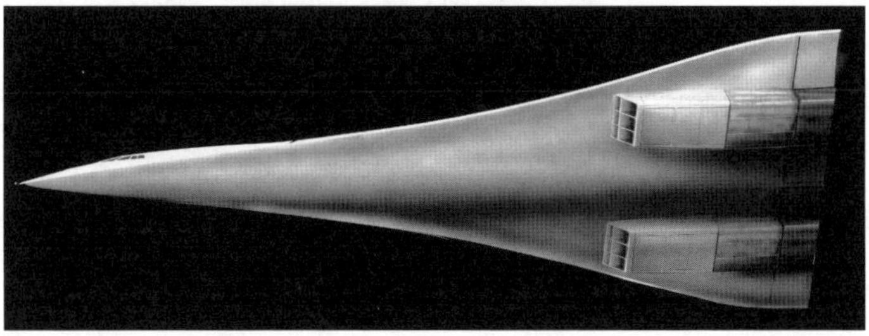

The passenger compartment was unusual in that it had no windows, this being due to the blended shape and the necessity to put tunnels through the structure for windows in such a design. Television screens were proposed to give the passenger a view, or selection of views or programs in another example of forward thinking. A view over the aircraft looking down from a small camera placed in the tail would seem an exciting prospect. Some conservatives involved in the selection process saw the lack of windows as something that would detract from passenger appeal.

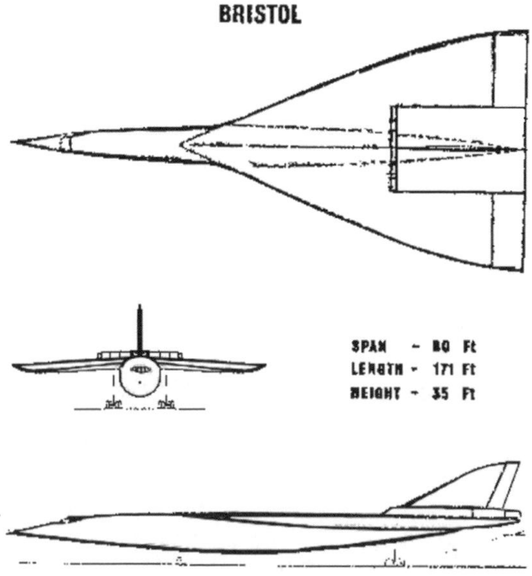

Bristol's SST design. This design was selected over the HSA.1000 yet the Concorde is what was actually built. (via Jim Floyd)

For whatever reasons, or combination of reasons, the Ministry of Supply awarded a contract to Bristol—and whatever other companies ended up in a consortium with them, to develop their design. This was at odds with Stuart Davies logical belief that since English Electric (soon to form BAC with Bristol, Vickers and others) had gotten the TSR.2 development while Hawker-Siddeley got nothing but cancellation notices, that they should have been able to win the SST contract if they produced a good design. As to whether it was a good design or not, one only has to look at the differences between the Bristol SST design, then the HSA-SST and finally the Concorde actual configuration to discover which was the most promising concept. The Hawker Siddeley team, through experience with pitch-up phenomenon through the Arrow program, also knew that the wing shape of the Bristol design was particularly prone to pitch-up and tip-stalling phenomena. Many suspect that BAC got the contract as a further inducement for the remaining independent British manufacturers to amalgamate into British Aircraft Corporation (BAC). The loss of both the TSR.2 and SST contracts certainly helped set the stage for the future amalgamation of Hawker Siddeley and BAC into British Aerospace.

In an effort to hedge their bets, once Hawker-Siddeley was cut out of all the contracts, the British establishment types approached first the U.S. then Germany and France to see if they'd join the development effort. France eventually joined after the U.S. refused—being into their own Mach 3 SST program—and Germany seemed largely disinterested.

By this time the French had been exploring a shape using a tube-fuselage and a low-ogival delta wing arrangement broadly similar to the HSA-SST and had termed it the "Super Caravelle". This was a much different aircraft design to the Bristol concept using a low-ogival delta similar to the wing of the HSA.1000 but a finite, tubular fuselage. The Concorde, of course, used this fuselage-wing design and four under-wing engines in installations identical to those proposed for the Hawker Siddeley design—leading to the obvious, and officially-unanswered, question; why wasn't Hawker Siddeley awarded the development contract in the first place?

Chapter 72

THE HSA.1011 NO BOOM SST

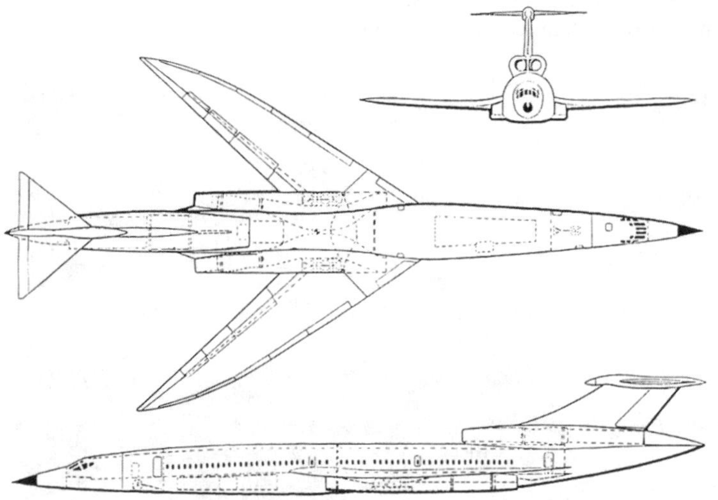

The Hawker Siddeley Aviation Type 1011, a swing-wing supersonic airliner that was designed to travel at Mach 1.15 to 1.2 without creating a sonic boom. Of course its top speed was much higher. There was a very promising military version of this aircraft. The only aircraft in service to use the theories of the HS-1011 is the B-1B which is now limited to Mach 1.25, mainly for stealth reasons. (image via Jim Floyd)

Some of the other conservatives at a high level of policy involvement were also showing more and more concern over the sonic boom and peoples' reaction to it. At the very beginning of the design work by the Hawker Siddeley Advanced Projects Group on the HSA SST a report was produced showing the sonic-boom theory that everyone had been designing too was wrong. On arrival in Britain the Avro team, particularly the former Arrow Chief of Performance John Morris, discovered that British industry and government had grossly underestimated the intensity of the sonic boom for aircraft cruising at 50-60,000 ft. They were neglecting to include the portion of the sonic boom added by the requirement of the aircraft to make lift—adding a further disruption of airflow. This was revealed to the industry during Jim Floyd's Roy Chadwick Memorial Lecture to the Royal Aeronautical Society in 1961. Floyd and the Advanced Project Group at HSA saw, early on, that this was a factor that could very possibly limit SST operations to over-ocean routes and undertook studies for a "no-boom" supersonic airliner.

The HSA.1011 was an interesting design for a transonic long-range airliner that would operate at Mach 1.15 to Mach 1.2 without producing a sonic boom when travelling in the stratosphere. Over ocean or uninhabited areas it could travel at up to about Mach 1.8, depending on the thrust available. The no-boom cruise speed of Mach 1.2 is about 25% faster than the 747 which appeared later and which is today still the fastest subsonic jet passenger plane of large capacity. The 747 actually achieves its high cruise speed, compared to conventional airliners by better "area rule" conformance by incorporating the upper deck "bulge" which ends where the wing joins the fuselage. The HSA.1011 incorporated the ultimate in volume distribution for high transonic flight, resulting in the minimum disruption of airflow at speeds around Mach 1. Studies and computer projections indicated that the shock wave would dissipate before it reached the ground, thus making no sonic boom at speeds of up to Mach 1.2. Concentration on low drag for this speed range meant it would be reasonably economical compared to a Mach 2+ aircraft was while still being able to fly faster than Mach 1.2 when permitted. The only aircraft developed using the concept of the swing-wing with a well-area-ruled fuselage is the Rockwell B-1 bomber which hit the drawing boards at North American Aviation a couple of years after the HSA.1011 was proposed. The Valkyrie, by the same company, was well along in design by this time but would never be adopted into service.

As time would tell, the eventual Concorde design was restricted from operating supersonically over land due to the sonic boom and would have few airports that would accept it due to engine noise on take-off. Some astute observers, such as a writer for the Atlantic Monthly, noted that Britain's secretive Central Policy Coordination Committee, then headed by Victor Rothschild, were particularly destructive to their country's SST project with continual prognostications of economic disaster for producer and operator alike and visions of public outrage over the sonic boom. Had all the carriers who initially expressed interest in purchasing Concordes done so, the economics would have been much more favourable for both the producer and the operators. Politics among the power elite notwithstanding, the Hawker Siddeley team had, in reality, anticipated the major cause of the commercial failure of Concorde and provided a solution before Concorde was even designed. This aircraft, the HSA.1011 and a military weapons carrier version of it were detailed in APG report 1011/104 of June 1961.

Author's concept of the HSA.1011 "no-boom" airliner.

With the award to Bristol's then BAC and Sud Aviation in France of the SST development contract, Hawker Siddeley was again left in the cold, and arguably not because their designs were deficient. In terms of government business at least Hawker-Siddeley seemed to have been "had" again, and by the time this switch was in the works Jim Floyd had already left the company in apparent distaste and in poor health. To have three world-beating designs cancelled was quite enough and the effort and disappointments had taken their toll. His intuition, as evidenced by a dubious letter to Stuart Davies before he took on the HSA-SST design task was proven correct once again. After the HSA-SST cancellation most of the Advanced Projects Group talents ended up, like their Avro Canada counterparts, employed in the United States. Jim Floyd decided he'd had enough of the big aviation concerns with their obvious vulnerability to political "swings and arrows" as he termed it and started his own firm. Peter Sutcliffe ended up at Boeing in charge of new product development, a position of monumental responsibility putting him front and centre with Boeing's later SST efforts. John Morris went to Douglas and became a senior company executive on the DC-10 jumbo-jet. Joe Farbridge went to join the ex-Avroites at NASA while Ken Cooke would go to McDonnell-Douglas and Colin Marshall ended up at North American-Rockwell. This seemed to be about the time the American SST program really began to gather steam, about three years behind the British as history would prove, and perhaps about five years behind Avro Canada.

Jim Floyd & Associates were contracted for economic studies for this project when BAC won out over Hawker-Siddeley in the SST competition. The Concorde was designed to the same maximum speed figures as the Arrow, and made use of the same kind of materials and construction technology. BAC actually sent a team to Avro after cancellation to acquire whatever technology from Avro they could that would assist them with their TSR.2 design. Without question this technology was also used in their Concorde design effort. It can be argued that Concorde owes many of its design elements to Avro and the Hawker Siddeley Group, however they received no contracts for the aircraft's development.

The stunning Concorde.

On November 29, 1962, Britain and France formed a treaty aimed at joint development and production of an SST. In shades of Kennedy's politicisation of the non-existent missile-gap during his first election campaign, Kennedy also viewed this European SST effort as a challenge to American prestige.

> "The United States viewed this Anglo-French effort as a challenge, and eight months later in June 1963 President John F. Kennedy announced a national project to develop a supersonic transport—the SST, as the American project would be called. It would go one better than the Anglo-French project by aiming for a Mach 3 giant of some 750,000 pounds, with seats for 290 passengers."[447]

Due to the perception that private industry, even in the United States, could not manage the challenge, the US government managed their effort. In 1966 a design competition between Boeing and Lockheed was finally decided in Boeing's favour. Over the years the Boeing SST design went through five distinct evolutions, most incorporating the variable geometry, or "swing" wing. These huge, elaborate designs posed design and production nightmares. After two-years trying to resolve the problems of the swing-wing on such a large aircraft designed to fly across such a wide speed range, it was abandoned in favour of a design similar to the one that Lockheed had proposed.

> "However simplified, even the revised SST design generated nightmarish problems. Structure weights went up, more thrust was required to carry the new weight, more fuel was necessary to feed the increased thrust, and at the rate of 675 pounds per hundred gallons the fuel invariably meant more weight. The design was trapped in an upward series of fuel-weight spirals with development costs estimated at about $5 billion when, in May 1971, Congress refused to appropriate any more funds for its development, and the SST was dead."[448]

Well, not quite. The Concorde went on to stellar service with an enviable safety record considering that the plane was never improved. The question isn't whether the SST is truly dead, but when the next one will be built and if it will be something along the lines of the "no-boom" SST or a Mach 2 or faster design. Boeing's proposal of a "sonic cruiser" seems to indicate the former.

Some, of course, argue that Concorde was a complete waste of taxpayer's money due to its extraordinarily high development cost and small production run of 14 aircraft. However, in the end the Concorde was operating in the black, indicating that a higher number of service aircraft and more routes would result in a viable market. It is also argued that such national ventures in the absence of an obvious market are folly. But what of the NASA space program? It was the result of technical competition and was undertaken for reasons of national pride and global prestige. Were the cultural and economic results of the space program a waste? Do we include the economic activity of movies, toys, clothing, books and other items spawned by the NASA programs in calculating the merits of the investment? One doubts, in restrospect, that the British consider the Concorde to have been a wasted effort considering its utility to the public and the uniqueness of its contribution to peacetime aviation. Is profit the only yardstick of human achievement?

447 ed. Greenwood, John T. Milestones of Aviation, New York, Crescent Books, 1991 p. 287
448 ibid. p. 290

POSTSCRIPT

While the Diefenbaker Conservatives may have benefited in their early elections from US assistance, manifested by their aversion to the national economic policies being promoted by the Liberals' Gordon Commission, by the beginning of Diefenbaker's second to last election campaign US favour had returned to the Liberals. Nash's *Kennedy and Diefenbaker* points out the US assistance given the Pearson Liberals due, in part, to Pearson's agreeing to reverse his earlier anti-nuclear position in favour of acceptance of US warheads.

Ironically, the Americans had helped elect a government that would make a sincere effort to reverse the buy-up of strategic resources and industry of Canada by naming Walter Lockhart Gordon as its first finance minister. Shortly after the election of Lester Pearson's minority Liberal Government in 1963, as part of the "60 Days of Decision," the Liberals rushed through a budget after just four weeks preparation. The norm was four months. Outside influence, especially by three "bright boys" from Toronto investment firms (in preference to Ministry of Finance specialists), and without proper vetting by legal experts in the Justice Department made, according to Peter C. Newman, an ill-advised and unenforceable budget. Newman doesn't suggest, however, that Gordon may have enlisted the help he used to prevent the intentions and measures of the budget from being leaked to agents and agencies that might oppose it.

In this budget, Finance Minister Walter Gordon tried to react to the ever-increasing buyout of the Canadian economy by American financial and corporate interests. His response to this was to impose a 30% tax on the sale of Canadian-owned corporate shares to foreign investors. Another measure was to demand that U.S. owned subsidiaries operating in Canada offer a minimum of 25% of their shares to Canadians. After the bitter relationship that Diefenbaker had had with the Kennedy administration, the prospect of dramatic improvement was promised by Pearson's long meeting with Kennedy shortly after being elected. As such this budget was seen as a severe slap to interests in the US. Without doubt retaliatory measures were under discussion not only on Wall Street, but at the Federal Reserve Board and within the US administration. Even Canadians, self-interested in protecting their U.S. sponsored jobs labelled Gordon as "some kind of Commie nut." This was a typical marginalisation tactic reminiscent of McCarthyism.

At the time the USA was experiencing a balance of payments deficit ie, more money was flowing out of the US and into other nations than was coming back in. The US was facing a money shortage at home even though this was caused, to some extent, by US money being absorbed outside the US while financing the buyout of other economies. Half of this deficit was accounted for by foreign borrowing in the New York money market. Two thirds of *this* amount was going to bonds from Canadian businesses, and provincial and municipal governments. Kennedy's administration imposed a 1.25% investment tax on US money entering Canada as a retaliatory measure.

In the business of forcing policy change, be they of corporate or national administrators, timing is everything. This measure came after the economic crisis brought on by the years of Diefenbaker rule that had paralyzed the economy. As a result Canada was in a poor position to withstand this measure.

Panic ensued when this measure was announced on July 18th 1963. In one hour the Toronto Stock Exchange fell over 8 points. Not only were just issued and future bonds at stake, but soon investors feared the Americans would dump all Canadian portfolios to escape the tax. The next day the T.S.E. recorded one of its biggest drops in history to this point losing over 15 points. Canada was facing rising interest rates, declining growth, and rising unemployment overnight. By Thursday the Canadian dollar was under heavy attack and in a day and a half some 110 million in Canadian reserves were sold eclipsing even the Diefenbaker government's 1962 devaluation crisis. This new devaluation crisis was a mirror image to the devaluation crisis of 1962, designed to slap down John Diefenbaker during his election campaign. (This last opinion is backed up by an American P.B.S. production on Kennedy and Diefenbaker that implies that the CIA was behind Diefenbaker's devaluation crisis.) Warnings were teletyped to Ottawa that by the following Monday Canada could be facing national bankruptcy! It is fortunate that Walter Gordon's autobiography *A Political Memoir* records the secret "back-office" dealings that went on to prevent the collapse of the Canadian economy. The lesson to be learned, of course, is how short-sighted and short-term policies lost for Canada the control of not only the Canadian economy, but also subserviated her global influence on every level.

On the following Saturday a council was assembled in the Finance Minister's office to discuss a means out of the fiasco. The only means available seemed to be to approach the Americans on bended knee, begging for an exemption to the tax. To this the Americans predictably agreed, with of course, specific demands of their own.

The resulting "agreement" was more akin to a hold-up! Canada was granted an exemption credit of up to 350 million a year in unbalanced trade. This was conveniently left open to revision at the President's discretion. Canada's own central bank reserves, the funds used during times of financial uncertainly to support the nation, were limited in size to a mere 2.7 billion dollars. This amount, used for among other things to protect the Canadian dollar from speculation devaluation, was steadily reduced thereafter. This is a key point. It meant that Canada would not be allowed to develop cash reserves to the point that it could protect Canada against even short term retaliatory economic measures of any magnitude. If Canada ever again instituted measures to reduce the buyout by American influences of its economy, it would face almost *instant* economic collapse under US retaliation. In essence Canada had handed the reigns of its economic independence to the owners of the U.S. Federal Reserve.

These measures placed a good deal of Canadian monetary and fiscal policy under the direction of the United States of America. The CBC mentioned that this one act had *"put into the hands of the US President more control over our economy than the past 20 years of growth of US investment in Canada represent."* A Globe and Mail financial columnist stated *"The major implication of the agreement is this - the Canadian Government now agrees that for the future Canada will be an economic satellite of the United States."* John Diefenbaker himself stated that this action was *"not in keeping with the sovereignty of this nation."* He was a man who would know.

Simultaneously, the Rockefeller dominated Citibank, then the 3rd largest bank in the world, tried to capitalise on the confusion of the new Canadian government by announcing its intention to acquire the Dutch Mercantile Bank and thus establish its Canadian base of operations. The Mercantile was the only foreign owned bank in Canada and a minor one at that, having its head office in Prince Bernhard's Netherlands. Rockefeller completed the deal on June 26th 1963 and then went to Canada on July 18th to test the reaction of the Canadian Government to a deal he stated had not yet been made! Gordon was rightly concerned about how a bank with reserves of 16 billion dollars (which dwarfed the Bank of Canada's reserves of about 2.5 billion) would affect government economic and fiscal measures. He stated that he might have to go as far as to impose retroactive ownership controls on this bank should the deal be finalised. Rockefeller was furious but later publicly announced the "done deal" anyway. This was a transparent attempt to pressure the Canadian government to grant him an exemption since the deal was already a publicly-announced *fait accompli*. He certainly had the cash reserves to topple the Canadian economy and the connections in Canadian "branch-plant" operations, not to mention connections in every sphere of corporate and political influence that would give him enough confidence to expect compliance.

In the U.S. what is good for the American political, corporate and financial "power-elite" is viewed to be good for the U.S.A. period. This is clearly shown in how the American State Department became involved on the side of Rockefeller/Citibank. A diplomatic note of protest was delivered to the Canadian Ambassador while connections all over Canada and the U.S.A. applied pressure to whomever would listen to have Citibank/Mercantile granted an exception to the Bank Act regulations demanding shares be issued to Canadians.

The result in Canada was a mirror image of the devaluation crisis response: capitulation! Mitchell Sharp took the place of Walter Gordon in finance and most of the nationalistic aspects of Gordon's budget quietly disappeared.

Distemper of Our Times asserts that *"not one line of any of the 4 Mitchell Sharp budgets enhanced Canadian fiscal or economic independence; quite the contrary."* Sharp's 1966 review of the Bank Act increased the limit on non-Canadian holdings in a Canadian Bank to 25% with no single holder to have more than a 10% share. This gave American interests more than a foot in the door. Still, Citibank was in violation of both clauses. At any rate they were granted a 5 year exemption to be reviewed annually to give time to comply. More likely the 5 years were to give the Canadian government time to further relax the bank act! Today there are Citibank owned banking operations in Canada with a corporate skyscraper figuring prominently in downtown Toronto. When the Toronto Dominion Bank and Canada Trust merged, Citibank took over all of Canada Trust's Mastercard customers. According to the master war strategist Von Clauswitz it is immaterial if one loses a battle as long as in the end, you win the war.

Mitchell Sharp's term as Finance Minister changed the direction of the Pearson government's economic policy 180 degrees from Gordon's crusade to buy back the economy. Peter C. Newman (*Distemper of Our Times* pg. 221) described official US policy which considered the development of Canada as a development of the "*...U.S. hinterland. In exchange for this development Canada gained quick, U.S. owned industrial development [such as the 1964 auto-pact] in return for control of Canadian resources such as the Columbia River.*" (In reality the Auto Pact was likely the low-tech bone thrown to Canada as a partial compensation for the earlier red-herring of Defense Production Sharing.) The Columbia River Treaty harnessed the development of this enormous resource to the benefit of the American western seaboard rather than to serve Canada's needs such as using this huge Canadian resource to irrigate the prairies to produce food with which to feed the planet. Quite literally the means to provide food for a huge percentage of the world's population was given away to provide cheaper drinking water to the US western seaboard, and for cheap water for US industrial purposes. Similar to later agreements on oil and natural gas production, the US was guaranteed that their percentage of this resource would never decrease no matter what Canada's needs were. Clearly concerns raised by Canadians about our fresh water during the Free Trade Agreement debate were somewhat *post-facto.*

What the world needs, in this writer's opinion, is a currency system that isn't based, as today, on the whims of the financial elite and subject to speculation and manipulation. The amount of currency in circulation should be based on the Gross Domestic Product of the nation in question with the value of a dollar (or whatever denomination) based on the average price of a loaf of bread in that nation. But this won't happen or even be discussed while the owners of the economy can control governments through currency speculation and devaluation crises. Preferred shareholder lists should be available to the public, and real competition should be ensured in every sector of the economy, particularly the media.

During the tenure of James Jesus Angleton as head of CIA counterintelligence there were repeated efforts to destabilise the Pearson government. Angleton had become personal friends with Kim Philby, the notorious Soviet agent working within Western intelligence, and the discovery that he had been so grossly deceived by Philby seemed to set off a paranoid reaction. The fact that these people viewed social democrats and socialists as merely shades of communist red didn't help. For far-right corporate interests related to the American military industrial financial complex, it was quite convenient to equate one with the other, especially where aspiring politicians were concerned. Being "soft on communism" became the new career-destroying attribute among civil servants.

By the end of the Pearson era, nearly two thirds of Canadian manufacturing facilities were foreign owned, mostly by the U.S.A.. The percentage of foreign ownership of key strategic industries such as automotive, petroleum, mining, chemicals and rubber ranged to the high 90's. Nine out of 10 Canadian factories employing 5,000 or more people were U.S. owned. Furthermore about 60% of Canada's energy resources were directly and inextricably owned by U.S. corporate interests while about half of our total manufacturing industries had the same masters. Canada, according to a US study, is the primary American source of 28 out of 32 *strategic* resources. Today US interests own the majority of these resources *in the ground* and the majority of any refining installations remaining in Canada. Of course the United States, through various doctrines, has always maintained that the nation is bound by duty and the Constitution to go to war to protect her vital interests. That she has done so, is well recorded even by popular history.

Observations of the deteriorating global political (and economic?) situation suggest that forces at play are very similar to those of the 1950s, and, in fact, throughout the 20th Century, but generally just below the 'radar' of the general Western public and media. Indeed, concentrations of media power by dominant cartels, along with concentrations of financial, industrial and military might, again resemble those at the dawn of the 20th Century. The growing gap between rich and poor and the destruction of the middle class continues apace. That people might be well advised to broaden their perception of the forms that political and economic offensives take, is the point of this book. Competition is a natural requirement of healthy Capitalism but is sadly lacking in the media and other sectors of the economy. Government complicity with the aims of the power elite is globally indicated by the lack of debate on this important subject.

The old adage 'Those who fail to learn the mistakes of history are doomed to repeat them" suggests that we cannot afford, as a species or as a planet, to continue along the same destructive paths as those practiced throughout the bloody 20th Century. As a wise American founding father once wrote: "the price of Liberty is forever vigilance". Freedom and democracy cannot exist without a properly-informed, *activist* citizenry. Wisdom and understanding do not preceed knowledge. It has already been shown that various special interests go to great pains to manipulate the media. But what of today when media control is concentrated in fewer and fewer hands—hands that are invariably attached to global capitalists interested in the triumph of their interests over all other political-economic models? With the corporate media having a virtual death grip on the culture of the United States, Britain and Canada particularly, the Anglophone nations are becoming increasingly disinformed in line with a movement to enshrine economic and political control in the hands of a global financial elite—i.e., monopoly capitalists. Since there are more than two political-economic systems, the public is therefore getting less than half the range of opinions available on important issues requiring their tacit support. This studied ignorance on the part of the West towards our own history and the outside world is a major cause of frustration on the part of, as an example, the Muslim people.

Through free trade agreements, which are really about unrestricted capital investment by non-residents on foreign nations, Canada, the United States and other nations are exporting jobs and money wholesale to nations with non-democratic governments and terrible human rights records. China used to be considered a Communist country. Now that they have embraced capitalism, but not democracy, what kind of nation are they? The answer appears to be that they are now following the 'state capitalism' model, i.e., they are now a fascist country. Yet the West exports jobs and money to them and our leading bankers and industrialists rush to invest in these nations thinking, as they did during the Nazi era, that the state will guarantee them a profit. But what of the jobs and welfare of the people who formerly worked for them in the nations in which they live? Apparently these wealthy elitists simply don't care about the wellbeing of anyone but themselves. What of the fact that the global environment simply cannot stand the industrialisation of nations such as China and India? What of the fact that the energy supply also cannot sustain their industrialisation? We have, arguably, already seen the first resource war: the second Iraq War. Is the power elite setting the world up for massive future wars by encouraging the industrialisation of non-democratic nations the way they did before WW II? Or do they even think beyond what they presume to be their own immediate self-interest?

The media, more concentrated in Canada than any of the G-8 nations, is doing an excellent job of mimicking the American myopic servitude to the corporate agenda by likewise ignoring the motives and powers behind America's new, militant, pre-emptive and, indeed, violent foreign policy. Insightful and popular foreign policy and history specialists are having their columns deleted from major newspapers and other media outlets throughout the West—in favour of 'patriotic' cheerleading designed not to inform, but to build support for a continued blind and arrogant approach to not only our national poor, but the poor of the world. Part of this campaign is to convince you that we need to subsume our national government's authority and our national sovereignty to undemocratic international bodies run by global capitalists and elitists, and to surrender all aspects of the operation of our society to private, for profit, corporations. This has been tried before, at the turn of the last century with two world wars the result. Once global capitalists secure near monopolies at home the only way to expand (since they are generally risk averted and are therefore lacking in innovation) is to expand globally. Eventually the interests of competing nations interfere and wars result. Perhaps the best way to preserve peace, democracy and capitalism are to enforce anti-combines legislation and break up huge corporations ensuring healthy, and innovative competition.

As Thomas Jefferson noted from Lord Kames' *Essays on the Principles of Morals and Natural*

Religion: "There is a principle of benevolence in man which prompts him to an equal pursuit of the happiness of all." Yet we have created a system that operates on debt to bankers by every element of Western civilisation from the governments on down to the working poor. With the pressures of daily life, a media dedicated to inciting peoples' material desires on behalf of their sponsors, layers of debt, interest and insurance on everything we do and buy, the principle of natural benevolence becomes replaced by survival of not the fittest but the *richest.* Self interest, which invariably leads to victors and losers, replaces teamwork and sacrifice for the betterment of others. While today's monetarist corporate and financial leaders love to quote from Adam Smith's *Wealth of Nations,* what they do not quote is Smith's assertion that corporations should be forbidden because they promote conspiracy among their leaders to the detriment of society at large. Also from Adam Smith's writings Thomas Jefferson noted: "All constitutions of government are valued only in proportion as they tend to promote the happiness of those who live under them."

It seems to me that the owners of media, wealth and real political power these days are self-serving, rather than promoting the happiness of those who are living under them. Jefferson also bears some responsibility for the passage "All men are created equal… [and] are endowed by their creator with certain inalienable rights…[including rights to] life, liberty and the pursuit of happiness… [In order to] secure these rights, governments are instituted among men, deriving their just powers from the consent of the governed, that whenever any form of government becomes destructive of these ends, it is the right of the people to alter or abolish it and institute new government." Very egalitarian thinking, however it stands somewhat in contrast to the opinions held by wealthy elitists and their sycophants, as proposed by Spencer in his Social Darwinist screed *The Study of Sociology:* "…I am simply carrying out the views of Mr. Darwin in their applications to the human race…all being subject to the increasing difficulty of getting a living…there is an average advance under the pressure, since only those who *do* advance under it eventually survive, [thus] these must be the select of their generation." In other words, greed is good for the species and those who are the richest must be the best. Help to the poor, sick, uneducated or disadvantaged was actually counterproductive to the advance of civilisation. John Kenneth Galbraith grasped the fundamental difference between American culture and that of Canada and Britain when describing Spencer's impact. "His numerous books were influential in England but in the United States they were very little less than divine revelations… Spencer was American gospel because his ideas fitted the needs of American [monopoly] capitalism, and especially the new capitalists… The rich man was the innocent beneficiary of his own superiority."

Perhaps it is the money system and its exaltation of greed that is responsible for bad government and the domination of society by morally-deficient people who are responsible for the decline of social democracy, civil society and the environment. Are ultra-rich capitalists the most evolved people as Spencer suggests or are they parasites on the backs of better people? Is it a characteristic of the evolved not to have the common sense to take only what they need and leave the rest? Are monopolies and monster corporations, richer than entire nations, a more developmental form of capitalism than smaller more flexible businesses practicing innovation and kept honest by competition? Real history provides unequivocal answers, yet the media and Western political system aren't discussing these things. Through banal, superficial and outright disinformative reporting by the monopolist corporate media the 'stupid idiotification' of society at large continues. Unfortunately what you don't know can hurt you.

References:
Books

Adams, Ian. *Agent of Influence.* Toronto: Stoddart Publishing, 1999

Andrew, Christopher; and Mitrokhin, Vasili: *The Mitrokhin Archive.* Middlesex: Penguin Books, 2000

Baglow, Bob. *Canucks Unlimited: Royal Canadian Air Force CF-100 Squadrons and Aircraft,1952-1963.* Ottawa: Canuck Publications, 1985

Bamford, James. *The Puzzle Palace, Inside the National Security Agency,* New York: Penguin Books, 1983

Baker, William. *The Life and Times of Bill Baker.* (private publication)

Brendon, Piers. *Ike: His Life & Times,* New York: Harper & Row, 1986

Bothwell, Drummond and English. *Canada; 1900-1945.*Toronto: University of Toronto Press 1990

Boucher, *Politics of Depression* (unknown)

Brooks, Courtney G., James M. Grimwood and Loyd S. Swenson Jr. *Chariots for Apollo: A History of Manned Lunar Spacecraft.* Washington: NASA Science and Technology Information Division, 1979

Burns, Gen. E.L.M. *Canada in the Age of the Superpowers* (unknown)

Buttler, Tony. *British Secret Projects, Jet Fighters Since 1950.* Specialty Publishers & Wholesalers, 2000

Campagna, Palmiro. *Requiem For a Giant,* Toronto: Dundurn Press, 2003

Campagna, Palmiro. *Storms of Controversy, the Secret Avro Arrow Files Revealed.* Toronto: Stoddart Publishing Co. Ltd., 1992, 1997

Campagna, Palmiro. *The UFO Files; The Canadian Connection Exposed.* Toronto: Stoddart Publishing Co. Ltd.,1997

Chernow, Ron. *The Warburgs, The Twentieth Century Odyssey of a Remarkable Jewish Family,* New York: Vintage Books, 1993

Collier and Horowitz. *The Rockefellers, An American Dynasty.*

Cook, Nick. *The Hunt for Zero Point.* Broadway, 2003

Corso, LCol (ret'd) Philip J. *The Day After Roswell.* Pocket Books, 1997

Crosby, Ann Denholm. *Dilemmas in Defense Decision-Making.* New York: St. Martin's Press, 1998

Coldicott, Helen. *Missile Envy.*

Cunningham, Randall. *Fox Two.* New York: Warner Books, 1989

Cuthbertson, Brian. *Canadian Military Independence in the Age of the Superpowers.* Toronto: Fitzhenry & Whiteside, 1977

Diefenbaker, John George. *One Canada, Vol.III, Ch. 2* Toronto: Macmillan, 1975

Dow, James. *The Arrow.* 2nd edition. Toronto: James Lorimer & Company, 1997

Deighton, Len. *Blood, Tears and Folly. An objective look at World War II.* 2nd Edition. London: Pimlico, 1995

Ethell, Jeffrey L, Robert Grinsell, Roger Freeman, David A. Anderton, Frederick A. Johnsen, Bill Sweetman, Alex Vanags-Baginskis and Robert C. Mikesh. *The Great Book of World War II Airplanes.* Tokyo: Zokeisha Publications Ltd., 1994

Epperson, Ralph. *The Unseen Hand* Tucson: Publius Press, 1985

Ferguson, Niall. *The Rothschilds, Money's Prophets.*

Floyd, Jim. *The Avro Canada C-102 Jetliner.* Erin: Boston Mills 1986

Francillon, Rene. *Boeing 707: Pioneer Jetliner.* Motorbooks International, 1999

Gainor, Chris. *Arrows to the Moon.* Toronto, Apogee Books, 2001

Galbraith, John Kenneth. *A Journey Through Economic Time.* Toronto: Houghton Mifflin, 1994

Gehlen, Reinhard: *The Service.* World Publishing 1972

Goodspeed, D.J. *A History of the Defense Research Board of Canada.* Ottawa; Queen's Printer, 1958

Gordon, Walter L. *A Choice For Canada,* Toronto: McClelland & Stewart, 1965

Gordon, Walter L. *A Political Memoir* Toronto: McClelland & Stewart, 1977

Granatstein, J.L. *The Generals: The Canadian Army's Senior Commanders in the Second World War.* Toronto: Stoddart Publishing, 1993

Griffin, Des. *Descent Into Slavery.* Emissary Publications, 1980

Griffin, G. Edward. *The Creature From Jeckyll Island: A Second Look at the Federal Reserve.* 3rd Ed., American Media, 1998

Ed. Greenwood, John T. *Milestones of Aviation.* New York: Crescent Books, 1991

Gunston, Bill.. *Stingers; The McDonnell Douglas F/A-18 Hornet,* New York: Mallard Press, 1990

Gunston, Bill (Editor in Chief). *Chronicle of Aviation.* London: Chronicle Communications Ltd., 1992

Gunston, Bill *Faster Than Sound.* Somerset: Patrick Stephens Limited, 1992

Hasek, John. *The Disarming of Canada.* Toronto: Key Porter Books, 1987

Hacker, Barton C. and James M. Grimwood. *On the Shoulders of Titans: A History of Project Gemini.* Washington: NASA Science and Technology Information Division, 1977

Hallion, Richard. *On The Frontier* [part of NASA history series] Washington: US Government Printing Office, undated.

Hastings, Stephen. *The Murder of TSR.2.* London: Macdonald & Co., 1966

Hotson, Fred. *The De Havilland Canada Story.* Toronto: Canav, 1983

Hoyt, *America's Wars and Military Excursions,* New York, McGraw-Hill, 1987

Kahn, David. *The Codebreakers, The History of Secret Writing.* New York: Macmillan, 1967

Kaiser, Robert G.. *Cold Winter Cold War.* New York: Stein & Day, 1974

Keating and Pratt, *Canada, NATO and the Bomb.* Edmonton: Hurtig Publishing, 1988

Strathern, Paul *Strangelove's Game.* Toronto: Knopf, 2001

McCullough, David. *Truman,* New York: Simon & Schuster, 1992

McQueen, Rod *The Money Spinners,* Toronto: MacMillan, 1983

Mellberg, Bill. *Famous Airliners.*

Milberry, Larry. *Aviation in Canada.* Toronto: McGraw-Hill Ryerson Ltd., 1979

Milberry, Larry. *The Avro CF-100.* Toronto: CANAV Books, 1981

Milberry, Larry. *The Canadair Sabre.* Toronto: CANAV Books, 1986

Milberry, Larry. *The Pratt & Whitney Canada Story.* Toronto: CANAV Books, 1989

Milberry, Larry. *The Canadair DC-4M North Star* Toronto: CANAV Books, 1982

Miller, Nathan. *FDR: An Intimate History,* New York: Doubleday, 1983

Miller, Jay. *Convair B-58 Hustler: The World's First Supersonic Bomber.* Aerofax Midland Publishing Ltd. 1998

Minifie, James M. *Peacemaker or Powdermonkey: Canada's Role in a Revolutionary World.* Toronto: McClelland & Stewart Ltd., 1960

Morton, Desmond. *A Military History of Canada.* Edmonton: Hurtig Publishers Ltd., 1985

Moseley, Leonard. *Dulles: A Biography of Eleanor, Allen and John Foster Dulles and Their Family Network.* New York: The Dial Press, 1978

Mullins, Eustace C. *Secrets of the Federal Reserve.* Bankers Research Institute, 1991

Nash, Knowlton. *Kennedy and Diefenbaker: Fear and Loathing Across the Undefended Border.* Toronto: McClelland and Stewart, 1990

Nesbit, Roy Conyers. *An Illustrated History of the RAF.* 7th Ed., Surrey: CLB Publishing, 1990

Newman, Peter C. *Renegade in Power: The Diefenbaker Years.* Toronto: McClelland & Stewart Ltd., 1985

Newman, Peter C. *Distemper of our Times.* 2nd Ed. Toronto: McClelland & Stewart, 1978

Newman, Peter C. *True North NOT Strong and Free.* Toronto: McClelland & Stewart, 1983

Orchard, David. *The Fight for Canada,* Toronto: Stoddart Publishing, 1993

Organ, Richard; Page, Ron; Watson, Don; & Wilkinson, Les. *Arrow.* Erin: Boston Mills 1980

Owen, David. *Hidden Secrets: A Complete History of Espionage and the Technology Used to Support It.* Toronto, 2002

Peden, Murray. *Fall of an Arrow.* Toronto: Stoddart Publishing Co. Ltd., 1987

Pincher, Chapman. *Too Secret Too Long,* New York: St Martins Press, 1984

Quigley, Carroll. *Tragedy and Hope; History of the World in Our Time.* Gsg & Associates, 1975

Regehr, Ernie. *Arms Canada: The Deadly Business of Military Exports.* Toronto: Lorimer, 1987

Rich, Ben. *Skunk Works: A Personal Memoir of My Years at Lockheed.* Little & Brown & Co. 1996

Roberts, John G. *Mitsui, Three Centuries of Japanese Business,* New York: Weatherhill, 1989

Rummel, Robert. *Howard Hughes and TWA.* Smithsonian Institute Press, p. 267

Shaw, E.K. *There Never Was an Arrow.* Toronto: Steel Rail Educational Publishing, 1979

Smye, Fred. *Canadian Aviation and the Avro Arrow,* unpublished

Stevenson, William. *A Man Called INTREPID.* New York: Harcourt Brace, 1976

Stevenson, William. *Intrepid's Last Case,* London: Joseph 1983

Stewart, Greig. *Arrow Through the Heart,* Toronto: McGraw-Hill Ryerson, 1998

Stewart, Greig. *Shutting Down the National Dream: A.V. Roe and the Tragedy of the Avro.* Scarborough: McGraw-Hill Ryerson, 1988

Stinnett, Robert. *Day of Deceit.* New York: Free Press, 2000

Stormer, John. *None Dare Call it Treason,* Florissant: Liberty Bell Press 1964

Scowen, Peter: *Rogue Nation: The America the Rest of the World Knows.* Toronto: McClelland and Stewart Ltd., 2003

Stursberg, Peter. *Diefenbaker, Leadership Gained 1956-'62.* Toronto: University of Toronto Press, 1975

Sweetman, Bill. *Aurora: The Pentagon's Secret Hypersonic Spyplane.* Osceola: Motorbooks International, 1993

Sweetman, Bill. *The F-22 Raptor.* Dedham Mass: Horizon House, 2001

Taylor, John R. (Supervising Editor). *The Lore of Flight.* New York: Crescent Books, 1978

Trubshaw, Brian *Concorde, The Untold Story.* Buckram: Suton Publishing, 2000

Thomas, Evan. *The Very Best Men; The Daring Early Years of the CIA.* New York: Simon & Schuster Inc., 2006

unattributed. *Aerospace Plane Technology: Research and Development Efforts in Europe.* Washington: United States General Accounting Office, 1991

Vesco, Renato. *Intercept But Don't Shoot* (publisher and date unknown)

Wilkinson, Paul H. *Aircraft Engines of the World* (publisher unknown, various years.)

Wright, Peter. *Spycatcher* New York: Viking, 1987

Whitcomb, Randall: *Avro Aircraft & Cold War Aviation.* St. Catherines: Vanwell Publishing, 2002

Wood, Derek. *Project Cancelled. The disaster of Britain's abandoned aircraft projects.* London: Jane's Publishing Limited, 1986

Wood, Derek. (Editor in Chief). *Jane's All the World's Aircraft (various years).* London: Jane's Publishing Limited,

Zuk, Bill. *Avrocar: Canada's Flying Saucer: The story of Avro Canada's secret projects.* Toronto: The Boston Mills Press, 2001

Zuuring, Peter. *The Arrow Scrapbook. Rebuilding a Dream and a Nation.* Dalkeith: Arrow Alliance Press, 1999

Letters, Reports and Periodicals

Avro Engineering Performance Group, Performance Report 15 for Avro Arrow Mk. 2, 3 December, 1958

Aide Memoire for MND George R. Pearkes, V.C., for discussion with John Foster Dulles and Secretary of Defense Neil McElroy, July, 1958

Aide Memoire for MND George R. Pearkes, V.C., "Advantages and Disadvantages of Continuing Production of the CF105, 25 August, 1958

Air Transport Board of Canada "Avro C-102 Jetliner Economics Vs. Canadair DC-4M North Star on Triangular Route" June, 1950

Aviation News. 10 November, 1958

A.V. Roe Canada Ltd. *Avro Newsmagazine: Special [Arrow] First Flight Issue.* Malton: Avro Aircraft Ltd., April 1958 –quotations from embedded article by Bill Gunston for *Flight* magazine on Arrow first flight.

A/V/M Hendrick quotations from his diary of 29 October, 1957

Bogolikos, Nikos. *Development of Surveillance Technology and Risk of Abuse of Economic Information, Scientific and Technological Options Assessment.* The European Parliament Luxembourg, October, 1999

Brame, Frank. Avro Technical Department report on SST studies to J.C. Floyd, 9 July, 1959

Braybook, Roy. "Fighting Falcon V Fulcrum." *Air International Vol.47, No.2.* Stamford: Key Publishing, 1994

Calloway, Oscar comments: Congressional Record, Vol. 54, p. 2947. 9 February, 1917

Canadian Ambassador to External Affairs regarding 30 January, 1958 air defense meetings between U.S. Secretary of the Air Force James Douglas and the Canadian Ambassador.

Canadian Aviation Industries, October, 1958

CAS A/M Hugh Campbell to MND George R. Pearkes, "CF-105 Supersonic Interceptor", 21 August, 1958

CDC: Record of Cabinet Defense Committee Decision, 21 August, 1958

Nixon, C.R., for Deputy Minister of National Defense, letter to MGen George R. Pearkes (ret'd) on fact that the government was not granting the CBC unclassified information on who ordered the destruction of the Avro Arrows.

CSC: Memorandum to the Cabinet Defense Committee: "Arrow Development Programme", 3 October, 1955

CDC minutes, 13 June, 1956: "The Development of the Introduction of the BOMARC Ground to Air Guided Missile and the MB-1 Air to Air Guided Missile on Canadian Manned Interceptors for the RCAF for the Defense of Canada"

CCSC Gen. Charles Foulkes: "Aide Memoire for the Minister; Advantages and Disadvantages of Continuing Production of the CF105" 25 August, 1958

Charyk, Joseph V. "Memorandum for the Deputy Secretary of Defense", 27 May, 1960

CIA: Wilber, Dr. Donald. "Overthrow of Premier Mossadeq of Iran, November 1952—August 1953, Chapter 10

Cohen, J.: Secret Avro Technical Department document titled: "Comparison of Arrow 2 and Bomarc in the Air Defense of Eastern Canada", 29 September, 1958

Cole, W/C W.R., memorandum to Air Member Canadian Joint Staff (Washington) "Iroquois Engine History and Status", 30 November, 1960

Congressional Record, February 22, 1963 Dr. Ralph K. White, head of the Soviet Division, U.S. Information Agency, speaking to the American Psychological Association, September, 1961

Crosby, S/L R.S., memorandum to Chief of the Air Staff at RCAF HQ, "Arrow Weapons System—Status of Aircraft 25206", 20 February, 1959

Dallyn, Gordon M. (Editor). *Canadian Geographical Journal. [Special Canadian aviation issue]* Ottawa: The Canadian Geographical Society, November 1953

DDP summary of bi-lateral air defense summit between Eisenhower, Diefenbaker *et al,* RG 49 Interim Vol. 67 File 151-9-1, part 3

DDP summary of summer summit between Eisenhower and Dulles and Diefenbaker and Pearkes. RG 49, Vol. 427, File 159-44-B, part 1

Douglas, W.A.B. for Deputy Minister National Defense: Note to File "CBC Programme on the Avro Arrow", 21 April, 1980

Earl, Marjorie. "How Roy Dobson Pushed Us Into the Jet Age", *Macleans,* 20 July, 1957

Eisenhower Library, secret Cabinet Paper describing sensitive political situation with Canada over the cancellation of the CF-105 and the failure of the Defense Production Sharing agreement. 3 April, 1959

Eisenhower Library, "Memorandum for Meeting With Prime Minister Diefenbaker" 1958

Engineering No. 5360 Vol. 206 (U.K. technical journal) "An Additional Use for the Arrow" (re: Anti-Ballistic Missile systems carriage on the CF-105), 17 October, 1958

Financial Post, 6 October, 1956, p.5

Floyd, J.C.. *Avro C-102 Jetliner,* lecture delivered to the Society of Automotive Engineers in January, 1950

Floyd, J.C. "The Avro Story." *Canadian Aviation* 50th Anniversary issue, 1978

Footit, Ray. Letter to Air Member, Canadian Joint Staff, Washington D.C., 18 February, 1959

Harasymchuk, Ted. (Editor). *Pre-Flight,* (various issues) Toronto: Aerospace Heritage Foundation of Canada.

Harding, Richard. "Say no to 'sissypolitik." *The Toronto Star,* 28 August, 2001

Henton, Darcy. "Avro Arrow: Right Stuff at the wrong time." *The Toronto Star,* 27 March 1988

Hunter, G.W., (Assistant Deputy Minister of Defense Production) to the Minister DDP Raymond O'Hurley "Arrow Termination – Status Report (undated, circa summer 1959)

Isinger, Russell and Donald C. Story. "The Plane Truth: The Avro Canada CF-105 Arrow Program." *The Diefenbaker Legacy, Canadian Politics, Law and Society Since 1957.* Regina: University of Saskatchewan, 1998

Javits, Jacob. (US Senator). Entry into Congressional Record re: Bilderberg Group,11 April 1964

Joint Report on an RCAF-DRB-NAE visit to NACA Langley: "Aerodynamic Problems of Avro CF-105 Aircraft", summary, 19 November 1954

Lukaseiwicz: Canada's Encounter with High-Speed Aeronautics, first published in *Technology and Culture*, Vol. 27, No. 2, April 1986

Michaels, Christopher. "Beyond the Horizon: A Test Pilot's Look At The Lockheed A-12/SR-71, From Mach 3 Plus To The Frontiers Of Space!" *Airpower.* Granada Hills: Sentry Books, 1993

McDowell, Donald R. "Five Years in a Phantom." *Vietnam Chronicles, Air War Over Vietnam.* Canoga Park: Challenge Publications Inc., 1991

NACA: Joint report re: Meeting to Discuss CF-105 Problems Held December 20 & 21, 1954 at N.A.C.A. 1512 H Street Northwest, Washington D.C."

NAE letter to A/V/M D.M. Smith, "A.V. Roe C/105 Design Study" 28 September, 1953

Norris, Geoffrey. "The Impossible Pilot." *Jet Adventure: Airmen Today and Tomorrow.* London: Phoenix House Ltd., 1962

Notes on Air Council Meeting to Consider 5981-111 (COR) d/22 August, 1957 Comparison of Air Defense Weapons Combination Held at 1415 hrs, 27 August, 1957

The Nye Committee Report (to the US government on arms makers and their geo-political entanglements)

Onley, David. "Zura Zaps Academics." *Aerospace Heritage Foundation of Canada Newsletter.* Vol.1 No.1, April 1990

Orenda News. A.V. Roe Canada Ltd. October, 1958

Pesando, Mario. *Jetliner Flight Trials and Other Things.* Unpublished, undated.

Phillips to Franklin Delano Roosevelt, November 7, 1935 Roosevelt Presidential Library PSF 25, Diplomatic Correspondence, "Canada."

Postol, Theodore A. "The Star Wars Conspiracy." *Harpers Magazine,* August 2000

Richardson, Doug. "Burning Desire for Power." [review of current and future turbofans and turbojets] *Air International Vol.47, No.2.* Stamford: Key Publishing, 1994

RCAF Air Council: Notes on Air Council Meeting, Comparison of Air Defense Weapons Combination, 1957

RCA: Astra 1 and Astra 2 progress reports, 1957

RCAF AMTS report: Notes of a Meeting to Review a USAF Appraisal of the CF-105 Held at Avro Aircraft Malton at 0900 hrs, 1 Nov. 1955

RG 28A, vol. 156, Public Archives of Canada.

Smye, Fred: personal letter to Dr. J.J. Brown on CF-105 cancellation, 13 May, 1968.

Speas, Dixon. "A USA Citizen's View of the Avro Jetliner" unpublished. 1994

Statistics Canada. *Quarterly Estimates of the Canadian Balance of International Payments, System of National Accounts.* Ottawa: The Queen's Printer, 1953 (pub.# 67-001)

Statistics Canada *Quarterly Estimates of the Canadian Balance of International Payments,*

Ottawa: The Queen's Printer, 1974 (pub.# 67-001P)

The Avro Organization. Toronto: A.V. Roe Canada Ltd., 1955(?)

The Orenda (Arrow first flight edition). Toronto: A.V. Roe Canada Ltd., March, 1958

unattributed: "Disc Shaped Vehicles Studied For Potential as Orbital Aircraft." *Aviation Week & Space Technology,* June 1960

unattributed: "Gloster's Grim Reaper" [on Zurakowski and his aerobatics] *Wingspan,* September/October, 1986

unattributed: "How Did the Company Get Its Name? Who was Hawker? Who Was Siddeley? (and Who Was A.V. Roe?)" A.V. Roe Canada Ltd., undated.

unknown: "Rocket Pioneer Von Braun Dies" *Arizona Daily Star,* June 18, 1977

unknown: Letter to Air Member, Canadian Joint Staff, Washington D.C., 29 April, 1957 unknown: Minutes of Hearings Before the Subcommittee on Appropriations, House of Representatives, Eighty-sixth Congress Second Session, Re: Air Defense Program Revisions in 1960 and 1961 Air Force Programs

unknown: Memorandum for the Cabinet Defense Committee "An Powerplant for the CF 105 Supersonic Aircraft" (circa 1954)

unknown: "Synopsis of Costs Applicable to CF-105 Programme" (circa spring 1959)

unknown: Memorandum to the Cabinet Defense Committee, "CF 105 Development Programme" 3 October, 1955

"Record of Cabinet Defense Committee Decision, 21 August, 1958

Westinghouse: Introductory service manual on the APQ-72 radar/fire-control, 1960

White House Cabinet Paper (re: sensistive situation regarding cancellation of the Arrow Weapons System and concurrent failure of Defense Production Sharing arrangements) 3 April, 1959

Young, Scott. *Jet Age: The Way Up. An account of the 10-year history of A.V. Roe Canada Limited.* Toronto: A.V. Roe Canada Ltd., 1955

Zurakowski, Janusz. (Introduction by Don Rogers) *Test Flying the Arrow and Other High Speed Jet Aircraft.* Ottawa: *The Canadian Aviation Historical Society Journal.* Vol. 17 No.4, Winter 1979

Diefenbaker Cabinet Minutes:

28 August, 1958 pages 6-11, 3 September, 1958 pages 2-5, 5 September, 1958 pages 16-18, 8 September, 1958 pages 6-7, 21 September 1958 pages 4, 9-11, 22 September, 1958 pages 2-3, 25 November, 1958 page 7, 22 December, 1958 page 7, 31 December, 1958 pages 3-4, 10 January, 1959 pages 8-9, 28 January, 1959 page 6, 3 February, 1959 pages 3-4, 4 February, 1959 pages 3-4, 14 February, 1959 pages 3-5, 17 February, 1959 pages 4-5, 19 February, 1959 page 2, 23 February, 1959 pages 2-4, 30 June, 1959 pages 2-4, 2 July, 1959 page 2, 7 July, 1959 page 5, 13 August, 1959 pages 3-4, 14 August, 1959 pages 4-6, 5 September, 1959 pages 11-13

Web Articles:

Baugher, Joe. "Convair YF-102" (http://home.att.net/~jbaugher/f102_7.html), 1999

Baugher, Joe. "McDonnell F-4E Phantom II," (http://home.att.net/~jbaugher/ff4_3.html), 1999

Baugher, Joe. "McDonnell YF4H-1 Phantom II." (http://home.att.net/~jbaugher/f4_1.html), 1999

Baugher, Joe. "Convair F-106A Delta Dart." (http://home.att.net/~jbaugher/f106_1.html),1999

Baugher, Joe. "Lockheed YF-12A." (http://home.att.net/~jbaugher/f12.html), 2000

Baugher, Joe. "General Dynamics F-111A." (http://home.att.net/~jbaugher/f111_1.html), 1999

Baugher, Joe. "Republic XF-103." (http://home.att.net/~jbaugher/f103.html), 1999

Baugher, Joe. "McDonnell F-15A Eagle." (http://home.att.net/~jbaugher/f15_6.html), 2000

Baugher, Joe. "McDonnell F-15C Eagle." (http://home.att.net/~jbaugher/f15_8.html), 2000

Baugher, Joe. "Grumman F-14 Tomcat." (http://home.att.net/~jbaugher/f14.html), 2000

unattributed. "AWG-9 Weapon Control System." (http://www.novia.net/~tomcat/AWG9.html), 2000

unattributed. "General Dynamics F-111A." (http://wpafb.af.mil/museum/modern_flight/mf51.htm) , 1999

unattributed. "General Dynamics F-111A." (http://intecon.com/museum/aircraft/f111.html), 1999

unattributed. "Hughes AIM-4F Super Falcon." (http://www.wpafb.af.mil/museum/arm/arm10.htm), 1999

unattributed. "McDonnell Douglas Air-2A "Genie" Rocket." (http://www.wpafb.af.mil/museum/arm/arm16.htm) 1999

unattributed. "Republic XF-103." (http://www.wpafb.af.mil/museum/research/fighter/f103.htm), 2000

unattributed. "North American XF-108A "Rapier"" (http://www.wpafb.af.mil/museum/research/fighter/f108.htm), 2000

unattributed. "Lockheed D-21B Unmanned Aerial Vehicle (UAV)" (http://www.wpafb.af.mil/museum/annex/an11.htm), 2001

unattributed. "General Electric J79 Turbojet Engine" (http://www.wpafb.af.mil/museum/engines/j79.htm), 2001

unattributed. "General Electric J47 Turbojet Engine." (http://www.wpafb.af.mil/museum/engines/eng49.htm) , 2001

unattributed. "Convair B-58A "Hustler."" (http://www.wpafb.af.mil/museum/modern_flight/mf33.htm), 2001

unattributed. "Convair B-58A 'Hustler.'" (http://www.wpafb.af.mil/museum/research/bombers/b5/b5-36.htm), 2001

unattributed. "B-58 Hustler." (http://www.afa.org/magazine/gallery/b58.html), 1999

unattributed. ""Satellite Killer" LTV Air-Launched Anti-Satellite Missile." (http://www.wpafb.af.mil/museum/space_flight/sf14.htm), 2001

unattributed. "Allison J35-A-35A Turbojet Engine." (http://www.wpafb.af.mil/museum/engines/eng46.htm) , 2001 unattributed. "Pratt & Whitney J57 Turbojet." (http://www.wpafb.af.mil/museum/engines/eng54.htm), 2001

unattributed. "Pratt & Whitney J58 Turbojet Engine." (http://www.wpafb.af.mil/museum/engines/eng55.htm), 2001

unattributed. "Arrow Decisions" [Pearkes re: cancellation reasons 1967] (http://collections.ic.gc.ca/uvic/pearkes/plv5/parrow.html), 2000

Gustin, Emmanuel. "BAC TSR.2." (http://www.csd.uwo.ca/~pettypi/elevon/baugher_other/tsr2.html), 1999

unattributed. "Project Suntan." (http://www.aemann.demon.co.uk/suntan.htm), 1999

various NASA articles and documents from http://www.nasa.gov, http://www.arc.nasa.gov, http://www.hq.nasa.gov.

Mattingly, Jack. Various information and diagrams from his Aircraft Engine Design website (http://www.aircraftenginedesign.com)

various. http://www.bilderberg.org

From the Jim Floyd collection;

Avro Engineering "Proposal: CF-105 Design and Development Program." Ad-15, Issue 2.

Secret Avro Brochure for the RCAF (16 pages), June 1955

Avro Engineering Division report to Avro Management Committee "Suggested Projects For Study, Other Than Those Presently On Contract." (advanced Arrows, missiles, SST's, anti-gravitics, nuclear and plasma propulsion etc.) (7 pages), 5 June 1958

Baker, Sir John W. Letter to Mr. Crawford Gordon from British Joint Services Mission in Washington D.C. thanking him for briefings (during BJSM team visit to Avro) by Grinyer, Frost and Floyd. (one page) 23 October 1954

Canadian Aviation Hall of Fame biography of J.C. Floyd (one page)

Floyd, J.C. "SST to Concord to Concorde, A look back at some of the untold history of the birth of Concorde. –unpublished(81 pages) 1990

Floyd, J.C. "Aide-memoire on Transonic Transport – Project 1011

Floyd, J.C. "The Canadian Approach to All-Weather Interceptor Development – The Fourteenth British Commonwealth Lecture." *Journal of the Royal Aeronautical Society.* (22 pages) December 1958

Floyd, J.C. "Some Current Problems Facing the Aircraft Designer." Roy Chadwick Memorial Lecture to the Royal Aeronautical Society. *Journal of the Royal Aeronautical Society,* (21 pages) September 1961

Floyd, J.C. "Reflections on the Manchester/Lancaster period at Avro Manchester" (unpublished, written for Stuart Davies) (5 pages) 22 May 1990

Floyd, J.C. text of speech for CF-100 reunion, (5 pages) January 2000

Floyd, J.C. "The Aftermath" 7 page article written June 1992

Floyd, J.C. "Reflections on the Arrow." Undated

Floyd, J.C. "Notes on Arrow Project' (answers frequently asked questions) (10 pages) 10 February, 1989

Floyd, J.C.. "Notes on Discussions With G/C Footit." Confidential letter to Fred T. Smye, 28 June 1957

Cohen, J.. "Comparison of Arrow 2 and Bomarc in the Air Defense of Eastern Canada" secret Avro Technical Department document (6 pages), September 1958

Floyd, J.C. Confidential letter to Sir Roy Dobson on his December 1955 visit to the UK. (19 December 1955)

Floyd, J.C. "Note on visit of Dr. Courtland Perkins, Chief Scientist, U.S.A.F., July 18/57" Memorandum to File (2 pages) 29 July 1957

Floyd, J.C. Letter to Sir George Gardner regarding the possibility of Britain receiving some of the flying Arrows for SST research. (2 pages) 2 April 1959

Floyd, J.C. Letter to John H. Parkin, Director NAE, regarding the NAE taking the Jetliner for research, rather than it being destroyed. (2 pages), 29 June 1956

Floyd, J.C. Letter to G.L. Humphrey (Avro UK-Canada liaison) regarding Floyd's autumn 1958 visit to the UK. (one page) 20 November 1958

unattributed "An Additional Use For The "Arrow"? *Engineering Vol.206, No.5360* October 1958

Floyd, J.C. Early sketch by Floyd of possible Arrow 4 configuration (undated)

Floyd, J.C. Letter to Sir Roy Dobson regarding suitability of Arrow for GOR. 339 (TSR.2 spec.), (2 pages), 19 February 1958

Floyd, J.C. Letter to Dr. Courtland Perkins (USAF Chief Scientist) regarding Arrow L/D max and other aerodynamic data which was enclosed with the letter. (one page) 6 March 1957

Floyd, J.C. Letter to J.A.R. Kay, General Manager A.V. Roe Manchester re: visit to UK, results of "Operation Sunbeam" interceptors vs. missiles tests and 1/2 scale Blue Steel for an RAF Arrow. (one page) 10 November 1958

Floyd, J.C. "Subject: Project Research Group" Memorandum to File (6 pages) 13 December 1956

Floyd, J.C. Letter to Air Chief Marshal Sir Thomas Pike re: disposition of flying Arrows after Black Friday. (2 pages) 2 April 1959

Floyd, J.C. Letter to Mr. J.L. Orr, Director Engineering DRB regarding DRB critiques of Avro wind-tunnel methods (open intakes vs. closed.) (2 pages) 30 August 1957

Floyd, J.C. Memorandum to File, Subject: Visit to West Coast Aircraft Companies, February, 1959 (2 pages) 4 March 1959

Floyd J.C. "Estimated Arrow Development Potential" (4 pages) 28 March 1989

Floyd, J.C. "Suggested Policy on CF-105" Confidential letter to Harvey Smith regarding Cook-Craigie production philosophy. (4 pages) 11 December 1953

Floyd, J.C. Private and Confidential letter to J.L. Plant (Avro Aircraft President at that time) regarding Floyd's concerns on charges to the RCAF for Arrow Mk. 2A modifications. (2 pages) 9 July 1958

Floyd, J.C. Strictly Confidential letter to J.L. Plant titled "The Arrow Controversy" detailing the British reaction to his visit to the UK in October 1958. (6 pages) 7 November 1958

Floyd, J.C. Memorandum to File (on possible post-Black Friday projects for Avro) (5 pages), 11 March 1959

Floyd, J.C. Memo to Robert Lindley, 19 June, 1957

Floyd, J.C. Confidential letter to Fred Smye titled: Complaint from D.L. Thompson on Avro's Over-Enthusiasm on Sparrow Program. 28 June, 1957

Floyd, J.C. Confidential report to Sir Roy Dobson on his December visit to England and France titled "Report on Visit to England and France", 15 December, 1955

Floyd, J.C. letter to Randall L. Whitcomb 6 June, 2005 (re: Avro/HSA SST designs)

Flight and Aircraft Engineer: "Ironclads and Arrows" 14 February, 1958

Floyd, J.C. Memo to A/V/M Hendrick (on missile possibilities for the CF-105), 30 August, 1957

Heirloom Books article: "James C. Floyd, Putting Canada at the Forefront of Aerospace Technology."

Heirloom Books article: "Canada's Gift to NASA, The Maple Leaf in Orbit."

Petterson, G.H. "Preliminary Proposal for Arrow 3," Secret Avro Technical Department document (91 pages) October, 1958

Pesando, Mario A. "Discussions on Ramjets With Curtiss-Wright at Woodridge, N.J., Jan. 31, 1958" Letter to Jim Floyd, 10 February 1958

Pesando, Mario A. "Curtiss-Wright Ramjets." Letter to Jim Floyd and Bob Lindley, 12 December, 1957

Pesando, Mario A. "Long Range Arrow" [Arrow PS-2 and Mk. 4), Secret Avro Project Research Group publication. (26 pages) September 1957

Pesando, Mario A. "Modified Long Range Arrow." Letter to Jim Floyd, 7 November, 1957

unattributed. "Ironclads and Arrows…" *Flight and Aircraft Engineer* Vol.73, No.2560 14 February, 1958

Pesando, Mario A. Avro Project Research Group study on Space Threshold Vehicle (STV), summer 1958

Pike, Sir Thomas G. Letter to Jim Floyd regarding possibility of UK acquiring the flying Arrows. (2 pages) 7 April 1959

Rummel, Robert W. Letter from Rummel (Trans World Airlines VP Planning and Research) to Jim Floyd re: Concorde sonic boom and route analysis. (one page) 5 December 1966

Shaw, Bill U. *"Arrow 2A Zero Length Launch Investigation."* Secret Avro Technical Department document (20 pages) October 1958

Shaw, G and E.K. Shaw Untitled report to undisclosed recipients on what was behind the Arrow cancellation. Conclusions were that it was done on behalf of American political and economic interests and that the real target was the company, not the Arrow. This document formed the basis of E.K. Shaw's "There Never Was an Arrow" (70 pages) 30 April 1959

Floyd, J.C. letter to Mr. J. McCulloch, Avro Aircraft Ltd., London England, 22 February, 1957 (re: German interest)

Other References:

Woodman, Jack. "Flying the Avro Arrow" Presented to Canadian Aeronautics and Space Institute, 16 May, 1978

Rogers, Don. Speech and video presentation to Ontario Society of Professional Engineers, 2001.

University of Victoria taped interviews between Dr. Reginald Roy and George R. Pearkes V.C., 1967

Air Transport Board Conclusions on Avro C-102 Jetliner Economics vs. Canadair DC-4M North Star on Triangular Route June 1950

Certain advantages will accrue to the airline which first employs a jet transport in domestic scheduled transport operations and these are believed to be sufficiently important to warrant a brief examination. Firstly there should be an increase in traffic due to the superiority of turbine-engined aircraft over conventional types, with respect to passenger comfort. Increased speed will also be an attraction. Both these factors assume greater importance as the stage length is increased. The very novelty of such a radical advance in type of equipment will also be of benefit. A temporary advantage in low fuel prices may also go to the first airline to introduce turbine-powered aircraft, though this advantage is expected to disappear as the demand for kerosene increases.

This study suggests that the Jetliner can be operated at a lower direct cost than the North Star for the route and schedule frequencies chosen even though the stage lengths are well below the optimum for the Jetliner. It is quite possible, however, that a comparable analysis of direct cost under the same conditions for a modern twin-engine transport powered by reciprocating engines (such as the Convair 240 or the Martin 404) would show lower direct costs than those estimated for the Jetliner. In comparison with such aircraft the Jetliner might still be more attractive, however if all factors are taken into consideration, since increased revenues are expected to result from the improved standards of comfort and speed which the Jetliner offers.

Conclusions.

Provided that the Jetliner in normal scheduled operations demonstrates the performance submitted by the manufacturer the comparative operating cost analysis of a 40 passenger version of the Jetliner and of the North Star when operated on the triangular route Toronto-Montreal-New York-Toronto with three daily flights in each direction indicates that:

1. The service requires three Jetliners (including one as reserve) as against four North Stars (including one as reserve).

2. The direct operating cost of the Jetliner, with the present price of kerosene in tank cars at Malton, varies between 79% and 81% of the North Star direct operating cost. Assuming the price of kerosene to rise to a level of $0.05 less per Imp. gal. than the price of high octane aviation fuel, direct operating cost of the Jetliner will still be lower than that of the North Star.

3. An equal indirect cost (as calculated from TCA data) was applied to the Jetliner and the North Star alike. On this basis, which is rather unfavourable to the Jetliner, the total operating cost of the Jetliner varies between 86% and 90% of the total North Star operating cost.

4. The introduction cost of the Jetliner in the proposed service will probably be of the order of $260,000.

5. Before any jet-engined transport is introduced on a particular route special studies with respect to traffic control and winds at cruising altitudes will have to be made. The calculated maximum wind at 30,000 ft. is indicated by the Meteorological Division, Department of Transport to be of the order of 250 mph. Such a wind will seriously affect

6. Increased frequency of service, or an increase in stage length up to 900 miles, either of which will result in a larger number of aircraft than specified in para. 1, will have the effect of lowering the direct operating cost of the Jetliner from the levels indicated in para. 2.

7. Due to the improved standards of comfort and speed which the Jetliner can offer, as well as the novelty of such a radically new type of transport, it is very probable that it will generate more revenue traffic than the North Star, so that the difference in net revenue will be appreciably greater than that indicated by the total cost figures given in para. 4.

8. It is very probable that under the basic route and schedule conditions assumed in this study, direct operating costs lower than those for the Jetliner would be achieved through use of a modern twin-engine transport such as the Martin 404 or the Convair 240, since the stage lengths involved are so far below the optimum for the Jetliner. The greater attraction of the Jetliner might, however, even out-weigh the higher cost level, particularly during the initial period during which no other North American operator would have jet transports in operation.

SYNOPSIS OF COSTS APPLI

SERIAL NO.	SUBJECT	C.D.	F.E.	COL. 1 PROGRESS CLAIMS AT SEPT. 23/58
ACDA-4	Airframe Development	DRB/AIR/ DEV./67	19368	$ 8,276,632
2-B-5-309	Airframe Development	DRB/AIR/ DEV.67	19368	52,372,008
	Sub-Total			$ 60,648,640
2-B-4-595	Airframe Tooling	462043	462043	$ 27,788,583
2-B-4-715	8 Aircraft Production	462043	462043	42,579,988
2-BX-7-1455	29 Aircraft Production	462043	462043	10,808,893
2-BX-8-27	A/ANS. Representatives	462043	462043	Nil
Misc.	Miscellaneous Airframe Spares	462043	462043	290,789
	Sub-Total			$ 81,468,253
2-BX-8-14	Blanket Airframe Spares	772778	772778	$ 30,497
2-BR-8-149	Repair & Overhaul Airframes	872801	872801	Nil
2-BR-8-146	Repair & Overhaul Airframe Components	872802	872802	Nil
2-BR-8-147	Repair & Overhaul Airframe Spares	872803	872803	Nil
2-BX-8-28	Airframe Electrical Systems	872476	872476	Nil
	Sub-Total			$ 30,497
	Total: Airframe Portion:			$142,147,390
2-B-4-717	Iroquois Development	DRB/AIR/ DEV. 109	21060	$ 46,699,165
2-B-5-846	B-47 Conversion	DRB/AIR/ DEV.109	21060	1,595,240
	Sub-Total			$ 48,294,405
2-B-5-585	Iroquois Tooling	562022	562022	$ 10,796,082
2-B-2-263	20 Iroquois Prototype Production	562023	562023	$ 38,278,292
2-BD-7-1484	87 Iroquois Pre-Production	562023	562023	5,837,022
2-B-7-1015	Iroquois Publications	562023	562023	94,099
	Sub-Total			$ 44,209,413
	Total: Engine Portion:			$103,299,900
2-USX-5-48	J 75 Engines (G.F.A.E.)	462044	462044	$ 8,859,522
2-USX-7-111	J 75 Spares (G.F.A.E.)	462044	462044	33,806
2-USX-7-166	J 75 Spares (G.F.A.E.)	462044	462044	9,900
	Sub-Total			$ 8,903,228
2-USV-8-336	MA-1 Electronic Systems (G.F.A.E.)	862021	862021	Nil
	Overall Total			$254,350,518

Legend

Column 3 equals column 2 minus column 1
Column 5 equals column 4 minus column 1

APPLICABLE TO CP-105 PROGRAMME

1959.

MS 8	COL. 2 PROGRESS CLAIMS AT FEB. 20/59	COL EXPENDI SEPT.23/58 TO FEB.20/59.	COL. 4 ESTIMATED PRE-TERMINATION EXPEND.	COL. 5 ESTIMATE OF PRE-TERMINATION EXPENDITURES FROM SEPT. 23/58 TO FEB. 20/59.
	$ 8,276,632	$ Nil	$ 8,276,632	$ Nil
	59,043,852	6,671,844	59,500,368	7,128,360
	$ 67,320,484	$ 6,671,844	$ 67,777,000	$ 7,128,360
	$ 30,137,453	$ 2,348,870	$ 30,300,000	$ 2,511,417
	50,450,109	7,870,121	51,500,000	8,920,012
	24,135,496	13,326,603	27,500,000	15,691,107
	Nil	Nil	24,000	24,000
	290,789	Nil	290,789	Nil
	$105,013,847	$ 23,545,594	$109,614,789	$ 28,146,536
	$ 53,835	$ 23,338	$ 75,000	$ 44,503
	382,663	382,663	407,663	407,663
	Nil	Nil	65,651	65,651
	29,288	29,288	50,000	50,000
	Nil	Nil	198,000	198,000
	$ 465,786	$ 435,289	$ 796,314	$ 765,817
	$172,800,117	$ 30,652,727	$178,188,103	$ 36,040,713
	$ 49,438,033	$ 2,738,868	$ 53,919,125	$ 7,219,960
	1,595,240	Nil	1,630,000	34,760
	$ 51,033,273	$ 2,738,868	$ 55,549,125	$ 7,254,720
	$ 13,233,958	$ 2,437,876	$ 13,500,000	$ 2,703,918
	$ 42,854,312	$ 4,576,020	$ 44,721,372	$ 6,443,080
	13,546,912	7,709,890	13,848,000	8,010,978
	99,000	4,901	99,000	4,901
	$ 56,500,224	$ 12,290,811	$ 58,668,372	$ 14,458,959
	$120,767,455	$ 17,467,555	$127,717,497	$ 24,417,597
	$ 8,859,522	Nil	$ 8,859,522	Nil
	33,806	Nil	33,806	Nil
	9,900	Nil	9,900	Nil
	$ 8,903,228	Nil	$ 8,903,228	Nil
	Nil	Nil	$ 1,750,000	$ 1,750,000
	$302,470,800	$ 48,120,282	$316,558,828	$ 62,208,310

umn 1,
umn 1,

SECRET

Cabinet minutes for 21 September, 1958

Government purchasing policy; purchase for defence programme
(Previous reference Sept.7)

6. The Minister of Finance said he had now had a chance to discuss the implications of the new government purchasing policy directive, which had been approved by Cabinet, with the Minister of Defence Production who had not been able to be present when it was considered. The Deputy Minister of Defence Production would be in Washington shortly to carry out negotiations and it would be desirable that he be in a position to explain that the new directive did not affect the pattern of government defence purchases based upon strategic consideration.

He hoped to be able to say something on this subject privately to the United Kingdom and to ask them not to press the Canadian government on this matter. The British had expressed some concern about the "buy in America" policy of the United States. He thought it preferable to soft-pedal the purchasing directive rather than jeopardize negotiations with the United States. Mr. O'Hurley was also of this opinion.

7. The Cabinet noted the report of the Minister of Finance on the recent government purchasing policy directive and agreed that it be withheld for some time.

Air defence requirements; recommendations of Cabinet Defence Committee
(Previous reference Sept. 7)

21. The Prime Minister reported that he had seen Mr. Crawford Gordon, President of A.V. Roe Company, who had also interviewed Mr. Pearkes and Mr. Fleming. Mr. Gordon had recommended that production of the Arrow aircraft and the Iroquois engine be undertaken but the programmes for the Astra fire control equipment and the Sparrow missile be cancelled. There was nothing essentially new in his proposal.

22. The Minister of National Defence and the Minister of Finance reported on their conversations with Mr. Gordon and noted that he had made certain assertions in regard to the willingness of the U.S. government to provide fire control and missiles that would be suitable for the Arrow aircraft. He had mentioned some large figures of possible savings that might be made by obtaining such equipment from the United States but had been unable to be precise about these and the figures appeared to be exaggerated.

23. In the course of a further long discussion on this matter, the following points emerged:

(a) Few ministers had changed their minds on the desirabilit of cancelling the contracts for the Arrow and its associated equipment. The Cabinet was clearly divided in its view on the central question.

(b) The chief concern of those who wished to have the Arrow contracts continued was the probable shock to the employment situation of such a major termination of work as would be involved in the cancelling of these contracts. It was recognized that the major impact would be psychological, not simply financial and it was very difficult to judge just how important an economic factor it would be.

(c) Some ministers felt, on the other hand, that the effect of continuing this work would be to impose an unnecessarily high cost upon the Canadian economy, which would contribute to the inflationary dangers and the high cost of exports that were handicapping Canada in securing and maintaining export markets. A decline in employment on these projects would be inevitable several years from now in any event, and that might be a worse time to suffer it than this year.

(d) If production of the Arrow and its associated equipment went forward, it was likely to become publicly known that this was done contrary to military advice and there was a danger that the government would be accused of wasting many hundreds of millions of dollars for what were political or economic reasons. That might seriously shake the confidence in the government of the man in the street.

(e) There was some question as to just what the views of the Chiefs of Staff really were on this issue and how much reliance should be placed upon them. Their recommendation for termination of the programme now appeared to be at variance with their views earlier, although it should be noted that only the Chairman of the Chiefs of Staff Committee was a member of that committee at the time the original recommendations were made. The Chief of the Air Staff recommended that the R.C.A.F. should have interceptor aircraft but preferred to purchase U.S. aircraft if the amount of money available to him for aircraft were fixed.

(f) The current international tension would make it appear foolhardy to cancel an important development programme such as that of the Arrow and Iroquois, although it was noted that, if in fact war broke out, it would be necessary to use current types of aircraft and possibly to concentrate on the CF-100 rather than proceed with the CF-105.

INDEX

A

B

D

E

F

G

H

I

N

O

P

T

U

V

W

X

Y

Z

Epilogue - email from Randall Whitcomb to Robert Godwin late 2007.

"I'm not strident I don't think in the text, I try to be laconic. But I quote primary sources, and then make conclusions, and yes, the verdict is fairly damning for John Foster Dulles and Allen Welsh Dulles (and the State Dept. in general).... but it is pretty darned hard on General Charles Foulkes and Minister of Defence Pearkes... and a guy named David Golden, Asst. Minister of Defence Production... and other Canadians. I point out that the guy who was cabinet secretary (and wrote the Arrow minutes I quote) was also head of the Parlimentary Security Commission (IIRC) and was quite possibly a Soviet Spy. There is plenty of "controversy" to go around in my book.

"The story isn't by any means just about the Arrow. The Jetliner emerges as an equally controversial cancellation, and this book makes the Arrow cancellation look a lot more sinister than what has gone before (and that's a lot of books).

"Fact is, I'm a bit scared of what I've created and maybe I'm at the point where I shouldn't mess with it until someone else reads it, lest I lose courage and water the text too much."